KT-117-432

TERROR AND CONSENT

THE WARS FOR THE TWENTY-FIRST CENTURY

PHILIP BOBBITT

PENGUIN BOOKS

PENGUIN BOOKS

Published by the Penguin Group
Penguin Books Ltd, 80 Strand, London wc2r orl, England
Penguin Group (USA), Inc., 375 Hudson Street, New York, New York 10014, USA
Penguin Group (Canada), 90 Eglinton Avenue East, Suite 700, Toronto, Ontario, Canada m4p 2y3
(a division of Pearson Penguin Canada Inc.)
Penguin Ireland, 25 St Stephen's Green, Dublin 2, Ireland
(a division of Penguin Books Ltd)
Penguin Group (Australia), 250 Camberwell Road, Camberwell, Victoria 3124, Australia
(a division of Pearson Australia Group Pty Ltd)
Penguin Books India Pvt Ltd, 11 Community Centre, Panchsheel Park,
New Delhi – 110 017, India
Penguin Group (NZ), 67 Apollo Drive, Rosedale, North Shore 0632, New Zealand
(a division of Pearson New Zealand Ltd)
Penguin Books (South Africa) (Pty) Ltd, 24 Sturdee Avenue, Rosebank,
Johannesburg 2196, South Africa

Penguin Books Ltd, Registered Offices: 80 Strand, London wc2r orl, England

www.penguin.com

First published in the United States of America by Alfred A. Knopf 2008
First published in Great Britain by Allen Lane 2008
Published in Penguin Books 2009
2

Copyright © Philip Bobbitt, 2008

The moral right of the author has been asserted

Due to limitations of space, permissions to reprint previously published material can be
found following the index.

All rights reserved
Without limiting the rights under copyright
reserved above, no part of this publication may be
reproduced, stored in or introduced into a retrieval system,
or transmitted, in any form or by any means (electronic, mechanical,
photocopying, recording or otherwise), without the prior
written permission of both the copyright owner and
the above publisher of this book

Printed in Great Britain by Clays Ltd, St Ives plc

A CIP catalogue record for this book is available from the British Library

978-0-141-01766-2

www.greenpenguin.co.uk

Mixed Sources
Product group from well-managed
forests and other controlled sources
www.fsc.org Cert no. SA-COC-1592
© 1996 Forest Stewardship Council

Penguin Books is committed to a sustainable future
for our business, our readers and our planet.
The book in your hands is made from paper
certified by the Forest Stewardship Council.

PENGUIN BOOKS
TERROR AND CONSENT

'Lapidary in its beauty . . . The Cold War had a dazzling pantheon of theorists . . . but the War on Terror has conspicuously failed to generate such scholarship – until now . . . This book is so important I hope the publishers have the civic spirit to send a copy to every parliamentarian, decision-maker and opinion-former in the land'
Matthew d'Ancona, *Spectator*

'Behind the pragmatic and unsparing struggles with how we are to manage all this frightening rapid change, there lies . . . an Augustinian Christian sense of the tragic obligation to achieve even a temporary and flawed good in the face of endemic untruthfulness and evil . . . the level clarity of its exposition allows us to look through to a depth that is neither consoling nor despairing but patiently hopeful'
Rowan Williams, *Daily Telegraph*

'This challenging, complex book . . . obliges us to think about all manner of issues vital to the security of the western democracies when too many people still cling to the hope that each terrorist horror will prove the last . . . Pervading Bobbitt's book is a deep moral belief . . . To possess any hope of defending ourselves . . . we need to possess faith in ourselves'
Max Hastings, *Sunday Times*

'The space of a review could not do justice to Professor Bobbitt's measured, civilized and pragmatic doctrine . . . This reviewer is convinced by the analysis and the remedy . . . Just as Pascal advocated that a person ought to "wager" as though God exists . . . I would wager Professor Bobbitt is right' Allan Mallinson, *The Times*

'Philip Bobbitt's *Terror and Consent* is a big book, enormous in concept and sweep, full of portent for transnational politics in the twenty-first century . . . it delivers more intellectual punch on the fraught relationship between state and society, terrorism and terrorists, than any book I know'
The Times Literary Supplement

'Always well-written, consistently provocative and intelligent on a grand scale . . . A celebrity conductor of an orchestra of talents, the greatest of them, it must be said, his own. While Wagnerian in its ambitions, requiring the reader to re-enter a Bobbitt-world created in an earlier blockbuster, *The Shield of Achilles* . . . the book is worth the effort'
Conor Gearty, *Independent*

'Philip Bobbitt is a latter-day philosophe . . . *Terror and Consent* is a banquet of a book . . . a work of high style and high politics. It is the most penetrating rethinking of these cardinal questions yet to appear. Specialists will be feasting on it for years to come. As seer and scholar in this realm, Bobbitt is without peer'
Alex Danchev, *The Times Higher Education Supplement*

'Powerful, dense and brilliant . . . Bobbitt shifts the paradigm for understanding terrorism' Edward Rothstein, *The New York Times*

'Magisterial . . . historically informed, meticulously argued and impassioned . . . "important" barely begins to characterize this book'
Craig Seligman, *Newsday*

'Intellectually stimulating . . . complex and challenging . . . Philip Bobbitt has been thinking broadly, deeply and innovatively about war for a long time. He has a sweeping grasp of international relations'
Steve Weinberg, *Boston Globe*

'Bobbitt's arguments are subtle and often sophisticated . . . There will be few readers who will not be enlightened in some important respects'
Stephen Fidler, *Financial Times*

ABOUT THE AUTHOR

Philip Bobbitt is Herbert Wechsler Professor of Federal Jurisprudence and Director of the Center for National Security at Columbia University. He has served as a senior adviser at the White House, the Senate and the State Department in both Democratic and Republican administrations, and has held senior posts at the National Security Council, including Director for Intelligence Programs and Senior Director for Strategic Planning. He was Anderson Senior Research Fellow at Nuffield College, Oxford, where he was a member of the Oxford Modern History Faculty, and March Christian Senior Fellow of War Studies at King's College, London, and is currently Senior Fellow in the Robert S. Strauss Center for International Security and Law at the University of Texas. He is a member of the American Academy of Arts and Sciences and has written books on nuclear strategy, social choice and constitutional law, as well as the celebrated *The Shield of Achilles* (Allen Lane/Penguin 2002). He lives in New York, Austin and London.

For
Lloyd N. Cutler
and
Sir Michael Howard

Law and strategy, American and Briton:
strongest and wisest when in concert

From *"A Poem for the End of the Century"*

When everything was fine
And the notion of sin had vanished
And the earth was ready
In universal peace
To consume and rejoice
Without creeds and utopias,

I, for unknown reasons,
Surrounded by the books
Of prophets and theologians,
Of philosophers, poets,
Searched for an answer,
Scowling, grimacing,
Waking up at night, muttering at dawn.

What oppressed me so much
Was a bit shameful.
Talking of it aloud
Would show neither tact nor prudence.
It might even seem an outrage
Against the health of mankind. . . .

—Czeslaw Milosz[1]

State of terror: gunmen execute Iraqi election workers at point-blank range on Haifa Street in Baghdad in an effort to prevent democratic elections to form the new Iraqi state. Photo by an Associated Press stringer, December 19, 2004.

CONTENTS

TERROR AND CONSENT

INTRODUCTION

Plagues in the Time of Feast

Oft expectation fails, and most oft there
Where most it promises; and oft it hits
Where hope is coldest, and despair most fits. . . .

—William Shakespeare,
All's Well That Ends Well, 2.1.145–47

THE WARS AGAINST TERROR have begun, but it will take some time before the nature and composition of these wars are widely understood. The objective of these wars is not the conquest of territory or the silencing of any particular ideology but rather to secure the environment necessary for states of consent and to make it impossible for our enemies to impose or induce states of terror. The source of these wars is not Islam but rather a fundamental change in the nature of the State and its evolving relationship to the new methods, purposes, and technologies of warfare.[1]

The wars comprise three different but related efforts at prevention and mitigation: an attempt to preempt attacks by global, networked terrorists; a struggle to prevent the proliferation of weapons of mass destruction; and the worldwide endeavor to protect civilians from natural catastrophes and nonnatural assaults that result in gross diminutions of humane conditions, including human rights. To put it summarily, we are fighting terror, not just terrorists.[2]

The first two elements of these wars are easy to relate to one another: if terrorists of a certain kind ever achieve their goal of getting nuclear or biological weapons, the risk to the civilian population of the democracies is almost incalculable. What is somewhat harder to see is that these risks are in several important dimensions almost indistinguishable from those imposed by the terror that is the consequence of genocide and ethnic cleansing and also of metropolitan earthquakes, pandemics, tidal waves, and hurricanes. Relieving the suffering and devastation that would be caused by such disasters calls on many of the same resources as the efforts against terrorism and proliferation. This fact will have important implications for the force structures and training of the armed forces of the democracies.

Chiefly, however, this relationship arises because civil trauma is a potential consequence of all three of these elements. The same globalizing factors that multiply the harm latent within each of these three threats also attack the legitimacy of the State. As one thoughtful commentator has concluded:

> Transnational terrorism, as represented by al Qaeda and its associated groups, has the potential to undermine the integrity and value of the state itself, destroying the domestic contract of the state by undermining its ability to protect its citizens from direct attack. This form of terrorism is a threat to the sovereignty and the legitimacy of the state itself.[3]

This observation is true of nuclear and biological threats, and of mass catastrophes. Moreover, these disparate sources of fear and chaos are further related because we must prepare to respond to their consequences when we do not immediately know into which basket of causality they fall. Indeed the most important feature of twenty-first century terrorist attacks may be that we often will not know their authors and must act in conditions of great uncertainty. If a power grid goes down we must respond without knowing whether it was the result of a terrorist attack, a lightning strike, or the act of a precocious California teenager. Acting in the face of uncertainty, with the greater reliance we must place on intelligence and planning, will call for a politics of maturity that will test our leaders, our institutions, and our peoples.

Finally, we must treat the three arenas of the Wars against Terror in relation to one another, because progress in any one often means a worsening situation in the other two. Managing this relationship will be the chief security problem for states of consent, such as the U.S. and Britain, in their struggle against terror.

So this is not a book about the "root causes" of terrorism unless we want to say that the enhanced vulnerabilities that are manifested in these threats are caused by the same globalizing forces that are changing the constitutional order of the developed states, that have brought the U.S. to a global preeminence, and that threaten that country perhaps most of all. Rather this book is about that change in the constitutional order—from nation state to market state*—and whether that change will result in the triumph of states of consent or states of terror.

*Market state: The emerging constitutional order that promises to maximize the opportunity of its people, tending to privatize many state activities and making representative government more responsible to consumers. It is contrasted with the current nation state, the dominant constitutional order of the twentieth century that based its legitimacy on a promise to improve the material welfare of its people. A brief description of the various constitutional orders of the State is given in chapter 1; the market state is described in detail in chapter 2.

TWENTY-FIRST CENTURY TERRORISM

I believe that almost every widely held idea we currently entertain about twenty-first century terrorism and its relationship to the Wars against Terror is wrong and must be thoroughly rethought. In this book I have tried to begin this fundamental rethinking. The looming combination of a global terrorist network, weapons of mass destruction, and the heightening vulnerability of enormous numbers of civilians emphatically requires a basic transformation of the conventional wisdom in international security.

This must be done now for the practical, insistent reason that while at present the United States, the United Kingdom, and our allies are making headway in many sectors[4] against al Qaeda in the First Terrorist War, there is no consensus of ideas about the underlying nature of the conflicts against terror. Ultimately, without a realistic and perspicuous understanding of these menacing phenomena on which we can agree, we cannot hope to cope with them successfully. Indeed we may not even be able to avoid falling out among ourselves, with deadly consequences.

Currently, we cling to ways of thinking that brought us success in the past but are ill-suited to our future. I have in mind especially our ideas about terrorism, warfare, and victory (the war aim). Among well-informed persons, a number of dubious propositions about twenty-first century terrorism and the Wars against Terror are widely and tenaciously held. Some of these assumptions are

- that terrorism has always been with us, and though its weapons may change, it will remain fundamentally the same—the weapon of the weak seeking to wrest political control from the strong;
- that because terrorism will always be with us, there can be no victory in a war against terror;
- that because there is no enemy state against which such a war can be waged, the very notion of a "war" on terror is at best a public relations locution, like the "war on drugs" or the "war on poverty";
- that terrorism cannot be an enemy, the subject of warfare, because it is a method, a technique, even if a sinister and brutal one;
- that because terrorism is a technique, not an ideology, it is therefore always a means to an end;
- that because terrorism is only a means to an end—that is, because it is not distinguished by the pursuit of any particular goal—"one man's terrorist is another man's freedom fighter";
- that the root causes of terrorism lie in conditions of poverty, eco-

nomic exploitation, neglect of health and education, and religious indoctrination that must be reversed before a war against terrorism can be won;

- that terrorism is best treated as a problem of crime, by law enforcement officials, and not as a matter for defense departments, which are inappropriate when there are no battlefield lines or armies to confront, and when the context requires constabulary forces and political measures;
- that if, on the other hand, terrorism is indeed a matter of warfare, there can be no place for the Geneva Conventions or other rules of law in war that are applied to conventional conflicts;
- that good intelligence provides the decisive key to defeating terrorism;
- that terrorism will not flourish in democracies;
- that the more power governments gain, the weaker the civil liberties that belong to the public;
- that terrorists "win" if they are able to force governments to enhance their powers of detention, surveillance, and information collection or if the citizenry significantly modifies its everyday behavior;
- that twenty-first century terrorism is the result of a clash of international cultures when medieval and backward worlds confront modern secular societies;
- that confronting hostile states can only make the Wars against Terror harder to win because it diverts resources and wins fresh adherents for the terrorist enemy;
- that the threat of terrorist attacks comes from the states of the Middle East or failed states in remote regions;
- that if the jihadist movements are defeated, the threat of terror will subside, at least for the foreseeable future;
- that terrorists will be confined to low-technology weapons for the foreseeable future;
- that because they will be so confined, terrorists therefore pose at most a modest threat to the stability of modern societies;
- that we should address this threat by concentrating on the likeliest assaults rather than preparing and organizing for the remote possibility that terrorists will pull off a truly catastrophic attack;
- that the forces required to deal with terrorists are completely unrelated to the forces required to deal with natural disasters such as tidal waves, epidemics, hurricanes, and earthquakes;
- and, above all, that the Wars against Terror really have nothing to do with such state-centric activities as ethnic cleansing and genocide or the proliferation and acquisition of weapons of mass

destruction or nonpolitical events like power outages, tsunamis, famines, and other civilian catastrophes.

Given these widespread notions, it is little wonder that most people do not believe that we are at war. As a reviewer in the *Times Literary Supplement* put it: "There is no war on terror. There is no enemy army and there can be no negotiation, no treaty and no peace. Terrorism is indeed a nuisance, a weapon of war, a technique of conflict as old as war itself."[5]

According to a CBS poll taken in May 2006 only 3 percent of Americans believe that terrorists pose the greatest danger to the U.S.[6] As if to confirm this assessment, since September 11 nothing much worse has happened. As another commentator has observed:

Given the vastness and apparent vulnerability of [the U.S.] and the seeming dedication of the terrorists . . . one would expect there to be a massive number of terrorist attacks . . . [W]hat's to stop terrorists from shooting at people in shopping centers, collapsing tunnels, poisoning food, cutting electrical lines, derailing trains, setting forest fires, blowing up pipelines, causing massive traffic jams . . . ?[7]

Interestingly, these two reactions are linked. If the events that take place are not those that experience has led you to expect to accompany warfare, then you are not very likely to believe you are at war in the first place. If you don't think you are in a war, you are not likely to attribute events to a well-considered strategy by your enemy. As we shall see, however, it is precisely our idea of war that must be adjusted for reasons that arise from the changed nature of states and their responsibilities.

Still, at present the most notable fact about the years that followed the attacks on the United States in September 2001 is how little violence and death then ensued. Despite the invasions of Afghanistan and Iraq there were fewer deaths in warfare in those years than at any time during the wars of the twentieth century.[8] Furthermore, despite a murderous campaign against Americans that began well before September 11, the number of Americans killed by international terrorists since the late 1960s[9] until December 2005 is about the same as the number killed during the same period by lightning or by allergic reactions to peanuts. One writer has calculated that the lifetime chance for an American of being killed by terrorists is about the same as being hit by a meteor.[10] Indeed despite a series of terrorist attacks on London, Madrid, Casablanca, New York, and many other cities, since 9/11 the total number of persons worldwide who have been killed by terrorists is about the same number as those who drowned in bathtubs in the U.S.[11] One could rationally conclude that it is little short of neurotic to worry about terrorism as a threat to the survival of the constitutional order of the democracies.

A similar situation obtains with respect to the threat posed by the proliferation of weapons of mass destruction. It seems highly implausible that the armed states of the West could face serious threats from North Korea or Iran, or from any state. It is now possible for the U.S. to determine within seconds the origin of any ballistic missile launch within an accuracy of ten meters. The leadership of a state that ordered such an attack would face the certainty of an immediate and annihilating retaliatory response. It would require of that leadership not mere irrationality, but something approaching a mass suicide pact to account for such an order. As the stocks of nuclear weapons as well as large quantities of biological weapons are held only by states, it would seem highly implausible that the citizens of the West will see the democracies collapse owing to WMD attacks. Even if terrorists got their hands on one or two nuclear devices, this would scarcely pose an existential threat to democracy. Indeed, highway deaths in America since nuclear weapons were developed in World War II have taken ten times the number of persons that died at Hiroshima and Nagasaki, and American political life has not been detectably changed thereby.

Finally, there can be no reason why citizens in the developed world need fear any truly significant curtailment of their human rights, much less mass violations of those rights of the kind entailed by genocide or ethnic cleansing. Although a prominent civil libertarian is reported to have said that "if a loudspeaker goes off and a voice says, 'All Jews gather in Times Square,' it could never surprise me,"[12] in fact it would be astonishing—and more astonishing still if anyone showed up (except possibly armed). Although the world is scarcely free of campaigns of ethnic cleansing and genocide, the democracies seem as safe from these horrors as there can be safety in an age of uncertainty. Whatever the intrusive and annoying nature of antiterrorist measures such as weapons screening at airports, carrying identity cards, data mining, closed-circuit-television monitoring of public spaces, the issuance of intelligence warrants, and even the convening of military tribunals, it is a grotesque exaggeration to claim that our citizens' civil liberties and civil rights have been grossly compromised by these measures, especially when these practices have been subject to independent review by the judiciary in the U.S. and the U.K. Where mass human rights violations have occurred—in Bosnia and Kosovo, in Chechnya, in Sudan, Rwanda, and Burundi to take the most recent—the concerns of OECD* states have been confined to discussions of how to

---

*The Organization for Economic Co-operation and Development (OECD) has thirty member countries drawn from the most highly developed economies.

ameliorate these catastrophes, not how to prevent them from coming home. The consequences of truly catastrophic natural events have not threatened the democracies of India and Indonesia when they were struck; why should they undermine the more secure democracies of the West? In any case, such catastrophes, though of potentially enormous impact, are highly unlikely.

The agonizing problems within each of these arenas only appear when we begin to reflect on the changes currently under way in the constitutional order of states—the transition from nation states to market states. This transition will change the nature of terrorism because terrorism, as we shall see in the next chapter, is an incident of the underlying constitutional order. Different constitutional orders spawn different terrorisms. Similarly, the emergence of market states will radically redistribute the availability of WMD owing to the development of clandestine markets. Finally the realities that are bringing this new constitutional order into being also render our infrastructures so much more fragile that even the wealthiest states— indeed, especially the wealthiest states—will face insecurities hitherto thought to be the domain of the poorest countries while the most insular states will be as exposed as the most porous and cosmopolitan. This book will examine what happens when these three consequences of constitutional and international change—the changing nature of terrorism, the widening proliferation of WMD, and the heightened vulnerability of the tangible and intangible infrastructures of developed states—interact. This interplay is one of the subjects of this book because the effort to preclude the interaction of these three elements is a motive force behind the Wars against Terror.

Terrorism will become a far more important security issue because market state terrorists, unlike their twentieth century predecessors, would actually use WMD against civilians. But how would they get these weapons, which are at present monopolized by a small number of states and require vast plant and expenditure to develop over many years? WMD will radically proliferate because nuclear weapons will become commodified* and offered for sale on an international clandestine market, while biological weapons will be easily and cheaply created owing to the Internet-assisted dispersal of knowledge, which will allow developers to bypass the difficult initial stages of recombinant DNA techniques, and even the need to culture viruses and bacteria.

But why would states *want* to acquire WMD and why in the world would they want to give them or sell them to terrorists? Proliferation by

---

*The *commodification* of WMD occurs when it is no longer necessary for a state to develop these weapons through a lengthy indigenous process, because the state can buy the necessary components and technologies in the marketplace.

and to states will occur because some states fear outside intervention. Fearing intervention by powerful states like the U.S., some countries will want weapons to deter interveners. Such intervention has occurred to pre-empt terrorists (as in Afghanistan) or to prevent human rights abuses (as in Kosovo) or to preclude proliferation itself (as in Iraq) or to enforce U.N. Security Council resolutions.*[13] Some states will share these weapons with terrorist networks[14] because these states cannot afford to confront the democracies or their military champion the U.S. directly, owing to over-whelming U.S. military superiority. Furthermore, some states will seek regional hegemony through "lateral" or "horizontal" deterrence—the strategy by which states like the U.S. are deterred from intervening in regional conflicts by the presence of WMD in the region.

Contemplating such eventualities, states such as the U.S. and the U.K., which have global interests that are quite vulnerable to unconventional, terrorist assaults, will come to believe that they must intervene in order to take precautions against terrorists developing ever more lethal attacks. States that are the target of intervention will conclude that they must ally themselves with and arm terrorists for otherwise they will surely be defeated conventionally. Therefore the states threatened by terrorists may conclude that they must intervene against terrorists and their collaborators before they are attacked. *We think terrorists will attack; so they think we think terrorists will attack; so they think we shall intervene; so they will attack; so we must.*

When states engaged in mass violations of human rights fear they will be the subject of humanitarian intervention, they attempt to arm themselves with WMD. Were terrorists to deploy WMD (acquired perhaps by stealth from states that dare not attack the U.S. and its allies directly), they would suddenly become really threatening. Thus when states fear campaigns against them for regime change either because they support terrorists or engage in terror against their own people, they seek WMD to deter those campaigns. *We think certain hostile states will seek WMD; so those states think we think they will seek WMD; so they think we will preempt; so they must acquire WMD; so we must preempt.*

A state's campaigns against its own civilians proceed at a rapid pace because they use organized violence against unarmed or lightly armed persons. When a state attacks another state, it attacks an army; when it attacks its own civilians it turns an army loose on an undefended populace. Before any humanitarian mission can act to protect these victims, hundreds of thousands can die. *We think certain oppressive governments will pursue genocide or ethnic violence among their own populations; so they think we*

*What Noam Chomsky sarcastically calls the "new military humanism."

think they will attempt genocide; so they think we will intervene; so they
must attempt genocide before we intervene; so we must intervene.[15]

It is the speed, scale, and irreversibility of adverse change that drives these whirlpools of reasoning. As we shall see, it is now possible for states and terror groups to arm themselves with WMD in a small fraction of the time it has hitherto taken. Once they are so armed, there is no undoing the danger, and the same is even true of mass violence with ordinary weapons when it is pursued against a defenseless domestic population.

For the past half century we could say that the states of the West and their peoples would remain remarkably safe from international violence as long as they could provide reassurance that they would stay out of the affairs of other states no matter how odious ("peaceful coexistence," it was called in the era that has just passed), and reassure their own publics that they would not significantly modify their customary liberties in a panicky reaction to what violence did ensue (reactions that, by and large, they were able to avoid).

The reason this reasonable course of action is not a realistic option has to do with the ending of that period—the end of the era of the constitutional order of the twentieth century nation state—and the change in the constitutional order that end is bringing about. The very success of the parliamentary democracies in the Long War* of the twentieth century has created the conditions for a new kind of conflict. Our control of the acute problem of superpower conflict has indirectly promoted chronic problems; indeed the better the technologies and strategies for the acute threats of the Long War became, the more severe have become the chronic consequences.[16] These consequences are bringing about a new constitutional order. As the 2005 Royal Dutch Shell Scenarios put it:

> [T]he gradual transition from the Nation State to the Market State model implies a redefinition of the state's fundamental promises: [from maximisation of the Nation's welfare] toward maximisation of opportunities for . . . civil society and citizens. States in the advanced market democracies do not define their own success in terms of being able to resist market forces, as in Europe not long ago, but in terms of

*The Long War of 1914–1990 embraced the First World War, the Bolshevik Revolution, the Spanish Civil War, the Second World War, the Korean and Vietnam wars, and the Cold War. See Bobbitt, *Shield of Achilles*, book I, part I. The Bush administration has used the term, interestingly, for the war on terror. See Bradley Graham and Josh White, "Abizaid Credited with Popularizing the Term 'Long War,' " *Washington Post*, 3 February 2006, p. A8. ("It also was a name proposed by . . . Philip Bobbitt to cover a collection of 20th century conflicts, from World War I to the Cold War, which resulted in democracy triumphing over communism and fascism.") See also Philip Bobbitt, "Get Ready for the Next Long War," *Time*, 9 September 2002, p. 84.

fostering market expansion to [provide] a wide range of public . . . goods.[17]

Market states undertake to change the bargain offered for power by changing the basis for legitimacy. The strategic raison d'être of the market state is the protection of civilians, not simply territory or national wealth or any particular dynasty, class, religion, or ideology. Of course, states have long sought to protect their populations from violence (though this was not their paramount objective). Had nation states been able to protect civilians successfully, had their conventional wisdom proved wise and prudent, such states might have survived with *their* basis for legitimacy—the promise of ever-improving material well-being—intact. During the era of twentieth century industrial nation states, however, the ratio of military to civilian casualties in war almost reversed, so that by the end of the century more than 80 percent of the dead and wounded in warfare were civilians. That failure is one factor driving the state's transition to a new constitutional order. As the British statesman Douglas Hurd put it:

> The world is run on a paradox. On the one hand, the essential focus of loyalty remains the nation state and there are nearly two hundred of these. On the other hand, no nation state, not even the single superpower the United States of America, is capable of delivering to its citizens single-handed the security, the prosperity and the decent environment which the citizens demand.[18]

Market states take up the challenge of protecting civilians and place it center stage in the life of the State. The stakes are achingly high. An avian flu epidemic—whether engineered by a state and given to terrorists or created by them (the genetic code of the 1918 avian flu that killed 50 million persons has now been posted on the Internet) or naturally occurring—could strike globally with an unprecedented velocity. Similarly a nuclear device detonated in a major twenty-first century city could dwarf the casualties at Hiroshima. These new vulnerabilities have important implications not just for diplomacy, but also for precautionary interventions and anticipatory preemptions. In addition to deploying these preclusive tactics, market states will be able to marshal many assets—relative nimbleness and dexterity in adapting to technological change, devolution, the use of private entities as partners, and global networks of communications—that were denied to nation states in their struggle against terror.

Waging wars against terror[19] is a historic struggle to preclude a world in which terror rather than consent establishes the State's legitimacy. What is at stake in the wars against terror is nothing less than building a basis of legitimacy for the new, emerging constitutional order.

If we want to defeat state-shattering terror in the twenty-first century, we will have to develop specific, comprehensive, and mutually entailed strategic doctrines that prescribe how we are to prevent the proliferation of weapons of mass destruction, mass terrorist atrocities, and humanitarian crises that bring about or are brought about by terror. If we want to maintain the rule of law domestically and restore the rule of law internationally, we will have to change the prevailing legal doctrines of sovereignty and universality in order to create a world in which law reinforces, and is reinforced by, the strategic position of the democracies.[20]

Many persons are at present quite properly concerned with the threat to constitutionalism, to rights and liberties, by their governments' reaction to the threat posed by terrorism.[21] Few of us consider, however, that terrorism itself might become a threat to the legitimacy of those states that depend upon the consent of the governed.[22] The twentieth century wars of which the Long War was composed taught us that *states* posed the principal, indeed the only, threat to our liberties, and now we remain trapped in this idea.

WINNING AND LOSING WARS AGAINST TERROR

The states of consent—"the West," broadly defined to include democratic states like Australia, Japan, Indonesia, Singapore, South Korea, South Africa, and India—are not winning the Wars against Terror though they have made considerable progress against al Qaeda.

Since the September 11 attacks, the United States has invoked the war power of the U.S. Constitution against terrorists. In an unprecedented action, American allies endorsed action on the basis of Article 5 of the North Atlantic Treaty, which provides that an attack on one member of the Alliance shall be treated as an attack on all.[23] The U.S. Congress, the British Parliament, and other governing bodies have passed various statutes aimed at making the prosecution and detection of terrorists easier. The United States has reorganized its bureaucracy and authorized vast new funding for fighting terrorism. Coalitions led by the U.S. and the U.K. have invaded and conquered Iraq in a campaign to prevent the proliferation of WMD (among other reasons), and the U.N. has sanctioned, for the first time, the invasion of a member state, Afghanistan, in order to suppress terrorism. Much of the senior leadership of al Qaeda has been killed or detained. Nearly 3,400 of its fighters are either dead or in prison. Two-thirds of the persons known to intelligence agencies at the outset of this war have been sequestered. The planners behind the al Qaeda attacks on American embassies in 1998, the USS *Cole* in 2000, and the September 11 atrocities have been killed or arrested, along with Osama bin Laden's regional coordinators in Southeast Asia, Europe, and the Middle East.[24] What remains of al Qaeda's leadership—the senior figures of bin Laden and his deputy Ayman al-Zawahiri—is in hiding. State practices of ethnic cleansing in Bosnia, in Kosovo and in Indonesia, as well as vicious religious repression in Afghanistan, were halted through concerted multilateral action.

Yet at the same time, al Qaeda has continued to strike; indeed there has been a drumbeat of violence, and far from abating since the invasion of Iraq, it has picked up momentum. Since 9/11, al Qaeda and its network of affiliates have carried out countless attacks. Among the most significant:

- On October 12, 2002, al Qaeda bombers killed 202 persons at nightclubs in Bali;
- On August 19, 2003, truck bombs destroyed the U.N. headquarters in Baghdad, killing 22, including U.N. envoy Sergio Viera de Mello, and injuring 200;
- On August 29, 2003, car bombers near the Imam Ali Mosque in Najaf killed at least 125, including Shiite cleric Mohammed Baqir al-Hakim, and injured 100;
- On February 27, 2004, terrorists attacked a superferry outside Manila, killing 116 persons;
- On March 2, 2004, suicide bombers linked to al Zarqawi, then leader of al Qaeda in Iraq, targeted Shiites celebrating Ashura; using improvised explosive devices (IED) and grenades they attacked the Holy Shrine of al Kadhamiya in Baghdad and the al Hussein and al Abbas Mosques in Karbala, killing nearly 200 and injuring hundreds;
- On March 11, 2004, bombers targeted the Atocha train station in Madrid, killing 191 and injuring 600;
- On July 7, 2005, suicide bombers targeted the public transport system in London killing passengers on the Underground and on a bus, killing 52 and injuring nearly 700 people;
- On September 29, 2005, al Qaeda coordinated three suicide car bomb attacks on a market and the surrounding shops in Balad, killing 103 and injuring 110;
- On November 9, 2005, suicide bombers targeted Western hotels in Amman, Jordan, killing 60 and injuring 115;
- On February 22, 2006, al Qaeda conducted its most successful strike since 9/11, destroying the Shiite al Askariya Golden Dome Mosque in Samarra, igniting sectarian violence that has killed thousands of Iraqi civilians, both Shia and Sunni;
- On April 11, 2007, suicide bombers in Algeria attacked a government building and police station in Algiers and Bab Ezzouar, killing 33 and injuring 222;

- On June 13, 2007, bombers once again attacked the Golden Dome Mosque, destroying both minarets.

Indeed, though we have made progress in many cases, one especially experienced commentator concluded in June 2007 that al Qaeda "is a more dangerous enemy today than it has ever been before."* Al Qaeda today is a sophisticated operation—with a sophisticated propaganda machine based in Pakistan, a secondary but independent base in Iraq, and an expanding reach in Europe. Its leadership is intact. Its decentralized command control structure has allowed it to survive the loss of key operatives such as Zarqawi. Its Taliban allies are making a comeback in Afghanistan, and it is certain to get a big boost there if NATO pulls out. It will also claim a victory when U.S. forces start withdrawing from Iraq. "The waves of the fierce crusader campaign against the Islamic world have broken on the rock of the Mujahideen and have reached a dead end in Iraq and Afghanistan," a spokesperson for the newly proclaimed Islamic State of Iraq said on November 29, 2006. "For the first time since the fall of the Ottoman caliphate in the past century, the region is witnessing the revival of Islamic caliphates."[25] The deadliest year of terrorist violence in two decades occurred in 2003. It was succeeded by an even deadlier year in 2004, and if we exclude terrorism waged by states, this was the deadliest year on record to date. In Bali, Kenya, Pakistan, Tunisia, Afghanistan, Iraq, Israel, and Morocco, as many people have been killed and wounded in terrorist attacks since September 11 as died on that day, itself the single most deadly terrorist attack in history. In the period from the defeat of the Taliban to mid-2004, more than 1,200 persons died in attacks from global jihadists *outside* Palestine, Kashmir, and Iraq. Virtually every week, American and British soldiers and Western civilians are killed in terrorist attacks. Arab television networks and al Qaeda websites show the beheading of innocent persons, a grotesque coup de théâtre never before depicted on television. U.S. and U.K. citizens, and noncitizens who are in American or British custody, have seen their rights diminish, some markedly. As Americans experience countless alerts, color-coded to indicate threat levels, they can reasonably conclude that they are less safe than before—if only somewhat so—and there are some who believe, unreasonably perhaps, that they are less safe than ever.

On October 9, 2006, North Korea announced that, despite six-power talks aimed at forestalling such an event, it had developed nuclear warheads and had conducted its first nuclear weapons test; this followed a provocative firing of a ballistic missile over the Sea of Japan. Iran is

*This was Bruce Riedel, former Senior Director for Near East Affairs at the U.S. National Security Council. See "Al Qaeda Strikes Back," *Foreign Affairs*, May–June 2007.

widely believed to be ardently pursuing the development of its nuclear arsenal. A commercial network has been exposed, though possibly not eliminated, that trades in Pakistani nuclear technology, Chinese warhead design, North Korean nuclear materials, and Ukrainian missiles. Genocide on a scale not seen since Rwanda is, at this writing, under way in Sudan while irregular warfare continues on a horrific scale in central Africa. In Iraq, a Sunni insurgency has used terror to attempt to prevent the creation of a democratic state. Terrorists in July 2005 murdered Sunni members of the committee drafting a proposed Iraqi constitution, kidnapped and killed Arab diplomats accredited to the new Iraqi regime, killed Saddam Hussein's defense attorneys, and exploded a truck bomb outside a Shiite mosque south of Baghdad. Shia militias in Iraq have responded with a sectarian campaign of assassinations, ethnic cleansing, and torture. A month before, in the U.S., Hurricane Katrina devastated coastal Louisiana, Mississippi, and Alabama, killing many thousands and causing more than $25 billion in damage while leaving 80 percent of New Orleans under water. The Iraqi violence and the hurricane, which at first glance seem so remote from one another and so unrelated, have exposed the inability of current U.S. force planning to protect civilians. As Richard Fallon has observed, "Market states may be particularly vulnerable both to some things that they in one way or another help to cause (maybe the proliferation of weapons of mass destruction) and to some things for which they bear no causal responsibility (such as earthquakes)."[26]

According to data released by the U.S. Central Intelligence Agency in the spring of 2006, there were 11,111 terrorist incidents in 2005, in which more than 14,600 civilian noncombatants were killed.[27] Figures in the State Department's annual report on terrorism disclosed a 400 percent increase compared with 2004.[28]

We are not winning the Wars against Terror because the developments that empower terror are gaining—as markets increase, as weapons technologies diffuse, as clandestine communications become more effective and infrastructures more fragile—at a faster pace than our defenses, our preemptive strategies, and our legal institutions are adapting. There is a widespread sense in the West of the unavoidability of further major terrorist attacks on the scale of the 9/11 atrocity, and many professional analysts expect that terrorists will acquire and use weapons of mass destruction, indeed that it is inevitable that they will do so. Yet the likeliest eventuality, at least in the near term, remains a natural disaster or conventional infrastructure attack that devastates a highly populated area.

"Strategy" concerns the role of the State in defending itself from violence from other states, while "law" has to do with the role of the State in monopolizing legitimate violence within its own borders. In the twentieth century it made sense to separate law and strategy; indeed, I will argue that this separation was a key to our successes in the fields of both national and international security during that century. Quite naturally, states of consent rely on habits of mind that are associated with the strategies by which the democratic nations in the past century successfully protected themselves from aggression and largely avoided domestic repression. Nevertheless, this particular habit of insulating law from strategy (and vice versa) can contribute to our defeat in the century we have just entered because the threats posed by twenty-first century terrorists do not arise from the politics of a hostile nation state—such threats were the domain of strategy, not law—nor do they arise solely from causes within a national polity.

We tend to associate terrorism with institutions that command power within but not among states, that is, in the domain of law, not strategy. Yet twenty-first century terrorism, as we shall see, is unlike that of the preceding century in that it possesses a significant strategic dimension. To combat twenty-first century terrorism, we shall have to think in terms of strategic doctrines that reinforce the legal institutions that command power among states as well as anticipatory legal institutions that operate strategically within our borders—that is, we have to think in terms of the confluence of strategy and law.

At present, however, the response by states of consent to all three of the essential theaters of the Wars against Terror—global, networked terrorism; the proliferation of WMD; and the increasing vulnerability of civilians to humanitarian crises—suffers from this separating of law and strategy. With respect to terrorism, the U.S. has greatly jeopardized its war aims by its lawless behavior at its penal colonies, while weakening the pursuit of its legal objectives through a persistent inability to persuade public opinion, in America and abroad, that the U.S. is at war and to develop the appropriate tactics for such warfare. Weapons proliferation has quickened in several states that are signatories to the Nuclear Nonproliferation Treaty (NPT), yet there is no consensus on a doctrine for preemption in the face of an NPT withdrawal (or cheating). Indeed at present states have been unable to agree to make the NPT mandatory or agree on what to do if the provisions of the treaty are used by a state as a halfway house on the road to weapons deployment or even if the treaty is openly violated. Finally, the legal response to the humanitarian crisis in the U.S. caused by Hurricane Katrina is perhaps epitomized by the Defense Department's reliance on a reading of the Posse Comitatus Act that forbids the use of American defense forces for law enforcement tasks (even though these essentially constabulary duties are precisely what much modern warfare will largely consist of), and by the aptly named Homeland Security Department, which was created at precisely the moment when the boundaries between domestic and foreign threats were being erased and the necessity to protect allies was intensifying.

Having detached strategy from law, military successes by the U.S. and its allies bring a loss of legitimacy in their wake—at Abu Ghraib, in Basra, at Guantánamo—while many efforts to rely on the architecture of our constitutional and international legal institutions actually weaken our strategic efforts—as we saw in Madrid in the spring of 2004 and repeatedly at the U.N. with regard to Iraq, Rwanda, Sudan, Iran, and North Korea. Without legal reform to bring international and domestic law into accord with the strategic context, and a thorough rethinking of doctrines of warfare to integrate regard for law into our strategic missions, we simply cannot win these wars. We wish to disorient those who would make us fearful; instead it is we who are disoriented. We bicker among ourselves, and the fear that might have united us will be the force that splinters our unity.

Our current strategy is to kill or capture the terrorists before a catastrophic attack happens. Yet Secretary of Defense Donald Rumsfeld questioned this approach[29] as ably as anyone in a memorandum of October 2003 that asked, "Does the US need to fashion a broad, integrated plan to stop the next generation of terrorists? The US is putting relatively little effort into a long-range plan, but we are putting a great deal of effort into trying to stop terrorists."[30] I believe we are misguided to ask only, "Who are the terrorists and why do they hate us?" Rather we should also ask, "Who are we and how have we organized ourselves such that terror could become an historical inevitability?"

Chief among our defenses are our ingenuity and adaptability, and yet it is there that we are most bereft. This is not a comment on the difficulties of formulating public policy or collecting intelligence. Rather, we do not sufficiently understand the symbiotic relationship between strategy and law—between what we do to protect ourselves from others, and what we do to protect ourselves from each other—and how that relationship is changing with the emergence of a new constitutional order.

We must step back and ask the most basic questions about the Wars against Terror. Do we know how to win such wars, in the way that we knew what we had to do to defeat the Axis powers in the Second World War? Are we developing new strategic doctrines of the kind[31] we had to develop to contain the Soviet Union in the context of mutual nuclear deterrence in the Cold War? Are we writing new international law and creating new institutions to cope with global problems in the twenty-first century, in the way we did when we faced similar global challenges after the First World War in the twentieth century? I think the answers to all these questions are dismayingly evident.

Time will bring forth new and more lethal terrorist groups long after al Qaeda is defeated. We must configure our forces to respond when we don't know, and can't quickly find out, whether the source of a catastrophic event is a natural event or one caused by terrorists because the political result—increasing terror and the delegitimation of government by consent—is the same in either case owing to the new bases for legitimacy arising with the twenty-first century constitutional order.

One cannot say precisely how long we have. We must urgently begin this fundamental rethinking. The terror that threatens states of consent is not exogenous. It hardly matters whether the forces of destruction arise from militant Islam, North Korean communism, or Caribbean hurricanes. Rather the sort of terror that threatens states arises not simply from ephemeral international politics but is endemic to the unique vulnerabilities of globalized, networked market states.

Yet as Henry Kissinger insightfully concluded, while "the U.S. administration has been right to recognize terror as a global problem that is deeply threatening, the U.S. has not been able to operationalize a response or develop a language to discuss it."[32]

Three days after the terrorist attacks of September 11, 2001, the United States authorized warfare "in order to prevent any future acts of international terrorism against the United States."[33] One year later, the U.S. Congress authorized the use of the armed forces to wage war against Iraq in order to "enforce all relevant United Nations Security Council Resolutions regarding Iraq," which included resolutions condemning Iraq's attempts to procure weapons of mass destruction and its mass human rights abuses. Two years later, in response to a devastating tsunami, the *Abraham Lincoln* carrier strike group led 18,000 U.S. troops in a relief effort on behalf of the Indonesian democracy.

These declarations and these actions by the armed forces compose elements of the Wars against Terror. This book attempts to set that struggle in a certain context: strategic, legal, and historical. It suggests a way to understand a war on terror, and, most important, why it is necessary to factor future possible worlds into decisions taken when waging such a war. Therefore this book is not principally about al Qaeda and the anti-Western revolution within Islam. Ultimately, it is about the changing nature of the use of force in establishing conditions of consent and legitimacy when confronting terror. This confrontation will transform the emerging constitutional order of the twenty-first century State.

It used to be that democracy, human rights, and international institutions were taken to be separate, detached terms. "Democracy" was a contested term among the parties to the twentieth century's ideological wars among nation states. Hitler, Mao, and Stalin claimed to govern "true democracies," and so there was no necessary link between democracy and the protection of human rights. Similarly, the domain of international institutions was believed to exclude the internal practices of states, including both their systems of governance and their behavior toward their own citizens. The U.N. Committee on Human Rights has room for the representatives of dictatorships, authoritarian monarchies, even theocracies. American racists in the 1950s, who were concerned that the U.N. Charter might interfere with racial segregation, were soothingly reassured that international institutions could not penetrate the sovereignty of their member nation states.

Moreover, whatever connections may have existed among these three subjects, none was thought to be relevant to terrorism. In the main it was a national problem; the U.N. couldn't agree even on a definition of terrorism for just that reason—that it was composed of nation states. Human-rights-protecting democracies like the U.K. were attacked by terrorists, but so were human-rights-abusing dictatorships like Liberia and Serbia.

Now, however, we are beginning to appreciate that states of consent are intimately connected to the protection of human rights—indeed, that protecting human rights is their reason for being—and that international institutions have a responsibility to protect persons from their own governments when these rights are grossly violated. We are beginning to see also that the security of democratic societies, the centrality of human rights, and the vitality of consensual international institutions are critical to combating terror. None can flourish in an atmosphere of terror, and each has a critical role in defeating this threat to governments that are based on consent. Robust democracies that enforce human rights guarantees and vigorous global institutions that support human rights will not of themselves assure victory in the Wars against Terror. Without them, however, we will surely lose that conflict. Indeed, they are what these wars will be fought over because, as we shall see, their evolution is what has brought about this conflict in the first place.[34]

In the next chapter, therefore, we will begin with a brief historical review of the differing modes of terrorism and how these correlate to the development of the constitutional order of the State.

PART I

THE IDEA OF A WAR AGAINST TERROR

Happiness depends on being free, and freedom depends on being courageous . . . But the man who can most truly be accounted [courageous] is he who best knows the meaning of what is sweet in life and of what is terrible, and then goes out undeterred to meet what is to come.

—Thucydides[1]

CHAPTER ONE

The New Masque of Terrorism

Morano: What are you, Friend?

Polly: A young Fellow, who hath been robb'd by the World; and I came on purpose to join you, to rob the World by way of Retaliation. An open War with the whole World is brave and honourable. I hate the clandestine pilfering War that is practis'd among Friends and Neighbors in civil Societies.

—John Gay, *The Beggar's Opera*, 2.5.21–22[1]

WARFARE and the constitutional order exist in a mutually affecting relationship.[2] Fundamental innovations in war bring about fundamental transformations in the constitutional order of states, while transformations in the constitutional order bring about fundamental changes in the conduct and aims of war. Terrorism has been, by contrast, merely a symptom, not a driver of this phenomenon. As we shall see, this accounts for the odd fact that terrorism surges after the end of the epochal wars by which the constitutional order is changed, after the peace congresses have convened to ratify that change. The difference in the current era is that now terrorists are about to acquire the weapons and strategies previously reserved to states at war, and they thus will acquire also the potential to affect the basic constitutional order.

It is a popular European retort to American policy since September 11 to say that the only thing new about the attacks on that day is that U.S. citizens were the victims. Societies that have endured assaults by the IRA, ETA, the PLO, and the FLN are skeptical about American perceptions of terrorism. It is natural, it is said, that the Americans, being unused to such incidents, should exaggerate their importance and their novelty. Older, wiser societies know how to handle such matters—and it is not with their defense departments.[3] Panic and overreaction are characteristic of a failure to put events in perspective.

In pondering these sometimes phlegmatic, sometimes shrill rebukes, one should bear in mind that approximately one-third of all the international terrorist attacks between 1968 and September 10, 2001, involved American targets. American diplomats, military personnel, and businessmen were murdered on several continents. In this period more American officials died from terrorist attacks than British during the same period of IRA depredations. One should also note that the onslaughts on New York and Washington on September 11, 2001, killed more persons than all terrorist attacks on British, French, and German targets since 1988 combined, and indeed fatalities were greater than all deaths from transnational terrorism during this period.[4] Finally, to miss the distinctiveness, the novelty of 9/11, as it has come to be called,[5] is to misapprehend what has happened to terrorism—its structure, its tactics and weapons, and its targets. When one fully appreciates this point, one sees al Qaeda in a way that reflects its singular deadliness and that redefines terrorism itself.

"Asymmetric warfare" is the use of unconventional means to attack a superior conventional force. It has existed at least since David and Goliath. Similarly the use of terror, associated with particular religious and ethnic groups, has a long history, and bands of holy warriors have killed civilians to achieve political objectives from ancient times. In first-century Judaea, Jewish terrorists struggled against the Roman occupation. One such group, known as the Sicarii (dagger wielders), often attacked Jewish collaborators. Another terrorist group, the Zealots, brazenly slit the throats of Roman officials. By striking in public places, like crowded markets, in daylight,[6] they seemed to underscore the inability of the Empire to ensure security. These groups had several advantages over their Roman occupiers, including especially initiative. They chose when to attack and then melted back into the non-Roman population that was indifferent or hostile to the occupation, and terrified of retribution by terrorists against anyone found to be a Roman informant.[7]

In seventh century India, the Thuggee cult ritually strangled travelers as sacrifices to the Hindu deity Kali. The terrorist's intent was to frighten his victim—an important element in the Thuggee ritual—rather than to motivate political action* by third parties. The cult endured over more than six hundred years and may have killed as many as 500,000 persons.[8]

In the eleventh century a Shia sect known as the Ismaili fedayeen attacked Christian occupiers and those Sunni officials who refused to adopt an especially ascetic version of Islam. These victims were often kidnapped and held captive and frequently killed. On occasion they might even be murdered at close quarters, surrounded by their bodyguards. These tactics revealed "a willingness to die in pursuit of their mission

---

*The political motive essential to terrorism includes more than simply a particular policy program. Inducing a state of terror is itself a political objective when its object is an entire society.

echoed by today's suicide bombers. While they are particularly remembered for attacking the Crusaders, most of their targets were other Muslims . . ."[9] Apologists of the ruling dynasty called these attackers
"hashshashin" because, it was alleged,[10] they would eat hashish before
murdering their victims and, in this state, were promised heavenly
rewards—including the abundant companionship of virgins. Our word
"assassin" is derived from *"hashshashin."*

These words from mankind's past—"assassins," "thugs," "zealots"— have
passed into modern English. It is not hard to see parallels between these
historical groups and those of the present; indeed, the references to
empire, religious fanaticism, the targeting of collaborators, ritual killings,
suicide missions, and the rest will be familiar to anyone who has lived in
the first decade of the twenty-first century. That does not mean, however,
that terrorism has existed essentially unchanged.

As we shall see, terrorism exists as an epiphenomenon of the constitutional order. This was true even in the medieval period, when the constitutional order had yet to metamorphose into the first modern states. The
terrorism of the Crusaders is a case in point. In his sacerdotal role, min-
gling military and ecclesiastical values, the Crusader was unlike earlier
and subsequent terrorists owing to his having arisen in the context of a feudal constitutional order. Yet a terrorist he was, though his "chivalric theatre
masked . . . many awful atrocities" including

> ferocious pogroms against Jews that were features of the preliminaries
> of many crusades, [and] gross examples of ethnic cleansing in which
> non-Christians were driven from towns of religious or strategic signif-
> icance by deliberate campaigns of terror . . .[11]

The failure to understand the unique motivations of the early Crusaders
has led generations of historians to make anachronistic assessments of the
Crusaders' motives. Each historian has tended to portray the Crusaders in
light of his [that is, the historian's] preoccupations—a not unusual phenomenon, but one that, ironically, is as period bound as the Crusaders' own
preoccupations. Nineteenth century interpreters thus described the Crusades as early examples of European economic expansion; their contemporaries characterized the Crusades as driven by imperialist motives. A
French historian of this period took the conquests of the Crusaders to be
"the first French empire."[12] Twentieth century Arab nationalists turned this
idea around and saw the Crusades as a species of ethnic exploitation.
Twentieth century Marxists proffered the theory that rising European pop-

ulations forced the landed aristocracy to take new measures to prevent the division of their estates, including primogeniture, which brought about a surplus of young males who had to be distracted by foreign adventures.

There is no evidence to support any of these claims, Jonathan Riley-Smith, professor of ecclesiastical history at Cambridge, has concluded.

> One should not criticise crusaders for being what they were not. They were not imperialists [of the nineteenth century state nation] or colonialists [of the eighteenth century territorial states]. They were not simply after land or booty [like the terrorists of the kingly states of the seventeenth century] . . . They were pursuing an ideal that, however alien it seemed to later generations of historians, was enthusiastically supported at the time by . . . St Bernard of Clairvaux and St Thomas Aquinas.[13]

That ideal—of sacred violence sanctioned by the pope, and penitential service in warfare—is a consequence of the feudal order, with its intermixture of knightly duties in war and religious obedience to the Church.

Modern terrorism thus arises with the birth of the modern state because terrorism is not simply tied to the use of violence to achieve political goals—that is, strategy—but is also linked to law. It is a necessary element in terrorism that it be directed against lawful activities. Modern terrorism is a secondary effect of the State's monopoly on legitimate violence, a monopoly ratified in law.

In each era, terrorism derives its ideology in reaction to the raison d'être of the dominant constitutional order, at the same time negating and rejecting that form's unique ideology but mimicking the form's structural characteristics. For example, if the State exists to forge the identity of the nation, its terrorists will deny all nationality and justify their works as necessary to forge an international identity, but they will be careful to adopt the meritocratic promotions and self-sacrificing ethos of the imperial state nation they attack. If the State exists to aggrandize the wealth of its territorial aristocracy, its terrorists will reject territorial definitions of citizenship and live in foreign climes while copying the State's mercantile methods and massacring natives with the professionalized forces that replaced mercenaries and were a watermark of territorial states. A state devoted to enhancing the sectarian perquisites of one particular prince will find it has evoked a permanent terrorist mercenary force—available to anyone—but one that, like this sort of state, reflects the most severe sectarian prejudices. A state whose constitutional order validates its actions by measuring them against the ruthless aggrandizement of dynastic glory by war will spawn a terrorism that is egalitarian but equally prone to aggrandizement by means of warfare based on claims of absolute sovereignty.

In the examples that follow, two dimensions should be borne in mind: what makes these various groups terrorists—their attacks on civilians and their adversarial relationship to states—and what makes them distinctive in each era—their relationship to the prevailing constitutional order of that era.

I.

The *princely states** of the Renaissance, the first modern states, created a distinctive form of terrorism. The consolidation of the state from its feudal and oligarchical origins drove Italian city groups like the *fuorisciti* to attack civilians as a political reaction to exclusion from power. The most important terrorists, however, were those drawn from the very forces the new states were compelled to employ to protect themselves. When the technology of warfare made feudal knights pathetically vulnerable, the mercenaries to which princely states turned were often liable to take their tactics of terror and turn them against innocent civilians in order to achieve the respectable war aim of enriching themselves and tormenting those religious sects they despised.

This was the case in the sack of Rome on May 6, 1527, by troops of the greatest of the princely states, that of Holy Roman emperor Charles V. Despite his historic triumph over the French army in Italy at Pavia in 1525, Charles's ally, the Bourbon Duke of Milan, found himself unable to pay his troops. Some 20,000 men, drawn from the mercenary forces of the emperor, rejected his command and turned against Rome, which was the object of hatred for the mercenary Protestant Germans known as the *landsknecht*s. Urged most pitilessly by these German mercenaries, this army attacked Rome—hitherto regarded as inviolable—in an orgy of rape, plunder, torture, and killing that lasted for more than seven months until it abandoned the city to plague.

All that happened cannot really be regarded with surprise because the imperial army and in particular Frundsberg's lansquenets, were ani-

---

*In this section—indeed throughout this chapter—I will offer only the briefest caricatures of the successive constitutional orders of the modern state from its birth in Italy at the time of the Renaissance. This depiction of the development of the modern state is pursued more thoroughly in *The Shield of Achilles: War, Peace, and the Course of History*. In the few pages I have available in the present work I can do no more than offer an instrumental sketch of these historical characterizations in order to show the contrasts between different modes of terrorism over time. See plates on pp. 190–91, infra.

mated by a violent spirit of crusade against the Pope. In front of Castel Sant'Angelo where the Pope had retreated, a parody of a religious procession was set up, in which Clement was asked to cede the sails and oars of the *"Navicella"* (boat of Peter) to Luther, and the angry soldiery shouted *"Vivat Lutherus pontifex!"* (Long live Luther, Pontiff!) The name of Luther was incised with the tip of a sword across the painting of the "Dispute of the Most Holy Sacrament" in the Rooms of Raffaello, out of disdain . . .[14]

Rome was reduced to fewer than 10,000 persons, and more than 50,000 were either driven from the city or perished. Cathedrals, churches, and shrines were pillaged. Of this mixture of amoral enrichment and intense sectarianism—so typical of the princely state itself—Luther wrote, "Christ reigns in such a way that the emperor who persecutes Luther for the pope is forced to destroy the pope for Luther." It wasn't the emperor who was in charge of these forces, however; after their mutiny, they became terrorists. This force separated itself from the state to which it owed only a contractual allegiance, and began attacking civilians and finally an undefended city for its own purposes.

Nothing was spared, sacred or profane. Clement VII's escape to and confinement within the walls of Castel Sant'Angelo until December, listening to the taunting of German mercenaries calling for his death and replacement by "Pope Luther," were the least of the indignities. Various cardinals and prelates, including one future Pope, Julius III, were humiliated and tortured, altars were ransacked, the Sistine Chapel used as a stable, riches confiscated, patients in hospitals and children in orphanages gratuitously butchered.[15]

Erasmus wrote to Jacopo Sadoleto (October 1, 1528) that not the city, but the world had perished.[16]

An almost equally infamous example of princely state terrorism occurred on November 4, 1576, when mercenaries from the Spanish *tercios* sacked Antwerp in three days of atrocities against the city's Flemish population. This time the mercenary force was composed of Catholics who hated and despised the thriving, Protestant merchant community. Motivated partly by lack of pay, and partly by rage at the wealthy, free-thinking city, they attacked the unarmed Protestant population, demanding money.

People who could not pay the soldiers were often hanged and tortured and to this day it is impossible to assess the number of people killed, raped or held to ransom. For as far as we can ascertain, some 8,000 people were killed. For many weeks Antwerp resembled one vast den of vice with troops gambling away their ill gotten gains in the Boarse.[17]

Known as the "Spanish Fury," the ensuing period of horror and cruelty toward the innocent was an event from which the city of Antwerp, formerly the most important financial city in Europe, never recovered. Of the city's 100,000 inhabitants in 1570, by 1590 no more than about 40,000 remained. Much as a mercenary force like the Protestant *landsknecht*s sacked papal Rome, *tercios* largely formed from Spanish Catholic recruits sacked Protestant Antwerp. "The Spanish troops who returned to Italy in May 1577, nine months after the notorious sack of Antwerp, took with them 2,600 tonnes of booty (and also remitted large sums of money, some of it derived from ransoms, by letters of exchange)."[18] The search for booty outside the laws of war, coupled with sectarian motives for violence entirely at odds with its putative client state, stains the Spanish Fury with the distinctive tincture of terrorism.

Perhaps the most striking example of princely state terrorism was provided by the Calvinist pirates who mixed fervent religious ideology with a taste for atrocities, very much as did the formidably sectarian princely state of the Habsburgs that was their target. In the years following the Treaty of Augsburg (1555), the Dutch revolt against Spain produced a number of violent refugees who made monasteries and clerical travelers their targets. Roving bands of these plunderers were called Wild Beggars or Forest Beggars. When they formed as corsair crews, they were called Sea Beggars. These murderous pirates preyed upon the Dutch coasts and estuaries, "pillaging, burning and slaying all whom they chose to treat as Catholic enemies. Priests and monks they put to death with horrible tortures; magistrates and officials of the government they held to high ransom." Suppressed for a time, in the latter half of the 1560s the Sea Beggars resurfaced as seafaring revolutionaries, winning an important victory over the Spanish fleet on July 10, 1568, at the Battle on Eems.

When William of Orange tried to form this group into a more regular naval force, he issued them letters of marque and reprisal. Such letters, issued by a sovereign, granted state authority to private parties to make war against the state's enemy and compensated them by promising them a share of the booty seized in warring. This early example of privatization allowed states to quickly put a naval force to sea without maintaining a permanent navy. In exchange for the prince's letter of marque, the Sea Beggars were required to conform to the Articles of War; to attack none but Spanish ships and carefully abate from molesting neutrals; to maintain a Protestant minister on each ship; to employ Dutch commanders; to receive on board only "folk of good name and fame," and to strictly punish all violence.

Disregarding these restrictions almost entirely, the Sea Beggars attacked vessels from any nation, terrorized fishing villages and committed numerous atrocities. "These irregular fleets, with ships procured in England, Holland, or Germany, were manned by mixed crews of refugees and desperadoes, French, Walloon, Dutch, or German, who soon carried on what was little less than miscellaneous piracy."[19]

Civilian vessels from the Dutch provinces were attacked. This, and diplomatic pressure from Spain, led to Queen Elizabeth's refusal in 1572 to allow the Beggars to refit in the English harbors to which they had repaired in the past. Forced to take refuge in the Maas, they seized the town of Brill by surprise, and, encouraged by their success, took the important seaport of Flushing. This ignited revolt in Holland, Zeeland, Utrecht, and Friesland, and proved to be an important turning point in the Dutch rebellion.

Each of these groups (the mutinous *tercios* and *landsknecht*s, the insurgent Sea Beggars) was associated with a state, but also separate from it;[20] each erupted with historic violence against unarmed civilians; and each could be characterized by the same sectarian motives that drove the princely state itself. They were terrorists owing to their violent attacks on civilians and the fact that they carried out such attacks in violation of the orders of the states with which they were allied, often using their assaults to gain leverage against the state that employed them; they were terrorists of the princely state because of their sectarianism and the mercenary character of their forces.

The *kingly state* took the Italian constitutional innovation—fundamentally, the objectification of the State—and united this with dynastic legitimacy. The result was a formidable creation that dominated Europe for the next century. The princely state had severed the person of the prince from his bureaucratic and military structure, thereby creating a state with attributes hitherto reserved to a human being. The kingly state—the constitutional order that by 1648 had superseded the princely state—reunited these two elements, monarch and state, creating an absolute sovereign and making of the king himself the State: *"L'état c'est moi."* [21]

The kingly state also bred its own terrorists. These we know as seventeenth century buccaneers, and although they were not wholly confined to harassing the Spanish trade from the Indies, they, like their twenty-first century counterparts, began by challenging the preeminent state of the day. Insofar as they were in league with one state or another—often Great Britain, France, or the Netherlands—we might call them today state-sponsored terrorists. Even though they had periods of legitimate privateering, they eventually turned their violence against noncombatants and neutrals in the service of their own remarkable political societies, which were notable for their ruthlessness, their egalitarianism, their racial and ethnic diversity, and their homosexuality.

Fissures in the façade of the kingly state appeared in the middle of the seventeenth century with the appearance of pirates both in Ireland and in the Scilly Isles. They were known as Sea Tories; the English state was too weak to suppress them. Then, with the English Civil War a body of men emerged who sailed to the East in order to plunder the poorly defended Moorish trade between India and Madagascar, selling their booty in New England or the Carolinas. They then turned their fabled covetousness toward the Spanish Main, which included Cartagena, Santiago, Porto Bello, Panama, and Santo Domingo. The enormous silver shipments of the second half of the seventeenth century went to Seville via the ports of the Spanish Main, then northward to the Yucatán Channel to catch the westerlies to Europe. This rich shipping vein was repeatedly opened by Caribbean pirates, the terrorists of the kingly state.[22]

As the Spanish military presence became overstretched, Spain's European rivals—who could not maintain fleets so far from Europe—employed "privateers," commissioned into an ad hoc navy with letters of marque, paid with a set share of whatever prizes they captured. These mercenary forces protected the local settlements from the Spanish and reaped lucrative sums by violating the Spanish embargo on trading with other European outposts. By the 1630s these had become known as "buccaneers." Using the mask of privateering they pursued the creation of an independent, non-dynastic sovereignty through terror. As terrorists, they became legendary for their cruelty to their defenseless civilian captives, and for their independent political agenda. This marked them as terrorists of the kingly state not simply because they served that constitutional order as mercenaries and preyed on civilians, but because they, like the kingly states that employed them, relied upon a nonsectarian ethos and claimed that the use of armed violence was lawful when authorized by a "sovereign."

The term "buccaneer" is derived via the French *"boucanier"* from "bukan," the Carib word for the method of preserving meat by smoking rather than salting; only the English used this word to refer to the pirates of the Caribbean. The French used *"filibustiers"* (from which our parliamentary term "filibuster" derives); the Dutch *"zeerovers,"* and the Spanish, tellingly, *"corsarios luteranos"* (Lutheran corsairs—a vestige of the terrorists who had attacked the Spanish princely state). These groups were composed of religious refugees, prisoners of war shipped to the Americas by Cromwell, exiled Huguenots, deported Irish, criminals, and runaway apprentices. Initially they were predominantly French, English, and Dutch but later they included large numbers of escaped African slaves.

By 1655, the buccaneers of Tortuga were calling themselves the Brethren of the Coast. Their armada had grown to the size of a state navy. These men were terrorists of remarkable savagery and bravery. More than 1,500 of various nationalities used Tortuga as their base, while the English pirates chose Port Royal, Jamaica. Between 1665 and 1671 the buccaneers sacked eighteen Spanish American cities, four towns, thirty-five villages, and captured countless ships.[23] Operating from Port Royal the Englishman Henry Morgan carried out a series of raids against virtually undefended cities on the Spanish Main, culminating with the dreadful sack of Panama in 1671. In 1697, however, Spain formally recognized all English and French occupied territories in the West Indies, ending the need for mercenaries to protect the islanders from Spanish attack. The status of privateer was withdrawn from the buccaneers by their state sponsors and the golden era of piracy and of kingly state terrorism began rapidly to wane.

What was the unique nature of this particular terrorism? When the buccaneer Samuel Bellamy invited the captain of a merchant vessel to join his pirate crew, the captain replied that "his conscience would not let him break the laws of God and man," to which Bellamy answered, "You are a devilish Conscience Rascal, damn ye. I am a free Prince, and I have as much Authority to make War on the whole World, as he who has a hundred Sail of Ships at Sea, and an Army of 100,000 men in the Field; and this my Conscience tells me . . ."[24] This remark ironically recalls Hobbes's idea of kingly state sovereignty by which he hoped to legitimate absolute rule. Without this foundation in sovereignty, Hobbes believed every man might think "himself to be so much master of whatsoever he possessed."[25] If Hobbes was the philosopher of the kingly state, Bellamy was its nemesis.[26] As one historian has noted, "[i]t is a common feature of . . . 'pirate ideology' that pirates thought of themselves as free kings, as autonomous individual [sovereigns]."[27]

Indeed, the pirates not only claimed sovereignty but practiced its prerogatives. When bounties were offered for their capture, the pirates responded by offering rewards for the kidnapping of officials. Pirate courts—called the "Distribution of Justice"—tried the captains and masters of merchant vessels "enquiring into the Manner of the Commander's Behaviour to their Men and those against whom Complaint was made [were] whipp'd and pickled."[28]

Each company lived under a written constitution, signed by every member of the crew to record his consent. The articles of Bartholomew Roberts's group began:

Every Man has a Vote in Affairs of Moment; has equal Title to the fresh Provisions, or strong Liquors, at any Time seized, and may use them at Pleasure, unless a Scarcity make it necessary, for the Good of all, to vote a Retrenchment.[29]

At this time the possession of firearms in Europe was restricted by law to members of the upper classes and their licensees. Weapons on a merchant ship were kept strictly under lock and key; the presence of armed marines in the states' navies was mainly to dissuade sailors from mutiny. But when the Dutch governor of Mauritius encountered a pirate company he recorded, in astonishment, that every member "had as much say as the captain and each man carried his own weapons in his blanket."[30]

. All booty was divided equally with the captain taking no more than one and a half shares. There was a formal system of compensation for the wounded ("If . . . any Man should lose a Limb, or become a Cripple in their Service, he was to have 800 Dollars, out of the publick stock, and for lesser Hurts, proportionately").[31] Pirate captains were elected and could be removed from office at any time by vote. All members of a crew had a vote regardless of previous social rank or occupation. A number of captains were Africans.[32]

B. R. Burg in his *Sodomy and the Pirate Tradition* chronicles the frequency of homosexuality among pirates.[33] Other scholars have argued that the homosexual pirate communities were a lure for men who "could not fit into the rigidly heterosexual model of a successful English citizen."[34] Whether or not this was the case, it is revealing that none of the pirate constitutions has any provision against homosexuality. It is known that the buccaneers of the period of the kingly state lived in male civil unions known as *matelotage*—possibly the origin of the word "mate"—holding their possessions in common with a right of survivorship should one partner die. Louis le Golif complained in his *Memoirs of a Buccaneer* that he was forced to fight two duels "to keep ardent suitors at bay."[35] These descriptions are consistent with the fact that the kingly state pirates—unlike, for example, the pirates of the South China Sea, who are organized in family groups—did not replenish their numbers with their children. Around 1650 the French governor of Tortuga imported several hundred female prostitutes to break the practice of *matelotage,* but it apparently continued with the adaptation that a partner shared his wife with his *matelot.*

In reaction to the discovery of the Americas and the vast riches this brought to Europe, kingly states without effective ocean navies had created the terrorists of the seventeenth century. In time, however, new technologies enabled ships to create a global network of exchange that dwarfed the previous trade in luxuries, and this in turn created a large population of seamen. When the *territorial states* of the eighteenth century began to achieve dominance, the partnership between terrorists and states collapsed. From roughly 1720 onwards, pirates were in open warfare with states that were determined to, and had the means to, capture and destroy them. European colonies on which the pirates had depended to fence the goods they seized were now more closely governed. The orderly mercantile spirit of the territorial states had little patience with the swashbuckling entrepreneurship of pirates. "Once British colonial and commercial dominance was established in the Caribbean, planters and merchants exerted pressure on the state to end the 'buccaneer era.' The pirates had served their purpose as terrorists . . ."[36]

Although a few decades earlier the British state had valued the terror that pirates spread through the Spanish-controlled Caribbean and South Sea islands and settlements, as Britain began to colonize some of these territories for itself, the British used laws, propaganda, and popular literature to vilify piracy and glorify imperial trade and colonial occupation.

As one commentator has observed:

> The decline of piracy in the Caribbean paralleled the decline of mercenaries . . . in Europe [and the creation of the professional armies of the territorial state]. Armies were codified and brought under Royal control and privateering was largely ended. . . . [N]avies were expanded and their mission was stretched to cover combating piracy.[37]

And another writer concurred that, with the Treaty of Utrecht in 1713, "the new, more powerful state consolidated its monopoly on violence. The state was fighting to allow commerce to flow unimpeded and capital to accumulate, bringing wealth to the merchants and revenue to the state."[38]

Territorial states had certain preoccupations that contrasted with those of the kingly state. Whereas a kingly state was organized around a person, the territorial state was defined by its geographical contiguity and therefore fretted constantly about its borders. For the territorial state, its frontiers defined its legitimacy, its defense perimeter, its tax base. Such states pursued similar diplomatic and strategic objectives, including rational borders; free seas and open markets (at least for their own colonial purposes); an international consensus that no state should be allowed to dominate the affairs of the others; secular state preferences in the international arena; and a continuous diplomatic dialogue.[39]

Piracy was transformed in reaction to the change in the constitutional order from kingly states to territorial states—with which it cooperated and contended, and on which it preyed. Territorial states had their pirates, to be sure, but these were no longer the terrorists of the era because the State had changed. Thereafter pirates were merely criminals. Henry Morgan had been knighted, Dampier had even become a patron of the Royal Society—but Captain Kidd was merely hanged after a trial by a special naval court.[40]

The eighteenth century terrorism of the colonial territorial states was in distinct contrast to that of the previous period. Two examples will suffice as illustrative: the use of Native Americans to terrorize colonists in the French and Indian wars of that century, and the organized extortions by the Barbary trading settlements that harassed shipping and enslaved captives seized at sea.

The war known in the U.S. today as the French and Indian War and almost everywhere else as the Seven Years' War began in North America and quickly spread to Europe when Britain declared war on France in 1756. It was the fourth and final major colonial war in a conflict composed also of King William's War (1689–97), Queen Anne's War (1702–14), and King George's War (1744–48). In all of these conflicts Native Americans were enlisted, principally by the French, to fight alongside colonial forces. The atrocities committed by these troops are well documented and may have increased the sense of fear among the Americans that led to the nineteenth century campaigns against Native Americans, at least some of which we would now call ethnic cleansing. For our purposes, it is significant that two great territorial states—Britain and France—used local indigenous tribes, mainly the Iroquois and the Algonquin, to terrorize the colonial population through a campaign of massacres, torture, and kidnapping. The motives of these states were essentially mercantile and commercial, not religious or dynastic. Whereas the kingly state had delegated campaigns to privateers and the earlier princely state to condottieri, when the territorial states privatized violence they carefully interpenetrated the chain of command with their own officers.

Any discussion of the terrorism of this era must also include an account of the Barbary settlements that menaced European and American trade through campaigns of terror directed against civilian commerce. Mediterranean pirates, operating from coastal ports under the nominal control of the Ottoman Empire, had long threatened European shipping. What had been common piracy, however, turned to a sophisticated form of economic extortion in 1662 when Britain negotiated an annual payment of gold, jewels, arms, and supplies in exchange for which the Muslim corsairs agreed to spare British ships. This practice, so characteristic of the emerging mercantile ethos of the territorial states, soon spread to all countries trading in the Mediterranean. The Barbary pirates had run an extensive trade in kidnapped persons for over a century, spanning different constitutional orders. Between 1580 and 1680 an average of 35,000 persons annually were seized by the Mediterranean pirates as they ranged as far north as the Irish coast. Those persons seized were then sold into slavery; only a few were ransomed. What made these pirates terrorists was the advent of the territorial states with which they developed an ongoing and routine relationship. Territorial states were well suited to institutionalized bribery; the Barbary pirates became accustomed to dealing with political institutions.

Owing to the payment of these fees by the British government, the vessels of colonial American merchants were rarely seized. During the War of Independence, France took on the role of guaranteeing U.S. shipping but after the peace of 1783 American ships became subject to predation. In 1785 the dey of Algiers seized an American ship and held its crew hostage for nonpayment of tribute.[41] The political arrangement sought was straightforward: states that did not pay tribute rendered their civilian shipping liable to seizure; once seized, the ships could be converted for use by the hostage takers (a Dutch renegade had persuaded the Muslims to abandon their galleys for sailing sloops that could go beyond the Mediterranean). Hostages could be ransomed if deemed important enough—an entire cottage industry of local credit grew up around moneylenders who would front the ransom in exchange for payments with interest—or if not, the hostages could be sold into slavery. Indeed, the principal work of the city-provinces Tunis, Tripoli, Algiers, and Salle was slave trading and religious conversion: if a hostage professed Islam he could be freed.[42]

The first American hostages were ransomed, but not until a decade had passed and eleven persons had died in an Algerian prison. Both France and Britain encouraged the harassment of United States trading, which they regarded as a commercial threat to their own interests.[43] By 1794, the dey of Algiers had seized eleven American ships and held 119 survivors for ransom (or conversion).[44]

President Washington's cabinet was divided. A proposal to organize a multilateral coalition of seafaring states to blockade North Africa and create a multinational force to combat terrorism had been rejected by the Europeans, who preferred to pay the extorted fees.[45] The vice president, John Adams, argued in favor of paying an annual sum in order to protect U.S. commerce and to avoid a war for which the United States was unprepared. The secretary of state, Thomas Jefferson, pressed for military action on the grounds that perpetual annual tributes were both degrading— "freedom from fear is worth fighting for"[46]—and would ultimately prove more expensive than warfare. It was characteristic of the intense nationalism of the emerging state nation that it would seek confrontation where its honor was challenged, in contrast to the sophisticated bargaining of the eighteenth century territorial state, which was more relaxed and less self-righteous about such matters.

During his presidency Adams pursued his policy of appeasement. In addition to making an annual payment, Adams agreed to build and deliver two warships to the Algerian corsairs. The U.S. paid significant sums: by

1800, more than $2 million had been paid, about a fifth of the annual revenue of the government.[47] The disgusted American consul in Tunis, William Eaton, wrote to the United States government in 1799 that "there is but one language which can be held to these people, and this is terror."[48]

In 1801 Tripoli declared war on the United States because the U.S. had rebuffed its demand that it be paid $225,000 in cash and $25,000 in goods annually—higher fees than those paid to the dey of Algiers. A new administration was now in power in Washington, and President Jefferson dispatched gunships to the Mediterranean when Congress was out of session.[49] When Sweden declared war on the Tripolitans, Swedish forces joined with American vessels to enforce a blockade on Tripoli. When Sweden made peace in 1802, however, the blockade collapsed.

In September 1803 the USS *Constitution* sailed into Tangier harbor. Its unexpected presence persuaded the sultan of Morocco to agree to refrain from molesting American shipping. That same year, however, the USS *Philadelphia,* under full sail, ran aground while pursuing a corsair. Three hundred and seven Americans were taken prisoner and quickly enslaved in Tripoli. The next American expedition against Tripoli was the largest: six frigates, seven brigs, and ten gunboats. The flagship also carried Eaton, the former consul, who had devised a plan to supplant the Tripolitan leader with his brother. Eaton met the brother in Alexandria and there organized a local mercenary force. They then marched seven hundred miles toward Derna in a daring maneuver. Although this force captured Derna, Eaton was unable to get reinforcements from the American expedition, whose commander feared the *Philadelphia* hostages would be killed in retaliation. Eaton's plan thus failed, but not before Tripoli had negotiated a release of hostages in exchange for a ransom of $60,000. A peace treaty was signed and the dey of Tunis, alarmed at the American action, also agreed to safeguards for U.S. shipping.

Some backsliding occurred—in 1807 Algiers detained three U.S. vessels, which were freed only upon the payment of $18,000—but generally the agreement held until the war between the United States and Britain in 1812. Once the American forces were preoccupied, the dey of Algiers announced "a policy to increase the number of my American slaves" and he captured the brig *Edwin* and its crew in August. On March 2, 1815, following the end of hostilities with the British, the U.S. dispatched ten ships to confront Algiers. Jewett recounts what happened next:

> The punitive expedition arrived off Algiers in June. [U.S. commander Stephen] Decatur promptly shot up the flagship of the Dey's fleet, capturing it with 486 prisoners. He then sent an ultimatum to the Dey: Free every slave at once, pay an indemnity of $10,000 to the survivors of the brig *Edwin*, and cease all demands for tribute forever.[50]

Algiers capitulated. This was followed by action against the dey of Tunis, who paid the Americans $46,000 to cease hostilities, and against Tripoli, which paid a $25,000 indemnity and freed its slaves. Thereafter attacks on American vessels ceased, although European ships were harassed until France occupied Algiers in 1830.

Were the Barbary pirates terrorists or simply resourceful, if criminal, entrepreneurs? Perhaps both. Because they were waging their predations against territorial states, they adopted many of the characteristics of those states, exploiting as well as copying the mercantile, cynical manners of the era, which were disinclined toward gestures of patriotic heroism. The Barbary corsairs used terror for political goals—to maintain their regimes, to earn revenue through slave trading and ransom, and to punish and humiliate infidels—and these goals were achieved by violence against civilians. Though sheltered within the state of the Ottoman Empire—Eaton, after all, was a consul accredited to a state—the corsairs were essentially non-state actors. Today we might call them state-sponsored terrorists, but they were quite unlike the privateers of an earlier period, being altogether more independent. Each local ruler had his own policy. And whereas the pirates of the kingly states had seized slave ships in order to free the slaves to create new sovereignties—by 1720 a large percentage of the pirate population was African—the Barbary pirates boarded vessels to find new inventory for their slave markets. They thrived not on confrontation, but on creating a climate of terror that would condition their state victims not to resist (for resistance could be expensive).

The constitutional order of the territorial state was replaced by a new one—the imperial *state nation*—in France shortly after it had been first created in America. In both societies, governments came to power that were based on the idea that legitimacy was a matter of fitness to rule, and that this fitness was properly judged by the national people. One corollary to this idea was the notion that government could be "purpose-built"—that is, constitutionally designed to provide the best governance. The territorial state, the previous constitutional order, had relied on custom for its legitimacy. Now citizens expected more of a reason for one group to govern another than simply the assertion that this is the way things had always been done.

The word "terrorism" seems first to have appeared during the French Revolution,[51] which is to say during the last decades when territorial states dominated Europe. Edmund Burke, contrasting the rule of the revolutionary leaders with that of the Bourbons, referred to the violence of the new French government as a "reign of terror," and it was he who first publicly used the word "terrorism" in 1795 to describe its acts. Maximilien Robespierre himself spoke of "virtue, without which terror is evil; [and] terror without which virtue is helpless."[52] Initially, revolutionary leaders called for "terror" to defend their new liberties against an invading alliance of territorial states that promised a restoration of the aristocracy that had governed France.[53] Terrorism was turned against a privileged class, partly to intimidate that class, and partly to isolate and expose those halfhearted allies in the revolution who could be expected to cavil at horrific measures. Far from shrinking from the label, Robespierre viewed "terror" as indispensable to the survival of the republic. "Terror is nothing other than justice, prompt, severe, inflexible; it is therefore an emanation of virtue; it is not so much a special principle as it is a consequence of the general principle of democracy applied to our country's most urgent needs."[54] What began as territorial state terrorism—elitist in structure, antimeritocratic in ideology—became transformed once the Jacobeans created a new state with a new constitutional order. It is redundant to observe that state terror, like other forms of terrorism, follows the constitutional order of its era: of course it does, as it is the State itself that is practicing terror.

> Robespierre's practice of using revolutionary tribunals as a means of publicizing a prisoner's fate for broader effect within the population . . . can be seen as a nascent example of the much more highly developed, blatant manipulation of media attention by terrorist groups in the mid- to late twentieth century. Modern terrorism is a dynamic concept, from the outset dependent . . . on the political and historical context within which it has been employed.[55]

The imperial state nation evoked a terrorist structure unique to that constitutional order. As Mark Burgess puts it:

> The newly defined notions of nationalism and citizenship, which both caused and were the result of a French Revolution [and, one might add, the American Revolution], also saw the emergence of a new [and] predominantly secular terrorism . . . The Italian revolutionary Carlo Pisacane's theory of the "propaganda of the deed"—which recognized the utility of terrorism to deliver a message to an audience other than the target and draw attention and support to a cause—typified this new form of terrorism.[56]

The use of the word "terrorist" to refer to an antigovernment fighter dates from this period. It is first recorded in 1866 (referring to events in Ireland) and 1883 (referring to acts taking place in Russia). Terror became a methodical technique to bring about revolution, not simply to maintain it. Terror was to be purpose-built. Like the state nation, terrorism was an attack on custom, on the conventions of the inherited society. In the case of state nation terrorism, that inheritance was the State itself. Like the constitutional order it assaulted, state nation terrorism addressed the nation, not simply its elites.

Pisacane's thesis[57] was first put into practice by a Russian anarchist group formed in 1878 to oppose the czarist regime.[58] Russian writers supplied an anarchist doctrine compatible with the notion that governments and indeed societies could be built by design. In this they reflected the constitutional order of the state structure they wished to destroy. David Rapoport describes anarchist doctrine as asserting four major points:

> 1) Modern society contains huge reservoirs of latent ambivalence and hostility. 2) Society muffles and diffuses them by devising moral conventions to generate guilt and provide channels for settling some grievances and securing personal amenities. 3) However, conventions can be explained historically and therefore acts we deem to be immoral, our children will hail as noble efforts to liberate humanity. 4) Terror is the quickest and most effective means to destroy conventions. The perpetrator frees himself from the paralyzing grip of convention to become a different sort of person, and society's defenders will respond in ways that undermine the rules they claim are sacred.[59]

Though descendants of these attitudes have often been invoked to rally attacks against the State in later eras, only the imperial state nation could have prompted this distinctive reaction because it was itself a constitutional rebuke to the conventions that determined the political mores of territorial states.[60]

A state nation is a state that mobilizes a nation—a national, ethnocultural, linguistic group—to act on behalf of the State. In contrast to the territorial state, it can thus call on the revenues of all society, and on the human talent of all persons. But such a state does not exist to serve or take direction from the nation, as does the subsequent constitutional order, that of the nation state. The state nation forged the identity of the nation by fusing it with a state. It was not responsible *to* the nation; rather it was responsible *for* the nation. The nation, for its part, provided the raw material with which the state nation powered the engines of state power.[61]

If it was the initial union of nationalism with the state that distinguished the imperial state nation, this union also created the anarchists who attacked this union.

> Why is our flag black? Black is a shade of negation. The black flag is the negation of all flags. It is a negation of nationhood which puts the human race against itself and denies the unity of all humankind. Black is a mood of anger and outrage at all the hideous crimes

against humanity perpetrated in the name of allegiance to one state or another.[62]

It is sometimes forgotten that the architects of the intensely national, imperial state nation forms—Napoleon and the American framers—also spoke in universalist terms. Like the heroic age of the imperial state nation, the anarchist period of terrorism had its idols, the Nathan Hales and General Gordons of the movement, and like their imperial counterparts these figures were praised as much, perhaps more, for their self-sacrifice as for their effectiveness. Sacco and Vanzetti were two such martyrs, but so were Albert Parsons and his hanged Haymarket co-conspirators; the fame of Pierre-Joseph Proudhon has survived, though few today remember Errico Malatesta or the assassins Gaetano Bresci or Leon Czolgosz. The Russian writer Sergius Stepniak described the terrorist as "noble, terrible, irresistibly fascinating, uniting the two sublimities of human grandeur, the martyr and the hero." When, on January 24, 1878, the anarchist Vera Zasulich shot and wounded the governor general of St. Petersburg, General Trepov, she threw her weapon to the floor of his reception room and cried that she was a *terrorist,* not a killer.[63]

Zasulich was tried for attempted murder and, despite the fact that there was no dispute as to the facts of the case, she was acquitted by a St. Petersburg jury. Her *advokat* had argued, and the jurors apparently accepted, that she "had no personal interest in her crime," but rather that she was "fighting for an idea." The public attending the trial applauded when the verdict was announced.

A year later a secret congress of the Land and Freedom Party decided on a policy of systematic terror with the aim of overthrowing the Czarist government. The majority of this group then reconstituted themselves as Narodnaya Volya (the People's Will) and on August 26, 1879, its executive committee condemned Czar Alexander II to death for crimes against the people.

Russian writers, including well-to-do intellectuals such as the émigrés Mikhail Bakunin and Prince Peter Kropotkin, as well as the odious Sergey Nechaev,[64] created an ideology of warfare against the State during the period of state nation terrorism. Their writings were universalist even as they sought to exploit nationalistic sentiment, and in this combination[65] too they mirrored the imperial state nation they wished to destroy.[66] This can be seen most clearly in the movements inspired in the territories of the former Ottoman Empire, which drew inspiration from their Russian predecessors.

Narodnaya Volya addressed the nation by systematically attempting to put terrorist murders at the service of nineteenth century, anti-imperial revolution. Its principal tactic was the assassination of Russian government officials, and on March 1, 1881, the death sentence it had pronounced was carried out with the bombing murder of Alexander II. In the ensuing decades, anarchists killed a French president in 1894 (Carnot), the president of Spain in 1897 (Canovas), an Italian king in 1900 (Humberto), an Austrian empress (Elizabeth) in 1898, an American president in 1901 (McKinley), a Serbian king (Alexander) in 1903, the Portuguese king (Carlos) in 1908, the Spanish prime minister in 1912 (Canalejas), the king of Greece (George) in 1913, and countless other officials. (An 1878 assassination attempt against the kaiser failed.) Gavrilo Princip, who was both an anarchist and a passionate nationalist, explained at his trial for the assassination of the Austro-Hungarian archduke Franz Joseph that he believed his political goals could be achieved "by means of terror. That means in general to destroy from above, to do away with those who obstruct . . ."[67] This tactic—to assassinate leaders in preference to terrorizing the general population—distinguished state nation terrorism from its successor, the terrorism of the nation state.

Anarchism was not defeated. Rather it simply faded away with the imperial state nations that were its targets when this constitutional order, shattered by the First World War, was progressively replaced by nation states. What destroyed the anarchist movement was not its failure per se, but the destruction of the constitutional order that gave it its birth and life. At the beginning of the twentieth century, the anarchist movement in Spain was the strongest in Europe. During the Spanish Civil War, it initially assumed a leading role, but by the end of the conflict it had been completely marginalized by the nation state ideologies of communism and fascism.

The nation state terrorist groups that succeeded the anarchists did not proclaim themselves to be terrorists; indeed, quite the opposite. They saw themselves as "freedom fighters" (the term comes from Menachem Begin, head of the Irgun which sought a Jewish nation state in Palestine) and were only called "terrorists" by the governments of the nation states they sought to intimidate. When Lori Berenson, an American woman convicted of collaborating with the Tupac Amaru group (MRTA) in Peru, held a press conference after her first conviction in 1996, she claimed that the MRTA was not a terrorist band but a "revolutionary movement."[68] The Irish Republican Army (IRA), the Basque Nation and Liberty (ETA), the Armenian Secret Army for the Liberation of Armenia (ASALA), the Corsican National Liberation Front (FNLC), the Algerian National Liberation Front (FLN), the Palestine Liberation Organization (PLO) and the Stern Gang, the Mau Mau in Kenya, the MCP in Malaysia, EOKA in Cyprus, and the Front de Libération du Québec (FLQ) were all twentieth century nation state creations. As Walter Laqueur points out,[69] the sensitivity of nineteenth century terrorists regarding nonofficial, civilian targets was replaced by the studiedly indiscriminate violence against civilians in the twentieth century. This too follows the pattern of the behavior of the nation state, whose total warfare against enemy societies reflects the constitutional order these states share. To destroy a state nation, one attacks its leaders; to destroy a nation state, one attacks the well-being of the national people.[70]

[I]t was Algeria's Front de libération Nationale, seeking liberation from France, that defined modern terrorism, deliberately spilling the blood of random French civilians. After France executed two Algerian rebels in 1956, the FLN slaughtered 49 Frenchmen in three days. FLN terrorists bombed beachside cafés where they knew families would perish . . . Their success inspired others: Basque and Quebecois separatists, Palestinian and Irish nationalists, Marxist cabals in Africa and Latin America. By the 1960s, the killing of civilians to sow fear and secure political gains was rampant . . .[71]

The industrial nation state sought the improvement of the material well-being of its people to confirm its legitimacy. If the state nation promised to forge the identity of the nation by uniting it with the State, the nation state promised to better the welfare of the masses. FDR said this, but so did Adolf Hitler and Joseph Stalin. All spoke from the point of view of the constitutional order that they shared. It brought us mass education, mass health care, the universal voting franchise, unemployment compensation, social security and old-age pensions. It set government against the free market, as one could see in the innovations of its earliest architects, Lincoln (who abolished the market in slaves) and Bismarck (who set up a program of unemployment compensation).

The terrorists of the nation state, including those national liberation movements that sought nation states for their peoples, used different tactics from their anarchist predecessors who aimed at high imperial symbols. The martyrdom celebrated in the nineteenth century was shunned in the twentieth, and targets changed. Rather than assassinating high officials, the terrorists of the twentieth century targeted the local officials, teachers and mayors, judges and hospital administrators, and civilians of a competing ethno-nationalist population (Catholics or Protestant, Greek Cypriots or Turkish, white planters or black protest organizers, and so on). When local officials were replaced by military personnel, counteratrocities occurred, increasing political support for the terrorists. Sympathy abroad generally favored those who used the methods of asymmetric warfare because they were, almost by definition, the weaker party without realistic military alternatives.[72]

These are the groups that contemporary Europeans have in mind when they assure Americans that terrorism is nothing new, and that, with proper police and investigative work, it can be managed. This assurance depends on a kind of category mistake. It assumes that terrorism is fundamentally unchanged, when in fact the history of terrorism displays a profound periodicity. The end of the ideological wars of the twentieth century nation states among parliamentarianism, communism, and fascism,[73] and with them the end of great power sponsorship of national liberation terrorism, coupled with developments in state evolution to be discussed in the next chapter, have brought forth a new form of terrorism, an unusually horrific homunculus, the unintended creation of the technology-wielding twenty-first century market state.

Just as earlier forms of terrorism reacted against the values while mimicking the techniques of the prevailing constitutional order, this new mode of terrorism reflects the new constitutional order coming into being, the informational market state. This process is not complete; in fact it has hardly begun. Most terrorist groups are indeed still nation state in form, like the IRA or the Tamil Tigers or ETA or the groups that seek national liberation in Aceh, Sudan, and Xinjiang. But, like the state itself, a new form of terrorism is also emerging, of which the group called al Qaeda is the initial, disturbing example.

So it was that princely states coexisted with fanatically religious mercenaries, kingly states flourished in the golden age of piracy, territorial states vied with the private armies of commercial consortia for overseas revenues and investment, imperial state nations struggled with international anarchists, and nation states attempted to suppress national liberation movements. And so it will be when the market state finds it has generated a terrorism that negates the very individual choice that the State exalts, and puts in service of that negation the networked, decentralized, outsourcing global methods characteristic of the market state itself.

II.

In chapter 2, we will take up a more extensive description of the market state. For now, here is a very brief sketch that will enable us to appreciate the sort of terrorism that this new constitutional order will generate.

> What are the characteristics of the market state? . . . [I]n contrast to the nation state it does not see the State as more than a minimal provider or redistributor. Whereas the nation state justified itself as an instrument to serve the welfare of the people (the nation), the market state exists to maximize the opportunities [of its citizens]. Such a state

depends on the international capital markets and, to a lesser degree, on the modern multinational business network [including the news media and NGOs] . . . in preference to management by national or transnational political bodies. Its political institutions are less representative (though in some ways more democratic) than those of the nation state.[74]

Market state terrorism[75] will be just as global, networked, decentralized, and devolved and rely just as much on outsourcing and incentivizing as the market state. It does not depend upon state sponsorship; indeed, in some cases it would appear that al Qaeda had more influence over the government in whose jurisdiction it worked than did that government over it. There will still be relationships between terrorist groups and states; but market state terrorists will be clandestine allies rather than mere agents, and market states will employ tactics, as we shall see in the next chapter, that are indistinguishable from those of terrorists.

Although states have long been supportive of terrorist activity, we are now seeing an evolution from state sponsors with leverage over their terrorist clients to international terrorist networks with increasing leverage over the associated states.[76]

The abrupt change from nation state terrorism to market state terrorism creates a difficult analytical transition for us to make.

Like generals, spies and policemen tend to fight the last war. In 1980s Japan, the security services were still worrying about Chinese and North Korean–supported communist groups when they should have had their eye on a crop of strange new sects blossoming at home. [The U.S. government] made a similar mistake with respect to al Qaeda. . . . Even now, its continuing determination to cast Islamic radicalism as an essentially state-sponsored phenomenon may be as much a product of an inherited way of viewing the world . . . Similarly, . . . until the bombing of a Madrid commuter train by Moroccan radicals in March 2004 [Spain's] focus was almost entirely on ETA, and its principal action the banning of the allegedly related Basque nationalist party Batasuna. Security services must learn to look forward to emerging threats, not backward at Cold War and separatist ones.[77]

Market state terrorism "neither relies on the support of sovereign states nor is constrained by the limits on violence that state sponsors have observed themselves or placed on their proxies,"[78] and as a result it is horrifyingly more violent. Its undiscriminating violence against civilians,

WORLDWIDE TERRORISM INCIDENTS 1996–PRESENT

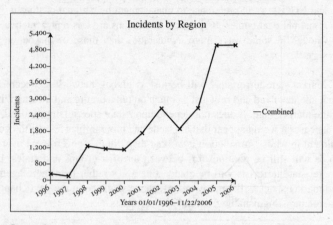

Courtesy of:
MIPT Terrorism Knowledge Base. "TKB Incident Analysis Wizard page."
Website, accessed November 22, 2006. Available from http://www.tkb.org/ChartModule.jsp

however, is not indiscriminate; it is calculated and carefully prepared. It is transnational, borderless, and prosecuted by virtual states (like al Qaeda) or by non-state actors (like the Colombian drug cartels) sheltering in weak states. It can be clearly distinguished in several important ways from nation state terrorism.

Market state terrorism is more lethal. The number of fatalities resulting from terrorist attacks has increased.[79] As Brent Ellis concluded in 2003, "[T]he trend towards increasing lethality of international terrorism is clearly apparent."[80] Similarly, writing in *Survival* in 2006, Anna Pluta and Peter Zimmerman observed that "since the early 1990's, the maximum violence in acts of international terrorism has steadily increased."[81]

Nation state terrorism was well described in a now-famous remark of Brian Jenkins in 1974: "Terrorists want a lot of people watching, not a lot of people dead."[82] There were many reasons for this. By their attacks terrorist groups wanted to achieve positive propaganda, which the report of large numbers of casualties might jeopardize. Sometimes terrorists feared the government suppression that could be triggered by a public backlash. Often the cohesion of the terrorist group itself was threatened by anti-civilian violence, leading to splintering or even cooperation by disenchanted members with the state security services.[83] Bruce Hoffman concluded that "[t]he more successful, ethno-nationalist/separatist terror-

ist organization will be able to determine an effective level of violence
that is at once 'tolerable' for the local populace, tacitly acceptable to
international opinion and sufficiently modulated not to provoke massive
governmental crack-down and reaction."[84] To put this in different terms,
violence had a declining marginal utility for terrorists as it increased
above a certain level.

Nation state terrorism,* however, like the twentieth century nation
state itself, began to wane with the end of the Long War of the twentieth
century—the conflicts that began with World War I and continued until the
Second Russian Revolution in 1989 and the end of the Cold War with the
Peace of Paris in 1990. As before in the history of the society of states—
after the Peace of Utrecht, after the Congress of Vienna—the end of an
epochal war and the ratification of an international constitution by a peace
congress paradoxically brought intensified terrorist activity and a new
modality of terror. Contrasting the announcement by the IRA of the end to
its armed campaign with the July 2005 bombings in London that occurred
the same week, the journalist Alan Cowell noted that

> [t]here is [now] no longer even a theoretical separation between "legit-
> imate targets" of traditional insurgency—like the armed forces or
> political leaders—and the "collateral damage" of civilians . . . The
> newest killing draws no such distinction . . . No one took responsibility
> or registered a demand. The sense of some proportion between the
> bombers' actions and their intentions seems to have been lost.[85]

As the U.S. National Commission on Terrorism found:

> A growing percentage of terrorist attacks are designed to kill as many
> people as possible. In the 1990s a terrorist incident was almost 20 per-
> cent more likely to result in death or injury than an incident two
> decades before . . . Today's terrorists seek to inflict mass casualties,
> and they are attempting to do so both overseas and on American soil.[86]

This conclusion was reached by the commission a year before the September 11 attacks. By 2006, Brian Jenkins summarized the situation:

*Compare the Boxer Rebellion to the Red Guards and the Cultural Revolution (all of which were
state-sponsored terrorism). See also the important work of Jessica Stern on this issue, and her view
that the acts of nation states, waging the total war so characteristic of nation states and deliberately
bombing civilians as a means of undermining public morale, amounted to state terrorism. Jessica
Stern, *The Ultimate Terrorists* (Cambridge: Harvard University Press, 1999), 14. Far more people
have been killed in the era of the nation state by state terror than by nation state terrorists. See Leon
Trotsky, *The Defence of Terrorism (Terrorism and Communism)* (London: Labour Publishing, 1921).
See also Fred Halliday, "Terrorism in Historical Perspective," *openDemocracy*, 22 April 2004, http://
www.opendemocracy.net/globalization-madridprevention/article_1865.jsp (accessed October 13,
2006).

The worst incidents of terrorism in the 1970s caused fatalities in the tens. In the 1980s, fatalities from the worst incidents were measured in the hundreds. By the 1990s, attacks on this scale had become more frequent. On September 11, 2001, fatalities ascended to the thousands—and the toll could easily have been higher. This is an order-of-magnitude increase almost every decade. We now look ahead to plausible scenarios in which tens of thousands could die.[87]

There is some disagreement as to whether it is in fact accurate to say that the number of attacks is declining; there is no dispute that the number of casualties and deaths is increasing. Partly this was the result of the growing reliance by al Qaeda on simultaneous attacks, which have become a watermark of market state terrorism. Because they make a greater impact through the magnifying lens of the international media, simultaneous attacks serve al Qaeda's global purposes better.

SINGLE VS. MULTIPLE SIMULTANEOUS TARGETS
(1998–18 MAY 2006)

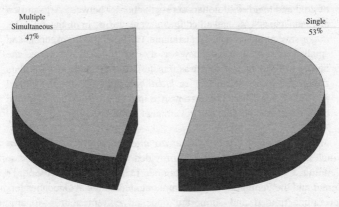

Multiple
Simultaneous
47%

Single
53%

Market state terrorists are much better financed than their predecessors, who relied mainly on local crime or on state sponsors to fund their activities. Because they can rely on a wider variety of sources for funding, market state terrorists have greater freedom of action.

[T]errorist organizations are broadening their reach in gathering financial resources to fund their operations . . . Sources of financing include legal enterprises such as nonprofit organizations and charities . . . legitimate companies that divert profits to illegal activities . . . and illegal enterprises such as drug smuggling and production . . . bank robbery, fraud, extortion and kidnapping . . . Websites are also important vehicles for raising funds.[88]

Al Qaeda seems to get much of its funding from two sources: charitable contributions[89] made by philanthropic and devout Muslims (who may not be aware of any diversion of their gifts), and the operation of legitimate businesses (such as bin Laden's network of companies).[90] These front groups, which include NGOs as well as multinational corporations, use the Internet and other global communications media as links. They enable the funding of legitimate enterprises—like the media—in ways previously reserved to traditional covert action by states. Because they are better financed, such market state entities can do precisely what market states themselves do: outsource operations, achieving greater efficiency and vastly greater reach.

The fluid movement of terrorist's [sic] financial resources demonstrates the growing informal connections that are countering the local fragmentation caused elsewhere by globalization. The transit of bars of gold and bundles of dollars across the border between Afghanistan and Pakistan as U.S. and allied forces were closing in on the Taliban's major strongholds is a perfect example. Collected by shopkeepers and small businessmen, the money was moved by operatives across the border to Karachi, where it was transferred in the millions of dollars though the informal *hawala** or *hundi* banking system to the United Arab Emirates. There it was converted into gold bullion and scattered around the world before any government could intervene.[91]

Market state terrorist operations are often outsourced to local groups, which are paid for their work and provided with infrastructure and some planning. Operations like the September 11 attacks on the World Trade Center and the Pentagon were not implemented by the al Qaeda leadership but rather funded and supported once an entrepreneur—Mohammed Atta—approached bin Laden with a daring plan. The actions in Bali, Morocco, Egypt, Turkey, Spain, Iraq, Britain, the Philippines, and elsewhere are characteristic. In each instance, local operatives linked up with al Qaeda representatives to carry out atrocities against civilians. Indeed that may be one reason why the U.S. has not, as of the winter of 2006, been hit again: except for sleeper cells, which are by definition not participants

*The *hawala* (or *hundi*) system relies on the deposit of funds with one person who will pay a person specified by the depositor from other funds controlled overseas by the person with whom the funds were originally deposited. It is an ancient system relying entirely on trust and has been used to move monies globally.

in current operations and therefore take more time to organize for actions, there is no extensive American network of terrorist operatives in the U.S. on whom al Qaeda can call to execute its plans. The fact that al Qaeda has begun using local groups that do not necessarily share its theocratic goals but are united with the al Qaeda leadership only in their opposition to the U.S. is a troubling turn, and it emphasizes yet again the critical role played by U.S. global power (and by anti-Americanism) in creating twenty-first century terrorism.[92]

The use of local groups has led some commentators to conclude that the terrorists involved in operations like the Madrid and London bombings are a few self-generated sympathizers who deeply identify with a distant struggle in Iraq, Afghanistan, or Palestine. Because al Qaeda is not structured along the lines of a nation state terrorist group, it is thought by some that angry Muslim bands spontaneously appeared and then managed to carry out the complex, synchronized bombings at Atocha and on the London transport system. In reality, as Peter Neumann has shown, "this is a ridiculous distortion."[93] We can see that when we compare the July 7, 2005, conspiracy in the U.K. with the terrorist plot that was interrupted in Miami in June 2006. In the latter, a true group of amateurish misfits tried to link up with al Qaeda and connected only with an FBI agent. Prior to this, the only known case of "self-radicalization" was that of Ahmed el Bakiouli and Khalil el Hassnaoui, two third-generation immigrants from the Netherlands who made their way to Afghanistan but, having failed to cross the border from Pakistan, headed for Kashmir, where they were shot dead by the Indian Border Security Force almost immediately after they arrived.[94]

In fact, we can trace the relationship between the complexity of an attack and the extent to which the terrorists had access to the financing, planning, weapons, and training of al Qaeda, even when this occurs through outsourcing to local groups. Marc Sageman's research on al Qaeda's global terror network has demonstrated that unless groups of potential terrorists were able to get access to the jihadist network, typically through someone who had gone through one of the training camps in Afghanistan, terrorist plots almost never materialized.[95]

Market state terrorist structures more greatly resemble VISA or Master-Card organization charts than they do the centralized, hierarchical structures of nation state governmental organizations, including nation state terrorist groups (or, for that matter, the twentieth century corporate business structures of the nation state). Here too we see a change from the nation state terrorist groups like the IRA, the Japanese Red Army, ETA, and the FLN. While the Provisional IRA reflected a "hierarchically organized authoritarian structure" with a "cellular base,"[96] for example, the

Canadian Security Intelligence Service more recently found a "reduced emphasis on a formalized group structure typical of terrorist insurgents in the past."[97] A RAND study noted that

> experts have begun to recognize the growing role of networks—of networked organization designs and related doctrines, strategies and technologies—among the practitioners of terrorism . . . [These structures comprise] loosely interconnected, semi-independent cells that have no single commanding hierarchy.[98]

Whether or not al Qaeda is likely to dominate the next quarter century or be superseded by even more dangerous groups,[99] if Osama bin Laden is studied in the political science classes of the future, it will be for his organizational innovations, which are his lasting legacy.[100]

Al Qaeda provides funding and infrastructure—planning, communications, and weapons—for operations that are carried out by local groups, often groups that have been at each other's throats for years. The almost universal presence of the United States, and the widely shared view among insurgents that the U.S. frustrates their plans for local regime change, facilitate these collaborations. According to one commentator, "driven now by a common enemy, old boundaries [have] eroded [and] individuals from different organizations [have come] together to carry out attacks."[101] According to Hoffman,

> The biggest change that's taken place is that the boundaries that used to differentiate groups are breaking down . . . I've seen transcripts of interviews with terrorists there, where they say it doesn't matter which Kashmiri extremist or Pakistani separatist group you join.[102]

This network links the Egyptian Islamic Jihad (EIJ) and al-Gama'a al-Islamiyya in Egypt; the Armed Islamic Group of Algeria (GIA); the Harakat al-Mujahideen based in Pakistan but operating principally in Kashmir; Jaish-e-Mohammed (also in India and Pakistan); the Islamic Movement of Uzbekistan; Jama'at al-Tawhid wal-Jihad (JTJ) in Iraq, known since September 2004 as al Qaeda in the Land of Two Rivers (the mujahideen network once led by Abu Musab al Zarqawi); Jemaah Islamiyah (which operates in Indonesia, Malaysia, and Singapore); and Abu Sayyaf in the Philippines. It is unlikely that all these various clans precisely share the millennial, global plans for a new caliphate that are said to animate bin Laden. What they and many other groups do share is a fear of and hostility to the West, and to the West's military champion, the United States. The director of the Global Terrorism Research Project at Monash University observed, "Anti-Westernism and anti-Americanism is emerging as a parallel link between organizations, allowing [the jihadists] to tap into a broader constituency." [103]

> [T]hroughout Asia, the Middle East, Europe, and Africa, domestic and sometimes dormant Muslim organizations began to poke their heads into world news. Angry words about repressive national governments changed to impassioned rhetoric about global institutions; local targets gave way to international ones; untrained gunmen became sophisticated bombers; innocent civilians surpassed guilty bureaucrats as the preferred targets; hard-to-get military hardware was abandoned in favor of trucks, cars, fertilizer, and cellphones; and suicide bombers proliferated.[104]

Yet even if the U.S.[105] had not been attempting to deliver aid in Somalia, had not stationed forces in Saudi Arabia in order to repel Iraq's invasion of Kuwait, had not attempted to pacify Lebanon in the midst of a civil war, had not removed Saddam Hussein by invading Iraq, and had not overthrown the Taliban, and thus not have presented vulnerable, extended, and inflammatory targets in all these states, al Qaeda would still have had a transnational terrorist agenda.

> [B]in Laden's achievement is also due to his ability to create an overarching religious ideology that has subsumed the particular agendas of the many groups. By redirecting much of the energies of these groups from unsuccessful efforts to cause upheaval in their home countries into a broader assault on the West, bin Laden has created a genuine strategic threat. . . . By operating transnationally, the groups have found a way to get out of the box of facing off solely against national police in isolated theaters—conflicts they usually lose. Instead, operational cells are small and typically attack third-nation targets.[106]

A global power like the U.S., which as an emerging market state that is increasingly less defined by its territorial boundaries and more by its nonterritorial interests, presents many local opportunities for terrorist attack. The suicide bomber is the ideal weapon for the outsourcing market state terrorist network to attack such targets. All the network advantages of redundancy, interoperability, diversity, and decentralized command and control are maximized by the outsourced suicide bomber.

Ellis believes that decentralized command structures make counter-leadership strikes less effective. Without the inspirational defiance, media, and financial acumen of a base, however, the decentralized force would dissolve and sink back into local struggles. Missions that require simultaneity, that are aimed to achieve broad disruption, and that are capable of using weapons of mass destruction cannot as yet be pulled off by local groups. Nor do I believe that a truly leaderless, sophisticated, spontaneous network will arise solely in response to American omnipresence and power to present a serious threat.

Networked structures have their own vulnerabilities. Travel and other communications arrangements are vulnerable to interdiction and yet are more insistently needed. The transmissions of electronic communications that are so potent for the market state terrorist group are also susceptible to intelligence collection and surveillance. As a RAND study pointed out, reliance by terrorists on the Internet makes them a potential target for information warfare—including deception.

Nevertheless, the international movement of terrorists has not only given them a global reach for their attacks, and made it easier for them to evade capture, it has greatly complicated prosecution if the attackers are captured and states confront a bewildering labyrinth of extradition laws that vary from state to state. Furthermore, the VISA-like, decentralized, franchised informational structure made possible by globalization also empowers the collection and dissemination of intelligence worldwide by terrorist networks, an activity that was once the province of states. Finally, it must be noted that this structure continues to expand. Although the Muslim states of the Middle East and Southwest Asia continue to be the locus of most terrorist activity,

> [j]ihadist structures have been uncovered in most major Western European countries, including the United Kingdom, Germany, France, Italy, Spain, the Netherlands and Belgium. While these countries are believed to be the main centres of activity, recent reports by Western intelligence services suggest that structures have also emerged in countries such as Poland, the Czech Republic and Bulgaria, not previously seen as likely bases for al-Qaeda-inspired groups.[107]

The most acute threats to the West, however, will be faced by the U.S. and the U.K.

> Al Qaeda's relocation to Pakistan has also provided new opportunities for the group to expand its reach in the West, especially the United Kingdom. . . . (By one estimate, Pakistan received 400,000 visits from British residents in 2004 . . . facilitating recruitment, training, and communication for jihadists.) The large communities of immigrants from Pakistan and Bangladesh living in the United Kingdom—and some disaffected Muslim British citizens—have become targets for recruitment; [and at present] the United Kingdom has become a focal point of al Qaeda's activities in the West.[108]

Moreover, al Qaeda's increasing links with Europe have rendered the
U.S. more vulnerable—an uncovered plot to blow up ten airliners in 2006
on the anniversary of 9/11 was linked to a British network—and opened
up a new front. John Negroponte, then U.S. director for national intelligence, testified that al Qaeda's leadership is "cultivating stronger operational connections and relationships that radiate outward from their . . .
secure hideout in Pakistan to affiliates throughout the Middle East, North
Africa and Europe." His aide, Robert Earle, later wrote, the "question is
not whether we are adapting and getting more adept. It's whether we can
do this fast enough to thwart the rising tide heading our way through
Europe."[109]

**JIHADI TARGETING BY GEOGRAPHIC LOCATION—TOTALS
(1998–18 MAY 2006)**

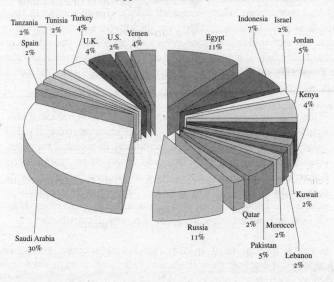

*Market state terrorists evade attempts to suppress them and enhance
their power through the adroit use of modern communications technology,
especially the Internet.*[110]

Paradoxically, the very decentralized network of communication that
the U.S. security services created out of fear of the Soviet Union now
serves the interests of the greatest foe of the West's security services
since the end of the Cold War: international terror.[111]

This is, however, no paradox. The various assets the West used to defeat fascism and communism—weapons of mass destruction, global communications, and a global market—are the same elements responsible for discrediting the nation state and bringing the market state into being. It is hardly surprising that each of these should be found in the service of market state terrorism.

> The Internet has become an important tool for perpetuating terrorist groups, both openly and clandestinely. Many of them employ elaborate list serves, collect money from witting or unwitting donors, and distribute savvy political messages to a broad audience online.[112]

Most countries, excepting the U.S., suppress to one degree or another radical Islamist newspapers, radio broadcasts, sermons, and books. Publication on the Web instantaneously evades this. The number of pro-terrorism websites is estimated to have increased from approximately 12 in 1998 to more than 4,700 by 2005.[113] Moreover, the Internet allows for global conversations with multiple partners, which also enables a dramatic increase in the sheer reach of indoctrination. According to Reuven Paz, director of the Project for the Research of Islamist Movements, "[t]he Internet is an open university."[114]

> [T]he tools of the global information age have led to enhanced efficiency in many terrorist-related activities, including administrative tasks, coordination of operations, recruitment of potential members, communication among adherents, and attraction of sympathizers. Before the September 11 attacks, for example, members of al-Qaeda communicated through Yahoo e-mail; Mohammed Atta . . . made his reservations online; and cell members went online to do research on subjects such as the chemical-dispersing powers of crop dusters.[115]

E-mail is heavily relied upon by market state terrorist groups, using cybercafés and discarding e-mail accounts after only a single use to avoid detection. Doctrine and strategy are debated in online discussion groups and chat rooms. A Saudi interior ministry spokesman estimated that the Internet is responsible for 80 percent of the recruitment of youths for the jihad.[116] Photographs are shared—the Abu Ghraib prison pictures were instantaneously provided worldwide—and responsibility for attacks may be claimed. Most of all, perhaps, the diverse rage of many hundreds of thousands is channeled rather than dissipated. Often overlooked is the participatory dimension of the Web: it's not just that the Internet allows remote leaders to reach thousands or hundreds of thousands of otherwise inaccessible persons, it's that it allows these alienated, often isolated people to speak back, to receive encouragement and reassurance as they separate themselves from society. "Islamists view themselves as fighting a global war to create or restore the big Islamic nation without borders or nationalism, and the Internet is the best tool for building their virtual *ummah*."[117] As we shall see, it is the Internet that allows al Qaeda to communicate its strategy even while its leaders are in hiding, and despite the loss of its territorial base, which once would have meant defeat and marginalization but is now easily overcome.

> Clandestine methods include passing encrypted messages, embedding invisible graphic codes using steganography,* employing the internet to send death threats, and hiring hackers to collect intelligence such as the names and addresses of law enforcement officers from online databases. All of these measures help to expand and perpetuate trends in terrorism that have already been observed. For example, higher casualties are brought about by simultaneous attacks, a diffusion in terrorist locations is made possible by internet communications, and extremist religious ideologies are spread through websites and videotapes accessible throughout the world.[118]

The Internet, however, also provides a useful window on the thinking of those who communicate via its websites. It is, as Robert Worth put it, "a two-way mirror, allowing outsiders a fuller view of the insurgents' ideas."[119] This use of a global communications technology is not limited to al Qaeda, however; we can expect other widely dispersed groups, united only by a particular alienation that would have otherwise withered through isolation, to organize and educate themselves by means of the Internet and eventually to turn this instrument against the State.

Having "lost their base in Afghanistan," Peter Bergen observed, "[and] their training camps [there] . . . [n]ow they're surviving on the internet . . . It is really their new base."[120]

> As well as propaganda and ideological material, jihadist sites seem to be heavily used for practical training . . . since the loss of the Afghan training camps. Sites like Al Battar contain hugely detailed information on how to [conduct kidnappings and] surveillance [and how to fire] rocket propelled grenades. Careful instructions were . . . posted on one jihadist website on how to use mobile phones as detonators for explosives, as was [done] in Madrid.[121]

---

*Steganography embeds messages, typically in pictures, such that they can be retrieved but cannot be detected by the naked eye.

No one, however, has made as dramatic a use of the World Wide Web as the mass murderer Abu Busab al Zarqawi. It was he who mobilized allies in dozens of countries through harrowing video clips of the bombings and beheadings his group carried out in Iraq. These were posted on multiple computer servers to avoid downloading delays; one version was even designed for viewing on mobile phones. Within hours of the release of each video, sophisticated sympathizers had translated his addresses into English, German, French, Dutch, and other languages. "While Osama bin Laden traditionally relied on al Jazeera and the media to disseminate his propaganda, Zarqawi went straight to the Internet, which enabled him to produce graphic videos that would never have been shown on the mainstream media," wrote Rita Katz, director of the SITE Institute, where many scholars go to study al Qaeda documents and videos.[122] In 2004 Zarqawi released a video in which a masked terrorist, possibly Zarqawi himself, beheaded the American businessman Nicholas Berg. This horrible video clip has been downloaded many millions of times.[123] Videos later posted in Thailand showed beheadings by terrorists who faced the camera and said one word: "Zarqawi."

Joseph Nye concluded that, by "moving from the physical sanctuaries of the 1990s to virtual sanctuaries on the internet, the terrorists reduce[d] their risk. No longer does recruiting occur only in the physical locations like mosques and jails. Instead alienated individuals in isolated national niches can make contact with a new imagined community of fellow believers around the world."[124] This corresponds to the similar movement in market states to bypass national advertising media in raising political funds, creating political commentary, and building political support via the Internet. Nye's use of the term "imagined community" is especially apt, for Benedict Anderson has argued, in a celebrated book of that name,[125] that it was once the conjunction of literacy and printing that enabled persons to identify themselves with larger units than the villages that had hitherto limited their worlds. Now we may say that literacy, satellite television, and the Internet have allowed a constructed identity based on a larger, imagined community of shared grievances.[126] A Pew Global Attitudes Project poll conducted in 2003 found that a large majority of respondents in Indonesia, Nigeria, Lebanon, Jordan, Pakistan, Kuwait, Morocco, and Palestine reported feeling increased solidarity with Islamic people living elsewhere.[127]

Market state terrorists are more likely to seek weapons of mass destruction, and should they manage to get them, these groups are far more likely to actually use them than their nation state predecessors would have been. The conventional wisdom from the 1970s onward was that terrorist groups would not seek WMD for the same reasons that led them to moderate the lethality of their conventional attacks. Fearing popular revulsion, international disapproval, local repression, and threats to their own cohesion, and facing active dissuasion by those states that monopolized WMD even when they were willing to arm terrorists with other weapons, these groups turned away from such acquisitions. If someone had said to either Gerry Adams or Yasir Arafat, "I can get you a ten-kiloton nuclear weapon," one can imagine the reaction. A cautious gasp, a quick turning away—reflecting the apprehension that one has met an agent provocateur. But suppose such an offer were made to bin Laden? He would say, "What will it cost?"[128]

Indeed, bin Laden readily acknowledges trying to obtain WMD for his jihad against the United States.[129] In May 1998, bin Laden issued a statement entitled "The Nuclear Bomb of Islam," under the banner of the "International Islamic Front for Fighting the Jews and Crusaders," in which he stated that "it is the duty of Muslims to prepare as much force as possible to terrorize the enemies of God."

James Campbell, in his study of changing terrorism and its relationship with WMD, concluded that "the 'qualitative rise' in terms of the casualties and damage produced by terrorist attacks provides an indication that terrorists may very well engage in more spectacular and sophisticated attacks that include the use of WMD."[130]

This won't be easy. When the millennial terrorist group Aum Shinrikyo attempted to spread sarin gas in the Tokyo subway system in March 1995, it was largely ineffective. Even though the group used "scores of highly skilled technicians and spent millions of dollars developing"[131] anthrax, sarin, and other toxins, their attack killed fewer persons than conventional explosives might have. Still, not many successes are required to do considerable harm with WMD, so that even a low-probability event becomes a concern.[132] The tremendous physical plant and investment required to weaponize such toxins or their nuclear counterparts, radiological or explosive, has meant that hitherto only states have been able to develop such arsenals. Now, as we shall see, a black market in the distribution and sale of WMD has emerged and potential customers like al Qaeda may have entered that market. This development is what is meant by the terms "commodification of WMD"—which occurs when states can buy the necessary components for WMD without having to create these themselves. It seems prudent to assume that this clandestine bazaar will grow. Currently, five of the seven countries the U.S. identifies as state sponsors of terrorism have programs to develop WMD. Moreover, there is also the continuing concern over the lack of adequate security for the biological and nuclear weapons of the former Soviet Union.[133] The acquisition of stolen weapons would represent a dangerous addition to this market's inventory. Finally, the assignment of Iran's apparently interrupted nuclear program to its

Revolutionary Guards and the uncertain relationship of Pakistan's Inter-Services Intelligence agency (ISI) to the Pakistani nuclear inventory raise the disturbing possibility of unauthorized access by jihadists to WMD.

Market state terrorism is more theatrical, producing vivid dramas and tableaux for the global network connected by the Internet, the World Wide Web, satellite television, and video technologies. Indeed, the theatrical nature of twenty-first century terrorism will become more important to such groups, just as the media are becoming more important to states. This has been evident in the activity of terrorists in Iraq.

Since his first communiqué appeared on a jihadist Web forum in April 2004, Mr. Zarqawi's media operation has posted hundreds of others, often with video clips. Lasting only a minute or two, the clips gave jihadist oratory far more immediacy: masked snipers shoot at American soldiers; a suicide bomber's car speeds toward an armored personnel carrier before disappearing in a fireball; a bomb detonates in a truck convoy, with the drivers fleeing the flames.[134]

Market state terrorists want a lot of people dead *and* a lot of people watching. The sheer drama of WMD makes them attractive weapons to terrorists even if more conventional weapons are often just as deadly and far easier to come by. Worryingly, the use of dramatic scenes like the beheadings in Iraq steadily raises the bar for new acts of terror to enthrall the easily jaded public imagination. We have to assume that atrocities like the Chechen attack on a Beslan school, where 186 children were murdered, and Zarqawi's practice of targeting Iraqi sites where candy was distributed to children will be succeeded by other scenes of deliberate, automatic-weapons fire on fleeing, screaming children. It is noteworthy that the footage we have of the terrorists who took the schoolchildren hostage in Russia was filmed on video cameras the terrorists themselves brought with them. This was also the case with the video images created when Chechens took over a theater in Moscow and held 800 persons captive, 129 of whom died. There, too, the terrorists brought minicams with them to the theater. We must assume that the visually shocking images created by the use of a weapon of mass destruction have an irresistible appeal to the twenty-first century terrorist. The global reach of such images has made all the world a stage.[135]

Market state terrorism is principally directed against the leading market states, the U.S. and the E.U. Nation state terrorism was bounded by national territories. Typically, it was directed against a dominant national group (e.g., the Tamil attacks on Hindu officials and civilians), or a national group that ruled as a foreign power (e.g., the Viet Minh attacks on the French). Market states, however, characteristically have interests that range far beyond their national territories but are not in any sense incorporated into the state (as with an imperial ruler and a subject territory).

Anti-Americanism is driven in large part by antiglobalization (and vice versa) because the U.S. is the leading emerging market state.[136] Globalization reduces the drive toward conventional warfare and intracommunal violence, while at the same time enhancing incentives for expressive violence, that is, the ritualistic, symbolic, and communicative violence of market state terrorism described above.[137] Because a global security system led by an American hegemon and an economic system led by the U.S. and the E.U. are perceived as threatening to destroy traditional values and cultures (through armed interventions as well as through intrusive cultural influences and manipulative financial institutions) while at the same time denying to other societies the benefits of globalized access to wealth, knowledge, and development[138] (a perhaps inconsistent view), the U.S. and Europe are becoming the main targets of international grievance.

JIHADI TARGETING BY NATIONAL INTERESTS—TOTALS
(1998–18 MAY 2006)

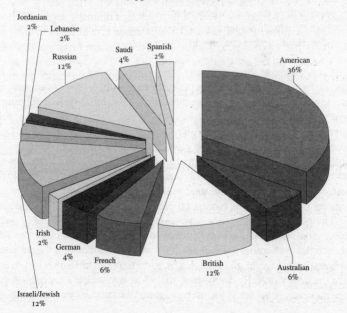

Attacks against American and European interests have steadily escalated in the last decade. The percentage of international assaults against
U.S. targets increased from about 20 percent in 1993–95 to almost 50 percent in 2000, i.e., before the September 11 atrocities. This shift was intensified by the gradual globalizing of terrorist networks as they shifted from
the Middle East. There are numerous Western targets in both Iraq and
Afghanistan, but even if American and British troops were not present
there, U.S. and U.K. civilians would still be killed by terrorists. Partly this
is because these countries have so many civilians abroad, and such far-
flung interests. These attacks also come in part, however, as a result of the
reverse side of globalization—not the centrifugal dispersal of American
and British or European outposts around the world, but the centripetal
return to the American and British homelands of hostilities whose nominal
focus may be international grievances but whose precise complaints arise
from disgruntled domestic, often immigrant, populations.

> Terrorism appeared as part of the underside of globalization. It was
> already becoming apparent that the consequence of the openness in
> the international system, economically, as much as politically, was
> taking certain things out of control. The result of globalization was the
> reduced power of states, the movement of capital and people around
> the world as governments opened up their borders. This created new
> opportunities for those who wished to inflict harm on the established
> order . . . On 11 September 2001 our advanced technologies and our
> vulnerabilities were combined.[139]

*Finally, market state terrorism is no longer simply a technique but is
also an end in itself.* Al Qaeda is pursuing an objective—the establishment
of a global caliphate—that is incompatible with a global system of human
rights. Unlike nation state terrorists, it does not simply want to seize the
governing apparatus of a particular national state; indeed, al Qaeda is a
reaction to the emergence of the globalized market states of consent. The
objectives of market state terrorism will inevitably evoke attempts to
achieve a constant state of terror because this is the most formidable alternative to a global order of state systems of consent and international
regimes of human rights. Nor will these attempts be confined to al Qaeda.
   The goals of ecoterrorists (whose desired world is incompatible with
the consumption patterns of the developed world, and indeed of the desires
of peoples generally throughout the world), animal-rights terrorists
(whose desired world gives a political voice to nonhumans that can override the democratically determined wishes of any society), antiglobalization terrorists (who define themselves against the currents that are bringing

the market state itself into being), and groups that have yet to gel have this in common: they cannot accept the existence of market states of consent, and thus will be at perpetual war with them. That makes terror an end as well as a means. The requirement for perpetual conflict translates in light of how armed conflict is developing (as we shall see in chapter 3) into a requirement for a continual state of terror.

III.

In all these various global aspects of market state terrorism, al Qaeda is the market innovator, so to speak, and as the perpetrator of the September 11 attacks is certainly worthy of study. Al Qaeda came first in part because Islam is a global religion[140] and because, derivatively, there were global financing institutions like the *hawala*s on which al Qaeda could rely. There is nothing, however, in the characteristics of the market state terrorist group—its lethality, global reach, independent financing, decentralized structure, and more deadly weapons—that is necessarily confined to al Qaeda. In fact, al Qaeda is probably a rather primitive prototype of the terrorism to come. Its importance lies in its being the first. Because it is very much a creature of postmodernity,[141] and the economic and political consequences of the end of the Long War, it is unlikely that it will be the last.

It is the postmodern, deterritorialized societies of Western Europe and the more cosmopolitan states of the Middle East that have bred the foot soldiers of al Qaeda. These young men find they must choose their identities. Global communications have made an Islamic identity behind a mask of terror one compelling option.

It took decades for Muslims in Africa and Asia to get upset about the plight of Arab Palestinians. Now Muslims react to events in Lebanon, Gaza, and Iraq while the events are under way, "in real time."[142] As noted above, recent research has found large and increasing majorities in Indonesia, Pakistan, Lebanon, Nigeria, and Jordan who feel solidarity with the Islamic population around the world.[143] Similar results will doubtless be found in surveys taken of European Muslim youth. The French scholar of Islamism Olivier Roy has observed that

[i]n fact, this new brand of supranational neo-fundamentalism is more a product of contemporary globalization than of the Islamic past. Using two international languages (English and Arabic), traveling easily by air, studying, training and working in many different countries, communicating through the Internet and cellular phones, they think of themselves as "Muslims" and not as citizens of a specific country.

They are often uprooted, more or less voluntarily (many are Palestinian refugees from 1948, and not from Gaza or the West Bank; bin Laden was stripped of his Saudi citizenship; many others belong to migrant families who move from one country to the next to find jobs or education). It is probably a paradox of globalization to gear together modern supranational networks and traditional, even archaic, infrastate forms of relationships (tribalism, for instance, or religious schools' networks).[144]

The story of al Qaeda's charismatic leader, Osama bin Laden, is well known.[145] What is less appreciated is the way bin Laden has studiedly transformed the nature of al Qaeda from the nation state terrorist model to a novel, market state form. In this evolution,[146] he has moved from the classic commando-style, nation state terrorism of the Afghan mujahideen fighting for the political goal of national liberation in Afghanistan to a global campaign against the West. Rather than denying they were terrorists, as nation state groups had consistently done, al Qaeda embraces the term.

Osama bin Ladin redefined the meaning of terrorism in the modern world. To understand this, it is helpful to compare his movement to the Palestinian movement. The PLO tried to become a state military organization, and it [had thus far] failed . . . Abu Nidal's [transitional] version of terrorism, on the other hand, used multiple support bases for Palestinian radicals. Instead of becoming a state, he moved within many states with many different . . . organizations, eventually hiring out his terrorists to state supporters. Osama bin Ladin differs in his approach from both forms of violence. With the wealth of his construction empire as backing, bin Ladin transcended the state and operated on his own.[147]

With his access to Saudi wealth and that of Muslim NGOs, bin Laden created a virtual market state, one that was not dependent on nation states for support. His goal is to transform the Muslim *ummah,* making the al Qaeda state the political expression of this global society of believers. This strategic objective is rooted in the legal goal of recognizing and enforcing sharia wherever Muslims can be found.

Is al Qaeda a market state terrorist group because it shares the structure of the market state and its practices while defining itself by its rejection of market state ideology, or is it a virtual market state that attempts to maximize the opportunities of its citizens—the faithful—by creating a global caliphate where they can find lifestyles denied them by human-rights-respecting states? Al Qaeda could be described either way, depending on the construction we give to the term "maximizing opportunities."* At this stage we may focus on its qualities as a terrorist group.

Olivier Roy vividly contrasts the characteristics of bin Laden's market state terrorism to nation state terrorism:

> Osama bin Laden . . . has been very critical of the Islamic movements of national liberation. He has been critical of the Palestinians, saying, "What use is it to create a Palestinian state? If you create a Palestinian state, it will be like many other states. You should try to mobilize the *umma,* the Muslim community, for your cause, but not for creating a Palestinian state." He is opposed to the idea of a Palestinian state. Bin Laden is a man who wants to unify all the Muslim population in the world against the world power, the United States of America. He doesn't care about Palestine. He doesn't care about Cairo, he doesn't care about Istanbul, and so on . . . Where is he fighting? New York, Bosnia, Kosovo, Chechnya, Central Asia, Afghanistan, Kashmir, Philippines, East Africa . . . Bin Laden is a man of global values. He is a product, a child of world values. He is not some kind of crazy man from the Middle East, coming from the desert to fight the crusaders. No, his battlefield is the modern world.[148]

Many have simply missed the revolution in terrorism presented by al Qaeda. Summarizing a U.S. Government Accountability Office (GAO) study of Canada, France, Germany, Israel, and the U.K., Anthony Cordesman concluded "that the United States has comparatively little to learn from the overall response its friends and allies are making to the emerging threats posed by mass terrorism, [weapons of mass destruction] attacks, and new forms of covert state and terrorist" attacks.[149] Yet because they do not appreciate this new form of terrorism, many commentators abroad are highly dubious of the American characterization of this threat and are therefore equally dismissive of the unique vulnerabilities of the U.S.

Nor does the only barrier to understanding market state terrorism come from those who claim that it is nothing new. A new front has opened up in this struggle for understanding in which it is claimed that al Qaeda is so novel that it is a mistake even to think of it as an organization at all, and some commentators even go further, to assert that the entire matter is an insubstantial nightmare foisted off on a credulous public.

Acknowledging that while once "al Qaeda functioned like a venture capital firm—providing funding, contacts, and expert advice to many dif-

---

*Which is not necessarily the same thing as maximizing choice, particularly for the doctrinaire. The Puritans came to America to create greater opportunities for a New Jerusalem, but not to increase choice per se.

ferent militant groups and individuals from all over the Islamic world,"[150] the journalist Jason Burke has concluded that now al Qaeda is less an organization than an ideology. This insight is easy to misconstrue. I would prefer to say that the kind of organization that al Qaeda represents is by its nature decentralized, devolved, outsourcing, networked, and global. Its "venture capital aspects"—which have been severely compromised by the invasion of Afghanistan—nevertheless are an essential feature of its structure. Al Qaeda is not "less an organization than an ideology," because that is the kind of organization it is: one that is less vertically controlled and managed than nation state terror groups but is nevertheless a coherent operational entity unlike a mere ideology or idea.

Still there are some for whom al Qaeda is merely an idea. It is a myth, concocted by governments to instill fear in order to increase the powers of the State. In January 2005 the BBC broadcast a three-part series, *The Power of Nightmares,* devoted to exposing the fact that the very "idea that we are threatened by a hidden and organized terrorist network is an illusion."[151] The series helpfully pointed to the "security services, and the international media" as the villains in perpetrating this delusion. The program offered this explanation of the government's motives in marketing this deception, which it termed a "dark illusion": "[I]n an age when all the grand ideas have lost credibility, fear of a phantom enemy is all the politicians have left to maintain their power."[152]

The *Guardian* further summarized the message of the series: "[Al Qaeda] is not an organised international network. It does not have members or a leader. It does not have 'sleeper cells.' It does not have an overall strategy. In fact, it barely exists at all, except as an idea . . ."[153]

It is important to treat these views seriously, not only because they come from a respected institution—the BBC—and because a television series of hour-long programs, nationally televised over three nights in prime time and devoted to persuading the public of the truth of these opinions, is bound to have a significant political effect, but mainly because understanding al Qaeda's "overall strategy" is absolutely crucial to its defeat. Postulating that it even has a strategy is one of the reasons I will offer in chapter 3 for naming the current struggle a "war." If there really is no strategy, no organization, no sleeper cells, etc.—if all the claims to the contrary are no more than a ruse to frighten the public into voting for the parties in power, this is real "news" and the BBC is after all perhaps the world's most respected purveyor of news.

Does al Qaeda have a strategy that is actually linked to the actions of the low-level terrorists who carry out murderous operations? Can al Qaeda maintain a strategy without a conventional system of command and control? Consider the following two narratives that relate the attempt by

Richard Reid to explode an American Airlines plane over the Atlantic and tell the story of Osama bin Laden and Ayman al Zawahiri's collaboration. These two examples, one operational, one strategic, ought to give us some guidance as to whether al Qaeda really only exists in the minds of propagandists for Western governments.

In late 2001, a young British citizen boarded American Airlines flight 63 from Paris bound for Miami.[154] When the plane was two and a half hours into its journey, and beyond radio contact with any land-based airtraffic controllers, Richard Reid struck a match and attempted to light the fuse to an explosive device that had been carefully constructed to fit inside the heel and sole of one of the athletic shoes he was wearing. The scent of the struck match caught the attention of a flight attendant, who directed him to extinguish the flame. She thought he was about to smoke a cigarette, which was against airline regulations. Reid complied and apologized; the flight attendant resumed her duties. Now concerned, however, that the passenger in the seat next to him would return, Reid began frantically trying to light the fuse. The attendant noticed the lit match, returned, and admonished him again about smoking on board an international flight. This time he ignored her, desperately trying to ignite the charge, and so she and another attendant tried to take away Reid's matches. When this happened, he bit her extended hand, she screamed and, in the post-9/11 environment, passengers rushed to assist the women and descended on Reid. This antic seriocomedy concluded with his being tied down by seat belts and further restrained by a 6'8" professional basketball player; the plane was diverted to Boston and he was arrested. This incident might not have ended quite so happily, however, for it was only by chance that Reid was unable to execute a well-thought-out plan that would have almost certainly cost the lives of everyone on the plane.

Reid grew up in southeast London, the child of a Jamaican father and an English mother. His father, born a Protestant, had converted to Islam while in prison. Reid himself became a petty criminal and left school at sixteen. Like his father he served several sentences in various institutions and prisons and also converted to Islam. Released from prison in 1995 he began to frequent the Brixton Mosque and became enamored with various radical imams, including the Egyptian Abu Hamza al-Masri, currently serving a prison term for incitement to murder.

In 1998, it was arranged that Reid would go to Afghanistan for training at a camp set up by al Qaeda, which by this time had been forced out of Sudan. After two years spent establishing his credentials and receiving training in more than one camp, Reid embarked on a six-month series of reconnaissance missions to scout targets for terrorist attack.

During this period Reid acquired a duplicate U.K. passport from the

British consulate in Amsterdam. He visited Tel Aviv, Cairo, Istanbul, and Karachi, making various reports to his al Qaeda controllers on airline security and on the location and arrangement of office complexes and transport links. We know all this from a detailed report written by Reid that was stored on a computer hard drive purchased by a journalist from a looter in Afghanistan. In December 2001 Reid obtained a fresh British passport from the consulate in Brussels; this would mask his frequent trips.

Once the target had been finally selected, the IED (improvised explosive device) was constructed. Using the explosive PETN—described in an al Qaeda manual seized in Afghanistan—the IED was fitted into the waffle structure of the bottom of one of Reid's athletic shoes. According to Sebestyén Gorka, an examination of an X-ray of the original shoe by *Jane's Terrorism and Security Monitor* disclosed nothing of the explosive, or the detonator and safety fuse. It was, in the words of the U.S. attorney, ingenious, hard to detect, and deadly. A subsequent examination revealed a palm print and hair residue found on the detonator that was not Reid's, suggesting that the device had not been made by Reid (who in any case had never revealed a sophisticated grasp of micromunitions). Gorka believes that the IED was probably built for Reid by Nizar Trabelsi, who is currently serving a prison sentence in Belgium for planning an attack against a U.S. military installation.

The subsequent investigation disclosed much of Reid's message traffic from various Internet cafés as well as calls made on his prepaid telephone cards. This and other evidence showed that he had received extensive logistical support from al Qaeda cells in Paris, and French authorities made arrests of persons believed to have assisted Reid. In Britain, police later apprehended Saajid Mohammed Badat, an associate of Reid's, who confessed that he had been planning a similar attack and had also acquired a duplicate passport through the Brussels consulate. Explosives and other paraphernalia necessary for an improvised explosive device were discovered at Badat's home.

Reid purchased a ticket for the Miami flight from Paris on December 21, paying with $1,800 in cash. Because he was carrying a newly issued passport (which did not disclose his trips to Afghanistan or his many reconnaissance journeys), had no luggage, and had paid for a one-way trip in cash, French authorities were suspicious. They refused to permit Reid to fly on the twenty-first while they investigated him. This delay probably saved the plane he was eventually allowed to board, because it meant that his athletic shoes were constantly worn for more than thirty hours during which the black-powder fuse of the IED became damp from perspiration. This was the fuse that Reid was unable to light once he was allowed by the French police to board the same flight the next day. Had the fuse been successfully ignited, there seems to be little doubt that it would have exploded with enough force to blow a hole in the side of the plane.[155]

In a letter to his mother, Reid explained the rationale for the attempted attack:

> . . . what I am doing is part of the ongoing war between islaam and disbelief . . . I didn't do this out of ignorance nor did i do just because I want to die but rather because I see it as a duty upon me . . . the message of islaam is the truth, this is why we are ready to die defending the true islaam rather than to just sit back and allow the American government to dictate to us what we should believe and how we should behave, it is clear that this is a war between truth and falsehood . . . this is a war between islaam and democracy.[156]

This uneducated petty criminal, whatever his limitations, accurately portrays the al Qaeda vision. This vision is a reaction to the globalization of human rights—democracy, the rule of secular law, the protection of women's rights. It seeks to universalize the legal rules and practices by which Afghanistan was governed under the Taliban. Like other terrorists from earlier eras, al Qaeda uses whatever weapons are at hand to terrorize civilians, but, interestingly, it uses the tactics of terror in order to be left alone to create a state of terror for its adherents. That is to say, al Qaeda seeks a state of terror, in one sense of the term, in order to frighten away other states, so that it may impose its own state of terror on those persons it governs. Its leaders believe that only such a state can offer Muslims the opportunity for devotion and orthodox practice that other states deny because only in such a state can the sharia be enforced.

Gorka draws five lessons from the Reid case:

- Considerable discretion is exercised at low levels in the chain of command: "the individual operative has a large sphere of mobility [and discretion]. Reid decided [on] an American [target] once the US had started to bomb Afghanistan."
- The use of classic intelligence gathering techniques for target acquisition reflects a practiced and informed method of operation, as does the use of modern means of communication.
- Finances apparently pose no problem, as Reid was "able to travel, sustain himself and pay in cash where necessary."
- Further attention should be paid to the young offender prison system to identify potential terrorists.
- Al Qaeda's wide-flung organizational network, distinct from the wider Muslim community, is the "pivotal influence" on ideology and terrorist training.[157]

I have dwelt on the Reid case because it seemed unfair to the views criticized here to discuss an incident of which the BBC producers could not have been aware: the bombings in London in the summer of 2005.[158] It is most unlikely that the perpetrators of this deadly bombing, in which fifty-two persons died, had the skills to create the cell-phone-detonated weapons that were so similar to those used to bomb trains at the Atocha station in Madrid. Although as of this writing the identities of any further conspirators are unknown, there were likely others, and it is already known that the chief suspect, Mohammed Sidique Khan, and a second conspirator were trained in Pakistan. Indeed, it may well prove to be the case that the fourth bomb, which exploded on a bus some forty-five minutes after the explosions on Underground trains on routes tracking three of the four points of the compass from Kings Cross station, was remotely detonated, killing the bomber who, for some reason, had failed to execute his planned attack on the fourth train. Finally, it seems unlikely that this particular group of men would have been the ones likely to select a date on which the U.K. was hosting the first day of the G8 summit, thus guaranteeing maximum media exposure shortly after Britain had assumed the presidency of the E.U.[159] On the contrary, such attacks seem well suited to the evolving strategy of al Qaeda, as expressed most clearly by its titular leader, Osama bin Laden, than to the impulsive behavior of the bombers themselves.

That strategy has developed in pursuit of a single, comprehensive goal: to enforce sharia, the code of law derived from the Koran, in those jurisdictions where Muslims reside or have historically resided. More than many Western intellectuals (think of the "Realist school" of American political scientists) and many Western leaders (think of President George W. Bush and Vice President Dick Cheney), bin Laden and his comrade, Ayman al Zawahiri, have realized that in the current era strategy and law must be tightly coordinated. The strategic goal of al Qaeda's jihad is a constitutional one, imposing the implacable, transnational jurisdiction of the sharia; and the constitutional goal, a caliphate of textualist clerics ruling via a market state of terror, is well suited to the tactical methods chosen, suicide bombings and careful exploitation of the media. Despite a shifting, and sometimes unpredictable, transformation of the strategic context, bin Laden and Zawahiri have managed to remain strikingly consistent in the pursuit of their objectives.

Each man came to this political vision by a different route. Osama bin Laden, born in 1958, was the son of a billionaire with close relations to the royal House of Saud. After dropping out of university bin Laden came to Peshawar in 1979, where he organized with others Maktab al-Khadamat

(MAK), which supported non-Afghan Arab fighters. Bin Laden's fortune provided air tickets, housing, training, and other support for these anti-Soviet jihadists.

In the early 1980s, Zawahiri—an Egyptian physician born to a distinguished professional family in 1951—also migrated to Peshawar. Zawahiri appreciated the value of an enormously rich idealist and began cultivating bin Laden. When the Soviets pulled out of Afghanistan, a heated debate ensued over what should be done with the jihadist forces trained in the Afghan conflict. Zawahiri wanted to overthrow the government of Egypt, while Bin Laden entertained visions of taking over Saudi Arabia and using its vast oil wealth to create a new caliphate. In August 1988, al Qaeda was formed as a loose alliance among various established jihadist groups. It was dominated by members of the Egyptian Islamic Jihad, Zawahiri's group, and funded by bin Laden.

The next period of both men's lives was devoted to their respective societies. Bin Laden worked in the family construction business; Zawahiri practiced medicine and conspired. In 1990, Saddam Hussein invaded and annexed Kuwait. Bin Laden, who was well known to the princes of the Saudi royal family, offered to organize a force of some 28,000 jihadists to protect the kingdom. It is hard not to think that he still believed he might assume power in Saudi Arabia some day, in some way, especially if he became responsible for the security of the country, was viewed as its savior, and commanded a dedicated force pledged to himself. These daydreams were dashed when the king rejected his offer and instead invited a U.S.-led coalition to deploy in the kingdom. After the First Gulf War ended, not in the removal of Saddam Hussein, but in a cease-fire, Western forces remained in what appeared to be a long-term deployment. It was at this time that bin Laden broke with the House of Saud and began open criticism of the regime. He defended his new stridency on the ground that the presence of unbelievers in the land of the two holy cities, Mecca and Medina, the protection of whose Muslim shrines was supposed to provide the basis for the legitimacy of the Saudi regime, contaminated this sacred trust. No doubt this was sincerely felt, but it may also be that the presence of a highly armed Western force made the possibility of the collapse of the regime (and its replacement by bin Laden) vanishingly remote. After a brief return to Afghanistan, bin Laden settled in Sudan in 1992.

Zawahiri was busy too. In 1990 Islamic Jihad had murdered the Speaker of the Egyptian parliament. Beginning in 1993 Zawahiri organized a series of assassination attempts. The first, in August, against the Egyptian interior minister, only succeeded in killing the bomber and his accomplice. The following November, his group attempted to kill the prime minister with a car bomb. The explosion did not injure the prime minister, but twenty-one others were hurt and a twelve-year-old schoolgirl was killed. This outraged Egyptians—some 240 persons had been killed by terrorists in the preceding two years—and a mass demonstration against terror seems to have shaken Zawahiri. The popular reaction and a brutal crackdown against the membership persuaded him that, as Lawrence Wright put it, "if Islamic Jihad was to survive, it would have to be outside Egypt."[160]

Still, despite far-flung contacts with jihadists, and ceaseless traveling by Zawahiri, both men focused on their respective countries. Bin Laden went into business in Khartoum, "investing heavily in Sudanese construction projects including an airport and the country's main highway; he also bought up the entire crop of Sudanese cotton and he occasionally picked up the tab for the country's oil imports."[161]

The Sudanese, however, under pressure from the U.S., Egypt, and Saudi Arabia, expelled bin Laden. In May 1996, bin Laden chartered a jet and, with two hundred colleagues and their families, flew to Jalalabad. In Afghanistan bin Laden was given the protection of the Taliban, and al Qaeda was partly integrated into the Afghan Ministry of Defense. Training camps were set up in Afghanistan for a broad, international group of jihadists who traveled there for instruction.

In August 1996, bin Laden issued the first of his most significant public pronouncements. This is the "Declaration of War Against the Americans Occupying the Land of the Two Holy Places," and it actually comes at the end, rather than the beginning, of bin Laden's first phase, in which he and Zawahiri were preoccupied with the national struggles to seize power in the great Muslim states of Saudi Arabia and Egypt, respectively.

> Through its course of actions, the [Saudi] regime has torn off its legitimacy: (1) Suspension of the Islamic Shari'ah law and exchanging it with man made civil law . . . (2) The inability of the regime to protect the country and allowing . . . the American crusader force to occupy the land. Today your brothers and sons, the sons of the two Holy Places, have started their jihad in the cause of Allah to expel the occupying enemy from the country . . .[162]

In 1997, Zawahiri rejoined bin Laden in Afghanistan and began the second phase of their collaboration.

This period broadened the scope of the confrontation with the United States. Whereas during the first period Saudi and Egyptian assets had been attacked directly, and American assets were targeted in those countries and in the proximate region, in the next phase the United States itself would be assaulted. Bin Laden and Zawahiri no longer saw the U.S. as simply propping up the regimes they wished to destroy. Now they asserted that the

U.S. was a worldwide threat to Muslims and had to be confronted in every part of the globe.

The February 1998 fatwa that followed was a watershed in two respects: it recognized the formal alliance between Zawahiri and bin Laden, and it laid out a rationale for a global war. It announced that the "ruling to kill the Americans and their allies—civilian and military—is an individual duty for every Muslim who can do it in any country in which it is possible to do it."[163]

There followed in August the horrific assaults against American embassies in Nairobi, Kenya, and Dar es Salaam, Tanzania. More than 220 people were killed and over 4,000 wounded in simultaneous truck bomb attacks. In 1999 a plot to attack the U.S. embassy in Tirana, Albania, was thwarted, but on October 12, 2000, al Qaeda struck again, killing 17 persons and injuring 39 in an assault on the American guided missile destroyer USS *Cole* in Aden harbor. As the ship was refueling offshore, a small craft with two men aboard approached the ship and exploded, tearing a forty-foot gash in the side of the vessel.

Now the audience for bin Laden's messages became worldwide—both Islam and the American presence were global, after all—and, interestingly, the intended recipients of this message were expanded to include the peoples of secular states like Iraq. They were to be enlisted in the struggle against the U.S. and the West, and against the international institutions that bin Laden believed served their purposes, including the U.N., the Red Cross, various humanitarian groups, multinational corporations, international corporations, and data exchange systems,[164] and especially those groups campaigning for human rights. The goal had crystallized into a global vision—well beyond even the restoration of an imagined caliphate—that stretched from Andalusia in Spain, across the Mediterranean to the Magreb, down through Somalia and across the Red Sea to the Gulf states and up to the Balkans, and thence across the Caucasus to Chechnya, Afghanistan, Pakistan, and Kashmir, now to include Indonesia and the Philippines. The new objective was a worldwide political structure of the faithful in which a state was created that had no historical precedents. It was to be built out of the practices of Sunni Muslims strictly adhering to Koranic laws; financed by petrodollars from the Gulf, the Middle East, and especially now from central Asia; and governed by a global theocratic network. Nation states and national borders would be rendered irrelevant.

In this vision, repeated references are made to the Taleban regime of Afghanistan being the model for future universal theocracy. This was soon followed by bin Laden's issuance ... of a fatwa against the US in which attacks against civilians were justified: "We call on every Muslim who believes in Allah and wishes to be rewarded to comply with Allah's order to kill the Americans and plunder their money wherever and whenever they find it."[165]

Then on September 11, 2001, al Qaeda struck New York and Washington with historic repercussions. Something approaching 3,000 persons were killed when New York's tallest structures were struck by hijacked passenger planes and the Pentagon was attacked by another seized airliner; a fourth plane bound for Washington went down in rural Pennsylvania.

The U.S. invasion of Afghanistan followed, despite bin Laden's repeated claims that he had nothing to do with the 9/11 attacks. The Taliban were routed. Bin Laden and Zawahiri fled. At their urgent request, other attacks followed, most notably in Bali, where 202 persons were killed,[166] in a futile effort to take pressure off the Afghan sector.

Whereas formerly bin Laden's public statements were addressed to followers and potential followers, as the Wars against Terror progressed the target audiences for these statements changed. Just before the invasion of Afghanistan, al Qaeda released a video of bin Laden addressing the U.S. political leadership and making various demands of the United States. These demands included a U.S. withdrawal from Saudi Arabia, the creation of a Palestinian state, and other ultimata. By 2004, however, bin Laden's public statements had shifted again: just before the U.S. election he was eager to appeal to the American public directly.[167] By 2005 these declarations shifted once more, addressing European publics on the one hand and the global Muslim community in its entirety on the other. Coupled with the terrorist attacks during these periods, a clear evolution of al Qaeda strategy emerges, including of course an evolving communications strategy, for al Qaeda has a communications council that carefully tailors messages to different constituencies and maintains relationships with influential media outlets.

Al Qaeda has moved from challenging local and national leaderships directly to attempting to destabilize them by attacking the U.S., which, it believed, would then withdraw from the Middle East, leaving its client allies to collapse. The U.S. response to September 11, including the destruction of the Taliban regime, confounded this strategy, which was then changed to accommodate adverse events. It has been reported that the al Qaeda leadership, recognizing that it would be difficult to follow up 9/11 immediately with even more spectacular strikes and believing that anything less would sacrifice the momentum gained by the World Trade Center and Pentagon assaults, cancelled a planned cyanide attack on the New York subway system. In any event, al Qaeda switched to outsourcing more numerous incursions all across the Muslim world, funding and assisting local groups to whom these attacks were assigned. As Riedel noted, "for the last several years, al Qaeda's priority has been to bleed the United States in Afghanistan and Iraq. Striking on U.S. soil has been a lesser goal."[168]

Paradoxically, the September 11 attacks—which do not appear to have had any connection to Saddam Hussein (despite his approaches to bin Laden)—allowed the Bush administration to pursue an invasion of Iraq. This considerably increased the stakes. Now al Qaeda faced the threatening prospect of a functioning state of consent in an Arab society. This challenge, however, could also turn out to be an opportunity for the jihadists because now their predictions of U.S. attacks on Muslims, the humiliation of captives, American imposition of certain legal norms—including women's rights and democratic practices—and the reports of riches stolen from the region by the colonial West all appeared to confirm bin Laden's portrait of a Muslim world under siege by the U.S. and its allies.

Accordingly, al Qaeda strategy shifted again. First, alliances were forged in Iraq. The psychopathic Abu Musab al Zarqawi was made emir of al Qaeda in Iraq, and he proceeded to conduct a vicious campaign of atrocities and torture, at first carefully singling out non-Iraqi targets. While it was puzzling to resistance sympathizers in the West, the targeting of humanitarian agencies, the U.N., and even local persons of Western descent involved in humane efforts for the Iraqi people was precisely in line with this strategy of forcing a struggle between local Muslims and everyone else. It was al Qaeda that ran the network of Internet sites recruiting suicide bombers from Saudi Arabia, Egypt, and Pakistan, paying for their travel through safe houses in Syria, and providing them with false documents and ultimately with explosives. A parallel campaign of terrorism by Sunni Baathists did not employ suicide terrorists; indeed, there were few Iraqis conducting those operations. What the Baathists had to lose with the coming of a parliamentary democracy was power, riches, and their deep identification with the Iraqi state; what al Qaeda could lose was far more significant. A human rights–respecting Iraq would be an attractive model for the coming change of generations in Saudi Arabia and Egypt. It would be an example of a successful state in the region that could co-opt the new Palestinian state as a secular ally, linking up with the pro-Western Afghan, Turkish, and Lebanese democracies. Iraq, rather than Egypt or Saudi Arabia, would be the laboratory for twenty-first century political renovation. The stakes were enormous for al Qaeda, which, in a tactical alliance with anti-U.S. Iraqi nationalists, now had to defeat the movement toward a revived Iraqi state.

This threat led not only to an intensified campaign against the U.S. occupation, but more importantly to a diplomatic and terrorist endeavor to force the U.S. to withdraw from Iraq by isolating it from its allies in the

Coalition. Hostages were carefully selected so they could be filmed in heart-wrenching scenes of torture and murder, desperately appealing to the governments of Coalition countries to withdraw. Arab diplomats accredited to the new Iraqi government were kidnapped and killed.[169] At the same time, attacks on Western states that had opposed the U.S.-U.K. Coalition had to be temporarily suspended. Attacks against states that sent troops to Iraq—Italy, Spain, the U.K.—had to be carefully timed and flawlessly executed. Anything less might backfire and result in increased resolve among the Coalition's partners. Finally, new conciliatory messages had to be delivered to democratic publics whose interest in Iraqi reform was slight.

Beginning in April 2004, audiotaped messages directed to Europeans proposed a "reconciliation initiative": al Qaeda would not target those European countries that withdrew forces from Muslim lands and broke with the U.S. In an obvious rhetorical move, bin Laden addressed Europeans as "our neighbors north of the Mediterranean," playing on the fears of many that the consequences of the American occupation of Iraq (including increased immigration) would be felt in Europe and not in America. While Zawahiri voiced criticism in February of the French decision to ban headscarves in schools—which he described as "another example of the Crusader's malice, which all Westerners have against Muslims"—bin Laden delicately attempted to split NATO with artfully crafted messages. The polls show, he said in one such taped message, that "[m]ost Europeans want peace . . . [I]njustice is inflicted on us and on you by your politicians, who send your sons—although you are opposed to this—to our countries to kill and be killed."[170]

While this message of conciliation and shared hostility to U.S. hegemony was being broadcast, al Qaeda was conducting its most successful terrorist operation in Europe to date, the Madrid bombings that killed 190 and seriously wounded 1,500, propelling into power a left-wing government that quickly allied with France and denounced the U.S.-U.K. Coalition before abruptly pulling its forces out of Iraq.

Thus the attacks on London on July 7, 2005—and the forbearance from spectacular attacks in the U.S.—should be seen as a plausible continuation of al Qaeda's anti-Coalition approach. This was confirmed by a Zawahiri videotape released through al Jazeera the first week in August, after the July 7 bombings.

> Blair has brought you destruction in central London, and God willing, will bring more destruction. O nations of the crusader alliance, we . . . offered you a truce to leave the house of Islam. . . . You, however, shed rivers of blood in our land so we exploded volcanoes of anger in your land. . . . If you don't leave today, then you shall inevitably leave

tomorrow but after scores of thousands of fatalities and double that
number of disabled and wounded people.[171]

Furthermore, in July 2006 a similar attack occurred in Mumbai (Bombay). On the eleventh of that month, bombs simultaneously exploded at
eight locations along the Mumbai commuter line that runs by the Arabian
Sea. More than 200 persons were killed. This attack, which was directed
against the financial and film center of India, came at a time when India's
political relationship to the United States had undergone a historic change.
India, which for decades had been aligned with the Soviet Union, and had
been Britain's most consistent adversary in the U.N., was now becoming a
Western ally in the region. I would be surprised if investigations did not
eventually confirm that elements linked to al Qaeda were responsible for
the bombing. Such a group, I surmise, will have been active in the Kashmir
conflict, but this unusual choice of target and the simultaneous attacks on
transport that are al Qaeda's signature mark it as something beyond the
usual Pakistani-Indian atrocities. As of this writing, the principal group
being investigated is Lashkar-e-Taiba (LeT), a group allied with al Qaeda,
which was set up with the assistance of the Pakistani intelligence services
a decade ago as a Kashmiri separatist organization. It has since expanded
to the international stage and its members have been arrested in the U.K.,
the U.S., and Australia. One of the London 7/7 bombers, Shehzad Tanweer, is believed to have stayed at a madrassa run by LeT in Mudrike, outside Lahore.

It is macabre to speculate, but we ought to expect similar attacks on any
state whose relations with the U.S. become close. If the U.S. and Russia
are able to cooperate more fully in international affairs, one consequence
would be to move Moscow up on al Qaeda's list of targets. Japan's alliance
with the U.S. has led some to speculate that it too will be added to the list.
When an attempt to bomb airliners leaving London airports was foiled in
August 2006, there was a widespread reaction in Britain that such schemes
were really the fault of Tony Blair's policies of close cooperation with
Washington[172] and the perhaps slightly discreditable suggestion that
Britain would be better off if somehow it could move the U.S. more
directly into the line of fire.

The evolution of al Qaeda's strategy can also be clearly seen in those
statements that do not emerge from Zawahiri and bin Laden but instead
emanate from the jihadist ideologues whose ideas have fueled al Qaeda[173]
and who have become the prime thinkers for the jihadist movement, figures such as Abu Musab al-Suri, a Syrian who has served on al Qaeda's
inner council, and the elusive Abu Bakr Naji,[174] who has been variously
identified as a Tunisian, a Jordanian, and the pen name for a collective of

various theorists.[175] Unlike the later declarations of the al Qaeda leadership, these statements are directed toward the radical faithful and are obviously not an effort to influence the wavering publics of American allies.

For our purposes, three important points emerge from these writers. First, the war aim for al Qaeda must be to kill civilians.[176] As al-Suri put it in his monumental work, *Call for Worldwide Islamic Resistance*,[177] the goal is "to bring about the largest number of human and material casualties possible for America and its allies."[178] Among other targets for extermination he lists Jews, "Westerners in general," citizens of countries belonging to the NATO alliance, Russians, Chinese, atheists, pagans, and hypocrites (Muslim apostates).

Second, the strategy called for is precisely that of establishing a state of terror. Lawrence Wright summarizes Naji's views as follows:

> [He] recommended that jihadis continually attack the vital economic centers of [the targeted countries]. Sensing weakness . . . the people will lose confidence in their governments, which will respond with increasingly ineffective acts of repression. Eventually the governments will lose control. Savagery will naturally follow, offering Islamists the opportunity to capture the allegiance of a population that is desperate for order. (Naji cites Afghanistan before the Taliban as an example.) Even though the jihadis will have caused the chaos, the fact will be forgotten as the fighters impose security, provide food and medical treatment, and establish Islamic courts of justice.[179]

Finally, the regimes that al Qaeda will establish have a remarkable market state quality to them that would be paradoxical if we mistakenly thought of the jihadists as nation state terrorists. Naji, for example, discusses this issue by addressing the question posed by a colleague: "Assuming that we get rid of the apostate regimes today, who will take over the ministry of agriculture, trade, economics, etc.?" His answer is that

> [i]t is not a prerequisite that the mujahid movement has to be prepared especially for agriculture, trade, and industry . . . As for the one who manages the techniques in each ministry, he can be a paid employee who has no interest in policy and is not a member of the movement or the party.[180]

In all these respects, it should be manifest that we are dealing with a new form of terrorism, and that this form reflects the emerging constitutional order of the market state.

Two important conclusions can be drawn from this evolution. First, there is a coherent strategy at work in both the bombings and the rhetoric of al Qaeda, and the most significant evidence for this is the fact that this strategy has changed to accommodate the initiatives of its enemies. It is most unlikely that these are the result of self-organized amateurs on the one hand, or an isolated and impotent leadership on the other. Second, while the rhetoric of al Qaeda has become more conciliatory—especially toward European publics it believes can be peeled away from association with the U.S.—the "ideological agenda of confrontation with the West and puritanical reform in the Islamic world"[181] has broadened since 1996.

Zawahiri, in his autobiographical *Knights Under the Prophet's Banner*,[182] described this evolution. In this work he explicitly recognizes that the decisive historical shift was not September 11, 2001, but the collapse of the Soviet Union in 1989, which increased the power and influence of the U.S., and thus also the stability of the regimes in Egypt and Saudi Arabia that were supported by the Americans. This unwelcome development was further strengthened with the deployment of U.S. forces in the region following the Iraqi invasion of Kuwait. The al Qaeda strategy had to be to attack the United States directly in the hope that it would abandon the states it had supported. Indeed, because the terrorists were drawn from these societies, Zawahiri believed the U.S. would become alienated from the regimes that were its clients, frustrated that they were unable to eliminate the terrorists they had spawned. Attacks on European societies would further weaken the U.S., which would be forced to draw on its own manpower and revenue alone to finance overseas commitments.

In many respects it was Zawahiri who made al Qaeda into the first market state terrorist organization: his use of outsourced suicide bombers; his choice of their targets (the Tamil Tigers had employed suicide units previously but mainly for assassinations); his use of heroic videos and tape recordings of the martyrs; his disdain for claiming responsibility for an attack, which was in accord with his efforts to make al Qaeda's role ambiguous, thereby fracturing any antiterrorist alliance (in contrast with nation state terrorists, who were only too anxious to claim credit for their atrocities lest some other group seize leadership of the national insurgency); his recognition that violence against the United States could be used as a rallying call to unite Muslims globally (while nation state terrorists rejected a transnational state), because the U.S. had a global presence and because the U.S. was, more than any other state, associated with the threats posed by globalization. Yet it was bin Laden whose shrewd use of abundant funds created worldwide clients that in turn made possible the conditions for al Qaeda's successes. Perfectly willing to overlook doctrinal differences—his pact with Shia Iran rivals the Ribbentrop-Molotov agreement in its cynicism (and in its ultimate fate, one imagines)—he was able to inspire groups that had been in conflict for decades to cooperate in actions against American interests. Because al Qaeda was a creature of globalization, it was easier for bin Laden adroitly to cite globalization both as a doctrinal spur, quickening anger against the U.S. and the E.U., and as an organizational saddle, spanning the broad stallion back of global Islam.

Bin Laden attacked the very basis for the society of nation states—its national orientation—and attacked, too, the principal institutions of that society, the United Nations and other nation state international organizations, and the systems of representative democracy of the nation state that had triumphed in the twentieth century. His own account of the moral responsibilities of the democracies recapitulates the market state assault on the legitimacy of nation states. This emerges from an examination of the justifications bin Laden offers for al Qaeda's actions in attacking civilians, the protection of whom, as we shall see in chapter 3, is the war aim of market states of consent.

To put bin Laden's problem in terms familiar from the Western tradition: he had to derive justifications for al Qaeda's decision to wage war (*jus ad bellum*) and its tactics in war (*jus in bello*). Bin Laden attempted to provide these concepts in the fatwa declaring war.

First, despite the fact that he was not recognized as having the theological authority that entitled him to issue fatwas, bin Laden argued that his literal reading of the Koran (a textual argument) was more consistent with the Koran's own account of its revelatory truths as unchanging and comprehensive than were interpretations by clerics whose readings of the Koran were legitimated solely on the basis of their official roles and education (a doctrinal argument); to do otherwise would be to "worship these men rather than the Book." Second, he described the role of the United States and its ally Israel as only the most recent example of a centuries-long effort to oppress the Muslims of the Near East, the "heart" of Islam. The Crusader invasion and the planting of a Crusader colony in the Holy Land in the late twelfth century[183] provide the paradigm of which the insertion of a Zionist state by Britain in the twentieth century is the most recent example. Israel is the European colony that the West intends to extend all the way to the ocean. Western intentions are manifested in an entire panoply of conspiracies: the support for corrupt regimes that, though nominally Islamic, do not respect the sharia in the enforcement of domestic law; the steady enrichment of the West at the expense of the Muslim nation through confiscatory energy deals, by which the wealth of the Near East is siphoned off to the West through sub-market clearing prices for oil; the refusal to permit the Muslim masses to elect Islamicist leaders, as evidenced by the cancellation of the Algerian elections when it appeared that fundamentalist candidates would have won and the West's refusal to support the validly elected Palestinian Hamas ministers; the indifference to Muslim suffering in Chechnya, Kashmir, and Bosnia; the U.N. sanctions imposed on Iraq that led to the deaths of countless innocents; the destruction of the fundamentalist Islamicist regime in Afghanistan; and most recently the overt invasion of Iraq by U.S. and U.K. forces on a deceitful pretext. Even though the Koran limits the legitimate grounds for jihad to defensive actions, it also enjoins every Muslim to protect every other Muslim, and thus bin Laden argues that he has ample grounds for declaring jihad against the Americans and their allies. On this basis he concludes there is a moral duty of every Muslim to wage jihad, and thereby provides the basis for an Islamicist doctrine of *jus ad bellum*.

This argument for *jus ad bellum,* however, does not resolve the problem of *jus in bello,* which is raised by the call in the al Qaeda fatwas for indiscriminate attacks on American civilians. Here too bin Laden had to overcome a theological obstacle: the Koran limits jihad to the destruction of combatants and strictly forbids the killing of innocents. Bin Laden addresses this issue by framing the problem in the context of Western consensual political practices:

> You may then dispute that [the rationale that justifies a fatwa for war] does not justify aggression against civilians . . . This [objection, however,] contradicts your continuous repetition that America is the land of freedom . . . Therefore the American people are the ones who choose their government by way of their own free will, a choice which stems from their agreement to its policies. Thus the American people have chosen, consented to, and affirmed their support for the Israeli oppression of the Palestinians . . . the armies which occupy our lands in the Arabian Gulf, and the fleets which ensure the blockade [and now the occupation] of Iraq . . . So the American people are the ones who fund the attacks against us, and they are the ones who oversee the expenditure of these monies in the way they wish, through their elected candidates.[184]

Note that this basis is not the conventional rationale for an attack on an enemy nation that was heard in the total wars of twentieth century nation states. Rather it is a market state approach because it addresses the responsibilities of citizens *as individuals* rather than as a vulnerable body politic. Consistent with market state parameters, bin Laden repeatedly refers to the results of polling (rather than elections) to establish the political intentions of a particular polity. Similarly, the war aim of al Qaeda is not national, though at one time Zawahiri and bin Laden may have thought in these terms with regard to Egypt and Saudi Arabia. Rather it is—though this may at first seem perverse—a market state claim for truly maximizing the opportunities of the individual, which can only be realized by using the tools God has given for the fulfillment of the individual, that is, opportunities to live under the sharia that the West and its human rights regimes would deny to Muslims. You Americans and the peoples of the West, charges bin Laden,

> rather than ruling by the Shariah of Allah in its Constitution and Laws, choose to invent your own laws as you will and desire. You separate religion from your policies, contradicting the pure nature which affirms Absolute Authority to the Lord and your Creator. You flee from the embarrassing question posed to you: How is it possible for Allah the Almighty to create His creation, grant them power over all the creatures and land, grant them all the amenities of life, and then deny them that which they are most in need of: knowledge of the laws which govern their lives?[185]

"Contrary to Bush's claim that we hate freedom,"[186] all we seek, bin Laden says, is freedom. Though market states in the West claim they endeavor to maximize opportunity, they would deny Muslims to live under divinely inspired law. "Leave us alone," he writes, "or else expect us in New York and Washington."[187] Very simply, al Qaeda seeks a free hand to establish a transnational market state of terror. If this sounds paradoxical, bear in mind that unless we take the appropriate steps in law and strategy for our own countries, we will some day make the same demand: that only a state of terror can allow us individual freedom by protecting our own constitutional preferences—the right to freedom of conscience—from attacks.

On September 20, 2001, President George W. Bush declared war on terrorism. His exact words are worth recalling. The war, he said, "will not end until every terrorist group of *global reach* has been found, stopped and defeated."[188] This remark has been ridiculed in some quarters; one critic expressed an opinion generally held that it "is misleading to talk of a 'war on terrorism,' let alone a war on 'global terrorism.' "[189] (Whether it is in fact misleading to use the term "war" in this context will be discussed in chapter 3.) If it does make sense, however, it makes sense precisely against a *global network,* as opposed to terrorism generally. The development of a global terror network is an example of market state terrorism, which is potentially more lethal than its predecessor, nation state terrorism, and is clearly distinguishable from it. The president was right to recognize this distinction.[190] As two commentators on terrorism—and persons who formerly held antiterrorism posts on the U.S. National Security Council—wrote in the summer of 2006,

> [t]he jihadists comprise a social movement, not just a cluster of terrorist organizations, and they are totally opportunistic and endlessly plastic in how they accommodate to circumstances. They thrive on our

preconceptions and our instinctive determination to come up with rigid schematizations, and we will get the better of them only when our thinking is as flexible and innovative as theirs.[191]

Market state terrorism is global terrorism. Markets, unlike nations, are often global. Indeed, it is becoming increasingly apparent that al Qaeda is not only a reaction to globalization[192] but that it is a manifestation and exploitation of globalization. To see that is also to see that market state terrorism is an unintended side effect of the globalization of international communications (including travel), rapid computation, and radical weapons development of the late twentieth century, which is to say the very strategic developments that are bringing into being the constitutional innovations of the market state. This suggests that al Qaeda will be copied by other globally networked infrastructures engendered by the emergence of market states. It is against these forms of global terrorism that war must be waged when we speak, as did President Bush, of a war against terrorists.

The unifying element among the groups to which al Qaeda outsources its operations is not a mystical, retrograde form of Islam but a shared hatred of the U.S. For this reason it is imperative that the U.S. not solidify that hatred among nation state terrorists but rather address their grievances generously. Casting America as a global, common enemy is one reason why the rising level of anti-Americanism should be of considerable concern to all; it is only a matter of time before an adolescent of European descent and no particular religious views is used as a suicide bomber.[193] If George Bush has done much to arouse anti-Americanism, many of America's friends have done little to suppress it.

"The notion," wrote the political scientist Richard Betts, "that the [twenty-first] century requires a whole new approach for a whole new ball game may seem intuitively right, but it is, in fact, wrong. The difference between the world of 2006 and that of 1999 is no more radical than the difference between the worlds of 1999 and 1992."[194] Actually, such a notion does not appeal to our intuitions, which are so heavily governed by the experience of the wars of the twentieth century. If we believe, however, that the post-1989 world is merely a continuation of the international environment that preceded it, we will be ill-equipped to take measures to cope with that new world. As Audrey Kurth Cronin put it,

[t]errorists have access to more powerful technologies, more targets, more territory, more means of recruitment, and more exploitable sources of rage than ever before. The West's twentieth century approach to terrorism is highly unlikely to mitigate any of these long-term trends ... The U.S. government is still thinking in outdated terms, little changed since the end of the Cold War ... The means and the ends

of terrorism are changing in fundamental, important ways; but the means and the ends of the strategy being crafted in response are not.[195]

IV.

In earlier centuries, liberationist, secessionist, and other political groups have used terror to gain or keep state power. In the twentieth century, terrorists did not customarily challenge the idea or the inevitability of the system of sovereign nation states; rather, they used violence to keep or to acquire power within that system. Terrorism represented national and nationalist ambitions, pitting established powers against nascent ones who wished to control or create states.

In the twenty-first century, terrorism presents a different face. It is global, not national; it is decentralized and networked in its operations like a mutant nongovernmental organization (NGO) or a multinational corporation; it does not resemble the centralized and hierarchical bureaucracy of a nation state. As in previous centuries, terrorism in this century will attack the legitimacy of the State, but terrorism in its new guise will increasingly have a less national focus and a less nationalist agenda. It will operate in the international marketplace of weapons, targets, personnel, information, media influence, and persuasion, not in the national arenas of revolution and policy reform. Its diplomacy will be theatrical and depend upon the new media of satellite television and Internet links. One might say that the televised terrorist pronouncement is a kind of démarche.[196] The greatest difference, however, will lie in the potential combination of a global terror network and access to weapons of mass destruction and therefore it is to that subject we now turn. This looming intersection of an innovative organization and a novel means of terror will require a fundamental rethinking of conventional doctrines in international security and foreign policy,[197] that is, in strategy and in law.

CHAPTER TWO

The Market State:
Arming Terror

This time Milo had gone too far. Bombing his own men and planes was more than even the most phlegmatic observer could stomach, and it looked like the end for him. High-ranking government officials poured in to investigate. Newspapers inveighed against Milo with glaring headlines, and Congressmen denounced the atrocity in stentorian wrath and clamored for punishment. Mothers with children in the service organized into military groups and demanded revenge. Not one voice was raised in his defense. Decent people everywhere were affronted, and Milo was all washed up until he opened his books to the public and disclosed the tremendous profit he had made. He could reimburse the government for all the people and property he had destroyed and still have enough money left over to continue buying Egyptian cotton. Everybody, of course, owned a share. And the sweetest part of the whole deal was that there really was no need to reimburse the government at all. "In a democracy, the government is the people," Milo explained. "We're people, aren't we? So we might just as well keep the money and eliminate the middleman. Frankly, I'd like to see the government get out of war altogether and leave the whole field to private industry. If we pay the government everything we owe it, we'll only be encouraging governmental control and discouraging other individuals from bombing their own men and planes. We'll be taking away their incentive."

—Joseph Heller, *Catch-22*

THE EMERGENCE OF the twenty-first century market state is the principal driver of the Wars against Terror. The same forces that are empowering the individual and compelling the creation of a state devoted to maximizing the individual's opportunity are also empowering the forces of terror, rendering societies more vulnerable and threatening to destroy the consent of the individual as the essential source of state legitimacy.[1] The chief example of this is the arming of terrorists with weapons of mass destruction (WMD). Bruce Ackerman recognized this development when he wrote:

> We are at a distinctive moment in history: the State is losing its monopoly over the means of mass destruction. And once a harmful technology escapes into the black market it is almost impossible for governments to suppress the trade. Think of drugs and guns . . . The root of our problem is not Islam or ideology, but this free market in death.[2]

I.

The *constitutional order* of the State is determined by the unique grounds on which the State claims legitimate power.[3] Thus the order of *princely states,* which flourished in the sixteenth century, legitimated its power by associating the prince with the structure of the modern state. Give us power, the State said, and we will better protect the person and the possessions of the prince.

The order within which most of the developed societies of the world live today is the *nation state*, a structure that dates from the second half of the nineteenth century, when the first mass voting franchise acts (including women's suffrage), large-scale free public education, social security programs, and industrial, "total" wars appeared. Its claim to power, too, can be described in a unique way.

The nation state bases its legitimacy on having undertaken the task of maintaining, nurturing, and improving the material conditions of its citizens whose equal rights to well-being derive solely from their membership in the nation itself. The nation state set itself against the unfettered market. Nation states asserted their legitimacy on the basis of a characteristic claim: give us power, they said, and we will improve the material well-being of the national people. The record of economic and material progress during the twentieth century amply justified this claim. Between 1947 and 2000 there was a twentyfold increase in the volume of world trade and a 700 percent rise in gross world product. Nevertheless, in the past decade, there has been an increasing recognition that, on account of challenges the nation state cannot successfully meet, we are entering the transition from one constitutional order to another—from the nation state to the market state.[4]

New strategic threats are arising owing to the proliferation of WMD and long-range delivery systems that make every state, whether it has nearby enemies or not, and whether or not its borders are otherwise secure, vulnerable to terrible attacks against which there can be little effective defense. The globalization of markets, owing to advances in computation, invites the rapid transience of capital, reduces the autonomy of the nation state to manage its own currency and economy, and encourages rapid economic growth that has transnational consequences like climate change and inequality. The universalization of culture (including universal human rights guarantees), which is the result of a global system of information that depends on recent developments in communications and transport, threatens the power of the State to preserve the culture of the nation through law, and links once-remote sources of infection and burgeoning epidemics. Each one of these developments challenges the legitimacy of the nation state by undermining its promise to continually improve the material well-being of all its citizens. These developments occurred, ironically, as a consequence of the greatest success of the society of nation states—the end of the Long War of the twentieth century and the triumph of parliamentary market-based democracies over the competing ideological forms of communism[5] and fascism. It was our success in building an international system of trade and finance, winning acknowledgment for norms of human rights, bringing rapid industrial development to virtually all northern-tier and many southern-tier states, achieving higher living standards and human reproductive control, creating international communications, and inventing and deploying WMD that defeated our competitors and discredited their systems.

Yet the very tactics, technologies, and strategies that brought us success in war between nation states have now brought us new challenges that cannot be met by the currently prevailing constitutional order of the nation state. Thus, at the moment of its greatest triumph, the parliamentary nation state is increasingly unable to fulfill its legitimating premise. States are finding it more and more difficult to assure their publics, that is their *nations,* of increasing equality, security, and community.

A new constitutional order that reflects these developments will eventually replace the nation state. That new order will treat these developments as challenges that it, and only it, can master. In part this is a matter of shifting the basis for the state's legitimacy away from assuring mass welfare and towards maximizing individual opportunity and by adopting methods of warfare and defense unavailable to the nation states. This is already happening. Some have speculated[6] that the new constitutional order will resemble that of the twenty-first century multinational corporation or NGO rather than the twentieth century state in that it will outsource many functions, rely less on law and regulation and more on market incentives, and respond to ever-changing and constantly monitored consumer demand rather than to voter preferences expressed in relatively rare elections.

Rather than attempting to control behavior through prohibitory regulation, the State will devise incentives for individual choices that generate positive spillovers* and externalities.[7] Some examples may be found in the proposals that switch default rules while preserving freedom of choice.[8] Other examples include "sin licenses," the market state version of sumptuary taxes and carbon-rights trading.

> Rather than charge a duty of $2 a packet, governments could [condition] the sale of cigarettes [on the purchase of] a smokers' ID, which might cost $5000 and entitle the holder to 2500 packets of cigarettes tax-free . . . By helping people to make forward-looking decisions for themselves . . . they enlarge their freedom, making it possible for them to do things they otherwise could not do. Giving Ulysses the rope with which to lash himself to the mast *adds to his choices*.[9]

Market states say: Give us power and we will give you new opportunities. In contrast to the nation state, the market state does not see itself as more than a minimal provider or redistributor of goods and services. States used to run airlines, telephone companies, and cable and wireless monopolies. Market states abandon these enterprises and see their role as enabling and assisting rather than directing the citizen's interaction with choice.[10] For example, poverty is to be alleviated by providing the poor with education and job retraining sufficient to permit them to participate fully in the labor market rather than by giving them welfare payments. Pension funds move from defined benefits protocols to defined contribution models—putting more responsibility on, and providing more opportunity to, the individual. Armies are to be raised from volunteers, compensated on a basis competitive with nonmilitary employment, rather than by mass conscription. The total wealth of the society is to be maximized, which will enrich everyone to some degree,[11] rather than enlarging the wealth of any particular group (like the poorest) through interventions in the market that tend to depress total economic performance and can sometimes bring impoverishment for all. Given the demographics of the developed world—its rapidly aging societies—and the competition for service-sector jobs from less developed societies, only such changes can

---

*Cass Sunstein and Richard Thaler's concept of libertarian paternalism is one prominent example of this phenomenon. Their theory is premised on the recognition that the design features of legal or organizational rules have a powerful influence on the choices made within those rules. The rule-making authority should therefore choose rules that will maximize choices that improve the general welfare. For example, an employer wishing to encourage increased savings by employees may automatically enroll employees in 401(k) plans unless they choose otherwise, or create plans that allow employees to prospectively allocate some proportion of future wage increases to savings. Such measures tend to generate a positive result (i.e., increased savings) while still allowing for maximum freedom of choice by the individual. See Cass R. Sunstein and Richard H. Thaler, "Libertarian Paternalism Is Not an Oxymoron," *University of Chicago Law Review* 70 (2003).

possibly fund even the more modest social programs of the future. This new constitutional order, the market state, has not yet fully arrived, but one can already see evidence of its approach.

States will not only deregulate vast areas of enterprise by repealing industrial statutes but will also deregulate the reproduction of our species by striking down antiabortion and anticontraception laws and by permitting new reproductive technologies like in vitro fertilization. States will make use of nongovernmental organizations and private companies as outsourced adjuncts to traditional government operations.[12] States will permit elected officials to be removed through ad hoc recall votes, and laws to be amended or repealed by voter initiatives and referenda* that bypass representative institutions like legislatures and collective bodies like unions.[13] Voluntary commitments may be used to qualify the generality of constitutional rights, for example, where the citizens of a gated private community consent to renounce the right to carry firearms as a condition of their residence. Eventually there may be a wider variegation of human rights within the state with more autonomy given to local, voluntarily composed communities. When these developments occur, we are witnessing the emergence of the market state.

Mayor Michael Bloomberg of New York City has proposed that the city experiment with a market state program that originated in Mexico and has been so successful at reducing rural poverty that it has been adopted by more than twenty countries. "Opportunity NYC" would pay parents $25 for each parent/teacher conference attended; $50 for obtaining a library card; $50 for taking the PSAT (a high school aptitude test); and $400 for graduating from high school. It would grant $20 to $50 per adult, per month, for maintaining health insurance and $100 to $200 per family member for preventative health screenings. It would add $150 per month for every full-time paycheck and pay bonuses for completing job training or educational courses. This sort of conditional cash transfer, in contrast to welfare rights, is characteristic of the market state.[14]

Operating through the nineteenth century imperial state, societies sought to enhance the nation as a whole; in the era of the nation state, societies took responsibility for the well-being of groups; in the market state, society becomes responsible for increasing the opportunities available to individuals. This means lowering the transaction costs of individual choice, which requires an increasing emphasis on risk, transparency, and accountability.

---

*Interestingly, these political efforts parallel the rise of private equity firms and for much the same reason: they are attempts to address the "agency problem" that arises when the interests of officials and taxpayers are not entirely aligned. See Michael Jensen, "The Eclipse of the Public Corporation," *Harvard Business Review* (September–October 1989).

It involves deregulation; the "franchising" of various sorts of provision—from private prisons to private pensions—and the withdrawal of the state from many of those areas where it used to bring some kind of moral pressure to bear . . . It means that government is free . . . to try and increase the literal and metaphorical purchasing power of citizens, but not to take for granted anything much in the way of agreement about common goals or social good . . . Government is now heard asking to be judged on its delivery of purchasing power and maximal choice.[15]

The market state is classless and indifferent to race, ethnicity, and gender, but it is also heedless of the values of reverence,[16] self-sacrifice,[17] loyalty, and family. From this perspective, one can see that Margaret Thatcher, for all her efforts to reduce taxes and make the economy more efficient, was—like Ronald Reagan—one of the last nation state leaders. These leaders tended to centralize power (despite rhetoric to the contrary) because they wished to use the authority of law to enforce moral norms. For this reason Reagan tried to criminalize abortion and Thatcher introduced the poll tax. Both favored enhanced penalties for drug abuse. Both successfully broke labor unions—a disfavored group in their respective political parties. Both successfully exploited divisive "wedge" issues in their political campaigns to energize their supporters (affirmative action in the U.S., industrial action in the U.K.), the opposite of the market state's focus on the individual rather than the group.

By contrast, a government like the one in the U.K. that is considering decriminalizing cannabis, charging a rational fee to students for their education—while subsidizing those in need of assistance in order to ensure that educational opportunities depend on merit—and requiring greater transparency for shareholders so they can evaluate executive pay practices, is a government that is, already, acting in part from market state premises. So, deplorably, also is the U.S. when its member states adopt organized gambling as a method of raising state revenue. In Japan, the government dissolved and called an election in 2005 over the privatization of the postal service. Indeed, in the U.S.,

[t]he federal government now spends about $100 billion more annually for outside contracts than it does on employee salaries. Many federal departments and offices—NASA and Energy, to name just two—have become de facto contract management agencies, devoting upward of 80 percent of their budgets to contractors.[18]

In addition to the roughly 130,000 American troops now serving in Iraq [in 2006], private contractors have their own army of approximately 50,000 employees performing functions that used to be the province of the military . . . [C]ontractors provide the bodyguards . . . and, in some cases, the armored vehicles and even helicopters that have become so necessary for the [protection of] foreign civilians in Iraq. Such protective services . . . are [even] responsible for the security of the American ambassador . . .[19]

Indeed, in Iraq private military forces have suffered more losses than the rest of the coalition of allied states combined. "American foreign policy, to a great extent," wrote Allison Stanger, "has been privatized. . . . In 2005, federally financed contractors were working in every United Nations–occupied country except Bhutan, Nauru, and San Marino."[20] Consistent with the history of the market state, Stanger notes that while contract spending has more than doubled since 2001, "serious federal efforts to outsource began under President Bill Clinton . . . for outsourcing is . . . a rational response to the . . . information age."

As the "state is becoming more driven by market dynamics and the corporate principles of operational effectiveness . . . the world of business is becoming more concerned and involved with social and cultural responsibilities previously left to government and non-profit institutions . . ."[21] A McKinsey survey found that 44 percent of U.S. executives polled thought businesspersons "should play a leadership role in efforts to address issues."[22] This political shift in responsibility reflects in part a shift in institutional wealth. Of the world's one hundred largest "economies" in 2000, only forty-seven were states; the rest were multinational corporations.[23] Wal-Mart's annual sales, for example, exceeded the GDP of all but twenty-one states.[24] If Wal-Mart were a country, it would be China's eighth largest trading partner, ahead of Russia, Australia, and Canada.[25]

The confrontation between old and new constitutional orders will bring a distasteful ferocity to politics,* and that too may provide fertile ground for twenty-first century terrorism. One might say that the Taliban represented a nation state's reaction to the emergence of market states while al Qaeda represents an attempt to hijack the new constitutional order.

Even in the developed countries, however, the backlash from this constitutional development can be felt. As the constitutional premise of governing changes, adherents of the old order feel betrayed, while their apparently inexplicable resistance to change is exasperating to the adher-

---

*One encounters a similar outrage in reaction to a thesis regarding market state terrorism, viz, that it is not caused by economic deprivation, for this reaction, too, is a symptom of the collision between nation state expectations and market state realities. Persons accustomed to thinking that the role of the State is to assure material well-being will naturally conceive of terrorism as a reaction to the State's failure in this regard. They have nothing to say to al Qaeda or ecoterrorists or animal-rights terrorists or even those antiglobalization terrorists who are aroused more by the threat to cultural identity than by unfair terms of trade.

ents of the new order. Those who cling to the old order can't quite credit the sincerity of those who advocate the policy proposals of the new order because these are so unresponsive to nation state assumptions about how a state serves the values of its society. Such proposals—like the legal recognition of same-sex unions, or attempts to privatize state pensions—seem simply pretense, perhaps a political gimmick or merely unprincipled.[26]

> The nation state saw its job . . . as looking after the welfare of the people and ensuring full employment; the market state seeks to maximise opportunity and sees employment as just another economic variable. [There is] a clash between these two visions of the state . . . Chirac's vision comes from an age (and a successful age it was) when politicians thought it was their duty to tame capitalism because only [then] could they achieve the economic and social goals they had set for themselves. This model had a different language. It talked about security from cradle to grave . . . The language of the market state, predictably, is the language of the market. It is about bottom line, throughput, innovation, opportunity and competition.[27]

These conflicts do not fall along party or left/right lines: nation state leaders support affirmative action (from the left) and antiabortion laws (from the right); they are suspicious of private schools (from the left) and hostile to the use of local languages (from the right); they support statutes against hate crimes and hate speech (from the left) and laws against narcotics consumption and pornography (from the right). In all these cases the common element is the use of law to enforce a national—which is to say, a particular historical, cultural group's—moral code.[28]

The threatening nature of the transition from the nation state to the market state invites violence, and this is not confined to particularly premodern or retrograde societies. It is notable that two of the most vicious American terrorists—the Unabomber, Theodore Kaczynski, and Eric Rudolph, the 1996 Summer Olympics bomber—were both protesting historic changes that can be associated with the transition to the market state (advancing technology and the deregulation of women's reproduction, respectively).[29]

For more than a century at a time, the constitutional order of the leading states typically remain stable. It happens, however, that we are entering one of those rare periods of seismic change—from the nation state of the twentieth century to the market state of the twenty-first. This transformation is partly evident in the use of market techniques as a supplement to and in some cases a replacement for legal regulation. Not only market-based incentives, however, but also many other innovations of governance from the devolution of power to networked localities and stakeholder groups to "benchmarking" government performance on customer service—all these are evidence of a new compact offered by the state to secure its legitimacy.[30]

One consequence of this devolution is the radical increase in the power of the media, which is why the dramaturgical elements of twenty-first century terrorism are bound to increase. As the media that inform and persuade publics become so much more powerful, movements of many kinds will seek to exploit them. In the preceding chapter, it was argued that terrorism will become the extension of diplomacy in the era of the market state. This will come via theatrical means.

Striking and largely unforeseen developments are transforming the strategic and legal context within which states must operate. First, as we saw in the previous chapter, a global terrorist network has emerged, creating a virtual state that more closely resembles the multinational franchising corporation than the centralized and militarized nation state. Just as previous terrorist groups uncannily mimicked the states they sought to destroy, so too this new type of terrorist organization looks like the states it proclaims to be enemies, the emerging market states. Like those nascent market states, this new terrorist network outsources operations; it depends on local groups to carry out warfare and pays them for it, supplying planning and infrastructure (including weapons). Like the market itself, this network is global and not territorial. Second, as nation states become market states, they vastly increase their wealth and inadvertently increase their vulnerability. Third, as the fabrication and control of biological and nuclear weapons begin to slip away from the rich and powerful states that have possessed a monopoly on them, and as the State begins to turn to markets in order to supplement the use of legal regulation as to which it holds a monopoly, these WMD are becoming *commodified*—that is, a clandestine market has developed, at first in the components, and then later in warheads and delivery systems. Having described the first of these developments in chapter 1, let us take up the remaining two.

II.

The emergence of market states has been fueled by, and itself propels, the growing global economy. Recent rates of economic growth have been highest in Asia, beginning with Japan, then Korea, Taiwan, and Singapore, and continuing at present with India and China—which some expect to grow by 7.5 percent and 8.4 percent per year respectively in the next twenty-five years. In 2006, 35 percent of global GDP was attributable to India and China. Some forecasters expect Brazil and Russia, two states whose GDP already puts them among the top ten worldwide, to increase their economies by 4.5 percent and 6.5 percent respectively per year during the same period and for the same reason: increased global integration. The number of persons living on a dollar a day has gone from 40 percent of the world's population to around 20 percent.

There are, nevertheless, at present only two economic superpowers, the United States and the European Union. During the last three decades their wealth has more than doubled, an achievement that is unprecedented for developed states. Within the U.S., real individual incomes have doubled since 1960, 70 percent of Americans now own their own homes, the average home size has doubled, people live twice as long as their nineteenth century forebears, the air and water are cleaner, and crime rates are decreasing.[31] "OECD economies have grown enormously in the past three decades, with gross domestic product per head growing up to tenfold since 1970 in the largest economies,"[32] but it is the economic relation *between* the U.S. and the E.U. that is driving this achievement. The E.U. and the U.S. account for 37 percent of global merchandise trade and 45 percent of world trade in services. There is more to come: even today, trade constitutes less than 20 percent of transatlantic economic activity.

> By a wide margin, EU and U.S. investment in each other's economies is what drives markets, jobs, innovation, and business activity. Bilateral trade between the EU and the U.S. in manufactured goods was $549 billion [in 2004], whereas "transatlantic" foreign affiliate sales [amounted to] $2.8 trillion. Add to this the foreign direct investment (FDI) by European companies in the U.S. and by American firms in the EU, more than $100 billion just in 2003, and the true picture of [the transatlantic economy] begins to emerge . . . The EU's total investment stake in the U.S. economy today exceeds $1.4 trillion, accounting for nearly 75 percent of all foreign investment in the United States.[33]

The emergence of market states will bring greater wealth to mankind than it has ever known, for such states extend the interconnectivity, the radical automation of infrastructures, and the lowering of the transaction costs of gathering information that are bringing this constitutional order into being. This new constitutional order will make life more abundant by enhancing productivity; more spacious by increasing accessibility to more varied environments; and more connected by means of a global network of telecommunications. It may bring important and unpredictable cultural challenges to societies, but as an engine of wealth creation, the market state surpasses all of its predecessors. It has the potential to bring a kind of perpetual feast to the developed world—the Edenic future of plenty promised by economists from Smith to Keynes—while its superordination of consumers can bring immense prosperity to the developing world. At the same time, the states of Europe and North America have experienced a tremendous growth in inequality and this development seems, in John Witt's words, "deeply related to the nation state transformation to market states, [because] the market state has abandoned the equality mandate of its predecessor."[34] This too is bound to stimulate antigovernment actions, some of them violent.

The emergence of market states not only excites terrorist reaction, as we saw in chapter 1, it also creates the conditions for a twenty-first century terrorism that is markedly more dangerous than its predecessors.

In the space of less than two decades, our basic infrastructures in banking and finance, oil and gas and electrical power, telecommunications and transportation, and government services themselves have all undergone a fundamental change. Where once it was only a nuisance if the lights went out in the middle of a banking transaction, it now can mean a complete interruption of financial services. Where previously transportation continued whether or not the telephone lines were down, now planes and tankers and air cargo are stilled, sometimes dangerously so, if communications are interdicted or otherwise interrupted. Infrastructures that previously were logically and geographically distinct have become interconnected and radically automated. This has led to an increase in national wealth comparable to that brought by the Industrial Revolution. With the dramatic rise in wealth, however, has come an equally dramatic rise in vulnerability. The nodes that connect these infrastructures, which are critical to their operation, now present far more lucrative targets than the simple bridges and power stations of previous decades. Using the tools of information warfare, attackers could overload telephone lines with special software. They could reroute and disrupt the operations of air traffic control, emergency calls, and shipping and railroad computers. In February 2003, three hackers disrupted logistics planning for U.S. operations in the Persian Gulf, and for many weeks it was thought the disruption was originating in the Gulf area because the hackers had cleverly routed their signals through computers in the United Arab Emirates. Hackers could alter, by remote control, the formulas for medicines in pharmaceutical plants. They could change the pressure in gas pipelines. In September 1998, a hacker group supporting the Mexican Zapatista rebels launched a denial-of-service attack against the Pentagon's primary Internet site in an attempt to shut it down.[35] The notorious Japanese group Aum Shinrikyo was working on developing computer viruses when it launched its sarin gas attack in the Tokyo subway.

Testifying before a congressional committee in 1997, the then director of Central Intelligence, John Deutsch, warned against an "electronic Pearl Harbor." A better phrase might be "electronic Agincourt," a battle that transformed the face of Europe when Henry V's yeomen, armed with longbows, defeated the French knights, the armored cavalry of the most powerful state on that continent. That kind of technological transformation of strategy and statecraft will soon be upon us. Not only have the targets become vastly more significant, the weapons of a new age are recasting the nature of the attacks on those targets. Information warfare specialists at the Pentagon have estimated that a properly prepared and well-coordinated incursion by fewer than thirty computer virtuosos with a budget of less than $10 million could shut down everything from electric power grids to air traffic control.

There is still no technology for determining the source of a disguised cyberattack,[36] so that the attack that ended up at the Pentagon that we can trace back to Austin, Texas, may not have begun in Austin, but may then lead us back to New York, or to Latvia, back to the Middle East, on to California, and there the trail may go cold, if we even get that far. Internet users now number about 120 million, 70 million of whom are in the U.S. Five years from now, it is estimated that about one billion persons will be online, two-thirds of them living outside the United States. The majority of students in graduate programs for applied mathematics in America are foreign, and a great many of them will return, highly trained, to societies that are hostile to Western interests.[37] Nor have these possibilities been lost on al Qaeda: Fouad Hussein describes the "fourth stage" of al Qaeda's twenty-year plan as lasting until 2013, by which time "al Qaeda will have completed its electronic capabilities and it will be time to use them to launch electronic attacks to undermine the US economy."[38]

In 1997 a red team—a team assembled by an intelligence agency to play a war game or execute an exercise as the adversary—pretended to be North Korean agents. Thirty-five men and women took hacker tools freely available on the World Wide Web, downloaded them, and managed to shut down large segments of the American power grid and completely silence the command and control system of the Pacific Command in Honolulu. In a red team attack, the Defense Information Systems Agency (DISA) launched some 38,000 computer attacks against its own systems, just to test them. Only 4 percent of the persons in charge of these systems ever realized that they were being attacked, and, of these, only one in 150 ever reported the intrusion.

Such assaults can render commercial aviation perilous, frustrate a week's trading on a major stock exchange, or freeze a natural gas pipeline to a large city in winter, but concatenating these sorts of events can trigger the economic and political panic that no recent war has ever brought to an advanced society. To these threats we must now add the possibility of bioweapons that are not delivered by bombers or missiles, but are dispersed by crop dusters, or low-yield nuclear weapons ferried into unsuspecting harbors by small boats and other craft.

Moreover, an age that has made it possible through global connectivity for persons and enterprises to locate anywhere has resulted in the increasing density and explosive growth of urban centers. It seems that wealth and the exchange of information are tightly linked and that an enormous amount of timely information can only be exchanged when the parties are in proximity. Thus the dramatic growth in wealth and productivity that is harnessed by the market state has as its concomitant a parallel growth in vulnerability. Partly this is due to the remarkable *Connectivity Paradox.*

The Connectivity Paradox holds that as electronic connectivity—which is a powerful engine of wealth creation—increases the scope and speed of communications, the requirement for human proximity does not decrease, and indeed with regard to key decision makers actually is heightened. As so enticingly rendered in countless television ads, it may be possible for an executive to sit on a remote beach and have access to his important files, correspondence, and immediate communications via the Internet but if he (or she) wants to be the first to learn of a new deal, or make new contacts for collaboration, or persuade others to follow his (or her) leadership, there is no substitute for proximity. As a wit once observed, "Nothing propinks like propinquity." As has been recognized widely, this has important consequences for a society's vulnerability.[39]

> [Connectivity] has sometimes made our technological, economic and social systems far less resilient . . . While greater connectivity allows companies larger profits, and gives society better ways to combine diverse ideas, skills and resources, it also harbours dangers. Most obviously, damage in one part of a system—whether it's a voltage surge in the electrical grid, a new disease in a far-off country, or the sudden devaluation of a key currency—can cascade farther and faster to other parts of the system.[40]

The irony is that this connectivity has not freed us from our need to coordinate and learn in person. This is true, by the way, of market state terrorists as well. As Peter Neumann observed, "the Internet may have made it easier for terrorist sympathizers to engage with the movement, but the core jihadist network continues to be based on personal relationships which need to be maintained and reinforced, especially among the key brokers without whose services large scale terrorist operations would be impossible."[41]

This year—2007—the world's urban population is expected to exceed that of its rural population for the first time; in 1900 the urban/rural ratio was 15/85. Today, the world's population living in cities is about the same size—more than 3 billion—as the total population of the earth in 1960. There are dozens of cities whose populations grew tenfold in the last thirty years. Sixteen cities have more than 10 million inhabitants, and they are heavily concentrated in the world's largest economies.* Generally speaking, it is the countries with the best economic performance that have urbanized most in the last fifty years, and as a general matter, the fastest-growing cities of that period have also had the highest standards of living within their countries. London was the first city to have a million persons; this occurred in the last half of the nineteenth century. By 2000, there were almost forty cities with populations exceeding 5 million.

> There is an obvious association between the world's largest cities and globalization. Growing cross-border flows of raw materials, goods, information, income and capital, much of it managed by trans-national corporations, underpin a network of what can be termed "global cities" that are the sites for the management and servicing of the global economy. Most international investment is concentrated in a relatively small proportion of the world's cities.[42]

It is no coincidence that Tokyo, New York, and London are also among the world's largest cities. If the metropolitan area of New York City were a country, it would rank tenth in the world's economies.[43] London by itself has an annual economic output comparable to Sweden, Belgium, or Switzerland.[44]

For the terrorist, as for the opportunistic microbe, these provide very tempting targets.[45]

III.

Market states not only supply the model for global, networked, and out-sourcing terrorism, they also enable the commodification of weapons of mass destruction. Furthermore, the access to information such states make available can empower malevolent individuals and small groups of persons. Finally, these developments operate synergistically: not only does technology empower hatred by providing access to weapons and easing complicated communications and logistics, it can also be used to inflame hatred via polished recruiting videos and what one commentator has called "terro-vangelism,"[46] the use of niche communications to reinforce prejudice and inspire a passion for spectacular, theatrical destruction.

---

*In 2000, the world's five largest economies (U.S., China, Japan, India, and the U.K.) had ten of the world's sixteen megacities, and almost half its million-person cities. All but two of the world's sixteen megacities were in one of the top twenty economies. Within each region, the largest cities tend to be concentrated in the largest economies—e.g., Brazil and Mexico in Latin America; China, India, Indonesia, Korea, and Japan in Asia.

**THE COMPARATIVE EFFECTS OF BIOLOGICAL, CHEMICAL, AND
NUCLEAR WEAPONS DELIVERED AGAINST THE UNITED STATES**

	Area covered (sq. km)	Deaths assuming 3,000–10,000 people per sq. km
Using missile warheads		
Chemical: 300 kg of sarin nerve gas with a density of 70 milligrams per cubic meter	0.22	60–200
Biological: 30 kg of anthrax spores with a density of 0.1 milligrams per cubic meter	10	30,000–100,000
Nuclear: One 12.5 kiloton nuclear device achieving 5 lbs per cubic inch of over-pressure	7.8	23,000–80,000
1.0 megaton hydrogen bomb	190	570,000–1,900,000
Using one aircraft dispensing 1,000 kg of sarin nerve gas or 100 kg of anthrax spores		
Clear sunny day, light breeze:		
sarin nerve gas	0.74	300–700
anthrax spores	46	130,000–460,000
Overcast: day or night, moderate wind:		
sarin nerve gas	0.8	400–800
anthrax spores	140	42,000–1,400,000
Clear calm night:		
sarin nerve gas	7.8	3,000–8,000
anthrax spores	300	1–3 million

Chart, Table 4.1A in Michael D. Intriligator and Abdullah Toukan, "Terrorism and Weapons of Mass Destruction," in *Countering Terrorism and WMD*, ed. Peter Katona et al. (New York: Routledge, 2006).

Advances in technology are rapidly lowering the thresholds for the development, deployment, and deliverability of WMD, particularly nuclear and biological weapons, as well as for weapons of mass disruption such as radiological, chemical, and cyberweapons. As Michael Intriligator and Abdullah Toukan have concluded, "with demand rising and marginal cost falling, as is . . . the case with . . . WMD technologies, it is only a matter of time before such weapons, including nuclear weapons, become available to terrorist groups."[47] The only reasonable targets of these weapons are civilians.

Radiological weapons, called "dirty bombs," are conventional explosives that are packaged with radioactive materials. Relatively little expertise is required to construct these bombs. It was reported in March 2002 that it was the consensus view of the U.S. government that al Qaeda probably possessed such often-stolen radioactive elements as strontium-90 and cesium-137 (which can be found in numerous civilian locations).[48] In January 2003, British officials found documents in Herat from which they concluded that al Qaeda had successfully built a small dirty bomb. As of this writing it has yet to be detonated.

Persons in the immediate vicinity of such a detonation would be killed by the blast effects; some might die of radiation exposure afterward. According to Richard Garwin and Georges Charpak, a dirty bomb containing one kilogram[49] of plutonium exploded in the center of Munich could lead to approximately 120 cancer cases ultimately attributable to the blast. While horrific, the small number of deaths suggest that the real effects of this and other weapons of disruption are psychological. The economic impact of introducing a contaminated area into the heart of a commercial center would of course be considerable.

By contrast, the blast effects alone of a nuclear explosion would be devastating to any society that suffered it. Once the world bears witness to a nuclear explosion directed purposefully at civilians and outside the context of conventional war, nothing in political life will ever be the same again. It's not that the stricken society will be utterly destroyed (like Carthage), but rather that the nature of such a society—particularly in attitudes toward consensual political norms and the rights of civilians—will be utterly changed (like the later Rome).

In May 2004, European officials conducted a simulation demonstrating that a nuclear device exploded at NATO headquarters outside Brussels could kill 40,000 persons immediately, overwhelming hospitals with hundreds of thousands of injured, spreading panic throughout Europe, roiling and disconcerting the world economy for a considerable period, and sending shock waves through the politics of every state. Former senator Sam Nunn, now chairman of the board of trustees of the Center for Strategic and International Studies, has repeatedly drawn attention to the "devastating, world-changing impact of [even a single] nuclear attack." And Arnaud de Borchgrave has written:

If a 10-kiloton nuclear device goes off in mid-town Manhattan on a typical work day, it could kill more than half a million people . . . Ten kilotons is a plausible yield for a crude terrorist bomb . . . [T]o haul that volume of explosives would require a freight train one hundred cars long. As a nuclear bomb, it could easily fit on the back of a pickup truck.[50]

Unlike radiological bombs, however, nuclear weapons are very difficult to build. While the basic blueprints are widely available, the specific detailed designs remain classified.[51] Enormous expertise would be required in a number of sophisticated areas, including metallurgy, hydrodynamics, electrical engineering, and physics.[52] Fissionable material such as highly enriched uranium or plutonium is difficult and expensive to create from naturally occurring uranium. There are some commentators who believe that there is no realistic risk from nuclear weapons not developed by states and that it is inconceivable that states would ever part with their weapons by delivering them into the hands of terrorists.

The Illicit Trafficking Database of the International Atomic Energy Agency has reported, however, some 540 confirmed incidents of illegal commerce in nuclear and other radioactive materials between January 1, 1993, and December 31, 2003. In the last ten years more than twenty-three attempts to steal fissile material have been thwarted. There are hundreds of tons of highly enriched uranium in Russia and additional tons in many other countries[53] enjoying varying degrees of protection. What is most disturbing is that fissile materials—once the province of a few great powers—have been connected to markets in bomb design and weaponry. The Pakistani scientist Dr. A. Q. Khan, whose operations will be discussed at greater length below, has now been linked to the Iranian, North Korean, and Libyan nuclear weapons programs. While it was originally thought that Dr. Khan had simply supplied designs for older Pakistani centrifuges, it is now believed that he also sold warhead designs. Moreover there are reports, discussed below, that experts, including a Pakistani nuclear weapons engineer, were asked to provide assistance to al Qaeda in its pursuit of nuclear devices.[54] It is at present unclear how extensive a role this particular network has played in North Korean nuclear development, but it is evident that that country's ballistic missile technology is now one element in a global market that includes nuclear technology. It may even be the case that North Korean fissile material will find its way to other states via a commercial network.

The U.S. Congress has appropriated almost $12 billion to secure scores of former Soviet and now Russian nuclear weapons and nuclear materials storage sites. The G8 has pledged another $20 billion. Nevertheless, of the forty-three countries and more than a hundred research reactors or related facilities that store highly enriched uranium sufficient to be weaponized, it is estimated that only about 20 percent are properly secured.[55]

Still more disturbing is the steady advance of biotechnology that makes biotoxins and viruses cheaper to create and easier to weaponize, and brings their deployment within the technical capabilities of many thousands of persons. Various technical complexities, however, mean that we have, for a while, a period in which it is unlikely that mass casualties will result from a biological attack by terrorists. Bacteria that cause plague and tularemia, and toxins that lead to botulism and hemorrhagic fevers such as

Ebola and Marburg, are deadly and contagious and are therefore difficult to work with. Smallpox poses an equally mortal threat but it no longer exists, so far as we know,[56] outside a few labs in Russia and the United States. Anthrax is found in nature but is not contagious and is technically challenging to mill properly for use as a deadly weapon, though this, as we have seen, is not impossible. In fact, we must conclude from the 2001 anthrax attacks* that, as the FBI stated, such biological strikes are well within the capabilities of non-state actors.[57]

This period of respite will shift as the techniques of microbiological intervention become more widespread. It will be possible for well-trained persons to alter the molecular structure of viruses in nature, producing a lethal infectious disease that, once exposed to human beings, can spread by contagion.

> By creating a virus from scratch, scientists are now able to change parts of the genetic material of a virus . . . Researchers have used this or similar techniques to create polio (entirely from synthesized DNA), Ebola, and pandemic flu, as well as other viruses . . . Using such technologies . . . there is no need for a bioweaponeer to isolate the virus from an infected patient, acquire it from a germ bank, or culture it from nature. All the required starting materials, such as cell lines and DNA synthesizers, are widely available . . . And the sequences for a growing variety of viruses that infect humans . . . including Ebola, pandemic influenza, and smallpox, are published in the open literature . . . Now such techniques require much less skill and time, thanks to the development of specialized "kits" purchased from biotechnology companies.[58]

Mail-order oligonucleotides (chemically synthesized DNA fragments) were used to build a functional polio virus genome for the first time in 2002.[59] Indeed in recent years, reputable, if ill-advised, scientists have posted the decoded genomes for both the 1918 avian flu and for polio on Internet sites.[60] In June 2006, the British newspaper *The Guardian* obtained a sequence of smallpox DNA through the Internet.

> The DNA sequence of smallpox, as well as other potentially dangerous pathogens such as poliovirus and 1918 flu are freely available in online public databases. So to build a virus from scratch, a terrorist

---

*Over the course of several weeks, beginning on September 18, 2001, a number of letters containing anthrax bacteria were mailed to news media and to the offices of two U.S. senators. Five persons died and seventeen others were made seriously ill.

would simply order consecutive lengths of DNA along the sequence and glue them together in the correct order. This is beyond the skills and equipment of the kitchen chemist, but could be achieved by a well-funded terrorist with access to a basic lab and PhD-level personnel.[61]

Writing in the journal *Biosecurity and Bioterrorism,* one scientist ruefully observed that

[t]he advent of the home molecular biology laboratory is not far off [as] the physical infrastructure of molecular biology is becoming more sophisticated and less expensive every day. Automated commercial instrumentation handles an increasing fraction of laboratory tasks that were once the sole province of doctoral level researchers, reducing labor costs and increasing productivity. This technology is gradually moving into the broader marketplace as . . . any cursory tour of eBay will reveal. [This] will soon put highly capable tools in the hands of both professionals and amateurs worldwide.[62]

Whereas the sheer length of the smallpox genome—185,000 letters long—might once have acted as a deterrent to production by non-state actors (polio has only 7,741 letters and the 1918 flu genome 13,500), the spread of this technology lowers this barrier. We can only assume that the pace of the proliferation of biological technologies will increase.[63] Thus the *acquisition* of pathogens will become easier for the terrorists. That still leaves *amplification*—the cultivation of the pathogen in substantial quantities.

Anthrax is a bacterium. It can be amplified by the same means of fermentation that are used in brewing; indeed, modern pharmacology originated in the brewing and dyeing industries. These techniques have been adapted by other industries, notably the makers of biological insecticides.[64] The necessary equipment is widely available and costs in the range of tens of thousands of dollars. Many brewpubs have fermenters that can cultivate the requisite deadly germs.

Smallpox is a virus. Here too the techniques for amplification are well known. Bacteria are grown in protein cultures, while viruses usually require media of living cells. Smallpox can be cultivated in eggs that are scrambled in a blender and the resulting product purified. As Richard Danzig notes, generations of medical students learned to do this before smallpox was eradicated.[65] Once synthesized, viruses can be grown in unlimited quantities. "The Rubicon has already been crossed and the process of creating novel genetically engineered orthopoxviruses [diseases including smallpox] is irrevocable," Ken Alibek, a former Soviet bioweapons scientist, wrote. "It is just a matter of time before this knowledge will result in the creation of superkiller poxviruses."[66]

Weaponization, however, remains a formidable obstacle. With respect to a contagious virus, the use of suicide agents simplifies the problem. Like most cities, Washington, for example, comprises various small communities. Its political leadership numbers in the hundreds. One suicide terrorist who posed as a verger handing out contaminated programs at the funeral of a prominent political figure could infect a great many of the persons known to the public as national leaders. A suicide agent at a Kennedy Center gala, or at a reception for Senate spouses—who are typically without security—could do the same.

Two additional properties of bioweapons, *reloading* and *dual use,* make the future prospects of the dissemination of information about them especially ominous. First, there is the aspect of "reload," as Danzig, a former secretary of the navy, has termed it.

> After inflicting a national trauma on 9/11, the attackers could not promptly repeat their achievement. They had consumed resources that were difficult to replenish (trained pilots willing to sacrifice themselves). Even more significantly, the modality that they used depended, in some measure, on surprise . . . [By contrast] the national security vulnerabilities made apparent by [the anthrax attacks] are greater than those associated with 9/11. This is because of reload. Attackers who use biological weapons probably can avoid prompt detection and stockpile or replenish resources that permit repeated attack . . . [A]bsent exceptional luck, [we do not have] effective means of interdicting a biological attack, even if we know that one has already occurred and that others are on the way.[67]

Making the matter more complex, there is the unavoidable dual use of the technologies that create medicines and vaccines as well as biological toxins. The tricky task of distinguishing between the use of enriched uranium for energy and for nuclear weapons[68] is child's play compared to the difficulty of maintaining a distinction between research for bioweapons and research for biotreatments.

> Consider a recently published breakthrough in aerosol technology that permits large molecules to escape the respiratory system's usual defenses and be inhaled into the deep lung. This advance could allow insulin to be inhaled rather than injected, a development that could increase compliance among diabetics and improve their quality of life. Yet this same breakthrough could theoretically make it easier for an

aerosolized bioweapon such as anthrax to be deposited into the lower airways, evading the immune system . . .[69]

The spread of WMD is an important strategic element in the Wars against Terror for several reasons: first, these weapons might be bought or otherwise acquired by terrorists; second, they might be used by states to terrorize their neighbors, compelling them to pursue courses of action they might otherwise lawfully reject (or vice versa); third, countries like the United States that have intervened for humanitarian purposes would be thoroughly deterred from such worthy projects by proliferated weapons.

The strategic implications of the potential spread of WMD are widely appreciated; they are the main reason behind the move to preempt this proliferation by military action including initiating changes in regime by force. These implications are also driving the increased size of military organizations needed to manage other states in a postconflict environment, the development of missile defenses, and efforts to strengthen international, nonproliferation legal protocols. Here too the victory sought is one of preclusion. We attempt to stop proliferation not by destroying the state that has acquired weapons but by preventing proliferation from occurring in the first place.

> *Unpredictability in every field is the result of the conquest of the whole of the present world by scientific power. This invasion by active knowledge tends to transform man's environment and man himself . . . to what extent, with what risks, what deviations from the basic conditions of existence and of the preservation of life we simply do not know. Life has become, in short, the object of an experiment of which we can only say one thing—that it tends to estrange us more and more from what we were, or what we think we are, and that it is leading us . . . we don't know and can by no means imagine where.*

—Paul Valéry, "Unpredictability"[70]

IV.

In December 2005 the International Institute for Strategic Studies published *Nuclear Terrorism After 9/11*[71] in its influential Adelphi Paper series. The paper challenged a number of assumptions that underlie much of the current discourse on this topic. This lucid and immensely informative essay provides a serious critique of the positions I have been urging. It argued:

1. No actual or aspiring nuclear weapon state has ever claimed to have nuclear weapons without also having all of the technical infrastructure necessary to produce them ab initio, *although, if the [argument that nuclear weapons technology was for sale was true] they could easily have bought a few on the black market.*

2. There is no evidence in the open-source literature of a true international black market in nuclear materials . . . To the extent that a market exists, it is almost entirely driven by supply; there appears to be no true demand, except where the buyers were government agents running a sting.

3. [T]he detailed plans and engineering drawings necessary to build a bomb are not easily available. It would also be very difficult, if not effectively impossible, to acquire sufficient quantities of suitable fissile materials . . . Developing nuclear weapons requires state-level resources . . .

4. Nuclear weapon states, even "rogues," are most unlikely to be foolish enough to hand nuclear weapons, which are among their dearest national treasures, over to . . . terrorists, especially when the chances of a suspected state sponsor suffering nuclear retaliation and annihilation are so good, and so blindingly obvious.

5. [T]errorists have not historically been particularly interested in WMD, and no terrorist use of WMD of any kind has resulted in mass casualties . . . [N]either al-Qaeda nor any of the organisations linked to it has ever used WMD, and the evidence that they have the will or the technical capacity to do so is limited and unconvincing.

6. [Contrary to those who believe that] "dirty bombs" could also be extremely dangerous, [t]he economic, social and psychological effects of a dirty bomb could be considerably more serious than its physical or radiological effects.

7. [Contrary to the claim that nuclear terrorism constitutes an existential threat to the United States and other potential target states,] to destroy the United States or any other large industrial state . . . would require a large number of well-placed nuclear weapons with yields in the tens or hundreds of kilotons.

These are important claims. Here we will refract them through the remarkable story of Dr. A. Q. Khan, the Pakistani metallurgist and director of the Khan Research Laboratory. This chilling saga can illuminate the future of all states when they must cope with an active market in WMD, for we now know North Korea, Iran, and Libya, among others, were participants in just such a market for nuclear technology and materials, to the surprise and dismay of officials who were inclined to discount such a possibility.

> From 1976 to 2004, Dr. Abdul Qadeer Khan was at the center of the global nuclear black market . . . For the first time in history all the keys to a nuclear weapon—the supplier networks, the material, the enrichment technology, and the warhead designs—were outside of state oversight and control.[72]

Khan was born in 1936 under the British Raj in Bhopal, now part of India. Several years after partition, his family, who were Muslims, immigrated to Pakistan. "The situation was relatively calm compared to what was happening in the rest of India and Pakistan," Khan recounted later, "but still I can remember trains coming into the station full of dead Muslims."[73] In Pakistan, he attended university in Karachi and then in 1961 he went to Europe for advanced education. He studied first in West Berlin, at the Technical University; in 1967 he went on to the Advanced School of Technology in the Netherlands at Delft, where he received a master's in metallurgical engineering, and subsequently took his doctorate in metallurgy from the Catholic University of Leuven in Belgium in 1972.

Khan then took up a post with FDO (Physical Dynamics Research Laboratory) at a time when FDO was a subcontractor for UCN (Ultra-Centrifuge Nederland), the Dutch arm of URENCO. URENCO was a European consortium at the frontier of developing the most sophisticated centrifuge technology for nuclear separation. Believing that nuclear power held the answer to Europe's energy needs, URENCO—a partnership between Germany, Holland, and the U.K.—had been founded to enable the production of enriched uranium fuel independent of the United States.[74] Thus Khan found himself at the epicenter of advanced research and development in the nuclear industry.

Over the next three years, he spent much of his time translating documents written in German about a new German-designed centrifuge (the G-1) and drafting engineering requirements. As a result of this work, he learned not only how the new technology functioned, but also the identities of the suppliers who provided the parts that were assembled to make the new centrifuges.

On May 18, 1974, India conducted a nuclear weapons test that it called a "peaceful nuclear experiment." Four months later, Khan sent a letter to the Pakistani prime minister, Zulfikar Ali Bhutto, via the Pakistani embassy in Brussels. He suggested that Pakistan should develop its own nuclear weapons; he proposed this be done by uranium enrichment; and he offered his services in accomplishing this. As a result, Khan went to Pakistan at the end of 1974 to attend secret meetings with various officials, including the prime minister.[75] On their instructions, Khan returned to FDO and began acquiring nuclear secrets in earnest. During this period, he stole the plans for almost every centrifuge then in production or design, and he collected a detailed inventory of where the components could be purchased. "Knowledge," Gordon Corera has concluded, "not physical material, was the essence of Khan's work and the secret to his success."[76]

There are two routes to creating fissile material. The avenue URENCO was pursuing used mined uranium and enriched it by a series of physical processes. Uranium ore is roughly 99.3 percent U-238,[77] which is not fissionable in ordinary circumstances; the remainder is the potentially fissionable U-235. Uranium "enriched" to contain 5 percent U-235 can be used as nuclear fuel for a reactor; a concentration of about 90 percent U-235 is necessary for weapons. One method of separating out the U-235 takes mined uranium ore and crushes, treats, and dries it into uranium oxide (called "yellowcake"), which is turned into a gas (uranium hexafluoride—UF_6) and then pumped into centrifuges. These spin, accelerating the particles of the uranium gas at high speeds so that the lighter U-235 can be siphoned off, and then are respun again and again to achieve higher concentrations. This requires a series of centrifuges connected by metal piping into a large configuration called a "cascade."

This method of uranium enrichment requires machinery of immense sophistication. Most countries that seek nuclear weapons choose the other principal route, which relies on plutonium. This involves reprocessing the spent nuclear fuel rods from a reactor. It requires only a reprocessing plant to separate the plutonium from the highly radioactive fuel rods in order to create fissile material that can be used either as fuel for a nuclear reactor or for nuclear weapons.

This second method provided the means by which India created fissile material for its "peaceful nuclear experiment." It was also the method chosen by Pakistan, which had obtained a reactor in 1972, and signed a contract with a French company in 1973 to build a reprocessing plant. With this plant, Pakistan could have had the fissile material to make up to fifteen or twenty bombs a year. But after the Indian nuclear test, fifteen nuclear supplier countries, known as the London Club,* banded together in Sep-

*Later the Nuclear Suppliers Group.

tember 1977 to restrict the export of nuclear technologies using a "trigger list" of banned exports, and conditioned imports on various undertakings and inspections by importing states. Reprocessing plants headed the list. The French cancelled the Pakistani deal. Canada refused to supply nuclear fuel, heavy water, or parts for the continued operation of the Karachi nuclear power plant.

Now the Pakistani prime minister turned to Khan, who had traveled to Pakistan in December 1975, allegedly for a brief vacation. In fact he never returned to Europe, and immediately began work with the Pakistan Atomic Energy Commission, which was pursuing a plutonium bomb. After quarreling with the PAEC leadership, Khan persuaded Bhutto to set him up at the Energy Research Laboratory to study a parallel enrichment method in complete secrecy, reporting only to the prime minister. When the plutonium avenue was foreclosed, Khan was able to step in and take up the fallen baton. By 1978 he had built G-1 prototypes. In April of that year he achieved a successful enrichment.

Whereas the PAEC's approach had been to acquire a major facility— a reprocessing plant—and to deal with the principal nuclear suppliers, Khan's approach

> was entirely different—viz, to get bits and pieces (components) of enrichment technology and equipment from small, high technology Western firms who deal with individual components; to bring the components together so as to achieve mastery over the enrichment cycle— from acquisition of yellowcake, gassification/solidification units and centrifuges to their operation; and to do the design work and the assembly of imported components in Pakistan by Pakistanis with some foreign technological assistance by selected foreign personnel from Europe and North America.[78]

Khan later said, "I took full advantage of the willingness of western companies to do business and decided to make purchases from the open market."[79]

> In Switzerland, Pakistan purchased key components for a uranium enrichment capability, including a massive unit to gasify and solidify uranium hexafluoride, so they could be fed into the centrifuges . . . In Germany, Pakistani diplomats purchased vacuum pumps and gas purification equipment . . . In France, Pakistani buyers may have been able to buy bellows for ultracentrifuges by routing the shipment through Belgium . . . In Britain, Pakistan purchased high-frequency inverters through a British front company, sometimes using a West German commission agent.[80]

In 1981, Bhutto's successor, General Mohammed Zia-ul-Haq, renamed Khan's facility the Khan Research Laboratory (KRL). Sometime that year, Khan had received a Chinese blueprint for a simple and effective nuclear warhead, and the various steps for making it, in exchange for the URENCO centrifuge designs. By the mid-1980s, less than a decade after Khan's clandestine flight from the Netherlands under the eyes of Dutch intelligence, Pakistan had produced enough highly enriched uranium for a nuclear weapon. It was a dazzling achievement. A country that could not make sewing needles, good and sturdy bicycles, or even ordinary durable metal rods[81] was about to be a nuclear weapons power.

By this time, KRL had produced the second-generation G-2, a centrifuge twice as fast as the G-1. This left KRL with an excess inventory of the G-1 (they were now called P-1s), which Khan augmented by ordering considerably more components from his suppliers than Pakistan required. Because an external procurement network had been necessary to create Pakistan's internal enrichment infrastructure, and because this had been undertaken in the greatest secrecy—including an entire funding channel run out of the prime minister's office—to avoid detection by other states, Khan now found himself the master of a commercial network, sophisticated intellectual property, and a substantial inventory that could turn KRL from importer to exporter.[82]

By the late 1980s Khan had established a relationship with Iran that led to the transfer of large amounts of nuclear technology, including the process for casting uranium metal. In 1987, three Iranian officials are said to have met several members of Khan's network in Dubai. Khan's intermediaries presented a program for Iranian nuclear weapons development. According to the International Atomic Energy Agency (IAEA),

> [t]his document suggests that the offer included a delivery of: a disassembled sample machine . . . drawings, specifications and calculations for a "complete plant"; and materials for 2000 centrifuge machines. The document also reflects an offer to provide auxiliary vacuum and electric drive equipment and uranium re-conversion and casting capabilities.[83]

Although the Iranians did purchase centrifuges, designs, and centrifuge technology, they apparently chose not to buy the entire package, and instead took the list of items needed to construct a nuclear weapon, which contained the names of equipment makes and companies, as well as the locations for shipment and the information as to how this equipment could best be procured, and simply went directly to Khan's subcontractors. IAEA officials believe that Iran also received a complete design for a nuclear warhead from the Khan network.[84]

This was Khan's first successful foray into the international market as an exporter. While there were Pakistani army officers—notably Aslam Beg, chief of staff from 1988 to 1991—who favored an alliance between Iran and Pakistan, it is hard to imagine that these transfers were authorized by the Pakistani state, whose history of diplomatic relations with Iran is a troubled one. Never has a state given its neighbor nuclear weapons. In 1990, however, the entrepreneurial A. Q. Khan offered to sell Saddam Hussein, Iran's bitter adversary, a nuclear bomb design and to guarantee the material support for its creation and production.

Following the defection of Hussein Kamel, son-in-law of Saddam Hussein and director of Iraq's Military Industrial Commission, which was in charge of Iraqi WMD, Iraqi officials turned over to the IAEA extensive documents about the country's WMD programs. These included a Top Secret memorandum concerning a meeting between Iraqi officials and a representative of A. Q. Khan:

> We have enclosed for you the following proposal from Pakistani scientist Dr. Abd-el-Qadeer Khan regarding the possibility of helping Iraq establish a project to enrich uranium and manufacture a nuclear weapons [*sic*] . . . He is prepared to give us project designs for a nuclear bomb. Ensure any requirements or materials from Western European countries via a company he owns in Dubayy . . . [and] request a preliminary technical meeting to consult on the documents that he will present to us . . . The motive behind this proposal is gaining profits for him and the intermediary.[85]

Other documents list items to be procured, similar to the requirements manifest that was provided to Iran, e.g., commission rates and pricing. The memorandum is dated October 6, 1990, two months after the First Gulf War began with the invasion of Kuwait by Iraq. Iraqi officials later claimed that they rebuffed Khan's overtures because they thought the offer might be part of an elaborate sting operation; they believed, they said, that Khan was acting as an agent provocateur working for Western intelligence agencies. In fact, he was only priming the market: as Corera observes, the "more countries that acquired nuclear technology, the more demand in the marketplace would be stimulated, leading others to follow suit and turn to the best known supplier. [In this way] Khan's business could become self-generating."[86]

By this time, KRL had gone well beyond simply mastering the most advanced centrifugal methods of uranium enrichment. In the 1980s, "Khan also had gained proficiency in developing the trigger mechanism, uranium reconversion, and bomb design and assembly."[87] India had tested the Agni ballistic missile in May 1989. When the U.S. cancelled the balance of a Pakistani order for F-16 fighter jets, KRL turned to the question of how to deliver a nuclear warhead to its target.

Khan's bureaucratic adversary, the PAEC, had worked assiduously to develop Chinese missile technology, specifically the solid-fueled M-11. A training missile had been received in 1990; by 1992 Pakistan had deployed thirty-four M-11s, but these had a relatively short range and could not reach New Delhi, the Indian capital. Khan began to pursue a separate track. Beginning perhaps as early as 1992, Pakistan started to cultivate a relationship with the North Korean military. In 1993, the Pakistani prime minister, Benazir Bhutto, closed a deal for missile technology during a December visit to Pyongyang.

What happened next has baffled analysts. Bhutto adamantly maintains that Pakistan paid cash[88] for the Nodong missile technology on which Khan was to rely for the development of the Pakistani Ghauri[89] missile. Yet subsequent events confirm that KRL centrifuge technology found its way to North Korea. Some have concluded that there was a swap of centrifuges for ballistic missiles;[90] to others it seems preposterous that Pakistan would trade away its "nuclear 'crown jewels'" for decades-old liquid fuel missiles . . . Assuming that Pakistan received liquid-fuelled missile technology and provided North Korea with cash, a testing site, and indigenous technological expertise, the [argument for] a centrifuge-for-missile barter does not make sense. Providing centrifuge technology seems gratuitous in such an exchange."[91]

Once again, however, our thinking has been confined by our expectation that all such transactions must be made state to state, and indeed that the state itself is a unitary actor. Khan probably did indeed trade away the centrifuge technology that he controlled to North Korea, but this was not done for Pakistan's benefit or with the knowledge of its leadership. Instead, Khan wanted two things: to hasten the delivery of Nodong technology so that he could best the PAEC in the competition to deploy a weapon that could reach New Delhi; and to begin a collaboration with North Korea for the benefit of the Khan network—a collaboration that would soon bear fruit when Khan's intermediaries negotiated a complete warhead facility with Libya. Only this explanation persuasively accounts for the fact that plutonium traces identified forensically as North Korean in origin were found in the technology that Khan sold to Libya. It would also account for the Inter-Services Intelligence search of a North Korea–bound chartered aircraft in 2000, which sought but did not find evidence of a clandestine KRL–North Korean collaboration. If the swap was made with Pakistani consent, there would have been no point in such a surveillance and search.

In the event, on April 6, 1998, the 1,500-kilometer-range Ghauri 1, a Nodong clone, was flight-tested. Pakistani television broadcast that "Prime

Minister Mohammad Nawaz Sharif has warmly congratulated Dr. Khan and his team of scientists and engineers, as well as the entire nation on this historic achievement."[92]

North Korea's relationship to the A. Q. Khan network was to prove fruitful for both parties, and is especially troubling for the rest of the world.

In 1993, U.S. concerns about a North Korean plutonium project led to a crisis that was narrowly averted by the 1994 Agreed Framework agreement. This agreement provided for the monitoring of a North Korean suspension of nuclear development in exchange for oil, assistance with light water nuclear reactors, and an enhanced diplomatic relationship with the U.S. Unlike plutonium projects, however, which require enormous plant and electrical energy, uranium enrichment is less vulnerable to satellite surveillance technologies. And so North Korea apparently began a parallel enrichment route to nuclear weapons within two years of signing the Framework Agreement.

> As Khan expanded his operations through the 1990s, his freedom was enhanced because of a lack of understanding in the West of just how ambitious he had become. Khan had always been on the radar of U.S. and European intelligence agencies and was understood to be a key player in Pakistan's own nuclear program . . . In 1996, the IAEA counted 12 nations being involved in the illegal nuclear business . . . It would not be clear for many years that Khan was actually at the centre of a web pulling the strings behind so many of the deals that would occasionally emerge into the light . . . Khan and his network had risen to become preeminent in the world of proliferation.[93]

Now Khan took a quantum leap forward in his operations. Hitherto, he had only supplied centrifuge designs, components, shopping manifests, and lists of willing suppliers, and, it is believed, uranium hexafluoride. This scale changed completely when he negotiated a program with Libya to provide a complete, turnkey nuclear weapons capability. For this project, he would have to manufacture or procure over a million components for ten thousand centrifuges, which would produce enough fissile material for up to ten bombs a year. He would ship almost two tons of uranium hexafluoride, relying on sources in both Pakistan and North Korea. He would provide a workable warhead design. He would train foreign scientists. But, perhaps most significantly, he would create his own global commercial enterprise, establishing factories in third-party states to evade the export restrictions that were increasingly hampering his suppliers. "Importing subcomponents from Europe and elsewhere . . . workshops in Turkey served as European mini-hubs, from which Khan's network could procure and supply centrifuge motors, power suppliers, and ring magnets from partially within the web of pan-European export controls."[94] These facilities assembled centrifuge motors and frequency converters that were sent with false end-user certificates to Dubai, where Khan had set up offices. There they were loaded onto German ships laden with other components from Malaysia, where Khan had his largest factories, including a nuclear centrifuge plant.[95] In South Africa, Khan's network was able to draw upon firms and individuals with experience from the former South African nuclear weapons program. There his affiliates began creating a massive system—it would have been two stories in height when completed—to feed and withdraw uranium hexafluoride gas into a centrifuge cascade.[96]

Libya had long sought nuclear weapons, but after twenty years it was no closer to success than when it had begun. The clandestine market was too fragmented for Libya to acquire the right equipment and matériel, and the country simply didn't have the indigenous technocracy to make or run the equipment when it was procured. A uranium-conversion facility purchased clandestinely in 1984 arrived without instructions for assembly and was left in storage for years. After more than a decade of trying, Libya had failed to construct a single centrifuge.[97] The Khan network offered a dramatic shortcut through these difficulties. "Rather than purchase piecemeal, a country would be offered everything on a platter—but at a price . . . [I]t would require a refocusing of the Khan network to a full service, private-sector model—a logical fruition of Khan's activities."[98]

The pace quickened. In 2001, Libya received 1.87 tons of uranium hexafluoride, flown in from Pakistan on an aircraft controlled by Khan. Later that year the Libyans were given validated—which is to say "tested"—nuclear weapons designs, accompanied by blueprints, sketches, instruction manuals, and other materials. The designs were for a bomb that would weigh around 500 kilograms. Though crude by the standards of the states with the most advanced weapons, the bomb was small enough to fit on a missile.[99]

By 2000, the American intelligence community had learned that the Khan network had provided Libya with a nuclear weapons design.[100] In 2002, the British Joint Intelligence Committee concluded that Khan had established factories in Malaysia and was using Dubai as his operational base, and that this network "was central to all aspects of the Libyan nuclear weapons programme."[101] Of course, intelligence information alone merely sets up the problem for decision makers; it doesn't resolve it. As Corera observed:

[C]onfronting governments suspected of proliferation . . . is not straightforward. Too little evidence and the country will simply deny its veracity or ask for more proof. But if too much evidence is shared, then the source of the intelligence*—usually either a human spy or electronic surveillance—will be all too obvious and open to elimination. Wait too long in watching a program and gathering intelligence, however, and it can be too late—a country can reach the point of no return with its nuclear program.[102]

In this case it was concluded by the U.S. and the U.K. that it was time for action to close down the network. As the Butler Commission put it (with some considerable understatement), "Khan's activities had now reached the point where it would be dangerous to allow them to go on."[103] Fortuitously, the U.S. and the U.K. had been engaged for some months in discussions with Libya about its reintegration into the world community. One precondition of this was the abandonment of any Libyan WMD programs, the existence of which the country had denied.

On October 4, 2003, the *BBC China,* flying a German flag, was diverted to port by its owners just after midnight, and put in at Taranto, Italy. The ship's owners had been directed by the German Federal Information Service (BND) to radio the vessel's captain and instruct him to change course as he exited the Suez Canal. A search was conducted in Taranto under the greatest tension: the search team had to identify five forty-foot cargo containers out of more than two hundred, with only serial numbers to go by. The *BBC China* was then to resume its voyage without disclosing its secret detour. The operation was jointly coordinated by American, British, German, and Italian authorities.

The search resulted in the seizure of containers packed with thousands of centrifuge components. The same day a senior British Secret Intelligence Service (MI6) officer initiated conversations with a Libyan counterpart, demanding an explanation. On December 19, 2003, the Tripoli government announced it would halt its efforts to produce or acquire WMD and would permit a series of inspections to confirm these undertakings.

> As a result of these [events], inspectors were able to speedily remove key materials related to missiles and weapons of mass destruction . . . —including centrifuges, an entire uranium conversion facility, nuclear weapons designs, uranium hexafluoride, and guidance pack-

*Here it seems that Khan's network had been penetrated by human spies, and its quarters extensively bugged. George Tenet described the CIA's role: "Working with British colleagues, we pieced together his subsidiaries, his clients, his front companies, his finances and manufacturing plants. We were inside his residence, inside his facilities, inside his rooms. We were everywhere these people were." Douglas Jehl, "C.I.A. Says Pakistanis Gave Iran Nuclear Aid," *New York Times,* 24 November 2004, A10.

ages of the Scud-C missile—and ensconce them safely in the United States.[104]

On February 4, 2004, Khan appeared on Pakistani national television and apologized to the nation for unspecified "activities which were based in good faith, but on errors [of] judgment related to unauthorized proliferation activities."[105] He was subsequently pardoned by the government, but remains under house arrest.

What does this astounding story say about the relationships among states, markets, and non-state actors? There are a number of lessons from the Khan affair: the need for greater U.S.-European coordination;* the need for greater security responsibility from the private sector; the requirement of new statutory authorities[106]; the difficulties of coordinating intelligence collection among states[107]; and the acute need to reevaluate the relationship between security guarantees and nonproliferation.[108] As Jason Epstein noted, "[t]here is enough fissile material in the world today for 300,000 bombs. . . . More than thirty states now have at least one metric ton of this material. Forty states, according to the IAEA, can now build a nuclear weapon while the eight or nine nuclear states themselves still possess 27,000 bombs."[109] Putting these lessons to one side for the moment, let us return to the conclusions offered in the Adelphi Paper that claimed that concern over proliferation to non-state actors was misplaced.

> *There is no evidence in the open-source literature of a true international black market in nuclear materials . . . To the extent that a market exists, it is almost entirely driven by supply; there appears to be no true demand except where the buyers were government agents running a sting.*

Examination of the case of the Khan black-market nuclear network, and other materials, should weaken our confidence in this assertion. From 1976 to 2004, Khan was able to create a global commercial network trading in nuclear warhead design, uranium enrichment technology, uranium hexafluoride, and long-range missiles.

> *No actual or aspiring nuclear weapon state has ever claimed to have nuclear weapons without also having all of the technical infrastruc-*

---

*The U.S. government issued about one hundred communiqués to the West German government alone over exports to Pakistan during the 1980s. Around seventy German firms are thought to have supplied Pakistan, but most U.S. complaints were simply ignored. In one 1986 West German Economic Ministry internal memo, an officer casually stated that U.S. intelligence warnings of planned nuclear exports to South Asia "usually land in my wastepaper basket." Corera, *Shopping for Bombs,* 35–36.

ture to produce them ab initio, *although, if the [argument that nuclear weapons technology were for sale was true] they could easily have bought a few on the black market.*

Iran and North Korea owe much of their current capabilities to the Khan enterprise. Libya was offered, and it accepted, a complete nuclear weapons program, using entirely external materials and know-how. Only the interdiction of a shipment of centrifuges, and the fortuitous diplomatic engagement of Libya in negotiations to return it to membership in the community of states, ultimately exposed and thwarted this purely commercial transaction. It's not so much that the italicized statement is entirely wrong, but that it is so complacent: if states with virtually no sophisticated technical infrastructure, like Libya, can, by means of a clandestine market, become a nuclear weapons power in a fraction of the time it took France or China, why can't we assume that a similar market will develop to serve those customers who, unlike states, do not require a large arsenal?

Nuclear weapon states, even "rogues," are most unlikely to be foolish enough to hand nuclear weapons, which are among their dearest national treasures, over to . . . terrorists, especially when the chances of a suspected state sponsor suffering nuclear retaliation and annihilation are so good, and so blindingly obvious.

We still do not know whether the Khan network functioned with or without the knowledge of the Pakistani leadership. The best studies of this question conclude that the evidence remains ambiguous.[110] For our purposes, it really doesn't matter. If the state was complicitous, it suggests that the italicized proposition is open to some doubt. It appears that nuclear weapons states will in fact hand over their "dearest national treasures" to persons who will convey them to a non-state entity—here, the Khan network itself. If the state was unwitting, the matter is even more damning. This would suggest that nuclear weapons states do not always entirely control their technologies (Pakistan did not want to arm its neighbor Iran with nuclear weapons); that they are willing to participate in a black market (North Korea swapped missiles and China provided warhead blueprints in exchange for centrifuge technology); that if a political entity has the funds it need not have the technocracy or technology necessary to build nuclear weapons in small numbers but can acquire this capacity off the shelf. There is no reason such an entity has to be a state, rather than an extraordinarily well-financed terrorist network. Khan planned to charge Libya less than $100 million for a complete "turnkey" operation that would produce a nuclear weapon. Finally, in a globalized market, there is unlikely to be a single state to which responsibility can be attached, and thus against whom retaliation might be directed. Finally, if thirty states or more have nuclear weapons, as has been predicted by some analysts, then the temptation increases for a state to give a warhead or atomic mine to a terrorist group rather than to send a weapon via a missile on the ground that its true provenance will be at best untraceable and at least vague or ambiguous.

> [T]he detailed plans and engineering drawings necessary to build a bomb are not easily available. It would also be very difficult, if not effectively impossible, to acquire sufficient quantities of suitable fissile materials . . . Developing nuclear weapons requires state-level resources . . .

It would perhaps be more circumspect to say that while developing nuclear weapons has, in the past, required state-level resources, once the hard work of experimentation and design is accomplished far fewer resources are required to copy, steal, or buy what was once innovative technology. There is no enforceable patent and licensing system on nuclear weapons.[111]

> [T]errorists have not historically been particularly interested in WMD, and no terrorist use of WMD of any kind has resulted in mass casualties . . . [N]either al Qaeda nor any of the organizations linked to it has ever used WMD, and the evidence that they have the will or the technical capacity to do so is limited and unconvincing.

The preceding chapters have implicitly questioned this historical observation. Indeed one of the key differences between nation state terrorism and market state terrorism is precisely the interest al Qaeda shows in acquiring WMD. In an interview with bin Laden conducted by *Time* magazine in early 1999, this exchange occurred:

TIME: The U.S. says you are trying to acquire chemical and nuclear weapons.
BIN LADEN: Acquiring weapons for the defense of Muslims is a religious duty. If I have indeed acquired these weapons, then I thank God for enabling me to do so. And if I seek to acquire these weapons, I am carrying out a duty.[112]

In November 2004, Michael Scheuer, former head of the CIA unit tracking bin Laden, disclosed[113] that bin Laden had solicited, and had received, a fatwa from a Saudi Muslim cleric stating that, despite prohibitions in the Koran against the harming of innocent persons,[114] the use of a nuclear weapon against the U.S. and other non-Islamic states was permissible. In fact, Sheikh Nasser ibn Hamed, a well-known Saudi cleric associated with al Qaeda, issued a fatwa in May 2003 entitled "A Treatise on the Ruling Regarding the Use of Weapons of Mass Destruction against the Infidels" on precisely this point. After quoting Koranic verses, he writes:

> Anyone who looks at America's acts of aggression against the Muslims and their lands over the recent decades will permit [attacks with WMD] based only on the section of Islamic law called "Repayment in Kind" without any need to indicate the other evidence. Some of the brothers have counted the number of Muslims killed with their direct and indirect weapons, and this number has reached nearly 10 million . . . The most recent case we saw with our own eyes is what happened in Afghanistan and Iraq . . . If a bomb was dropped on them that would annihilate 10 million . . . that is permissible, with no need to mention any other proof. Yet if we want to annihilate a greater number, we need further evidence.[115]

Al Qaeda spokesman Suleiman abu Gheith has stated that the group's objective is "to kill 4 million Americans—2 million of them children—and to exile twice as many and wound and cripple hundreds of thousands."[116] It is hard to imagine that this objective could be achieved by any other method than the use of WMD.

Even here, however, the Khan experience has relevance.

The precipitous collapse of the Taliban resulted in an intelligence trove for the U.S. and its allies. Documents and disks disclosed al Qaeda's biological weapons program, including the location of several sites containing commercial production equipment and cultures of a biological agent. This came as something of a shock, as this capability had been entirely unknown to the CIA.

What was even more disturbing were documentary reports of contacts between al Qaeda and Pakistani nuclear scientists who met to discuss the development of nuclear weapons. Two scientists formerly with the PAEC (one of whom had previously worked at the KRL under Khan and who subsequently became chairman of the PAEC) had left the Pakistani program to found a charity, Ummah Tameer-e-Nau, dedicated to relief work in Afghanistan. While visiting Kabul in 2000, one of these scientists, Sultan Bashiruddin Mahmood, was summoned to a meeting with bin Laden. A series of meetings with bin Laden ultimately took place in a Kabul compound over several days in August 2001.[117]

We have no conclusive reports of the content of these conversations. Mahmood's son later said, "Basically, Osama asked my father, 'How can a nuclear bomb be made and can you help us make one?' " In any event, the

invasion of Afghanistan brought an abrupt halt to this dialogue. Both scientists, along with the entire board of directors of the charity, were arrested
by Pakistani authorities. Mahmood was interrogated; he failed a series of
lie detector tests.[118] Months of further interrogation have not further illu-
minated this incident; as of this writing, Mahmood is under house arrest
and his name is among those designated as terrorists by the U.S. Those
who doubt that Mahmood had the technical skills to build a nuclear warhead[119] are missing the point of the Khan narrative: it's not simply what
technical facility the scientist or manager has, but rather his (or her)
knowledge of where to find corruptible, cooperative, and capable co-
conspirators. Mahmood had been removed from his position with the
PAEC because of his vociferous advocacy of the "massive development of
weapons-grade [nuclear] material to help arm other Islamic countries."[120]
At his interrogation he is reported to have disclosed that bin Laden insisted
that he already had sufficient fissile material to build a bomb, having
obtained it from former Soviet stockpiles through a militant Islamic group,
the Islamic Movement of Uzbekistan.

> *[Contrary to those who believe that] "dirty bombs" could also be
> extremely dangerous, [t]he economic, social and psychological effects
> of a dirty bomb could be considerably more serious than its physical
> or radiological effects.*
>
> *[Contrary to the claim that nuclear terrorism constitutes an exis-
> tential threat to the United States and other potential target states,] to
> destroy the United States or any other large industrial state . . . would
> require a large number of well-placed nuclear weapons with yields in
> the tens or hundreds of kilotons.*

These objections go to the issues to be addressed in the remainder of
this book. If, as I believe, warfare is changing, as will be argued in chapter 3, and the aims of warfare are undergoing a transformation, as will be
discussed in chapter 4, it is a mistake to assume that the conquest of land or
the total destruction of a society constitute the only criteria for victory or
defeat in the Wars on Terror. At stake in these wars is the capacity of market states to maintain systems of consent and to avoid becoming states of
terror. Threats such as those posed by dirty bombs, to say nothing of even a
handful of nuclear detonations,[121] are precisely the sort of attacks that
could lead to the moral and psychological defeat sought by our enemies. In
fact, because biological terrorism has the potential for repeated attack
without appreciably destroying the terrorists' resources and need for planning, it is particularly useful, as Richard Danzig observes, in "undermining confidence and forcing ever-escalating investments of resources to
achieve a modicum of defense."[122]

As long as we continue to think in twentieth century, nation state terms, we will not be able to develop doctrines and capabilities sufficient to address this new threat. The principal reason that North Korea was able to evade the detection of its ardent violation of the Agreed Framework treaty was the neglect of the capabilities of the Khan enterprises owing to U.S. and British incredulity. The same is true about proliferation to Iran. In both cases Khan's commercial network allowed these countries to pursue uranium enrichment programs in addition to the larger and more easily detected (and attacked) plutonium plants. In a telling and disquieting report, Iranian officials were said to be present at the North Korean missile launches in the summer of 2006 that threatened Japan, and North Korean officials have been observed at what Syria concedes was a facility for strategic missiles and what Israel claims was a nascent nuclear weapons program when it was attacked in the fall of 2007.[123]

Ultimately the A. Q. Khan story is about the difficulty of curtailing the exchange of knowledge. Khan acquired his skills, and precious centrifuge technology, as the employee of a Dutch engineering firm. Is it so unlikely that there is a similar young man or woman today, working for Pfizer or GlaxoSmithKline or another international pharmaceutical company, who will one day use the knowledge acquired there to create biological weapons? And for what reason must it be that, were this capability to be sold, the only willing buyers would be states?

> Modern DNA sequencing technology permits absolute characterization of any organism's genetic material . . . All this information is stored in digital data files that are commonly accessible via a currently nonattributable manner over the Internet . . . The recent production of infectious poliovirus . . . is merely the tip of the iceberg when it comes to potential implications of this technology . . . As the number of commercial DNA synthesis enterprises and the prevalence of this technology in smaller laboratories increases, standard approaches to monitor [biowarfare agents] will become less effective. Many of these new approaches are specifically designed to decrease the technical expertise necessary to produce quantities of biological agents that would be sufficient for a group with nefarious intentions . . . Emerging biotechnologies likely will lead to a paradigm shift in [biological weapons] development; future biological agents could be rationally engineered to target specific human biological systems at the molecular level.[124]

We are about to witness a revolution in biotechnology that will take us far from the familiar, naturally occurring agents of twentieth century state labs. These agents will be more accessible to terrorists as developments in bioinformatics become widely commercialized,[125] and at the same time pose far more complex threats.

V.

The Adelphi Paper discussed above, *Nuclear Terrorism After 9/11*, begins with this observation: the "point Karl-Heinz Kamp made nine years ago applies just as well today: if all these [concerns] were [justified], why is it that terrorists still do not possess nuclear explosive devices?" Similarly, one might ask: if the concerns voiced in the preceding pages have a realistic foundation, why haven't we seen WMD, including biological agents, used by al Qaeda?

One answer is that the acquisition of WMD by a twenty-first century, globally networked terror group like al Qaeda—a group, that is, that would use such weapons—is no less likely an eventuality because it is difficult in the short run. One might also add that the market state itself is still emerging. Because it is driving market state terrorism, it will have to mature before its symptoms, of which al Qaeda is one, become fully developed. Perhaps the best answer, however, is that it is simply unrealistic to shape a policy of dealing with future threats according to the threats we have faced in the past. We do not know whether al Qaeda or its successors will acquire WMD. In such uncertainty, we must nevertheless decide whether to structure our defenses around unlikely but horrific attacks, or in anticipation of less preventable but more predictable conventional assaults.

This is a controversial matter. Many analysts believe that the small-scale conventional bombings associated with terrorism will continue to be the norm. "Bombs are every [terrorist's] favourite," one analyst at the Center for Strategic and International Studies was quoted as saying. "They're tried and true." Biological weapons are a different matter: "If there's snow, the germs all die in the cold, and no one notices a thing. Terrorists aren't going to rely on weapons that are difficult to use or that will fizzle at the last minute."[126]

Many observers believe that the U.S. and the U.K. should concentrate on the most probable attacks. Right now "Washington," it has been said, "is the capital of imaginary threats," which divert attention from measures that could prevent the most likely of terrorist attacks.

This criticism goes to the subject of chapter 4: what is at stake in the Wars on Terror. In my view, we must address some low-probability events because of their potentially high impact.[127] Terrorists can murder many thousands of Americans through small acts of attrition: suicide bombing, sniper assaults at shopping centers, sabotage of power lines, train derailments, pipeline explosions, and the like. We have learned that societies adjust to repeated small-scale assaults, however, even if cumulatively they take 40,000 lives—the number lost on U.S. highways every year. Rather it is the theatrical, mass-scale attack that has the potential to disrupt the political culture of the target society. The increasing emphasis on the citizen as spectator, as a consumer of entertainment however shocking, is characteristic of market state societies. Market state terrorists are heroes of autonomy who maximize their own options by terrorizing those who would restrict them. They are consumers of opportunity, who compete to seize the attention of the otherwise distracted public. As we saw in the previous chapter, it has been reported that at least one attack on New York was stood down by the al Qaeda leadership after 9/11 because it was deemed too unspectacular.

This chapter has argued that the market state terrorists of the twenty-first century will arm with weapons of mass destruction. This will come about through clandestine markets, the radical redistribution of hitherto secret information on a universal scale, and the ever-lowering costs of WMD.[128] The next chapter will relate these developments with respect to terrorism to the changing nature of twenty-first century warfare.

As we have seen, it is the global presence of the United States, the first and most dynamic of the emerging market states, that has been the main target as well as the chief precipitating factor of twenty-first century terrorism. American military power, American empathy and ideals, and American ubiquity have brought forth both American hegemony and al Qaeda, and will bring forth other global, networked terrorists in the future. The appearance of mutated market states like al Qaeda represents the emergence of a form of plague, propagated by the very conditions that brought us feasts. Such states of terror take the structure of the new form—the constitutional order of the market state—but renounce its mission of freeing the individual the way a virus might inhabit the structure of a normal cell but take over its nucleus.

Of course we have had states of terror in the past. For them, terror was a means to an end. Robespierre (see page 39) might have been speaking for Josef Stalin, Adolf Hitler, or Mao. What is interesting is that some states, like market state terrorists, will now seek something like perpetual terror. With respect to WMD, this is manifested in the state's desire to use these weapons in order to enforce lateral, or horizontal, deterrence—that is, the use of WMD to prevent defensive interventions on behalf of local allies. Iran or Iraq did not plan to attack Washington or London; rather, they sought WMD to prevent the U.S. and the U.K. from intervening when they attacked their weak regional neighbors. This is the use of WMD for compellance and it too is not entirely new. The report that Eisenhower threatened the use of nuclear weapons to bring China and North Korea to the negotiating table in 1953, if true, is an example of compellance by means of WMD; so are Hiroshima and Nagasaki. These incidents are to be contrasted, however, with the subsequent "balance of terror" achieved by the U.S. and the USSR in the 1960s, which served the objective of deterrence. What the state of terror in the current era seeks is a perpetual standoff not to prevent a mutual annihilation but to protect its predations. The terror becomes, in a globalized era, an end in itself.[129]

This transition from one constitutional order to another will occur over many decades, and there are many forms that the market state might take. If the past is any guide, the transition will not be completed without violent conflict. In the past, decades-long epochal wars brought about these transitions. It may be that the wars against al Qaeda, the Taliban, and Saddam Hussein's regime were the first engagements of this new conflict, the epochal war of the market states, the Wars against Terror.

I.

> Last year I called this world of gain-givings
> The darkest thinkable, and questioned sadly
> If my own land could heave its pulse less gladly,
> So charged it seemed with circumstance whence springs
>   The tragedy of things.

II.

> Yet at that censured time no heart was rent
> Or feature blanched of parent, wife, or daughter
> By hourly blazoned sheets of listed slaughter;
> Death waited Nature's wont; Peace smiled unshent
>   From Ind to Occident.

—Thomas Hardy, "At the War Office"

CHAPTER THREE

Warfare Against Civilians

. . . By a name

I know not how to tell thee who I am:
My name, dear saint, is hateful to myself,
Because it is an enemy to thee.
Had I it written, I would tear the word.

—William Shakespeare,
Romeo and Juliet, 2.2.1–2

STATES WERE NOT "at war" with terror groups like the IRA. There are many good reasons to think that the concept of war is inapplicable to an adversary that has no territory to defend, no capital to seize, no army to surround, no citizenry that can be menaced—whether that adversary is twenty-first or twentieth century, a market state or nation state terrorist group.

From the time when the first modern states began to emerge, only states have made war.* Children and animals may fight, but they cannot make war. When crime syndicates fight—often lethally—they do not make war and their crimes are not war crimes. Since the Renaissance, brigands, pirates, feudal and religious orders, even corporations (like the Dutch East India Company) might fight but only states could sanction violence as war. War is a matter between states—constitutional entities created by and wielding law—and war carries with it the constitutional evolution of five centuries of interstate conflict. For half a millennium it has taken the resources of a state to destroy another state by war. In such a world, every country knew that its only lethal enemies would be drawn from a small class of potential adversaries. Only states could muster the huge revenues, hire or conscript the vast armies, and deploy the complex technologies required to threaten the survival of other states by defeating their armies. Indeed, it was to respond to such a threat—from France in 1494—that the

---

*"Civil war" is, as international law recognizes, a conflict for control of a state; sometimes it arises from secession, the motive for which is to create yet another state. Civil wars are waged by states, or following the collapse of a state, by more than one entity that claims the right of statehood.

rich, weak walled cities of the Italian plain were compelled to innovate constitutionally, bringing into being the first modern states. It should not surprise us that warfare has been an affair of states; it has been as influential in shaping the state as the state's constitutional development has been in shaping the evolution of war. Revolutions in military affairs have acted in a mutually affecting relationship with revolutions in constitutional affairs. Indeed, twenty-first century global terrorism is one consequence of this interaction.[1]

On August 23, 1996, the terrorist group al Qaeda declared war on the United States;[2] on September 14, 2001, the United States obliged by authorizing the use of military force against global terrorism, of which al Qaeda was the only cited exemplar. If only states make war, is al Qaeda perforce a state?

A case can be made. The Italian oligarchies of the fifteenth century became states when they developed permanent legal relationships with other states (hitherto treaties had expired with the deaths of their feudal signatories), standing armies (though composed almost entirely of mercenaries after the disastrous failure of Machiavelli's scheme to create a citizen army in Florence), consistent sources of finance (to pay for war and the construction of fortresses), and bureaucracies, including the first permanent legations. The territories of these states were ill-defined; that would come later with the need to set up customs cordons. National peoples were not especially identified with any particular state; indeed, their rulers might not speak the local language and might rule over many disparate national groups. The notion that a nation deserves a state—the idea of "self-determination"—came much later. The State has undergone many transformations in the constitutional order—the basis for the state's legitimacy—in the ensuing five centuries. Now it is about to undergo another. Could al Qaeda be an example of this new form?

The terror network that bin Laden has assembled might be described as a new and mutated form of the State, a terrorist market state. Market states of consent will no doubt be manifest in a number of forms (mercantile, entrepreneurial, managerial) just as nation states came in various ideological manifestations (communist, fascist, parliamentary); the state of terror[3] will come with different valences.*

In a sense, al Qaeda attempts to enlarge the choices available to individual Muslims, regardless of nationality, by creating a global state that enforces the sharia† and to which Muslims can repair in a world that

---

*The *valence* of a constitutional order is its affinity for a particular mode of governance, e.g., the valence of an entrepreneurial market state is characterized by seeking international leadership through the production and marketing of collective goods that the world's states want.

†*Sharia* refers to the body of Islamic law derived from the Koran and the sunnah, which are the deeds, remarks, and approbations of the Prophet Muhammad.

would deny them this means of governance. Al Qaeda makes no pretense that its principal objective is to better the material well-being of Muslims and indeed disdains the economic benefits of an open trading system, credit based on market interest rates, and economic relations based on state equality. It does not aspire to be a nation state. Like other states, it has a standing army; like those of market states, this army is partly a framework provided by the state, and largely an outsourced, mercenary collection of units assembled for particular operations. Al Qaeda has a treasury and consistent source of finance; like market states it raises a significant amount of its revenue not from taxation but from voluntary contributions, either through donations or through business transactions. Like other states, al Qaeda has an intelligence collection and analysis cadre. It even runs a rudimentary welfare program for its fighters, their relatives and their associates. Like a market state, however, it provides financial incentives in lieu of regulation; thus, instead of nation state conscription to recruit fighters, as, for example, practiced by the Taliban, al Qaeda offers bounties to suicide bombers and to professional kidnappers. It makes alliances with other states by using its financial power adroitly. It promulgates a recognizable system of laws, the sharia. It declares wars. What it lacks, at the moment anyway, is contiguous territory, and while this omission may not necessarily mean that al Qaeda is not a state—perhaps it is a virtual state— it does mean that traditional strategies of deterrence and retaliation will have to be rethought.

It's not only that a global terrorist network cannot be deterred through threats of nuclear retaliation in the way that Soviet ambitions were checked. It's that threats of U.S. retaliation are so much more powerful today that they force hostile states to outsource aggression to terrorist networks (as we saw in the summer of 2006 when Hezbollah, armed by Syria and Iran, attacked Israel). As already noted, the U.S. has highly accurate systems that can locate a hostile missile launch within seconds. No state would reasonably target the U.S. without assuming certain retaliation. All this doesn't mean the end of war, however, so much as the end of the complete reliance on retaliatory threats and the beginning of disguised attacks using surrogates. This will give a network like al Qaeda something like the status of a state insofar as it can make alliances and extract concessions. This is not to insist that al Qaeda is a certain kind of state and thus that we can be said to be at war with it. It simply suggests that we are in a certain kind of war and thus al Qaeda cannot be said to be a typical twentieth century nation state terror group (with which a state could *not* be at war).

Unlike conflicts with earlier nation state terrorist groups, global war *can* be waged by a market state terrorist network (whatever al Qaeda's proper organizational nomenclature, that is, whether we choose to regard it as a state or not) precisely because the capability to wage such a war is not confined to a nation state in part because the technology of warfare hitherto reserved to states is becoming more widely available to such networks. Owing to advances in the development of international telecommunications, rapid computation, and weapons of mass destruction, it will someday be possible for small groups, acting either for themselves or covertly on behalf of nonattributable state sponsors, to deliver devastating blows to the infrastructure and the populations of even the greatest countries. When the motivation for these strikes is not criminal but political; when the targets are military in nature and the operations carried out with a disregard for the survival of the attackers; and above all when the nature of the assaults is such that, previously, they could only have come from states because the assaults are sustained and global in scope—then it may not be unreasonable to regard them as acts of war.

But is it wise to do so? That can only be answered by a careful attention to the legal implications for our societies of calling such conflicts war, and also, of course, the implications for war itself. It can be said that al Qaeda is engaged with many states, including the U.S. and the U.K., in a kind of armed conflict that will set the pattern for early-twenty-first century wars. We might wish to call it "war" simply because that's what it is. As we shall see, our failure to recognize this transformation of war has been a costly one. Nevertheless, many respected authorities disagree with this position; the most distinguished of them is the eminent historian Sir Michael Howard.

I.

In "What's in a Name?," a characteristically trenchant and elegantly argued essay for *Foreign Affairs,* Sir Michael draws two conclusions.[4] First, as a prudential matter, calling the struggle against terrorism a "war" has significant costs. Second, the struggle against terrorism is analytically distinguishable from war. It is not even close, analytically, to the metaphorical "wars" on crime or poverty or drugs.

Sir Michael supports his first conclusion with four practical reasons: to label terrorists enemy combatants gives them legitimacy they would otherwise not have; to label the fight against terrorism a "war" forces states to look for other states to attack because warfare is a matter of state conflict; taking these two consequences together, the "war" appellation tends to legitimate the use of force as a priority rather than making it the last resort of state action; and finally, because the preceding three developments are mutually reinforcing, we find as a result that the domestic debate is polarized. Violence abroad turns political discourse at home into charges of warmongering and countercharges of appeasement.

Moreover, Sir Michael argues that because the means and methods of war are so likely to be counterproductive in the struggle against terrorism, we should not permit ourselves to think of being at war with al Qaeda. We are engaged in a struggle for the "hearts and minds" (a phrase he reminds us that was born in the Malaysian antiterrorist campaign) of a vast Muslim civilization already challenged by modernity, diversity, and economic failure. This struggle cannot succeed unless we have the cooperation of the members of that civilization; the techniques of warfare, however, are bound to alienate them. Because "one man's terrorist is another man's freedom fighter," he can be suppressed "only if public opinion . . . supports the authorities in regarding them as criminals rather than heroes." Denominating a struggle as a war implies the terrorists are warriors, not murderers. Furthermore, when the terrorist provokes the authorities into retaliating with overt armed force, he wins: either he escapes or he is martyred. Aerial bombing compounds this on a large scale, and drains legitimacy and empathy away from the legal order that is responsible for such destruction.

Shifting from the prudential to the analytical, Sir Michael comes down heavily on the "crime" side of the question whether terrorism is an act of war or a crime. He notes, astringently, that the "British in their time have fought many such 'wars'—in Palestine, in Ireland, in Cyprus, and in Malaya . . . [b]ut they never called them wars; they called them 'emergencies.' " He observes that in an ideal world a police operation would have been conducted by the U.N. against the terrorists who attacked Washington and New York, and the perpetrators tried before an international court. He concludes that we are not at war, simply as a definitional matter, and should be careful not to pretend otherwise lest we bring into play the many negative dimensions that inevitably accompany war.

"What's in a Name?" is a concise, logical, and frank essay that will be especially persuasive to those who don't need to be persuaded of its premises. If we reject those premises, however, we will find that its many penetrating observations support conclusions diametrically opposed to those drawn by the author.

Sir Michael says that those means appropriate to warfare were out of place in past struggles against terrorism. He acknowledges no important differences[5] between the terrorist techniques of postcolonial national liberation movements and those of al Qaeda. Therefore we cannot be at war with al Qaeda. Reverse these assumptions, however—consider that al Qaeda's nonnational, global network presents a different sort of terrorism, and that the methods of twenty-first century warfare (even apart from wars on terror) will require factoring in complex social, psychological, and political contexts that in the past have not been thought part of the battlefield—and we will reach rather different conclusions. Put aside the unquestioned assumption about the continuity between the fields of Malaysia, the streets of Belfast, and the hurtling airliners over New York and Washington. Then recognize that warfare that is *augmented* by counter-recruitment of terrorists, by prosecutions, and by police work is not a kind of "category mistake" but is in fact the way warfare is likely to occur in many theaters in the twenty-first century.

Giving terrorists rights as enemy combatants does indeed legitimate them as warriors, though, as we shall see, it need not legitimate their tactics, which can be war crimes. In a global struggle against an overwhelming superpower, however, all armed conflict is likely to be asymmetric. Are we to call all the fighters against the West criminals, whatever their tactics? And if we do, can we expect our publics and everyone else's to go along with this designation? Legitimacy is not ours to bestow in the global context, though it might well have been in Northern Ireland or Malaysia, or any confined jurisdiction where criminal process was controlled by the besieged government. Perhaps, in Sir Michael's ideal world, a U.N. force would have invaded Afghanistan and put bin Laden and Mullah Omar on trial before the International Criminal Court. Perhaps, in that world, a global consensus on the application of law and a global monopoly of the means of violence would deny us the use of the term "war" when we fight terrorists, just as we do not war on insider traders or drunk drivers. But that is not the world in which we live.[6] Nor is it likely to be, so long as its most powerful state is too strong not to excite competition, too ever present not to excite hatred, and too vulnerable to ignore threats before they materialize into faits accomplis.

It is true that characterizing the conflict with the terrorist network as "war" does tend to focus attention on states. Renaissance states were created to manage the wars of the Renaissance, much as Gothic arches were erected to support Gothic buildings; the one exists to buttress the other. But in the context of asymmetric warfare, a context in which the global network often must rely on the covert aid of states and can be used by them clandestinely to accomplish attacks states would never dare do openly, isn't a focus on the relationship between states and terror one we should more sensitively cultivate rather than renounce? In the future, we may be astounded that we permitted a state, Afghanistan, openly to recruit, train, and arm guerrillas to kill Americans and British subjects, limiting ourselves to the occasional arrest in a Pakistani hotel—at a cost of millions—or, when our casualties began to mount, the occasional vague (and expensive) cruise missile attack. Even at present, it is to be regretted that the world community tolerated two states, Iran and Syria, setting up their own terrorist group within another state, Lebanon, that was powerless to suppress it, using that group, Hezbollah, to plunge Lebanon into a war with Israel the plan for which war Lebanon's democratically elected government was not even informed of. Hezbollah's role closely tracks the use of terrorist proxies predicted in the previous chapter: Iran and Syria are arming and directing a non-state group because Israel's overwhelming strength makes them unwilling to risk a direct confrontation.

Sir Michael fears that a frank assertion of war legitimates the use of force as something other than a defense of last resort. "The fault in Bosnia," however, as Robert Cooper has reminded us, "was precisely that we used force as a last resort."[7] We ought to be aware that, sometimes, failing to resort to force risks exposing our societies to attacks for which post-event prosecution or even retaliation seems pathetically ineffectual and tardy, while hopelessly destructive. A state that must choose between careful police work and high-intensity warfare is not likely to be very effective in either domain against a global network that moves easily from protected enclaves in remote mountain redoubts to sophisticated urban centers and back again.

Sir Michael's two fundamental conclusions might be characterized as having to do with means (calling the struggle against terrorism a war is counterproductive) and ends (our objective in this struggle pertains to criminal prosecutions, not warfare). Both judgments, however, depend upon assuming away what makes the problem so novel and so difficult. Just as he sees no need to entertain the idea that something new is happening with regard to terrorism, so too he declines to discuss the possibility that warfare is changing in a way that forces it to transgress the hitherto well-defined distinctions between police behavior and military campaigns.

It is true that reliable intelligence is easier to obtain from a populace that regards terrorists as criminals rather than as heroes. But does this observation bear on the distinction between war and crime? There are criminals who remain heroes to their publics (Dick Turpin, for example, or Billy the Kid) but who disdain warfare; and there are war criminals who are despised by some (Saddam Hussein) and lionized by others (Saddam Hussein, again), and much-admired warriors who are betrayed for police rewards (Emiliano Zapata) in much the same way that criminals are (the Tamil bandit Veerappan). It doesn't seem to matter much to the population quite what the authorities choose to call the culprit. Warrior or criminal, Pancho Villa or Robin Hood, an alienated populace will shelter its heroes and reject its villains as it sees them.

Nor is it obvious that the terrorist has his adversaries in the double bind Sir Michael describes. It is true that Mullah Omar and his ally bin Laden did succeed in provoking the U.S. and its allies into action. But as they scuttle from cave to cave, remembering the good old days when a child could be shot for flying a kite or a woman stoned for reading a magazine, one wonders whether they do feel they have in fact taken the "first trick," as Sir Michael puts it, by having been thrown out of Kandahar and Kabul by a campaign in which aerial bombing played a decisive role.

Aerial bombing, like suicide bombing, can delegitimate its practitioners. It did in Vietnam. The reason, however, was not that Vietnam did not constitute a theater of war and was, instead, a conflict in which only police action could have defeated the North Vietnamese army and the Vietcong. When Saigon fell, it did not fall to the Vietcong, but to the tanks and regular forces of the North Vietnamese and it fell because the U.S. declined to supply aerial support for the beleaguered Army of South Vietnam.[8]

Today, for many individuals, suicide bombing is a way to become a soldier. A suicide mission, which is often venerated by society in conventional wars, has become, for these persons, equated with suicide bombing.

Both terrorism and warfare are undergoing a radical transformation. The large-scale, "industrial" warfare of nation states is being replaced by the targeting of civilian populations as a direct objective, rather than a collateral cost. The purpose of this warfare is not to seize territory per se but rather to terrorize a civilian population into acquiescence. Mary Kaldor's thesis of the "new war" that is replacing the conventional wars of the twentieth century has been summarized as arguing that

> [t]he "new war" is a phenomenon of our time, just as the great conflicts between national armies dominated the first half of the century and ideologically-fuelled guerilla wars the post-1945 decades. . . . In a "new war" a motley mixture of paramilitary groupings, local cadres, and army units with no defined command structure [skirt] major battles, but seek . . . control in different ways: they shape the local population in their own image . . . by terrorizing [them] or by killing en masse . . . The militias pay their own wages by extorting money . . . , by looting . . . , by trading . . . on the black market, but also by exploiting the opportunities of an increasingly global community, for example in gifts from wealthy émigrés abroad or by diverting humanitarian aid. . . .[9]

Kaldor thinks that we have not yet adequately grasped the different and unique character of "new wars," and that we try to extinguish them with tried and trusted "old war" methods. How very right she is. Even the Pentagon has now recognized that warfare is changing, and not necessarily in the direction for which it had planned.[10]

The long-standing strategy of the U.S. has required that American forces be configured so that they could fight two major conventional wars at the same time. That model anticipates two wars like the Gulf War of 1991 or the invasion of Iraq in 2003, while maintaining enough reserves to fight a similar conflict, for example, in Korea. Now, however, the Quadren-nial Defense Review mandated by Congress is considering a drastic reno-vation of this strategy.

> In effect, the unusual mission in Iraq, which could last for years, has not just taken the slot for one of the two wars; it has upended the cen-tral concept of the two-war model. It is neither a major conventional combat nor a mere peacekeeping operation. It does not require the full array of forces . . . necessary for a conventional war, and it takes far more troops than peacekeeping ordinarily would.[11]

That is why the phrase "a war on terror" is not an inapt metaphor, but rather a recognition of the way war is changing. As Sir Michael Howard observes, the "war on terror" is not like the metaphorical wars on crime or drugs or poverty because these enemies of mankind do not have "much of a constituency."[12] The terrorist networks with which we are engaged do have their political and ideological partisans—perhaps millions of them—and in this too their commanders are unlike criminals and very much more like political leaders.

The initial Coalition intervention in Afghanistan was a striking military success—in three weeks the Coalition accomplished what the forces of the Soviet Union had been unable to do in ten years—though as yet an incom-plete one. No new atrocities have yet occurred in the U.S.—in part, I have argued,[13] because al Qaeda was forced to change its strategy, but the infor-mation and personnel rounded up in Afghanistan, plus the disruption of the al Qaeda command and its harassment in the field, must also be assumed to have played some part in this. The cross-border platforms have been replaced with in-country ones. Training camps that had provided more than 20,000 fighters, according to the International Institute for Strategic Studies,[14] and by other estimates up to 60,000,[15] are now closed. The Tal-iban were not cemented in power, as some commentators predicted would be the result of bombing. Support from the Pakistani government for the U.S. did not wane in the months following the rout of the Taliban. Indeed, the clandestine Pakistani trade in nuclear technology was exposed and compromised. Is it likely that support for the pro-Western Pakistani regime that accomplished this would have been strengthened if the Taliban had been able to defy the West successfully? The mass riots, the hostage tak-ing, the refugee exodus—none of this happened to any significant degree. In fact, some three million Afghan refugees have returned. Elections were successfully held in October 2004.

Was the innovative military campaign in Afghanistan warfare? Obvi-ously. Against whom? The Taliban, in part, but mainly against a terrorist

group, al Qaeda. I would go further, in light of the elections and the campaign to protect civilians that is ongoing as I write: it is a war against terror
itself, its staging camps, its sadistic quotidian regimes, its desire to cow a
entire people and to intimidate others abroad.

II.

Any redefinition of war will have to take into account the causes of war. In
one sense, these haven't changed for millennia: fear, greed, envy, anger,
and the desire for vengeance, but also humane concern and empathy for
suffering, as well as doctrine—religious or political or ethnocentric—
aggressive leaders and passive societies (or vice versa), and many other of
mankind's least changeable traits all play their part in moving states and
societies toward organized violence. These unaltered motivating elements
do not account for what is new about warfare now. Its causes lie not so
much in man's fellows, or his gods, or his passions as in his intricately
evolving infrastructure. As Bruce Ackerman quite perceptively puts it,
"The root of our [current] problem is not Islam or any ideology but a fundamental change in the relationship between the state, the market, and
technologies of destruction."[16]

There are many motivating factors that animate al Qaeda's forces.
What caused the Wars against Terror, however, was a war *for* terror, and
what caused that onslaught was the emergence of market states, a development that enraged and empowered those who created al Qaeda.

Two new factors brought forth the asymmetric attacks in Nairobi, Dar
es Salaam, New York, Washington, and elsewhere. First was the overwhelming conventional strength of the United States and its allies. The
very capabilities that permitted us to tame the acute problem of continental
annihilation posed by the Cold War have brought us the chronic problem
of twenty-first century terrorism. As Jeffrey Record has observed:

> Perversely, the West has become the victim of its own conventional
> military success. Unchallenged mastery of conventional war is driving
> the competition into asymmetric strategies at both the supra- and the
> sub-conventional levels of warfare . . . It is no coincidence that the
> attractiveness of both [terrorism and weapons of mass destruction] to
> Islamic states and groups hostile to the West has increased in the wake
> of each Arab conventional military defeat.[17]

The second factor was the source of that strength: a relatively open and
increasingly globally linked society whose wealth derives from its exploitation of information. Both of these factors are a consequence of the

victory of the parliamentary states in the Long War[18] of the twentieth century that defeated fascism and communism.

The U.S. and the U.K.[19] were the principal beneficiaries of that victory, although many states shared in its fruits and some—notably Russia, Japan, and Germany—could not otherwise have existed in their present form. Britain currently has access to the protectionist markets of the European Union, which will, after its enlargement is completed, constitute the largest single economic market on earth, while at the same time Britain has cemented its security alliance with the strongest military power on earth. Thus with less than 17 percent of European GDP,[20] and a defense budget that is less than 2½ percent of its own GDP,[21] Britain has managed to have access to the largest economic and military structures extant. It has accomplished this in part by undeviatingly pursuing the destruction of both fascism and communism in Europe, often at mortal risk.

In that struggle the U.S. extended its security perimeter to include both Europe and East Asia, thus magnifying the risks it ran. But for this extension of its own jeopardy, there can be little doubt that at least some states, Germany foremost among them, would either have been absorbed into the communist camp, giving a new lease on life to a lethal ideology, or would have acquired their own nuclear weapons, with incalculable consequences for multipolarity and deterrence. For five decades America was willing to risk nuclear annihilation in order to defend West Germany, Japan, and South Korea.

"Extended deterrence," as this came to be known, required historic courage, steadfastness, and foresight. The benefits of the global peace that followed the Soviet capitulation accrued to all states, but to none more than the U.S. In the period following the Peace of Paris in 1990, America's portion of total gross world product actually increased despite the vigorous growth of competition from many newly capitalist states. By 2002 the U.S. share of the world's total wealth approached what it had been in the 1950s when America's principal competitors were recovering from the devastation of World War II. This economic bounty funded an even more overwhelming military strength. In 2002, the *increase* in U.S. defense spending alone was greater than the entire U.K. defense budget (and three-fourths the size of China's) even though the total cost of defense was about half what (as a percentage of GDP) the U.S. recorded during the Cold War. The consequence of this development for warfare was profound: it meant an acceleration of the search for weapons of mass destruction by hostile states, the cultivation of links to terrorist groups, and above all the rising threat of asymmetric attacks as groups and states antagonistic to the U.S. and the U.K. turned away from conventional challenges that it would have been absurd to press.

The consequence of this, in turn, was to increase the urgency of preempting the proliferation of WMD and destroying the supporting frameworks for global terrorism. Action against Iraq and Afghanistan represented a profound shift from the legal and strategic ideas dominant in the twentieth century when preventive war was rejected on both strategic and legal grounds.

The United States National Security Strategy, which is discussed in some detail in chapter 9, relies on "the inherent obligation to defend our nation against its enemies as the first and fundamental commitment of the Federal Government."[22] To do so, the Strategy contends, "We must be prepared to stop rogue states and their terrorist clients before they are able to threaten or use weapons of mass destruction (WMD) against the United States and our allies and friends . . . [T]o forestall or prevent such hostile acts by our adversaries, the United States will, if necessary, act preemptively."[23]

Two categories of anticipatory self-defense are commonly recognized, preemption and prevention. One standard distinction defines preemptive acts as those initiated on the basis of an expectation that an enemy attack is imminent and defines preventative acts as those initiated in the belief that armed conflict, while not imminent, is inevitable, and that delay would involve great risk.[24]

Preemptive war as a doctrine has an ancient lineage. Francis Bacon was not the first political advisor to disdain academic counsel when he wrote:

> Neither is the opinion of some of the Schoolmen to be received: that a war cannot justly be made, but upon a precedent injury or provocation. For there is no question, but a just fear of an imminent danger, though no blow be given, is a lawful cause of war.[25]

In the twentieth century preventative war was associated with unprovoked aggression. Hitler's occupation of Norway, for example, was justified on the grounds that if unoccupied, Norway would eventually have been invaded by Britain, to Germany's disadvantage. Preventative war was especially disparaged during the Cold War when it threatened the stability of nuclear deterrence. Thomas Schelling captured this concern brilliantly when he wrote that

> [f]ear that the other may be about to strike in the mistaken belief that we are about to strike gives us a motive for striking, and so justifies the other's motive . . . [A] modest temptation on each side to sneak in a first blow—a temptation too small by itself to motivate an attack—[changes] expectations, with [an] additional motive for attack being produced. . . .[26]

In the case of self-defense against imminent attack, the U.N. Charter makes an exception to its otherwise absolute bar against the use of force absent an authorizing Security Council resolution. This might authorize armed preemption (as in the case of Israel's attack on Egypt in 1967) but not preventative attack (as in the case of Israel's attack on the Iraqi nuclear facility at Osirak in 1981, which was condemned by the Security Council). What has changed? And how are anticipatory warfare and precautionary threats different from the categories of preemption and preventative war?

At the outset, we should be clear that anticipatory warfare is not the result of the development of WMD or delivery systems[27] that allow no time for diplomacy in the face of an imminent reversal of the status quo. That might have been President Kennedy's justification for threatening a preventative war against Cuba to prevent it from deploying ballistic missiles with nuclear warheads, but it would have been folly to have made a similar argument for action against the Soviet Union. Rather it is the potential threat to civilians—a market state concern, as we shall see in the next chapter—posed by arming, with whatever weapons, groups and states openly dedicated to mass killing that has collapsed the distinction between preemption and prevention, giving rise to anticipatory war. We could have stopped the genocide in Rwanda had we acted preclusively; by the time the killing was imminent it was too late. Those inspectors who were shocked by the progress of the Iraqi nuclear weapons program in 1991—by some accounts Saddam Hussein was a year away from deployment—must have been quietly thankful for the Osirak raid ten years earlier.[28] Had Saddam Hussein acquired nuclear weapons before he invaded Kuwait, the option of disarming him would have been infeasible. Michael Walzer once asked whether "the gulf between preemption and prevention has now narrowed so that there is little strategic (and therefore little moral) difference between them." As with all moral questions, one would have to know a good deal about the facts of the case under consideration. As to the law, however, it seems clear that a transformation is well under way.

This transformation does not necessarily mean that the use or precautionary threat of using force is the best way of challenging proliferation, for example, in every case or even in many cases. Theater missile defenses, alliances, economic sanctions, extended deterrence, and regional denuclearization all have a role. We must recognize, however, that as the threats to the states of consent, including the U.S. and the U.K., have changed, our ideas about war must also change.

One way to articulate this change is to say that developments have increased the role of *preclusion* in warfare, moving us away from traditional tactics like deterrence or depleting the enemy through the attrition of its forces, toward other tactics like paralyzing enemy initiative and halting the acquisition of WMD. Such warfare attempts to apply the full range of military and nonmilitary capabilities to preclude hostile acts and the development of capabilities in hostile hands that, once acquired, are unlikely to be voluntarily disgorged. This is the meeting point between market state terrorism and war. The war aim is to protect civilians and their officials so that, behind this military shield, the political development of governance based on consent can take place outside a climate of terror. Preclusion is the "new deterrence," i.e., it will be the central doctrine of warfare for the states of consent.

III.

To enable this sort of anticipatory warfare in the context of market state terrorism, however, we must first put aside the dichotomy between law enforcement and war as the structuring template for understanding the struggle against twenty-first century terror. It isn't only that "war" makes a more appropriate label for our struggles against market state terrorism than "crime"; it's also that rigidly separating the two frustrates an effective response. Here are some examples:

> [A] terrorist group bombed New York City's World Trade Center in 1993. Their purpose was to spread cyanide gas throughout the area and topple the skyscraper into other buildings, causing them to tumble like dominoes. Fortunately, the plot failed, and the bomb caused minimal damage and death . . . [W]hen the police first began investigating the incident, they handled it like a typical crime. Even after they classified it as terrorism, they limited the scope of the investigation to a small group. Some months later, law enforcement officials and prosecutors were embarrassed to find they had stumbled on an international terrorist organization with an extensive religious ideology and a worldwide support network.[29]

Justice Department guidelines prevented the FBI or the prosecutorial team from communicating what they had found to anyone else in the government. Treating terrorism as a law enforcement matter activated these guidelines, which were meant to insulate the criminal process from political influence in ordinary prosecutions.

In any event, by 2002 it was abundantly clear that a law enforcement approach alone was insufficient. The U.S. had dealt with the 1993 attack on the World Trade towers through a successful criminal prosecution that, in Lawrence Freedman's conclusive phrase, "had palpably failed to stop a second attack."[30] The calls from al Qaeda apologists for "hard evidence" of bin Laden's involvement, like the proposals that al Qaeda itself, a militant movement with global participants, could be arrested and prosecuted, were now simply ignored.

Nor is it sufficient to say that the pursuit of terrorists should be done on two parallel tracks, law enforcement and military. Consider this second example:

> The ambiguity of American counterterrorist policy emerged in the wake of the [African] bombing. Was this a military matter, or should it be handled as a breach of international law? The U.S. responded in two ways. First, FBI antiterrorist task forces composed of federal agents, state, and local police officers went to both scenes. In the subsequent investigation, two arrests were made and a fuller picture of al-Qaeda began to emerge. Task force investigators testified before a federal grand jury and arrest warrants were issued for bin Ladin . . . and other members of al Qaeda.
>
> President Clinton, however, had another response as well. Armed with intelligence of possible locations of bin Ladin's bases, and with possible evidence of chemical weapons production in Sudan, Clinton ordered cruise missile attacks against selected targets. The missiles destroyed a factory in Sudan, although subsequent reports questioned the material being produced there, and missiles also landed on six bases in Afghanistan. Bin Ladin escaped.[31]

An avalanche of criticism and hostile interrogation befell the Clinton administration. Was there sufficient proof that the chemical factory in Khartoum had really been shipping weapons (the owner's lawyers in Washington denied it) regardless of the ample evidence of Sudanese collusion with bin Laden and the Sudanese government's eager efforts to get chemical weapons? What about bin Laden's right to a fair trial before punishment? Was the administration trying to distract attention from the scandal involving the president's extramarital sexual activities? And so on—questions that would have been absurd regarding a traditional war, but that had an important place in the context within which this sort of war was being fought.

Peter Neumann, writing in *Survival,* gives further examples:

> Adopting the "war" doctrine . . . continues to be politically unacceptable [in Europe] yet it is equally obvious that the criminal justice model with which most European states have . . . aimed to tackle the [terrorist] threat is ineffective. The cases of Mounir el Motassedeq and those responsible for the Madrid bombings demonstrate that, even in

the most obvious and dramatic instances of terrorist involvement, substantial convictions cannot always be achieved.[32]

The twentieth century's emphasis on the distinction between war and crime is an artifact of that era's separation of law and strategy, which enforced rigorous isolation on both and reached its apogee in the era of the highly professionalized nation state that carefully segregated different disciplines. This attitude led to popular notions such as "only military personnel are capable of taking military decisions" (you wouldn't want an amateur conducting brain surgery, would you?) and its particularly American variation, "only courts should make constitutional determinations" (the rule of law privileges the judiciary to tell us what the law is; you wouldn't want the president doing that, would you?). Not only is this approach stultifying for fighting a borderless war against twenty-first century market state terrorism, it isn't even helpful as an account of our military and constitutional history in other eras[33] when the victorious side often owed its ultimate triumph to political intervention, such as Lincoln's in the American Civil War[34] or Churchill's in the Second World War (or interference and guidance by Richelieu or Bismarck,[35] for that matter), and the greatest constitutional decisions were not only not made by courts but were nonjusticiable (the American purchase of Louisiana from France,[36] the decision to suppress Southern secession in the U.S., and in Europe the royal abdications that followed World War I).

Most importantly, however, this attitude has distorted our appreciation of what war has become.

> Rapid and dramatic advancements in the technology of warfare during the rise of the mechanized age of warfare drove a bureaucratization of warfare, and consequently, a trend toward specialization and division of labor that persists and defines western military doctrine today. The extent of this division of labor is reflected in our . . . doctrine, the design of our armed services, and the distinctiveness of our military strategies. . . . [T]he need to master the growing complexities of warfare through specialization [has] led to the unintended consequence of adopting a truncated national idea of what constitutes war and what does not. [The gap] between our prevailing theory of war (how and what war "should" be) and the . . . practice (what and how war "is") [has] created a seam between our security strategy and our war-waging methodology that . . . is being exploited by our adversaries[.][37]

The solution for the twenty-first century is to integrate legal practices with action by the armed forces. Such integration is fraught with the most difficult questions. When should intelligence gained in the investigation and prosecution of a crime be passed on to the intelligence agencies, including the defense agencies? And, in a frontless war, how can we avoid militarizing the domestic environment, including the passing of information collected by the intelligence agencies through extraordinary means to the institutions of ordinary criminal prosecution? Can persons alleged to be terrorists be seized within the U.S. or the U.K. as if they were soldiers on a battlefield and held indefinitely as prisoners of war?

The American attempts to halt terrorism by arrest, rendition, and trial may even have inadvertently weakened our defenses against the attacks of September 11 because, as noted above, this approach prevented information being shared between prosecutorial agencies like the FBI and the Department of Justice and other agencies such as CIA and the White House. Realizing we are fighting a war and not just pursuing criminals shifts the focus to strategy, which does not seek to correct matters after the fact, as do prosecutions, but rather tries to anticipate and neutralize hostile action before the fact. Such a characterization suggests that controlling and diminishing the revenue stream to bin Laden's network is far more important, for example, than capturing or killing any particular individual. It emphasizes the need for cooperation among allies and international consensus building, which law courts are free to ignore. It also means that the Geneva Conventions—which apply to all combatants, whether or not they are in uniform[38]—must be invoked.

Finally, we have the third and perhaps most telling example, the debacle that followed the Coalition capture of Baghdad in 2003. U.S. military doctrine clearly divides operations into four linear and sequential phases: Phase I covers the preparation for combat; Phase II embraces the initial operations that prepare the battlefield, including the suppression of anti-aircraft weapons, and other damage-limitation strikes; Phase III is combat; Phase IV comprises post-combat or stability operations. There have been countless criticisms of the Coalition's failure to plan adequately for Phase IV operations, but in fact the fault wasn't that there was no plan, but rather that this rigid, linear concept was followed rigorously. There was a plan, and it was terribly wrong.

After the dramatic seizure of the center of the Iraqi capital by no more than 4,000 Coalition troops—a daring and incredibly courageous assault—the demoralized Republican Guard units defending the city collapsed. What happened next simply did not fit the Coalition's rules of engagement:

> Almost immediately, tens of thousands, maybe millions of Iraqis came out of their homes and, first, in a haphazard way but then very meticulously over time, began to destroy all of those institutions that the U.S. Air Force had been so careful to preserve during the [Phase II] bomb-

ing campaign—all of the ministries, hospitals, universities, museums, libraries . . . In two or three weeks [during which time the provisional authority was confined to its headquarters], the looters did more damage than all of the combat operations.[39]

The combat teams that had seized the city were far too few to conduct patrols. The troops that poured in after Baghdad was captured did not see law enforcement as one of their tasks; and indeed they were not trained and equipped for, nor experienced at, such tasks. That is strange—indeed, it would be inexplicable if one did not appreciate the tenacious grip our ideas about what constitutes "war" have on operations—because the U.S. had ample experience with similar situations following armed interventions.

In 1990, U.S. forces defeated the Panamanian Defense Force in Operation Just Cause in only three days. Looters immediately appeared on the streets of Panama City and in a few days did more damage to the Panamanian economy and to the city than had actual combat operations.[40] In 1994, Operation Uphold Democracy brought U.S. forces to Haiti. On the second day of the intervention, U.S. troops were welcomed by mass demonstrations celebrating their arrival. These same troops then stood by and watched as Haitian police beat to death demonstrators who had turned out to acclaim the U.S. action.[41]

In Bosnia we sat through weeks and weeks of the burning of the Sarajevo suburbs, where once again the U.S. military, smartly organized, well armed, but with no order to intervene, watched the destruction of towns and cities that had survived the conflict. When NATO forces went into Kosovo after the war, they found the place fairly intact. Then we witnessed two years of unbridled lawlessness that saw more deaths and conflict [including] the ethnic cleansing of the Serbs and other ethnic minorities.[42]

The problem has been that increasingly military operations cannot be adequately framed as a linear development from high-intensity combat to progressively lower intensity law enforcement.[43]

It is true that there is little consensus as to whether the attacks of September 11 were acts of war or simply crimes. The answer is not a legalistic one: under U.S. constitutional law, the Congress does not have to pass a declaration of war for a state of war to exist; nor under international law do acts have to be either crimes or acts of war—they can be both, as the defendants at Nuremberg learned. Nor do historical precedents necessarily govern. We are in the process of redefining both terrorism and war.

Nor is the inquiry purely a strategic one, for there are legal consequences, both domestic and international, of saying we are at war. These must be carefully worked out, because, in the present state of confusion, denominating the conflict against al Qaeda as a war can lead to some ludicrous conclusions. On January 25, 2005, for example, an Italian judge dismissed criminal charges against five North Africans on the grounds that their alleged terrorist activities constituted wartime "guerrilla" acts. In an especially revealing passage the judge observed that "[h]istorically, the activity of the cells in question coincided with the United States attack on Iraq"[44] and therefore could not be prosecuted even though at least one of the suspects had connections to the terrorist cell responsible for planning the September 11 attacks. It seems to have escaped the court that acts of war directed against innocent civilians are punishable as crimes.

The traumatic events of September 11 certainly resembled acts of war. The devastation of the battlefield, the precision of the attacks, the inclusion of military headquarters as a target along with other subjects of national symbolism, the self-sacrifice of the attackers, and the political interpretation of the events by their authors are all characteristics of war. If, as Justice Grier said in the *Prize Cases,* a war is defined "by its accidents—the number, power, and organization of the persons who originate and carry it on,"[45] then the network bin Laden heads is certainly at war. As Christopher Coker concluded, "[a]ssassination, ambush, sabotage and assault may all be criminal acts but when systematised they form part of a larger picture that can be interpreted perfectly well through the traditional discourse of war."[46]

IV.

Terrorism involves the use of what would otherwise be ordinary criminal acts—arson, kidnapping, extortion, murder—for political goals. We have long since learned how to quarantine warfare, which otherwise would also encompass many criminal acts, as a special province of law. We did not prosecute soldiers for acts that would be criminal outside war; indeed we sometimes gave them medals instead. We hanged terrorists.[47]

In the twentieth century, terrorism was wielded for domestic purposes; it was the extension of internal politics, as it were, by criminal means. With the creation of al Qaeda, terrorism has internationalized, and it has become the extension of diplomacy by other means.

This has meant that counterinsurgency and counterterrorism are merging. Hitherto, insurgents sought a change of regime, while terrorists typically sought a change of policy. Mao Zedong and Zhou Enlai were insurgents who sought to replace the government of China with themselves. The terrorists who murdered Israeli athletes did not wish to govern Israel; they sought a change in Israeli policy with respect to issues disputed by the Palestinians. Al Qaeda brings these two elements together in seeking to replace various regimes—in Saudi Arabia, in Egypt, in Jordan, in Iraq—by using terror to force a change in U.S. policy and that of U.S. allies supporting these regimes.

This should be clearer, not less clear, when bin Laden uses the international media to conduct diplomacy, because the use of these media is also a characteristic of the diplomacy of the twenty-first century. Consider this message delivered by bin Laden, dressed in the formal robes of a head of state, aired on satellite television in October 2004:

> People of America this talk of mine is for you and concerns the ideal way to prevent another Manhattan and deals with the war and its causes and results . . . [T]hinking people when disaster strikes make it their priority to look for its causes in order to prevent it happening again. But I am amazed at you even though we are in the 4th year after the events of Sept 11th. Bush is still engaged in distortion, deception and hiding from you the real causes. And thus the reasons are still there for a repeat of what occurred. So I shall talk to you about the story behind those events and I shall tell you truthfully about the moments in which the decision was taken for you to consider . . . If you were to avoid these reasons, you will have taken the correct path that will lead America to the security that it was in before September 11th . . . The events that affected my soul in a direct way started in 1982 when America permitted the Israelis to invade Lebanon . . . And as I looked at those demolished towers in Lebanon, it entered my mind that we should punish the oppressor in kind and that we should destroy towers in America in order that they taste some of what we tasted and so that they be deterred from killing our women and children. And that day, it was confirmed to me that oppression and the intentional killing of innocent women and children is a deliberate American policy. . . . This means the oppressing and embargoing to death of millions as Bush Sr. did in Iraq in the greatest mass slaughter of children mankind has ever known and it means the throwing of millions of pounds of bombs and explosives at millions of children—also in Iraq—as Bush Jr. did . . . So with these images and their like as their background, the events of September 11th came as a reply to those great wrongs . . . [Y]ou may recall that for every action, there is a reaction.[48]

The contrast of this ultimatum with bin Laden's 1996 declaration of war could not be greater. That proclamation, explicitly addressed to other Muslims, deemed the *casus belli* to be the American presence in Saudi Arabia, which was presumed to defile the holy shrines of Islam. The Palestinian cause or that of Lebanon or Iraq had never been a principal interest of bin Laden when speaking to Muslims, whom he addressed on essentially theocratic grounds. But the 2004 ultimatum is aimed at the American people. It shrewdly picks up the popular filmmaker Michael Moore's ridicule of President George W. Bush's apparently placid reaction to news of 9/11 ("because it seemed to him," bin Laden said, "that occupying himself by talking to the little girl about the goat and its butting was more important than occupying himself with the planes and their butting of the skyscrapers, we were given three times the period required to execute the operations") and some of the more shrill accusations against the Bush administration by American critics ("he took dictatorship and suppression of freedom [and] named it the Patriot Act under the pretense of fighting terrorism"). Bin Laden's electronic white paper is not meant to persuade diplomats, as in the nineteenth century, or pivotal interest groups, as in the twentieth, but is targeted directly at the people, and relies on popular culture and the global system of communications. Diplomacy, like terrorism and warfare, is changing with the change in the constitutional order. Bin Laden's language is menacing but not especially violent; indeed it is at pains to seem more in sorrow than in anger, more aggrieved than aggressive. His acts are worse than crimes; they are high politics.

We can see the transition from nation state terrorism to global, networked terrorism, from insurrection and crime to war, that is, in the evolution of Hezbollah, the Iranian-backed Shia terrorist group in Lebanon. Having succeeded in expelling Israeli occupation forces from south Lebanon, and having captured twenty-three seats in the Lebanese parliament, Hezbollah turned from its pursuit of national power. When a kidnapping campaign across the Israeli border, followed by a botched rescue attempt by Israel, unleashed terrible retaliatory Israeli assaults on Lebanon on July 12, 2006, Hezbollah's leader Hassan Nasrallah, who has previously proclaimed that "[i]f Jews all gather in Israel, it will save us the trouble of going after them worldwide,"[49] explained that "Hezbollah is not fighting a battle for Hezbollah, or even for Lebanon. We are now fighting a battle for the [Islamic] nation."[50]

For at least some persons, what seemed like the evolution of terrorism into something resembling conventional warfare was actually welcome, simply because it clarified a matter that has been so difficult for many to come to terms with. The Israeli novelist Etgar Keret wrote, after a Hezbollah missile attack:

> Suddenly, the first salvo of missiles returned us to that familiar feeling of a war . . . We long[ed] for a real war to take the place of all those exhausting years of intifada when there was no black or white, when we were confronted not by armed forces, but only by resolute young people wearing explosive belts . . .[51]

What Keret was actually witnessing was the beginning of the transformation of conventional terrorism into war. From separate national liberation terrorist insurgencies against Israeli occupation, an alliance between the Palestinian terror group Hamas and Hezbollah had emerged, and it began to coordinate attacks on the southern and northern borders of Israel even though Israel had withdrawn from Gaza and Lebanon.

Terrorism has become war, and that is one reason why it makes sense to describe the conflict against terrorism as war. Another reason is that war is becoming a struggle against terrorism, and, as we shall see, our failure to recognize it as such has been very damaging indeed.

V.

In several important respects warfare is changing with the transformation of the nature of the State from nation state to market state. Accordingly our ideas about how to wage war will have to undergo considerable change. Once we see how war has changed, we will notice its "accidents," as Grier put it, are indistinguishable from those that characterize the Wars on Terror.

Deterrence through unavoidable nuclear retaliation and deterrence through sufficient conventional force together laid the basis for the victory of the parliamentary nation states in the era of the Cold War. These strategic options cannot provide a similar stability in the era to come because the sources of the threats will be at once too ubiquitous and too easy to disguise. States will face threats that can come from everywhere and yet cannot be attributed to anyone, anywhere. It will prove immensely difficult to deter an attacker whose identity or location is unknown and, as we shall see, the very massiveness of their conventional and nuclear forces makes it unlikely that the U.S. or the U.K. will be challenged openly. What is far more likely is that asymmetric warfare will become the norm when great powers are confronted. Of what use is a tank battalion against a motorboat tied up at Wall Street with a clandestine nuclear device on board? Asymmetric warfare can include covert attacks by countries, the overt use of proxies, and unattributed attacks by independent terrorist groups, whether linked by a network or acting in isolation.[52]

This change in warfare is captured with great insight in a series of addresses[53] and a powerful book[54] by the British general Sir Rupert Smith. Smith was the commander of the British Armoured Division in the first Gulf War in 1991 and gained worldwide attention (and respect) in 1995 as the leader of UNPROFOR, the U.N. Protection Force in Bosnia. "Our bane today," he writes, "is a conception of force and formulated forces within the paradigm of interstate industrial war, whilst our conflicts are those of the paradigm of war amongst the people."[55] Transposing these ideas for my own purposes, we can see that the important features of twenty-first century warfare that Smith identifies are linked to the transformation of the nature of the State. Indeed appreciating the changes in warfare helps us understand why the methods of fighting terrorism and ethnic cleansing, as well as intraconflict stabilization, have now become the activities of war.[56]

First, a shift is occurring from the industrial, total war of nation states that attacked the national infrastructure of cities, to fighting wars that either target or seek to protect civilians. This shift comes about when the enemy uses the people to conceal or protect itself, as has been characteristic of terrorists. It was clear that the precision and care of the Coalition air plan against Iraq in 2002 took into account that battles would be fought in towns and cities; the air campaign produced many fewer casualties than some had expected. Reacting to attacks using human shields, suicide bombers and enemy fighters concealed in civilian clothes, Coalition ground forces showed considerable restraint, and the result was that civilian casualties attributable to Coalition forces have been comparatively low.[57] Nevertheless the inability to quickly establish civil order, to prevent looting and killing, and to suppress the emergence of private militias also showed that this lesson of future wars had not been entirely learned. As Coker concluded, "Armed forces will increasingly have to learn how to conduct high intensity combat, counterinsurgency, peace support and reconstruction *simultaneously*."[58]

The task of the armed forces of the U.S. and the U.K., as Mary Kaldor put it, will be "to protect people, provide security so a political process can get going, and act in support of the rule of law. For this role, forces are needed that combine soldiers, police and civilians with the capacity to undertake various humanitarian and legal activities"[59] because the "new wars," as she terms them, are "fought by networks of state and non-state actors, where battles are rare and violence is directed mainly against civilians . . ."[60]

Failing to appreciate this in Iraq, such tasks were considered peacetime duties—"post-conflict stabilization"—and not the stuff of war or warriors. As we shall see, the U.S. administration simply could not bring itself to believe that more regular forces were needed once Baghdad had been taken. In testimony before Congress that he must surely regret, Deputy Secretary of Defense Paul Wolfowitz claimed that it was inconceivable that the Coalition would need more troops in Iraq after the fall of the Iraqi state—"after the war," as it were—than during it. As a direct result of this inadequate conceptualization of war, as of November 2007 at least 80,000

Iraqis had died since May 1, 2003, when President Bush spoke from the deck of the USS *Abraham Lincoln* and proclaimed the end of "major combat operations" in Iraq.

A reconceptualization of war, however, requires a redefinition of victory. If the capture of the national capital and the defenestration of the national political leadership characterized the victories of the nation state, as we will see in the next chapter, how do we know who is winning when the conflict manages to continue despite conventional battlefield successes? Body counts can provide a comparative arithmetic, but as we learned in Vietnam, they tell only a deceptive part of the story. In every war, it's not what you do to the enemy, but what he can do to you as you pursue your political objectives that determines victory.

In the conflicts of market states, media and public relations will play a decisive role in determining who is winning. Partly this is owing to the fact that warfare that alienates a local population among whom it is fought will be more difficult to conclude successfully. Every night of the ongoing war in Iraq, Arab television is filled with images of wounded civilians and ruined buildings. "[W]e fight in every living room in the world as well as on the streets and fields of a conflict zone," Smith writes.[61]

The role of the media is critical too because the democratic population at home will know nothing of the war except what they learn from the media. Their support for the allegedly "discretionary" and certainly "speculative" wars of the future—because they aim to prevent future, uncertain atrocities—will wax or wane with the media's assessments. Smith writes, "Whoever coined the term 'Theatre of Operations' was very prescient. We are conducting operations now as though we are on the stage . . ." This was not the case with secret counterterrorist operations in the past or generally even with the massive operations of the conventional twentieth century warfare that carefully managed access by journalists.*

What is true for our own forces is of course also true for those of our enemies. The interconnections among satellite television and sites on the World Wide Web have allowed terrorists to wage warfare in a novel way, adroitly exploiting the theatrical nature of war in the twenty-first century.[62] Peter Bardazzi, director of new media development at New York University, has observed that the beheading videos, for instance, are set up "like a stage."[63] Michael Ignatieff has written brilliantly about this phenomenon, calling it "The Terrorist as Auteur."[64] One is tempted to think that if politics in the market state tends ever more toward entertainment, then warfare cannot be far behind.

---

*Which contrasts sharply with the process of "embedding" journalists used in the Second Gulf War.

Second, twenty-first century warfare is unlikely to witness decisive battles because large-scale battles are not likely to be joined—the insurgency in Iraq, for example, has resolutely refused to mass, and the Coalition has never lost a platoon—and because the objectives of this warfare are different from those of earlier conflicts. In the future, wars will rarely be directly related to national survival but rather to the prevention of intolerable situations. As Robert Leitch writes:

> [T]he aims of the nation state characteristically produce unambiguous objectives for military force to take, hold or destroy [whereas now] forces are deployed not to decide the matter but to establish the conditions [of consensual government] . . . reached by other political, economic and social means.[65]

As the American general John Abizaid has often said of Iraq, the mission of Coalition forces there is to enable the indigenous political process to go forward to establish a state of consent, not to dictate its politics. Multinational forces will be required to fight such wars, just as they are needed to fight global terrorism, with each state contributing according to its interests and its judgment of risk, and this will lead to complex rules of engagement and constraints on the use of force as these coalitions confront non-state enemies. This also represents a change from the paradigm of the nation state at war. Now, Smith observes, "we tend to conduct our conflicts and confrontations in some form of multinational grouping, whether it is an alliance or a coalition . . . against some party or parties that are not states."[66] Super-state arrangements confront sub-state groups.

Third, the shift to a market state has largely replaced conscription with an all-volunteer, which is to say market-based, force. Traditional tasks like peeling potatoes are outsourced to McDonald's because it is cheaper to do so. Conscription, "the human production line" as Smith terms it—in another industrial, nation state metaphor—is being phased out in many countries, and there is no longer a seemingly infinite number of persons whose cost to the State is confined to their maintenance. This has led to much greater professionalization of the force, but also to greater emphasis on force protection. "We fight," Smith writes, "so as not to lose the force, rather than fighting by using the force at any cost to achieve the aim."[67] For many reasons, the citizens of a market state are more sensitive to the value of individual life and less tolerant of sacrifice. Accordingly, there is "a greater emphasis on force protection including body armor, heavily armored vehicles and well protected bases."[68] The implications of this change for the Wars against Terror are considerable if not widely appreciated, for these measures distance the force from the people amongst whom they operate who may conceal the adversary, who are the primary audience and the source of information . . . [Indeed] most armed forces deploy with very large administrative structures designed for wars of maneuvering large mass. They require guarding and fortifying [but in a war against terror the] more they are secured, the more isolated and the more of a target they become.[69]

Against terrorists we will want to deploy only those persons necessary, including sophisticated personnel capable of gaining local knowledge and dealing with NGOs and the media. This is facilitated by the move to an all-volunteer force (AVF) that can bring technicians, scientists, and other specialists to the fight. The market state move to an AVF has now gone further to include private military companies.[70] At present, several hundred such companies operate in over a hundred countries on six continents, generating over $100 billion in annual revenue.

The distinction between "military" and "civilian" in a Stryker brigade combat team . . . may be clear administratively, but in functional terms it's . . . based mostly on the Pentagon's interest in savings in an era in which the nation state is morphing into a market state . . . "Approximately 120 specialized contractors are an integral part of the [Stryker brigade combat team's] highly complex systems maintenance, sustainment, and technical support . . . In addition to saving dollars, military outsourcing can also keep casualty figures down."[71]

A further aspect of outsourcing involves quiet cooperation with local proxies. U.S. surveillance planes at present assist local forces in sub-Saharan Africa tracking jihadists; elsewhere, training missions by U.S. Marines and Army Special Forces act as force multipliers, and American humanitarian efforts in conjunction with local authorities often result in intelligence collection.[72] As previously observed, Iran's support of Hezbollah in Lebanon has outsourced the Iranian confrontation with Israel.

Outsourcing also means different roles for different national forces within the Alliance. For many states, this will mean the shift from a "boutique" force, which has small capacities in a wide range of areas, to a "niche" force, which can contribute decisively to protracted coalition operations in a narrow set of roles.[73] Alex Tewes draws this proposal (for Australian forces) directly from the emergence of the market state:

[W]hile nation states can be seen as self-contained . . . entities . . . , market states are inherently dependent on other states behaving according to an explicit and common rule set . . . [O]nce a nation accepts the globalisation rule set, it is transformed from a nation state to a market state. The interdependency of market states—and Australia is now one of them—has significant implications for national defence and security planning . . . A role-based approach to national security would turn the focus away from concentric geographic circles to specific and high-value niche roles that the [Australian Defense Forces] . . . perform in our region or within a larger coalition on a global basis.[74]

Australia's role in pacifying Timor and its law enforcement deployments following the Bali bombings and in the Solomon Islands provide models for the sorts of capabilities so necessary in the kind of conflict that war is becoming.

Fourth, campaigns are becoming longer because we are seeking a condition, freedom from coercion, "which," Smith argues, "then must be maintained until an agreement on a definitive outcome, which may take years or decades."[75] As with the transformation of constitutional structures by states, so too armies tend to mimic those military practices that are successful for their opponents.[76] Just as terrorists typically must localize the use of force and give priority to preserving that force, antiterrorist forces must give battle only when there is a clear advantage in doing so. The time when a commander for the nation state like Ulysses Grant could be successful simply by having the ruthlessness to attack positions until they could be stormed is past, as was evident in the massive Russian assault on Grozny, which proved counterproductive. This means a move away from very large forces commandeered for a relatively short period of time to reliance on large reserves that can be used to sustain a long campaign.

This also means different training and tasks for military forces, as has been argued in many quarters with respect to constabulary forces. And, too, defense capabilities once thought relevant only to the military sector will be called on for a variety of tasks. Only the Department of Defense can set up a 10,000-bed field hospital of the sort that a biological attack, or a humanitarian crisis, or a region contaminated by a reactor meltdown would require. U.S. airlift and sealift capabilities have made notable contributions in the aftermaths of the Pakistani earthquake in 2005 and the tsunami in the Indian Ocean in 2004, as will be discussed subsequently.

Fifth, the use of technology is changing. In Joint Vision 2010, the Pentagon outlined a program it hoped would leverage new technologies in the private sector on behalf of U.S. and allied armed forces, but the real impact of technological innovation, I fear, will be exploited by unconventional military organizations. Access to markets in weapons of mass destruction and cyberterrorism could well bring the terrorist to technologically even ground with conventional forces. As Leitch notes, making the GPS*[77] available on the open market "was a free gift to terrorists."[78] Because private-sector technology is not only more advanced than that possessed by most defense units, and is also upgraded more quickly, this situation is likely to grow worse.[79] By contrast the favored weapons of nation state conflict—the main battle tank and heavy artillery pieces— are often vulnerable to terrorists in close proximity with relatively simple weapons.

Though we continue to build tanks, the last battle in which armored formations maneuvered against each other supported by artillery and air forces and were the deciding force, took place in the 1973 Arab-Israeli war.[80] Armaments procurement ought to stimulate the development and deployment of novel nonlethal weapons that disable the enemy without killing. In earlier wars, killing an enemy was the objective;[81] in twenty-first century warfare, temporarily disabling an enemy soldier without killing is much the preferable outcome.[82] Only then can he be interrogated for vital information; only then can he be released if he was not in fact an enemy combatant; only then can the human costs in suffering that are inseparable from warfare in any century be mitigated.

Sixth, the transparent operation of law, monitored by international observers, will be crucial in the Wars against Terror because establishing the legitimacy of these wars is essential to their success. Smith categorically, and rightly, states that "if we are to operate amongst the people . . . we must do so within the law. To do otherwise would be to undermine our own strategic objective, to establish and uphold the law."[83] Obedience to the rule of law by the government is an essential feature of the preservation of human rights, the conditions for which are, after all, what the states of consent are fighting to maintain. Not understanding the nature of the victory sought—the preclusive victory that protects rights from coercion— we are apt to undermine our own fighting.

> [I]f one is operating amongst the people, and the object is to achieve and maintain a situation of order in which political and economic measures are to take hold, then by implication one is seeking to establish some form of rule of law. Indeed this may be defined as a strategic objective—which means that to then operate tactically outside the law is to attack one's own strategic doctrine. This is effectively what hap-

*The Global Positioning System (GPS) uses an arrangement of satellites orbiting the earth to enable a GPS receiver to accurately determine its location, speed, and direction. Perhaps equally helpful to terrorist forces has been the availability of accurate satellite maps via the Web.

pened with incidents of abuse by US soldiers in Abu Ghraib prison in Baghdad or British soldiers in Basra in 2004—or of course the US-administered camp in Guantanamo Bay, Cuba. . . .[84]

In all the half-dozen respects Smith identifies, warfare is changing in ways that are remarkably similar to the way the struggles against terrorism are developing. That is because twenty-first century warfare is both a cause and an effect of the change in the constitutional order of which twenty-first century terrorism is itself a manifestation. Market states are devolved, outsourcing, and networked, and they rely on market incentives rather than legal regulation (which is, after all, deterrence); market state terrorists are also devolved, outsource their operations, and depend upon voluntary contributions and business transactions; market state wars rely on coalitions, outsourcing, and supplement deterrence with precautionary incentives and the anticipatory use of force.

William S. Lind summarizes this development well:

In broad terms, [twenty-first century] warfare seems likely to be widely dispersed and largely undefined; the distinction between war and peace will be blurred to the vanishing point. It will be nonlinear, possibly to the point of having no definable battlefields or fronts. The distinction between "civilian" and "military" will disappear. Actions will occur concurrently throughout all participants' depth, including their society as a cultural, not just a physical, entity.[85]

All of Smith's six propositions come together in the conclusion that our current force structure is inadequate owing to our failure to appreciate the "new war" of which Mary Kaldor and others have written. The forces in Iraq, Afghanistan, and elsewhere simply are not configured, trained, or deployed principally to protect civilians;[86] to battle street by street with light arms; to mingle with the population. Instead, they are exhausted because they are too few to carry out these tasks, they rely on large platforms—tanks and planes—that mass firepower, and they are not trained for this kind of war. Finally, and most importantly, they are not the sort of force required to restore and maintain law and order.

VI.

We think in these embattled theaters that we are dealing with what have come to be called "failed states." Viewed as nation states, they appear to have grossly failed the state's obligation to better the material well-being, including the safety, of the national people. A better characterization, however, would be that they are struggling market states, in the grip of the criminality that markets bring in the absence of law.

> Afghanistan, Bosnia, Haiti (twice), Iraq, Kosovo and Liberia . . . were not failed states. They were rogue governments engaged in massive human rights abuses. And they were governments that on the surface appeared to be police states [but in reality were] kleptocracies. They were organized criminal enterprises that engaged in a multitude of criminal activities. The revenue from these criminal activities was used to keep the regime in power and to pay off the security services and key individuals.[87]

In Afghanistan, the Taliban taxed opium cultivation, taking 20 percent of the crop. When they then enforced a ban on production altogether, they were able to sell their own stocks at a lucrative premium. The Milosevic regime in Yugoslavia, Charles Taylor's government in Liberia (which traded diamonds, timber, and rubber for arms and cash), and preeminently the Saddam Hussein regime in Iraq, which may have earned more than $10 billion through an orchestrated scheme of kickbacks and smuggling that manipulated the U.N. Oil-for-Food Program, all provide similar examples.[88] After intervention, in each of these cases, lawlessness ensued and the armed forces that believed they had won the war found themselves helpless to protect the civil society they had come to defend. That is, they were unable to establish what was mistakenly regarded as "postconflict" stability in the midst of a conflict.

Michael Dziedzic and others have observed that the military is a "blunt instrument . . . capable of imposing a most basic, rigid form of order"[89] even though "in a sensitive period of occupation, one false step by a soldier using excessive force can have catastrophic consequences."[90] It is certainly true that the armed forces, as we currently conceive of them, are inappropriate for the protection of civilians. They are trained to mass force in order to destroy the enemy; they are not trained to preserve order and to protect civilians.[91] Nevertheless, that is now, I will argue in the next chapter, their most important function.

Perhaps in recognition of this, the U.S. has been using its elite Special Operations forces to maintain civil order in these theaters. The result has been exhaustion on their part and frustration on the part of their commanders.[92]

> While combat forces are effective in neutralizing hostile forces and providing initial stability . . . such units are typically neither trained nor equipped to handle long-term security problems such as looting, rioting, crowd control, crime, civilian disturbances, restoring

basic services, and local law enforcement, all of which require increasingly nonlethal countermethods. These latter types of critical skills can often make the ultimate difference between mission success and failure.[93]

The problem is the picture of warfare to which we cling. This picture unfolds in this way: peacemaking by diplomats; war-making by the armed forces; peace-building by aid and reconstruction personnel.[94] The reality of twenty-first century warfare, however, is that all these tasks must be performed simultaneously, and that war-making itself now must include not only elite forces to neutralize hostile, organized adversaries but also constabulary forces to handle crowds and lower levels of organized violence.[95]

Constabulary forces are "organized along military lines, providing basic law enforcement and safety in a not yet fully stabilized environment."[96]

> They are trained in military skills, but their focus and equipment is on minimal/nonlethal use of force . . . Unlike traditional soldiers, the goal of constabulary units is to defuse potentially violent situations . . . rather than to "neutralize" the enemy or destroy a target . . . [C]onstabulary forces are highly skilled in the tactics and doctrine of light infantry, including rapid deployment . . . [Their] training includes martial arts, use of firearms and light weapons, intelligence-gathering and interrogation techniques . . . use of communications equipment, and foreign languages and cultures. Most European constabulary forces also have specialized . . . sniper teams. Their equipment reflects a hybrid of police and military gear as well: flak jackets, shields, batons, tear gas, and automatic weapons. They are able to secure and protect traffic routes [and] set up and manage prisons . . .[97]

Already mentioned here is the exceptionally successful role played by Australian forces in situations that fall between conventional war fighting and local law enforcement. It remains to be noted that a number of European countries—most notably France, Italy, Spain, Portugal, and the Netherlands—have well-established constabulary forces. The Multinational Specialized Unit in Bosnia was headed and staffed largely by Italian *carabinieri* but included constabulary forces from seven countries. The French *gendarmerie* have been involved in constabulary operations in Haiti, El Salvador, Cambodia, the western Sahara, and elsewhere. Dutch, Portuguese, and Spanish constabulary forces have been deployed in operations in Africa and the Balkans.

Condoleezza Rice was no doubt right when she remarked that "[w]e don't need to have the 82nd Airborne escorting kids to kindergarten,"[98] but in fact the safety of children is now an objective of warfare and unless troops are trained and equipped for these tasks, the 82nd and other similar forces will be pressed into service inappropriately.

A 2004 study by the U.S. Defense Science Board concluded that U.S. constabulary capabilities were grossly inadequate, but it made the mistake of relegating these tasks to the "postconflict" phase.[99] One unfortunate consequence of looking at the problem this way is that it makes cooperation with the U.S. so difficult for other states; it appears that the Americans intervene and create the mess, and then call on others to clean it up.[100]

If, however, from the outset of an intervention, Coalition forces included NATO and E.U. teams that could deploy these capabilities, the opportunities for joint political action would be greatly enhanced. Indeed, on September 17, 2004, the E.U. presidency announced that several European governments* had decided to create a multinational European *Gendarmerie* Force (EGF) that would act as a light expeditionary force, configured to keep public order within a conflict zone. The drawback to relying on such cooperation is that it limits American discretion. Suppose the states of the EGF oppose intervention, as they did in Iraq? This, however, will always be a risk when we rely on coalitions of the willing, and, furthermore, raising the bar to discretionary interventions—those that do not implicate the vital interests of the U.S.—may be, at this point, the only way to resurrect the American-led alliance after the debacle in Iraq. The alternative is to create U.S. forces for these tasks.[101]

That option is reflected in a proposed Pentagon directive of late 2005 that explicitly states that "[s]tability operations are a core U.S. military mission" [that] "shall be given priority comparable to combat operations and be explicitly addressed and integrated across all [U.S. defense] activities." The previous locution, "Phase IV," is nowhere to be found in the document.[102] It remains to be seen whether, whatever the official rhetoric, the experience of Afghanistan and Iraq has persuaded Washington that just as terrorism has become war, the conduct of war must now embrace the struggle against terror.

At present the EGF is far too small, and the alliance too divided, for a European constabulary force to play much of a role in Iraq. The transformation of American forces that is under way will come too late to be of help in the near future. In both cases, however, efforts at reform are not sustainable within the inherited conceptions of what constitutes war.

The days of a preponderance of conventional force-on-force operations have given way to more complex challenges of asymmetric warfare, urban counterinsurgency, extensive civil affairs/public diplomacy

---

*France, Italy, the Netherlands, Portugal, and Spain.

work with the state's publics [and] stabilization . . . Our greatest
enemy is complacency with old stereotypes of conventional attrition
warfare . . . The Armed Forces must be . . . capable of seamlessly shifting focus from combat operations to dealing effectively with the rigors
of . . . establishing security and law and order . . . This transformation
would also require tailored rules of engagement . . .[103]

As General Smith writes, the new warfare "is not a better paradigm
than interstate industrial war, it is simply different—and understanding
difference, and accepting it, must become a central part of our way
ahead."[104] We must be sensitive to these profound innovations when we
decide whether the Wars on Terror are properly called "wars."

Were there sophisticated critics who did not think they were hearing
music when they first heard Louis Armstrong play jazz, or that they were
reading poetry when they first came across "The Love Song of J. Alfred
Prufrock," or like the three friends in Yasmina Reza's play *Art,* were undecided whether Man Ray, to say nothing of Andy Warhol, was really doing art?

It's not only the innovative, however, that throws us when we confront
an unfamiliar claim on a familiar term. It's also our lack of acquaintance
with the past. Bruce Ackerman, in his valuable *Before the Next Attack,*[105]
writes: "Classical wars traditionally involve a battle against sovereign
states . . . Classic wars come to an end. Some decisive act of capitulation,
armistice or treaty signals the moment of termination and in a way all the
world can see."

Actually, Ackerman's model is not the one generally prevalent in history and certainly not in classical history. As Chris Brown notes, the war
against terror is

actually much more typical, as are the kind of long struggles with exte-
rior barbarians that characterized Imperial China's wars or the wars of
the later Roman Empire. Moreover, and this is the crucial point, these
latter wars are also more typical of the post-Westphalian international
order . . . Very few modern wars have ended with a surrender and/or a
peace treaty . . . [A] war on terror would not be appropriate for all vari-
eties of terrorism, but it is for the variety against which the present war
is being, or ought to be, fought. . . . Such a war will look very like the
kind of wars that have been characteristic of most of human history.[106]

And John Witt writes that in the accounts of Vittoria, Gentili, Grotius,
and Vattel "there are many different states of war. War is a multifarious
condition for them: *guerre publique, guerre couverte, guerre mortel,* . . .
[and] in the U.S. in the 1820s perfect and imperfect war. But . . . by the

time of Lieber and his code . . . the age of nation states [is left] with only a single, monolithic paradigm of warfare. . . . The rise of the nation state and the winnowing out of the early modern variants . . . of war are coincident in time."[107]

VII.

In the end, what difference does it really make? What *is* in a name?

Broadly speaking, the refusal to recognize the new character of warfare has been felt in two dimensions: one, within conventional war itself, where a too narrow definition of war has had a crucial impact on how U.S. wars have been fought; and two, within counterterrorism, where the refusal to recognize that a war is being fought has needlessly imperiled civilians whose protection is the chief aim of market state wars. The Coalition invasion and occupation of Iraq is an example of the first dimension, the retaliation against Hezbollah in Lebanon of the second.

THE WAR IN IRAQ

The Coalition invasion of Iraq began on March 20, 2003.[108] Troops from the United States and the United Kingdom made up 98 percent of the invading forces. More than forty other states[109] provided noncombat support, as well as special forces. The total number of ground troops, about 200,000, was less than half that deployed in the first Gulf War. Partly for that reason, the Iraqi army was taken by surprise. This meant that oil wells were not set on fire by the Iraqi forces, and defensive deployments were not complete by the time of the actual invasion.

General Tommy Franks's war plan envisioned the U.S. Army's 5th Corps advancing from Kuwait, proceeding west by northwest along the Euphrates and then attacking Baghdad from the desert to the west. The U.S. Marine Corps would go east of the river in a parallel advance. The British would seize Iraq's second largest city, Basra.

British forces quickly reached the edge of Basra on March 21 but met with stiff resistance from Iraqi regular troops and the fedayeen, a militia force. The British surrounded the city and allowed civilians to leave. U.S. Marines under British command—for the first time since World War II—captured the Gulf port of Um Qasr.

By the 22nd, forward elements of the 3rd Infantry were 150 miles inside Iraq, roughly halfway to Baghdad. On the 23rd, marines met with heavy resistance around the city of Nasiriya, even while to the west, 5th

Corps forces were heading toward Baghdad. By the 25th the forward momentum had stalled.

On the 26th American forces surrounded Najaf, where units of the 3rd Infantry Division had been engaged in fierce combat. That same day, paratroopers from the army's 173rd Airborne Brigade landed in northern Iraq, linking up with Kurdish troops.

On April 1, the army's 101st Airborne Division began the final assault on Najaf. The next morning, members of the 3rd Infantry advanced on Baghdad through the Karbala Gap, crossing the Euphrates. By April 3, advance elements had reached Baghdad International Airport on the western edge of Baghdad, having circled past the main elements of the Iraqi Republican Guard massed to the south of the city. Hit unexpectedly from the north, the Iraqi Medina Division collapsed.

On April 5, the 2nd Brigade of the 3rd Army Division launched a daring raid into Baghdad, encountering stiff fire and returning to the airport around noon. The next day, after two weeks, the British took Basra, where they were greeted with wild celebration. Looting, however, soon began.

That same day, marines driving from the south prepared to assault Baghdad from the east. This sector was virtually undefended. The next day, another raid was made by the 2nd Brigade, which headed directly for the center of the city. Its commander decided that the Iraqis would be unprepared for a force that refused to fight street by street but instead headed straight for the city center. Accordingly, he set up camp in a large parade ground and park near the Republican Palace, which offered free lines of fire, though the U.S. troops were completely surrounded by Iraqi forces. He spent the night in Saddam's palace. "Nineteen days after crossing the Kuwait border, less than a week after the breakthrough at the Karbala Gap, the Americans [had] penetrated to the very heart of the regime."[110]

In Baghdad, U.S. forces encountered resistance from the fedayeen and Baath Party militia, but the regular Iraqi army had largely melted away. Rather than surrendering, as U.S. commanders had hoped, its soldiers had simply deserted and returned home. On the afternoon of April 9, the statue of Saddam Hussein in Firdos Square was pulled down. There were some scenes of rejoicing, but in the main the city was undemonstrative. As in Basra, extensive looting began.

At a press conference on the 11th, the U.S. secretary of defense was asked about the looting. He replied that "freedom's untidy and free people are free to make mistakes and commit crimes and do bad things." It is plain that he anticipated the end of the war, and that afterward these crimes would be prosecuted, but that they formed no part of the conflict relevant to U.S. armed forces. The same day, Mosul fell to Kurdish *peshmerga* and

U.S. Special Operations forces. Reflecting on the course of the conflict to this date, James Fallows later said that "the ousting of Saddam Hussein's regime will be studied for years as a success, as a brilliant combination of movement, firepower, deception, speed, unconventional tactics. This was a brilliant moment for the US military."[111]

On April 16, General Franks flew into Baghdad to congratulate his commanders on their dazzlingly rapid victory. On May 1, the U.S. president landed on the deck of an American carrier, the *Abraham Lincoln,* which had been festooned with a banner inscribed, "Mission Accomplished." He announced the end of combat operations in Iraq. Fewer than 150 American troops had been lost; more than 4,000 would die in the coming years.

Throughout the summer the Coalition forces directed their efforts at capturing the fugitive former leaders of the regime. Saddam's two sons were cornered and killed in July. In total, more than three hundred top Baathist officials were killed or captured.

Toward the end of 2003, however, an insurgency had jelled, drawing on fedayeen and Baathist loyalists, and exploited by sectarian militias, like the Shia Mahdi Army and al Qaeda Sunni elements led by Abu Musab al Zarqawi. For the first time since April, Coalition forces were compelled to use air power in an attempt to quell the opposition. The most difficult areas were concentrated in Anbar province and the city of Fallujah, to the west of Baghdad, and Baghdad itself, as well as poorer districts of the Shia stronghold of Basra, in the south.

In 2004, following the capture of Saddam Hussein the preceding December, the insurgency actually became more violent. The impact of Sunni attacks on Coalition and Iraqi security forces was intensified by assaults by the Shia Mahdi Army. In reply, the Coalition and the Provisional Authority set up to manage the restoration of Iraqi sovereignty attacked the Sunni insurgent stronghold of Fallujah and the Mahdi Army headquarters in Najaf. In both cases, successful Coalition incursions were ultimately blunted by the mounting horror of civilian casualties. In Fallujah, in response to a demand by the Iraqi Governing Council, Coalition troops were withdrawn, and ultimately the cities of Fallujah, Samarra, Baquba, and Ramadi were left in insurgent control. Similarly, though Coalition troops took back the cities of Najaf and Nasiriya in the summer of 2004, the Mahdi Army leader, Moktada al-Sadr, was able to remain in control of his Shia militia following negotiations brokered by the Shia leader, the Grand Ayatollah Sistani, after the Imam Ali Mosque—a holy Shia shrine where al-Sadr's forces were massed—was attacked by Coalition forces.

In the ensuing two years, violence against the agents of the new Iraqi state, which had taken formal power in June 2004, steadily increased. In 2006, this was surpassed by sectarian warfare in which Shia militia and government personnel were both targets and perpetrators of violence against a gruesome Sunni insurgency. The society seemed to fractionate as Coalition troops kept more and more to their compounds, unable to assure security to the country they had invaded.

There have been many Coalition triumphs in this war, beginning with the striking successes of the initial invasion. The aftermath of those successes has been so disheartening, however, as to call into question whether or not the final judgment on the intervention will be positive.[112] It brings to mind the so-called American paradox: that the U.S., as Isaiah Wilson put it, has a "propensity to win all the battles but still lose the wider war."[113] Much of this failure can be directly attributed to American and indeed Western ideas of what actually constitutes "war." Each important mistake in the intervention in Iraq can be related to this misconception. Indeed, the paradox itself is a "by-product of an institutionalized western idea and practice of war and warfare that has become obsolete, in some critical respects, in the face of a new geostrategic . . . operating environment of war [that] has prevailed [since 1990]."[114]

Let us review what in hindsight appear to be the critical mistakes made by the Coalition after the fall of Baghdad.

Coalition forces failed to establish civil order in the aftermath of the collapse of the Baathist regime because this was not seen as a military responsibility.

It had been U.S. policy not to target Iraq's physical infrastructure, especially its power plants and electrical grid, but American air strikes had inadvertently damaged power lines and also the fuel lines to power plants. This led to a system shutdown, but it was the looting in Baghdad that made the job of restarting the system so difficult.

The computerized control center in the capital was stripped bare . . . Even the transmission lines, which contained copper and aluminum, were stolen. "They just started at one end of the transmission line and worked their way up, taking down the towers, taking away the valuable metals, smelting it down, selling it into Iran and Kuwait," [an AID official said]. "The price of metal in the Middle East dropped dramatically during this period of time."[115]

The absence of power made the security situation more acute and made it almost impossible for the Coalition representatives to communicate with the public over television and radio. As the situation deteriorated it became obvious that there were simply too few troops to secure Baghdad, much less the entire country.

In allocating his forces [the Coalition commander] continued to view
Baghdad as the political center [but even] so, the US military was hard
put to keep order in the capital.

[The] 3rd Infantry Division had plenty of tanks and [armored vehi-
cles] but relatively few infantry. [Of the division's] eighteen thousand
troops, only ten thousand or so were in a position to patrol Baghdad . . .
Of these just twelve hundred would be dismounted infantry . . . "We
simply did not have enough forces for a city of six or seven million,"
[said one commander]. "The forces were stretched too thin and the
troops . . . often did not understand the significance of the stuff they
were guarding."[116]

By comparison, New York City has a force of 38,000 police, and it,
despite some depictions in the movies, is not a war zone. But then neither
was Baghdad, in the conventional sense. The "war" was over. The looting
and civil disorder that followed were not tasks for the military, whose
numbers were too small and whose composition was inappropriate to the
task: "The problem was not just one of numbers. The United States also
lacked the right sort of troops for the [next] phase: it needed to have more
civil affairs units, military police, and interpreters."[117]

The U.S. government had been warned of the possibility of mass looting after initial hostilities had taken down the regime, but it had rejected a
plan for sending 5,000 American police personnel into the city. It had no
wish to divert resources from the reconstitution of the Iraqi police.[118]

This is hard to understand unless we appreciate that securing law and
order in the city of Baghdad was not seen as a military matter. Had it been,
the U.S. would never have been willing to relinquish the primary role it
had sought for the Coalition with respect to warfare. Instead, as Defense
Secretary Donald Rumsfeld asserted in the passage quoted above, the looting and killing was put down to score settling by Shia and petty crime,
matters that a "free society" dealt with after the fact, not preventively,
through its civil not its military institutions. Although the U.S. Defense
Department had been advised that "if we don't establish the rule of law
first [with] a constabulary force, legal teams and corrections officials . . .
then our experience tells us that nothing else happens. We don't get economic reconstruction, we don't get political reconciliation,"[119] these were
Phase IV matters.

One official Army historian of the war has been quoted as concluding
that

U.S. war planners, practitioners and the civilian leadership conceived
of the war far too narrowly and tended to think of operations after the

invasion "as someone else's mission," [while in fact,] those later operations were critical because they were needed to win the war rather
than just decapitate Saddam Hussein's government.[120]

When, after some weeks, L. Paul Bremer took over as head of the Provisional Coalition Authority, one of his first acts was to order a zero tolerance
policy with respect to crime and looting in Baghdad. Bremer's position
surprised commanders, who simply made it clear they had no intention of
enforcing this policy. The American commanders of both the 3rd Infantry
Division and the 1st Marine Division indicated that Bremer's views should
not be confused with orders to the forces.

Coalition forces were vastly undermanned.

Before we celebrate the wisdom of the retired generals who warned
that an insufficient number of troops were sent to Iraq in 2003, we should
look behind this correct conclusion to the assumptions it reflects.[121] As one
prominent general put it, the U.S. needed more troops because "that's how
our doctrine reads." Defense Secretary Rumsfeld was familiar with their
arguments; they were precisely what he had come to the Pentagon to transform. Rumsfeld was an advocate of speed, agility, precision weapons, and
a leaner, more highly trained force as opposed to the mass and firepower
favored by conventional American doctrine. The use of more troops in the
2003 invasion of Iraq would have prevented the "rolling start" that "sent
units into battle as they arrived in theater, rather than waiting to concentrate them"[122] which, though contrary to doctrine, allowed Coalition forces
to surprise the Iraqis. This prevented the destruction of the Iraqi oil fields
and minimized losses to Iraqi civilians. Because Rumsfeld and his generals saw this, they thought they had resolved the issue of troop numbers.
What they did not see—because they weren't looking for it—was the
number of troops required for the war that followed the fall of Baghdad.
Had they seen this problem they would also have seen that such numbers
could not be found in the U.S. force structure for the lengths of time such a
conflict would require. That would have meant either an indispensable
need for partners (Coalition allies supplied 400,000 troops in Gulf War I,
most of them from Muslim nations) or a reintegrated Iraqi army which,
instead, was disbanded.

[a] lack of sufficient troops was a consequence of the earlier, larger
problem of failing to understand that prevailing in Iraq involved more
than just removing Hussein. "This overly simplistic conception of
the 'war' led to a cascading undercutting of the war effort: too

few troops, too little coordination with civilian and governmental/ non-governmental agencies . . . and too little allotted time to achieve 'success,' " . . .[123]

This meant that when Coalition forces first detected the fedayeen resistance, they were ordered to streak past to Baghdad. In late March 2003, U.S. commanders wanted to attack the fedayeen rather than leave them in their rear. These were the fighters who would ultimately form the core of the insurgency.

> Rather than slowing the rush to Baghdad to wipe out the fanatically committed Fedayeen, Franks forced his commanders to forge ahead . . . on the continuing assumption that the real fight would be against the Republican Guard around the capital. Instead, the Guard offered almost no resistance and evaporated into the populace. Meanwhile, once the American forces had moved on, the Fedayeen in the south did the same. Both groups [Republican Guards and fedayeen] are thought now to have reappeared as insurgents.[124]

A lack of troops meant that forces could not be detached to deal with the fedayeen. It also meant that the counterinsurgency was doomed: "Numbers count. One of the truisms . . . is that if you are forced to shift forces around in an insurgency to plug holes, you lose. [You sacrifice] cooperation from the locals who need the presence and security."[125]

In the summer of 2006, the Coalition faced two principal threats: an insurgency (of which a part, the smallest and most vicious, was affiliated with al Qaeda) and a general condition of lawlessness, especially in Baghdad where sectarian militias had seized control of various parts of the city. To address these threats, the Coalition relied on a counterinsurgency strategy that sought to deny the enemy sanctuaries outside Baghdad, and attempted to steadily bring order to the capital city by sending troops to the most insecure sectors in the country generally and in Baghdad. With the prevailing force levels, this strategy could not succeed: indeed it was in conflict with itself.

That is because a statewide pacification strategy, attempting to bring security simultaneously to the entire country, demands enormous numbers of troops, at least four or five times the number then in the country. With then-current force levels, Coalition troops went from hot spot to hot spot, each of which they had to abandon so that they could go to another. Reinforcing Baghdad, which ought to have been the primary objective, only meant weakening even further the numbers available for countrywide operations.

As Kenneth Pollack has noted, with the numbers then available,

[a]gainst a full-blown insurgency such as the one we are facing in Iraq, offensive operations cannot succeed and are ultimately counterproductive. The guerilla does not need to stand and fight but can run or melt back into the population, thus avoiding crippling losses. If the [counterinsurgency forces] do not remain . . . for the long term, the guerillas will be back . . .[126]

They will return as soon as Coalition forces are moved to the next trouble spot, and when they return they will exact vengeance on any collaborators.

[T]here is no way that a [counterinsurgency] force can gather enough intelligence on insurgent forces through traditional means to exterminate them. The only way to gather adequate information is to convince the local populace to volunteer such information, which they will only do if they are . . . safe from retaliation.[127]

By concentrating its few forces on the towns and provinces of greatest unrest, the Coalition deprived Baghdad and Basra of sufficient security. When these cities too erupted in sectarian violence—prompted in part by the fact that only the militias could assure safety—the Coalition was forced to draw down even further the manpower from the offensive search-and-destroy missions. This meant a greater emphasis on firepower in these missions, which in turn further alienated the local peoples. We were, in Pollack's words, "failing to protect those Iraqis who most want reconstruction to succeed, and we [were] further antagonizing the community that [was] most antipathetic to our goals. We [were] reinforcing failure."[128]

It needn't have been this way. Based on recent experience in the Balkans, a number of studies[129] had made remarkably similar estimates as to the number of troops that would be required to subdue Iraq. NATO had deployed about 200 soldiers for every 10,000 civilians. For Iraq, this rough ratio would have meant a stabilization force of more than 450,000—three times the number commanded by the Coalition.[130] Once Baghdad fell in 2003, however, a previously planned deployment of an additional 16,000 troops to augment the 130,000 in the theater was cancelled. After all, the war was over.

The Coalition Provisional Authority's decision to disband the Iraqi army made the problems caused by the already inadequate troop levels of the Coalition even worse.

On May 16, the CPA issued Order No. 1, "De-Baathification of Iraqi Society," barring the top four levels of the Baath Party from government posts. By the CIA station chief's estimate this removed some 30,000 personnel from administrative agencies. This was followed, on May 23, by Order No. 2, "The Dissolution of Entities," formally abolishing the army, the Defense Ministry, and Iraq's intelligence agencies. This affected some 300,000 persons who were cashiered, en masse, into a society with a soaring unemployment rate.

Violent demonstrations erupted, and the CPA then decided to pay the Iraqi troops a stipend, a move that seems to have brought the worst of both worlds into being: "[The US] was paying money to a bitter, demobilized army but was getting nothing in return, and had created a situation in which the soldiers were unsupervised, had no stake in the new order, and were free to create mischief, or worse."[131]

This decision was even more catastrophic than the decision not to send a coalition force comparable in size to that which the First Gulf War coalition fielded. The difference is well-captured in an interview with Dr. David Kilcullen, a political anthropologist who formerly served as a counterinsurgency advisor to the American commander in Iraq, David Petraeus.

> If we were to add 50,000 troops, just hypothetically, that would give us an extra 50,000 people to feed, people to move around, people to support. It would probably give us an extra 10,000 bayonets on the ground. So, an advantage of 10,000. If we win 50,000 Iraqis from [the insurgency] it gives us an advantage not of 50,000 but of 100,000 because we get 50 and they lose 50. . . . So it is all about partnering with the [indigenous] population. . . .[132]

This has important implications for the future, when the training of foreign allies will assume greater significance. U.S. Defense Secretary Robert Gates has grasped these requirements to a degree not shown by some of his predecessors. In a 2007 speech, Gates stated that the army needs to prepare for other unconventional conflicts it is likely to face in the coming decades. The army must get better at conducting wars like those in Iraq and Afghanistan, which, he said, "will remain the mainstay of the contemporary battlefield for some time." He asked the army not to treat the current conflicts as anomalies and thereby retreat into the more familiar ideas of conventional combat, as it did after Vietnam. Success in future conflicts, he said, "will be less a matter of imposing one's will and more a function of shaping behavior of friends, adversaries, and most importantly, the people in between."[133]

The decision to disband the army was scarcely an irrational one, though it has been portrayed as such.[134] The old Iraqi army was intensely distrusted and hated by the Kurds and the Shia against whom it had been deployed and against whom it had used chemical weapons. It had disinte-grated, and there was no organized group on which the CPA could depend, even if it had decided to do so. Finally, the presence of veterans of the Republican Guard and other units would have been a barrier to reform and the effort to create a law-abiding, nonsectarian force.

Rather the problem was that, with an inadequate number of Coalition troops, the dissolution of the Iraqi army meant that there were now far fewer soldiers who could be called on to maintain order, and that the insur-gency would be swollen with disaffected men who had been trained to use munitions.

As Gordon and Trainor note: "Rumsfeld and Bremer each contributed to the security problem. Rumsfeld limited the number of American troops in Iraq, and Bremer limited the number of Iraqi forces that were immedi-ately available. The two decisions combined to produce a much larger security vacuum."[135]

From a conventional perspective, however, both decisions made sense: the "war" had ended, so there was no need for new men from the Coalition countries, and disbanding a hostile army is usually considered a conven-tional objective of warfare, not a misstep in its prosecution.

The Coalition strategy of killing terrorists rather than protecting civil-ians, a strategy that inflamed the insurgency and made it more difficult to suppress, followed from a mistaken impression as to the nature of the insurgency.

The principal objective of nation states at war was not to protect civil-ians, and certainly not civilians of a hostile if defeated state. U.S. antipathy to proposed amnesties, to bribes for local sheikhs, to the reappointment of former Sunni officials who were no more than nominally Baathists, all reflect a certain attitude about the objectives of warfare. Put simply, it wasn't only that the U.S. administration misjudged the extent and scope of the war it had initiated—that "postconflict" operations were in fact an active part of that war—it was also that the kind of war the administration thought it had on its hands was misapprehended.

The attacks by the Fedayeen on the road to Baghdad demonstrated that the . . . coalition was contending with a decentralized enemy that was fanatical, not dependent on rigid command and control, and whose base of operations was dispersed throughout the towns and cities of Iraq. The "center of gravity" was not a single geographic location—the Iraqi capital—but the entire Sunni [region] and more broadly the Iraqi people themselves.[136]

In other words, this was a war on terror. "Decapitation" and "departure"—the killing or capture of the regime's leaders followed by a quick drawdown of Coalition forces—could not win this war. Nor, given the troops available, could a strategy of directly assaulting the most dangerous and recalcitrant areas. The concentration of forces required for such sweeps exposed the civilians in Baghdad to confrontations with Coalition military; the sweeps themselves—breaking down doors, ordering families to lie on their floors while their heads were held in place by boots, men searching women for weapons while in the presence of other men, shouting and firing—antagonized the civilian population and, because those civilians were unwilling to provide accurate information to a force they saw as hostile occupiers, were too often without profit.

There are now, it has been estimated, perhaps as many as 200,000 in the insurgents' network, with 40,000 active fighters. The insurgency has no center of gravity, no obvious chain of command, no unifying ideology or single identifiable organization—which is only to say that it is not characteristic of a nation state (where Baghdad and the Saddam Hussein regime were the "center of gravity") nor is it characteristic of nation state terrorism. As Christopher Coker writes, "[t]he insurgency is taking place in an ambiguous and constantly shifting environment with constellations of cells gravitating to one another from time to time to carry out armed attacks, trade weapons and engage in joint training, and then disperse, often never to cooperate again."[137] He might also have added that much if not most of the kidnapping and murder is done for hire, with bounties on the heads of American and British soldiers, on Iraqi ministers, policemen, and ordinary construction workers. In all of this, war has become a conflict not confined to the former official state apparatus, but a struggle to defeat (or impose) terror.

Secretary of Defense Donald Rumsfeld came into office determined to bring the benefits of the revolution in military affairs* (RMA) to U.S. operations. Using sophisticated reconnaissance and surveillance systems, precision weapons (including unmanned aerial vehicles), and high-tech communications, relatively small forces and mixed units[138] could dramati-

---

*Hereinafter "the RMA"; also sometimes referred to as the MTR (military-technical revolution) although strictly speaking the MTR refers to the impact of new technologies and systems on preexisting concepts of warfare, while the RMA denotes the application of those technologies to new ideas about tactics, doctrine, and organization, culminating in a new concept of warfare altogether. See the discussion in Edward A. Smith, *Effects Based Operations: Applying Network Centric Warfare in Peace, Crisis, and War* (Washington, D.C.: Department of Defense Command and Control Research Program, 2002). *The Shield of Achilles* presented the thesis that revolutions in military affairs induced transformations of the constitutional order *and* that transformations in the constitutional order bred revolutions in military affairs. For the historian, it is an arbitrary choice where one steps into this river of causal currents: the interaction between these two phenomena is mutually affecting such that nothing fundamental happens in the constitutional realm that does not have fundamental consequences in the strategic arena, and vice versa.

cally increase the lethality and effectiveness of fire while greatly reducing mass. Rumsfeld's first term as secretary of defense, in the Ford administration (1975–1977), had been frustrated by the Pentagon's resistance to reform. His second term (2001–2006) was marked by a strenuous effort to transform the U.S. military into a lighter, more agile force, and he was sharply criticized for running roughshod over the uniformed services.[139] Over Iraq, criticism eventually focused in large part on the lack of plan for postcombat operations.

This criticism is misplaced. It is not that the U.S. had no plan, but rather that it studiedly followed a mistaken plan. After a daring and triumphant campaign to seize Baghdad and rout the Iraqi army—effectively employing the rapid tempo that enabled U.S. forces to seize critical bridges before they could be destroyed and enter the Iraqi capital before defenses could be reinforced, impressively coordinating different combat arms, in short adroitly using the benefits of the RMA—Coalition commanders and the CPA carefully followed a war plan that shortly after the fall of Baghdad was revealed to be wholly inappropriate. As Gordon and Trainor conclude, "The violent chaos that followed Saddam's defeat was not a matter of not having a plan but of adhering too rigidly to the wrong one . . . [A]fter the fall of Baghdad . . . the requirements were reversed: mass, not speed, was requisite for . . . victory."[140]

Rumsfeld and his colleagues were right about the RMA, but neglected to appreciate how its emergence would affect constitutional matters, devolving power to networks of insurgents and militias. This lapse in foresight is particularly surprising because the intervention had been justified on the basis that the Iraqi regime was linked to terrorist groups like al Qaeda, including a relationship with Zarqawi, and that Iraq possessed WMD. If either of these claims were true, Coalition forces would have to have been prepared to mount a vigorous counterterrorist campaign in Iraq as part of the war and would have put on the ground numbers of troops sufficient to seal Iraq's borders so that WMD could not be removed and then fall into the hands of terrorists abroad.

If, on the other hand, the intervention had been justified out of concern that Saddam Hussein would, sooner or later, acquire WMD, then the preparations for a long occupation and carefully prepared transition to stable government—as well as regional denuclearization[141]—would have been even more urgent. Otherwise his successors might have pursued the same course as quickly as the occupation withdrew. These preparations would have required the Coalition to accept that the prevention of proliferation is valid as a war aim. Again, this is something the U.S. administration urged, at great cost to its standing in world opinion, but, paradoxically, refused to act on once Baghdad was taken. The paradox, however, is not inexplicable. The U.S. simply had a too narrow conception of war, whatever its rhetoric.

THE WAR IN LEBANON

If "war" is a necessary term for what ensued after the fall of a regime to conventional arms in Baghdad, it is no less necessary for what will be required to resist twenty-first century unconventional terrorism.

Hezbollah is a Lebanese umbrella organization of Islamicist Shia groups, including military and terrorist personnel as well as political figures who participate in Lebanon's new democracy. "Hezbollah" means the "party of God."

In 1982, Iran dispatched some 2,000 Revolutionary Guards to the Bekaa Valley to fight against Israeli forces that had entered Lebanon to confront elements of the Palestine Liberation Organization and al-Fatah quartered there after their expulsion from Jordan. At that time, Iran trained and began to fund Shia terrorist groups. Hezbollah was formed in that same year by a group of Shia clerics sworn to resist the Israeli occupation of largely Shia south Lebanon and to bring an Iranian-style theocracy to all of Lebanon. Over the next decade, the group carried out a series of kidnappings and murders in the country. In 1983 a group later identified as associated with Hezbollah executed a suicide bombing attack on the American embassy in Beirut and on a U.S. Marine barracks, killing some 241 persons including French paratroopers. Hezbollah is thought to be responsible for more than two hundred attacks that have killed roughly a thousand persons.

From its inception it was allied with the state of Iran, which provided training, funds, and weapons to the group. As its attacks on Israel and Israeli forces escalated, its funding from Tehran was increased.

With its base in Lebanon's Bekaa Valley, some poorer sections of Beirut, and south Lebanon,* Hezbollah was at the center of the national resistance to the Israeli occupation in the zone of Lebanon adjacent to the Israeli border. Its attacks on Israeli forces are widely believed to have forced Israel out of Lebanon in May 2000. With this success it has steadily grown in influence, and is now a major provider of social services, running schools, hospitals, and various welfare programs. It also operates the al-Manar satellite television channel and radio station.[142] In the elections in 2005, Hezbollah won 14 seats in the 128-member Lebanese parliament, and gained two ministries in the government.

Thus far this description might fit any of a number of nation state terrorist groups. But with the Israeli withdrawal, Hezbollah began to take on a new character. This was confirmed on July 12, 2006, when Hezbollah launched Katyusha rockets across the Lebanese border, hitting the Israeli town of Shlomi and various Israeli outposts in the Golan Heights, a region

---

*Shia comprise some 40 percent of the Lebanese population.

of Syria occupied by Israel since its capture in the Six-Day War of 1967. That same day, Hezbollah mounted an attack on Israeli forces in northern Israel, killing several soldiers and civilians, kidnapping two troops, and ambushing an Israeli attempt to recover them. It seems likely that these attacks were in part an effort to replay earlier captures of Israeli troops, which had prompted the mass release of prisoners held by Israel pursuant to an exchange; the attacks may also have been reprisals for Israeli attempts to pick off Hezbollah activists. Crucially, these abductions came on the eve of a proposed vote by Palestinians for a two-state solution and were doubtless intended to subvert that goal (reflecting, again, Hezbollah's larger, regional objectives). In any case, many persons, including the Israeli leadership, believed that Hezbollah was wholly unprepared for an Israeli invasion and did not intend to provoke one.

The next day, Israel imposed a blockade on the state of Lebanon; it attacked Beirut's international airport, damaging two runways; it hit a Lebanese air base in the Bekaa Valley; and Israeli naval warships bombarded an electric power station less than twenty miles south of Beirut. Hezbollah replied by shelling two Israeli towns with 9K51 Grad rockets.

The following day, Hezbollah launched dozens of rockets into northern Israel, reaching Haifa, and fired two Iranian-built C-802 cruise missiles (of Chinese design) at an Israeli missile boat and an Egyptian civilian craft. Iran and Syria both denounced Israel.

In the next few days, Israel bombed the airport road from Beirut and the main highway between the city and Damascus. The al-Manar television station was attacked but it continued broadcasting. Israeli warships blockaded the Beirut harbor, cutting off fuel deliveries, and bombarded Beirut's lighthouse and four ports. Air strikes and artillery shelling hit hundreds of Lebanese targets. Hezbollah fired rockets into Haifa, Tiberius, Nazareth, and Afula, its farthest penetration yet.

On July 17, U.N. Secretary General Kofi Annan and U.K. prime minister Tony Blair proposed an international stabilization force. Saudi Arabia supported the proposal the next day but fighting continued until the 30th when an Israeli air strike hit a three-story building in Qana, southern Lebanon, killing almost 60 persons, including 17 children hiding in its bomb shelter. At this point, Israel declared a forty-eight-hour cease-fire.

Israel had made the move to war because it was unwilling to allow Hezbollah to attack Israeli forces and civilians. It saw, correctly, that the terrorist group had crossed the border in order to excite an Israeli political reaction—the exchange of prisoners, and the intimidation of the public. No state can tolerate such attacks without compromising its sovereignty. The July 14 statement by the Hezbollah leader, Hassan Nasrallah, that Hezbollah was now ready for "open war" against Israel only confirmed the fact that this was an act of war, not a mere terrorist incident.

Moreover, the Hezbollah assaults coincided with those of Hamas operating out of Gaza. Hamas, too, was once a nation state terrorist group, fighting to establish an Islamicist Palestine. Its alliance with Hezbollah, however, may be indicative of a now larger agenda. For this alliance, and the aid it receives from Tehran, is globally oriented. It now claims to seek the restoration of "an Islamic Waqf," that is, the reoccupation of any lands ever held by Muslim rulers on the grounds that these territories were "consecrated . . . to Muslim generations until the Day of Judgment."[143]

Finally, the role of the state of Iran which coordinated these attacks to coincide with its potentially embarrassing indictment by the U.N. Security Council for proliferation deceptions, suggests an international agenda, not a national uprising. To the contrary, Iran hopes to split the Council, and public opinion, by isolating its adversary the U.S. as the enemy of Palestinian national rights. Wrapping itself in the Palestinian flag is a shrewd public relations gesture, but the means by which this has been done indicates that the ultimate agenda is by no means limited to Palestine.

Iran did not want to provoke war; neither did Hezbollah.* It was Israel that took the opportunity to attempt to change the balance of forces by striking at Hezbollah. If Israel was correct, however, that terrorists can make war, it was mistaken in believing that it confronted nation state terrorism and that it could somehow discipline that terrorism by striking at the weak nation state in which it was sheltered.

Furthermore, Israel misread the kind of war it must now fight. As a result, its reaction—hundreds of air strikes, many hundreds of civilian casualties, the destruction of Lebanese infrastructure without which a modern society cannot function in a civilized way—was horribly off the mark. By bombing Beirut, closing its ports, and crippling the Lebanese economy through air strikes, Israel essentially did al Qaeda's work for them, for al Qaeda wants to destroy the secular economies, frighten off tourists, and isolate the societies of the Middle East. Israel's strategy caused reaction from potentially supportive states, like Jordan, Egypt, and Saudi Arabia—who had initially denounced the Hezbollah attacks—to turn sharply against it, when this support might have mitigated hostile European responses. The Israeli attacks undermined the Blair government, which had been far more attentive to Israel's vulnerabilities than its predecessors. Most of all, however, it revealed a state that had no plan for this kind of war. In this, it was eerily like the U.S. in Iraq, but as a reversed mir-

*When Hezbollah fighters kidnapped two Israeli soldiers on July 12, they doubtless had in mind a prisoner swap like ones in the past: in 1985, 1,150 Arabs (mostly Palestinians) were traded for three Israeli soldiers; in 1996, 123 Lebanese for the remains of two Israeli soldiers; in 2004, 433 Palestinians and others for an Israeli businessman and the bodies of three soldiers. This plan appears to have been coordinated with Hamas in Gaza, where Palestinians dug a tunnel under the security barrier that surrounds Gaza and assaulted Israeli soldiers, killing two and kidnapping one. They offered to exchange the kidnapped soldier for 95 women and 313 children held in Israeli prisons.

ror image: whereas in Iraq, the U.S. didn't realize it was at *war* with terrorists after Baghdad was seized, Israel knew it was at war, but mistook the kind of war that twenty-first century, networked terrorists oblige their opponents to wage.

The wars in Iraq and Lebanon are two vivid and historic examples of the failure to recognize the unique form of war that is upon us in this era. There are countless other consequences of this failure.

One result of rejecting the notion of a "war on terror" was the refusal by the U.S. to use the assets of the Defense Department against al Qaeda before 9/11 and to focus instead on the terrorists' arrest and extradition, to assign responsibility to the CIA, and to spare the defense budget.[144] Another bureaucratic consequence was to tighten the grip of the CIA on the conduct of covert action, rejecting the recommendations of the Robb-Silberman Commission, as well as those of the 9/11 Commission, which had urged that the agency's special paramilitary unit be transferred to the Pentagon. This would have allowed U.S. armed forces a larger role in carrying out intelligence, reconnaissance or sabotage missions that are more secretive than the clandestine operations already carried out by U.S. Special Operations command. Such a move would reflect a recognition of the change in warfare that is under way.

Another consequence of the refusal to acknowledge the Wars against Terror is that we disparage those military persons who are enlisted in these wars. Here is Simon Jenkins, the most articulate and compelling of the journalists writing opinions opposed to those expressed here:

> To describe what should be a relentless campaign against criminal terror as war is metaphor abuse. By hurling resources and media attention at some distant theatre, it deflects effort from the domestic front. It also insults those who fought and died in real wars, when territory was threatened and states were at risk.[145]

On the contrary, when we recognize that warfare is changing; that we very much need to fight abroad no less than at home, indeed that it cannot be successfully fought by confining ourselves to either front; we will then see that the men and women who have died on our behalf in Afghanistan and Iraq and countless other places deserve the honor of soldiers for all the reasons I have given. A war against terror is not a misplaced metaphor; indeed it is not a metaphor at all.

Additionally, the refusal to recognize this change in the nature of warfare patronizes and condescends to our publics (to say nothing of our political leaders). Both Bruce Ackerman and Philip Heymann, two of the U.S.'s most thoughtful academics, have expressed concern that the very use of the term "war" simply unhinges the public, which is then easily goaded into irrational and self-destructive decisions. But if this is true, surely the resolution lies in nurturing a more mature citizenry that is prepared for the worst and not taken by surprise when the technology hitherto reserved for battlefronts begins to explode among us.

The resolution of the issue cannot lie in an absurd nominalism that holds that if we simply don't use the word "war," whatever the reality, that the challenges that come to democracies at war will be mitigated or even avoided.[146] This approach reached a certain apogee in a powerful article by James Fallows, who decided that the entire matter could be resolved if the Americans simply declared victory in the war on terror.[147] Fallows, like Ackerman, identified a number of destructive results of being at war: war encourages fear; war predisposes the U.S. to think too narrowly about using its formidable nondefense assets; worst of all, war is an open-ended invitation to defeat. How true, but how fanciful to think that a unilateral declaration of victory will cause all these difficulties to vanish. In the end, reality will determine these matters, not nomenclature, for, as one thoughtful commentator put it, "the present and prevailing US (western) construct of what constitutes 'war' is rapidly being overruled by the contemporary realities of 21st century warfare."[148]

Nor is this nominalism confined to the U.S. administration's critics. In his conduct of the war in Iraq, George W. Bush has cast considerable doubt on whether he actually does consider operations there as part of the Wars on Terror,[149] for he has chosen to fight in Iraq as if it were a theater of conventional operations. It is as if he, too, has been using a word for practical political reasons—to rally the public, to gain support for appropriations—without regard for the reality the word is supposed to reflect. Had the president believed that the use of the term "war" was compelled by reality and not just by the instrumental purposes to which he put the word, he would surely have raised taxes (not significantly lowered them), brought Democrats into the cabinet, enlarged the army, and ardently sought American alliances abroad. These steps have invariably characterized the measures taken by U.S. presidents who have led the U.S. in war since 1917.

Yet another result of this reluctance to acknowledge this particular state of war came when families of victims of the 9/11 atrocities applied for wrongful-death compensation. Like ordinary tort victims, they were compensated on the basis of an expected earnings stream that was cut off by the murders. Stockbrokers' families received more than the families of janitors. This can be a very sensible rule for tort law. It is a very poor rule, however, for warfare, when the victims have been chosen by the murderer on no other basis than their identity with the wartime enemy. The firemen who died, died not as firemen but as Americans, that is, they died for the reason that the fires were set in the first place.

Finally, an important adverse effect of refusing to recognize the struggle against terror for what it is, a war, is that it prevents us from appreciating the strategy of our enemy. To paraphrase Mao, we must respect our enemy's strategy, and despise his aims for law. Criminals do not think about how to discombobulate the police; criminals are thinking about the bank. But war fighters devote their energies to responding to the initiatives of their adversaries, trying to throw their plans off balance, adapting new tactics as the armed struggle ebbs and flows. Because there have been no successful attacks on the U.S. since 9/11, it is comforting to conclude that the atrocities of that September day were a fluke, a one-off. If a serial killer suddenly stops his crimes, we don't look for a *tactical* reason to account for this. But since 2002, al Qaeda affiliates have killed citizens from eighteen of the twenty countries that bin Laden has identified as supporting the Coalition invasions of Afghanistan and Iraq, while at the same time avoiding spectacular attacks on the American homeland. There is every reason to think that this is a deliberate shift in strategy. It would be deplorable if we failed to recognize this shift and thereby inadvertently contributed to its success. The same point can be made with respect to the war in Iraq. In the first years of occupation, the goal of the insurgents was to isolate Coalition forces—from the Iraqi people, from the U.N.—and to isolate the U.S. within the Coalition and from potential allies abroad. This strategy largely succeeded but did not, however, prevent the well-attended and internationally monitored elections in 2005 and the formation of an indigenous, multiparty government. As a result, the strategy was changed to concentrate on dividing the society along sectarian lines in order to make governing impossible. This strategy began to succeed with the bombing of the Samarra mosque in February 2006. Between that time and the end of March, some 6,000 bodies were found in the streets of Baghdad, the victims of sectarian executions.[150]

In late 2003, the Norwegian intelligence service came across an al Qaeda strategy paper posted on an Islamicist website. The paper argued that attacks on the U.S. homeland would, at this point, be counterproductive and that instead it was necessary to target American allies in Europe in order to force their governments to withdraw support for the liberation and occupation of Iraq. This, the paper urged, would intensify economic and military pressure on the U.S. as it bore more of the burden of the invasion. Of great interest is the discussion of the relative advantages of striking Spain, Poland, and the U.K. Spain, it was concluded, was the most promising target:

It is necessary to make utmost use of the upcoming general election in Spain in March next year. We think that the Spanish government could not tolerate more than two, maximum three blows, after which it will have to withdraw as a result of popular pressure. If its troops still remain in Iraq after these blows, then the victory of the Socialist Party is almost secured, and the withdrawal of the Spanish forces will be on its electoral programme.[151]

The success of this strategy—the Parti Popular that had supported the Coalition was defeated after murderous attacks on Madrid—has important implications for the future and indeed has guided terrorist attacks since then. The al Qaeda report went on:

Lastly . . . we emphasize that a withdrawal of the Spanish or Italian forces from Iraq would put huge pressure on the British presence (in Iraq), a pressure that [Tony] Blair might not be able to withstand, and hence the domino tiles would fall quickly.[152]

It was therefore to be expected that London would be struck, not by a massive, 9/11 blow but by an attack on mass transit trains in the mode of the 3/11 strikes in Spain. These are the deliberate steps of an international military and political campaign of organized violence—which is to say a war. This has been confirmed by the public declaration of Ayman al Zawahiri in a videotape following the first London bombings. This performance was analyzed by one commentator:

Several audiences are intended in the [Zawahiri] video. For the Western audience, now grappling with the issue of whether to connect the London bombings with Iraq, and whether to take the route of Madrid, this message was intended to isolate the policymakers via inspiring foreboding among civilians and changing the political language among the intellectual elites. For British citizens: "Blair has brought you destruction to the heart of London, and he will bring more destruction, God willing."[153]

Such statements have far more in common with Hitler's threatening political broadcasts—rallying supporters, dividing adversaries, promising peace on reasonable terms—than they do with the extortion demands by kidnappers or serial killers or even the "nonnegotiable demands" of the Weathermen, or the KKK, or the IRA, for that matter. They are the televised front for a careful international diplomatic and strategic plan.

The refusal to acknowledge a new era is manifest in many quarters, but especially in Europe. "Europeans tend to find the idea of a 'war on terrorism' unappealing, nor do they think it an appropriate description of the situation," Peter Neumann concluded. "This has stopped European governments from over-reacting, but has also encouraged a sense of complacency."[154] The following passage is from Lord Justice Hoffmann—a widely and rightly acclaimed British jurist—in an appeals case reviewing the detention of alleged terrorists, the legal status of which turned on whether the British government had valid grounds to invoke a treaty provision on the basis that it faced a national emergency:

> I do not underestimate the ability of fanatical groups of terrorists to kill and destroy, but they do not threaten the life of the nation. Whether we would survive Hitler hung in the balance, but there is no doubt that we shall survive Al-Qaeda. The Spanish people have not said that what happened in Madrid, hideous crime as it was, threatened the life of their nation. Their legendary pride would not allow it. Terrorist violence, serious as it is, does not threaten our institutions of government or our existence as a civil community.[155]

The main thing wrong with this conclusion, apart from its profound misunderstanding of the events in Madrid, is that it omits one word at the end of the paragraph. That word is "yet."

We are at war no less than when a conventional state surprised the U.S. with an attack in 1941, and we have been attacked now for much the same reason. Now, as then, the U.S. aroused fear that its global presence could threaten the ambitions of messianic movements that only wanted a free hand in their drive for regional subjugation and domination. Then as now we face a long and bitter struggle. We should make no mistake: this is war.

Lawrence Freedman has summarized with his customary lucidity the principal challenge this new form of warfare poses. Noting "the difficulty the U.S. armed forces face in shifting their focus from preparing for regular wars, in which combat is separated from civil society, to irregular wars, in which combat is integrated with civil society," Freedman emphasizes that success in these wars will require that "the purpose and practice of Western forces be governed by liberal values [despite the fact that] the integration [of warfare] with civil society makes the application of liberal values so challenging."[156]

This chapter has argued that, in light of developments in warfare and in terrorism, it makes sense to speak of a war against terrorists like al Qaeda and the Iraqi insurgents.

Getting important actors such as the military leadership and the legal community to change their ways of thinking will not be easy. Many senior army officers in the U.S. and the U.K. have been trained that war necessarily involves the overwhelming use of force and firepower. Two especially thoughtful observers, Daniel Benjamin and Steven Simon, finally concluded that the "record demonstrates that our military is simply incapable of adapting its culture to embrace . . . highly mobile, highly lethal counterterrorism operations. . . . The missing ingredient for success with the most important kind of counterterrorism mission is not courage or technical capability—our uniformed personnel are unsurpassed—but organizational culture."[157] That would be a pity for, as General Petraeus's own counterinsurgency manual concluded, "[t]he military forces that successfully defeat insurgency are usually those able to overcome this institutional inclination to wage conventional war against insurgents."[158]

Nor is this conceptual inertia confined to the military. A law professor at a prominent university was reported to have concluded that it was "nonsensical to go to war with terrorists," offering this analogy: "The Colombian drug cartels have airplanes and bombs and boats, and it shoots down American airplanes," this professor said. "They're criminals. You can't go to war against the Colombian drug cartel. . . . If you could, then when they shot down an American military plane, they wouldn't be guilty of anything. They'd have combat immunity [and therefore couldn't be sued or indicted]."[159]

Putting aside the question of what is precisely the right response to a well-armed state-within-a-state that shoots down an American plane, isn't there something slightly comic—and a bit depressing, too—about assuming that because someone cannot be sued or charged with a crime, there really is nothing that can be done? Apparently law professors can be as fixated on conventional ways of addressing problems as generals. Both will be hard to persuade about new forms of warfare (although I am inclined to think of the Pentagon as a roiling sea of intellectual ferment compared to law faculties).

In this chapter I have argued that the conditions that have caused the rise of the market state, conditions that are neither ephemeral nor transitory, have brought this change in warfare. Henry Kissinger has captured this reality in this acute observation:

> [These wars] are not temporary interruptions of a beneficent *status quo*.
> They signal instead an inevitable transformation of the international

order resulting from changes in the internal structure of many key participants, and from the democratization of politics, the globalization of economics, and the instantaneousness of communications.[160]

The next chapter will try to explain why a war not just against terrorists, but against terror itself makes sense.

> *I lived in the first century of world wars.*
> *In the day I would be reminded of those men and women,*
> *Brave, setting up signals across vast distances,*
> *considering a nameless way of living, of almost unimagined*
>   *values.*
> *As the lights darkened, as the lights of night brightened,*
> *We would try to imagine them, try to find each other,*
> *To construct peace, to make love, to reconcile*
> *Waking with sleeping, ourselves with each other,*
> *Ourselves with ourselves. We would try by any means*
> *To reach the limits of ourselves, to reach beyond ourselves,*
> *To let go the means, to wake.*
>
> *I lived in the first century of these wars.*
>
> —Muriel Rukeyser, "Poem"

CHAPTER FOUR

Victory Without Parades

O, now, for ever
Farewell the tranquil mind! farewell content!
Farewell the plumed troop and the big wars
That make ambition virtue! O, farewell!
Farewell the neighing steed and the shrill trump,
The spirit-stirring drum, the ear-piercing fife,
The royal banner, and all quality,
 Pride, pomp, and circumstance of glorious war!

—William Shakespeare,
Othello, 3.3.347–50

AS WE CURRENTLY understand this potent phrase, "the war against terror," it is hard to imagine quite how we could win such a war. Are all terrorists everywhere to surrender? Will they sign a peace treaty that binds all future fighters who would resort to terrorism? And what of terror itself? How would it be vanquished? Will we cease to speak of "the terrors of this night"? Will neurotics abandon their phobias? Will the Hitchcock film fail to frighten the moviegoer, and the final exam cease to terrify the student? To state the problem in this way shows its absurdity. The only possible outcome is captured by the satirical headline, *Flash from War on Drugs: Drugs Win.*[1]

Yet this absurdity may have more to do with how we've stated the problem, or at least our understanding of that statement, than with the problem itself. This isn't a semantic quibble. Often when our understanding of the issues insufficiently reflects the reality of the problem, we configure our problems in ways that make them insoluble. Key factual elements are ignored or dismissed, and needed concepts are not developed. The false problem we construct cannot be treated by the methods at hand, yet it keeps us from developing new approaches.

One missing concept is a description of the current evolution of the State because, as we saw in chapter 1, terrorism is a function of the prevailing constitutional order. Only if we understand the constitutional order that has evoked a particular form of terrorism can we also understand that unique terrorism. Another crucial concept is an appreciation of the threat posed by twenty-first century terrorism because, as we saw in chapter 2, this new constitutional order, the market state, has the potential via markets in WMD and WMD-related information to supercharge the danger posed by terrorists such that states can be imperiled to a degree hitherto the exclusive province of states themselves. We also must have a realistic apprehension of contemporary warfare. We cannot successfully wage war if we don't understand how warfare is changing. If, as we saw in chapter 3, warfare is to be fought among civilians rather than on desolated plains between states, the appropriate force structure, its training and weapons, will need to change. Finally, the objectives to be achieved or avoided will, like war itself, also be transformed. We must develop a comprehension of the war aim of market states in this new environment: what would it mean to win the Wars against Terror? We must grasp what is at stake—what we may lose—in a war against terror. Otherwise we may be inclined simply to assume away the problem, believing that only conventional wars can actually threaten the institutions of government or jeopardize our civil community, and we may not therefore notice when we ourselves take steps that compromise the very patrimony that is at stake.

Even if the Reader is prepared to entertain the idea that twenty-first century terrorists are a proper subject of warfare and not just law enforcement; and that the proliferation of WMD makes states that are otherwise not an imminent, immediate threat the proper subject of anticipatory war; and that the wars of the future will encompass measures against non-state actors—even if one can be persuaded to consider these premises, they would justify a war against terrorists and against a certain sort of terrorism, but not a war against terror itself. That is, even if market state terrorism is more than just a technique, available to all, and is actually a twenty-first century geopolitical reaction to globalization, even then it would still be absurd to make war against an *emotion*. This chapter will argue, however, that it is precisely against terror—and not simply against terrorism or the arming of terrorists—that war must be waged if the war aim of market states of consent is to be achieved.

I.

We often use the term "representative democracy" because it is familiar, but today there is far more to this form of government than simply elections that confirm the will of a majority. It stands for a whole system of the rule of law that respects human rights as well as providing representation according to the popular will. Twenty-first century democracy, in this larger sense, is the latest version of the state of consent.

Ever since the emergence of modern states at the time of the Renaissance, there have been *states of consent* and *states of terror*. Indeed, Thucydides characterized the ancient city-states of Athens and Sparta in something like this way, though both had representative institutions.[2] States of consent govern on the basis of authority freely derived from the unfettered consent of the governed, authority that must be regularly and frequently renewed and that can be withdrawn; states of terror govern by means of repression and are not bound by the freely given decision of the public or indeed any particular set of public representatives, nor can their regimes be peacefully replaced involuntarily. If Thucydides' Sparta is an ambiguous case, Herodotus's Persia is not.

Each category must of course be applied relative to the prevailing constitutional order of the day. A princely state of consent, like Machiavelli's Florentine republic, would appear pretty oligarchical to parliamentarians today; a kingly state of terror, like Henry VIII's England, nevertheless was rather mild compared to the totalitarian nation states of the twentieth century.

In the vanguard of the transition from nation state to market state, two states of consent—the United States and the European Union—are emerging as market states along somewhat different lines. States of terror will also come in several forms: some will be market states like the virtual caliphate of al Qaeda, but there will be others, including nation states like Saddam Hussein's Iraq (which sponsored terrorists), or the Taliban's Afghanistan (which was sponsored by terrorists) or Kim Jong Il's North Korea (which embodies the three elements of terror—terrorism, crimes against humanity, and WMD proliferation—to a degree that is, at present, unique). The United States and the European Union, if they lose the Wars against Terror, might also become states of terror, for, as we shall see, that is how wars of this kind are lost: not by conquest and the surrender of territory but by the compromise of the fundamental conditions for consent in the face of awful civilian suffering. As Audrey Kurth Cronin concluded:

> International terrorism is not dangerous because it can defeat us in a [conventional] war, but because it can potentially destroy the domestic contract of the state by further undermining its ability to protect its citizens from attack. The . . . greatest danger is not defeat on the battlefield but damage to the integrity and value of the state . . . The use of terrorism implies an attempt to de-legitimise . . . the structure of the state system itself.[3]

Yet if they do not lose—if the U.S. and the E.U. endure without compromising the basic ethos and practices of consent—they will steadily and surely prevail over states of terror that depend upon a climate of fear not only to intimidate other states, but to establish their own authority with respect to the persons they seek to govern. The states of consent will prevail if they endure because their enemy must win. States of terror can maintain themselves in power only by fresh threats that, if successfully resisted, steadily erode their legitimacy. States of consent don't need to win; they simply need not to lose. Indeed for such states, not losing amounts to winning.

It will be crucial in such a struggle to develop legal indicia that allow one to determine when a state, including one's own state, threatens to become a state of terror. We must be able to say when an act of violence represents a legitimate effort to preclude terror and when it is itself an act of terrorism.

It is also important to be clear about what we are fighting for. A state of consent in the current era is not merely one whose elections reflect majoritarian practices but one which rests on the protection of certain fundamental rights—*inalienable* rights, a legal term that means rights that cannot be ceded, or bartered, or sold. These rights inhere in the individual and are not granted by the State that is created to protect those rights. Because consent is not merely a matter of saying Yes, but also of having the option to say No, consent depends upon the possibility of alternatives. Inalienability is one way—the law's way—of creating the necessity of citizens having to choose among alternatives.

One cannot freely choose, however, in an atmosphere of terror. It is the objective of the twenty-first century state of terror to bring about just such an environment of terror because this is the basis on which it claims the legitimate right to govern. Like all market states, the market state of terror says: Give us power and we will increase your opportunities. Characteristically, however, it also adds: And this can only be done if you allow us to protect you with methods and practices that are not subject to consent. Thus such states cannot coexist with consent whether it is that of their own societies or that of others.

It may at first appear implausible that a market state could ever be a state of terror; how does such violent repression "maximize opportunity"? This would appear especially the case with any market state that was seized or created by Salafist fundamentalism, which condemns choice in elections, in matters of religion, criminal sentencing, sexuality, and other decisions. Nevertheless, al Qaeda is in fact an excellent example of how this might come about. Muslims now face an unprecedented and to some persons a disturbing array of political choices by virtue of the same forces that are creating market states, viz, the globalization of trade and finance, the internationalization of culture, a global system of human rights, various transnational threats, and the diffusion of WMD. This bewildering menu of choices is an example of one corollary to Parmenides' Fallacy. It will be recalled that Parmenides' Fallacy occurs when a decider contrasts a proposed option with the present context rather than with other possible contexts that will eventuate if other options are exercised; things change, and so indefinitely extending the present is never a realistic option. A corollary to this idea is that when we do choose, we are often haunted by the possibility that the option we choose will bring about a future less appealing than an option we forswore.[4]

The result is that the expansion of options does not necessarily mean "maximizing opportunity" but instead can simply paralyze the person asked to choose. Truly maximizing the opportunity for such persons means submission to a comprehensive set of choices. By choosing the entire package, the citizen/consumer is able to navigate the otherwise debilitating course of abundant but disconcertingly numerous options and the consequences or the corollary described above are avoided.

Al Qaeda offers just such a package. It "maximizes opportunity" by assuring the chooser that the right choice has been made. Outside such dogmatics, how can one know that one's choices have in fact created a better world than the one another set of choices might have brought into being?

This is perhaps best understood by those who would impose a state of terror. A videotape of Osama bin Laden in December 2004 proclaimed Abu Musab al Zarqawi to be al Qaeda's emir for Iraq. As the head of the al Qaeda franchise in Iraq, Zarqawi claimed responsibility for numerous car bombings and the beheadings of foreign and Iraqi hostages in 2004 and 2005. Drawing on an informal network of foreign al Qaeda fighters, former Baathist party members, and local criminals who were paid for kidnappings, Zarqawi assumed the principal leadership of the most lethal elements in the anti-Coalition insurgency in Iraq. A $25 million bounty (the same amount as that marked for bin Laden) was put on his head, and he was eventually killed. From the time when he was designated emir until his death in June 2006, Zarqawi "led a murderous campaign unmatched in the history of al Qaeda."[5] Prior to this period, al Qaeda had killed some 3,200 persons; under Zarqawi's leadership, al Qaeda forces probably killed twice that many.[6] Bruce Reidel concluded that, "even by the ruthless standards of al Qaeda, Zarqawi excelled."[7]

On the eve of the historic Iraqi elections in 2005, Zarqawi released an audiotape threatening those who might attempt to vote and explaining the reason for his opposition to those elections. "We have declared a bitter war against democracy and all those who seek to enact it."[8] Islam, he said, requires the rule of God and not the rule of "the majority of the people."[9] He explained furthermore that democracy was based on other objectionable beliefs beyond simple "majority rule, [beliefs] such as freedom of

religion, rule of the people, freedom of expression, separation of religion
and state, forming political parties."[10] In his statement Zarqawi declared
that democracy's principles of majority rule and respect for individual
rights "allow infidelity and wrong practices to spread . . . "[11] "Anyone who
tries to help set up this system is part of it."[12] Freedom of expression is
allowed in such states, "even cursing God. This means there is nothing
sacred in democracy."[13] Most important, Zarqawi announced that, because
democracies are states of consent, every member of the society is culpable
for the state's actions and therefore every citizen is a legitimate target for
violence. It's not simply that civilians are to be terrorized in order to bring
pressure on their governments, as in the era of the "total wars" of the
nation states. Rather, attacks on civilians are an end in themselves because
the civilians are being punished for their very existence as the constitutive
participants in democracies. "This is how our ethical stances are dictated,"
said bin Laden's deputy, Ayman al Zawahiri, after the London bombings in
July 2005. "Your democratically elected governments continuously [make
war] and your support of them makes you directly responsible . . . Until we
feel security [for our practices], you will be our target."[14]

These attitudes are not unique to the jihadists. The war aim for all states
of terror, and all would-be states of terror, is the

> achievement of a separate . . . community in which all . . . share the
> same identity . . . cemented together by fear, isolation and suspicion . . .
> The creation of an atmosphere of fear and hatred is particularly attrac-
> tive for so-called militias . . . The militias pay their own wages by
> extorting money from the [terrorized] population, by looting deserted
> buildings, and by trading goods on the black market, but also by
> exploiting the opportunities of an increasingly global community, for
> example in gifts from wealthy émigrés abroad or by diverting humani-
> tarian aid shipments . . . [For] the powers-that-be [in a state of terror]
> to remain in power, [they must] sustain an atmosphere of dread.[15]

Zarqawi and Zawahiri saw clearly that the war against al Qaeda, the
war against the Taliban, the war against the insurgency in Iraq and the
heroic efforts there and in Afghanistan to prevent the murder of innocent
Afghan and Iraqi civilians and officials, ultimately concern the creation of
states of consent, replacing former states of terror and warding off the
imposition of new ones. Elections are only a part of this. Fundamentally it
is a matter of recognizing certain human rights of conscience, the inalienable rights that so disgusted Zarqawi and without which, as we shall see,
neither national nor international systems of law based on consent can
long endure. But the reverse is also true: in the current global environment,

examples of systems of consent are highly threatening to regimes of terror. The latter can never find the security Zawahiri demands as long as the former exist.

Terrorists can do fatal damage to the conditions that underlie consent either with attacks using WMD or simply by rolling infrastructure attacks using conventional explosives: either can coerce policy changes from a democratically elected government (as happened following the Madrid attacks) or create the demand for an authoritarian regime. That is the answer to the question posed by Ronald Dworkin:

> Is the danger really so great? Religious fanatics bent on murder are not the only enemies of society. We face serial killers, drug dealers, muggers, industrial polluters, train operators that skimp on safety, and white-collar criminals. . . . It is unclear that the dangers these people pose to our security is any less than the danger of terrorism.[16]

These threats are in fact modest by comparison precisely because they do not, in our contemporary life, have the ability to change the nature of the State.*

But states of terror can't coexist with states of consent either: the conditions that underwrite repression are vulnerable to intervention (as in Iraq or Panama) or the demand for democracy (as in Ukraine, Lebanon, and elsewhere).

This is what Mario Vargas Llosa has in mind when he writes of

> the various sects and movements bent on provoking the Apocalypse in order to prevent Iraq from soon becoming a free and modern country . . . a perspective that rightfully terrifies and drives insane the gangs of murderers and torturers [of Saddam Hussein's regime] along with fundamentalist commandos from al Qaeda . . . All of them, totaling only a few thousand armed fanatics, but with extraordinary tools for destruction, know that if Iraq becomes a modern democracy, their days are numbered.[17]

II.

Here is an account of the reception of the news in America that Germany had agreed to an armistice, ending hostilities in World War I:

---

*One can imagine, however, a society where criminals do pose such a threat, for example, Colombia or parts of West Africa.

So the tidings spread throughout the country. In city after city mid-morning found offices half deserted. . . . people marching up and down the streets again as they had four days previously, pretty girls kissing every soldier they saw, automobiles slowly creeping through the crowds and intentionally backfiring to add to the noise of horns and rattles and every other sort of din-making device. Eight hundred Barnard College girls snake-danced on Morningside Heights in New York; and in Times Square, early in the morning, a girl mounted the platform of Liberty Hall, a building set up for war-campaign purposes, and sang the "Doxology" before hushed crowds.[18]

And this is an account of how Britain took the news, broadcast on German radio the day before, that Nazi Germany had surrendered to Allied forces in World War II:

As midnight ushered in May 8th [1945], one of the bigger ships in Southampton docks let out a deep throated V sign. Others, large and little, joined in cacophonously with their raucous or piping notes, and searchlights flashed out V in morse across the sky.

But London had earned the honour, which would have fallen to it in any case, of providing the center of rejoicing. The weather was dull in the capital next morning; a light rain, inappropriately, fell. Many houses displayed Union Jacks . . . The Daily Mirror, fulfilling a faith long held in the fighting services, rejoiced by disrobing completely the hitherto tantalizing "Jane." Crowds massed, on the other hand, at St Paul's Cathedral which was packed with worshippers all day.

In the afternoon, the sun came out to play over the dense crowds in the main streets. . . . At three o'clock, Churchill broadcast to the nation, and the many crowding outside the House of Commons heard his familiar voice relayed over loudspeakers, and joined in fervently with "God Save the King" when it was played at the end. Immediately afterwards, Churchill proceeded from Downing Street to the House, and his car was pushed the length of Whitehall by the sheer weight of the mobbing people.[19]

These accounts seem uncannily similar, and it is tempting to think that victory has always been like that: official announcements, thronging crowds, bunting everywhere, and that is to a large extent true. Similar scenes were enacted in London after Waterloo. It is also tempting to think that victory itself is defined by such scenes, but that is not altogether true. Victory is not simply the defeat of the enemy; it is the achievement of the war aim. A state can fail to defeat its enemy but win victory by gaining its war aim, as happened to the United States in the War of 1812; or a coalition of states may defeat its enemy, as the U.N. force did the North Koreans in 1950, but fail to win victory. Furthermore, because the war aims of states are determined by their constitutional and strategic situations, it is not quite right to think that victory itself has been the same from age to age.

Since the Renaissance victory in armed conflict has been periodically redefined by the war aims of the states in conflict, as we shall see. The aims of warring states were structured by their shared constitutional order, which provided the basis for their legitimacy. When we are able to appreciate the new basis for legitimation of the State, we shall also be able to portray the changing nature of victory in the period ahead. A war on terror is coming into being owing to the market state's requirement that it be able to prevent or mitigate certain otherwise unavoidable and intolerable civilian catastrophes. As a result, our war aims and therefore the nature of the victory required to achieve them will be redefined once again, bearing in mind that a new period is not wholly new but is marked by what is innovative, unprecedented, and constitutionally significant.[20]

There have always been cheering crowds in the capitals of the victors, but what exactly they were cheering about has changed from era to era. The modern state did not spring fully formed as it is today when it first emerged at the end of the fifteenth century. In the interim, several different constitutional orders achieved dominance in the governance of what became known as the Great Powers. These distinct orders of the State not only fought different kinds of war, they sought different kinds of victories. Just as warfare in the modern era is a matter of conflict among states, so victory in war has been defined by the objectives of states.

Each constitutional order was founded upon a unique claim to legitimacy.[21] Each achieved hegemony through an epochal war, which proved the new form to be strategically dominant and began a period of imitation by states that wanted to adopt the new, more successful constitutional model. Each constitutional order was recognized as the legitimate order for other states by the peace congress that concluded the epochal war of the period and sorted out the winnings. It should not be surprising that what amounted to success changed as each order redefined the appropriate goals for warfare and then ratified these goals for the victorious side at the resulting peace conference. The convening of these congresses marked more than the end of belligerency; the treaties they drafted became the new constitutions for the society of states re-created by war. By this method the new, strategically dominant constitutional order enshrined itself in a new international legal order.

A glance back at previous constitutional orders discloses some marked differences in the war aims, and hence the indicia of victory, for each form.

Therefore to understand the changing nature of victory we must first study the shift in the constitutional order that determines the war aim. To vastly oversimplify, the sixteenth century princely state sought to aggrandize the personal possessions of the prince; the seventeenth century kingly state attempted to enlarge the holdings of the ruling dynasty; the eighteenth century territorial state tried to enrich its country as a whole (and its aristocracy in particular) by acquiring trading monopolies and colonies; the nineteenth century state nation struggled to consolidate a dominant national people and sought empire; the twentieth century nation state fought from 1914 to 1990 to establish a single, ideological paradigm for improving the material well-being of its people. To put it in slightly more technical terms, victory achieved in pursuit of these various (and sometimes overlapping) goals could be characterized as *perquisitive* (princely state), *acquisitive* (kingly state), *requisitive* (colonial territorial state), *exclusive* (imperial state nation), and *inclusive* (nation state). Victory is defined by the war aim. The victory sought by twenty-first century market states will be *preclusive*.

III.

The leaders of the princely states of the late Renaissance pursued perquisitive victories that would enhance their personal status. Charles V and François I seriously contemplated a personal duel as a way of resolving the Habsburg-Valois wars. Above all, these princes desired the perquisite of determining the religion of their subjects. This is reflected in the most important constitutional concept of the era, *cuius regio, eius religio,** enshrined in the Peace of Augsburg. Perquisitive victories, like princely perquisites generally, were personal to the ruler. His successors, the absolute monarchs of kingly states, sought acquisitive victories, conquests that would enlarge their familial, dynastic inheritances and consolidate a contiguous patrimony. Warfare was regarded as a perfectly legitimate means of aggrandizing the holdings of the dynasty. We have only to compare the careful preparations of Louis XIV—the very apotheosis of the leader of a kingly state—for the War of the Spanish Succession with those of Frederick the Great, the quintessential territorial-state sovereign, preparing for the War of the Austrian Succession forty years later to see the difference in their respective constitutional orders and to appreciate the contrast between kingly states and their successors, the territorial states. Where Louis went to great lengths to establish a dynastic basis for warfare in order to place a Bourbon prince on the throne of Spain—the thwarted

---

*He who rules determines the religion of his subjects.

PLATE I: THE CONSTITUTIONAL ORDERS

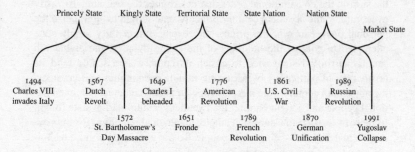

There have been six distinct constitutional orders of the
State since it first emerged during the Renaissance.

PLATE II: THE EPOCHAL WARS

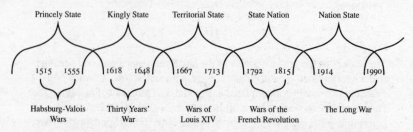

Each epochal war brought a particular constitutional order to primacy.

PLATE III: THE INTERNATIONAL ORDERS

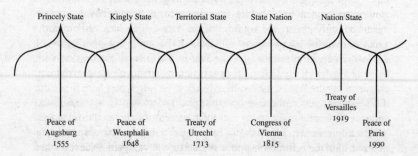

The peace treaties that end epochal wars ratify a particular
constitutional order for the society of states.

PLATE IV: BASES FOR LEGITIMACY

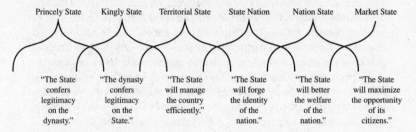

Princely State	Kingly State	Territorial State	State Nation	Nation State	Market State
"The State confers legitimacy on the dynasty."	"The dynasty confers legitimacy on the State."	"The State will manage the country efficiently."	"The State will forge the identity of the nation."	"The State will better the welfare of the nation."	"The State will maximize the opportunity of its citizens."

Each constitutional order asserts a unique basis for legitimacy.

PLATE V: HISTORIC STRATEGIC AND CONSTITUTIONAL INNOVATIONS

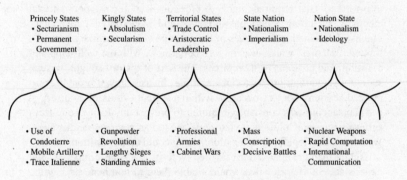

Princely States	Kingly States	Territorial States	State Nation	Nation State
• Sectarianism • Permanent Government	• Absolutism • Secularism	• Trade Control • Aristocratic Leadership	• Nationalism • Imperialism	• Nationalism • Ideology
• Use of Condotierre • Mobile Artillery • Trace Italienne	• Gunpowder Revolution • Lengthy Sieges • Standing Armies	• Professional Armies • Cabinet Wars	• Mass Conscription • Decisive Battles	• Nuclear Weapons • Rapid Computation • International Communication

*A constitutional order achieves dominance by best exploiting the strategic
and constitutional innovations of its era.*

dowry, the Spanish wife, the secret agreement with the other principal contending family negotiated by the family heads—Frederick disdained the
color of dynastic legality in his annexation of Silesia, first offering to sell
his vote as imperial elector to Austria in exchange for territory and, when
this was rejected, launching an aggression in defiance of the Pragmatic
Sanction to which his father was a signatory.

Territorial states like Frederick's Prussia or George III's Britain were
preoccupied with "the country," the territory of the state, for essentially
mercantile reasons. They sought proprietary yet requisitive victories in
order to gain the commercial, taxing, and trade advantages achieved when
they annexed the territory or colonies of the defeated state—within a
carefully maintained, that is, *required,* balance of power. The Treaty of

Utrecht, which ratified the hegemony of the territorial state, contained the first international recognition of this requirement; it also contained the first agreements fixing duties levied at frontiers and diminishing the role of internal customs duties. The "most favored nation" clause made its first important appearance in this treaty. The preeminence given to commercial matters—the treaty was accompanied by an extensive series of commercial agreements among the signatories—was characteristic of territorial states. In place of the communities and towns that defined the boundaries of the kingly state, the territorial state attempted to fix a frontier boundary, a line that marked its jurisdiction. Such lines were necessary to enable territorial bartering in order to maintain the requisite balance of power. This bartering frankly derogated dynastic rights.

The age of the territorial state was the period of the ancien régime. Its wars were characterized by the adroit use of strategic and tactical maneuver that forced the opponent into abandoning indefensible ground and thus into retreat. This required highly professionalized forces; non-national elements, including individual officers[22] and men (but not mercenary armies), flourished in the forces of the great powers. Its military aspect— limited, "cabinet" wars—was in perfect harmony with the well-tempered constitutional customs of its regimes. The sort of victory sought by such states mirrored their proprietorial ambitions. Success in war brought commercial cessions. Victory occurred within a system—think of an orrery— and rebalancing was constantly required to prevent any losing state from suffering too great a loss or a victorious one too great an aggrandizement. Winning meant legalized annexation; losing could mean partition.

Rather than the annexations favored by territorial states, imperial state nations sought victories that would enable them to dominate by law the civil life of the societies they conquered without incorporating them into the national polity. Such a state mobilized a nation, an ethnocultural group, to act on behalf of the state. Unlike the territorial state, it could thus call on the revenues of all society, and on the human talent of all persons (because rank was open to all). This constitutional order did not exist, however, to serve or take direction from the nation, as does the nation state, but rather to give the nation identity and direction. This is quite clear in the case of Napoleonic France, which incorporated many nations within its territory, but suppressed nationalism wherever it encountered it outside France. It was equally true of the British and Dutch empires.

It is important to appreciate the characteristics of such a state in order to understand the nature of the warfare it waged and the kind of victories it sought. Napoleonic warfare eventually compelled every territorial state to conform itself to the state nation model if it was to survive French predations.

The prodigious effects of the French Revolution abroad were evidently brought about much less through new methods and views introduced by the French in the conduct of War than through the changes which it wrought in statecraft and civil administration, in the character of Governments, in the condition of the people, etc. That other Governments took a mistaken view of all these things; that they endeavoured, with their ordinary means, to hold their own against forces of a novel kind and overwhelming strength—all that was a blunder in policy . . . We may say, therefore, that the twenty years' victories of the Revolution are chiefly to be ascribed to the erroneous policy of the Governments by which it was opposed.[23]

Armies of conscripts, meritocratic and bourgeois ministries, broad-based taxation without exemptions for the nobility, all spread across Europe just as the international officer class of the territorial state vanished. Most importantly for our current purposes, state nations sought victories of far greater scope than had territorial states. If the warfare of the territorial states was characterized by concerted efforts to minimize risk, the warfare of the state nation can be said to have sought the high returns that only come from accepting great risks.

The victories pursued by the imperial state nations were exclusive in nature because the winning state looked to dominate the loser without incorporating it into the metropole. It was neither necessary nor desirable to incorporate conquered lands into the victorious state. Inclusion would have been unwelcome to the dominant national group and could even have threatened its domestic hegemony. Instead the state nation desired, by treaty or conquest, control over both the internal and external relations of the subject society—that is, the property rules, educational systems, and cultural institutions (including language), as well as the treaties, borders, and armed forces of the imperial possession. This is the definition of empire: the control, by law, of the civil life and the political relations of another society. This kind of victory enhanced the prestige of the national people that triumphed in war. In the year 1800, Europeans controlled 35 percent of the land area of the world; by 1878 this figure had risen to 67 percent; yet the size of the principal imperial state nations had scarcely materially changed.

The constitutional transition to the state nation should therefore not be confused with that which resulted in the nation state. The nation state takes its legitimacy from putting the State in the service of its people; the state nation asks rather that the people be put in the service of the State. The state nation did not derive its legitimacy from maintaining the welfare of the people; rather it was legitimated by forging a national consciousness, by fusing the nation with the State. Its victories, like its wars, served this goal.

Nation states, by contrast, achieved victories when they were able to include the defeated states within their own ideological camp; for parliamentary nation states, that meant granting self-determination to nationalities. For fascist states this meant inclusion in a military alliance and the division of spoils; for communist states this meant inclusion in an international bloc whose leadership was connected by an ideological affinity (or valence) based on class violence. In every case, the total warfare of the nation state demanded total constitutional victory—scrapping the *Kaiserreich* in 1919 and replacing it with the Weimar constitution, stripping the emperor of Japan of his divinity in 1945, absorbing ancient European states of Central Europe into the Soviet system after World War II.

The nation state exists to determine what will promote the well-being of the national people and to realize this through legal action. The flow of legitimacy is from the people's sovereignty to the State; hence the importance to the nation state of broadening suffrage and the vexing problem of self-determination, that is, the people's judgment on statehood itself. The question posed by self-determination is: When does a nation get a state? Such a question was nonsense to the state nation. One might say that the process of decolonization in the early twentieth century was the confrontation of nascent nation states like Ireland or India or Indochina with decaying state nation forms, like Britain and France; while that of the century's middle period was the confrontation of competing national claims to a state. British diplomats were completely flummoxed[24] by Hitler's Sudeten claims in 1938, when he threw in their faces the rhetoric of national self-determination* enshrined in the Versailles Treaty that Germany despised but had been compelled to ratify.

The transition from state nation to nation state brought a change in constitutional procedures. The plebiscite, the referendum, and indeed the whole array of participatory procedures do not derive from the American or French revolutions that ushered in the era of the imperial state nation. Quite to the contrary, in Federalist Paper 63 James Madison wrote that the distinction of the American government "lies in the total exclusion of the people, in their collective capacity, from any share" in the government. By the end of the American Civil War, however, the requirements of legitimation had changed. Similarly, in Europe it was once again the relation between constitutional change and strategic innovation that made a transformation both necessary and possible. Mass education, the

---

*Ninety percent of the Sudeten Germans lived in parts of Czechoslovakia in which they were 90 percent of the population.

broadest possible widening of the franchise, and social security systems all followed.

The successful nation states of the decades-long conflict of the twentieth century sought national liberation for China, France, Italy, and for the peoples of other countries only insofar as they could be included within the victor's ideological camp. When Japan and Germany were utterly prostrate at the feet of the victorious Allies, a Carthaginian peace was proposed and rejected. Instead, these states were incorporated within the economic and security systems of the victors. During the war in Vietnam, President Lyndon Johnson promised postwar aid to North Vietnam while hostilities were still under way; a Mekong River hydroelectric plan, among other ideas, was proposed to the incredulous Communists. The post–Cold War history of aid to the states of the former Soviet Union confirms this inclusive approach to victory by the parliamentary nation states.

The armies of the market state, like the Coalition forces in Iraq, do not claim the right to determine the precise outcome of a political process but rather try to provide that process with sufficient security so that its citizens can develop within their polity in their own way.

> The task of legitimate security forces is to protect people, provide public security so a political process can get going, and act in support of the rule of law. For this role forces are needed that combine soldiers, police, and civilians with the capacity to undertake various humanitarian and legal activities.[25]

Market states will gain victories when they can maximize the freedom of each citizen to achieve his or her preferred world. For each market state precisely who is a citizen and what limits are put on permissible freedom may vary enormously. For some states the only citizens will be the faithful; for some, freedom may mean the expansion of the opportunity to pursue a variety of crimes and predations without interference from the State (other than being taxed); for others, the freedom sought will be the opportunity to achieve the shared, voluntary cooperation that precludes coercion and establishes legitimacy via consent. It is notable that in his November 2004 international address, bin Laden stressed that all he really sought was noninterference from the Western governments. If there were a cosmopolitan "godfather" who could speak on behalf of an international criminal conspiracy, doubtless he would say the same.

At the beginning of the twenty-first century, we still live in nation states and their legitimating mission—to better our material well-being—still defines the contemporary state. Yet this mission is becoming harder and harder to fulfill, and publics know this. Few contemporary national groups, except those such as the Palestinians, Tamils, Basques, or Kurds, who are without states, seek their fulfillment in a relationship between their nation and the nation state. It is increasingly difficult for the nation state to execute the functions that it added to its portfolio when it superseded the state nation: not simply the maintenance of an industrial war machine of immense cost that is able to assure the physical security of its citizens, but also the preservation of civil order by means of bargaining among constituencies, the administration of juridical norms that embody a single national moral tradition, the control of the economy of the society in order to provide a continuous improvement in the material conditions of life for all classes—a control that has passed to markets—and an ever-widening scope of material benefits through government entitlements.

It can hardly be surprising that nation states face historically low levels of citizen and civil servant satisfaction. Similar dissatisfaction can be observed with the twentieth century corporation, a creation of the regulating nation state. Market regulation (and the regulation of private life, including personal matters like sex and reproduction) by the State has become increasingly unpopular. Many citizens feel they have been effectively marginalized in the political life of their societies, and political parties, unions, and elected officials themselves seem ever more marginal to the government of society. Private business organizations* have taken the initiative regarding job creation, energy policies, and even international development. It is they who determine whether the economic policies of a state merit the confidence and credit without which no state can develop. At the same time, there are new security demands on the State that require ever greater executive authority, secrecy, and revenue. The constitutional shape that will emerge from this latest phase of transformation could be configured in several different ways—as was the nation state—but these varying forms will eventually achieve a consensus as to the basis of their shared legitimacy. That basis will define the new market state.

The nation state's mission of material improvement led it to seek managerial, inclusive victories that harnessed the conquered society to the mass production and consumption of the victorious coalition. Total warfare demanded total surrender. As George Kennan put it,

> the precedents of [the American] Civil War . . . and of our participation
> in the two world wars of this [twentieth] century created not only in
> the minds of our soldiers and sailors but in the minds of many of our
> people an unspoken assumption that the normal objective of warfare

---

*See the McKinsey survey cited in chapter 2 indicating that 44 percent of U.S. business executives think businesspersons "should play a leadership role" in efforts to resolve public issues.

was the total destruction of the enemy's ability and will to resist and
his unconditional surrender.[26]

The citizens of market states will not expect the State to assure their
material success; in fact they are bound, across the many variations of
this constitutional order, to the belief that states are not especially good at
creating wealth. Rather these citizens will look for infrastructure that
increases their opportunities. As one commentator observed:

> The Nation State was defined and legitimated, in part, by its ability to
> ensure the material well being of its citizens. In contrast, the Market
> State earns its legitimacy by providing the opportunity to its citizens to
> advance their own well being. The Nation State is characterized by
> top-down, government centric solutions . . . that make absolute guar-
> antees about the material outcome of its charges. The Market State . . .
> guarantee[s] a set of basic tools and an open playing field . . .[27]

Market state warfare is directed toward civilians. For market states of
consent, the principal defense aim will be to prevent catastrophic loss of
civilian life, irrespective of the source of such losses, in order to allow
society to develop and maintain consensual government. The objective of
a society composed of information-based market states of consent is the
maintenance of a pluralistic[28] global community (as opposed to the rela-
tivism of the society of the industrial nation states, or the exceptionalism
of the imperial state nations, or the elitism of the colonial territorial states).
Thus, with respect to terrorists, the war aim is not simply the attrition of
conventional military capabilities but of the terrorists' legitimacy. A recognition of this war aim ought to govern the tactics of warfare. "Dramatic
cruise missile attacks, for example, play into the mindsets of developing
countries (and even of some US allies) affirming the belief that the US is
too powerful . . . The ironic result is an overall increase in political sympathy for the terrorists or their cause."[29]

A secondary defense goal seeks to preserve the opportunity-maximizing
assets of the State—principally infrastructure (transportation, energy,
information connectivity, and the like) as well as the institutions of education (including freedom of inquiry) and health—from depletion in warfare, which can come about either from direct attacks or through poorly
planned responses to the threats such attacks pose. For this reason states of
consent must be wary that they do not bankrupt themselves confronting
terrorism where the advantages of cost greatly favor the suicide bomber.
Interestingly, bin Laden is aware of this risk. In his winter manifesto of
2004, he urged a strategy of economic attrition against the United States

by forcing the U.S. to respond to threats (even while he decried restraints on his freedom of action as American "terrorism").

The war aims of market states of terror will be to achieve independence to coerce their own peoples, and to prevent states of consent from providing attractive examples to which the publics of the states of terror might turn for models.

The rise of market states has prompted the emergence of twenty-first century networked terrorism, and the potential for arming these terrorist networks with WMD, and an increasing vulnerability to disasters of various origins. The Wars against Terror are a response to the evolution of these threats (including the opportunities they present to states of terror), and these threats are themselves driving the growth of market states in part because they are so damaging to the legitimacy of nation states. The outcome of these wars will determine whether this new constitutional order—the market state—will be composed of states of consent or states of terror.

IV.

If market states are indeed emerging, such states' terms for victory in warfare can best be described as preclusive. The goal, whether for the market state of consent or for the market state of terror, is to preclude a certain state of affairs from coming into being. For the state of consent, it is terror itself that must be precluded, chiefly by the protection of innocent civilians. For the state of terror, it is individual self-assurance that must be prevented from spreading within a society, for once enough people refuse to be cowed it will be difficult to return them to a condition of submission. The line can be fine, of course, between protecting someone and preventing her from developing as she wishes (as every parent knows).

In the Book of Genesis, when the murderer Cain is asked where his brother Abel can be found, he replies, notoriously, with the irritated question, "Am I my brother's keeper?" Many generations (and countless sermons) have understood this phrase to mean that Cain is disclaiming responsibility for the well-being of his brother. "Am I supposed to look after my brother's well-being?" goes this reading. But this exegesis does not sound quite right; the question put to Cain was not about Abel's situation (which God already knows, as is made clear in the next verse). The Hebrew word *shamar,* which we translate as "keeper," would be better understood as "jailer"—like the keeper of a zoo, or the warden of a medieval "keep" or prison. Cain is not disclaiming a duty of care so much as sarcastically replying that Abel is free to do as he pleases—which reinforces Cain's implicit claim that he has no knowledge of what has befallen his brother.

When we consider the paradigmatic case of preclusive humanitarian intervention to prevent genocide or ethnic cleansing, we must consider these two elements, domination and responsibility. To the person, or the peoples, for whom others would assume responsibility, the exercise of that duty sometimes looks like simple authoritarianism and even exploitation (as indeed it often is). This is one legacy of nineteenth century imperialism; and there are many beneficiaries of the altruistic late-twentieth century humanitarian interventions in Somalia or Haiti or Kosovo who seethe with resentment. The intervenor has preempted the right of the suffering people to act for themselves. Though this may be justified on the grounds that without outside intervention these peoples will have no real alternative in their circumstances, yet a preclusive victory has inadvertently stimulated resistance, even hostility, to the intervenor.

These concepts are important to keep in mind when we try to understand how humanitarian intervention is related to the Wars against Terror. It is obvious that some conditions of civil chaos can breed terrorists and that the environment of a lawless state is especially propitious to harboring terrorists. Doubtless intervention against Afghanistan could have been justified on these grounds alone. But the deep connection between the Wars against Terror and the struggle to prevent crimes against humanity, such as those brought on by campaigns of genocide or ethnic cleansing, lies elsewhere: in the changing nature of the State.

Genocide and ethnic cleansing threaten world order by creating vast and unpredictable refugee flows; by embittering minorities that are easily radicalized and then turn to the global theater to exact their revenge; and finally by robbing the society of states of its self-respect because they demonstrate the unwillingness of states to enforce international norms of human rights. Palestinians, Chechens, Bosnian Muslims, and Kashmiris provide ample examples of all of these phenomena: refugee camps and destabilizing inflows into other societies, al Qaeda foot soldiers and leaders, and eloquent television images that, replayed over and over across the global media network, sicken persons in more comfortable circumstances.

Furthermore, states of terror, whether in Rwanda, Burma, or Guatemala, inevitably embroil their neighbors in conflict and become transit points for international crime[30] that must some day eventually include the lucrative clandestine trade in WMD (whether they desire to become possessors like North Korea or mere facilitators like Sudan).

Regimes that use terror to keep themselves in power legitimate themselves by arguing that they have de facto control and that this state of affairs is sufficient for legal recognition of their sovereignty and autonomy under international law. This indeed was the legal basis for the recognition of nation states in the twentieth century.[31] What is wrong with this claim—as a strategic or legal matter—in the twenty-first century? Do they threaten their neighbors, much less world order, simply by asserting such a basis for legitimacy and relying on it? To take an analogy from the Long War of the twentieth century, does the mere presence of a fascist regime in Paraguay or Portugal render it illegitimate as a legal matter and therefore liable to lawful strategic attack in the absence of any actual alliance with the fascist belligerents in Japan, Germany, and Italy?

Even if the answer is No, that does not entirely settle the point and may only underscore the difference between the Long War of the twentieth century and the Wars against Terror of the early twenty-first. The issue in the Long War had to do with whether communism, fascism, or parliamentarianism would bear the mantle of the legitimacy of the nation state. The mere presence of fascist and communist states did not necessarily threaten the parliamentary states, but when parliamentary states were attacked by revolutionary forces, as in Greece in 1947, attempting to change the basis on which the state governed, the U.S. reacted with military assistance. The issue in the Wars against Terror also has to do with the preservation of consent as a basis for the legitimacy of parliamentary states. Such states cannot thrive—perhaps cannot even survive as states of consent—in conditions of terror. That is why they pursue victories of preclusion: trying to prevent terrorist acts before they unpredictably occur, trying to preempt the proliferation of WMD before they are irrevocably deployed, trying to avert humanitarian crises before their momentum becomes irresistible. The mere development of certain threats can require precautionary diplomacy and even anticipatory military action.

A state that maintains itself by terrorizing its own people plays a pivotal role in the global twenty-first century struggle between states of consent and states of terror. One corollary of the argument that intervenors may justifiably act when people have no real choice about their affairs is that humanitarian intervention is illegal against rights-respecting consensual states that do not formally request intervention (as for example after an earthquake or famine or when the democratically chosen regime is under threat from insurgents). Another corollary is that it is impermissible to use air strikes and missiles to terrorize the civilian population of such a state; such tactics define the state of terror.

V.

In the wars of territorial states, civilian casualties were practically negligible. During the American Revolutionary War, British and American forces suffered 34,000 military casualties; civilian deaths were almost insignificant. With the arrival of total wars in the late nineteenth century this began to change. As the twentieth century progressed, the numbers of civilians killed in wars escalated. Whereas approximately 80 percent of the victims of warfare in the early twentieth century were military personnel and 20 percent were civilians, by the turn of this century this ratio had been completely reversed[32] and the percentage of civilian deaths in the early twenty-first century is approaching 90 percent.[33] Sir Lawrence Freedman has identified the crucial element—targeting civilians—that creates the war aim of preclusive victories. The objective of such victories is to reduce the capacity to do harm. He thus draws our attention to the

> important links between the acts which prompt humanitarian intervention and those that prompt a war on terrorism. In both cases the victims are most likely to be defenseless civilians. The moral objection lies in the use of violent means against non-combatants for political objectives . . . Even famine and disease, on close inspection, often turned out to be the result of "political" as much as "natural" disasters. To mitigate the effects of these disasters . . . mean[s] acting to stop large-scale abuses of human or minority rights by repressive states, calm civil wars and other forms of intercommunal violence.[34]

Here the intervening state seeks a victory for human rights that precludes both the exclusive subjugation and the inclusive incorporation of the people of the losing state. Warfare is not "pushed" by the fear aroused by the nation state, but "pulled" by the empathy evoked in the citizens of the emerging market states. Elites do not alone define the terms of victory; rather this is done in conjunction with the media, NGOs, and other private actors. Even the alliances waging war are different: in the place of the legalistic institutions of the nation state, like the United Nations and NATO, the market state seeks "coalitions of the willing,"[35] that is, consensual and voluntary groups of states who are acting not because they are bound by law to do so but rather because they choose to collaborate.

The same sort of victory is sought by states attempting to prevent the proliferation of WMD to states or groups that would use them for compellance[36] rather than deterrence.[37] Here, too, the aim is to preclude the achievement of an objective by violence against noncombatants.

The kind of victories market states will seek in the wars against global terrorism will be measured in large part by the prevailing sense of psychological well-being of their citizens. It is commonly said that terrorism does not pose "an existential" threat to societies, by which is meant that, unlike the nuclear megatonnage targeted at countries during the Cold War that could have totally destroyed a society, the terrorists mount at most, even with WMD, an attack against a few targets. It is ironic that this particular word "existential" should be chosen to express this argument, because if by "existential" we mean the attitudes typified by that grouping of philosophers that includes Nietzsche, Kierkegaard, and Heidegger, then that is precisely the sort of threat that terror poses. That is, it threatens to change the way we experience our lives, draining meaning from relationships of trust and community, and coloring life with the awful hues of suspicion, intimidation, and fear. Victory over an existential threat of this kind is never finally established because it has no essential element.

Such victories would be reflected in ever-shifting polling and media groups instead of occasional elections, and thus would be more volatile; it might be possible to "win" on the battlefield but lose before various advocacy groups, including civil-libertarian ones. Victory in a war against global, market state terrorism would be decentralized, and self-configuring. There would be no surrender, no occupied capital; there would be no victory parades. There would be the kind of peace that comes from recognizing what we have avoided rather than the release that comes after the passage through a dark period to a safe, sunlit station.

Fundamentally, victory in such a war would be a matter of precluding states of affairs that in themselves amount to losing. Victory, to be gained, must be shared, including with our adversaries in order to preclude recidivism. Unless former adherents of the terrorist network can share in a post-war security regime—be safer than they would have been had they continued the struggle—they will never leave us or themselves in peace. Plea bargains, amnesties, bribes, and other market state approaches will be more important than public relations campaigns aimed at "hearts and minds." As we saw in the preceding chapter, the war in Iraq provided a striking example of how such struggles should not be fought.

Interestingly, it was precisely a preclusive strategy that most alarmed the sinister terrorist Abu Musab al Zarqawi,[38] who directed that al Qaeda attempt to frustrate such a program by using suicide attacks on Shia civilians in order to alienate them from the U.S.—which could not protect them—and force the Sunnis to close ranks to safeguard themselves from reprisals. He, as well as others,[39] seemed to realize that the Coalition forces were too few to protect civilians, even in Baghdad, against such tactics.

VI.

The war aim of the market states of consent must be to prevent attacks on civilians. Unlike the warfare of nation states, the killing of civilians cannot be excused as "collateral" to the strategic or tactical objective either because civilians are colocated with military targets (as at Hiroshima) or because it is believed civilian casualties will weaken the will of the government to carry on (as in the firebombing of Tokyo). For states of terror, targeting civilians is the point; for states of consent, protecting them is the objective even when they may sympathize with our enemies. Or to put this the other way around: the changed war aim of market states is a consequence of the nation states' inability to protect civilians. Aspiring market states of terror attack civilians so that they can establish their legitimacy and discredit that of states of consent: they will protect civilians by ceasing their attacks. Market states of consent must change their tactics to confront this threat.

An appreciation of this changed war aim long eluded Coalition forces in Iraq. Anger at insurgent attacks provoked kinetic responses that, in any case, could not be followed through to their conclusion owing to the political backlash that resulted. Lawrence Freedman quotes a British brigadier that

> the inclination to intimidate opponents rather than to win over waverers has been a feature of pacification operations in Iraq. One analysis that he cites of operations conducted from 2003 to 2005 notes that most were reactive to insurgent activity—seeking to hunt down insurgents. Only 6% of ops were directed specifically to create a secure environment for the population.[40]

The move to a different agenda will not be an easy transition for U.S. forces to make. On the one hand, the powerful inertia of past success in conventional warfare will make it difficult for American commanders to adjust to a regimen so focused on civilians.* This is one more reason why it is imperative that we recognize that we are at war with terror.

> Without an audience to which to appeal, terrorists have much less power over time. Yet, the military campaign that the U.S. seems temperamentally and bureaucratically compelled to carry out is likely to enhance and perpetuate the anti-Western, anti-secular, anti-materialist hatred that the al Qaeda network is disseminating.[41]

---

*The Coalition in Iraq appears, however, to have finally found just such a commander. David Petraeus has been widely quoted as arguing for "a greater American combat role in protecting the Iraqi population." Michael R. Gordon, "In Troop-Level Debate, Some Would Do the Same with Less, Some Less with Less," *New York Times,* 11 September 2007, at 418. As Petraeus's own counterinsurgency advisor put it:

> Conventional war is binary. . . . It has two sides. And it's enemy-centric. What you're trying to do is figure out what the enemy is trying to do and defeat the enemy by . . . outmanoeuvring them or removing their war-making power. . . . Counterinsurgency is not like that. It's not enemy-centric. It's actually population-centric. And I think we have found over the last three or four years of evolution of the conflict in Iraq that the more we focus on the population and protecting them, the easier it is to deal with the enemy. The more we focus on the enemy, the harder it is to actually get anything done with the population.

See David Kilcullen, interview with Charlie Rose, *Charlie Rose Show* (PBS), 5 October 2007.

On the other hand, the very viciousness of terrorists tempts many other-wise sober persons into a violent rhetoric of retaliation. In an article sent to the American commander just prior to the Second Gulf War, General Charles Horner wrote:

> In the end, if we are going to lead then we must be considered the madmen of the world, capable of any action, willing to risk any thing to achieve our national interests . . . If we are to achieve noble purposes we must be prepared to act in the most ignoble manner.[42]

Such conclusions arise from a resolute refusal to recognize the sort of victory we must aim at. Their authors seem heedless of what we are fight-ing to achieve, and thus propose tactics that are easy to merge with the tac-tics of the state of terror we wish to avoid. Far from pursuing ignoble methods, we must ardently seek weapons and tactics that reflect our war aims (which must include developing a system of justice that will provide a model for states of consent under the stress of terror). Preclusive victo-ries, by their very nature, lend themselves to the use of economic and trade embargoes, inspection regimes, no-fly zones, and other uses of force short of war because these victories attempt to prevent violence with its atten-dant civilian horrors.

This has led some thoughtful individuals to examine the possibilities of developing and deploying nonlethal weapons. At present a debate is being waged between those who argue for the development of weapons that will contain violence at a minimum level, and those who contend that the emer-gence of non-state actors bent on atrocities counsels against measures that convey anything less than the message that terrorism will be met with overwhelming force.[43] In many ways this is a false debate, because the addition of nonlethal weapons (NLW) to the arsenal of the armed forces does not rule out the use of devastating force when that is appropriate. Attacking a massed force of fighters, or even a training camp, can be easily differentiated from trying to neutralize a sniper hiding in a crowd, or ter-rorists using human shields.

The U.S. Department of Defense defines NLW as "weapons systems that are explicitly designed and primarily employed so as to incapacitate personnel or material while minimizing fatalities, [and] permanent in-jury."[44] NLW include stinger grenades; 12-gauge shotgun rounds using bean bags, rubber pellets, and wood bits; 40 mm foam rubber and wood rounds; sticky and restraining foam; barrier foam; gastrointestinal convul-sives; calmative agents; malodorous agents; adhesives; superlubricants; and caustic agents.[45] Grenades, land mines, and other explosives can be adapted to fire nonlethal projectiles such as clusters of rubber balls or sponges. A number of countries, including the U.K., France, Russia, Israel, and Italy, have developed these weapons.

Many of these systems are far from deployment, and the ones with which we have experience are far from perfect. In three decades of conflict in Northern Ireland the British Army employed a range of NLW, including rubber and plastic bullets. Hundreds of injuries were reported during this period and seventeen deaths were attributed to these weapons between 1970 and 1994.[46] Plastic and rubber bullets may hit a vulnerable area of the body. Sticky foam can cover a person's mouth and nose, blocking airways. Several deaths have been attributed to electric guns, like the Taser.[47]

Some promising new technologies, like acoustic rays* and directed energy rays† may be useful in combat situations. Others, like projectile netting,‡ may be employed to prevent suicide bombings or to stop civilians mistakenly fleeing checkpoints. Still others, like the calmatives used by the Russians to rescue hostages held in a Moscow theater, are especially useful in confined spaces like an airplane (where firing bullets is problematic) or even an underground railway (where going from car to car can be deadly).

In 1996, Lieutenant General Anthony Zinni ordered a variety of NLW for the 13th Marine Expeditionary Unit assigned to cover the withdrawal of 2,500 U.N. peacekeepers from Somalia. His weapons included caltrops (sharp-edged pyramids that can puncture tires, which are especially effective against pursuing vehicles); flashbang and stinger grenades; low kinetic energy rounds that fire wooden plugs; and various chemical crowd control agents.[48] Operation United Shield was a success, and Zinni—later the general who preceded Franks as head of Central Command—was quoted as endorsing the development of NLW, saying, "I think the whole nature of warfare is changing."[49]

VII.

The war aim of the market state of terror is to bring about an environment of terror within which consensual choices—the selection of representatives and policies in a democracy, the operations of the market, the exer-

---

*This NLW emits an inaudible sound wave that disrupts internal organs with unfamiliar harmonies, causing uncontrollable nausea.

† This NLW employs millimeter waves that can, at a distance of more than a kilometer, stimulate the nerve endings in human skin, producing a powerful sensation of heat but not burning or damaging tissue. It is effective through heavy clothing and can be directed in ways that acoustic rays cannot be.

‡ This is netting embedded in a roadway (perhaps near a contested military checkpoint) to entangle a vehicle's undercarriage and tires. It can stop a 7,500-pound truck traveling at 45 miles per hour within 200 feet.

cise of religious freedom and other human rights (especially the rights of women but also the rights of vulnerable racial, religious, and ethnic groups[50])—cannot be maintained. The state of terror justifies this war aim on the grounds that, in a state of consent, there are no innocent civilians. The process of consent implicates every citizen in the decisions taken by governments in their names. Preclusive victory by states of terror attempts to preempt individual choice; preclusive victory by states of consent tries to prevent that preemption.

Thus, whether we are fighting a terrorist network, or a conventional state, or an unconventional state for that matter, the nature of "winning" will be redefined. One sees this most clearly in the cases of territories that have been attacked by U.S.-led coalitions in the last decade and that are, at this writing, in various stages of occupation, for example, Bosnia, Kosovo, Afghanistan, and Iraq.

In each of these more or less conventional states, all but one of which are members of the United Nations, success on the battlefield has not led to peace in the civil society. As of this writing, war continues at a considerable level of violence in both Afghanistan and Iraq, and whatever peaceful relations pertain in Kosovo and Bosnia are owed to the persisting occupation.[51] This does not mean, as some critics of the U.S.-U.K. alliance would have it, that we have lost these wars or even that we are losing them. It simply means that our war aims—to convert these societies to self-functioning, rule-abiding, human-rights-respecting states that do not fall back into violence—are not ultimately achievable through organized violence alone and that the battlefield is not confined to a temporal or spatial front.

From this fact some commentators are apt to conclude that the warfare in Iraq and Afghanistan really has had no impact whatsoever on the terrorist network against which the warfare is allegedly at least partly directed. This depends on equating "winning" with "eradicating terrorism," and on making the further assumption that if you are not winning *in these terms,* you must be losing. In fact, in this kind of war, not losing constitutes a kind of victory if it can be maintained at an acceptable cost.

The war against a global terror network, al Qaeda, is in an early phase. Yet already owing to the Coalition invasion of Iraq, terrorists from this network or any other cannot someday call on Saddam Hussein to supply them covertly with weapons with which to attack the West when he would not have dared to have done so directly, and when he, but not they, had the resources to buy into a clandestine market in WMD. Owing to similar warfare by an ad hoc coalition, Afghanistan can no longer shelter al Qaeda training camps, or the import of weapons (including nuclear isotopes), or travel, or the conduct of financial transactions within the cloak of state sovereignty—the usual moves by a state sponsor of terrorism. Critics of the American and British governments may be impatient that terrorism has not been eradicated, but these actions are steps toward isolating and marginalizing al Qaeda not only from what was an important ideological ally (in Afghanistan) but just as importantly from what could have become an important tactical one (in Iraq).

Perhaps most significantly, the U.S. and the U.K. have a chance to better the lives of Afghans and Iraqis in ways that can—though it is far from clear that they will—preclude those societies from returning to brutality. If, as Robert Wright has observed, "too few who opposed the war [in Iraq] understand the gravity of the terrorism problem, and too few who favored it understand the subtlety of the problem,"[52] both these elements are present when we ignore either the perilous risks run by not removing Saddam Hussein or the complex and difficult challenges posed by his removal. Yet, both risks and opportunities must be coolly gauged for victory to be achieved. States must be forthrightly assessed in order to forestall the dispersal of WMD; this is no less true, indeed it may even be more urgent, when such weapons are being sought by a regime like Saddam Hussein's than when they are already deployed. Publics in these states must also be confronted and persuaded—a task that is not possible when they are held in thrall by pitiless regimes such as ruled in Baghdad and in Kandahar.

Preclusive victory in such a war consists in preventing more dangerous weapons or more vulnerable targets from becoming accessible to terrorists or to states that might exploit them. Winning will amount to making the world safer than it otherwise would have been, which will require long campaigns and patient ones, including ongoing involvement with the defeated country. Making the world safer than it would otherwise have been might strike some commentators as a pathetically modest, even commonplace goal, but it is hardly that. The most remarkable feature of preclusive victory is precisely this anticipatory, precautionary attention to possible futures, which relies heavily on intelligence and analysis, and therefore puts enormous burdens on trusted communication with the media and the public.

The single greatest failure of the checkered course of the Coalition's intervention in Iraq has been the inadequacy of the force structure (Coalition and Iraqi) deployed there to protect civilians. Once the decision was made to dismantle the Iraqi army—a conventional war aim—it should have been clear that as many as four times as many Coalition troops were required in order to achieve the true victory of preclusion rather than the illusory victory of mere conquest. This failure arose in part because many states refused to become involved, even to the extent that France initially blocked NATO training of Iraqi policemen. Mainly, however, it is the consequence of misunderstanding what sort of victory we were seeking, with all the collateral results of this misunderstanding that were evident at Abu

Ghraib and in Guantánamo. President George W. Bush put it exactly right when he said on May 1, 2003, that "[i]n the images of falling statues we have witnessed the arrival of a new era [of warfare]."[53] But what he had in mind,* it seems, was not the era we have actually entered. Indeed the falling statue of Saddam Hussein did not mark victory—as it might have in earlier eras—but rather entry into a new era of warfare that is composed almost entirely of attacks on civilians, or assaults on those forces that attempt to prevent those attacks.

Inevitably critics will ask: Was it really a good idea to press ahead with such costly interventions when victory (as they conceive it) seems impossible to achieve? Weren't we better off with the status quo with which we lived comfortably? In reaction to such questions, political leaders will inevitably be tempted to exaggerate the clarity and imminence of threats, to stress the definitive nature of alarming prewar intelligence estimates, even to promise that traditional expectations of victory are about to be realized.

Consider the October 2001 invasion of Afghanistan. Are we better off now than we were the day before we intervened? Probably not. Before that war we knew where al Qaeda had its bases. It had not struck since September 11, 2001. A number of American and allied soldiers who became casualties were then alive and unwounded. Public opinion in Pakistan was less hostile to America. There was a greater measure of sympathy around the world for our losses in New York and Washington. We had not spent the immense sums required to fight a war halfway around the globe and then support a fragile postwar government.

There is, however, a more relevant question: Are we—the states of consent, including the U.S. and the U.K.—better off today than we would have been if we had let the Taliban continue arming and sheltering our al Qaeda enemies, many of whom we killed and captured in our intervention? Would we have been able to interdict the subsequent operations we thwarted through the interrogation of captives and the capture of documents and disk drives? My judgment (for it is a matter of judgment) is that we, and the Afghan people, are vastly better off for our having acted. We may not be better off than we were (though a great many Afghans unquestionably are)[54] but rather than we would have been had we not acted.

Similarly, as we look to the future, we must not simply ask whether our having invaded Iraq will result in our being worse off than we were before the invasion. This is Parmenides' Fallacy,[55] which compares present states of affairs not with each other (the worlds that would be actual today if we had acted differently in the past) but with the past. For we do not have the

---

*Though the president recognized a new sensitivity to the role of civilians ("[w]ith new tactics and precision weapons, we can achieve military objectives without directing violence against civilians"), he failed to acknowledge that warfare would be waged against an enemy in the midst of civilians, as in Fallujah.

option of holding time still. The urgency of removing Saddam Hussein, for example, lay in the fact that every day he stayed in power, he grew richer, and the chance of his acquiring nuclear and biological weapons increased, international inspections notwithstanding (as we subsequently saw in North Korea, Libya, and Iran, all of which were subject to IAEA inspections). Those who say sanctions were working are essentially assuming that time would stand still—that the sanctions would be continued indefinitely (with all the consequences for Iraqi civilians), that Coalition forces would credibly threaten invasion indefinitely in order to win Saddam Hussein's grudging cooperation, that the no-fly zone would have been policed indefinitely without any Iraqi success at shooting down U.S. and U.K. planes. To avoid Parmenides' Fallacy, the question we should ask is, Are we, and the Iraqi people, better off now that Saddam Hussein and his sociopathic dynasty have been removed, or would we be better off if they had not been? As Rolf Ekeus, former head of UNSCOM and one of the most distinguished diplomats of his generation, put it, it "trivializes" the Coalition's intervention against Iraq to say that it was about finding and seizing Saddam Hussein's *existing* stocks of WMD.

Those who believed that the status quo could have been indefinitely extended in Iraq through inspections thus had an obligation to tell us how the inspectors would have prevented Saddam Hussein from buying a weapon from, say, North Korea or Pakistan—which would have caused a rather dramatic change in the status quo. Supporters of the indefinite presence of inspectors focused on large weapons like missile launchers that they said we would have been able to detect (although our experience hunting for Scuds in the First Gulf War would lead one to question that assumption). Were they also considering that in the future we might have to detect and capture weapons no larger than a case of beer?

Whether they admit it or not, those who favored containment were asking for an armed American presence in the region, threatening enough to ensure continuing Iraqi compliance, as well as perpetual sanctions that would have crushed innocent Iraqis even further (mainly children, whose premature deaths owing to Saddam Hussein's manipulation of U.N. sanctions were put by UNICEF at 3,500 per month). That is because without troops on his borders, Saddam Hussein would not readmit inspectors, and without the sanctions and inspectors, he could have quickly replaced whatever outlawed weapons we were lucky enough to find and destroy. He had, we now know, diverted funds from the U.N. Oil-for-Food program, which was intended to mitigate the harsh consequences of sanctions,[56] and had received more than $10 billion in illegal profits derived from oil smuggling.[57] In testimony before Congress, the former head of the Iraq Survey Group reported that Iraq's illegal military procurement budget increased a hundredfold from 1996 to 2003, to half a billion dollars, most of which funds came from illicit oil contracts. He testified, moreover, that it was indisputable that Saddam's ambitions for Iraq included renewing his quest for WMD once sanctions were lifted.

We now also know that Saddam Hussein would have had access to a clandestine market in nuclear weapons technology. Iraqi preparations for just such a volte-face have been confirmed by the buried centrifuges uncovered and the testimony of the tightly controlled teams of Iraqi scientists interviewed after the invasion and recorded in passages seldom quoted from the report of the Iraq Survey Group.[58] This conclusion accords with the judgment of Dr. Mahdi Obeidi, Iraq's chief nuclear scientist. Obeidi was forced to work in Saddam Hussein's nuclear weapons program while his family was held hostage. "Our nuclear program could have been reconstituted at the snap of Saddam Hussein's fingers," he wrote. "Iraq scientists had the knowledge and the designs needed to jumpstart the program" when sanctions were lifted.[59] It is why Dr. David Kelly concluded that the only effective means of assuring the nonproliferation of WMD was, in his words, "regime change" *whether or not* Iraq possessed such weapons before the intervention.[60]

The war in Iraq, which is only a part of the effort to protect states of consent from states of terror, is far from over. Following the capture of Saddam Hussein, there were hopes that the anti-Coalition insurgency would subside, hopes that ignored the nature of the conflict we have entered and that confused "winning" this sort of war with the victories in past conflicts. Instead, the number of U.S. troops—and of Iraqi civilians— killed and injured has actually grown since "victory" was declared.

The bombing of Iraqi police stations, the killing of officials of the new regime, including the assassination of the president of the Iraqi Governing Council, the kidnapping and murder of civil contractors, the ambush of American and British patrols, have continued undiminished. What has materially increased is the constant predation of innocent civilians by local militias and sectarian terrorists. If these cannot be halted—if civilians cannot be protected—then we will have lost the war in Iraq. Then the question of whether it was wise to invade becomes easy to answer: it is never wise to commence an anticipatory war that is lost.

Similarly, in Afghanistan, Taliban attacks have increased, directed as in Iraq not only or even primarily against Coalition forces but against Afghan army units, international aid groups, and Afghan police and other civilians. As in Iraq, security in Afghanistan remains precarious, especially for those local persons who are trying to establish a democratic state.

Terrorist incidents have not been confined to the active theaters of war, Afghanistan and Iraq. In December 2004 there were bombing assaults on Riyadh and Istanbul, followed by an al Jazeera broadcast from bin Laden's chief associate, Ayman al Zawahiri, threatening further attacks and calling format..

for the ouster of Pakistan's pro-American president, General Musharraf. Ominously, two assassination attempts were made on the general in a ten-day period; both were near misses, and both occurred in a militarized zone that had evidently been penetrated by the plotters.

The most salient fact about these attacks, taken together, is how shrewdly they target the links between Western Coalition forces and the local groups with which those forces wish to ally. As Paul Rogers wrote in *openDemocracy*:

> In Iraq, oppositional forces demonstrate an ability to target the weaknesses in US security. Sufficient attacks on well-armed US patrols are conducted to limit American engagement with ordinary Iraqis, while much greater emphasis is placed on killing Iraqi police and security forces, politicians and public service managers, together with sustained sabotage of energy facilities . . . What is striking about all three [theaters]—Afghanistan, al-Qaida and Iraq—is the manner in which [U.S. and U.K.] opponents learn to respond to overwhelming US military superiority. In Afghanistan, the Taliban regime is terminated within three months, but two years down the line its guerrilla forces are resurgent, targeting the weak links in the Karzai administration while building relations with self-serving warlords. Meanwhile, al-Qaida [apparently retains] an ability to act that requires the United States to warn its own citizens of the potential for an attack as devastating as 9/11.[61]

We should not therefore conclude, however, that things are worse than they otherwise would have been had Coalition armies not forced a change of regime in Baghdad and Kabul, and routed the al Qaeda state-within-a-state quartered in Kandahar. We are tempted to do so if we have not made the transition in our expectations about victory that will be crucial for understanding twenty-first century warfare.

Free elections have been held for the first time in decades to choose representatives of more than 50 million persons. Events in Lebanon, Syria, Libya, Saudi Arabia, and Palestine all reflect this movement in different degrees. In Afghanistan, elections for a president and subsequently for a parliament have been successfully held. In Iraq, a new constitution has been ratified in popular elections and elections for a parliament in late 2005 brought 58 percent of the voters to the polls, despite bombings* and death threats. As the Druze leader Walid Jumblatt—no ally of the West—put it after the first set of Iraqi elections:

*There were some forty-four deaths around polling stations and at least nine separate attacks on election day.

It's strange for me to say it, but this process of change has started
because of the American invasion of Iraq. I was cynical about Iraq. But
when I saw the Iraqi people voting three weeks ago, 8 million of them,
it was the start of a new Arab world. The Syrian people, the Egyptian
people, all say that something is changing. The Berlin Wall has fallen.
We can see it.[62]

Whether this will lead, via elections or otherwise, to states of consent
or states of terror—for elections can bring regimes of terror to power, as
they did in Germany in 1933—one cannot at this point say. Surely, however, it is a necessary beginning and it recognizes what is at stake in the
Wars on Terror. In an earlier era, it would have been sufficient to put into
power mere stakeholders for Coalition states. Saddam Hussein would have
been replaced by Ahmed Chalabi,* perhaps, whose pro-Western and pro-
Israel rhetoric had captivated much of Washington. Instead, the current
prime minister of Iraq, Nouri al-Maliki, chosen by an elected parliament,
has sharply criticized the U.S. and the U.K. for not supporting an immediate cease-fire in Lebanon, a sentiment that happens to be shared by the vast
majority of his people.

It would not have been justified to invade Afghanistan or Iraq to bring
democracy to those societies. The Wars on Terror will not be won by conquest. Having invaded these countries for strategic reasons, however, there
cannot have been much choice about what sort of regime we could legitimately bring into being. In the end, we alone cannot sustain foreign states
of consent; that must be done by the peoples of those states themselves. If
we are attentive to what victory means in the Wars on Terror, however, we
will know with assurance what kind of state we must leave behind, when
we do seek regime change, and what forces† are required for a successful
transition.

VIII.

A redefinition of what winning means is not unprecedented in the history
of states. The evolution of ideas about what constitutes victory has paralleled the evolution of warfare and the constitutional order of the State. It is

*Director of the Iraqi National Congress, the umbrella organization of anti–Saddam Hussein
exiles.

†It is encouraging that Secretary of Defense Robert Gates is on record as saying, "Army soldiers
can expect to be tasked with reviving public services, rebuilding infrastructure and promoting good
governance. All these so-called nontraditional capabilities have been moved into the mainstream of
military thinking, planning and strategy, where they must stay." David S. Cloud, "Gates Says Military
Faces More Unconventional Wars," *New York Times,* 11 October 2007, http://www.nytimes.com/2007/
10/11/washington/11gates.html.

not only the Pentagon planners or the diplomats at Whitehall, however, who are trapped in an archaic attachment to large platforms, tons of ordnance, vast armies—the characteristics of the nation state at war. Rather it is also their critics who have not understood the changes taking place about them. They expect victory to be like the liberation of Paris in 1944—roses strewn, pretty girls kissed, summary justice dispensed.

In the wars of the nation state, battle deaths and casualties, including the collateral deaths that inevitably accompanied the campaigns that preceded the triumphal marches into European capitals, were measured in many hundreds of thousands, not in mere hundreds or thousands. In the current era, victory means not going back to that warfare. Yet the new kind of warfare is unlikely to yield the old kind of victories. When this expectation is frustrated, some conclude that things are worse than ever. Perhaps that is true and perhaps it is almost beside the point.

In the warfare of the twenty-first century it is unlikely that we will gain victory through battles or even through decisive attrition from small engagements. Other indicia of winning must be developed, when winning amounts to not losing in order to enable the steady expansion of zones of consent, which will be both territorial and non-territorial. To take one example, we are winning the wars against global terrorism when no successful attacks occur on our critical infrastructure—those computer-dependent links between telecommunications, banking and finance, transportation, energy, and government services without which contemporary life in the developed societies cannot be sustained—because we have made that infrastructure so resilient that attacks, when they inevitably come, are not successful. That protection involves a number of tactical methods that not only include "hardening" targets, making them more deceptive and difficult to attack, but also preempting attacks and preventing hostile elements from gaining the weapons, communications, and access necessary for a successful attack. Infrastructure, as we have seen in Iraq, is a crucial element in the creation and preservation of a state of consent.

Such "preclusive victory" has more in common with deterrence than with compellance, with reassurance than with reconquest, and yet it is novel too. It requires us to begin again each day, without the prospect that, once al Qaeda has disintegrated and bin Laden found the martyrdom he seeks, warfare will cease. On the contrary, we can see that al Qaeda is but a precursor of future market states of terror.

Our situation is well summed up by an American lieutenant colonel:

The war against al Qaeda and other terrorist groups of global reach represents the first conflict of the 21st century in which the characteristics of globalization—the enhanced mobility of people, things and ideas—have come into play . . . [C]ontrary to what historians such as

Martin van Creveld have argued, therefore, the proliferation of weapons of mass destruction and the emergence of powerful non-state actors, such as al Qaeda, do not mean the end of decisive warfare or of major wars among states. Instead we find a general shift toward less overt and more protracted forms of conflict. . . .[63]

Many things will change before we again know the peace we took for granted before September 11. For that day we learned an awful lesson about our vulnerability, which is unlikely to diminish, and we began to ponder the risks we face, which are likely to grow. These risks compel us to preclude situations so desperate that were they to come about our situation would become irretrievable.

States have long contemplated surprises that might threaten their forces—even, during the nuclear era of the Cold War, a surprise attack that would have meant the annihilation of whole societies. The possibility of such an attack, however, sat within a well-understood context of great power conflict out of which the theory of deterrence—and the ultimately successful victory of inclusion—came. We do not as yet have a new theory that deals with our new situation.

What we can say at this stage is that the logic of the war aim of the market states—to protect civilians—and the concomitant rejection of approaches like strategic bombing and "total war" that had characterized the wars of nation states inexorably leads to the conclusion that the United States and her principal allies should seriously consider regional denuclearization.[64] This controversial conclusion will be discussed in more detail subsequently.

IX.

Princely, kingly, and territorial states, and imperial state nations and nation states, all had distinctive elements in their conceptions of victory, just as they were distinguished in the ways they made war. The coming market state will fulfill this pattern because its constitutional order responds to the State's deepest requirements of legitimacy. We should, however, keep one additional thought in mind: what will be true of the U.S. and the U.K., should they develop along market state lines, will also be true of al Qaeda and other as yet unnamed terrorist organizations. They, too, will employ self-financing operations, rely on coalitions of the willing, and seek preclusive victories.[65] They, too, will be pulled by public opinion, and will be organized in a nonvertical, constantly reconfiguring way. In some ways, they are already showing us how to organize ourselves for victory. What they cannot show us is what our goals would be. Among the war aims of preclusive victory must be the preparation for, mitigation of, and effective response to many forms of terror, whether or not they originate with terrorists.

It is difficult to argue that the Wars against Terror must embrace the struggle to prevent mass terror arising from the violation of human rights by genocide and ethnic cleansing. After all, these atrocities occur in states that are profoundly not states of consent, and thus their relationship to the fear of those who live in consensual societies is highly attenuated. They may be the proper subjects of warfare, or "humanitarian intervention" as it is commonly called, but they have little to do with bringing about those conditions of terror that would delegitimate the states of consent and cause their citizens to force fundamental constitutional change. Those citizens may feel empathy with the victims, even guilt if they do not intervene, but they do not feel terror.

It is even more difficult to explain the view, much less justify it, that the Wars against Terror must also include the effort to preclude terror arising from nonvolitional sources, like earthquakes and other natural disasters. These catastrophes may indeed spread terror but they are hardly the traditional subjects of warfare. It is fanciful enough to declare war on terrorism; are we now to declare war on tsunamis and hurricanes?*

Yet advancing these arguments is one principal purpose of this chapter, for I will endeavor to show that because the market state of consent replaces the provision of security promised by nation states with the commitment to manage risks, and because market states of consent assert that pluralism grounded in human rights distinguishes them from other forms of the market state, protecting civilians from the risks of catastrophes that threaten such pluralism is a proper defense aim of those states. Indeed, safeguarding civilians from catastrophic harm is crucial to achieving such pluralism within and among such states. Furthermore, the elements of twenty-first century warfare—force structure, logistics, and weapons and matériel, as well as the law that must undergird war—are not only germane, but critical to achieving this goal. The preclusion of the worst effects of catastrophe, just as much as the preemption of terrorism and the prevention of the proliferation of WMD, is a valid objective of the Wars against Terror. Indeed, in a world where weapons can widely proliferate, only preclusion could bolster what value deterrence might still retain; if an attack could come from anyone, untraceably, then a retaliatory threat is effective against no one.

---

*In prosecuting a war against terror that mitigates and precludes civilian catastrophes arising from natural or ambiguous sources, we are not "at war" with earthquakes and typhoons any more than we were at war with bridges and railway stations in World War II. They are simply incidental objects of our strategy. We cannot preclude earthquakes but we can preclude their worst effects, including most notably the collapse of effective democratic government.

The reasons have to do with the commonalities that such preclusion shares with the struggle to preclude terrorist attacks and coercion by means of WMD. First, we cannot deter natural catastrophes or the mass violation of human rights through threats of retaliation, just as we cannot deter al Qaeda by such means. No more than Canute could command the natural tides, we cannot wholly prevent (though we can often halt) ethnic cleansing because it arises within polities and on the basis of emotions that we do not control. All these catastrophes, tsunamis and terrorist attacks alike, share two horrible traits: inevitability and unpredictability. There is a general consensus that London, for example, will be struck someday by a serious terrorist attack, bringing casualties in the thousands; the same must be said for the destruction that would follow an earthquake along California's San Andreas Fault. Like death itself, these events can be mitigated, even perhaps postponed, and their worst effects precluded, but they cannot be finally avoided.

Second, we lack strategic warning in all these cases, unlike the situation that prevailed during twentieth century conventional war. Stalin may have been stunned when the Nazis mounted Operation Barbarossa and suddenly attacked their Soviet ally, but he was not astonished. FDR was surprised by the timing of the Japanese attack on Pearl Harbor, but the reaction in Washington would have been quite different if the Canadians had attacked instead. In both cases, leaders had some sort of warning owing in part to the necessity of the enemy to mass his forces for attack and in part to the developments in political context that led to war.

Third, the effects of natural disasters and campaigns of ethnic cleansing mimic those of catastrophic military attacks. As the *New York Times* observed after a hurricane hit New Orleans in 2005:

> Total allocations for the wars in Iraq and Afghanistan and the war on terror have topped $300 billion. All that money has been appropriated as the cost of protecting the nation from terrorist attacks. But what was the worst possible case we fought to prevent? Losing a major American city.[66]

In September 2005 President George W. Bush asked Congress to provide a larger role for U.S. armed forces in responding to natural disasters within the United States based on just such a relationship. "Clearly, in the case of a terrorist attack that would be the case, but is there a natural disaster—of a certain size—," he asked, "that would then [require] the Defense Department to become the lead agency in coordinating and leading the response effort?"[67]

Fourth, the aftermath of natural catastrophes—the apparently inevitable looting, collapse of law and order, the sheer barbarism—is quite similar to the behavior we observe in the wake of warfare. Whether Rome was depopulated by barbarian attacks or by the plague, the behavior of the few remaining within the city walls was notable for its depravity and brutality. In this too natural catastrophes resemble the aftermath of armed humanitarian interventions.[68] The first effect of the earthquake in Pakistan in 2005 was widespread looting and violent anarchy, just as in New Orleans in 2005, and just as in Baghdad in 2003. Unless those who would help the victims can achieve a monopoly on violence, any reconstruction and relief will be thwarted. Achieving such a monopoly often requires armed forces.[69]

Fifth, and of increasing importance, we may be unable to determine whether a catastrophe is man-made. If an avian flu pandemic does strike in the next decade, will we be certain that the actual viral strain is not one slightly altered from the genome posted on the Internet in 2005? If we may be uncertain, at least initially, it is important that we devise responses that don't depend on certain knowledge of the true origin of the disaster. Indeed, as of this writing, we still don't know the origin of the anthrax attacks in 2001 (though we can assume that the anthrax involved in those attacks was cultured—an assumption we might not be able to make in the case of influenza). Even obviously natural disasters are not entirely free of human agency.

> . . . Hurricane Katrina feels more like a man-made disaster than a natural one. The levees, built by engineers, didn't hold; development destroyed much of the area's protective wetlands; local, state, and federal governments failed to provide a quick rescue . . . "So far as I can tell [said Yale sociologist Kai Erickson after extensive research] there's not a single person living in New Orleans who truly thinks this was a natural disaster."[70]

Sixth, the Wars against Terror have already markedly increased the capability of U.S. and U.K. forces to perform humanitarian relief, and in critical instances victories in the Wars against Terror have come as a result of successful humanitarian missions following natural disasters.

> The fact is, the Navy of the 1990s could not have responded nearly as quickly and efficiently to the tsunami as did the post-9/11 one. This is largely because of structural changes made to fight the war on terrorism. . . . September 11 has also encouraged America's blue-water (oceanic) Navy to become more of a green water, street-fighting force, adept at littoral operations, whether that means infiltrating coastal terrorist hideouts or providing onshore assistance to disaster victims.[71]

Humanitarian work in the Indian Ocean, in the Philippines, and in Pakistan has, in Robert Kaplan's words, "provided a major victory in . . . the war on terrorism."[72] Nor is this collateral benefit confined to overseas catastrophes. "Homeland security should also provide a basis for renewing America's crumbling infrastructure. Improving the nation's public health and emergency care systems are two obvious examples."[73]

Seventh, natural disasters are acute but they are also the result of slow buildups, concatenations of small events not dissimilar from the lead-up to and sudden catastrophe of WMD proliferation or terrorist attacks. The American jurist Richard Posner has pointed out that a catastrophic scenario for global warming "would happen abruptly; in the span of a decade, rising ocean levels would drown the world's coastal cities and a disrupted Gulf Stream would turn Europe to ice."[74]

Eighth and finally, like twenty-first century global terrorism or the clandestine market in WMD, the vulnerability of civilians to natural catastrophes and campaigns of genocide has been markedly increased by the globalizing forces that are ushering in the market state.

With the global population now at six billion, humans are living in urban concentrations in an unprecedented number of seismically, climatically and environmentally fragile areas. The earthquake-stricken region of Pakistan saw a doubling of its population in recent decades, certainly a factor in the death toll of more than 20,000. The tsunami in Asia last December showed the risks to the rapidly growing cities along the Indian Ocean. China's booming population occupies flood zones. Closer to home, cities like Memphis and St. Louis lie along the New Madrid fault line, responsible for a major earthquake nearly 200 years ago when those cities barely existed; and the hurricane zone along the southern Atlantic Coast [as well as the Gulf coastal regions like the New Orleans estuary] and earthquake-prone areas of California continue to be developed. More human beings are going to be killed . . . by Mother Nature than ever in history.[75]

When catastrophes of this magnitude occur, democratic societies are put under a degree of stress similar to that experienced in wartime. Lawlessness, the forming of militias, and other indicators of state collapse often follow. As argued in chapter 3, such conditions represent a challenge that only armed, constabulary forces can cope with. For the market state, the purpose of whose defense forces is to protect civilians, such events can threaten a loss of legitimacy; and for the market state of consent this invariably poses the prospect of the rise of forces of terror who present themselves as the guarantors of safe havens for the victims. In the case of the tsunami, terrorist forces were strengthened, and the conflict intensified, in Sri Lanka, but such outcomes are not inevitable. Despite al Qaeda efforts to recruit after the tsunami struck Aceh, the aftermath of that catastrophe—including especially the relief efforts by U.S. defense forces—proved to be a catalyst for rebels in the province and officials in the Indonesian government to sign a truce agreement that ended thirty years of fighting.

Even if we grant, however, that there are certain similarities between the reactions to natural catastrophes,[76] state atrocities, and the phenomena previously brought within the scope of the Wars against Terror, what do these links mean for warfare? Why is war the appropriate response? Are we going to declare war against the Janjaweed?[77] Against Mother Nature or, rather, not against catastrophes per se, but against the State's preparations for and response to catastrophes? Against FEMA? It's absurd.

Consider again, however, the arguments offered in the preceding chapter. Suppose twenty-first century warfare will consist not only in devastating and precise air strikes and other high-intensity, high-technology tactics but also in the stability operations that come in their aftermath. As the intrepid journalist Robert Kaplan has observed, "because of our military's ability to move quickly into new territory and establish security perimeters, it is emerging as the world's most effective emergency relief organization . . . undertaking relief work in places like the southern Philippines and northern Kenya to win goodwill and, informally, to pick up intelligence on America's terrorist enemies."[78]

Indeed, one reason to recognize that stability operations are a valid part of the Wars against Terror is to compel defense chiefs to reorganize their forces—and the training, composition, and equipment of those forces—as well as to oblige greater cooperation with civilian agencies, including NGOs.

If American soldiers want to be more effective . . . they'll have to be able to work in a coordinated way with, or even alongside, nongovernmental groups like Doctors Without Borders and International Red Cross. The Pentagon is a big fan of peacetime "combined ops" with foreign militaries, and this term should be expanded to include training with civilian . . . groups as well. . . . [T]he Navy [already] has plans to [embed] personnel from NGOs on its hospital ships.[79]

The American failure to stabilize and rebuild Iraq after the rapid defeat of the Iraqi army and the capture of Baghdad has given new impetus to this effort. Similarly, the apparent refusal of the Pentagon to rely on State

Department planning for a postwar Iraq has underscored the need for transdepartmental cooperation in managing what are misleadingly called "post-conflict or Phase IV[80] operations."

The previous chapter argued that in conducting warfare in the coming century, it is the *combination* of military and law enforcement means, the intermingling of the strategic and the legal, that will be decisive. This chapter goes further and suggests that relief and mitigation operations are an essential element in the stability operations that all now recognize must be part of the defense mission. Kaplan saw this early on when he wrote:

> The distinctions between war and relief, between domestic and for-
> eign deployments, are breaking down . . . [T]he disaster relief pro-
> vided by the aircraft carrier *Abraham Lincoln*[81] during the Indian
> Ocean tsunami probably did more to improve America's image in
> Asia in relation to that of China than any conventional training deploy-
> ment . . . There is no better example than Pakistan [where] hunting
> down al Qaeda in its lair will be impossible without the goodwill of the
> local population. That attitude can be generated by the relief work tak-
> ing place in [Pakistani] Kashmir . . . And it's what the future of the
> American military will be increasingly about.[82]

That is because relief operations, like stability operations, occur at the intersection of the two chief war aims of the market state of consent: the protection of civilian lives and the preservation of the rule of law (where the latter includes the maintenance of human rights). But what these operations comprise has not always been well understood.

Former U.N. secretary general Boutros Boutros-Ghali expressed the conventional understanding in his White Paper Agenda for Peace, published in 1992.[83] Peace operations come in three phases: peacemaking, which is the task of diplomats; peacekeeping or peace enforcement, which is the aim of military operations; and finally peace-building, which is the province of aid and reconstruction personnel. In a similar vein, though from a different perspective, the U.S. Department of Defense[84] concluded that peacekeeping operations occurred in this sequence: combat operations, post-combat stabilization, and reconstruction.[85] In fact, as we have most recently learned in Iraq, these various stages are by no means distinct. Perhaps more than anything, the failure of reconstruction in Iraq has undermined support there for the U.S.-led intervention, but this reconstruction could not take place without the large constabulary force the U.S. was unwilling to commit owing to the mistaken assumption that internal security would be assured once the conventional war had been won by a small, high-intensity force. At every stage of Boutros-Ghali's sequence there ought to be interpenetration of the officials and personnel involved in the other stages; at every part of the DOD's sequence there had to be armed units capable of collaborating with other armed forces as the tasks shifted backward to sieges like Fallujah, forward to stop the looting in Baghdad with less than overwhelming firepower, backward again to interdiction along the Syrian border, forward even further to setting up courts and restoring electricity.

The important relationship between preserving the rule of law and maintaining the legitimacy of states of consent in the face of awful human suffering can illuminate some of the often-misunderstood aspects of intervention. As we saw in the preceding chapter, it is not usually the case that interventions take place in failed states. Such states are not "failed" in the sense that simple disorder reigned;[86] it was rather that *law* was missing, not merely order. This is important to recognize because it helps us to see clearly the mission of the armed forces in such interventions: it is not to establish democracy but rather to legitimate the rule of law and maintain its operation. As Lord Ashdown, the successful U.N. high representative for Bosnia-Herzegovina, put it:

> In Bosnia we thought that democracy was the highest priority, and we measured it by the number of elections we could organize. In hindsight, we should have put the establishment of the rule of law first, for everything else depends on it—a functioning economy, a free and fair political system, the development of civil society, and public confidence in the police and courts.[87]

The protection of human rights falls within the ambit of the market state of consent's wars on terror for much the same reason as does the protection of civilians from natural disasters. In both cases, twenty-first century military establishments—augmented with constabulary units and reconfigured to undertake these tasks, but recognizably armed forces—are to be used to preclude situations that undermine the legitimacy of consensual governance. Criminal states terrorize their own peoples, who have no recourse to the rule of law; natural catastrophes bring terror to the people of every state, no matter how rights-respecting. In both cases the establishment (or restoration) of the rule of law is a predicate for the emergence (or maintenance) of market states of consent.

Such a mixed role for the armed forces is not without precedent. As noted in the preceding chapter, the Italian *carabinieri,* the French *gendarmerie,* and Spain's *guardia civil* all are constabulary forces that have evolved from royal army garrisons. Indeed, this is one reason why Americans were so wary of creating a standing army when their constitution was framed: just such military units had been used as tools of domestic repression. A similar sentiment lies behind the 1878 Posse Comitatus Act, which largely forbids the use of federal defense units in domestic operations, a statute that has in the past sometimes bedeviled the use of U.S. forces to aid in disaster relief and to suppress riots—just as, ironically, the 1994 U.S. statute that banned police assistance to foreign states has hamstrung U.S. efforts to develop foreign constabulary capabilities.

Yet such a role is not unheard-of even in the American context. As Robert Perito reminds us, the U.S. Army was both an enforcer of the civil peace and a protector against attack when it patrolled the American West and fought the Plains Indians. "The Texas Rangers," he says, "are the quintessential constabulary force. They fought in the US Army in the Mexican War, in the army of the Confederacy in the Civil War [and] fought Native American tribes on the frontier. [T]hey policed the US-Mexico border and were . . . law enforcement agents in the Old West [arresting] outlaws."[88] A similar role has been played in Canada by the Royal Canadian Mounted Police. Nor should we neglect the creation of homeland forces to respond to domestic catastrophes when the U.S. National Guard is deployed overseas. Lawrence Korb has proposed a Home Guard, consisting of "doctors, nurses, construction workers, firefighters, police officers, communications experts, city planners, engineers, and social workers" that would train on a voluntary basis (though paid like soldiers when deployed).[89] Some states, notably Virginia and California, already have begun such programs but this is clearly a national, not a local, problem.

X.

The Human Security Centre at the University of British Columbia issued a report in 2005 that noted a decline in every form of political violence since 1992 except terrorism. The total number of conventional wars and armed conflicts had dropped by more than 40 percent and the deadliest wars by 80 percent. The average number killed per conflict fell from 38,000 in 1950 to just over 650 in 2002.[90] But if we adjust these figures to take into account deaths by genocide and ethnic cleansing and from natural disasters, however, the trends are reversed. Consider these civilian catastrophes.

On December 26, 2004, a series of earthquakes registering 9.0 on the Richter scale struck the western littoral of northern Sumatra. These quakes, the largest since 1964, were so powerful that they slightly altered the rotation of the earth. The two strongest of these shattering subterranean events caused tsunamis[91] whose waves reached from Somalia and Kenya to Malaysia and engulfed the coasts of twelve countries, leaving more than 220,000 persons dead and another 4 million refugees. Vacationers' cameras recorded three-story waves washing persons out to sea, crashing upon

Hindu ritual bathers celebrating Full Moon Day, demolishing a prison and erasing entire villages.

U.S. military aircraft began flying search-and-rescue missions immediately after the event and military units were on the ground within three days, even before the central operations headquarters in Thailand was set up. At the height of the effort, there were almost 18,000 American military personnel deployed to the region. More than 2.4 million pounds of supplies and equipment were delivered, including U.S. Air Force drops of more than 261 tons a day for 47 days. Eighteen ships and 35 helicopters were dedicated to the mission. U.S. military medical teams treated almost 3,000 civilians.[92] Perhaps most interestingly, the U.S. command in Honolulu was able to create an innovative communications network, linking satellite systems and networks cobbled together from a wide range of civilian and military systems. This network provided text and voice messaging, collaborative software, and broadband services not only to the armed forces deployed but also to various NGOs such as Project Hope and the Red Cross.

Contrast this effort with those with which the U.S. confronted Hurricane Katrina, the sixth strongest hurricane ever recorded in the Atlantic basin.[93] It first made landfall as a Category 1 hurricane north of Miami on August 25, 2005, and, after killing a dozen persons and giving birth to several tornadoes, returned to sea. In the Gulf of Mexico the storm strengthened to a Category 5 hurricane with winds of 175 mph, then weakened as it hit land along the Louisiana coast on August 29 with 125 mph winds and slammed into the levee system that protected New Orleans from Lake Pontchartrain and the Mississippi estuarial Delta. The levees were breached and 80 percent of the city was subsequently flooded (largely by the now unbridled lake), in many places up to twenty feet deep. Whole sections of the only major freeway leaving the city were destroyed.

The official death toll stands at 1,833, the fifth highest number for a hurricane in the country's history. As of this writing, more than 500,000 persons are said to have been affected, including many who have been displaced. Over 1.2 million persons were ordered evacuated. The damage is estimated to be about $75 billion, which would make Katrina the most expensive natural disaster in history. Nor is this likely to be the worst for a while; scientists agree that we are entering an era of "superhurricanes," perhaps caused by greenhouse gases from intensifying economic development.[94]

But the meteorological data scarcely capture the full story of the catastrophe. What really occurred in late August was the abandonment of a great American city owing to the mingled incompetence and neglect of the federal officials to whom responsibility for national security, but not for relief, is principally given. Shootings, carjackings, looting, and rapes were reported, including some crimes by policemen. Shelters set up in the New Orleans Superdome became squalid and dangerous. Outside, thousands of people, most of them poor, were stranded for days; many died waiting for rescue.[95] Snipers attacked rescue workers; police deserted the city, fleeing in their patrol cars.

New Orleans is a poor, largely black city and so were many of its victims, suggesting that federal neglect was partly the result of indifference to a marginalized group. Contrary to the widely disseminated reporting at the time, however, the dead were not disproportionately poor or black. Persons over sixty—who account for about 15 percent of the population of the city—accounted for 74 percent of the deaths. Nearly half were older than seventy-five. Many were in nursing homes or hospitals—where nearly 20 percent of the victims' bodies were recovered—that were simply abandoned by their staffs. The abilities of the executive leadership of the Federal Emergency Management Agency (FEMA) were called into question after they repeatedly claimed to have been surprised by the severity of the hurricane and appeared unaware of reports of several thousand displaced persons trapped in the Superdome and the New Orleans Convention Center.[96] This made FEMA, and the Department of Homeland Security of which it was now a part, appear feckless and callous, but actually indicated flaws in these agencies that went much deeper. The failure to anticipate and prepare for an evacuation—and the vile events in the two consolidation centers—reflect profound misunderstandings of the crisis and the policies necessary to cope with it.

Katrina provoked the city's first mandatory evacuation. Although 80 percent of New Orleans residents left, as many as 100,000, including tourists, remained and 70 percent of the area's fifty-three nursing homes were not evacuated. Many of these persons had no means of exit, and the FEMA leadership decided not to assemble a fleet of buses until it had a formal request from the state (which did not come until August 31).

The hurricane struck New Orleans on Monday the 29th. On Tuesday the city began sending evacuees to the Superdome and the New Orleans Convention Center. On entering the Superdome evacuees were searched for weapons, but there was no time to do this at the convention center, which quickly filled with urban poor, prosperous but displaced hotel guests, and hospital workers and their patients. Armed groups of fifteen to twenty-five men terrorized the population, robbing evacuees at gunpoint; women were seized and raped by gangs; gunfire became routine. Police were unable to use their weapons among the dimly lit crowds that fled from hall to hall or cowered when there were muzzle flashes. When the SWAT teams that stormed the center nearly every night did apprehend some of the criminals, they were merely moved to other parts of the hall and released because the jails were flooded and there were no temporary holding cells. At one point the police simply decided to evacuate its men by helicopter, abandoning the convention center and its 15,000 persons. Only the timely arrival of 100 National Guardsmen restored order. Ultimately 10 regular police officers stationed at the Superdome and 15 to 20 at the convention center completely abandoned their posts, following the example of hundreds of policemen in other parts of the city.

The last buses arrived on Saturday, September 3. By that time, several bodies had been dumped near an exit at the convention center, a number of infants had died of dehydration, and some children were so dehydrated they had to be carried out by guardsmen. Several adults died walking to the buses at the Superdome where ten are known to have perished. At the convention center, about two dozen bodies were found, including one with multiple stab wounds. In the meantime, photographs of this disgrace were televised and broadcast around the world, along with plaintive scenes of stranded persons crying out to be evacuated.

How in the world did this occur? FEMA had been reorganized in a way, and with an agenda, that attempted to marry it to the larger purposes of the Department of Homeland Security, which was created to wage wars against terrorism on the domestic front. But far from enhancing FEMA's capabilities, these were diminished because the Bush administration took the view that FEMA's control of the preparedness budget for natural disasters had turned it into another agent of the federal entitlements programs that administration partisans, including the first FEMA director, despised.[97] This view resulted in the relinquishment of budget control ($800 million in preparedness grants since 2003[98]) and was combined with another article of political faith: that the federal government should defer to states and localities where domestic matters were concerned. Once the incentives by which FEMA had persuaded local governments to prepare for catastrophes were removed, local plans foundered. Yet it was the execution of these plans that FEMA now deemed a prerequisite for federal action.

If the American government—realizing that the Wars against Terror had no defined, foreign battle front—had never created a "homeland" security department; if the government had appreciated that maintaining order and safety in the face of a natural disaster was a crucial element in its Wars against Terror and thus could never be delegated to, or predicated upon, action by subnational political units like cities or counties; if, in other words, it had thought through the logic of its own rhetoric about the threat of twenty-first century terror, the debacle in New Orleans need not have happened. In the absence of such forethought, it became inevitable.[99]

Under the Bush administration, FEMA redefined its role offering assistance but remaining subordinate to state and local governments. "Our typical role is to work with the state in support of local and state

agencies," [said the FEMA spokesman]. . . . Rather than initiate relief
efforts—buses, food, troops, diesel fuel, rescue boats—the agency
waited for specific requests from state and local officials . . . Telephone
and cell phone service died, and throughout the crisis the state's special emergency communications system [failed, rendering officials]
unable to fully inventory the damage or clearly identify the assistance
they required from the federal government.[100]

By separating the "demand" side of terror (whose responses are activated by threats) from the preparedness and recovery "supply" side,* the
administration had unwittingly assured that when a catastrophe came the
government would be working at cross-purposes with itself so that, for
example, monies would be available for biochemical suits but not for
emergency operations centers that link communications. This observation
was made in July, before the hurricane, by the head of the National Emergency Management Association in a letter to Congress.[101]

In fact, FEMA itself had issued a report prior to September 11, 2001,
concluding that the three most likely catastrophic disasters that might
befall the U.S. were a terrorist attack on New York, a hurricane hitting
New Orleans, and an earthquake in San Francisco. One hopes that when
the third of these catastrophes occurs, the administration in power will
have learned from U.S. failures with respect to the first and second.

What was lacking was a general sense of how these threats fit in the
larger scheme of federal responsibilities[102] to combat terror, a sense not
advanced by the election of a president who had never held federal office,
and of the leadership of both houses of Congress by a party that had won
power through the sustained disparagement of federal programs. And, too,
there was little understanding of how a program of preclusion and mitigation of these threats might be implemented as part of the Wars against
Terror.

Despite the presence of the USS *Bataan* and the USS *Iwo Jima,* with
helicopters, pilots, doctors, hospital beds, and ample supplies of fresh
water[103] and deliverable food rations, these vessels were not engaged for
days but sailed offshore observing the crisis. It was not until four days after
Hurricane Katrina hit that the White House authorized sending federal
troops to New Orleans and three more days before they arrived in significant numbers.

The administration thought that FEMA's role was limited to coordinating local and state authorities.[104] When the resources of these authorities
were quickly overwhelmed, FEMA moved decisively—if unbelievably—

*See chapter 8.

to turn back offers of assistance from the private sector and other government agencies[105] (on the theory that aid would encourage persons to stay in the area that was supposed to be evacuated), and tried manfully to organize the collapsing state and local response by proposing that the state governor sign a memorandum requesting the federalizing of all relief assets. FEMA had no authority to order an evacuation, and the Department of Homeland Security had no prepared plans to use military assets for search-and-rescue missions. By failing to grasp that this was an issue of national security, the government's abundant military assets were sidelined and, it must be added, a command structure of incompetents[106] was put in place that would never have been tolerated within the national security establishment.[107]

Compare this response to that which occurred six weeks later. On October 8 an earthquake registering 7.6 on the Richter scale struck the portion of Kashmir that is within Pakistan, less than sixty-five miles from the capital of Islamabad. The major cities of Muzaffarabad, Mansehra and Balakot and numerous villages in the region were completely destroyed. The death toll, at this writing, is thought to have exceeded 73,000 with a similar number seriously injured. About 3.3 million persons have been made homeless. Owing to the difficult terrain—made more so by the destruction of roads and countless landslides—and the proximity of harsh winter weather, the provision of food and shelter for the refugees was an immediate priority. Because of the location of the affected area, it was in many ways far more difficult than providing relief to the coastal areas hit by the tsunami or the hurricane.

After two weeks, the international response was so inadequate that the leading U.N. aid official called on NATO to stage what became an awe-inspiring airlift. Jan Egeland[108] proposed "a second Berlin airbridge" and added, "We are humanitarians, we don't know how to evacuate hundreds of thousands of people in the Himalayas. But the most efficient military alliance in the world should be able to."[109] In the event, it was the U.K. and the U.S. that provided Chinook transport helicopters to ferry hundreds of tons of tents, blankets, food, and other supplies three weeks later. As in the related cases of the need for armed force to protect tsunami relief vessels from Somali pirates, or the need for a similar force to protect against predatory gangs in the aftermath of Hurricane Katrina, so too in Pakistan there was a significant role for the military in protecting the delivery of humanitarian aid to the victims of the earthquake.

Reflecting on the efforts by U.S. armed forces to provide tsunami aid to Indonesia, U.S. deputy secretary of defense Paul Wolfowitz pointed out that it was these actions that gave Indonesia's new democracy "a chance to succeed" by safeguarding the infrastructure that is critical to democracies.[110] James Fallows noted that some 79 percent of Indonesians said that their opinion of America improved because of the relief effort, and that there was a similar turnaround in Pakistan after U.S. troops helped to feed and rescue villagers in the aftermath of the earthquake there.

Now consider two final cases.

As of this writing, a conflict in the Darfur region of western Sudan has been going on for three years, most recently between the Janjaweed, a government-sponsored militia recruited from local Arab tribes, and non-Arab tribes that the Janjaweed has attempted to drive from the area. There continues to be some debate whether the government's attacks amount to genocide, but there is little doubt that there is ample factual evidence to sustain a charge of ethnic cleansing. After the horrors of Cambodia and Rwanda, there was some momentum near the end of the twentieth century for international intervention to halt such catastrophes. Why then has the world community been so reluctant to intervene in Sudan?

The answer partly has to do with the twenty-one-year-long civil war in southern Sudan between an Islamic dictatorship based in the capital, Khartoum, and Christian and animist African tribes. This war was finally terminated by an agreement in January 2005 but while it was under way, relations between "Arab"[111] and "African" tribes in the west deteriorated in a competition over arable land and water that was intensified by advancing desertification throughout the Sahel. An African insurgency found initial success in its attempt to keep the central government at bay, controlled in recent years by the National Islamic Front. In 2003 the central government changed tactics and empowered local paramilitary militia to terrorize the African tribes in Darfur, just as Belgrade had armed and supported the Serbian militias that "cleansed" Bosnia of Muslim villagers. As one commentator observed, the Janjaweed forces were "dramatically different in character, military strength and purpose from previous militia raiders. Khartoum ensured that the Janjaweed were extremely heavily armed, well-supplied, and actively coordinating with the regime's regular ground and air forces . . ."[112] Indeed, the tactics employed in Darfur are eerily reminiscent of those used in Bosnia against Muslims and by Saddam Hussein against the Kurds:

> Janjaweed assaults, typically conducted in concert with Khartoum's regular military forces (including helicopter gunships and Antonov bombers), have been comprehensively destructive of both human life and livelihood: men and boys killed *en masse*, women and girls raped or abducted, and all means of agricultural production destroyed. Thriving villages have had buildings burned, water sources poisoned, irrigation systems torn up, food and seed stocks destroyed and [orchards] cut down.[113]

Darfur's prewar population was approximately 65 percent African, or a little more than 4 million. Of these, the U.N. has been able to account for only a million, and it is widely believed that hundreds of thousands have died, as much from malnutrition and disease owing to displacement (90 percent of all African villages in the region have now been destroyed) as from violence. This combination of studied displacement and the deliberate destruction suggests a campaign that might be termed either ethnic cleansing or genocide.[114]

Before the 2004 tsunami, the U.N. termed the Darfur conflict the world's worst humanitarian crisis. Since, perhaps more than another 200,000 persons[115] are believed to have died. Why hasn't the international community put a stop to this?

Partly it is the politics of the nation state that paralyzes international institutions. The U.N. Security Council has repeatedly refused to go beyond sanctions on Sudan and the unrealistic proposal to put Janjaweed personnel on trial by the International Criminal Court if they are arrested. China wants oil from the region and has negotiated contracts with the regime in Khartoum. As the Russian military has weakened as funding has plummeted from Cold War levels, Moscow has become increasingly apprehensive about authorizing armed interventions. The North Atlantic Council, like the U.N. Security Council, has a unanimity rule. Thus France, which opposes multilateral action in Africa (though not French unilateral intervention) for fear of diluting its influence in the region, has blocked NATO from any direct role. The E.U., though its combined armed forces are more numerous than the Americans', can readily deploy only about 6 percent of its ground troops. That would doubtless be sufficient to rout the Darfur militia but there seems little political will among the member states to get involved.[116]

And why should they? As nation states define their national interests, in precisely whose interest is it to protect these destitute and vulnerable victims? Market states, however, require a common ethos in a way their predecessors did not. The Australian official Alex Tewes wrote that while nation states may be seen as fully sovereign creations "much like billiard balls bouncing off one another on a billiard table, market states are inherently dependent on other states behaving in [a way that] enables commercial and [political intercourse] to occur in a predictable fashion."[117]

Market states must demonstrate the worth of global markets and the globalizing principles—including the rule of law—that underlie such markets. In several important respects this brings situations like that in Darfur within the scope of their national interests.

First, it is very much in the interest of the emerging market states to enhance the rule of law, without which markets cannot flourish. Capitalism may thrive in corrupt, monopolistic commercial societies but efficient markets do not, for they demand not only the security of property rights, but the transparency of commercial operations, broad access to capital, and stable labor relations—all of which depend on the rule of law. Nor is this mission simply a matter of principle. Few things would validate the market state more persuasively than alleviating poverty in Africa, a task that cannot ultimately be done by direct transfers or debt relief. All the best intentions in the world cannot sustain economic growth in Africa through programs like End Poverty Now, Live 8, and the like. True, the developed world could end poverty in Africa tomorrow through direct aid—for a while. Then high birth rates, destruction of the environment, armed conflict, and corrupt regimes would bring into being a new poverty, which, it is true, could also be eradicated—temporarily—by the wealthy developed world. But at some inevitable point that world would decline to continue its ever-increasing aid to the other world it had brought into being, a world of swollen cities and ruined countrysides, without economies that can be sustained in the absence of direct transfers. Then the misery of hundreds of millions would cascade into irremediable agonies one can scarcely envision. If, however, with the opening of American and European markets, greater foreign direct investment, the security of property rights, and the changes in the role of women and family size that come in the wake of economic opportunities, sustainable economies come into being, then there is no reason why poverty cannot continue to decline. In the past decade, global poverty has been reduced by 40 percent—not by direct transfers but by global trade.

Next, the leading market states need to recognize that preventing mass brutality against civilians, as in Darfur, is an important element of the Wars against Terror. It's not only that genocide and ethnic cleansing create breeding grounds for the recruitment of terrorists, and embitter groups against the states that had the resources and did not come to their aid. It is also that these wars against civilians destabilize entire regions. In Darfur, more than a million refugees have fled to camps in neighboring countries. If the strategic principle—the war aim—that links market states of consent is the protection of civilians, nothing can lower the number of civilian deaths as dramatically as protecting the most vulnerable.

More importantly, a state that turns on its own citizens is a state of terror no matter what its constitutional evolution, and as such it will always pose a challenge to states of consent, to their self-respect, and to their legitimacy in the eyes of their own citizens. Sudan does not threaten the E.U. or the U.S., any more than Serbia did when it conducted its massacres in Kosovo. But these states of terror do threaten the fundamental premise of the market state—that it will maximize the opportunity of its people—because they suggest that that opportunity is bought at the price of allowing terror to triumph (if elsewhere), and once that bargain is struck it is a short step to the demand that a state of terror replace one's own state of consent when the going gets rough. If maximizing opportunity was worth the price of terror elsewhere, surely—at least in principle—it will seem worth the sacrifice of a few luxuries like the rule of law at home.

Finally, it may well be that the conflict in Darfur is an example of one of the many unintended consequences of globalization. If desertification has been greatly intensified by climate change, as has been recently argued,[118] then this is at least partly responsible for the heightened violence between farmers and nomadic herding tribes.

The best prospect for mitigating the catastrophe in Darfur lies with intervention by a mixed force, with soldiers drawn from the states of the African Union (which had pledged to increase its forces there to possibly 12,000 by spring 2006 though, as of the late summer 2007, only 7,000 were deployed), relying on logistical support from NATO. This is precisely the sort of cooperation that will be necessary to penetrate other No-Go areas where terrorists flourish. Darfur could be a prototype of market state success just as it has been thus far of nation state failure.

I have suggested that, using the elements of twenty-first century armed forces, market states of consent should preclude or mitigate civilian catastrophes whether they are the result of natural disasters or of state programs of genocide and ethnic cleansing. In the last example presented in this chapter I will briefly touch on a threat that could possibly be the result of either of these sources of terror.

The threat of a biological virus, such as the sort of avian flu called the "Spanish flu" that killed an estimated 25 million persons in 1918, will in the twenty-first century add ambiguity to its defining trait of lethality. Microbiologists have now pieced together the virus from fragments found in tissue samples of the flu's victims. This virus was injected in laboratory animals with horrifying results: the virus produced 39,000 times more copies of itself than regular flu and killed all the infected laboratory mice in under a week.[119] The experimenters then published the flu's genetic blueprint—its genome—on the Internet. If a virus were created from these plans, which is by no means out of the question, it could kill more persons if released than would a nuclear weapons attack on a major city.

Influenza is mankind's most contagious pathogen. It does not need to be weaponized, as it passes easily by sneezing and coughing and is capable of living for many hours outside a host, for example on door handles or in the fabrics of furniture. We have no present immunities to the Spanish flu, unlike the usual seasonal flu, and this accounts for the high mortality rates among those persons recently infected with the related avian flu, H5N1. An outbreak in any one country could engulf the world in successive waves of infection in less than twenty-four months.[120] Borders would be sealed, "people would confine themselves to their homes, global supply chains would break, and [above all] confidence in government would erode."[121]

Nor is this threat limited to viruses and other pathogens with which we are familiar. The notion that the biowarfare programs of the past will determine the template for future programs is one of several commonly held but highly dubious assumptions. Writing in the *New England Journal of Medicine,* an analyst recently concluded that this assumption—that only a certain few agents pose a plausible threat—is largely an artifact of weapons programs that predated our current knowledge of molecular biology.[122] It was once the case that certain agents were selected for biowarfare based on their natural properties and the limited technical expertise available. Anthrax and smallpox are examples. The explosion of new techniques and of automated methods will change this premise.

Moreover, large-scale industrial processes, the creation of which it was once assumed posed a barrier to the development of bioweapons, are no longer necessary for the development of potent lethal agents.

> Increasingly, the means for propagating biologic agents under controlled conditions are being made accessible to anyone . . . [M]any relevant procedures require far fewer resources than ever before . . . Today, anyone with a high school education can use widely available protocols and prepackaged kits to modify the sequence of a gene or replace genes with a microorganism; one can also purchase small, disposable, self-contained bioreactors for propagating viruses and microorganisms. Such advances continue to lower the barriers to biologic-weapons development.[123]

Nor can we rely on the customary understanding of "weaponization"—the process by which pathogens are made into usable weapons. Now scientists can resort to the mechanisms for packaging and preserving infectious agents that nature itself provides because they can manipulate the properties of those agents through genetic and biological engineering, for example, by enhancing the virulence of naturally sporulating organisms or by simply using self-replicating agents that are highly transmissible among humans.[124]

This convergence of biological terrorism and infectious diseases seems inevitable. It will bring new problems to the free flow of information on which science depends, including the science that might lead to treatment and antidotes, an issue that will be discussed in a subsequent chapter. Here I only wish to argue that public health surveillance of, and response to, emerging infections and biological terrorism should not depend upon identifying the origin of the pathogen, a task that may prove insuperable. Rather, by assimilating our response to such diseases into a broader strategy to preclude terror—including, of course, the necessary steps taken for force protection (because infectious diseases are already associated with urban warfare and low-intensity conflict)[125]—we can develop an integrated strategy that is not frustrated by ambiguities about the origin of a pathogen. This strategy must include defenses in forward areas like African, South Asian, and Latin American societies. According to the U.N. Food and Agriculture Organization, should such diseases become endemic in these states, which have at present little ability to detect or respond to disease, the emergence of a related strain easily transmitted to humans becomes almost inevitable.[126]

As with the previous subject of ethnic cleansing practiced by states of terror, there can be no tolerance for No-Go areas allegedly rendered off-limits by the sovereignty of regimes that have demonstrated no desire or capability to protect their own people. Refusing to recognize the suppression of potential pandemics as within the scope of the war aims of states of consent in their struggle against terror may seem commonsensical, but it is a dangerous, perhaps fatal policy. Disease shares with global terrorism the disturbing qualities of inevitability and unpredictability, as well as the potential to destabilize states of consent. Both are acutely threatening to the market state, the global interconnectedness of which makes it vulnerable.

Finally, seeing that the protection of the "disastered," as one writer[127] has aptly called the vulnerable community of refugees, victims, evacuees, and sheer survivors, is an important element of the Wars against Terror will enable us to better assess policy proposals to provide that protection. The linkage between twenty-first century terrorism, the proliferation of WMD, and the protection of civilians from genocide, natural disasters, and gross violations of human rights is not merely conceptual. Rather it helps us come to terms with the awful fact that progress in one dimension of this struggle often comes at the expense of success in another.

XI.

Much has been asked of the Reader in this chapter. But much also will be familiar: that with the end of the Long War, the U.S. and the U.K. no longer face the prospect of a totalitarian superpower intent on territorial cessions for ideological reasons; that this conclusion is far from utopian because it must also be said that in some ways the societies that emerged in triumph from that war, the epochal war of the twentieth century, are more vulnerable today than they have been since the end of that war, and can expect further increases in their vulnerability.

The U.S. Department of Homeland Security has prepared scenarios for fourteen plausible threats to U.S. national security: the detonation of a ten-kiloton nuclear device by terrorists; a biological attack with aerosolized anthrax; an outbreak of pneumonic plague; a flu pandemic originating in South Asia; the release of a chemical agent over a football stadium; an attack on an oil refinery; the explosion of a chlorine tank; a 7.2 magnitude earthquake; a major hurricane in a metropolitan area; three cesium-137 dirty bombs detonated in three different cities; the explosion of improvised explosive devices in sports arenas and emergency rooms; the contamina-tion of ground beef by liquid anthrax; an outbreak of foot-and-mouth dis-ease; and a cyberattack on the U.S. financial infrastructure. Every one of these scenarios represents a threat to the consensual basis of market states of consent because any one has the potential to impose a climate of terror within which consent cannot take place. The ensuing environments could jeopardize the rule of law, which is the basis for a state of consent. Each of these scenarios is a possible defeat for the strategic aims of market states of consent, and therefore precluding every one comes within the objectives of the Wars against Terror. The speed, scale, intensity, and irrevocability of these events require preclusive strategies.

On the morning of August 30, 2005, President George W. Bush deliv-ered a speech at a U.S. naval base in California. The war in Iraq, he said, was part of a global struggle against terrorists and the U.S. had no choice but to win that war or find itself at the mercy of fanatics. That same morn-ing, American television sets—indeed, the television sets of the world—were showing the immediate aftermath of Hurricane Katrina, which would ultimately prove the costliest natural disaster to date in American history. Neither the president nor the TV commentators saw much connection. But the economist and columnist Paul Krugman did. Referring to the debacle taking place in New Orleans, he wrote:

> I don't think this is a simple tale of incompetence. The reason the mil-itary wasn't rushed in to help along the Gulf Coast is, I believe, the same reason nothing was done to stop looting after the fall of Bagh-dad. Flood control was neglected for the same reason our troops in Iraq didn't get adequate armor. At a fundamental level, I'd argue, our current leaders just aren't serious about some of the essential func-tions of government. They like waging war, but they don't like pro-viding security, rescuing those in need or spending on preventive measures.[128]

The security environment of the U.S., the U.K., and other states of consent will remain complex and will include many different kinds of threats, but the principal danger will come from those threats to the globalizing principles that lie at the core of our national interests.[129] Among those threats we must now count civilian catastrophes of diverse and sometimes unknowable origins.

It is a bitter irony that the U.S. and the U.K., in the pursuit of high moral aims like the liberation of Afghanistan from the draconian nightmare of the Taliban, the release of Iraq from its captivity under Saddam Hussein and his court, and the pursuit of the murderous gang associated with bin Laden and Zawahiri, should find themselves the object of moral contempt by so much of the world. Sir Richard Dearlove, the former head of Britain's Secret Intelligence Service (MI6), has even said of America that its "cause is doomed unless it regains the moral high ground."[130]

Whether or not this is entirely fair, it does state the right goal. The states of consent, including especially the U.S. and the U.K., which have extended themselves on behalf of other societies, must have moral authority to prosecute the Wars against Terror, partly because it is necessary to win converts to our cause in order to isolate terrorists, and partly because our own self-respect is a predicate to the waging of any difficult struggle. This chapter has offered reasons why the concept of victory that is relevant to our constitutional era ought to be focused on the protection of civilians. That war aim would embrace not only the preemption of the proliferation of weapons of mass destruction, and the prevention of terrorist attacks, but also the protection of victims of catastrophes whose origin may or may not lie with terrorism.

Our moral authority can only be enhanced by this war aim, so long as it is pursued by methods that are sensitive to this goal. The Pentagon appreciates this. In February 2006 it briefed a new white paper on the Wars against Terror that was reported to state that the "way we conduct operations—choosing whether, when, where and how—can affect ideological support for terrorism."[131] Pentagon officials acknowledged that the American military's efforts to aid disaster victims in Southeast Asia and Pakistan "did more to counter terrorist ideology than any attack mission."[132]

Are these methods consistent with winning? "I know we're killing a lot, capturing a lot, collecting arms," Donald Rumsfeld, then secretary of defense, reportedly told a meeting of defense analysts. "We just don't know yet whether that is the same as winning."[133] That was 2003, and if we didn't know the answer then, we certainly do now.

Establishing and maintaining the rule of law is a strategic objective. This means, as General Rupert Smith observed, "that to operate tactically outside the law is to attack one's own war aim."[134] We must understand the larger context of what is at stake in the Wars against Terror in order to define the war aim correctly and thus provide the indicia of victory. Whereas wars in previous eras aimed for the capture of particular leaders or territory by means of battle, in the coming period conventional battles will be rare, violence will be directed almost entirely at civilians, and victory for states of consent in such wars will lie in precluding such attacks in the first place. Pursuit of the war aim of protecting civilians will require that governments use their defense forces to preclude mass terror arising from many sources, including not only market state terrorism, and nuclear and biological weapons proliferation, but also from genocide, ethnic cleansing, and even natural catastrophes. By this means—wars on terror—the states of consent can preserve their civil institutions and the environment of consent on which these institutions depend.

SUMMARY OF PART I

To summarize: Terrorism follows the constitutional order and so is therefore in the midst of a transformation (chapter 1); the new constitutional order, the market state, will arm terrorists with more lethal weapons, including nuclear and biological weapons, and more effective communications (chapter 2); a war against terror makes sense, as an idea, because terrorism has become more warlike, and war is becoming indistinguishable from counterinsurgency and counterterrorism operations (chapter 3); the war aim of the U.S. and the U.K. is to preserve states of consent by protecting civilians, and this means that the Wars against Terror will pursue three intertwined objectives: to preempt twenty-first century market state terrorism, to prevent WMD proliferation when these weapons would be used for compellance rather than deterrence, and to prevent or mitigate genocide, ethnic cleansing, and the human rights consequences of civilian catastrophes (chapter 4).

The threats we will soon face are such that we cannot afford to lose, yet to win we must reconceive victory; now that war must aim at victory newly conceived, we must change our ideas of what counts as war: the new warfare attacks innocent civilians because it challenges rights and opportunities, not nationhood or wealth or territory; finally, war is changing because states go to war on behalf of their legitimacy and the basis for legitimacy is changing.

For market states, legitimacy is based on the state's promise to maximize opportunity. For states of consent, opportunity depends upon respect for human rights and the rule of law. Indeed, that is why the new warfare of twenty-first century terrorists attacks opportunity, not territory. And that is why it is opportunity that must be defended, and why its maintenance constitutes an ongoing victory. Both states of consent and states of terror are evolving into market states. Al Qaeda no less than the United States and the European Union is becoming a devolved, decentralized, outsourcing, privatized, global, and networked entity.

In waging the Wars against Terror, states of consent suffer at present from the twentieth century's tendency to separate law and strategy. One can see this most obviously with respect to the struggle against terrorism: creating a lawless zone like Guantánamo while at the same time resisting even the appellation "war" for fear of its untoward domestic consequences have brought defeats that are perhaps best appreciated as lost battles. The same thing is true, however, in our efforts to resist the proliferation of WMD. The voluntary nature of the nonproliferation treaty (a legal matter) has been detached from the doctrine of preemption (a strategic issue) so that we approach the acquisition of nuclear weapons by Iran, for example, with neither an effective legal policy nor any real strategic options that, in the absence of lawful undergirding, would not bring a preemptive intervenor into global contempt. The fact that we do not have large-scale constabulary forces represents both a neglect of the humanitarian side of these wars as well as a refusal to recognize the emerging war aim of protecting civilians. The Lebanese invasion by Israel—a state whose security is daily under threat by Hezbollah—shows how far wrong a state of consent can go when it misapprehends the war aim and the changes under way in warfare.

If we fail to see how these three dimensions of terror together form the structure of the threat we confront in the Wars against Terror, we will make an important strategic and moral error that, ultimately, will dwarf the tactical mistakes I have called attention to in Part I. That error is a failure to appreciate how progress in each of the three different areas— against terrorism, WMD proliferation, the consequences of humanitarian catastrophes—is necessary to win those wars. Whenever one hears an argument that, for example, resources in the struggle against al Qaeda have been diverted to Iraq, one must bear in mind that that observation is not in itself a decisive criticism on the policy. We must operate in all three dimensions of these wars. It may be that the "diversion" of resources to tsunami relief will ultimately prove to have been an important move in the Wars against Terror. Moreover, we must prepare ourselves for the unwelcome possibility that these three dimensions are in some ways antagonistic, and that progress in one area increases the difficulties in another area. That, in some ways, is a good description of the human condition and of tragic choices generally.

> *Write it. Write. In ordinary ink*
> *on ordinary paper: they were given no food,*
> *they all died of hunger. "All. How many?*

It's a big meadow. How much grass
for each one?" Write: I don't know.
History counts its skeletons in round numbers.
A thousand and one remains a thousand,
as though the one had never existed. . . .

Hands come floating from blackened icons,
empty cups in their fingers.
On a spit of barbed wire,
a man was turning.
They sang with their mouths full of earth.
"A lovely song of how war strikes straight
at the heart." Write: how silent.
"Yes."

—Wislawa Szymborska, "Hunger Camp at Jaslo"

PART II

LAW AND STRATEGY IN THE DOMESTIC THEATER OF TERROR

Law was brought into the world for nothing else but to limit the natural liberty of particular men, in such manner, as they might not hurt, but assist one another, and join together against a common enemy.

—Thomas Hobbes, *Leviathan*, chapter 26

CHAPTER FIVE

The Constitutional Relationship
Between Rights and Powers

When the ignorant are taught to doubt they do not know what they safely may believe.

—Justice Oliver Wendell Holmes, Jr.[1]

I.

THERE IS A virtually universal conviction that the constitutional rights of the People and the powers of the State exist along an axial spectrum. An increase in one means a diminution of the other. On this spectrum we imagine a needle oscillating between two poles, moving toward the pole of the State's power in times of national emergency or toward the pole of the People's liberty in times of tranquillity. One recent symposium put it this way:

> The tension between national security and civil liberties fluctuates from normal times to crises; a crisis often forces the reassessment of civil rights and liberties. When people fear their security is threatened, they often are willing to acquiesce in incursions of civil liberties as a perceived trade-off to gain a sense of greater personal safety. Conversely, when people feel secure, they are inclined to bridle at even minor constraints on their personal liberties.[2]

A corollary to this conviction is the widely held belief that intelligence and law enforcement agencies constitute a threat to civil liberties. As one critic put it:

> Today everyone agrees that cooperation between the CIA and FBI is a key to preventing future terrorist attacks. But what if CIA-FBI intelligence sharing isn't about terrorist threats? What if the CIA is telling the FBI about people who criticize the president and speak out against an unpopular war?[3]

And finally, there is a third idea associated with the first two: that the courts are the chief protectors of our civil rights and civil liberties.

There is something to all of these intensely and sometimes unthinkingly held assumptions. Governments do claim more authority for law enforcement and for executive action generally in times of crisis and our liberties are correspondingly curtailed. Conscription, heightened scrutiny at airports, and restraints on battlefield reporting all offer vivid examples. Courts do, on occasion, hold the government in check in such periods. The *Pentagon Papers Case*,[4] *In rè Endo*,[5] and the recent cases arising from the Wars against Terror, *Rasul v. Bush*,[6] *Hamdi v. Rumsfeld*,[7] and *Hamdan v. Rumsfeld*,[8] are historic instances. But the spectrum view and its corollaries are so radically incomplete, and so thoroughly and unquestioningly pervasive, that they must be supplemented with a realistic link to the strategic context within which our constitutional liberties are situated, a context from which such views are often antiseptically and unreflectively disengaged.

II.

Legitimacy in governance is a constitutional matter. The reverse is also true: constitutional governing is a matter of maintaining legitimacy. In the U.S., courts affirm the legitimacy of government operations by insisting that they conform to the provisions of the American Constitution. No act by government is lawful unless it comports with the letter and spirit of the Constitution.

Among other resources for the interpretation of the U.S. Constitution, we rely on two great foundational documents: the Declaration of Independence (1776) and the Federalist Papers (1789). It is hard to overstate the importance of these eighteenth century works; each is crucial to the operation of one of the conventional modalities of constitutional interpretation, that is, to one of the key ways in which the Constitution is applied. The Declaration of Independence provides the fundamental framework of limited sovereignty that is the basis for *ethical* argument, the form of constitutional argument[9] that is most associated with the assessment of human rights claims against the government. *The Federalist* is a collection of eighty-five essays[10] that instruct us on how the ratifiers of the original, unamended Constitution understood the compact to which they were agreeing. This understanding is the basis for *historical* argument, another important form of argument by which the provisions of the Constitution are construed. Both of these classic documents bear on the subject of the relationship between rights and powers in time of war. Both address the fundamental issue of sovereignty.

Thomas Jefferson and the editorial committee to whom he grudgingly submitted his draft of the Declaration of Independence wrote the following immortal passage in the convention's open letter to the king of England:

> We hold these truths to be self-evident: that all men are created equal; that they are endowed by their Creator with certain inalienable rights; that among these are life, liberty and the pursuit of happiness; that to protect these rights, governments are instituted among men, deriving their just powers from the consent of the governed.

The Declaration directly addresses the British sovereign and is, in fact, an attempt to redefine the *sovereignty* of states. To understand "sovereignty" it is helpful to remember the origin of this concept in the body and will of the prince. Just as a man's will is sovereign as to the conduct of his body, so the prince (and later the State) were thought sovereign as to the instruments of government, that is, its internal law and external strategy.[11] The first modern states succeeded to the sovereignty of the princes who preceded them.

With this context in mind, we might read the Declaration's phrases this way:

> We hold these truths to be self-evident: that all men are created equal [that is, that no man can be another's sovereign]; that they are endowed by their Creator with certain inalienable rights [that is, that certain powers inhere in the individual and cannot be sold or given away—"alienated"—to the State, which as a consequence can therefore never be more than a limited sovereign]; that among these rights are life, liberty and the pursuit of happiness [that is, that a partial list of the necessarily retained rights over which government cannot be sovereign are those personal decisions that govern individual identity—whom to marry, where to live, what livelihood to pursue, how to worship, what to think and write, etc.]; that to protect these rights, governments are instituted among men [that is, that the purpose of government is not to grant rights, but to protect them], deriving their just powers from the consent of the governed [that is, only those delegable powers that are in fact allocated to government by the People can serve as the basis for legitimate action by the State].

For our current purposes, the crucial passage is "that to protect these [inalienable] rights governments are instituted among men, deriving their just powers [the means to protect rights] from the consent of the governed." It cannot be consistent with this fundamental idea that the appropriate exercise of the proper powers of the government can ever come at the expense of the rights of the People. Yet everybody seems to assume that they do. If the purpose of constitutional government is to protect rights, how can the State ever claim legitimacy for its acts when these acts compromise rights? Is the Jeffersonian idea unrealistic or idealistic to a contradictory degree, or is it simply misunderstood—as is the familiar phrase "all men are created equal" when it is taken to assert an unrealistic claim that talents and abilities are equally apportioned among all persons?

It will be recalled that in part 1 the fallacy of comparing present states of affairs to past ones when assessing public policy (Parmenides' Fallacy*) was discussed. Bearing that discussion in mind, the question here, in the Wars against Terror as with any decision to prosecute a war, becomes: Are the rights of the People greater or lesser than they *would otherwise have been* if the decision to go to war had not been taken? It is obvious, but no less a half-truth for being obvious, that the rights of the British people were less in 1940 than in 1936, owing to the decision of their government to oppose Nazi aggression in Europe. The appropriate analysis, however, asks whether the rights of the British were less in 1940, not than they were in 1936, but than they would have been in 1940 if their government had decided to give Hitler a free hand in Europe.

With this background, let us turn to Paper No. 1 of *The Federalist Papers,* written pseudonymously by Alexander Hamilton. In this essay, Hamilton asserts that "the vigor of government is essential to the security of liberty; . . . [in fact] their interests can never be separated."[12] This observation links the passage quoted from the Declaration of Independence to our current dilemma. It is human rights, and only such rights, that can justify increasing the vigor and power of the State because it is the purpose of the State to protect the rights of its People.† It would appear to follow from this that any increase in the "vigor" of government that comes at the expense of public liberty is illegitimate. And that would seem to suggest the apparently paradoxical conclusion that some increases in the power of the State may increase, or at the least do not diminish, the liberties of the People.

Consider the danger states of consent face from warfare waged by a global terrorist network. Al Qaeda is a network linking tens of thousands of persons worldwide—counting only those who have been through the Afghan training camps—and outsourcing operations to an unknown number of local groups. In the U.S., the U.K., Spain, and many other states these persons can infiltrate society, avoiding attention until they strike and possibly avoiding detection even after they have committed an atrocity.

---

*Parmenides' Fallacy is discussed in chapter 4. See pp. 183–184, 209.
†And thus the concept of "due liberties" also changes with the constitutional order.

Should they be able to acquire nuclear or biological weapons, terrorists from such a network could kill many thousands, even many hundreds of thousands, without disclosing their true identities.

This threat is by far the gravest we currently face to our civil rights* and civil liberties.† The Commission on the Continuity of Government's first report,[13] for example, dealt with the potential disruption of democratic government by a massive attack on the U.S. House of Representatives, depriving that body of a quorum for many months and thus crippling representative government. The vulnerability of the House poses the greatest possible threat to our civil rights, because a House deprived of a legitimate quorum couldn't pass legislation; indeed, it couldn't even declare war on its attackers until new elections were held many months later. In the meantime, the Speaker of the House—number three in the line of succession for the presidency of the United States—would be chosen by a rump session.[14] The consequences for the civil rights of U.S. citizens could scarcely be greater and would likely include the imposition of martial law.

To take another example, the judge in the 1993 World Trade Center case is still under police protection, because terrorists in Egypt—in a murderous attack on largely Swiss tourists mistakenly thought to be Americans—issued a death threat against him. What impact does attempted intimidation of the judiciary have on the right of trial by jury and the separation of powers, to say nothing of the civil rights and liberties of the judge himself? Or consider the consequences for freedom of movement of lockdowns in schools; or the effect of the bombings of synagogues and churches on the freedom of worship; or the impact on the freedom of speech of assassination threats like the one against the author Salman Rushdie. As Michael Lind has observed:

> Paradoxical as it may seem, a strong state is the precondition for individual liberty. We can go about our business unarmed only because we are confident that we are adequately protected by the government. In countries where government has crumbled or been smashed, like Afghanistan and Iraq, . . . life reverts to anarchy. People who are afraid to venture out of fortified homes are not free, whatever their abstract legal and political rights may be.[15]

If we are to protect our civil rights and civil liberties against such threats, the aggressive use of informants, surveillance, wiretaps, searches, interrogations, and even group-based profiling must be measured not only

---

*Such as rights of voting and representation, the conduct of an independent judiciary, the system of consent to governance.

†Such as the rights to free speech, the free exercise of religion, and rights of personal autonomy and individual development.

against the liberties these practices constrict, but also with respect to the liberties they may protect. Against the menaces posed by a global terrorist network, we at present have law enforcement practices more suited to apprehending burglars, drug dealers, and bank robbers. It is simply not sufficient to say that augmenting these practices with laws and practices more appropriate to counterterrorism is necessarily inconsistent with protecting our civil rights and civil liberties. Worst of all is the cant one hears that *any* significant change in our current practices means "the terrorists have won." Such remarks reflect that we really haven't thought through not only what "winning" is but also what "losing" really means. Inconvenience and annoyance occasioned by more rigorous law enforcement are to be distinguished from realistic constitutional concerns about government intrusion. Only when broadly shared constitutional understandings are breached by government can we justifiably claim that the legitimacy of that government is at risk.

In addition to strengthened law enforcement, we will need armed forces that have been reconfigured to cope with asymmetric threats. For all the good work they do, the chief protector of American constitutional rights is not the Lawyers Committee for Civil Rights or the American Civil Liberties Union or even the Supreme Court; it is the 101st Airborne Division.

III.

Will empowering the government weaken our rights? Here let us take up four hypotheticals suggested by the legal commentator Stuart Taylor.[16]

1. An anonymous informant tells the FBI about an apartment in Trenton, New Jersey. This is the city from which terrorists mailed some of the anthrax-laced letters that convulsed Washington in the autumn of 2001. Now, the informant claims, they are said to be planning more of the same. Indeed, it is said that they are about to commence an anthrax attack on New York City. Could the FBI get a search warrant? Would they get approval for a wiretap? It is unlikely, Taylor writes, because under the Supreme Court's interpretation of the Fourth Amendment, an anonymous tip usually falls well short of probable cause standards for ordinary criminal surveillance.

Or suppose the FBI learns from a wiretap that an al Qaeda terrorist, driving an orange truck, has a bomb, and plans to detonate it somewhere in Manhattan in two hours. The FBI and the local police want to search all orange trucks in the area. The chance that any one of the dozens or hundreds of orange trucks could be the one with the bomb would be far too small to amount to "probable cause" with respect to any particular truck. For this reason Taylor concluded that the FBI couldn't get a search warrant to inspect all the orange trucks in Manhattan. The Court has recently made clear, however, that government can act without probable cause or even reasonable suspicion in cases of "special needs, beyond the normal need for law enforcement." In *Indianapolis v. Edmond,* the Court struck down a roadside checkpoint program but stated that random, suspicionless checkpoint stops would be permissible when the primary purpose is not ordinary crime control.[17] The "Fourth Amendment would almost certainly permit an appropriatedly tailored roadblock set up to thwart an imminent terrorist attack." This suggests that there is a jurisprudence developing wholly outside the individualized model of suspicion that applies in ordinary crime situations (though the *Edmond* rule applies only if the government plans to use testimony from the person detained to incriminate that person at trial).[18]

2. An FBI agent stakes out the apartment, and he sees two men emerge from it and head off in opposite directions. He follows one to a mailbox, watches him mail an envelope, approaches him, grabs him when he tries to flee, and arrests him when he resists. What should the FBI agent do next? Can he aggressively press the man for information about where his companion was going? Supreme Court case law has been interpreted by a virtual consensus to say, "The agent must read him his *Miranda* rights and the agent can ask no questions if the man requests a lawyer, and unless there is probable cause linking him to criminal activity that has already been committed, the agent has to release him and let him go about his business."

3. Through a miraculous stroke of good fortune—a fire in the Manila apartment of one of the conspirators—Philippine police in January 1995 thwarted a plan to blow up eleven airliners over the Pacific using nitroglycerine pressure-sensitive bombs. In dry runs, the terrorists had already successfully smuggled packages onto these airliners. As of January 2007, the U.S. government had not yet met the January 2005 deadline that all bags carried on airlines be screened. Suppose another nineteen al Qaeda terrorists tried to smuggle nineteen bombs in checked bags onto nineteen airliners on any given morning. How many would get through? Taylor speculates perhaps somewhere between ten and fifteen, if the administration's public statements that national-origin profiling will not be tolerated are consistent with its classified instructions to security screeners. It may be true that it's bet-

ter to let a hundred guilty persons go free than to have one innocent person be detained. But is it also true that it's better that one hundred innocent people die so that one innocent person not be detained? That's the world we enter when we go from mere crime to the mass murder of twenty-first century terrorism.

IV.

Most of the rules that have hamstrung U.S. agencies in the wars against global terrorism are not constitutional in nature. Many date from the 1970s. At that time, investigations into the Watergate affair disclosed a number of very ugly executive practices: FBI spying on politicians, the wiretapping of Martin Luther King Jr., the COINTELPRO activities that began with the infiltration of the Ku Klux Klan and proceeded to the harassment of antiwar activists, and rather absurd CIA plots to embarrass and even assassinate Fidel Castro. Congress, the courts, and the executive branch itself fashioned new regulations to forbid such practices. One result of these disclosures was the extension of restrictions on the governmental power to search, wiretap, and interrogate suspected persons, including terrorists.

Government scrutiny of American citizens and resident aliens is limited to situations in which demonstrated facts, not suspicion or tips, establish probable cause that a crime has been or is about to be committed. In 1976, the attorney general issued detailed rules (not held to be required by the Constitution) that curtailed FBI agents from infiltrating and monitoring certain groups even at public meetings. No investigative scrutiny is allowed based on political activity or religious affiliation, for example. At the same time, the CIA was forbidden to spy on Americans and, with few exceptions, to conduct any intelligence collection within the United States, and NSA was forbidden to collect intelligence against U.S. "persons," including the foreign subsidiary of an American corporation. The CIA could share no foreign intelligence wiretaps with the FBI. As a result, the FBI and the Justice Department did not seek material from the CIA because it could taint prosecutions and thus cause judges to throw out cases. The FBI could not share intelligence with the CIA that the FBI gained in the course of an ongoing criminal investigation. Perhaps just as important, the Justice Department cannot, by its regulations and Supreme Court holdings construing Rule 6 of the Federal Rules of Criminal Procedure, share grand jury information with any other government agencies.

The same rules that govern a routine search for stolen goods or marijuana applied to a preventive search for a bomb or anthrax spores. To examine a dwelling, obtain a wiretap, or thoroughly inspect a car or truck, the government had to be able to persuade a judge that the search was likely to uncover evidence of a crime that had already been committed or was imminent. The FBI couldn't interrogate Zacharias Moussaoui[19] even after the September 11 crimes because he had asked for a lawyer. Everyone knows the drill: you have the right to remain silent; you have the right to a lawyer. Once a lawyer has been requested, the police can't ask any questions until the lawyer arrives, and he will immediately tell his client to shut up and not say anything. This is not a constitutional rule against the collection of evidence per se, but rather against the introduction in any subsequent trial of incriminating evidence that is the fruit of a collection the courts have declared improper on nonconstitutional grounds.[20] Nevertheless its effect is to render such questioning presumptively unlawful. What purpose, it is assumed, could such information lawfully serve if not for use in trial?

Such restraints do not apply to U.S. operatives collecting intelligence abroad, and this has led to a culture of separation between domestic and international intelligence activities. As one critic of U.S. practices explained before September 11, "Essentially, the FBI is constrained by constitutional protections and dedicated to gathering evidence and enforcing the law. The CIA specializes in stealing secrets, skirting the law and not getting caught."[21]

Al Qaeda, however, moves in real time between these two spheres, and while U.S. agencies may not play by rules of law when they are abroad, the domestic jurisdictions within which they find themselves when abroad will ultimately limit them sharply. Two cases come to mind.

First, in the summer of 2006 an Italian appeals court ordered the arrest of nineteen CIA agents. Overturning a lower court decision, the court of appeals issued arrest warrants arising from the abduction of the radical Muslim cleric Osama Mustapha Hassan, also known as Abu Omar. It was alleged that American intelligence agents had followed Hassan, an Egyptian who had been living as a refugee in Italy since 1997, and kidnapped him, taking him to the U.S. base at Aviano, from which he was flown to Egypt. Hassan also asserted after his release that, while in the custody of Egyptian police, he had been tortured with electric shocks.[22]

Such an operation is an example of the practice of "extraordinary rendition" by which a possible terrorist is returned to his native country and interrogated there, presumably because the methods of interrogation are more severe than in the host country and because the laws of the host country, in this case Italy, would not permit an extradition by ordinary legal means precisely because of concern over the conditions of custody. As of this writing, the Americans sought by Italian authorities are still fugitives.

Second, in late 2003 a German judge in Hamburg freed a Moroccan charged with having been a co-conspirator of the September 11 hijackers. The judge acted when he received a letter from the German national police, the Federal Criminal Agency, that included testimony by an unnamed witness who asserted that only four members of the Hamburg cell responsible for the 9/11 attacks—three of the pilots and the acknowledged co-conspirator Ramzi bin al-Shibh—knew of the attacks in advance. This claim, if true, would have exonerated the Moroccan, Abdelghani Mzoudi. Mzoudi lived with bin al-Shibh in Mohammed Atta's Hamburg apartment, had visited Afghanistan, and had transferred money to a co-conspirator.

By simple deduction, the judge concluded that the one person who could have truthfully made the assertion that only four people in Hamburg knew of the cell's mission had to be Ramzi bin al-Shibh, the other three having died in the attack. Bin al-Shibh had been arrested in Pakistan one year after September 11 and was in American custody. The German judge assumed, not implausibly, that the Federal Criminal Agency had received reports of bin al-Shibh's interrogation from the Americans who had seized him in Pakistan.

Despite what he conceded to be strong doubts about the reliability of such exculpatory claims, the judge felt compelled to discharge the prisoner on the grounds that the actual truth of the statement could not be judged in the absence of testimony by bin al-Shibh himself, whom the Americans had no intention of bringing to Germany and producing in open court. The judge stated, "[We] have many questions about the credibility of this information, but there is no possibility to verify bin al-Shibh's statements," and thus he granted the defense lawyers' request for an immediate release of Mzoudi.[23] This action was taken despite evidence that members of the cell—including Mzoudi, bin al-Shibh, and another Moroccan, Mounir el-Motassadeq—had fled Hamburg in the weeks before September 11, and knew of the plans for the attacks. Motassadeq was the only person who has been tried and convicted in connection with September 11 and that conviction has now been overturned on similar grounds by the German courts.[24]

To avoid such fiascoes in U.S. courts, the American government undertook a number of measures to facilitate the war against global terrorism. These measures have been the subject of considerable adverse comment.

V.

In the immediate aftermath of the September 11 attacks, the U.S. government introduced extensive legislation and also acted through executive orders on the basis of preexisting authority. The president declared various statutory states of emergency.[25] On September 18, he signed Joint Resolution 23 authorizing the use of military force.[26] Like a declaration of war, a joint resolution is passed by both houses of Congress and signed into law by the president. It is one of several constitutional routes by which the Congress can take the country to war.[27] Pursuant to this authority, the U.S. deployed 29,000 military personnel in two carrier battle groups as well as an amphibious ready group and several hundred military aircraft. A U.N. resolution supporting the invasion of Afghanistan was sought by the U.S. and adopted unanimously by the Security Council. Warfare commenced on October 7, 2001, against Taliban and al Qaeda forces, leading to a number of traditional wartime legislative measures. For example, the 2002 Appropriations Act was amended to include war bonds. Other bills dealt with war profiteering, farm credit to reservists, and pensions to veterans who saw active duty. Congress initially provided $320 million for aid to the Afghan people. Sanctions were lifted against Pakistan and India, which had been imposed after these two states conducted nuclear weapons tests,[28] and $100 million in aid was sent to Pakistan. The U.S. signed a free trade agreement with Jordan (only the third country ever to enjoy such status), and Indonesia was designated as a "beneficiary development country" with various trade benefits.

Some of the statutory, regulatory, and executive steps taken at this time by Washington have proved highly controversial, including an extensive program of detentions and interrogations. The USA Patriot Act, signed on October 26, 2001, provided for a number of law enforcement reforms, as well as criminalizing aid to designated terrorist organizations. There is little point in subjecting this complex statute to detailed analysis here.[29] Three aspects of this law, however, are worth scrutiny because they reflect genuinely difficult problems that arise when twenty-first century terrorism must be addressed by twentieth century law enforcement. Whatever the fate of the bombastically named Patriot Act, these questions are likely to be with us for some time. They arise from the insistent need to fashion rules governing the investigation of suspects in order to prevent further terrorist atrocities without infecting the ordinary processes of the criminal law.

(a) Section 218 of the USA Patriot Act amends the Foreign Intelligence Surveillance Act (FISA), which was originally enacted in 1978 to provide a second, national-security track for the authorization of wiretaps. Before the post-Watergate revelations of abuses of FBI authority, wiretaps for intelligence purposes had simply bypassed the standard procedure for criminal investigations, which required a showing that a crime had probably been committed or was impending, and for searches also generally required prior notice to the person whose premises were to be searched. As a reaction to the disclosures made during the Watergate hearings, this uninhibited track for intelligence surveillance was closed (until it was reopened without public notice by the Bush administration after 9/11), and a period ensued when intelligence surveillance came within the standard criminal procedures. This situation was plainly untenable: imagine notifying an embassy that the FBI planned to search its wastebaskets before the search could be conducted.[30] FISA was an effort to redress the many problems that resulted from this mésalliance between counterespionage and ordinary criminal prosecution.

FISA granted the FBI authority to carry out searches and electronic surveillance against the agents of foreign governments when permission to do so was granted by a special FISA court that reviewed applications by the Department of Justice. The traditional requirement of "probable cause" to believe that a crime has been or is being committed was relaxed. If there was probable cause that the target of surveillance was a foreign power or the agent of a foreign power, regardless of whether the target was suspected of a particular crime—unless the target was a "U.S. person"— surveillance without prior notification was permitted. Surveillance against "U.S. persons" (citizens or resident aliens in the U.S. or U.S. businesses) still required probable cause that the target was engaged in espionage in violation of U.S. criminal provisions. The collection of foreign intelligence had to be the sole or primary purpose of the surveillance and, by regulations pursuant to FISA, "minimization" rules (designed to prevent the disclosure of the identities of U.S. persons) made it exceedingly difficult for prosecutors to collaborate with intelligence collectors.[31]

One can see the problems terrorists pose for such a statute. First, many terrorists are not accredited to a foreign power. Second, they may be U.S. persons who, though gathering information or assisting terrorists, are not conducting espionage. Third, even if the "primary" purpose of the surveillance was to uncover a crime, so long as a significant reason for the intrusion was to prevent terrorism it made sense to permit surveillance without prior notice, and without the assurance that the crime had already been committed. Terrorists were not simply criminals, but they were not foreign spies either. A new statutory model was needed.

This led to Section 218 of the Patriot Act, amending FISA to include wiretaps on international terrorists, and requiring only that the collection of intelligence be a "significant" purpose of the investigation. This change led to fears that the new national security track for wiretaps and searches would be used by prosecutors trying to evade the Fourth Amendment's probable cause requirements for ordinary criminal warrants. In what sometimes seems to have been an obtuse pattern, the administration did in fact take an aggressive position by claiming that the new procedures would "allow [FISA] to be used primarily for a law enforcement purpose."[32] This was too much for the Foreign Intelligence Surveillance Court, the court that reviews applications for surveillance in secret. In an unprecedented public opinion, the court found that such a proposal would lead to criminal prosecutors having "a significant role in directing FISA surveillance and searches from start to finish . . . guiding them to criminal prosecution."[33] The court unanimously rejected the government's proposed procedures, holding that "law enforcement officials shall not make recommendations to intelligence officials concerning the initiation, operation, continuation or expansion of FISA searches or surveillances."[34]

This went too far for the special FISA court of review. Their opinion held that while it was absurd not to permit FISA warrants for intelligence collection on terrorists as well as their prosecution, FISA warrants could not be used to seek evidence of ordinary crimes.

While it is deplorable that the Department of Justice is so tone-deaf to the need for public approval of its actions in an uncharted area of the law, FISA reform is urgently needed.

> We were at war with terrorists who were armed with disposable cell phones and encrypted emails buried in a global multibillion-communications-per-day system. It seemed crazy to require [a separate warrant to intercept] each communication under a legal regime that was designed before technological revolutions brought us high-speed fiber-optic networks, the public Internet, e-mail, and ten-dollar cell phones.[35]

(b) Following the September attacks, the government rapidly compiled a list of all males ages eighteen to thirty-three of Middle Eastern and European origin who had entered the U.S. after January 2000. More than two hundred American universities were later contacted for the names of students from Islamic countries. By September 17, 2001, the Immigration and Naturalization Service had tasked more than half its investigators to track down persons who it believed might be terrorists or who might have information about terrorists. Subsequently the government questioned more than 5,000 noncitizens and held more than 1,200 for further interrogation.

The Patriot Act mandates the detention of any alien determined by the attorney general to be connected to terrorism. No term for this detention is provided, and thus it could last either until the suspect is deported or is determined no longer to be a threat. In fact, only a handful of those detained were considered material witnesses with regard to acts of terrorism; the rest were either charged with criminal offenses unrelated to terrorism, released, deported, or held on immigration violations.

Three elements of this procedure attracted the most negative reaction: the refusal to publish the names of the persons detained; the order by the Bureau of Prisons that communications between prisoners and their attorneys might be monitored;[36] and the lack of any adjudicatory process by which a fixed term of detention was determined.

The refusal of the government to disclose the names of the detainees was given immense publicity and was repudiated in an opinion by a federal district court. It raised the specter of someone simply disappearing from society without anyone knowing that an arrest and detention had taken place. This widespread portrayal of the detentions may have been at odds with the true context. According to the government and some well-placed observers,[37] the detainees themselves were in fact free to disclose their identities to anyone they wished.[38] Rather it was the media that, having filed demands for lists of those detained, were not provided with names. In the course of the ensuing outrage from the media, it was not reported that the disclosure of such lists without the consent of the detained puts detainees in jeopardy, especially deportees whose personal security might be threatened when they were returned. If, however, the administration has misled the public and some detainees were not allowed to inform other persons of their detention, as other observers have charged,[39] then the procedures fail to meet minimum standards of due process.

And, too, there were legitimate grounds to fear that attorneys might be used as accomplices. An al Qaeda training manual captured in Manchester, Great Britain, discusses at some length how American legal protections can be exploited, including the use of counsel.[40] But there are also, in the ordinary criminal context, well understood regulations by which orders can be sought to monitor attorney-client conversations so long as the evidence generated is not admissible at trial. These rules ought to be sufficient in the context of the detention of alleged terrorists.

The nature of the actual detentions posed a more serious problem. It was not simply the dragnet that preceded them but the conditions of arrest and confinement that were troublesome. Many hundreds of Middle Eastern men, almost all of whom were innocent of anything but minor immigration violations, were imprisoned with criminals and treated as such. It may well be that these detentions disrupted al Qaeda networks and the communications within and among cells. This may have bought the U.S. time: when a member of a terrorist group is detained, the group typically disbands, flees the country, and destroys its plans, having assumed, as it must, that it has been compromised.[41] If this was the case, then this was an undeniable benefit to the U.S., purchased at the price of hugely disrupting the lives of a great many innocent persons. Almost all the detained men had less in common with ordinary criminals than with draftees who had been conscripted to provide a service to the country's security; they should have been treated accordingly. Among other things, they should have been compensated financially when no evidence of complicity in terror attacks was found.

The creative lawyering by which immigration statutes and rules governing material witnesses were stitched together to capture a group of aliens on grounds having nothing to do with immigration is likely to prove a troubling precedent. Governments ought not to be relieved of constitutional standards for action merely because they choose to act against aliens. Rather, aliens and citizens should be subject to the same rules where terrorism is concerned, barring some particular reason to do otherwise. This will check the government when it attempts to act too aggressively against aliens, and it will reflect the reality of the war on terror, especially in Europe: "enemy aliens" who might serve in the armies of hostile states are no longer necessarily the problem.[42]

Many suspected terrorists cannot be brought to trial owing to the sensitivity of the evidence, the required standard of proof, and the exclusion of hearsay gathered from foreign interrogations. Furthermore, there is the risk of disclosing the identity of undercover agents and informants. What is needed in the U.S. is a preventive detention statute perhaps similar in some respects to those of the Netherlands, Great Britain, Spain, and France. Because such a statute would be limited to terrorists associated with al Qaeda or a global network, because the conditions of confinement would be considerably better than those of ordinary prisoners, and because there would be an independent judicial assessment of the possibility of bringing the suspected terrorists to trial and of the evidence supporting confinement, such a statute would be more restrictive of government than is the current British, French, or German law.[43]

On December 16, 2004, in Britain, the Law Lords found the British Anti-Terrorism, Crime and Security Act to be impermissibly discriminatory against foreign nationals—sixteen of whom were being detained—because the provisions of the Act did not also apply to British citizens. This not unreasonable holding,[44] however, was buttressed by a much more troubling finding that the British government's exercise of an "opt-out" clause from the European Human Rights Convention for national emergencies was unjustified. Such a holding, in its small way, brings us closer to a time when something truly dreadful happens and law is swept aside because it has been rendered irrelevant by flamboyant acts of judicial self-satisfaction. Only Monty Python could do justice to the judicial expressions of complacency that, remarkably, cited the reaction to the train bombings in Madrid as supporting its conclusions of how modest a threat terrorists posed to the political order.

In fact, in Spain terrorist suspects can be held for up to thirteen days without charge and as long as four years without trial. In France, persons suspected of merely associating with terrorists can be imprisoned. After the murder of filmmaker Theo Van Gogh in 2004, the Dutch government sought to allow prosecutors to use intelligence reports as evidence without revealing their source and to lower the threshold required for police to hold suspects without charge.

The solution must lie in some mixture of contested hearings—trials with evidentiary rules tailored to the context of terrorism—appeals, and surveillance. As a *Guardian* editorial pointed out after the Law Lords' opinion came down, "technology has given governments much greater capacity to keep suspects under surveillance,"[45] and this ought to be part of the response to this problem. Persons—whether citizens, residents, or aliens—should not be arrested in the U.S. and jailed unless they have committed some serious offense.[46] If the government wishes to detain a person on other grounds, some statutory provision should be created that specifies a certain period—perhaps forty-five days[47]—after which the government would have to charge that person or release him; that specifies daily payment—perhaps $500[48]—and nonprison conditions; and that requires an initial hearing at which the government would record its grounds for reasonable suspicion. Additionally, there must be some intermediate step between detention and prison, relying on the technologies that are available to limit a person's access to certain buildings, financial instruments, weapons, foreign travel, and communications, upon a showing of just cause by the authorities. Finally in July 2006, in the wake of an adverse Supreme Court ruling, the Bush administration asked Congress for legislation that would clarify the rights owed to detainees. It is disgraceful that the Congress had not acted prior to this executive branch nudge, but it may be that the responsibility for this dereliction is partly to be laid at the steps of the White House, which for some time actively discouraged legislation on this matter.

(c) Usually, when a person's private habitat is searched, law enforcement officials must announce themselves before entering. In the U.S. this is a court-recognized requirement of the Fourth Amendment's guarantee against unreasonable searches and seizures, but the "knock and announce" requirement actually antedates the American Bill of Rights.[49] Nevertheless, there are precedents[50] recognizing that when the intent is to deter criminal behavior—the destruction of evidence, for example—the standard notice that is otherwise given when a suspect's property is searched for evidence of a crime that has already been committed can be delayed. Such searches are called "sneak and peek," and Section 213 of the Patriot Act codifies this federal case law.

Section 213 allows federal agents covertly to enter a person's home or office when the government can show it has "reasonable cause" to believe that providing immediate notification of the execution of a warrant may have an adverse result. There has been an enormous outcry in the civil liberties community and in the defense bar over this provision. This reaction provoked a vote in the House of Representatives to suspend Section 213.

As with other controversial measures proposed by the Department of Justice in the aftermath of September 11, codification of "sneak and peek" warrants has long been sought by prosecutors. The government simply took advantage of the political momentum provided by the terrorist atrocities to win passage of a law it much desired. The difficulty is that, while these powers are not limited to antiterrorism investigations, there is plainly ample justification for their use in legitimate antiterrorist activities. In such cases, it is the prospective prevention of harm that is paramount, rather than the retrospective punishment for harm that has already occurred. In this instance, one may question whether we have been well served either by the government that aggressively overreached or by the civil liberties lobby that appears to be in a state of denial about the global terrorist threat. Each community sometimes seems mesmerized by the other and by their shared history of past struggles.

(d) As observed earlier, the customary practices and habits of law enforcement and prosecution are ill-suited to fighting the wars against global terrorism. Conducting such a war also requires measures that go against the grain of the increasing transparency we expect from the State and the increasing privacy we wish for ourselves, both of which are functions of the ubiquity and penetration of the communications media. The debate over national identity cards[51] reflects the latter concern about privacy and the carefully chosen, rather than inherited or assigned, nature of individual identity in the market state, while the use of public threat warnings reflects concern about transparency in government. In a market state all persons are presumed to be sovereign consumers, and they are therefore dependent on information to make their individual decisions.

No other liberal, democratic state has so openly shared its fears about possible attacks with its public as has the U.S.[52] Bizarrely, the governor of California at one time went so far as to issue a warning against the use of public bridges throughout his state. The principal culprits, however, were the attorney general and the secretary for homeland security, two prominent Republican politicians—one a defeated U.S. senator, the other a former state governor—without any significant experience handling intelligence or planning global warfare. It is they who implemented the system of nationwide alerts, usually announced by themselves on national television, until they risked becoming figures of ridicule and delegated these tasks to their subordinates.

The first nationwide alert came precisely one month after the attacks of September 11, 2001. This was followed by a similar alert two and a half weeks later, called a "credible threat warning" of indefinite extension. In other words, the public was told that the government had plausible, believable information of an attack, the precise location or nature of which it could not share (if in fact it knew). Eventually, the FBI would issue five nationwide alerts, none of which was followed by a terrorist incident.

Perhaps recognizing the uselessness from any point of view (except that of the terrorists who were trying to frighten the country, and of the administration, which did not want to be caught napping a second time), the government devised a system that permitted the alarm bell to be shut off and the seriousness of the threat to be calibrated, or at least appear to be calibrated.

This was the color-coded Homeland Security Assessment System (HSAS). It had two parts: an alert that could be raised or lowered depending on the threat assessment, and a series of suggested measures that accompanied each level of alert. It was described by the government this way:

> Threat Conditions [the colors] characterize the risk of terrorist attack. Protective Measures are the steps that will be taken by government and the private sector to reduce vulnerabilities. The HSAS establishes five Threat Conditions with associated suggested Protective Measures.[53]

This "system," if that is the right term for a congeries of unsystematic ideas, was announced jointly by the attorney general and the secretary for homeland security on March 12, 2002. On September 10 of that year, they raised the threat level from Yellow ("elevated") to Orange ("high"), noting that communications intercepts had indicated the desire by terrorists to commit some outrage on the anniversary of the previous year's atrocity. Nothing happened, and so two weeks later the level was reduced to Yellow. Since the initiation of the HSAS, the U.S. has oscillated between Yellow and Orange levels of concern. Presumably none of the protective measures of Yellow remain to be done when shifting back to that status, and state, local, and federal governments have already undertaken all of the recommended protective measures when the country goes back to Orange status. The vagueness and generality of these recommendations and their permissive language—"may be applied"—makes one wonder precisely what coordinated, effective guidance is intended. In any case, at those threat levels none of the recommended measures apply to the citizenry at large, whose benefit, if any, is simply to be told that things have gotten worse (or somewhat better).

On February 7 the following year, the level was raised again to Orange, apparently on the basis of intercepts indicating plans to perpetrate terrorist acts at the end of the hajj, the annual Muslim pilgrimage to holy sites in Saudi Arabia, in mid-February. These warnings came after the bombings in Bali and the attacks in Mombasa. But nothing new occurred, and the level was reduced again to Yellow.

On March 17, 2003, the attorney general and the secretary announced another move to Orange status. One month later, the threat level was reassessed at Yellow. On May 20, it was raised again to Orange, then, on May 30, lowered to Yellow.

Only the alert on December 21, 2003, was accompanied by any specific, visible measures. This time, sixteen international flights were cancelled, and scores of passengers were interviewed. It was estimated that the alert cost state and federal governments as much as $3 billion, but this figure was contested by the administration.[54] Sectors like aviation were given explicit priority, and some regions were put on higher alert, resulting in what security officials called the "Yellow-and-a-half" decision to put additional police, bomb-sniffing dogs, and more intensive vehicle inspections in place for some cities. Nothing untoward occurred, no arrests were made, and on January 9, 2004, the level was reduced again to Yellow.

One hopes that the reason no new attack on the American homeland has occurred is because the detentions in the U.S., the captures in Afghanistan and Pakistan of senior al Qaeda figures, and the interrogations that accompanied these arrests have blocked the plans of terrorists. It may be, also, that al Qaeda strategy has changed, at least for the time being. And, of course, one knows that sooner or later, regardless of the color of the alert, new attacks will come. The issue remains, however, what positive contributions such national alerts actually make to the well-being of the public.

Both the U.S. and British governments have come in for criticism about how they alert their publics to impending terror attacks. In London, then minister for home affairs David Blunkett was accused of keeping the public uninformed as to the extent of the terrorist threat to Britain. Tory opponents challenged him to release as much detail as the Bush administration had in the United States. In the U.S., the secretary for homeland security, Tom Ridge, was accused of playing election year politics by ratcheting up the alert level while praising "the President's leadership in the war against terror." The problem reached such a crisis that it now appears that a substantial intelligence asset was compromised in one official's desperation to convince the media that yes, there really was information about an imminent attack even though some of it was years old.

There was a time when societies at war were willing to trust their leaders to decide when, from a strategic point of view, information could be safely released to the public. In a way, this trust was responsible for the famous Coventry legend, the false story that Winston Churchill permitted the city of Coventry to be attacked without warning, despite his knowing through decoded intercepts that the city was about to be bombed, so that he could keep the secret that the British were reading encrypted German radio signals.

Different attitudes prevail today in Britain and the United States. It is simply intolerable that officials might know about an impending attack and not make this knowledge public so that individual citizens could decide for themselves whether to run risks that, in the past, were calculated by governments alone. No one, official or otherwise, is allowed to have potentially lifesaving information and not share it.

One must have some sympathy with the governments of both countries. On the one hand, no official wants to neglect to give a warning that might save lives; on the other hand, the strategy of asymmetric warfare is to use the target's strength against itself. If a terrorist network can, through the deceptive use of communications, including debriefings, cause a state of alarm without actually having to do anything, it has scored a minor success. If the attacker through the costless tactic of making threats can force the target state to multiply defensive measures, the attacker has, for the time being, won a relative victory when those measures cannot be indefinitely maintained at a reasonable cost. If officials then try to minimize the impact of the warning with suggestions that the public go about its business as usual, they dilute the effectiveness of the announcement and encourage a complacency that they were trying to dispel in the first place.

While there are no perfect solutions to this conundrum, we could vastly improve our rules for warning if we stepped back and looked more closely at the strategy of alert systems.

First, we should distinguish between informing, warning, and alerting.[55] *Informing,* in this context, means simply putting into the public domain as much of what the government knows as it can without compromising intelligence sources and countermeasures. *Alerting* means contacting public officials and managers of the infrastructure in the private sector when there is a good reason for them to be on the alert. *Warning* means cautioning the public at large when there is something specific to warn them about and when the government can couple that warning with advice about how to substantially reduce risks. How would this play out in practice?

If the government believes it knows something is coming, but not where or when, it should inform the public about the nature of the ongoing threat—for example, general information about al Qaeda's activities and its expressed intentions. "Osama bin Laden has openly discussed his desire to acquire nuclear weapons and has, on at least one occasion, attempted to purchase nuclear materials." If the government thinks something is about to happen and believes it knows either where or when, but not both, it should alert federal, state, and local officials as well as private-sector operators of the critical national infrastructure (banks, hospitals, energy links, power grids, etc.) that, for example, "we believe al Qaeda has targeted the Statue of Liberty but the attack could come five years from now." If the government feels it knows an attack is coming, and where *and* when it will occur, it should warn the public directly through the sort of press conference it has been using to announce general changes in the color-coded system.

The rationale for these distinctions arises from the strategic costs imposed on the U.S. and the U.K. by terrorists. If we confuse the terms "inform," "alert," and "warn," we inadvertently shift the calculus of costs to the terrorists' advantage. For example, if we alert when we should be informing, we increase costs to the infrastructure on the basis of knowledge that can't justify these costs, and we make the long-term (or widespread) precautions that are imposed impossible to sustain. If we warn when we should be alerting, we invite the "Chicken Little" (or perhaps the "Boy Who Cried Wolf") costs of making real warning more expensive to achieve. If we merely inform when we should be warning, we lose the trust of the people and make them prey to conspiracy theorists of all kinds, including the calculatedly malevolent.

The terrorists want the maximum effect with the minimum of risk. By confining our costs, we force them to escalate theirs—we force them, that is, to be more specific—and sooner or later we learn how to crosshatch their threats to track down their operatives and thwart their plans.

The general approach of empowering millions of persons by putting them on the lookout is a good one. It was, after all, a shrewd Customs agent and not anyone in Washington who foiled the Millennium Plot to bomb Los Angeles airport on December 14, 1999. But the color-coded system is so broad and indiscriminate that it is both costly and ineffective. The underlying problem is not so easy, but it is amenable to more careful thinking.

(e) While a good bit of sarcasm could also be lavished on the airport screening processes—the absurd reluctance to use profiling methods, the endless lines that in themselves levy a substantial cost on the economy, the refusal to outsource screening to a private company—nothing was quite as mindless in the frenzy after 9/11 as the fate of the unfortunately-named Total Information Awareness (TIA) project.

In May 2003, the Pentagon announced that it planned to fund a number of research projects that would respond to the 9/11 Commission's recommendation that government develop methodologies for "(1) think[ing] about how surprise attacks might be launched; (2) identify[ing] telltale indicators connected to the most dangerous possibilities; (3) where feasible, collect[ing] intelligence on these indicators; and (4) adopt[ing] defenses to deflect the most dangerous possibilities or at least trigger an earlier warning."[56]

One of these projects was a cluster of research grants that would provide technological support for imagining scenarios in which terrorist attacks occurred, developing hypothetical profiles consistent with those scenarios, and then testing those profiles through data mining—the sys-

tematic canvassing of immense quantities of publicly available information. The objective of this research was to develop a program that marshaled technology to identify activities that indicated terrorist preparations
(for example, the purchase of flying lessons with cash[57] or buying chemicals useful in bomb-making[58]) so that actual attacks could be prevented.
"Before terrorists strike, they must enter the country, receive funds, case
their targets, buy supplies, and send phone and e-mail messages. Many of
those activities will leave a trail in electronic databases."[59]

Databases containing financial, educational, travel, medical, housing,
and communications data, fingerprints, photographs, and biometric eye-
scan information would be sifted through the complex algorithms of pattern analysis for the "electronic footprints" of terrorist preparations, and
crosshatched with intelligence leads.[60] In a sense, "pattern analysis" is
only conventional crime-solving (think of the pins on a crime map) or the
stuff of epidemiology (think of the famous map correlating cases of
cholera with London water cisterns) but raised to an astronomically higher
level by computers. TIA's data would have been confined to that to which
the government, following Supreme Court precedent, was lawfully entitled—that is, to material as to which there was no legitimate expectation of
privacy. The claim by a prominent columnist that "every public and private
act of every American" would be accessible was an exaggeration, though it
proved to be a widely influential riposte nevertheless.

In fact, as part of the project TIA would also have funded proposals to
develop methods of "anonymizing or blinding" the data in order to prevent
their misuse, to reassure the public with respect to concerns about privacy,
and to develop protocols that, in the words of the respected former deputy
secretary of defense John Hamre, would be "much stronger than the privacy protection we have now."[61]

Perhaps more revolutionary than data mining was the office's research
into privacy protection . . . "[S]elective revelation" of data . . . would
give only small amounts of information at a time. For example, an initial search might count how many people traveled a certain route in a
certain time period, say by plane from Hamburg to Kuala Lumpur during a given week. The answer might be just a number, say 10. The analyst would then combine that number with additional intelligence and
make the case to an independent authority, maybe a judge or foreign
intelligence board, in order to get a go-ahead to learn more about the
make-up of that group of 10 people. . . . Combined with even more
information from other sources, the analyst could make a new case to
this outside authority to obtain greater access to the characteristics of
[some of the ten]. It would take several such iterations before an analyst could learn names and other key identifiers. An electronic audit

trial would record the use of such a system, and a technological self-policing system would comb through the searches to identify outliers that might signal misuse of the system . . . It was TIA technology applied to privacy protection.[62]

TIA never got past the research concept phase.[63] Its director, Admiral John Poindexter, was forced out, and Congress killed the project completely in a rare act of alacrity and finality. Inept public relations brought the program to a crash, aided by the failure of the media and Congress to educate the public and by the exquisite if inevitable alliances between left- and right-wing privacy groups. Poindexter, who as former national security advisor had been indicted[64] for his role in the Iran-Contra affair, was made the scapegoat.[65] The *New York Times* described the entire program, in a phrase both trite and erroneous, as an "Orwellian project" when in fact it was precisely the sort of methodology the problem of terrorism—which includes the problem of protecting privacy—requires. Electronic privacy groups argued that the project violated the U.S. Constitution's Fourth Amendment guarantee against unreasonable searches and seizures because information was being collected without a warrant—a manifestly spurious argument in light of definitive judicial holdings to the contrary and the fact that the information to be assessed was in the public domain or had been voluntarily submitted to private companies without restriction. If the government unlawfully enters a house to search it, it is in the position of a private person who commits the tort of trespass. Yet private parties routinely collect and sell the data that was to be mined by TIA, and there is no suggestion that this is unlawful.

In a lapse of public relations judgment worthy of James II, TIA officials chose as their symbol the pseudo-Masonic all-seeing eye* that blazes forth from the pyramid depicted on the Great Seal of the United States. The Latin motto *scientia est potentia* ("knowledge is power") can hardly have been reassuring to the agency's critics. Even the name of the project was a little threatening, summoning up as it did a menacing ever-presence.[66] But nothing done by Poindexter and his team could possibly excuse the irresponsible barrage of criticism that befell them.

Defenders of the program, and there weren't many, asked whether someday the failure to use data mining might also mean a failure to catch a deadly terrorist conspiracy. On the basis of reports in the *New York Times* in late summer of 2005, some claim that it already has. These reports alleged that in September 2000 a U.S. Army military intelligence program code-named "Able Danger" used data-mining techniques to identify a

---

* Once the badge of the "Illuminati," to the alarm and delight of generations of conspiracy theorists.

U.S.-based terrorist cell, one of whose members was Mohammed Atta, and recommended that his name be referred to the FBI. The recommendation, which it is claimed also identified three other 9/11 hijackers by name, was not pursued, allegedly owing to opposition by Defense Department lawyers.[67] It is true that Atta had entered the U.S. on a tourist visa and, once he was in the country, any previous CIA surveillance would have stopped, but the rest of these allegations should be treated with some skepticism. In any case, they underscore the potential for data mining when *combined* with intelligence from human sources.

The pervasive distinction in intelligence collection between "foreign persons" and "U.S. persons"—which term includes U.S. citizens, green-card holders, and U.S. corporations—is, I will argue in the next chapter, unsustainable in a globalized era.[68] Here, however, I only wish to make the claim that without innovative computer-assisted techniques like data mining it will simply be impossible to cope with the volume of information that must be analyzed in order to prevent rather than prosecute terrorist acts. Congressional action to ban these techniques is a questionable contribution to achieving victories of preclusion in the Wars against Terror.

(f) Nothing, however, has drawn as much adverse comment as the detentions at Guantánamo Bay, Cuba, where the U.S. has created a prison colony holding hundreds of men as unlawful combatants without access to lawyers, familial visits, or judicial scrutiny. For the most part, these were men seized on the field of battle in Afghanistan, arrested there or in Pakistan. At least one, however, was taken in the U.S., and there were two detainees, both U.S. citizens, who were being held in a Navy brig in South Carolina likewise as "unlawful combatants." There were also an undisclosed number of prisoners held in Afghanistan and allegedly elsewhere.

Like prisoners of war, these persons may be held indefinitely without formal charge. Like criminals, they can be tried and sentenced for planning or carrying out acts of violence for which soldiers are not prosecuted. In the government's view, no court could require that the government choose between these alternatives, or have the power to enjoin such captivity, or, for that matter, to prohibit torture or even summary execution. How did this happen?

Partly it was a matter of the U.S. administration's apparently irresistible desire to overreach where legal questions are concerned.* This has led to the claim that, because the land on which the U.S. base is located is leased rather than held as sovereign American territory, no U.S. court has jurisdiction over events there. This claim was rejected in *Rasul v. Bush*.[69]

---

*For example, Patriot Act provisions have been used in child pornography prosecutions that have nothing to do with terrorism. See Kenneth Anderson, "Law and Terror," *Policy Review* 139 (October–November 2006), 14.

The whole theory of the U.S. Constitution is that it applies law to the acts of the State. Without a constitutional authorization, there can be no lawful acts of State. It follows from this that simply changing the location of government action cannot release the State from the requirement to follow its fundamental law. Insofar as Congress has made the federal courts the locus for enforcing claims that the government has acted unconstitutionally and has not created an exception for overseas suits or suits during wartime, it would be absurd to conclude that the government could evade this commitment to judicial scrutiny by manipulating where it acts rather than changing what it does.[70]

Partly, however, the government's actions are explainable by the sheer novelty and difficulty of the problem. Prior to the current conflict, combatants seized in battle or in preparation for warfare were either prisoners of war or common prisoners. The Geneva Conventions address the former classification; domestic law covers the latter.[71] The conventions were an international effort to enforce the laws of war, which themselves were a kind of bargain brokered between armies. In exchange for acting under certain rules—including the wearing of uniforms and insignia, acting within a recognized chain of command, conforming to other indicia of formal armed service, and above all, allowing for the humane evacuation of the wounded and observing the laws of war—soldiers were given various legal guarantees of respectful treatment. Among these was the promise that they would not be tried for crimes (other than war crimes) and would not be required to provide information beyond the simple identification of their names and units. Partisans and spies who refused to come within the designation of lawful combat still had to be treated humanely, of course. These individuals had to be fed and sheltered as well as given medical attention and access to the Red Cross and religious representatives, but unlike lawful combatants, they could be interrogated and tried as common criminals for killings, espionage, sabotage, and other crimes that were not necessarily war crimes.

Al Qaeda members are not ordinary soldiers. It is not simply that they defy that classification by adopting civilian clothes, false identities, and a chain of command that does not take orders from any conventional state; rather, they studiedly exploit that defiance as a means of causing terror. Hiding away in the civilian population, taking hostages, murdering noncombatants, and answering to a clandestine commander are tactical imperatives for terrorists.

But if al Qaeda members do not qualify for POW status, they are not ordinary criminals either. Nor are they spies for foreign governments. When they are captured on the field of battle in Afghanistan among Taliban troops, it seems unreasonable to try them all as murderers, and, in any case, the process due for law enforcement is too cumbersome and inappo-

site. Moreover, there is the vexing fact that, with respect to a global terrorist network that has mounted offensive operations in many theaters, there
is no forward battlefield line and thus the al Qaeda operative captured in
civilian clothes on the way to a meeting where he will deliver instructions
to his colleagues is neither quite a mere criminal nor quite entitled to the
full protection the Geneva Conventions accord to soldiers. Even if he is
believed to be armed, he could not be shot on sight as in warfare; yet even
if he is not armed, we would not want to release him so that he can commit
overt acts of war.

If such a person is seized at an airport rather than on a more conventional battlefield, it makes little sense to try him for a crime. In all likelihood the crime has yet to be committed, and indeed that is the point of
seizing him in the first place. On the other hand, if he is held as a combatant in war—the war against global terrorism—when is he to be repatriated? And to which state? With whom can he be traded in a prisoner
exchange? Because there are no satisfactory answers to these questions,
because simply releasing such a captive is fraught with dangerous consequences, and because trying him as a criminal is unlikely to succeed
within the current rules of trial practice and evidence, the U.S. administration has taken the position that he can simply be held indefinitely, like
other prisoners of war who await the end of the conflict in which they participated, yet be interrogated like a spy or partisan and tried like a criminal
before a military tribunal (which of course no ordinary criminal could be).
This simply amounts to a refusal to follow existing law or create new law
that is more responsive to our new situation. It doesn't answer questions
such as who is an actual combatant when non-dangerous associates of terrorists travel without arms; what is an appropriate period for detention,
what judicial body should determine this, what methods of interrogation
are permissible, and what forum recognized by international law can try
these persons. It doesn't answer any of these questions because the American administration's position was not to ask them in the first place. The
result was an historic defeat for the U.S.

About 10,000 prisoners were taken in Afghanistan in the initial fighting
in late 2001. This number was winnowed down to about 700 detainees at
Guantánamo.* They came from over thirty-five countries. Photographs
showing them shackled with their eyes and mouths covered spurred criticism in these countries, which include U.S. allies whose cooperation is
indispensable in the war on global terrorism. Some states—like Great
Britain, nine of whose citizens were detained at Guantánamo—lodged

---

*As of this writing, 377 Guantánamo detainees—about half of the total that have been held
there—have been released or transferred to other governments. Fourteen prisoners (termed "high
value" detainees) have been transferred to Guantánamo from confinement at undisclosed locations.

protests with the U.S. government. As of this writing, all but two British citizens have been bound over to British custody. Four French detainees were sent to France where they continued to be held.

In early 2006, a Seton Hall law professor issued a report, based entirely on U.S. government documents, that provided a detailed picture of the Guantánamo prison population.

- 55 percent of detainees have not been determined to have committed any hostile acts against the U.S. or its allies.
- 8 percent were definitely characterized as al Qaeda fighters, 40 percent were determined to have no connection to al Qaeda, and 18 percent had no definitive connection to either al Qaeda or the Taliban.
- While 8 percent were detained as "fighters" and 30 percent as "members," some 60 percent were detained on the grounds that they were "associated with" groups believed to be terrorist organizations.
- Only 5 percent were captured by U.S. forces; 86 percent were arrested either by Pakistani or Northern Alliance forces and turned over to the U.S. in exchange for significant bounty payments.
- Many of the Taliban detainees were conscripts.[72]

This picture scarcely justifies the statement of the U.S. defense secretary in June 2005: "[T]hese are people all of whom were captured on a battlefield. They're terrorists, trainers, bomb makers, recruiters, financiers, [bin Laden's] bodyguards, would-be suicide bombers, probably the 20th hijacker, 9/11 hijacker."[73] Some of the detainees certainly fit this description, including Mohammed al-Kahtani, whose fingerprints have implicated him as the twentieth hijacker, who was turned away by a skeptical immigration officer a few weeks before the 9/11 attacks. But much of the secretary's statement has not been verified and indeed has been sharply attacked by a group of highly respected lawyers in private practice—many who are partners in rather conventional large firms—who have volunteered to represent the detainees *pro bono publico*.*

One alternative to holding the detainees indefinitely is to have military tribunals assess the factual claims that are bound to arise as to whether

*In January 2007 the deputy assistant secretary of defense in charge of detainee affairs denounced their efforts in a radio interview, naming more than a dozen law firms and adding, threateningly, that "when corporate CEOs see [this, they] are going to make those law firms choose between representing terrorists or representing reputable firms." He then added that while "some will maintain that they are . . . doing it pro bono . . . others are receiving moneys from who knows where and I'd be curious to have them explain that." See Neil A. Lewis, "Official Attacks Top Law Firms Over Detainees," *New York Times,* 13 January 2007, http://www.nytimes.com/2007/01/13/washington/13gitmo.html (accessed October 25, 2007). Later, after a halfhearted apology, the official resigned.

those detained really were al Qaeda assets or were simply the victims of
bounty hunters, battlefield confusion, or other misidentification, perhaps
owing to score-settling among informants. Such adjudications would discharge some men and convict others to fixed terms. The U.S. government
has claimed that it may try such individuals by military tribunal—for
which there is a perfectly plausible rationale and some precedent—and
that neither the detentions, regardless of where they occur, nor the process
of the tribunals is reviewable by a civilian court pursuant to a writ of
habeas corpus—a claim that, in the absence of congressional action, is
extraordinarily unpersuasive in light of the changes in warfare that have
taken place since the precedents that support this argument were decided.
This claim was rejected by the U.S. Supreme Court in *Hamdi v. Rumsfeld*.[74] The initial executive order by the president issued on November 13,
2001, evoked a general outcry from the legal community. This order suspended the use of the domestic criminal courts. Specifically it allowed for
detention and prosecution outside the U.S. by a tribunal of five uniformed
officers applying a relaxed standard of proof in proceedings conducted in
secret from which there was no appeal. The death penalty could be ordered
by three of the five members of the court. Civilian attorneys were barred.
In light of the kind of warfare in which we are engaged, as described in
chapter 3, and the sort of war aims we must pursue, as described in chapter
4, a plan better calculated to buttress the claims of our enemies and alienate our allies could hardly have been devised.

In March 2002, the administration modified its original proposals for
military tribunals. The modifications were crafted in large part by a distinguished advisory group of civilian lawyers that included the late Lloyd
Cutler. The new guidelines were far more reasonable. These guidelines
restored the presumption of innocence and required that guilt be proven
beyond a reasonable doubt. A unanimous verdict was necessary for the
death penalty. Defendants were allowed to choose civilian attorneys.
While the evidentiary rules permitted the introduction of hearsay testimony and material gathered without a warrant (for example, papers seized
in Afghanistan during and after the war and intelligence intercepts of communications), the trials were to be open to the public and the press except
for specific evidence whose disclosure compromised national security as
determined by a court (as is similarly done with such evidence in the civilian courts), and a three-judge appeals panel was created.

Civilian courts are plainly insufficient for prosecuting acts of international terrorism, owing in part to the hostility jurors are likely to feel for
such defendants. Interrogations and searches conducted on the battlefield
yield evidence that could not be admitted under traditional civilian rules.
One can't imagine *Miranda*[75] rules being read to a captured prisoner during a firefight. More importantly, the need to protect the sources and meth-

ods of intelligence so far outweighs the need for any particular conviction that a civilian court becomes the arena for blackmail by the defendant who must be set free or allowed to confront witnesses whose presence in court means the end of their usefulness as sources.

As of this writing, the U. S. Supreme Court has thrice rebuffed administration efforts to restrict the due process rights of persons detained as unlawful enemy combatants.[76] In response, the Congress passed the Detainee Treatment Act of 2005 and the Military Commissions Act of 2006. The latter statute,[77] which stripped detainees of the right of habeas corpus,* has now been struck down by a circuit court on the grounds that "the Constitution does not allow the President to order the military to seize civilians residing in the United States and detain them indefinitely without criminal process, and this is so even if he calls them enemy combatants."[78]

But is this so if they *are* enemy combatants? A good thought experiment is this: If the passengers aboard the fourth airliner hijacked on September 11 had successfully landed that plane after having wrested control from the hijackers, would the government have been able to detain the hijackers as enemy prisoners of war? If the rule provides otherwise, then it clearly does not come to grips with the changing nature of warfare. The question ought to be framed: by what process do we determine whether a detained person out of uniform is in fact a combatant at war with this country? Designation by a military tribunal, without more, is not sufficient, but insisting on the processes due in ordinary criminal prosecutions is not sufficient either.

It ought to be plain—from all that has been argued thus far—that providing civilian judicial review for such designations is crucial to waging the Wars against Terror. It is not a civil libertarian's conceit but rather an essential element in the arsenal of the states of consent.

There are important constitutional limitations on the use of military tribunals, moreover. The attorney general's poorly expressed statement that "foreign terrorists who commit war crimes against the United States . . . are not entitled to and do not deserve the protection of the American Constitution"[79] expresses a profound misunderstanding of the role of the U.S. Constitution. The rights of terrorists are scarcely the issue; it is the power of the government that is in question. It's not that alleged terrorists deserve

*The Suspension Clause of the U.S. Constitution allows Congress to "suspend" habeas corpus in the case of invasion or rebellion. One would be hard pressed to conclude that our current situation fits those conditions. Moreover, a textual case can be made that the Suspension Clause implies that Congress must make habeas corpus relief available. See *Ex Parte Bollman* 8 U.S. (4 Cranch) 75 (1807) (Marshall, C. J.). It is no answer to say that the statute only provides for a "temporary" suspension; as one Congress cannot bind another, any explicitly temporary suspension can easily be made effectively permanent. Nor is it sufficient to say that the Guantánamo detainees are alien enemy combatants. Both the U.S. and the U.K. provide habeas corpus writs to aliens and the matter of whether they are in fact "enemy combatants" is precisely what is at issue, unlike the battlefield case of an enemy in uniform.

or do not deserve constitutional rights; rather it is that, without giving them such rights, the government is powerless to try them in the first place. Furthermore, any protection for the rights of defendants can be adapted to the exigencies of the society prosecuting them. There have, after all, been literally thousands of military tribunals conducted in past wars.

In such a context, the concern must be that the government not be permitted to militarize the domestic environment, shunting aside civilian institutions owing to the frontless nature of the global war. Seeking specific statutory approval of Congress, guaranteeing civilian review through habeas corpus, and wherever feasible repatriating prisoners for trial in their own countries would be necessary elements of any statutory system of successful military tribunals. Imposition of the death penalty for those foreign nationals who are not repatriated and whose countries do not have capital punishment is an option likely to do far more harm than good because it alienates other societies whose help we need, frustrates extraditions, and creates an international cause célèbre with each death sentence. Finally, civilian appellate review, which is provided under the Uniform Code of Military Justice for courts-martial, is indispensable to assure the legitimacy of these tribunals.

POWs in World War II were detained by the hundreds of thousands. They were not charged with crimes, were not told when they would be finally discharged and repatriated, did not have access to lawyers, and were not allowed to bring habeas corpus suits to challenge their detention. This precedent could mislead us into thinking that today it would comfortably cover persons alleged to be terrorists. Further, it might lull us into believing that we do not need to craft new laws for our new strategic situation. But when we realize that the World War II precedents are paradigmatic of nation state warfare, when there was little doubt as to the identity of the enemy or that he was affiliated with a state with which we were at war, when we could expect a final end to battle, when the soldiers detained were plainly POWs and therefore could not be tried for crimes—when, that is, a strategic situation dramatically different from the one we now face pertained—no administration should want to rely on those precedents. It would merely add another element to that resistance to reform so evident in every quarter, including that of the administration's opponents.

(g) Just before Christmas 2005, congressional officials announced plans to investigate the disclosure that the National Security Agency had used access to the public switched network to trace and analyze large volumes of phone and Internet traffic. Owing to the globalization of the telecommunications industry, many international-to-international calls as well as those with a U.S. party are routed through this network. It was alleged[80] that NSA had been gathering clues to possible terrorist activities based on pattern analysis of this traffic. Such analysis might determine not only who contacts whom, but from which locations, how frequently, at what time of day, of what duration, and so on. Calls from pay phones in Afghanistan might be of particular interest. When an NSA supervisor believed there was an actual link to al Qaeda, the agency had been authorized by the president to intercept the conversation and collect intelligence without a warrant so long as one party to the connection was outside the U.S.

This disclosure sent shock waves through Washington because the national security establishment had insisted that such collection would not operate against U.S. persons unless there was a specific warrant issued by the Foreign Intelligence Surveillance Court.[81] It appeared that, at least where the conversation included a foreign participant outside the U.S., this is exactly what had been done.

In the next chapter, there will be an opportunity to discuss this program in more detail and to explain how the U.S. government found itself in a position that seemed, to the White House at any rate, to require action that at least appeared to be in direct defiance of the law. In the present section, however, I wish only to treat the legal rationale offered for this decision.

The administration's legal argument was not a moving target, as was widely charged at the time, shifting from one basis for the president's power to another, but rather one of three interlocking parts: (1) the executive has inherent power to authorize this surveillance; (2) the surveillance did not violate the explicit provisions of FISA that no surveillance of this kind can be made unless by statute, because that requirement was satisfied, so the government argued, by the authorization for use of military force after 9/11 (which as a joint resolution had the status of a statute); and (3) if (2) was a controversial reading of FISA (as the government's lawyers realized), FISA should nevertheless be construed this way on the basis of the doctrine that all statutes should be read so as not to implicate constitutional problems, like those arising from the plausible assertion of (1) if FISA is read to prohibit this surveillance.

The U.S. president's power to take domestic action in time of war is usually analyzed, at least on a doctrinal basis, by reference to the concurring opinion of Justice Robert Jackson in *Youngstown Sheet & Tube v. Sawyer,* decided in 1952. Facing a steelworkers' strike in the midst of the Korean War, President Truman authorized the takeover and operation of U.S. steel mills by the army. In holding this action contrary to law, Justice Jackson offered a simple three-part test: the president's powers were (1) at their height when he acted pursuant to statute; (2) less when he acted on his inherent, concurrent powers; and (3) least when he claimed inherent, exclusive power, that is, when Congress had already rejected giving the executive the power it now claimed to exercise. Because Congress had considered, but then refused to enact, an amendment to the Taft-Hartley Labor Relations Act that would have given the president the power to use the armed forces in the way Truman had ordered, Jackson argued that only the most definitive allocations of power to the executive could justify the president's actions.[82]

President Bush's claims to an inherent power to conduct intelligence operations in time of war are not without merit. There is ample precedent for this, going back to John Adams's presidency. But the further claim that this power is exclusive—that it cannot be constitutionally regulated by congressional action—seems to fly in the face of many statutes, including the Patriot Act and its provisions for amending FISA, that give the executive greater power to conduct surveillance, provisions requested by the president in the first place.

These countervailing examples tend to push the administration's position back to its statutory claim that Congress's action in passing the Authorization for Use of Military Force (AUMF) in the wake of 9/11 included, implicitly, an authorization for expanded electronic surveillance. This too is not implausible on its face, but runs into difficulties with the subsequent Patriot Act provisions amending FISA. If the Congress intended to allow the executive leeway to surveil U.S. persons without a FISA warrant, what could have been the point in expanding the scope of executive power to seek such warrants, as provided in the Patriot Act, a bill ardently sought by the president, and passed well after the AUMF?

This in turn takes us to the claim that FISA should be construed to permit the president's practices because if it is not, a court would necessarily have to confront the argument that the statute, if not so construed, is unconstitutional. This is a somewhat technical claim having to do with the judiciary's recognition, in many opinions, of the wisdom of avoiding statutory constructions that invalidate the statute sought to be applied. If there is a reasonable way to apply the statute—to save it, as it were—courts would be imprudent to insist on a reading that requires them to strike down legislative action.[83]

In this context, however, this prudential claim proves too much. If the constitutional issue to be avoided is based on the president's claim of an inherent, exclusive power, then construing the statute to avoid confronting this issue simply eviscerates the statute. Such claims would make congressional regulation a nullity without actually deciding the issue in the president's favor. Moreover, this constitutional argument is based on a judicial doctrine of deference that has no application when a nonjudicial actor such as the Congress is evaluating the executive claim.[84]

Nor, even if as a prudential matter such a step were wise to protect the institutional position of the Court, could it possibly be recommended as a policy to be applied by other branches of government. With a single claim—undecided by any party other than the branch of government making the claim—the two other branches of government would be preempted. This rebuttal is a structural argument,[85] and if it were not definitive, there is a more profound structural point to be made.

In the U.S. constitutional system, the People and not the State are sovereign. Thus the legitimacy of acts of the State must derive from acts of the People, notably elections. When elections are fought every biennium, the policies of the current administration are debated. The outcome of these elections is the result, therefore, of a dialogue between candidates and the voters.

Imagine, however, that the discussion of an important issue was simply a sham because the administration held a view contrary to what it professed, and that there was no way for anyone to know this. This crucial element of our constitutional structure would be subverted.

This is what happens when secret operations are confused with secret policies.* Every government conducts secret operations, and every branch within government is entitled to the secrecy of its deliberations.[86] What the American system does not tolerate is secret policies.

In April 2004, President George W. Bush stated publicly:

> Now, by the way, any time you hear the United States government talking about wiretap, it requires—a wiretap requires a court order. Nothing has changed, by the way. When we're talking about chasing down terrorists, we're talking about getting a court order before we do so. It's important for our fellow citizens to understand, when you think Patriot Act, constitutional guarantees are in place when it comes to doing what is necessary to protect our homeland, because we value the Constitution.[87]

This could be understood as committing the government to request warrants from the judiciary as a condition of electronic eavesdropping. That is a policy, not a particular operation. Had the president disclosed to the public that he opposed such a policy, he might still have refused to say what, if any, intelligence programs were under way that reflected his views. But when he secretly decides not to enforce a statutory provision because the measure is, in his view, unconstitutional and neglects to say so (much less why), he sacrifices the legitimacy that comes from the public's

---

*An important exception might be policies with regard to covert action conducted in foreign states. Without deciding this point, I will simply say that covert actions (which should be rigorously defined as efforts to change the political decision making of other states without disclosing the hand of the United States government) cannot be undertaken against the U.S. public.

understanding of his decision and undermines our system of public consent. Moreover, when secret policies are exposed, the appearance of an indifference to law is heightened, which can only damage U.S. war aims in the Wars against Terror.

Testimony on this matter by the attorney general in February 2006 failed to correct this impression. Brilliantly satirized by Jack Balkin, it is summarized thus:

> We won't answer hypothetical questions about what we can do legally or constitutionally. We also won't tell you what we've actually done or plan to do; hence every question you ask about legality will be in effect a hypothetical, and therefore we can refuse to answer it.[88]

Whether or not the president can order warrantless collection against suspected terrorists and their interlocutors is an important question with significant constitutional dimensions, including whether a president is obliged to make an independent constitutional analysis of a statute and on that basis can decline to enforce it (as presidents have repeatedly done with the War Powers Resolution). The president does have an independent obligation to assess the constitutionality of the statutes he takes an oath to execute, but he must discharge this obligation by giving public reasons, stated in legal terms. This may be made clearer in the discussion to follow.

(h) In a welcome departure from the passive-aggressive attitude of the U.S. Congress, Senator John McCain proposed legislation that would ban "cruel, inhuman or degrading treatment" of prisoners. Why this was necessary takes some explaining.

In 1994, the U.S. explicitly made torture a federal crime.[89] For the purposes of that statute, however, "torture" is confined to such severe actions as beatings, electrocutions, and the like. Coercive interrogations of prisoners that include the denial of blankets, books, warm clothing, quiet surroundings, and company, or involve such practices as hooding, sleep deprivation, manacling, and even forced stress positions, are not generally held to fall within that law.[90]

In 1996, the U.S. gave domestic jurisdiction to U.S. courts over crimes arising from grave breaches of the Geneva Conventions and provided that violators of the conventions could be sentenced to death. But while the 1949 Geneva Convention does forbid subjecting a prisoner of war to threats, insults, or any "unpleasant or disadvantageous treatment" or form of coercion, these proscriptions apply only to valid prisoners of war—those persons within a transparent chain of command, in uniform, carrying openly displayed weapons, and obeying the laws of war. These provisions do not protect terrorists. Such persons are protected, it is true, by the U.N. Convention Against Torture and Other Inhuman or Degrading Treatment or Punishment. But that convention defines "torture" narrowly as the intentional infliction of severe pain or suffering, to which the U.S. Senate, in consenting to the convention, added the specification that torture was confined to "universally condemned" methods such as "sustained systematic beating, application of electric currents to sensitive parts of the body, and tying up or hanging in positions that cause extreme pain."[91] The Senate further qualified its consent to the convention by a reservation providing that "cruel, inhuman and degrading treatment" was limited to behavior that would violate the U.S. Constitution's Fifth and Fourteenth Amendments, which behavior, under some precedents, seems to be limited to methods of interrogation that shock the conscience, considered in light of all circumstances (including presumably the importance and likelihood of discovering information).

Nevertheless, it is unlikely that the abuses that have taken place at Guantánamo and at Abu Ghraib prison* in Baghdad would have occurred, at least on the scale that is now being publicly reported, if the existing regulations governing the treatment of prisoners had not been trumped by an executive claim of inherent constitutional authority to conduct torture, or at least highly coercive interrogations approaching torture, in spite of the prevailing statutory and regulatory framework.

It is certainly true that the usual conditions of a war against terrorists create complexities for what used to be simply a murky area of constitutional law. Most scholars assume that the president's power as commander in chief governs tactics on the battlefield and that Congress cannot regulate them; but suppose that coercive interrogations take place on the battlefield; suppose the battlefield is everywhere?

The U.S. Army Field Manual on Human Intelligence Collector Operations (FM 2-22.3) provides the legal regulations that govern the conduct of military interrogators. It explicitly applies to all detainees including insurgents and civilian internees. It prohibits acts of violence or intimidation, including threats, insults, or exposure to inhumane treatment and also provides that the violation of these prohibitions is a criminal act punishable under the Uniform Code of Military Justice. It gives these examples of prohibited acts:

- Forcing the detainee to be naked, perform sexual acts, or pose in a sexual manner.
- Placing hoods or sacks over the head of a detainee; using duct tape over the eyes.
- Applying beatings, electric shock, burns, or other forms of physical pain.

*Apart from the abuses attributable to poorly trained and supervised units.

- "Waterboarding" [a name for various methods that frighten a prisoner by leading him to believe he is drowning].
- Using military working dogs [to threaten or inflict injury].
- Inducing hypothermia or heat injury.
- Conducting mock executions.
- Depriving the detainee of necessary food, water, or medical care.

The manual also asks the following two questions: (1) If the interrogation technique was used by the enemy against one of your fellow soldiers, would you believe the soldier had been abused? (2) Could your conduct in carrying out the interrogation technique violate a law or regulation? "If you answer yes to either of these tests, the contemplated action should not be conducted. If the [interrogator] has any doubt that an interrogation approach . . . is consistent with applicable law, or if he believes that he is being told to use an illegal technique, the [interrogator] should seek immediate guidance from the chain of command and consult with the [staff judge advocate] to obtain a legal review of the proposed approach or technique."[92]

These regulations are promulgated pursuant to a federal statute based upon the U.S. Constitution's provision that the Congress shall have the power "[t]o make Rules for the Government and Regulation of the Land and Naval Forces."[93] Subsequently, however, the U.S. Army Field Manual on Interrogation was revised by the secretary of defense to include "extended interrogation techniques" that could be used on captives who fell outside the Geneva Conventions' definition of a prisoner of war and who were therefore deemed to be unlawful combatants.* This was done pursuant to the president's reserve constitutional authority as commander in chief of the armed forces.

These techniques were first used against detainees captured in Afghanistan and others held in Guantánamo. The director of interrogation of detainees at Guantánamo then went to Iraq to assist interrogators there. General Ricardo Sanchez, the commander of U.S. forces in Iraq, after consultation with the Guantánamo team and military intelligence forces who had been using these techniques in Afghanistan, issued his own set of permissible methods, despite the fact that many prisoners held in Iraq were indisputably prisoners of war and all detainees from that conflict came within various provisions of the Geneva Conventions. There can be little doubt, now, that a number of interrogation methods that would have been deemed unlawful were practiced owing to the exercise of executive authority predicated upon the president's claim of exclusive constitutional power.

*This revised provision was later dropped.

In a later chapter, I will discuss the issue of torture in the Wars against Terror more fully. At present, as with the previous discussion of electronic surveillance, my concern is with the constitutional issues on which the present chapter has focused. These were brought into the public discourse with the passage by Congress of the McCain detainee amendment to the Defense Authorization Act. That amendment prohibited the inhumane treatment of any detainees, including prisoners at Guantánamo, by requiring military (though not CIA or other non–Defense Department) interrogators to follow the standards outlined in the U.S. Army Field Manual.

At the signing of the bill by the president the White House issued the following statement:

> The executive branch shall construe [the McCain amendment] relating to detainees, in a manner consistent with the constitutional authority of the President to supervise the unitary executive branch and as Commander in Chief and consistent with the constitutional limitations on the judicial power, which will assist in achieving the shared objective of the Congress and the President . . . of protecting the American people from further terrorist attacks.[94]

This language is meant to inform the public, and the Congress, that the president reserves the right to decline to enforce an otherwise valid statute should he deem such nonenforcement to be necessary to protect the American public. Moreover, the president will not be bound by any judicial determinations to the contrary. Is this lawful? Can a president arrogate to himself such a supervening role, and if he does, does this mean he is "above the law"? The answers are not obvious, but there are answers, and they are, we can be thankful, legal answers.

Suppose Congress passes a statute that requires the dishonorable discharge of all HIV-positive military personnel. Or suppose the president is asked to enforce a statute that purports to permit the use at trial of unwitting statements by persons in custody, despite the Fifth Amendment's provision against self-incrimination. Or what if a joint resolution of Congress, which has the status of law, requires that the president withdraw U.S. forces from a particular deployment if a subcommittee of the Congress demands this redeployment? In all these instances, there are recent and authoritative Supreme Court opinions that would suggest that enforcement would be unconstitutional. The president could scarcely discharge his oath to uphold the Constitution—the supreme law—if he chose to carry out laws that he conscientiously believed to be unconstitutional, and this belief was well-grounded in constitutional jurisprudence.

This issue has been thoughtfully addressed in an opinion by the U.S. Department of Justice's Office of Legal Counsel[95] and in a series of articles by H. Jefferson Powell, who formerly served at OLC. Roughly, the conclusion of these elegant essays is that the president should enforce (or decline to enforce) statutes consistent with his best judgment of the resolution the Supreme Court would reach were the question of the constitutionality of the statute put before it in a justiciable case.[96] But what if the president believes the Supreme Court jurisprudence on the particular question is wrong? At least some judicial doctrines of constitutional construction are specific to the judiciary and defer, for example, to the other branches of government in ways that are inappropriate for the executive to apply by simply deferring to itself.* If we appreciate that doctrinal argument for the executive is not simply court precedents, but also the precedents set by previous executive decisions—the Messages and Papers of the Presidents being for the executive what the United States Reports are for the judiciary—then we may want to visit previous presidential decisions in similar contexts.

The most celebrated of these was Andrew Jackson's veto in 1832 of Congress's authorization of the national bank, an early version of an American central bank. Although the Supreme Court, in the case of *McCulloch v. Maryland,* had ruled that Congress did in fact have the constitutional power to create such a bank, Jackson disagreed. His veto message laid out the various constitutional arguments to the contrary in much the same way such arguments are deployed in Marshall's sublime opinion for the Court. There is little doubt that the president may veto a statute whose provisions infringe upon what he takes to be the constitutional authority of the executive. But suppose the Congress then repasses the statute over his veto. May he then simply decline to enforce the statute—or some particularly offensive provision within it—even when it is clear that a court would uphold the statute?

This was the issue Thomas Jefferson discussed in his letter of September 11, 1804, to Abigail Adams when he declined to enforce the Alien and Sedition Acts that had proved so controversial in her husband's administration:

> You seem to think it devolved on the judges to decide on the validity of the Sedition Law. But nothing in the Constitution has given them a right to decide for the Executive, more than to the Executive to decide for them. Both magistracies are equally independent in the sphere of action assigned to them. The judges, believing the law constitutional, had a right to pass a sentence of fine and imprisonment; because that

*As we saw with the claim in the preceding discussion of FISA, the judicial doctrine of avoiding constitutional claims in construing a statute would be ridiculously broad in the hands of the executive who would both provoke the conflict and then decorously defer to his own construction in order to avoid conflict—with himself.

power was placed in their hands by the Constitution. But the Executive, believing the law to be unconstitutional, was bound to remit the execution of it; because that power has been confided to him by the Constitution. That instrument meant that its coordinate branches should be checks on each other. But the opinion which gives to the judges the right to decide what laws are constitutional and what not, not only for themselves in their own sphere of action, but for the Legislature & Executive also, in their spheres, would make the judiciary a despotic branch.[97]

And though it might surprise some, this view is consistent with that taken by Chief Justice John Marshall in *Marbury v. Madison,* which recognized the judiciary's power to decline to enforce a statute it determined to be unconstitutional. Marshall's argument has been frequently neglected owing to the ambiguity in an oft-quoted phrase that, wrenched from its argumentative setting, can easily be taken to mean something other than its import within the opinion. When Marshall writes that "[i]t is emphatically the province and duty of the judicial department to say what the law is,"[98] he is not saying that the Court is the definitive expositor of constitutional interpretation but rather is making the following argument for the judicial review of statutes for their constitutionality: (1) in order to decide cases, courts must look up the law to be applied; (2) no validly passed statute is in fact lawful unless it is consistent with the Constitution, which is the supreme law; (3) courts must therefore *necessarily* undertake an inquiry into the constitutionality of every law that is sought to be applied. Only then will the courts be able to enforce statutes lawfully.

A similar argument can be made on behalf of the executive. This does not mean that the president may decline to enforce laws with which he simply disagrees. That was the issue with President Nixon's impoundment of authorized expenditures that, he believed, were fiscally irresponsible. His refusal to spend appropriated funds was one of the bases—in my view, the strongest basis—urged for his impeachment. Rather the Marshallian-Jeffersonian argument is the following: (1) in order to act lawfully, each branch must act in accord with the supreme law, the Constitution; (2) when called upon to apply law that it believes to be unconstitutional, each branch must decline to do so on the simple grounds that the purported law to be applied is not in fact "law"; (3) each branch must therefore undertake an assessment of the constitutionality of its own decisions to act. This is especially the case when the constitutional question at issue is not justiciable, and therefore must be decided by the responsible branches even if they are generally inclined to defer to the judgment of courts; otherwise, the Constitution would simply be ignored. Whether this is a matter of Congress determining the constitutional parameters of impeachment, or the Senate setting the constitutional parameters for the confirmation of judges, or the president fixing the constitutional parameters for the issuance of pardons, to fail to address the constitutional basis for action is irresponsible.

Lawyers know how to do this. They simply appropriate the modalities of constitutional argument as these have been developed over two centuries. Arguments from the original intent of the ratifiers of the Constitution, from the text as it is commonly understood today, from the structure of government, from the costs and benefits of a particular reading, from the precedents appropriate to each decider, and from a general assessment of the ethos of the American state of consent and that state's sovereignty as limited by our custom of inalienable rights—these six forms provide the means of independent constitutional review even when there is no case on point in the United States Reports.

Thus the president's signing statement issued at the time of the presentment of the McCain amendment was at once encouraging and disappointing. It was far more acceptable than his action with respect to the constitutionality of FISA restraints on executive surveillance because it is public and not secret. It could have, therefore, provided the basis for public consent (or rejection) of the president's policies. But it is disappointing because it is simply a formulaic statement of the conclusions of the president; it gives no reasons. It does not confront adverse arguments from the text (the Congress's power to regulate the armed forces, for example) or even bother to cite precedents helpful to its conclusion (the consistent position of the presidents with respect to the unconstitutionality of the War Powers Resolution, for example, which was passed over President Nixon's veto).

Now, unfortunately, it appears that there was a reason why no reasons were given and it was not a constitutional one. Before the passage of the McCain amendment, the White House had solicited, and the Office of Legal Counsel had obligingly provided, a secret legal opinion reasserting the legal authority to conduct a variety of coercive interrogation techniques that were widely thought to violate the McCain amendment, should it be adopted. Because this secret opinion followed a highly publicized withdrawal of an earlier OLC opinion taking much the same permissive approach—the withdrawal had been posted on the Justice Department website that proclaimed, "Torture is abhorrent both to American law and values and to international norms"—there can be little doubt that one purpose of maintaining the secrecy after the amendment was adopted was to deceive the public. This impression is confirmed by the refusal to allow access to secret legal opinions even to officials such as the deputy attorney general and the general counsel to the NSA.[99]

The administration desperately needs to rely on law because this reliance gives legitimacy to its actions. Law is not simply an obstacle to the execution of good policy. It can be a helpful buttress, a strong undergirding, a firm foundation for policy, but only if it is conscientiously employed.[100] Nowhere is this truer than with respect to the policies being developed to wage the Wars on Terror, both because the problems are difficult and novel and therefore test legitimacy, and because establishing the rule of law is a principal war aim. As the pertinent Army manual observes, "[u]se of torture by US personnel would bring discredit upon the US and its armed forces while undermining domestic and international support for the war effort."[101] If the administration insists that the enforcement of these legal rules is unconstitutional we must be told precisely why this is so, in the language of the law. This is the responsibility of the president, the attorney general, and the counsel to the president. Then the administration must promulgate new rules or go to Congress for statutory authorization to provide for new rules.

(i) Finally, consider the difficult case of Jose Padilla. This case brings together a number of the issues arising from the unique problem of a frontless war waged by terrorists who defy the rules and customs of ordinary, conventional warfare. In such a war, there is no localized theater of operations; and the usual indicia for the identification of enemy forces are not available. Suppose intelligence collected in such a war implicates an apparent civilian who is present in the U.S. or even happens to be an American citizen. He is detained but is carrying no weapons. He has met with the leaders of the enemy conspiracy, and made telephone calls to al Qaeda paymasters but the only evidence of his complicity in planned attacks is the hearsay collected from the coercive interrogation of detainees held outside the U.S. The government is loath to release him, as would a military commander be to release a prisoner of war who might be rearmed by the enemy. As a prisoner of war he can be detained until the end of hostilities. There is insufficient admissible evidence to try him for treason or conspiracy to commit a crime. On the other hand, holding him indefinitely without any adjudication of whether the intelligence implicating him is accurate amounts to giving the military the authority to arrest any unarmed citizen who falls under suspicion. It is the natural outgrowth of the Guantánamo problem (prisoners of war who do not qualify as protected POWs under the Geneva Conventions; prisoners who cannot be repatriated or exchanged; prisoners who must be held with no prospect of eventual release because the war in which they have fought has no final end), and just as the Guantánamo practices of coercive interrogation migrated to Abu Ghraib, so the Guantánamo conundrum of indefinite detention has migrated, with Jose Padilla, from Cuba into the domestic life of the American city.

Jose Padilla,[102] the son of Puerto Rican parents, was born in Brooklyn in 1970. After moving to Chicago, he became a gang member and was repeatedly arrested. During his last prison term, he was converted to Islam. Upon his release he went to a mosque in Fort Lauderdale, Florida, in the company of the registered agent for the Benevolence International Foundation, a charity that has been accused of funding terrorist activities.

In 1998, Padilla moved abroad, traveling to Egypt, Pakistan, Saudi Arabia, and Afghanistan. In 2001, it is claimed, he met with Abu Zubaydah, a senior al Qaeda coordinator. Abu Zubaydah allegedly sent him to Pakistan to learn terrorist tradecraft, including bomb-making, after Padilla had offered to detonate a bomb that would disperse radioactive material in an American city. He would have seemed an attractive recruit: he had an American passport; he didn't look Middle Eastern or use an Islamic name; he was enthusiastic. True, he had a criminal record, but persons who want to become mass murderers cannot be presumed to have unblemished pasts.

It is alleged that early in 2002, Padilla discussed an attack on the U.S. with other al Qaeda operatives in Pakistan; again the matter of the radiological bomb came up. Abu Zubaydah later claimed that at that time Padilla was instructed to return to the U.S. to carry out reconnaissance on American sites in preparation for the attack. In March 2002, however, Abu Zubaydah was taken into custody by intelligence agents in Pakistan and intensively interrogated. When Padilla flew from Pakistan to the U.S. on May 8, the American government faced a difficult dilemma. Federal rules of evidence do not permit the consideration of intelligence reports as proof in a criminal trial, no matter how reliable the informant. Yet the planning disclosed in the intelligence debriefings was the only serious crime Padilla had as yet committed. Unlike an ordinary soldier, he was not traveling with a unit, not in uniform, and not carrying weapons. His threat, if any, was inchoate but it was nonetheless potentially deadly. Any effort to hold Padilla as a grand jury witness was bound to be temporary because he could not be forced to testify without a grant of immunity.

When Padilla arrived at Chicago's O'Hare Airport, he was arrested and initially held as a material witness. To continue detaining him, he was not unreasonably classified as an "enemy combatant" by order of the president on June 9, 2002, and sent to a Navy brig in South Carolina.[103] The order purported to be based on the authority granted the commander in chief by the Authorization for Use of Military Force passed by Congress on September 18, 2001, in the immediate aftermath of the 9/11 attacks. That joint resolution authorized the president to "use all necessary and appropriate force against . . . organizations or persons."[104]

On December 18, 2003, the U.S. Court of Appeals for the Second Circuit disagreed with this interpretation, noting that the resolution only authorized force against persons whom the president "determines planned, authorized, committed, or aided the terrorist attacks that occurred on September 11, 2001, or harbored such organizations or persons,"[105] and ordered Padilla released. The U.S. Supreme Court vacated this decision the following February, however, on the technical grounds that Padilla's petition ought to have been filed in the Fourth Circuit. In a controversial decision delivered in September 2005, the Fourth Circuit court of appeals upheld the president's order. This set the stage for a Supreme Court decision on the merits.

Apprehensive about just such a decision, the U.S. government then decided to release Padilla into civilian custody, where he was promptly charged with a number of crimes (none of which include planning attacks against the U.S. or indeed terrorist activity of any kind). That explains why Padilla's attorneys actually resisted this move though they had hitherto repeatedly called for his release or indictment, and initially prevailed before the court of appeals, which commented dryly that the "shifting tactics in the case threatens [the government's] credibility with the courts." On January 3, 2006, however, the Supreme Court reversed the court of appeals and granted the prosecutors' request to transfer Padilla from military to civilian custody.

The absurdity of the legal farragoes by which Padilla was held for five years before being indicted on charges unrelated to 9/11 is thrown into high relief by the parallel case of a Qatari citizen pursuing university studies in Peoria, Illinois, Ali Saleh Kahlah al-Marri. In December 2001, al-Marri was arrested in Illinois and charged with the relatively minor offenses of credit card fraud and making false statements to financial institutions. As in Padilla's case, information extracted from detainees abroad persuaded the government that al-Marri had traveled to Afghanistan, met with the al Qaeda leadership, and volunteered to conduct terrorist operations in the U.S. Like Padilla, he was arrested without any evidence that he possessed weapons or explosives (though it was claimed that al-Marri surfed the Web looking for dangerous chemicals and collected information about U.S. targets). But in this case, prosecutors' apprehension over a looming suppression hearing[106] moved the government to request that all criminal charges against him be dismissed with prejudice,[107] and the president signed an order directing that al-Marri be transferred to military custody. The president's order stated that al-Marri's detention was "necessary to prevent him from aiding Al Qaeda in its efforts to attack the United States or its armed forces, other governmental personnel, or citizens."[108] Thus, al-Marri traversed the same legal no-man's-land as Padilla, only in the opposite direction.

It must be obvious that neither of these solutions is satisfactory. Indictment and prosecution are bound to founder when the key evidence is inadmissible, and the actual crimes that have been committed (as opposed to those that have been planned) are relatively trivial. But neither is it acceptable to arrest unarmed persons and to hold them for years without any independent assessment of the government's judgment that they do in fact represent "a continuing, present and grave danger to the national security."[109] Taking these two cases together with those of the hundreds of detainees at Guantánamo, one can see the difficult problem global terrorism poses for a constitutional system of consent in the twenty-first century.

Eventually Padilla was convicted, though not of the horrific crimes with which he was originally charged as planning, and his conviction was taken in many quarters as a vindication of the criminal mode of fighting terrorism. As Judge Michael Mukasey, the presiding judge in the Abdel Rahman case, noted, however, precisely the opposite was true: when examined closely, the Padilla case shows the criminal process is not well suited to resolve such matters.

First, terrorist prosecutions provide terror groups with a rich source of intelligence. As a consequence of Abdel Rahman's prosecution for the 1993 World Trade Center bombing, the government was required to turn over a list of unindicted co-conspirators, which included bin Laden's name. We now know that within ten days the list had reached Khartoum, alerting bin Laden that his connection to the bombing had been uncovered. During the Ramzi Youssef trial what seemed at the time to be innocuous testimony about the delivery of a cell phone battery actually tipped off terrorists still at large that one of their communications links had been compromised. That particular line had provided the government with extremely valuable intelligence; it was immediately shut down by the terrorist network.

Second, the demand on prosecutorial resources is enormous. Despite al Qaeda attacks and attempted attacks going back to 1993, criminal prosecutions have yielded only about three dozen convictions, and even these, according to Judge Mukasey, "have strained the financial and security resources of the federal courts to the limit."

Third, the rules used to protect the rights of ordinary criminals strike a balance between the interests of the person prosecuted and the potential harm to public safety. The scales of justice are not calibrated so that a terrorist threat can be accommodated as if that threat posed the same risk to society as a common burglar. Khalid Sheikh Mohammed is reported to have initially told his captors that he wanted a lawyer, wouldn't speak until he consulted one (if then), and that he would see them in court. The result of his interrogation doubtless owes much of its value to the fact that his wishes in this regard were not gratified.[110]

There remains an obscure statute, the Non-Detention Act passed in 1971, that provides that "[n]o citizen shall be imprisoned or otherwise detained by the United States except pursuant to an Act of Congress,"[111] and it may be that future Court action, should it rely on this statute, could galvanize Congress to address the anomalous situation posed by the global

terrorist, a soldier without a country, in a war with no prospect of a definitive end. Up to now, Congress's refusal to take up this question has been
little short of irresponsible. There is no reason why such figures as al-
Marri and Padilla should not be allowed to present a defense before a specially convened tribunal that is allowed to consider affidavits drawn from
classified interrogations. If found to be irregular soldiers in the al Qaeda
forces, as claimed by the government, they can be electronically tagged,
their passports revoked (or expelled if that is appropriate, as was done with
Hamdi[112]), and their transmissions monitored without the need for a warrant, for some specific time that could only be extended after a new hearing. The usual features of such hearings—a written record, the right to
counsel, the right of appeal, and so on[113]—ought to be provided to satisfy
the constitutional requirements of due process, and because the perception
of decent treatment is an important element in maintaining the legitimacy
of the efforts of states of consent to protect themselves.

The rules of evidence, rights of confrontation, and public access should
conform to those used by the Yugoslavia Tribunal established by the U.N.
to prosecute war crimes.*

VI.

The legitimacy of a government's actions turns on its constitutional practices. The current U.S. administration's position that it can arrest anyone it
believes to pose a terrorist threat and hold them without charge for an
indefinite period cannot be correct because it dissolves the rule of law on
which detention itself must rest. Yet it does respond to novel and real problems that must be satisfactorily and creatively addressed by Congress.

It is possible that the government may increase its powers, and, as suggested in this chapter, the people may increase their rights as well. And it
is also possible that the government can weaken its powers—as, for
example, by the recent legislation that has stripped the federal courts of
the power to conduct habeas corpus proceedings arising from detentions
abroad, or by the congressional action that halted DARPA's pilot program
to protect civilian identities—and at the same time the rights of the People
will decrease. That this is not commonly understood should be a cause
for concern. My thesis is likely to provoke bewilderment and amazed
incredulity, yet at bottom it depends upon a premise that all who are committed to government by consent do in fact share: that respect for the rule

*Compare the excellent proposal by Jack Goldsmith and Neal Katyal for a specialized "national
security court" that would oversee preventative detentions. See "The Terrorists' Court," *New York
Times,* 11 July 2007, http://www.nytimes.com/2007/07/11/opinion/11katyal.html (accessed October 25, 2007).

of law is the indispensable element in legitimate governance because protecting our rights is the purpose that empowers government in the first place.

In January 2006 the U.S. attorney general, Alberto Gonzales, went to the Georgetown University Law School to deliver a speech. There he encountered a number of law students who wished to protest the administration's use of warrantless wiretaps. Among them were four persons holding a banner that read, "Those who would sacrifice liberty for security deserve neither." This is a statement often attributed to Benjamin Franklin.

The statement is pithy and contrapuntal and in this it sounds like the epigrammatic Franklin, the author of *Poor Richard's Almanac* ("eat to live, not live to eat"), but it doesn't sound quite right. It is actually rather crude and is unlikely to have been uttered by the man who endorsed conscription to protect colonial settlements. What Franklin actually wrote was, "Those who would give up essential liberty to purchase a little temporary safety deserve neither liberty nor safety,"* a comment that might more aptly apply to someone censoring a cartoon out of fear of the reaction to it than to a requirement that citizens carry identity cards.

In each of the instances discussed above, real and difficult strategic problems confronted the U.S. In each case, the White House relied on constitutional arguments that would, if accepted, remove the legitimating force of law from its efforts by making statutory law irrelevant to executive action. In each instance, the result was to deepen the impression of the U.S. government as one indifferent to the rule of law. This is a staggering tactic in a war that is, at bottom, about the preservation of the rule of law. About the best defense one can offer is that other legal institutions—the U.N. Security Council, NATO's North Atlantic Council, the U.S. Congress—were not offering much help in bringing law to bear against the threatening forces facing the U.S. and that to rely on them for legitimating action would have been futile.

If, as argued in part 1, victory in the wars on terror is gained through the protection of civilians, and that this will require the reconnection of strategy and law, it is disheartening to record how studiedly the U.S. administration has cultivated a reputation for contempt for law. Disdain for law is an appealing posture to some persons, though why they should seek government office—in a government of laws—is something of a puzzle. In the present historical hour, the role of scofflaw was not a hard one for the president to land: novel and threatening problems were unsuitable for many of the laws as they stood and crafting new ones would be politically costly.

---

*The passage comes from Franklin's reply to the governor, addressed to the Pennsylvania Assembly, November 11, 1755; slightly altered, it is also inscribed on a plaque in the stairwell of the pedestal of the Statue of Liberty.

Enervated market state politicians—Gerhard Schroeder comes to mind—would be eager to excuse their own faltering visions by focusing on the shortcomings of the U.S. in realizing its conceptions and would lose no opportunity to publicize American lapses. Even so, the administration of President George W. Bush will be seen as notable for the panache with which it seized this role and thereby unintentionally brought discredit to the actions of American forces and disparaged the foresight of many U.S. policy makers.

In these pages, I have repeatedly called for congressional action and other initiatives by government. FISA reform, preventive detention statutes, rules governing coercive interrogation, the merger of national and international intelligence agencies (without the FBI), a thorough renovation of the classification of information (including meaningful penalties for unlawful disclosure, which can only make sense if far, far less information is classified in the first place and if the standards for classification are rigorous and clearly defined), military tribunals whose jurisdiction is limited to persons captured on conventional battlefields, a federal terrorism court with specialized rules of procedure and Article III judges, legal protection for companies that collaborated in good faith with U.S. intelligence agencies, indemnities to protect interrogators (including the provision of legal counsel), and compensation for persons wrongly detained—all these are measures the Congress (and mutatis mutandis, the British parliament) should urgently evaluate. There is also much the public can do. Indeed, there is even something that professors of constitutional law can do.*

In the last few years, there has been a "strategic turn" in constitutional law, analogous in some ways to the fabled "linguistic turn"[114] taken by Anglo-American philosophy in the second half of the twentieth century. Prominent constitutional academics have begun to infuse their legal work with efforts to appreciate the strategic context for law. This is not unprecedented. The first several essays by Alexander Hamilton in *The Federalist* explain the need for a new constitution largely on geopolitical grounds. But in recent decades these papers, and this point of view, have been neglected.

Now, important constitutional scholars like Sanford Levinson,[115] Bruce Ackerman,[116] Akhil Amar,[117] Jack Balkin,[118] Jack Goldsmith,[119] Martha Minow,[120] Jed Rubenfeld,[121] Philip Heymann,[122] Stephen Holmes,[123] Norman Ornstein,[124] Richard Pildes,[125] David Golove,[126] Noah Feldman[127], and others have begun a movement that would infuse constitutional and international law with a much-needed attention to strategy. It is precisely the strategic dimension that is neglected when we view the interface of constitutional rights and the powers of the state as a zero-sum game.

*See Kenneth Anderson's proposals in "Law and Terror," 21–24.

There is a final reason why it is a blunder to think of rights and powers in a two-dimensional way—a reason that forms the basis for the discussion in chapter 7 of ends and means in the Wars against Terror. When we come to believe that any necessary improvement in the powers of government to fight terror comes at the expense of our rights, we forsake the basis for distinguishing our goals from those of terrorists—we cannot say we are waging wars on terror in order to protect our rights—and thus we sacrifice the ability to define terrorism in any nonarbitrary way. For just as it is possible to increase the powers of government and, at the same time, increase the rights of the people, it is also possible to decrease human rights and, at the same time, enfeeble the ability of the state of consent to defeat terror. This is well captured in the following excerpt from an essay by the director of Human Rights Watch:

> [I]gnoring human rights as part of the fight against terrorism is likely to breed resentment that undermines international cooperation. The people whose cooperation is most important to defeat terrorism are the people who live in countries that are generating terrorists [as well, one might add, as the people in marginal communities in the developed world]. They are needed to report suspicious activities and to dissuade would-be terrorists from embarking on a path of violence. Yet these individuals are also the most likely to identify with the victims of a counterterrorism strategy that ignores human rights. When they see their compatriots detained in violation of the Geneva Conventions at Guantanamo, subjected to "stress and duress" interrogation techniques at Bagram air base in Afghanistan, or mistreated by an authoritarian government whose repression is overlooked or even encouraged in the name of fighting terrorism, they are less likely to lend their support to the counterterrorism effort. Again, the advantage of ignoring human rights proves short-lived.[128]

As we shall see in the balance of part 2, the only effective strategy in the Wars on Terror requires a scrupulous adherence to the rule of law, and where the law is inadequate, a vigorous and transparent effort at law reform. Guantánamo was an important battle in the Wars against Terror, and we lost it.

CHAPTER SIX

Intelligence, Information, and Knowledge

Where is the wisdom we have lost in knowledge?
Where is the knowledge we have lost in information?

—T. S. Eliot, "Choruses from 'The Rock' "[1]

WHAT IS AN "intelligence failure"? The compromised agent? The credulous acceptance of disinformation? The neglect of standard tradecraft? These are all failures in the methods of collecting secret information by the clandestine intelligence services, to be sure. In the aftermath of the terrorist attacks on New York, London, and Madrid and the surprising inability to locate expected WMD in Iraq, many critics asked whether these events were evidence of intelligence failures. What these critics had in mind was actually a miscarriage of the intelligence process, a complex bureaucratic enterprise that has most signally fallen short when the political and strategic judgments it produces are inadequate to cope with the threats to the societies it protects. There may be insufficient information owing to mistaken priorities, inadequate funding, unavailable sources, or penetration by the enemy that leads to a failure of the intelligence process but is not attributable to the mishaps of secret intelligence collection operations per se.[2]

Two of the most damaging failures of the intelligence process of the recent period, the inability to give adequate warning of the 9/11 attacks and the apparently erroneous conclusion that Iraq possessed a substantial arsenal of WMD, may in fact be the result of the ways in which we tried to solve the most difficult intelligence challenge of all: how to develop rules that will effectively empower the secret state that protects us without compromising our commitment to the rule of law. These mistakes, however, pale beside a much larger failure, which arose from public reliance on intelligence reports that could not withstand public scrutiny. *This* failure provides an overture to future challenges that will arise when governments are compelled to rely on secret intelligence in order to craft public policies that anticipate threats and to attempt to neutralize them before they mature. What is most interesting, however, is the ways in which these two challenges are linked.

I.

It is much in fashion after 9/11 and after the mistakes of the Iraqi intervention to pillory the intelligence services. "The terrorist attacks on the United States, Spain and Britain and . . . the war on Iraq . . . have been frequently described as [the result of] 'intelligence failures' . . . The result has been an outpouring of critical books and articles on the failings of American intelligence."[3]

What has failed, and if not addressed will continue to fail, is the *intelligence process*. Here are six misadventures of the intelligence process, including the political judgments based on the intelligence product, one can expect in the future:

- We—the states of consent—will suffer an attack by a weapon of mass destruction and not be able to persuade much of the public that we have correctly determined its true origin.
- We will fail to interdict attacks by terrorist cells within the U.S. and the U.K., despite apprehensions in American and British agencies that identified the terrorists beforehand.
- We will not predict a foreign government's unexpected financial collapse, with significant consequences for our own economies.
- We will not detect a foreign government's unexpected acquisition of a weapon of mass destruction.
- We will not provide warning of a surprise attack against one of our allies or on our forces overseas.[4]
- Indeed when Europe is struck by an attack of 9/11 proportions, the U.S. will be accused of failing to alert the targeted country on the grounds that U.S. intelligence actually wished for (or connived in) the attack.

We will have these setbacks owing to our continued reliance on the *antinomies*[5]—two opposing concepts used to allocate responsibilities—described below because, up to now, maintaining these antinomial rules permitted us to manage both a robust intelligence security apparatus and a free, democratic state of consent.

These antinomies were crucial to American success because they enabled us to maintain the rule of law in an essentially private society without sacrificing national security. They have worked so well that we cling to them, neglecting to see that this success was linked to the world out of which these dichotomies grew and not realizing how time-bound our problems, and therefore their solutions, have been.[6] In this chapter, we will see how the operation of these antinomies led to the 9/11 and Iraqi WMD failures of the intelligence process.

We will have to do more than simply reject the legacies that are crippling us and replace them with methods more adapted to the problems we face. We will have to find new ways to protect civil society without sacrificing its values or delegitimating the methods by which our values are protected. If politicians and their publics will have a greater need for intelligence estimates about alternative futures in order to anticipate and preclude threats, as argued in part 1, then the strictest scrutiny as well as the weightiest reliance will fall on the work of the intelligence agencies.

We will have to develop standards that justify both collection of intelligence and the uses to which such intelligence is put. We will want to have an open debate about the limits that might be appropriate in the selection of targets for clandestine intelligence gathering—*jus ad intelligentiam*—and also with respect to the methods used—*jus in intelligentia*—in Sir Michael Quinlan's insightful analogy to the standards applied to warfare.[7]

II.

Taking decisions to preclude a state of terror—whether by arresting a would-be terrorist who has yet to commit a crime, by preempting a state that has yet to complete its acquisition of WMD, or by preventing the displacement of people in order to forestall an irreversible cascade of mass migration—depends upon estimates about the future. Rarely before have governments had to rely so heavily on speculation about the future because a failure to act in time could have such irrevocable consequences. This will bring the role of estimative intelligence into new areas of controversy, as policy becomes more dependent on intelligence estimates and the requirement that the public be informed (and persuaded) becomes more exacting.

Intelligence estimates are based on the careful analysis of immense amounts of information, sorting out the true from the false, assigning probabilities to information that might be either true or false, guessing what the future would be like if all the relevant facts were available to the analyst. The problem for estimative intelligence in the current environment is its reliance on a relatively stable world from which to extrapolate. In such a world, states confront one another across sharply demarcated territorial lines, and vast armies are conscripted and equipped with mechanized weapons. The readiness of these forces, their composition and equipment, are observable and traceable and thus are the subject of intense scrutiny. With the overwhelming dominance of U.S. arms, however, new threats are emerging. New forms of warfare reflect this development, which is rendering the stable world of conventional armies an anachronism and is steadily replacing that world with a host of uncertainties. This is not a secret; everyone knows it. But it doesn't fit the world of our achievements, and though we pretend to recognize the changed world we insist on repeating the strategies that brought us victory in the old world because, after all, they were successful strategies.

In a report done in 1983 for the U.S. director of central intelligence, a group of senior advisors were asked when national estimates were likeliest to go astray. They concluded that,

> in the estimates that failed, there were a number of recurrent common factors which, in retrospect, seem critical to the quality of the analysis. The most distinguishing characteristic of the failed estimates—the Sino-Soviet split, the development of the ALFA submarine, the Qadhafi takeover in Libya, the OPEC price increase, the revolutionary transformation of Ethiopia, the Soviet invasion of Afghanistan or the destruction of the Shah's Iran—*was that each involved historical discontinuity . . . The basic problem in each was to recognize qualitative change and to deal with situations in which trend continuity and precedent were of marginal, if not counterproductive, value.*[8]

The chief reason given in 1947 for the creation of the CIA was to prevent another surprise attack on the United States like the one at Pearl Harbor.[9] For sixty years the U.S. succeeded. Yet on September 11, 2001, a date that might truly be said to "live in infamy," another surprise attack on the United States occurred with greater loss of life than at Pearl Harbor. With an annual budget that is twice the defense outlays of Iran, Iraq, Syria, North Korea, Cuba, and Libya combined, the U.S. intelligence community was not able to thwart or even give sufficient warning of this attack, which has been estimated to have already cost the United States $90 billion. To quote the national security analyst Desmond Ball:

> The terrorist attacks on the World Trade Center and the Pentagon on September 11 involved the worst intelligence failure by the US intelligence community since Pearl Harbor in 1941. It was a failure at all phases of the intelligence cycle, from the setting of priorities and tasks, through the gamut of collection activities, to the analytical, assessment and dissemination processes which should have provided some warning of the event—and it befell not only the traditional national security and military intelligence agencies but also the myriad

law enforcement and specialized agencies involved in counter-terrorist activities. US and allied intelligence agencies had been watching Osama bin Laden closely (albeit fitfully) since 1996, and were well-informed about his intentions towards the US, but were unable to discern his operational plans and preparations.[10]

The result was an historic failure of the intelligence process, not because a part of the system collapsed and especially not simply because that part devoted to acquiring secret information was unsuccessful. Rather, it was a failure of the system by which priorities are set, resources are allocated, and above all, political decision-makers are sufficiently alerted to a potential threat so that they can shape policy accordingly.[11] When a government's intelligence systems fail to enable its leadership to anticipate events of potentially lethal significance for vital national interests, it is then that they invite a catastrophic intelligence failure.

Here are a few examples of such disasters. In each case, the U.S. and U.K. governments were surprised by these events.*

- The Japanese attack on Pearl Harbor in 1941
- The acquisition and testing of the Soviet atomic bomb in 1949
- The Chinese attack on Korea in 1950
- The Hungarian revolution in 1956
- The Berlin Wall in 1962
- The Arab-Israeli war in 1973
- The Iranian revolution in 1979
- The August coup and subsequent collapse of the Soviet Union in 1991
- The Iraqi invasion of Kuwait in 1990
- The Indian testing of a nuclear weapon in 1998
- The Rwandan genocide in 1994
- The al Qaeda attacks in 2001

The ultimate consequences of these catastrophic intelligence failures were not always completely negative. The Hungarian revolution caused the U.S. to abandon a strategy of liberation of the Soviet satellite states—a strategy called "rollback"—and this was probably just as well. The creation of the Berlin Wall erected a visible rebuke to Communism, demonstrating its essential undesirability to the peoples it claimed to benefit. The

---

*Although in some instances—e.g., the Berlin Wall and the Indian nuclear test—they were generally expected by the intelligence services but the precise timing was not known and thus the political leadership had not prepared for the events.

Egyptian surprise attack on Israel ultimately failed, permitting Egypt to detach itself from the Soviet Union—a process begun by President Sadat some months before the 1973 war—once it became clear that only the United States could save the Egyptian Third Army from annihilation. The Iraqi invasion of Kuwait enabled the United States to assemble a global coalition, including Russia, with which to establish American credentials as a vigorous but not monomaniacal world leader. The al Qaeda attacks may yet prove to be the first battle in a long war against terror in which the United States and the United Kingdom will act in concert with other states to create successful anti-terror coalitions. These coalitions might unite the U.S. and the U.K. with states like China and Russia that otherwise might be our adversaries. Even skeptical political figures in France and Germany may come to believe that the U.S. and the U.K. can lead the democracies without putting them at unreasonable risk.

Nevertheless, these dozen cases were serious fiascoes. The fact that the U.S. and its principal allies recovered from them speaks well for their resiliency; still, it would have been preferable if these events could have been correctly anticipated and their costs thus avoided or minimized.

Yet the U.S. has had notable intelligence successes during this same period. Interestingly, many of them have come in the wake of devastating failures.

- The destruction of the Japanese fleet at Midway was made possible by breaking Japanese naval codes, thus providing information of a kind that the U.S. had failed to collect before Pearl Harbor.
- The detection of Soviet missiles in Cuba was accomplished by a spy plane, the U-2, which was developed to prevent the U.S. from being surprised by the Soviets' nuclear development as it had been surprised by their A-bomb test.
- The Chinese were not drawn into the Vietnam conflict owing in part to the careful, though much criticized, calibration of U.S. warfare in Vietnam in light of the Korean experience.
- The fruitful clandestine links between the West and the Solidarity movement in Poland helped avoid the tragedy of Hungary, which was uppermost in the minds of both parties.
- Though the U.S. was surprised by the building of the Berlin Wall, its existence led to covert action that facilitated the flow of German refugees through Budapest and resulted in the wall being torn down by Germans instead of by American forces.
- Though the U.S. did not predict the precise timing of the 1973 war in the Middle East, it used that conflict to convince the Soviet Union that the United States was prepared to intervene and thus persuaded Moscow to abandon its Egyptian ally.

- In light of the shah's overthrow, which the U.S. did not predict, Washington was prepared for the collapse of the Marcos regime in the Philippines, in which the armed forces were skillfully managed to encourage democracy.
- Though the U.S. missed the attempted coup against Gorbachev by Kremlin hardliners, it was able to enforce restraint in the Baltics by covert means, thereby preventing violence that might well have brought Soviet reactionaries into power before Yeltsin's democratic regime could be consolidated.
- Though the U.S. leadership failed to conclude that Saddam Hussein was about to invade Kuwait, the Bush administration used that invasion to marshal virtually the entire international community to redress that invasion, strengthening the rule of international law, providing a successful example of East-West collaboration under U.N. auspices, and even achieving tactical surprise of its own when Iraqi forces were fooled into expecting an amphibious counterinvasion.
- Failure to dissuade the Indian and Pakistani governments from acquiring nuclear weapons gave greater impetus to the proactive, counterproliferation regimes that successfully halted the Libyan nuclear program—whose supplier, A. Q. Khan, had been at the heart of the Pakistani program—and uncovered clandestine nuclear weapons efforts by North Korea and Iran that were also aided by the A. Q. Khan network.
- The covert cooperation with local forces to stop ethnic cleansing in Kosovo was in part a reaction to the U.S. having left prevention to others in Rwanda.
- The U.S. achieved a respite from successful terrorist attacks on the U.S. homeland, if only temporarily, through the aggressive disruption of al Qaeda cells in Afghanistan and elsewhere following the tragedy of September 11.

If, as the cliché goes, experience is an expensive way of learning, perhaps it is an effective one as well. Success can derive from failure.

But can failure also derive from success?[12] In each of its misfortunes, the United States had the information in hand to prevent the catastrophe,[13] but this information was misframed[14]—by which I mean the information was fitted into a frame of reference that proved to be inappropriate. Often that framework was determined by a prior success. For example, it was hard for the U.S. to doubt the surveillance regime that had accurately caught the Indians preparing for a nuclear test the first time, when in fact the Indians, having been detected, changed their procedures to cope with American scrutiny.

Success determines how we frame our experiences. We rely on strategies that have worked in the past to succeed for us in the future. That's why success often leads to failure when we do not appreciate a genuinely new situation. Only failure, it seems, then forces us to reevaluate our strategies.

In the Vietnam War, it was difficult for the United States to adapt the tactical methods that had won the war in Europe a quarter of a century before and that had saved South Korea from being overrun a little more than a decade earlier.* The threats that the West will face in the twenty-first century are so unlike those of the Long War of the twentieth century that it must be obvious that intelligence operations must also change. That we won that war, however, with such methods as we now have enshrined, will prove a significant obstacle to reform.

III.

Over the seventy-five years of the Long War, the U.S. and the U.K. developed creative methods for reconciling the need to respond to global threats with the need to preserve their constitutional habits of limited government, personal liberty, and political freedom. In the United States, these methods were built of legal elements often mistakenly believed to be fundamental to our constitutional and strategic well-being because for so long they assured that well-being. Rigorously applied regulations dealt with the difficult paradox of a law-abiding, open government that had to employ secret intelligence methods to protect its national security, methods that when practiced abroad were often illicit. Many of these hitherto successful regulations must now be modified or radically redefined if the U.S. is to avoid attacks like the one on September 11, for it can be shown that some of these now-calcified regulations played a crucial role in the events of that awful day. In a larger sense the U.S. and the U.K. must overcome the separation of law and strategy that has overregulated domestic intelligence through law while abandoning[15] lawful behavior overseas as a dimension of international intelligence operations.[16]

A half-dozen basic antinomies[17] provide the foundation for the American nation state's approach to the collection and use of intelligence. Up to now, they have defined the interplay between our constitutional order and the intelligence activities that serve that order.[18]

These opposing distinctions are (1) the division between the public and private sectors; (2) the separation between the domestic and the interna-

---

*Perhaps similarly, the failures of U.S.-led forces to quell the Iraqi insurgency reflects a refusal to train for this sort of dispersed warfare in the wake of Coalition successes in the First Gulf War. The slogan "No More Vietnams" has thus left a bitter legacy for the preparation of our forces.

tional; (3) the different rules we apply to law enforcement and intelligence operations; (4) the different reliance we place on secret as opposed to open sources (newspapers, articles, and monographs, or interviews with their authors); (5) the distinction between intelligence collection and analysis; and finally, (6) the differing roles of intelligence producer and intelligence consumer.

The United States and Britain have kept the public sphere separate from the private in order to maintain a robust civil society and cabin the scope of the State (unlike totalitarian states). They[19] have sharply separated the roles of the military and the police in order to avoid militarizing the domestic environment. The U.S. has kept the national separate from the international in order to maintain a federal state in America; the U.K. has done so most recently, in order to avoid a federal state in Europe. The U.S. has sequestered law enforcement from national security, and by this means, it has provided expansive due process to accused persons while maintaining a cloak of secrecy protecting the secret agencies. By maintaining intelligence analysis separate from collection, the U.S. and Britain have enhanced the professionalization of both. By keeping intelligence consumers apart from producers, we have reduced, if not entirely removed, the politicization that can corrupt both. By relying on the government to find and maintain secrets while leaving publicly available information to academics and journalists, we have attempted to protect BBC journalists from being arrested overseas and CIA analysts from penetrating university journals.*

Each of these antinomies, which we take more or less for granted, contributed to the events of September 11. Remember, however, that before the U.S. had that catastrophic failure, it had important successes.

Before September 11, George Tenet, CIA director from 1997 to 2004, often described America's counterterrorist program as keeping bin Laden's network off-balance and anxious about its own security. The U.S. had a strategy—arrest and prosecution, coupled with efforts to frighten and disorient bin Laden and his team—that seemed to be working.[20] The U.S. enjoyed successes in identifying, tracking down, and bringing to justice many terrorists. The arrest and prosecution of Ramzi Youssef, the organizer of the World Trade Center bombing, was one such achievement. More than two dozen terrorists have been brought to trial since the summer of 1998, more than half of them associates of the bin Laden organization.

In 1993, the U.S. apprehended Omar Ali Rezaq for the hijacking of an

---

*Rules protecting journalists and academics from involvement with intelligence activities evolved most rigorously in the late 1970s; consider the experience of CIA with *Encounter* magazine and the National Education Association in previous decades.

Egypt Air flight in which fifty-eight people died. Subsequently, the U.S. arrested Mohammed Rashid for the 1982 bombing of a Pan Am flight and in 1996 captured Tsutomu Shirosaki for a rocket attack on the American embassy in Jakarta. In one of the most sensational examples, FBI and CIA agents, in a daring 1997 raid, captured and arrested Mir Amal Kansi, the assassin who killed two CIA employees in a 1993 attack near Agency headquarters at Langley, Virginia. The U.S. acted with remarkable alacrity after the 1998 bombings of its embassies in Kenya and Tanzania: within twenty-one days of the bombings, the first suspects, all linked to the bin Laden network, were behind bars.

Al Qaeda was wholly frustrated in its Millennium Plot in late 1999,[21] and hundreds, perhaps thousands, of lives were saved. Many terrorist acts have been thwarted, and the work of the intelligence services behind these successes has not been made public.

These achievements depended upon the fundamental distinctions mentioned above: the work of arrest, extradition, rendition, and trial was done by governments, not by the private sector; the cases were prepared for prosecution and trial principally in order to achieve legal, not strategic objectives; complex arrangements were required for the handoff between CIA and FBI; and, it should be noted, none of the terrorists were U.S. citizens, so some of the restraints on the National Security Agency[22] and CIA did not apply; secret intelligence, frequently augmented by offers of rewards and cooperation with foreign services, was decisive rather than the mining of open sources of information; the collectors could safely be separated from the analysts once bin Laden's fingerprints on operations had been identified; and the ultimate consumers of the intelligence product—the National Security Council—had a structure in place, established by Presidential Decision Directive 62, that put the national coordination of counterterrorism in the hands of one person, a sophisticated and experienced user of intelligence, Richard Clarke.

Then the attacks of September 11 came despite many warnings, including Clarke's.[23] It was in some ways a more menacing setback than Pearl Harbor, because while the Japanese bombing did prefigure four years of bitter struggle in the Pacific, the al Qaeda attacks are the harbinger of wars that offer little promise of peace even in a decade.

IV.

With the events of September 11 in mind, let us revisit the basic antinomies, those purposeful distinctions that have given us a mooring in the past.

(1) The private/public distinction is written into the U.S. Constitution

in the Fourth Amendment's search and seizure provisions, in the Ninth Amendment's guarantee of unenumerated rights, and also generally in the fundamental idea of the Declaration of Independence that the people retain certain rights that cannot be delegated to the government.

> The Constitution, federal privacy laws, and stringent Justice Department counterintelligence guidelines all focus on protecting individual civil rights. [We accept that this] emphasis hinders crime prevention by severely limiting the surveillance of suspicious individuals and groups, the interception of mail and phone calls, and the seizure of evidence, such as computer hard drives.[24]

Americans are willing to pay this price in part because the cost of ordinary crime does not cripple their society.

Equally significantly, as a consequence of the public/private distinction, corporations are put in charge of much security even though it is not always in the interests of shareholders to take the maximum precautions necessary to protect the public, but rather only to insure against reasonable loss. For example, before 9/11, American airline companies bitterly fought the recommendations of the Gore Commission (which provided for intelligence sharing among the CIA, the FBI, and the Federal Aviation Administration) because of the extra costs the adoption of these recommendations would have imposed.

This division between public and private explains in part* why the FBI did not provide the airlines with the names of two persons it had been warned about by the CIA, even though nothing would have prevented the hijackers' banks from reporting to the airlines that the hijackers' credit cards were overdrawn and that therefore they would be denied passage. Proposed government programs that were to collect no more than commercially available information on travelers to the U.S. have recently been repudiated by Congress as an impermissible invasion of privacy by government, and there has been widespread outrage at reports that the private communications company AT&T and various banks have collaborated with the U.S. government in conducting secret surveillance. As one of the most insightful and experienced observers of U.S. intelligence, Gregory Treverton, has noted:

---

*But only in part: the FBI took the position that it needed dates of birth or passport numbers to alert the airlines and that names alone were insufficient; the CIA, which had this further information, refused to provide it and indeed for quite some time refused even to alert the FBI that two al Qaeda agents, al Hazmi and al Mihdhar, were in the U.S., a blunder that arises from yet another antinomy, the division between the national and the international. See Lawrence Wright, "The Agent," *The New Yorker*, p. 62 et seq., 10 and 17 July 2006.

[P]rivate financial institutions have vastly more information about [terrorists and their networks] than government . . . I was in the CIA building during the mole-hunt that produced CIA spy Aldrich Ames, and it was striking that his creditors knew so much more about his finances than his employer did.[25]

Similarly, this division between public and private sectors has made it harder for governments to cut off bin Laden's financing than to stop the flow of funds to terrorists when these were supplied by governments. Among other factors, the U.S. and the U.K. treasuries didn't want to weaken the confidentiality among private international banks and their clients, fearing that this would damage the system of commercial banking as a whole.

Sometimes this antinomy works in perverse ways. Thus, the Immigration and Naturalization Service was not able to take advantage of the substantial upgrades in computer performance in the private sector because it was barred from installing a fingerprint-identification system at U.S. entry points that was incompatible with the FBI's less advanced computers. Yet in an effort to appease the private sector (including passengers), the INS was required by law to clear all international passengers within forty-five minutes.

(2) The distinction between the national and the international—that is, between domestic and foreign—is equally basic to current intelligence operations.

This distinction is responsible for the fact that the CIA cannot, with certain very minor exceptions, track persons in the United States, or even follow foreign persons once they arrive in America, and that the National Security Agency cannot collect intelligence from intercepted conversations between U.S. individuals, or even U.S. corporations, or resident aliens.

The CIA is reported to have had information in 1999 about a planned al Qaeda session to be held in Malaysia in January 2000. The Malaysian government was notified by the CIA and photographed the meeting, thereby enabling the identification of two men, Nawaf al Hazmi and Khalid al Mihdhar, who became 9/11 hijackers.

A few days after the Kuala Lumpur meeting . . . the CIA tracked one of the terrorists, Nawaf Alhazmi, as he flew to Los Angeles. Agents discovered that another of the men, Khalid Almihdhar, had already obtained a multiple-entry visa that allowed him to enter and leave the United States as he pleased . . . [D]uring the year and nine months after the CIA identified them as terrorists, Alhazmi and Almihdhar lived openly in the United States,[26] using their real names, obtaining driver's licenses, opening bank accounts and enrolling in flight schools—until the morning of September 11 when they walked aboard American Airlines Flight 77 and crashed it into the Pentagon.[27]

The CIA wouldn't have followed these men within the United States.[28] Though the CIA informed the FBI, it neglected until August 23, 2001, to alert the State Department so that the department, through the INS, could place these names on a watch list to prevent their entry into the U.S. By that time, both men were in the country. For its part, at this point the FBI neglected to pursue information about al Hazmi and al Mihdhar.* Questioned about its failure to follow up on a cable[29] alerting the bureau to their presence, one FBI official said, "If the cable says, 'Don't let them in the country,' and they were already in the country, what's the point of bringing this up now?"[30] Nor did the CIA have access to a July 5, 2001, FBI memo warning that several Islamic radicals under surveillance in Phoenix were enrolled in aeronautical school and might seek to infiltrate the civil aviation system. That, after all, was a domestic matter, outside the agency's foreign jurisdiction.

Before September 11, the "standard FBI line" according to one source who spoke to *The New Yorker* writer Joe Klein, was that "Osama bin Laden wasn't a serious domestic security threat," presumably because his attacks theretofore had been in foreign environments.[31] An internal FBI review, after 9/11, has concluded that "everything was done that could have been done."[32]

The United States has no intelligence agency fully devoted to internal security, like the British MI5 or the French Direction de la Surveillance du Territoire (DST).[33] The FBI is primarily a law enforcement institution.[34] For reasons regarding the third antinomy, discussed below, this complicates the picture even further, but for now it is sufficient to appreciate the difficulties arising from the water's edge separation between the CIA as an overseas agency and the FBI as a domestic body. Eighty percent of FBI personnel are devoted to solving crimes. There are counterterrorism and counterespionage divisions, but their officers rotate between them and the much larger criminal division.

Not surprisingly, the FBI is a "downstream" organization devoted to

---

*Here, too, another antinomy was involved: part of the FBI's failure was attributable to "the Wall"—a Department of Justice policy intended to regulate the exchange of foreign intelligence information between intelligence agents and criminal investigators. Intelligence agents were forbidden to share information with agents investigating criminal matters on the grounds that future prosecutions would be tainted because collection standards were lower for intelligence agents; criminal investigators were forbidden to share information with intelligence personnel. On August 29, a New York–based FBI agent requested authority to use his office's "full criminal investigative resources" to find al Mihdhar. This request was denied because al Mihdhar was not under criminal investigation. The agent replied, "Someday someone will die and Wall or not, the public will not understand why we were not . . . throwing every resource we had" at the problem.

reviewing past events as a basis for prosecutions. As Charles Cogan puts it, "What is deficient in the US system is the same kind of *upstream* intelligence [perspective] applied inside the United States, in the manner of MI5 and the DST" (emphasis in original).[35] That is unquestionably true, but what deepens this deficit is the exclusivity of FBI jurisdiction domestically, and this goes back to the domestic/foreign antinomy. Cogan has concluded that

> if we had a fully functioning internal security service . . . acting in seamless coordination with the CIA, it seems likely that [Al Hazmi and Al Mihdhar] would have been picked up on their arrival in the United States. This in return would have had a major effect on the unfolding of [the 9/11] operation, perhaps even to the extent of wrapping it up before it could have taken place.[36]

In a troublingly similar recapitulation, the domestic/foreign distinction may have been responsible for the failure of a special operations intelligence group, mentioned in the last chapter, to share results of data mining that uncovered Mohammed Atta's al Qaeda cell. Lawyers for the Defense Department are alleged to have intervened to prevent this information from going to the FBI because Atta was designated a "U.S. person on the grounds that he was present in the U.S." When frustrated intelligence analysts bitterly initiated a review after 9/11, the result was that they were told, "We did everything by the book." And so everyone had; that was the problem.

One other important effect of this division between the domestic and the foreign is the sequestration of U.S. defense budget resources from border control and security. Despite concerns about homeland surveillance that led to the destruction of DARPA's* TIA pilot program, it must be recognized that only the Defense Department has the funds and the infrastructure to pursue the new technologies that will make post-entry tracking effective.

Another effect of the division between national and international is the difficulty of coordinating domestic antiterrorist initiatives with the intelligence services of other countries. As one European official put it, "those we have been arresting [since September 11] are people we knew about before but never thought were particularly dangerous to us inside our national boundaries."[37] The most important tactical al Qaeda base for the attacks on America wasn't Afghanistan; it was Hamburg, Germany.

---

*The Defense Advanced Research Projects Agency is a U.S. Department of Defense component responsible for the development of new technology for military use. Among other technologies, the Internet originated with DARPA's predecessor.

(3) This brings us to what has become the most significant and perplexing of these fundamental dichotomies, the antinomy that results from the differing imperatives of law enforcement and intelligence activities.

Before 1978 and the regulatory fallout from the Watergate affair, U.S. law provided that the president could, on his own authority, order the interception of electronic communications in the U.S. for national security purposes. At the time of the September 11 attacks, however, such action had to either satisfy the criminal standards for establishing probable cause before an ordinary judge (there must be proof that a crime had been committed or was about to be), or the government had to go to a special Foreign Intelligence Surveillance Act court and show probable cause that the person was the agent of a foreign power.[38] Although groups engaged in international terrorism now come within FISA's definition of "foreign powers," "[it was] not clear that there [was] any legal authority . . . that empower[ed] the United States to conduct electronic surveillance or physical searches for intelligence purposes against a target who has not been shown to be an agent of a foreign power . . . but who may be planning a major [terrorist] assault in the United States."[39]

FBI agents were forbidden to create an intelligence-gathering file—that is, one based solely on suspicion that someone poses a threat to the United States. The bureau's handling of Zacarias Moussaoui is instructive. Justice Department officials felt compelled to turn down a request by the CIA to seek a warrant enabling the FBI to conduct surveillance on Moussaoui even though the CIA had provided evidence of his link with bin Laden. FBI field agents had seized Moussaoui's computer in mid-August after learning he had sought flight training for the Boeing 747–400, a commercial airliner, and had inquired about flight patterns over New York City. Without a warrant, FBI agents couldn't look at the contents of the computer. The Justice Department was convinced, possibly on dubious grounds, that no judge would issue a warrant on such a basis. Absurdly, Moussaoui was going to be deported on a U.S. government jet to France (he is a French national), where his computer, transported separately, could be examined by the French. The events of 9/11 intervened.

As Jeffrey Smith, former CIA general counsel, put it:

The question is: is this particular investigation . . . a law enforcement investigation that's going to lead to a trial? Or is it an intelligence investigation designed to produce intelligence which might lead to some other action, a military action, a diplomatic response, or an arrest overseas, or intelligence activities to disrupt it? And the law now is such that, when you start down one course, it's very hard, if not impossible, to shift to the other course, because [wiretaps developed and put in place for criminal prosecutions are] designed with a very specific set of rules governing the manner in which wiretaps will be conducted, ultimately, to be introduced in court, [and these rules are] designed to protect the rights of the defendant. With an intelligence wiretap, it's very different. The fundamental purpose is to collect as much information as you can . . . and there's never the intention that it will be used in prosecutions.[40]

One consequence of this was that if the FBI installed an ordinary wiretap for counterterrorist purposes because it intended to prosecute someone, it would refuse to share any results with the CIA. So, as we have seen, no one other than the prosecutors and a few persons in the FBI and the Justice Department had access to the information generated by the investigation of the World Trade Center bombing, in 1993, until after this evidence was presented in court. That meant that for almost six years the White House and the CIA were denied information that should have been used to alert intelligence operatives overseas.[41]

Similarly, the FBI refused to provide the State Department's Bureau of Consular Affairs, the agency which approved Mohammed Atta's visa despite the fact he was on an FBI watch list, with access to its National Crime Information Center Database on the grounds that the Bureau of Consular Affairs is not a law enforcement agency.[42]

Sometimes multiple antinomies concatenate. Thus in the case of Mohammed Atta, once the CIA finally reported his identity in a cable to the INS, it was discovered that Atta had already entered the country. The case then ceased to be a foreign intelligence matter and went to the FBI. The FBI refused to give the watch list names to the FAA because the FAA was not a law enforcement agency; or to the airlines because they were private, not public; or to the State Department because it was a domestic issue.

These bureaucratic border wars may sound as if they are nothing more than turf battles among agencies. In fact, they are the result of the carefully structured ways that intelligence was organized before the appearance of the phenomenon of strategic terrorism. Thus neither the appointment of a new administrator nor the promulgation of a new executive directive demanding cooperation will much change things.

In retrospect, one of the most serious charges about the September 11 events is that the U.S. refused to accept the 1998 offer by the Sudanese to hand over two men suspected of involvement in the East African bombings of American embassies and that it was reluctant to accept a Sudanese proposal to arrest and extradite bin Laden himself. These accusations have been emphatically denied, but in any case, it is not hard to understand why the U.S. would have been wary of managing an extradition and prosecution. It is highly unlikely that, at that stage, there was sufficient admissible evidence that could be introduced in an American court for any U.S. administration to be confident of a successful formal prosecution. Law enforcement was, as it was expected to be, completely detached from foreign policy. We don't have political prisoners in civilized countries. At the time, bin Laden was not a common criminal who could be convicted of any ordinary crime in an ordinary trial.[43]

In early 2006, the antinomy between law enforcement activities and the collection of intelligence was fused with the antinomy arising from contrasting rules for domestic and foreign surveillance when a heated dispute erupted in the U.S. following the disclosure of the NSA's warrantless wiretapping of international conversations of U.S. persons. A brief review of the historical background to the political and legal crisis that ensued may illuminate how that crisis directly arose from American practices.

The interception of messages in order to protect the State is as old as the modern state itself. In the early nineteenth century, the term "black chamber" applied to secret rooms in the sorting offices of the main postal links in Europe where mail was brought so it could be opened and read.

> London's was in Abchurch Lane, near St Paul's. Black chambers resembled laboratories. Kettles spouted steam to soften wax seals. Experts took impressions of seals with a soft amalgam to make the new ones in case they broke the originals while sliding hot wires under them. Specialists slid thin flat needles with a long slit in them into envelopes and twirled the letter around them so they could be extracted without breaking the seals.[44]

Diplomatic mail was opened, dispatches were copied, and the envelopes resealed. This was done in all capitals. When an outraged British ambassador complained to the Austrian foreign minister, Metternich, that he was now getting copies rather than originals of his correspondence from Britain, Metternich simply sighed and said, "How clumsy these people are!"[45]

Furthermore, there is nothing new about governments pledging to stop reading their citizens' correspondence. Regulations requiring postal secrecy were passed as early as 1532 in Austria, and 1685 in Prussia, and were present in the oath of succession taken by the future Holy Roman emperor Joseph I in 1690. In the United States, the first federal postal statute included a provision forbidding federal agents from illegally opening the mail.

In every case, however, there was presumed to be an exception for the surveillance of foreign correspondence. British statutes passed in 1711 and 1837 required warrants to open domestic mail but did not apply to diplomats' messages or to the reports of spies. Against this historical background, it is hardly surprising that for a long time U.S. chief executives simply assumed they had constitutional power to conduct surveillance of the agents of foreign governments, either acknowledged or clandestine.

In the U.S. the interception of foreign intelligence communications is done by the National Security Agency. Created by the Truman Memorandum in 1952, the NSA is the largest American intelligence agency. Typically, about 60 percent of the president's daily briefing comes from NSA signals intercepts. From 22,300 miles above the earth, U.S. satellites with 2,000-square-foot antennae swept Soviet microwave communications between the strategic rocket forces headquarters in Moscow and ICBM sites in western Siberia. The same technology could pick up conversations among Americans. It was assumed that this would not be done without warrants.

As with so much in the field of contemporary U.S. law governing the executive, this assumption ran aground in the Watergate affair. FISA (the Foreign Intelligence Surveillance Act, which was discussed in the previous chapter) was the outcome in 1978 of negotiations between the executive and the Congress that sought a workable compromise that would enable the U.S. government to conduct intelligence operations against foreign-based threats while preventing the abuse of that power for domestic political goals. The NSA (or the FBI) would need FISA warrants to intercept communications with U.S. persons, including resident aliens.

On September 10, 2001, the NSA intercepted two messages: "the match begins tomorrow," and "tomorrow is zero hour." Those intercepts came from suspected al Qaeda general locations; they were intercepted randomly from Afghan pay phones. Not surprisingly, these messages—among an enormous number of others—were not translated until September 12.

"[P]rior to September 11th, certain communications weren't considered valuable intelligence," General Michael V. Hayden, the deputy director of national intelligence and former head of the NSA, acknowledged in a speech on January 23, 2006, but after the attacks, Hayden had "exercised some options [he'd] always had."[46] In addition to these unspecified options, the president asserted authority to collect intelligence against anyone in the United States, whether validly present or not, as well as U.S. corporations, including those operating overseas who were in communication with persons abroad believed to be connected to terrorism, without going to the FISA court.

Before the September 11 attacks, the NSA typically eavesdropped on very few persons in the U.S., often fewer than a dozen. It was the FBI, with its far less intrusive low-tech wiretapping, that requested most of the FISA warrants.[47] General Hayden was insistent that his fresh authority for warrantless collection was approved by NSA and Justice Department lawyers and was signed off on by the attorney general. The debate in 2006 turned on the legality of the president's action and was enriched by a lengthy Department of Justice memorandum defending the president and a pithier letter by a group of distinguished law professors attacking the decision.

It is easy to get lost in these important questions, however, and lose sight of the revolutionary political and technological events that are transforming the very basis of warrants in the first place.

Signals intelligence in the twentieth century meant intercepting analog signals carried along dedicated voice channels, connecting two discrete and known target points. In the twenty-first century, communications are mostly digital; they carry billions of bits of data, are dynamically routed in packets, and are globally networked.

General Hayden was particularly at pains to insist that the NSA collection procedures at issue were "focused" and did not involve a vast "driftnet . . . that we then sort out by these alleged keyword searches or data-mining tools."[48] Still, data mining that builds on known and confirmed information about a terrorist group can prove extraordinarily valuable.

If the U.S. government had taken the names it already had on its terrorist watch list and swept airline reservations, it would have caught two hijackers, Nawaf al Hamzi and Khalid al Mihdhar, with reservations on the same flight on 9/11. If airline records had been checked, it would have been learned that both persons purchased tickets for American Airlines flight 77 using their real names, addresses, phone numbers, and frequent flyer numbers. If the government had then cross-checked the street addresses of the two, it would have discovered that Salem al Hazmi and Mohammed Atta shared a street address with Nawaf al Hamzi and that they too were flying on September 11, on American Airlines flights 77 and 11. Using publicly available address information would have also disclosed the identity of a third man, Marwan al-Shehhi (who shared an address with al Mihdhar), and a further check of airline information would have revealed that he had purchased a ticket on the same day for United Airlines flight 175. Research of telephone numbers would have identified four more hijackers—Fayez Banihammad, Mohand al Shehri, Waleed al Shehri, and Abdulaziz al Omari—who shared a phone with Atta, and a return to airline records would have shown that all six men were scheduled to fly on 9/11 on American Airlines flights 11 and 77 and United Airlines flight 175. A search of postal records would have shown that Satam al Suqami shared a post office box with al Shehri, and a quick check with American would have shown that he too had purchased a ticket on flight 11. Also booked on flight 77 was Hani Hanjour, a former roommate of al Hamzi and al Mihdhar. If the FBI had scanned INS watch lists for expired visas and cross-checked that information with the passenger lists of the four flights, it would then have picked up the name of Ahmed Al Ghamdi, booked on United flight 175. Address information for al Ghamdi would have disclosed that he used the same address as Hamza al Ghamdi, Saeed al Ghamdi, Ahmad al Haznawi, and Ahmed al Nami. The first two were booked on United flight 175, and the second two on United flight 93, all for 9/11. Al Haznawi was a former roommate of Ziad Jarrah, who was also booked—in his own name—on United flight 93 for that day. A further scan of frequent flyer numbers would have added the name of Majed Moqed to the list. Moqed had used al Mihdhar's number to purchase his ticket for American flight 77. Elementary data mining, that is, would have easily picked up all nineteen hijackers, though only two were actually suspected terrorists, all flying on the same day on only four different flights.[49] These links, in themselves innocent, would not have been enough, however, to yield a finding of probable cause before most judges. Yet within two weeks of the 9/11 attacks, the U.S. had located hundreds of e-mails linked to the hijackers, in English and Arabic, sent four to six weeks before September 11, some of which included operational details of the planned terrorist assault.[50]

In August 2007, Congress passed, and President Bush hurriedly signed, a law that amended FISA, the legal framework for the electronic interception of various kinds of communication with foreign sources. This precipitated vehement attacks—notably by the *New York Times* editorial board—on the legislation and those who had voted for it. Commentators put it about that the law was wholly unnecessary, that it authorized a lawless and unprecedented expansion of presidential authority, and that Democrats in Congress cravenly accepted all this for the basest political reasons. None of these widely broadcast conclusions is likely to have been true.

All sides agreed that some legislative fix is required because of changes in telecommunications technology. Where once it made sense to require warrants when communications passed through America's public switched network (virtually all domestic calls once traveled on landlines), this ceased to be the case when American routers became the transit points for foreign conversations that might or might not involve a person in the United States and fiber-optic cable replaced satellite transmission for international calls.

Communication that formerly had been linear, analog, and point-to-point has been replaced by the disaggregated packets of the Internet. Two persons talking to each other in Europe could find their conversations going through American switches. It also became difficult to determine the true origin of any communication that was routed through the United States. If a terrorism suspect in Pakistan is having conversations with someone on a computer with a New York Internet protocol address via a chat room run by an Internet service provider in London, where exactly is the intelligence being collected? If the answer is in the United States simply because the servers are located there, of what possible relevance could that be to the protection of the rights of Americans?

Amending the statute to focus on protecting American people rather than an American address, however, would not have dealt with a larger and more profound problem. The change in the global communications infrastructure is both a driver and a consequence of a change in the nature of conflict. The end of the Cold War was brought about in part because of technologies that empowered the individual and whetted people's appetites for more control over their lives. These same developments also empower networks of terrorists, and the war they will soon be capable of waging has little in common with the industrial warfare of the twentieth century. Accordingly, foreign intelligence tasks will also change.

It once made sense to require that the person whose communications were intercepted be a spy when the whole point of the interception was to gather evidence to prosecute espionage. This makes much less sense when the purpose of the interception is to determine whether the person is in fact an agent at all and when prevention, not prosecution, is the objective. This sort of communications intercept tries to build from a known element in a terror network—a person, a telephone number, a photograph, a safe house, an electronic dead drop—to some picture of the network itself. By cross-hatching vast amounts of information, based on relatively few confirmed elements, it is possible to detect patterns that can expose the network through its benign operations and then focus on its more malignant schemes.

For this purpose, warrants are utterly beside the point. As Judge Richard Posner has put it, "[O]nce you grant the legitimacy of surveillance aimed at detection rather than at gathering evidence of guilt, requiring a warrant to conduct it would be like requiring a warrant to ask people questions or to install surveillance cameras on city streets." Warrants, which originate in the criminal justice paradigm, provide a useful standard for surveillance designed to prove guilt, not to learn the identity of people who may be planning atrocities and discarding their cell phones frequently.

A statutory fix that simply waived the warrant requirement when both parties to a conversation were foreign would scarcely address this problem. Technology is changing the nature of the threat, not merely the mechanics of collection. The statutory change is unnecessary, I suppose, if one believes that there is in fact no real threat, that it's all hype by the White House to expand its powers—presumably to some other end—and that all we have to fear is fear itself. Doubtless, some people do believe this. If the editorialists and columnists in the news media make this assumption, they should frankly say so.

Furthermore, there is an unstated assumption that warrantless surveillance is lawless surveillance. There is, however, judicial precedent for warrantless searches, even if you can't tell this from the public debate. The president of the American Bar Association objected to the new statute by sarcastically observing, "The last time I checked, the Fourth Amendment is still in the Bill of Rights," which he doubtless believed to be a withering salvo.

In fact, there are many instances in which warrantless surveillance has been held to be permissible under the Fourth Amendment. Searches in public schools require neither warrants nor a showing of probable cause. Government offices can be searched for evidence of work-related misconduct without warrants. So can searches conducted at the border, or searches undertaken as a condition of parole. Searches have been upheld in the absence of a warrant where there is no legitimate expectation of privacy. The Clinton administration conducted a warrantless search—lawfully—when it was trying to determine what the spy Aldrich Ames was up to. The day after Pearl Harbor, President Roosevelt authorized the interception of all communications traffic into and out of the United States.

The legislation passed in August 2007 was a statutory effort to legitimize efforts by NSA that had been called into question by a FISA judge. The head of NSA had testified that this reversal, requiring warrants, had had a staggering effect on collection efforts. Moreover, General Hayden, director of the Central Intelligence Agency, had stated that the program was of such importance that, had it been in effect prior to 9/11, it was his "professional judgment that we would have detected some of the 9/11 al Qaeda operatives in the U.S. and we would have identified them as such." To put this in context it seems clear that NSA couldn't have gotten a warrant to tap a particular line used by al Mihdhar or al Hamzi, but could have traced them when they had conversations with their co-conspirators overseas.*

If there was a flaw in the legislation it was that the judiciary was taken out of the loop, but this too was partly the result of the obsessive focus on warrants. The real role for judicial intervention ought to be post hoc—not granting warrants but rather in close supervision of the surveillance that is undertaken once the government has done so. This would have subjected the government's programs to more timely scrutiny and thus conferred greater legitimacy to the undertaking. It has always seemed a bit absurd that some civil libertarians defend the warrant requirement by arguing that

*Remarks by Lt. General Michael V. Hayden, National Press Club, 23 January 2006. And, significantly, the U.S. director of national intelligence, Adm. Mike McConnell, testified in September 2007 that the crucial arrest of a German jihadist cell preparing to attack Frankfurt airport was a direct consequence of the relaxed rule dispensing with warrants for the interception of a communication abroad (though this occurred, at least in part, before this program was sanctified by the new statute). See Eric Schmitt, "New Law Credited in Arrests Abroad," New York Times, 11 September 2007, http://www.nytimes.com/2007/09/11/washington/11terror.html (accessed October 25, 2007).

it can't really impede intelligence collection because warrants are routinely granted anyway.

The kind of attacks with which this book is concerned—those that truly threaten the state of consent by undermining its institutions and sense of well-being—require complex organization and effective communications. To prevent such attacks it is axiomatic that methods for acquiring access to these communications must be facilitated. Market state terrorists are empowered by communications technology; it would be idiotic not to exploit this technology to defeat them.

FISA depended on certain boundary rules—it is triggered by activity "within the United States" or involving "U.S. persons" (either citizens or corporations legally resident within the U.S.)—that do not conform to the realities of a global, networked terrorist threat that moves easily, both personally and electronically, in and out of U.S. territory. Because contemporary communications are broken into packets, even targeting a specific communication will require scanning and filtering an entire communications flow. When FISA was held to require a warrant for any surveillance that "occurs in the United States" when there was a substantial likelihood of intercepting the contents of a communication to or from a person in the U.S., this required warrants for surveillance of wholly foreign communications if the intercept were accomplished by means of a telecommunications switch on U.S. soil. In fact, one can acquire a voice-over-Internet protocol from anywhere in the world, so some jihadist websites have suggested acquiring VoIP with U.S. telephone numbers.

If an automated machine is initially collecting hundreds of thousands of conversations, e-mails, credit card charges, airline reservations, addresses, and the like looking for particular patterns or trying to cross-check leads, it is not obvious that warrants specific to particular persons make any sense. Until these patterns intersect with hard leads about specific persons there is no point, and much to be concerned about, in intelligence personnel having access to the results of this analysis. Yet once such intersections are established, it would nevertheless be difficult to imagine getting warrants in such situations, not only because they are time-consuming and eat up resources, but mainly because the standard of probable cause to conclude that the target is a terrorist agent cannot be met. Indeed, trying to determine just who is such an agent is the point of collection. Requiring a finding of probable cause makes little sense for pattern analysis. In the globalized world of telecommunications, the distinction between persons present or not in the U.S. doesn't make sense either. Yet both were cornerstones of FISA. As Posner puts it: "FISA's limitations are borrowed from law enforcement. When crimes are committed, there are usually suspects, and electronic surveillance can be used to nail them. In counterterrorist intelligence, you don't know whom to suspect—you need surveillance to find out."[51]

FISA's shortcomings are related to the same developments that are driving the emergence of market states. As the director of the Center for Advanced Studies in Science and Technology Policy summarized the problem,

> FISA simply did not anticipate the nature of the current threat to national security from transnational terrorism and nuclear weapons proliferation, nor did it anticipate the development of global communications networks or advanced technical methods for intelligence gathering. FISA is no longer adequate to address certain technology developments, including the transition from circuit-based communications to packet-based communications; the globalization of communications infrastructure; and the development of automated monitoring techniques, including data mining and traffic analysis.[52]

At bottom, the FISA reform debate is an outgrowth of the foreign/domestic antinomy. When FISA was first enacted, most domestic calls were done by wire; most international calls were done via satellite. To protect domestic users, the statute required a warrant as a precedent for wiretap interception. Today, most international calls and messages go by means of fiber-optic cable; an increasing amount of domestic phone traffic is wireless, in great measure owing to cellular phones.

But the real problem is the antinomy itself. As Gregory F. Treverton puts it, "[O]f the implications of the market state for intelligence, . . . [the] first is the draining of meaning from 'foreign' and domestic,' " and he gives this example:

> [T]he National Security Agency's vast capacity to monitor signals is as close as the world has to a capacity to monitor the movements of money across borders. It might do so not just in the interest of the American state but for the sake of global transparency in capital movements. . . . [T]hat task [however] would upend every distinction on which U.S. intelligence is based—the movers of money have, in general, not committed a crime, nor do they pose a specific "national security" threat to the United States, many of them would be Americans, and NSA would be hard-pressed to share its take without revealing its capacity. Its international purposes would conflict directly with its national ones.*

---

*Treverton is the former vice chairman of the National Intelligence Council and the author of *Reshaping National Intelligence for an Age of Information* (Cambridge, 2003). The quoted passage is from his "Intelligence and the Market State," an unclassified paper prepared for the CIA; see *Studies in Intelligence* 10 (Winter–Spring 2001): 69–76.

Not everyone agrees that the foreign and the domestic antinomy is, in Tre-verton's apt phrase, "the vanishing divide." Responding to the provision in the Intelligence Reform and Terrorism Prevention Act that requires the DNI's approval of the FBI's choice of the head of the National Security Service (within FBI), the national security legislative counsel for the ACLU stated that "it's *alarming* that the same person who oversees for-eign spying will now oversee domestic spying, too."[53]

(4) There has also existed for some time a struggle within the intelli-gence agencies over whether their primary business should be directed at acquiring secrets or mining the increasingly abundant open-source envi-ronment. "Open sources" are simply unclassified papers like newspapers and books, and assets like the journalists and academics who produce them.

Many CIA analysts are prisoners of a single set of sources, virtually all of them secret. This means that while agency analysts might do an expert job on, say, the collapse of the Argentinean currency, they will often do so without a systematic collection of what the very best Wall Street or other private sector analysts are doing. Most of the expertise on Afghanistan, North Korea, Iran, or the like is no longer to be found inside the intelli-gence agencies, or inside government for that matter.[54] Indeed, according to the Aspin-Brown Commission, "In some areas, such as economic analy-sis, it is estimated that as much as 95 percent of the information utilized now comes from open sources. . . . [But an] adequate computer infrastruc-ture to tie intelligence analysts into open-source information does not appear to exist."[55] Systematically accessing these outside sources, how-ever, requires a considerable change of approach.

They might have added that the human infrastructure—mainly linguists—does not sufficiently exist. Americans don't become linguists and U.S. intelligence agencies often refuse to hire persons with close rela-tions abroad, though such persons are far likelier to possess fluency in a foreign language and familiarity with a foreign culture.*

The tendency to disparage open- or foreign-source material is under-standable. As every careful reader of a newspaper knows, information finds its way into print because someone with his own agenda wants it there. More importantly, intelligence analysts want to add unique value to their product, creating a comparative advantage that can come only from secret sources. Also, information about terrorist activities is so closely guarded by the terrorists themselves that there are few open sources that have enough facts to be of real help—although al Qaeda has cultivated media outlets and indeed has a minister for media affairs.[56] Finally, even

*I am indebted to Harold Edgar for this pertinent observation.

abundant open source material cannot set the collection agenda: there is just too much of it. The collector must already have made the political judgment that will determine relevance. As one of the most thoughtful intelligence officials in the U.K. has noted, "[t]he failure to appreciate the significance of radical Islam since the Second World War was largely a consequence of our mindset that Arab nationalism was the key issue. We were just looking the wrong way."[57]

Al Qaeda is a very complex target for clandestine collection. Fundamentalist Muslims are unlikely to be "turned" by offers of money or sex, or even fear of incarceration, and at present, it is hard to believe that U.S. policy has tempted many to forsake their current allegiances. Insinuating a spy into al Qaeda is also difficult. The core around bin Laden and Zawahiri has been together for some time. The peripheral groups to whom most operations are outsourced are easier to penetrate, but each is only responsible for executing a few plots.

Secret sources are necessarily hard to corroborate. This is one reason, as we shall see, to reform institutional intelligence arrangements to encourage more sharing: it can better expose the possibility of concerted deception. One sometimes wonders whether the chorus that calls for a greater emphasis on human source intelligence (HUMINT) has reflected on the lack of such reliable information where North Korea or, it turns out, Iraq were concerned—targets that are no more difficult than the al Qaeda leadership. Indeed, the principal reason to place greater reliance on opensource materials when these are available is to allow intelligence collectors to focus their budgets more exclusively on the collection of secrets from the most difficult targets.

(5) Another classic antinomy in intelligence work is the distinction between collection and analysis. Not surprisingly, after September 11 there were numerous calls for greater efforts at intelligence collection, including the relaxing of some of the legal restraints on collection. It is true that, no matter how much information was ignored by analysts before September 11 because it did not fit into the prevailing set of expectations, still more information might have been better. The difficulty is that more information, without more analytical resources to assess it, simply compounds the problem. It builds the haystack ever higher even if it adds a needle or two in the process. About the events of September 11, one writer concluded, "It's becoming increasingly clear, however, that September's intelligence failure stemmed not from the inability to collect data, but from law enforcement's inability to analyze and act on information already in hand."[58] Information overload may actually inhibit the conversion of information into knowledge, to say nothing of the reflection required to acquire understanding. NSA estimates that by the end of 2007, the Internet will carry 647 petabytes of data each day (by comparison, the holdings of

the entire Library of Congress—130 million items, including 30 million books—represent only .02 petabytes).

Once it was worthwhile to pay a building janitor to empty the contents of a wastebasket in a foreign ministry and deliver them to an agent. It was profitable to pay a handsome sum for a military manual for a particular weapon. The information thus gained fitted into a larger picture about our adversaries—chiefly the Soviet Union, about which it was difficult to learn even the most basic facts—and we knew what to make of the information we gained. Nowadays two things have changed. First, a single Zip drive downloaded by an agent can provide more information than a roomful of analysts can sort out in a year. For instance, a scientist at the Los Alamos nuclear lab was alleged to have downloaded more than 400,000 pages of highly classified material and then parked the information on an accessible e-mail site.[59] One consequence is that our enemies could overload our collection efforts rather easily by, for example, using hot words like "explosive" in thousands of innocent or even nonsensical conversations. If the intelligence services are being systematically misinformed, for example, about allegedly pending airline attacks, immense resources can be commandeered by an enemy who does little more than place a telephone call on a line he suspects is being tapped. This would soak up analytic capabilities and thus disable us just as thoroughly as if the NSA were bombed.

Second, it is not so clear precisely where our adversary now resides. Because the terrorist is in a sense stateless—or perhaps the agent of a virtual state—data about him ebbs and flows in a sea of information about ordinary people in non-hostile countries. The larger tides are obscured by the myriad ripples of information. This is no less true of the domestic terrorist.

If the culture of secrets can sometimes be the enemy of understanding the broader picture (the open source problem), the culture of collection, hermetically sealed off from analysis, creates its own problems. We must be able to achieve greater intimacy between analysts and collectors. Only then can collectors explain the availability and quality of sources and analysts can ask for missing pieces. Collection will be more fruitful and the intelligence product more discriminating.

(6) Finally, attention must be drawn to the differing roles of intelligence producer and consumer that create yet another antinomy. For some time, it has been assumed that the producer is rather like a scientist[60] who gathers facts impartially, heedless of the use to which they will be put and uncontaminated by any passion other than the pure love of knowledge; whereas the consumer of intelligence is animated by the political and policy imperatives of the day. If the producer becomes infected with the preferences of the consumer, then the risk is that intelligence will be politicized; if the consumer attempts to govern production, then the risk is that

worthwhile, if inconvenient facts will not be brought forth. It is a picture that owes as much to the scientistic ambitions of social science as to any reality, but it is a picture that nevertheless has many in its thrall. Just such a picture animated the Butler Report, commissioned to inquire whether political pressures on the U.K. Joint Intelligence Committee had corrupted its assessment of Iraqi weapons of mass destruction.[61]

With regard to terrorism, this has resulted in a number of barriers to sharing information. More importantly, these principles have interrupted the mutual process of learning by which catastrophic errors can be avoided. Thus it has been reported (and heatedly and authoritatively denied) that a member of the Clinton administration, pressed by an aggressively skeptical media to prove that U.S. attacks on al Qaeda camps in Afghanistan really were legitimate efforts to stop bin Laden and not, as it was alleged, attempts to distract the public from the president's impeachment woes, revealed that we had been listening to bin Laden's satellite phone traffic and therefore had good reason to know his location at the time of the attacks. It has been claimed that al Qaeda's leadership stopped using this means of communication almost immediately after this was recklessly reported in the *Washington Times*.[62] Similarly, a Bush administration official, anxious to confirm that the Orange alert of August 2004 was in fact supported by intelligence collection, announced to the press that a Pakistani member of al Qaeda had been arrested and then unfortunately proceeded to name him. This indiscretion ended the usefulness of the Pakistani, who in fact had been "turned" by the authorities and was acting as a double agent following his arrest. Doubtless there was some misunderstanding about the ground rules between the journalists and the officials in these cases, but the immediate consequences were devastating. This was the result of the separation between producer and consumer, where the latter (often under pressure from a skeptical media) is insufficiently sensitive to the needs of the former.

Usually, it is the other way round. Producers often create intelligence products of little use to the policy makers who need relevant information. Recent experience with the President's Daily Brief provides an instructive example. The PDB is a small magazine produced by the CIA for the president's use. It is an effort—originally by the CIA, now under the auspices of the director of national intelligence—to provide the president with international intelligence warranting his attention. The first PDB was produced in 1964 for President Johnson. New presidents devour it in their first months in office. It is an amalgam of secret news, largely military and political, enlivened by occasional descriptions of foreign personalities.

Here are two examples, the first from the Clinton presidency and the second from George W. Bush's first term. The brackets indicate redactions.

SUBJECT: BIN LADIN PREPARING TO HIJACK
US AIRCRAFT AND OTHER ATTACKS[63]

1. Reporting [—] suggests Bin Ladin and his allies are preparing for attacks in the US, including an aircraft hijacking to obtain the release of Shaykh 'Umar 'Abd al-Rahman, Ramzi Yousef, and Muhammad Sadiq 'Awda. One source quoted a senior member of the Gama'at al-Islamiyya (IG) saying that, as of late October, the IG had completed planning for an operation in the US on behalf of Bin Ladin, but that the operation was on hold. A senior Bin Ladin operative from Saudi Arabia was to visit IG counterparts in the US soon thereafter to discuss options—perhaps including an aircraft hijacking.

- IG leader Islambuli in late September was planning to hijack a US airliner during the "next couple of weeks" to free 'Abd al-Rahman and the other prisoners, according to what may be a different source.
- The same source late last month said that Bin Ladin might implement plans to hijack US aircraft before the beginning of Ramadan on 20 December and that two members of the operational team had evaded security checks during a recent trial run at an unidentified New York airport. [—]

2. Some members of the Bin Ladin network have received hijack training, according to various sources, but no group directly tied to Bin Ladin's al-Qa'ida organization has ever carried out an aircraft hijacking. Bin Ladin could be weighing other types of operations against US aircraft. According to [—] the IG in October obtained SA-7 missiles and intended to move them from Yemen into Saudi Arabia to shoot down an Egyptian plane or, if unsuccessful, a US military or civilian aircraft.

- A [—] in October told us that unspecified "extremist elements" in Yemen had acquired SA-7s. [—]

3. [—] indicate the Bin Ladin organization or its allies are moving closer to implementing anti-US attacks at unspecified locations, but we do not know whether they are related to attacks on aircraft. A Bin Ladin associate in Sudan late last month told a colleague in Kandahar that he had shipped a group of containers to Afghanistan. Bin Ladin associates also talked about the movement of containers to Afghanistan before the East Africa bombings.

- In other [—] Bin Ladin associates last month discussed picking up a package in Malaysia. One told his colleague in Malaysia that "they" were in the "ninth month [of pregnancy]."
- An alleged Bin Ladin supporter in Yemen late last month remarked to his mother that he planned to work in "commerce" from abroad and said his impending "marriage," which would take place soon, would be a "surprise." "Commerce" and "marriage" often are codewords for terrorist attacks. [—]

During the Clinton presidency, the problem arose of providing items to the president that he felt were relevant to the development of his thinking. Reading the PDB item above, it is hard to see how its disparate bits of scanty information would be of much use to a president. Early in his first term, President Clinton met with the director of central intelligence, James Woolsey, and asked for a PDB briefing that might resemble an article by Robert Kaplan that the president had been reading. This vivid essay ran for twenty-four pages and discussed the plight of several West African countries, drawing on issues of crime, social development, health, demography, education, and tribal conflict. These were addressed against an historical background of colonial geopolitics which, Kaplan argued, had ignored the ethnic complexities of Africa. The colonial process, by ignoring traditional West African cultural, social, and tribal boundaries, had contributed to a burgeoning crisis that foretold future problems including those of Western inner cities.

> It was [the] cultural colour, specialist understanding and a unique perspective that Bill Clinton was looking for from the CIA. . . . What he was asking for was not what the CIA assumed; to them it was just a particular briefing on a particular issue but from the president's perspective the article reflected deeper trends.[64]

Woolsey felt the CIA community failed to appreciate President Clinton's need for the sort of background report typified by Kaplan's essay.[65]

The Bush administration seems to have overcorrected for this problem by instituting daily, intensive meetings between the director of central intelligence and the president, during which the director orally delivered the PDB. As a result, the PDB became far too sensitive to the president's preoccupations, with the briefers reporting back to the editors every raised eyebrow or crossed leg in an effort to appeal to this audience of one. In its review of the colossal intelligence failure regarding Iraqi WMD, the Commission on the Intelligence Capabilities of the United States Regarding Weapons of Mass Destruction (the Robb-Silberman Commission) concluded:

As problematic as the October 2002 NIE [National Intelligence Estimate] was, it was not the [intelligence] Community's biggest analytic failure on Iraq. Even more misleading was the river of intelligence that flowed from the CIA to top policymakers over long periods of time in the PDB . . . [These daily reports] with their attention-grabbing headlines and drumbeat of repetition, left an impression of many corroborating reports where in fact there were very few sources . . . In ways both subtle and not so subtle, the daily reports seemed to be "selling" intelligence in order to keep its customers, or at least the First Customer, interested.[66]

Regarding the al Qaeda threat, this process created its own, more perilous pitfalls, for even when the president does request specific information, unless the PDB provides context its information is apt to be misinterpreted. During the spring and summer of 2001, President Bush several times asked the briefers delivering the PDB whether any of the threats mentioned were directed toward the American homeland. In response, the CIA decided to include an item in the PDB. The two CIA analysts involved in drafting the item believed it was their chance to communicate to the president their view that the threat of an al Qaeda attack in the U.S. was serious. This was the result:

SUBJECT: BIN LADIN DETERMINED TO STRIKE IN US

Clandestine, foreign government, and media reports indicate Bin Ladin since 1997 has wanted to conduct terrorist attacks in the US. Bin Ladin implied in US television interviews in 1997 and 1998 that his followers would follow the example of World Trade Center bomber Ramzi Yousef and "bring the fighting to America."

After US missile strikes on his base in Afghanistan in 1998, Bin Ladin told followers he wanted to retaliate in Washington, according to a [—] service. An Egyptian Islamic Jihad (EIJ) operative told an [—] service at the same time that Bin Ladin was planning to exploit the operative's access to the US to mount a terrorist strike.

The millennium plotting in Canada in 1999 may have been part of Bin Ladin's first serious attempt to implement a terrorist strike in the US. Convicted plotter Ahmed Ressam has told the FBI that he conceived the idea to attack Los Angeles International Airport himself, but that Bin Ladin lieutenant Abu Zubaydah encouraged him and helped facilitate the operation. Ressam also said that in 1998 Abu Zubaydah was planning his own US attack.

Ressam says Bin Ladin was aware of the Los Angeles operation.

Although Bin Ladin has not succeeded, his attacks against the US Embassies in Kenya and Tanzania in 1998 demonstrate that he prepares operations years in advance and is not deterred by setbacks. Bin Ladin associates surveilled our Embassies in Nairobi and Dar es Salaam as early as 1993, and some members of the Nairobi cell planning the bombings were arrested and deported in 1997.

Al-Qa'ida members—including some who are US citizens—have resided in or traveled to the US for years, and the group apparently maintains a support structure that could aid attacks. Two al-Qa'ida members found guilty in the conspiracy to bomb our Embassies in East Africa were US citizens, and a senior EIJ member lived in California in the mid-1990s. A clandestine source said in 1998 that a Bin Ladin cell in New York was recruiting Muslim-American youth for attacks.

We have not been able to corroborate some of the more sensational threat reporting, such as that from a [—] service in 1998 saying that Bin Ladin wanted to hijack a US aircraft to gain the release of "Blind Shaykh" 'Umar 'Abd al-Rahman and other US-held extremists. Nevertheless, FBI information since that time indicates patterns of suspicious activity in this country consistent with preparations for hijackings or other types of attacks, including recent surveillance of federal buildings in New York.

The FBI is conducting approximately 70 full field investigations throughout the US that it considers Bin Ladin–related. CIA and the FBI are investigating a call to our Embassy in the UAE in May saying that a group of Bin Ladin supporters was in the US planning attacks with explosives.[67]

President Bush subsequently testified that the import to him of the August 6 PDB was historical in nature. He said the article affirmed that al Qaeda was dangerous, which he said he had known since he had become president. He said bin Laden had long been talking about his desire to attack America. He recalled some operational data about the FBI and remembered thinking it was heartening that seventy investigations were under way. Exhibiting a profound indifference to what would become his own professed strategy of preemption, he concluded that there was "no actionable intelligence" in the PDB. He did not recall discussing the August 6 report with the attorney general or whether his national security advisor had done so. Without more context and some realistic description of the significance of this report, the president believed he had been presented with little more than a *Newsweek* article.

Instead of producing the PDB for a small circle around the president, and then adapting this daily paper to create a more widely circulated[68] document—formerly called the NID (National Intelligence Daily), now the SEIB (Senior Executive Intelligence Brief)—one study[69] has proposed that the initial draft be created for middle managers. This would be the outcome of an ongoing, constant dialogue between intelligence consumers and producers. It would then be enriched to make the PDB—the opposite of the present process, which strips information away from the PDB to produce the less closely held publications. This might sacrifice the effort to reflect the president's preoccupations in favor of a more contextualized portrait of what the bureaucracy is thinking, including differing opinions held and some assessment of the sourcing behind the reporting. After the debacle over weapons of mass destruction in Iraq, this has a certain appeal. The real problem, however, is not choosing which constituency to inform, but rather to make consumer and producer more sensitive to each other. One cannot criticize the White House for neglecting to act on fragmentary but cumulative evidence before 9/11, and then also criticize it for acting on fragmentary but cumulative evidence of Iraqi weapons of mass destruction.

The notion of cultivating a closer relationship between consumers and producers is, to put it very mildly indeed, a highly controversial idea. The Hutton Inquiry and the Butler Report in the U.K. were premised on the notion that there is something fundamentally wrong with close relations between the political consumers of intelligence and its bureaucratic producers. Richard Helms, the highly (and rightly) respected former U.S. director of central intelligence (and head of the clandestine service before that), made it a practice to present his intelligence findings to the president and the National Security Council and then leave the room, in order to be certain not to become involved in the policy debate that followed. The same factors that are changing the state that Helms and other admirable men and women served are also, however, changing the role of intelligence. In the twenty-first century, enormous political weight will be borne by the intelligence product as consumers take decisions in environments of great uncertainty and as these decisions must be publicly defended as consistent with intelligence estimates.

V.

These then are the fundamental constitutive distinctions that govern the practice of intelligence by American and British agencies as they attempt to fight terrorism. It is important to remember that these distinctions are very much the product of the twentieth century nation state and are by no means fundamental to the historic constitutions of either the U.S. or the U.K. though they have now hardened into unassailable antinomies.

There are countless instances of the pernicious effect these antinomies have had on warning in areas other than terrorism. For example, at the time of the Iranian revolution it would have been very significant to know that Iranians were sending vast amounts of money out of the country to California, but the U.S. government was not permitted to track bank transfers once they entered America or even when they entered a branch of one of its banks overseas. The former deputy national security advisor James B. Steinberg has testified that, excepting the millennium terrorist plot, the FBI wholly refused to share investigative information with the NSC on the grounds that the White House had to be kept out of the loop with regard to criminal investigation in order to preserve propriety.[70]

The horrific potential of terrorist atrocities throws this issue into stark relief because the losses that result from such attacks can be so high and the categorizations on which these distinctions depend in such cases can be so unclear. Such catastrophes may be simply the consequences of crimes, or military attacks, or even the result of natural events. Indeed we may not know, in some cases, precisely how to characterize a particular event or determine who is responsible for it.

"To meet such a wide variety of needs," Russ Travers concluded,

> [the role of the intelligence community] should be that of an information clearinghouse capable of addressing all the security issues of the early 21st century . . . [This] will require us to be far better attuned to the work being done in the academic community, other governmental institutions, industry, and the myriad of other entities that collect and analyze data . . . We could introduce rotationals from academia into the midlevel ranks of the Intelligence Community . . . We should have a much closer relationship with responsible journalists, extending beyond the "backgrounder process" to a more routine give-and-take among professionals interested in accurate information.[71]

Such proposals make us uncomfortable because they blur the lines between public institutions and private industry, international actors like foreign services and domestic ones, law enforcement agencies and intelligence operators, and they introduce collection by journalists and analysis by academics—in short, violating all the important distinctions we have relied on in the recent past for our successes and which structured what at the time were the only acceptable practices. In the U.K., "Michael Herman expressed surprise that Lord Butler did not recommend following the American example of appointing distinguished academics to their [own] National Intelligence Council."[72] But Len Scott and Gerald Hughes concluded that in "Britain such a relationship would be antithetical to longstanding traditions in both academic and political culture."[73]

In fact we should go even further. There must be some "assigning executive" or "managing partner" or "directing controller"—none of these sounds quite right—that sorts out what elements of a problem are best treated by covert action, clandestine or open collection, diplomatic and military action, or investigation and prosecution. That marshaling director must have the statutory authority to determine that action be taken and to have the bureaucratic authority to enforce those decisions. Something like this has been created in the 2005 Intelligence Reform Act, which provided for "mission managers." These have now been assigned to counterproliferation, counterterrorism, North Korea, and Iran. Such guiding persons or groups could coordinate cooperation with the many private-sector assets that Treverton and Herman have identified.[74]

Finally, it must be possible to move seamlessly back and forth among various approaches to "treatment" of the problem so that initial commitments to one approach do not dictate its continued pursuit. That counsels in favor of a single director for almost all the U.S. intelligence agencies and their budgets (before the latest reorganization that created the post of director of national intelligence, the director of central intelligence controlled less than 50 percent of intelligence funds) or at least a series of directorates that have at their apex such a general officer.

This was the finding of the U.S. 9/11 Commission, which adopted the Goldwater-Nichols paradigm of defense reform as its model. For most of the twentieth century, the U.S. armed forces were organized by the various services, and from World War II onward these service commands reported to the Joint Chiefs of Staff (JCS). The chairman of the JCS was elected by the service chiefs, and he reported to the secretary of defense and to the president, who held the military role of commander in chief.

This system led to intense service rivalries and tended to sacrifice cooperation in doctrine, weapons development, and organization. Warfighting was also planned and executed—and even evaluated independently—by each of the services. The inability of defense forces to realize the doctrinal goals of the AirLand battle doctrine, and the fiasco of the Iran rescue mission of 1980, were testimony to the consequences of this division of effort along service lines. To correct this, the Goldwater-Nichols Act of 1986 reformulated the chain of command and introduced combined arms at the command level.

Instead of reporting to a service chief (e.g., the army chief of staff), when operating abroad each service component deployed overseas now reported to a regional or functional commander, originally known as a commander-in-chief, now called a combatant commander. This commander is responsible for fielding a combined arms force composed of all the military assets available. Thus for example, Central Command is headquartered in Florida and commanded by an army four-star general. His

area of responsibility includes twenty-five countries in the Arabian Peninsula, the Horn of Africa, south and central Asia, and the northern Red Sea
regions. Reporting directly to him are the U.S. Army forces headquartered
in Georgia; an air force command in South Carolina; marine forces in
Hawaii; naval forces out of Bahrain; and a special operations command
(also in Florida). Or for example, the Pacific Command is headquartered at
Honolulu and commanded by a four-star navy admiral. Army Pacific,
Marine Forces Pacific, the Pacific Fleet, and Pacific Air Forces, all at different bases in Hawaii, report to him.

These combatant commanders in turn report, for operational purposes,
directly to the secretary of defense and thence to the president. There are
five geographically defined commands and three functional ones (plus one
unified combatant command that has both a geographic and a functional
area of responsibility).

It was this model, which by general consensus has been a success in
Bosnia, Kosovo, and Afghanistan, that impressed the members of the 9/11
Commission. They recognized in the divisions of the intelligence community some of the same structural defects that had hampered joint defense
operations. According to the commission's report:

> The problem is nearly intractable because of the way the govern-
> ment is currently structured. Lines of operational authority run to the
> expanding executive departments, and they are guarded for under-
> standable reasons: the DCI [director of central intelligence] com-
> mands the CIA's personnel overseas; the secretary of defense will not
> yield to others in conveying commands to military forces; the Justice
> Department will not give up the responsibility of deciding whether to
> seek arrest warrants. But the result is that each agency or department
> needs its own intelligence apparatus to support the performance of its
> duties. It is hard to "break down stovepipes" when there are so many
> stoves that are legally and politically entitled to have cast-iron pipes of
> their own.[75]

The commission recommended a National Counterterrorism Center
(NCTC), led by a civilian and staffed by personnel from the various agencies that would combine strategic intelligence and joint operational planning. The commission followed the model of the combatant commands in
providing that the NCTC should not direct the actual execution of operations; it was to leave that job to the agencies just as the combatant commands rely on the individual armed services. Indeed, the commission
proposed a number of national intelligence centers with both geographical
(China/East Asia, Middle East, Russia/Eurasia) and functional (WMD
proliferation, international crime, and narcotics) responsibilities.

Goldwater-Nichols did little to help resource allocation, however; this continued to be governed by the priorities of the individual services. For example, if the air force were to recommend a delay or scaling back of the C-17, a large transport aircraft, to satisfy its budget cuts (or the Navy a similar reduction in sealift), the impact would be felt on joint operations, but the decision would be made largely by the individual service. The 9/11 Commission recognized this problem when it recommended unified budgetary authority for the entire intelligence community—which would include agencies far larger than the CIA, with budgets that are at present governed by other departments, notably DOD.

The result was the passage by Congress of the Intelligence Reform and Terrorism Prevention Act of 2004. This statute created the office of director of national intelligence (DNI). Congress might have opted for a strictly coordinating DNI with limited staff and circumscribed statutory authority, much like the early national security advisors. Or Congress might instead have created a DNI who was more like a cabinet secretary for intelligence, with complete statutory authority over the principal intelligence agencies (including the NSA and the NGA, the National Geospatial Agency) and responsibility for their budgets, though this too could have been achieved with a modest bureaucratic structure. Instead, the Congress chose to create an office with broad responsibility for oversight but limited statutory authority.[76] Its first occupant, John Negroponte, was an experienced official of consummate skill who with the backing of the White House might have been able to master this new system, but even at this stage, it is clear that the Pentagon has managed to thwart fundamental institutional reform. Negroponte himself has moved on to serve as deputy secretary of state.

VI.

There have been many recent commissions and studies on intelligence reform:[77] the Aspin-Brown Commission,[78] the Hart-Rudman Commission,[79] the Hutton Inquiry,[80] the 9/11 Commission,[81] Lord Butler's Report,[82] the Robb-Silberman Commission, and others. In the United States these have been uniformly critical.[83] Legislation has been proposed that would take the Department of Justice out of the intelligence business, put the Defense Department entirely in control of paramilitary operations, and consolidate the sixteen agencies that at the present have intelligence responsibilities. On December 17, 2004, the president signed the Intelligence Reform and Terrorism Prevention Act.[84] Though a welcome step, it will prove to be insufficient. Why?

It is because, in the words of one analyst, "[a]ll significant proposals . . . assume . . . that many, if not most, of the processes that define the intelligence discipline remain sound. These processes are just being executed incorrectly, and the solution to that is new and better management and oversight."[85] If we had had a centralized system, reform commissions would have recommended decentralization; because we had a decentralized system, they recommended centralization.

Centralization can encourage the rationalization of resources and reduce duplication, but it has costs as well. As Anne Joseph O'Connell noted, centralization can destroy "needed safeguards and eliminat[e] beneficial agency . . . competition." Decentralization

> may combat "group think." [It] may prevent "capture" of agencies or overseers by particular interest groups, decreasing the politicization of intelligence. . . . [I]f [decentralization] produces competition, it may yield better outcomes than coordination. [Finally, decentralization] may increase reliability by decreasing the chances of the system failing entirely. . . . [C]ompletely independent but redundant structures yield the greatest increase in reliability.[86]

In fact, neither centralization nor decentralization is particularly linked to the changing nature of the threat. It is the intelligence *process* that needs reform.

> This process is locked in the pre-electronic industrial process of a factory environment. Raw material is pushed in at one end and the finished product emerges at the other. No part of the process needs to communicate with any other, and each knows its function. And while whatever is produced may or may not be relevant to the user and their environment, this is not the production line's problem.[87]

The most fundamental aspects of the prevailing intelligence processes of collection and analysis can be traced to the industrial, nation state environment from which they emerged.[88] Though we unthinkingly assume that Mata Hari and Major André were doing essentially the same sort of things as a twenty-first century spy who has infiltrated al Qaeda ("the second oldest profession," it is sometimes called), in fact the tradecraft of intelligence necessarily varies with the geopolitical context. "For the intelligence producer and their consumer, significant shifts in geo-politics or technology can have (and will) result in delayed reactions and unforeseen and unintended consequences."[89] The Robb-Silberman Commission concluded that

> [t]he imagery collection systems [for example] that were designed largely to work against the Soviet Union's military didn't work very well against Iraq's unconventional weapons program, and . . . they

aren't working very well against other priority targets, either . . . That's because our adversaries are getting better at denial and deception [but mainly because] what we can see doesn't tell us what we need to know about nuclear, biological, and chemical weapons.⁹⁰

Twentieth century warfare required industrial plants that could be surveilled by overflight and satellite. Twenty-first century warfare will have to be more subtle, less conspicuous.

Our current methods of clandestine collection, the targeting of important officials likely to know critical secrets, even the assumption that we can usually forecast our collection requirements, all originate with the kind of war we fought in the twentieth century. It made sense to have undercover persons assigned to embassies or military bases abroad when government officials were themselves the targets of collection by the agencies of hostile states. That is not true when the objects of collection move to the street or the media center because the threat has shifted, and with it the locus of the information we need. In the Cold War there were perhaps fewer than a hundred Soviet "illegals" in the U.S.—spies operating without diplomatic cover. Today, who can say how many persons enter the U.S. with some operational link to al Qaeda? Nor is this problem confined to intelligence operations against terrorists. Even with respect to states, traditional methods and locales may fail us: if we want to anticipate the overthrow of a government by a mass movement, it seems clear that paying attention to events at a palace is unlikely to give us warning.⁹¹

For almost 50 years . . . the Intelligence Community's resources were overwhelmingly trained on a single threat . . . By comparison today's priority intelligence targets are greater in number (there are dozens of entities that could strike a devastating blow against the United States) and are often more diffuse in character (they include not only states but also nebulous transnational terror and proliferation networks) . . . [S]ome of the weapons that would be most dangerous in the hands of terrorists or rogue nations are difficult to detect. Much of the technology, equipment, and materials necessary to develop biological and chemical weapons, for example, also has legitimate commercial applications. Biological weapons themselves can be built in small-scale facilities that are easy to conceal, and weapons-grade uranium can be effectively shielded from traditional detection techniques.⁹²

Given the increasing sophistication of identification technologies⁹³—biometrics, surveillance technologies, and the use of linked databases—that have been developed to expose terrorists, it probably makes sense to use expensive secret personnel principally against WMD proliferation, global terrorism, and mass atrocities whose prevention can justify the expense of maintaining a clandestine identity. What is wanted in the current era for the great mass of reporting is a network of well-connected and thoroughly vetted persons who are linked by secure Internet sites but who are no more than stringers, paid by the item. Indeed this is the system on which al Qaeda largely depends. Concurring with Carmen Medina's suggestion about collection, Treverton proposes a parallel network that would link police and analysts:

> The final challenge in assembling the network is . . . sharing information with the 18,000 law enforcement agencies in the United States, not to mention with private citizens. There, the challenge is to play on the comparative advantage of the different levels of government: local law enforcement, for instance has lots of eyes and ears but little capacity to do . . . sophisticated analysis of collected information.[94]

Not only collection but the craft of intelligence analysis would benefit from such an appreciation of the changed circumstances. When the U.S. and the U.K. faced closed and duplicitous states like Nazi Germany or the Soviet Union, it made sense to give priority to efforts to divine the significance of recent events. The massive forces our enemies marshaled would usually provide us with strategic warning of an attack if we were careful to listen to government chatter. This has conditioned generations of twentieth century analysts. As Medina writes:

> 90% of the tradecraft of analysis concentrates on how best to understand what just happened . . . Analysts are quite experienced . . . in writing instant histories. In their first writing assignments, they are usually provided with a stack of cables—almost all of them describing an event in the past—and asked to write a concise piece describing the development and its import. The analytic profession has never devoted as much attention nor has it developed as much technique to address the future. [It is] often said that the primary job of the analyst is to explain not predict.[95]

This is very sensible in dealing with well-understood problems like the confrontation with communist states or anticipating the policies of allied governments. With respect to our allies, much analysis can be outsourced, but the threat posed by the rather staid and predictable Soviet group has been replaced with threats that must be anticipated from the barest fragments and often from secret sources. Because of the strategic nature of the threats, the policies it prompts will require that a new weight be given to alternative futures.

One recent proposal recommends "the identification and recruitment into the analyst corps of those well-established students of foreign affairs who have a track record of being ahead of their peers when it comes to insights, rather than the untried and unproven graduates who are typically recruited into the analytical ranks."[96] This is probably impossible for many reasons, not the least of which is that "well-established students of foreign affairs" are not hanging around waiting to take modestly paying jobs in Langley, Virginia, but have careers of their own. On the other hand, this suggestion, like those of Treverton and Medina, points the way to the increased outsourcing of analysis. This is controversial in itself (noncareer personnel are often denied access to sensitive materials even when their security clearances would otherwise permit such access) and would become even more so if the proposals suggested earlier about greater collaboration between analysts and collectors were acted upon.

Medina endorses the use of scenario planning and suggests that analysts should create "a master list of scenarios concerning all relevant international and national security issues, [which would] serve a clearing function for government agencies wanting to plan strategically."[97] This proposal has the merit that it also addresses the issue of better communicating intelligence to consumers.

VII.

September 11 wasn't the only recent catastrophic intelligence failure. "While the intelligence services of [France, Germany, and Russia] also thought that Iraq had weapons of mass destruction [in 2002], in the end it was the United States that put its credibility on the line, making this one of the most public—and most damaging—intelligence failures in recent American history."[98] Much the same charge can be leveled at the failure of the British intelligence process, which of course includes the bureaucratic and ministerial leadership that relies on the assessments of its services, and the costly reliance of the British government on claims about Iraqi WMD.

With the release of the final report of the Iraq Survey Group, many asked, how could the intelligence agencies of the U.S. and the U.K. have gotten it so wrong?[99] Why did these two states (and many others) express such confidence in a proposition—that Saddam Hussein had significant quantities of WMD he was concealing from U.N. inspectors—that turned out to have been without a scrap of hard evidence?

There have been extensive investigations in both countries. In the U.K., the Butler Report echoed the Hutton Inquiry, which exonerated the government from charges of lying, but concluded that Britain's Joint Intelligence Committee might have been unconsciously influenced by proximity to persons from 10 Downing Street who were eager for reporting that could be used to justify the prime minister's policies. In the U.S., the Senate Intelligence Committee blamed "collective groupthink" and a shortage of human intelligence assets. A further U.S. report came when the Robb-Silberman Commission gave its account in March 2005. "Groupthink," a lack of "HUMINT," and "unconscious political pressures" all seem plausible candidates for blame. But how could these phenomena also be responsible for the fact that the same erroneous conviction was shared by the intelligence agencies of France, Germany, and Russia, which are reported to have concurred in the U.S.-U.K. Iraqi WMD assessment even as their political masters strongly swerved away from the policy of regime change favored by the U.S. and Britain? As their governments disagreed, these various national agencies can't all have been unconsciously pressured to reach the same conclusion; they didn't all lack human assets in Baghdad, as we know; they didn't all belong to one intimate, self-reinforcing group. Moreover, some believe that it is the separation of intelligence producers from intelligence consumers that is pernicious, not their occasional and often infrequent contacts.

Earlier, six antinomies were discussed with respect to the failures of the intelligence processes around 9/11. Let us now review the same antinomies while looking at the Report of the Commission on the Intelligence Capabilities of the United States Regarding Weapons of Mass Destruction (the Robb-Silberman Commission)[100] and its discussion of the Iraqi WMD fiasco.

COLLECTION AND ANALYSIS

According to the Robb-Silberman Report, "Our collection agencies are often unable to gather intelligence on the very things we care the most about. Too often, analysts simply accept these gaps; they do little to help collectors identify new opportunities and they do not always tell decision-makers just how limited their knowledge really is."[101] It is true that between September 11, 2001, and the invasion of Iraq in March 2003 collaboration in the U.S. between collectors and analysts improved substantially. This was largely due to the creation of the Terrorist Threat Integration Center (now the National Counterterrorism Center) and to the co-location of collectors and analysts. But this helpful step had not reached the counterproliferation units responsible for the Iraqi WMD assessments. Even co-location, while a positive step away from the antinomy of opposing collection and analysis, still depends on personal contacts and office space, rather than simply the aspiration to integrate the two groups. Information deemed "operational" by collectors at the FBI or CIA is withheld as a matter of routine, though analysts frequently stress its importance.[102]

Analysts are, in the words of the Robb-Silberman Report, "the repositories for what the Intelligence Community [IC] *doesn't* know."[103] They are therefore crucial in tasking collectors and in guiding them to fill in these gaps. But collectors are repositories of *how* the IC knows what it thinks it knows, and they are thus critical elements in informing the analysts of how much weight to put on any particular source. This was made plain in the commission's discussion of HUMINT derived from an Iraqi chemical engineer known as Curveball.

In early 2000, the U.S. IC obtained information about Iraqi WMD programs indirectly from a source code-named Curveball. The U.S. did not have direct contact with Curveball, who was an agent for the German intelligence service, which denied access to him by American intelligence personnel. Claiming that Curveball would refuse to speak to Americans, the Germans would debrief him and then pass the debriefing notes to the Defense Intelligence Agency (DIA), whose Defense HUMINT Service was a collection entity within the U.S. Department of Defense (DOD).

DIA, though hampered by a lack of direct access, could have provided some assessment of the value of the information it was getting—specifically, by assessing the credibility of the source. Testifying before the Senate Select Committee on Intelligence, Defense HUMINT Service officials responsible for disseminating the Curveball material stressed instead that it was not up to them to assess the source's credibility, but rather was the responsibility of the analysts who read the reports to judge their accuracy. This service took the view that it had no responsibility for vetting or validating Curveball's information. "[A]sset validation is solely the responsibility of analysts—if the analysts believe the information is credible, then the source is validated."[104]

The culture of separation also proved pernicious from the other end. When the CIA became concerned about the veracity of the Curveball reporting, it wasn't only the withholding of these doubts from analysts that led to the resulting fiasco; it was also the insistence of the analysts that Curveball's information must be true that paralyzed further inquiry about the source of this information. Indeed, the analysts themselves at the CIA (the DI) never informed the collectors (the DO) that the DI was relying so very heavily on the Curveball material in its assessments of Iraqi WMD. When Secretary Powell's speech to the U.N. was being scrubbed for accuracy, the DIA HUMINT official present was not told that the information being fed to Powell was from an Iraqi National Congress source which the DIA knew to be a fabricator.[105]

There were four sources for the allegation that Iraq maintained a mobile biological weapons lab. Accordingly, the National Intelligence

Estimate (NIE) attributed the judgment that Iraq "has transportable facilities for producing bacterial and toxin BW [biological weapons] agents" to "multiple sources." In fact, Curveball provided approximately one hundred detailed reports on this subject; the second and third sources each provided one report and the fourth—the Iraqi National Congress source—had been exposed months earlier as a fabricator. Because the analysts didn't know their sources, they didn't realize how dependent they were on a single, dubious asset. Because the collectors didn't know the degree to which the analysts were basing their decisions on this source, they saw no urgent reason to validate that source or to pass along information that came their way that Curveball was also a fabricator. A division chief in the DO, alerted by a contact with a foreign agency to Curveball's problems, thought this information was "no big deal" because he did not know the extent of the analysts' reliance on Curveball's reporting. He assumed there must be ample other sources and could not imagine, he testified, that Curveball was "it."[106]

This antinomy—collectors must be kept separate in order to protect their sources and the methods of collection, and analysts must be isolated in order to dispassionately assess information—runs deep on both sides. The NSA largely refuses to share raw intercepts with anyone outside the agency. The DO won't provide operational information even within the CIA, much less to any other agencies.

The Robb-Silberman Commission review of the intelligence community's performance on Iraq sharply criticized the way analysts and collectors share information:

> First, the source descriptions on raw human source reporting often provided insufficient detail and clarity to allow analysts adequate insight into the source's reliability. For example, the CIA report on the alleged uranium deal [with Niger] that was sourced to Ambassador Wilson described him (unhelpfully) as "a contact with excellent access who does not have an established reporting record."* . . . Second . . . analysts were often unable to determine whether a series of raw human intelligence reporting came from the same source. For most reporting, there is currently no way to determine . . . whether a series of reports represents one source reporting similar information several times or several different sources independently providing the same information . . . Finally, analysts often obtain insufficient insights into the operational details bearing on the reliability of sources.[107]

---

*Wilson had been a senior director at the NSC for Africa, ambassador to Gabon, and had a distinguished record in African diplomatic affairs.

Among scholars who write about intelligence failures, blame is most often attributed to analytic lapses. Within the community of professional intelligence officers, the fault is more often laid on insufficient—not inept—collection. In fact, the actual responsibility for failure seems to vary with the situation:

> In the Yom Kippur War . . . it does seem that sufficient evidence was available for US analysts to warn Washington of the approaching Arab attack on Israel . . .With the famous pre–Cuban Missile Crisis [NIE] of 19 September 1962, a fair judgment would be that there was insufficient intelligence available to the drafters, at the time of publication, to permit them reasonably to conclude that the Soviets were placing offensive nuclear missiles in Cuba.[108]

With the National Intelligence Estimate on Iraqi WMD, it seems clear that it wasn't either the analysts or the collectors who were responsible but rather the ethos that kept them from effectively collaborating.

PRODUCTION AND CONSUMPTION

Sherman Kent, the Yale historian who became the legendary head of the Office of National Estimates at the CIA, the precursor of today's National Intelligence Council, laid the basis for this antinomy when he warned: "When intelligence producers realize that there is no sense in forwarding to a consumer knowledge which does not correspond to preconceptions, then intelligence is through."[109] Yet while Kent famously cautioned about the dangers from a too-close association between producers of intelligence and consumers, he also wrote that "of the two dangers—that of intelligence being too far from the users and that of being too close—the greater danger is the one of being too far."[110]

In the Iraq WMD case, the ethos of arm's-length dealing between producers and consumers undermined the use to which policy makers put the intelligence provided to them. This was largely because analysts were unwilling to admit what they didn't know, and thus the policy makers hopelessly overstated to the public the basis for the confidence with which their judgments were held and were recklessly exposed to discredit. For their part, with respect to Iraq, consumers gave the impression to producers that they were not interested in uncertainties and qualifications on the intelligence judgments that analysts rendered. This may have produced a kind of politicization of intelligence, but it did not result from the too-close association between producers and consumers but rather from the uncommunicative distance separating them. Only producers can educate intelligence consumers not to expect greater precision than the evaluated data permits, and only consumers can cultivate trust and confidence that the judgment rendered will not remove the producer from the playing field if that judgment is politically inconvenient.

In its overall commission finding, the Robb-Silberman Commission concluded: "The Intelligence Community's performance in assessing Iraq's pre-war weapons of mass destruction programs was a major intelligence failure. The failure was not merely that the . . . assessments were wrong. There were also serious shortcomings in the way these assessments were made and communicated to policymakers."[111] The crucial October 2002 NIE was not candid in disclosing its reliance largely on one human source and ambiguous (or even contradictory) imagery and SIGINT.

The NIE did offer several caveats, noting, for example, that "[t]oday we have less direct access and know even less about the current status of Iraq's nuclear program than we did before the Gulf War."[112] But if that caveat had any impact on the reader, it would have been to remind him (or her) that in 1991 the IC had completely missed a burgeoning Iraqi nuclear program. In any event, this effort at modesty came on page 13 of the NIE, and thus follows at least two other firm statements that Iraq was reconstituting its nuclear weapons program and could have fissile material sufficient for a device in the next few years.

Only an ongoing dialogue between producers and consumers can adequately educate each in the needs and limitations of the other. Richard Betts, one of those most skeptical of the producer-consumer antinomy, has ruefully observed that "everyone knows that 'politicization' is bad. It is assumed to damage the credibility of intelligence. Some are unconcerned because they believe it seldom happens, or matters little when it does. Virtually no one, however, believes that it is a *good* thing."[113]

If politicization is one risk of closer relations between intelligence producers and consumers, when we see the costs of distance in this relationship perhaps we may conclude that it is a risk worth running. Only a close relationship can allow for informed interrogation, on the one hand, and informed, if sometimes inconvenient, candor on the other.

Intelligence consumers are not simply skilled implementers of policy; they are also shrewd judges of trends and intentions. Few analysts can match the personal contacts that senior policy makers have with foreign leaders; fewer still have the wide experience of the world that many policy makers bring to their roles. What these consumers want are facts against which they can test their own intuitive judgments. In that, they are more like judges, who tend to be drawn from the worldly practice of politics and law, and less like law professors and law clerks, who resemble the analysts who write intelligence products. At the same time, there are too many "facts" for the unguided producer to provide unless he or she has a pretty intimate and current view of what the consumer's prejudices, preconceptions, and preferences are. In the case of Iraqi WMD, the producers confronted a cadre at the highest level who had decided to use the emotion generated by 9/11 to solve a largely unrelated but critical problem, the apparently entrenched dictatorship of Saddam Hussein, that had proved impervious to previous action. That meant that the producers' job was to apply stringent scrutiny to the evidence that would support this policy, so that when the day of reckoning came the U.S. would not be discredited.

It is widely quoted—indeed, it has been referred to above—that President Truman created the CIA in order to prevent another Pearl Harbor.[114] What is less widely quoted is how he expected this to work:

> Therefore, I decided to set up a special organization charged with the collection of all intelligence reports from every available source and to have those reports reach me as President without departmental "treatment" or interpretations. I wanted and needed the information in its "natural raw" state and in as comprehensive a volume as it was practical for me to make full use of it.[115]

In other words, Truman sought to overcome the notions that kept the collection and analysis, as well as the production and consumption, of intelligence at a distance from each other. As Robert Earle concluded, "There is no question that unless analysts point collectors into the agreed-upon gaps, they will keep analyzing what gets collected, not what's most needed."[116]

PUBLIC AND PRIVATE

The October 2002 NIE focused closely on the technical signatures of an Iraqi WMD program but had little to say about Iraqi politics and the culture of the Saddam Hussein regime. The Robb-Silberman Commission speculated that "[i]t seems unlikely . . . that weapons experts used to combing reports for tidbits on technical programs would ever have asked: 'Is Saddam bluffing?' or 'Could he have decided to suspend his weapons programs until sanctions are lifted?' "[117] The commission faults the imagination of the analysts but that seems less than fair. One can hardly reprove a weapons expert, having been chosen to exercise his expertise, for failing to be a regional expert who specializes in Baathist politics and the psychology of sociopaths.

Yet there are such experts, and a great many of them can be found in the private sector companies that had dealt with the regime, among journalists who had interviewed Saddam Hussein, and among academics who specialized in the study of the internecine power politics of the region. How can their expertise be made accessible to the analysts and collectors working in the public sector?

The crucial pieces of evidence that should have been sought were not about Saddam Hussein's disintegrating caches of WMD (the sort of secret the Cold War had trained intelligence agencies to look for) but about illicit maneuvers behind the Oil-for-Food Program. Here Saddam Hussein was able to skim vast sums through a system of kickbacks from favored vendors, and to amass even greater funds through illicit oil sales. The case to be made for intervention in Iraq was not what weapons Saddam Hussein had managed to deploy, but what weapons he could assemble with such enormous funds. A. Q. Khan rather than al Qaeda should have been the threat model. Here the evidence was to be found not only in complex technical imagery or the testimony of defectors, but also in the humdrum records of private commercial transactions.

The most difficult aspect of the increasingly dysfunctional public-private distinction with respect to the intelligence debacle over Iraqi WMD, however, was the strange relationship that emerged between the intelligence agencies and the media. In 1987, the U.S. Senate Select Committee on the Iran-Contra affair published a report, "Covert Action and the Constitution."[118] Part of that report's conclusions dealt with the charge that the Reagan administration had misused intelligence procedures in order to persuade itself that a significant Iranian faction of moderates existed with whom the U.S. could deal to secure the release of American hostages. The administration accomplished this self-hypnosis through the National Intelligence Estimates. As we have seen, these estimates, official papers that assess specific issues, are crafted by the National Intelligence Council, a group serving the entire intelligence community and drawing information from it. The council produced more than one estimate that poured cold water on the White House's idea of negotiating with "moderates" in Iran. But the administration continued to seek an estimate that would bolster its position and eventually got one, which gave decisive momentum to what became a quite unconstitutional and amateurish project. The ensuing humiliation has given force to the fears of politicization noted above.

Although the U.S. and the U.K. differ in many constitutional respects, the charges against the Blair government—that it had "cooked" the intelligence product in order to build a false case for intervention in Iraq—are similar to those leveled against the Reagan administration over the Iran-Contra debacle. These charges were the subject of both the Hutton Inquiry and the Butler Report, which in many ways paralleled the investigations of the Senate Select Committee conducted after the exposure of the Iran-Contra affair. Not surprisingly, there are lessons to be learned from this earlier inquiry into intelligence and its use by government, but interest-ingly the most significant of these have to do with the media and the need for public sophistication.

First, the public should know that the press will always be able to find a "reliable senior person" (or persons) who disagrees with the official esti-mate, arrived at by community processes. Roughly speaking, there are two kinds of secrets:[119] those that someone knows (whether Saddam Hussein had WMD or whether, as the *New York Times* put it, "Iraq really did destroy virtually all of its weapons and toxic agents, retaining only the ability to start banned programs up again once the world stopped looking") and those secrets that nobody really knows (that is, what Iraq would do with such weapons, and how other regional actors would react if Sad-dam Hussein acquired nuclear weapons on the clandestine market).[120] "Strategic warning" depends upon assessments of both capability and intentions—that is, upon both kinds of secrets. Because the crucial ques-tions about intentions are a matter of intuition and judgment, it is not sur-prising that dissenters can always be found. Indeed, good intelligence organizations try to encourage dissent as a way of sharpening their esti-mates and preventing the mindless consensus that seizes so many institu-tions (including the press or, for that matter, the academy).

So it is not whether an investigative journalist can find dissenters, but rather what the intelligence community, through its collaborative proce-dures, ultimately produces. In Britain, the Joint Intelligence Committee (JIC) was the vehicle for those procedures, and it was generally well regarded among intelligence officials. The conclusions reached by the JIC on Iraqi WMD were adopted unanimously by its members. Unless this committee had completely gone off the rails in an effort to propitiate the prime minister, the media charges of a cooked estimate, which were based on an unidentified dissenter's leak, were misplaced. In the end, the Butler Report confirmed that such charges were wholly unfounded. By contrast, the Senate Select Committee investigating the Iran-Contra matter con-cluded that the White House had repeatedly refused to accept the consen-sus judgment of the intelligence community.

Second, intelligence assessments do not deal exclusively with secrets, nor do they rely only on clandestine sources and methods. The controversy over the "dodgy dossier" used by the British government to support its analysis of Saddam Hussein's intentions seems to arise at least in part because one of the intelligence estimates was prepared using unattributed material from a decade-old doctoral dissertation and not because the mate-rial was false.[121] This objection betrays a broad misunderstanding of the intelligence product. There was a time when a large section of CIA analysts was devoted to things like estimating Chinese rice production, but reliance has been increasingly put on information gathered from "open-source" materials. Indeed, there should be greater reliance upon open-source materials precisely so that intelligence agencies can focus their limited resources on collecting and analyzing secrets. Therefore, if the criticism is that the unacknowledged use of academic materials is, in itself, wrong because it gives the impression that the conclusions and analyses therein were the product of the intelligence community, then this is no criticism at all. In the Iran-Contra affair, it was the president's refusal to inform the public of his true policies (trading arms in order to ransom hostages) that raised constitutional concerns, rather than his efforts to persuade the public by using intelligence materials without specifying their source.

These points do not mean, however, that the entire controversy was a tempest in a teapot, for these issues prefigure some of the conflicts to come as we learn to cope with new security threats and the emergence of a new constitutional order that demands more transparency in government.

The fraught relationship between the intelligence agencies and the press is mutating, with each taking on some of the other's characteristics. The media are under the intense competition imposed by the twenty-four-hour news cycle and the pressures of investigative journalism, on the one hand, and there are new demands on intelligence agencies arising from the Wars against Terror and the emergence of market states, on the other. As a result, the press will have to learn to be as skeptical of its sources, and as shrewd in triangulating facts that confirm or disconfirm the accounts it collects, as any good intelligence agency. At the same time government agencies must learn the techniques of collaborative information sharing that characterize the best editors and journalists.

Both the press and the agencies will have to change in these circumstances. The idea of a communications director who is knowledgeable about actual operations is anathema to intelligence professionals. They know, as few in the public credit, that even the simple disclosure by governments of generally reported information can have disastrous consequences. But a skeptical public will not be satisfied by the complacent murmuring of talismanic phrases like "sources and methods." Rather, skilled communications directors—the despised "spin doctors" who are accustomed to dealing with the press openly—will play an increasing role as a critical part of the intelligence apparatus. It seems that not only does warfare take place in the public theater, as Rupert Smith notes, but so now do intelligence operations.

This mirror-image description of the press corps and the intelligence community is evident in the British controversy over the decision to invade Iraq. The BBC was criticized in the report of the Hutton Inquiry for an insistence on using single-source material simply because it was highly inflammatory, sexy, fitted the prejudices of the reporter, and fulfilled the insistent requirements of management—which are the very elements of

the indictment the BBC leveled against the government in the first place
when it accused the government of perverting the intelligence process.

In late 2007 the U.S. released a National Intelligence Estimate (NIE)
reversing its own 2005 report that Iran had an active nuclear weapons program. Only weeks earlier, officials had announced that the release of NIEs
would be ended to protect analysts from the prospect of public disclosure.
Now portions of the new NIE were publicly released on the grounds that
the new estimate was at odds with the 2005 assessment and contradicted
statements by U.S. officials to the public. The debacle of the Iraqi WMD
NIE may yet lead to success.

SECRETS AND OPEN SOURCES

Intelligence, though indispensable to fighting a war against terror, or any
war for that matter, cannot decide a course of action for a government. In
complex political matters of war and peace, there are no "killer facts"—
evidence so probative that it sweeps away the need for judgment. The
apparent knowledge that Iran suspended its nuclear weapons program yet
has paradoxically continued to conceal this from U.N. inspectors tells us
very little about Iran's ultimate intentions. It does not yield any obvious
policy that will insure the continuation of this suspension or compel compliance with the NPT, to which Iran is a party. Nor can the mere release of
intelligence information settle a key issue of legitimacy that besets governments waging twenty-first century warfare—namely, how to communicate
to the questioning public the bases on which decisions are taken when
these decisions crucially rely on intelligence. Because there are no "killer
facts," intelligence does not make decisions for leaders any more than a
photograph, however accurate, decides for a painter what pigments to use
or what perspective to adopt. Therefore, the disclosure of intelligence to
the public, which is fraught for many reasons, is not as likely to resolve the
crises of legitimacy brought on by a lack of transparency as one might be
inclined to believe. At the same time, it must be conceded that greater
reliance on nongovernmental, open-source material might, paradoxically,
have exposed the most influential flaw in the intelligence community's
methodology in dealing with Iraqi secrets.

In large part, the intelligence failure over Iraqi WMD goes back to a
mistaken assessment of what counted as "proof." Many think of proof—at
a trial, for example—as a fact that stands apart from judgment. But there is
no fact that determines a murderer (as distinct from the killer), or the existence of God, or whether someone loves you. It is always and only a matter
of judgment applied to proof. Regarding Iraq, judgment within the "intelligence community"—a dangerous portmanteau phrase, I realize—had been

decisively warped by earlier intelligence failures that caused all the agencies involved to shift the burden of proof.

In the summer of 1995, U.N. inspectors were only weeks away from submitting a report to the U.N. Security Council that would have given Saddam Hussein a clean bill of health on the charge that he was pursuing WMD. This report was of considerable importance because investigations after the first Gulf War had stunned Western intelligence agencies with the discovery that Iraq's nuclear weapons program went far beyond what had been assessed by any intelligence organization. Before the war, the U.S. intelligence community had decided that because no formal, coordinated nuclear program could be detected, it was unlikely that Iraq would have a nuclear device before the end of the decade. Shocked by the breadth of the Iraqi nuclear program it discovered after the war, the community now reversed itself and concluded in 1993 that Iraq might have been only a year away from deploying a nuclear weapon. The significance of this intelligence failure could have been catastrophic; it would have meant that Iraq possessed a "counterdeterrent"—that is, a capacity to preclude an expeditionary force like the Gulf War coalition.

So one can imagine the consternation in Washington, London, and elsewhere in 1995 when Saddam Hussein's son-in-law, Hussein Kamel, defected and brought with him knowledge of clandestine Iraqi WMD programs that had been concealed from the inspections. Kamel described where the materials and facilities were, what had already been built, the existence of an extensive biological weapons program, the plans to reconstitute nuclear weapons development, hidden nuclear blueprints, as well as centrifuges and other technology. His debriefing[122] left no doubt that the U.N. inspectors and the intelligence agencies that fed the U.N. tips had been fooled. He even named who was running Iraq's deception operations and described in detail how they worked. He further declared that deployable Iraqi stocks of WMD had been destroyed in order to persuade the Security Council to lift sanctions (after which, he said, the programs would be resumed). Following this crucial defection, the Iraqi government hastily turned over an avalanche of documents that confirmed a biological weapons program that had been greatly underestimated by the U.S. intelligence community.[123]

These revelations had a decisive effect on intelligence agencies worldwide, and why should they not have? In the futile search for evidence of WMD programs inside a totalitarian society, the intelligence services had twice been fooled. Absence of evidence, as the saying goes, had been mistakenly judged to be evidence of absence.

The effect was to shift the burden of proof[124] from the requirement of affirmative evidence of the presence of WMD programs to affirmative evidence of their dismantlement and permanent discontinuation. This was in accord with U.N. Security Council resolutions that required confirmation by Iraq of its abandonment of its WMD programs. With this shift in the burden of proof, intelligence collectors now had to find affirmative evidence not just of the destruction or desuetude of stocks, but evidence that no clandestine programs were under way. The affirmative proposition that Saddam Hussein was clean could be disproved; indeed, it had been, with traumatic results. But how could the intelligence agencies ever disprove the proposition that Saddam Hussein was, somewhere, busily working away at a WMD program? According to the Robb-Silberman Commission, CIA analysts

> explained that, given Iraq's history of successful deception regarding the state of its nuclear program and evidence that Iraq was attempting to procure components that *could* be used in a uranium enrichment program, they could not envision having reached the conclusion that Iraq was *not* reconstituting its nuclear program.[125]

Historians will find that there was much more to the motives that led to the invasion of Iraq than concern over WMD. For some, it was the failure of sanctions that fueled the prospect of Saddam Hussein's future acquisition of nuclear weapons, which would have long-term consequences for terrorism, proliferation, and the stability of the region. Such a conclusion about the future can never be definitively settled by facts in the present. It is a matter of judgment, not least of the parameters used by those who conscientiously try to provide proof. Greater testing of its judgments by dialogue with non-secret sources might have been fruitful; instead, the analysts determined that only "specific information from a very well-placed, reliable human source" could have caused them to question their judgment.[126]

The Robb-Silberman Commission recommended the creation of an Open Source Directorate at the CIA. It was appalling that there was no entity that collected, processed, and provided open source information to analysts.[127] An Open Source Directorate that would, at a minimum, gather and store "digital newspapers and periodicals that are available only temporarily on the Internet and giv[e] Intelligence Community staff easy (and secure) access to Internet materials" is unlikely to actually "help improve the Intelligence Community's surprisingly poor 'feel' for cultural and political issues in the countries that concern policymakers most."[128] It remains to be seen whether the creation of an open source director in the office of the DNI will have the resources to fulfill this function. It is clearly not enough to simply make documents available. There are now 28,000 newspapers, 26,000 radio stations, 21,000 TV stations, 108 million web-sites, and 45,000 daily podcasts. What is required is the cultivation of trusted experts worldwide who are linked by secure Internet networks.

An officer in the Directorate of Intelligence (DI) has recently proposed a "Google" for intelligence customers.* This would revolutionize "the way customers interact with DI analysts . . . Instead of first tasking DI ana-lyst, customer would just log on to a secure system and search for the latest products, including charts and graphs, on any topic."[129] This would, of course, greatly lower the barrier between producers and consumers and is bound to be resisted accordingly. It could, however, also be used to pro-vide open-source information organized around specific areas of concern.

LAW ENFORCEMENT AND INTELLIGENCE

The Robb-Silberman Commission drew attention to the fact that the Depart-ment of Justice, reflecting an entrenched antinomy, separated the Office of Intelligence Policy and Review (which handles the FISA warrants) from the counterterrorism and counterespionage sections of the Criminal Divi-sion. Indeed, they reported to two different deputy assistant attorneys gen-eral. The commission concluded that this separation had, in some cases, "contributed to errors that hampered intelligence gathering."[130]

This division of responsibility is further reflected in the limited authority given the new director of national intelligence (DNI) over FBI intelligence operations. Although the Intelligence Reform and Terrorism Prevention Act mandates that the DNI lead the entire sixteen entities of the U.S. intelligence community, which specifically includes the FBI's "intelligence elements," the DNI has no power to initiate, terminate, or redirect any collection undertaken by the FBI's agents. Nor does he have control over the bureau's portion of the National Intelligence Program budget or personnel.

The ability of the FBI is further compromised by yet another antinomy, the division between the foreign and the domestic. It is hard to see how a law enforcement agency dedicated to catching criminals after they have committed a crime is well suited to conduct preventive intelligence collec-tion, but even if the culture of the FBI were miraculously to transform

---

*A related and promising innovation is the development of Intellipedia, a user-driven network of individuals with similar security clearances in sixteen different U.S. intelligence agencies that creates various entries in the way that Wikipedia does for the general public. This allows persons working on the same problem but in different agencies to jointly contribute to its description and analysis via the Internet. See Clive Thompson, "Open-Source Spying," *New York Times,* 3 December 2006, and Cass R. Sunstein, "A Brave New Wikiworld," *Washington Post,* 24 February 2007, A19. If Intellipedia were made available to policy makers—in the Google-like way suggested above—they would be able to search for an up-to-the-minute product created by multiple agencies.

itself, its overwhelmingly domestic mission is at variance with the global nature of the threat.

In summary, two ideas drove intelligence communities in the period before the second Gulf War: in the U.S., the conviction that Iraq was reconstituting its nuclear program, and in the U.S. and the U.K., the consensus that a mobile biological weapons capability had been deployed. Contrary to many claims, Hussein Kamel's testimony that he had overseen the destruction of the remaining Iraqi WMD did not resolve the matter; rather, his testimony tended to increase concern because it showed that U.N. inspectors and the intelligence community had been so thoroughly duped. This shifted the burden of proof so that when, some years later, the community was divided as to the suitability of intercepted aluminum tubes for uranium enrichment, the balance tipped toward those who were more alarmed. Technical evidence couldn't, however, resolve the mobile lab issue one way or the other; to a satellite camera, one white van looks like another. A human source might resolve this, however, and thus the community was eager for material from Curveball, questions about whose reliability[131] were unknown to the analysts who seized on his reports.

The 9/11 and Iraqi WMD intelligence failures appear at first to have little in common. *The 9/11 Commission Report* criticized the intelligence community for its failure to share information among agencies and concluded that this failure materially contributed to the larger failure to "connect the dots"—that is, to the analytical lapse that prevented the U.S. from anticipating an attack and thwarting it. "With each agency holding one or two pieces of the puzzle, none could see the whole picture."[132] The Iraq WMD failure presented a different problem. It wasn't so much that analysts were unaware of what their counterparts in other agencies were thinking; it was rather that, with some exceptions,[133] all the analysts were thinking the same thing. Information inconsistent with this widely shared thesis was discarded or, tellingly, reclassified as the result of Iraqi deception.

Once we see, however, that the consequences of these analytical shortcomings were magnified by the various antinomial divisions we saw in the 9/11 tragedy, we can appreciate that the Iraqi WMD intelligence failure was indeed very similar in its causation to that of 9/11. But for the mistakes introduced by pitting collectors and analysts, producers and consumers, public and private sources, and so on against each other, the analytical shortfalls of the October NIE would have been mitigated. The real loss, we must remember, wasn't occasioned by an American or British mistake in assessing Iraqi WMD capability.[134] The colossal loss was the result of repeatedly and vehemently claiming to the world that this capability justified intervention by the U.S. and the U.K. This was catastrophic because the legitimacy of the kind of anticipatory war waged by the coalition led by the United States and the United Kingdom depends on persuading the public of the urgency of a hypothetical.* This places immense burdens on the intelligence agencies and radically shifts the political dialogue.

"To be sure," the Robb-Silberman Report finally concluded, "the Intelligence Community is full of talented, dedicated people. But they seem to be working harder and harder just to maintain a *status quo* that is increasingly irrelevant to the new challenges presented by weapons of mass destruction."[135] What is less easy to see is that it is the status quo that is making it impossible to cope with these challenges. Summing up, Desmond Ball concluded simply that

> the sorts of fundamental changes which might improve intelligence about strategic surprises . . . are unlikely to be implemented . . . [Such] reforms are inhibited by the ingrained philosophies and operational habits which dominate Western intelligence agencies—the surrounding secrecy, the self-defeating compartmentalization, and the sovereignty of the principle of protection of sources and methods. They seem constitutionally unable to . . . exploit the growth in open-source intelligence or to harness the technical skills available in the private sector . . . [W]ithin another decade there will be another crisis or calamity of strategic proportions which will have caught the new intelligence establishment unawares.[136]

It has been more than twenty-five years since Richard Betts's seminal 1978 article[137] on intelligence failures appeared. There is now something of a consensus[138] that such failures are inevitable. The U.S. is at an impasse today in the reform of the intelligence system, however, because it has constructed the problem of twenty-first century intelligence in such a way—the twentieth century American configuration that is the result of the six antinomies described here—as to render it insoluble. Once we realize that we must radically change the structuring ideas, we will have taken the first step to successful reform. The second step will take more time. As Sir Mark Allen has observed, there is an important connection between

> the "market state" and [the] shift in the locus of secret intelligence work in the operations of government. Secret intelligence has moved much closer to the surface of policy and so there is greater reliance on

*See Rwandan example infra, p. 335.

it. The strain of this shift is very great. It has enormous implications for the public appreciation of government, of risk assessment and societal permission for government action.[139]

Coping with these implications will involve cultivating the judgment of sophisticated men and women, both the analysts who handle intelligence and the public who will have to assess that judgment when they are called upon to endorse political action based on the hypothetical. Partly this will be done in our universities, which will some day have intelligence schools much as they have schools of law, business, and journalism. I surmise that the need for students trained in this discipline will far exceed the small numbers required by government agencies.

Partly this coping must be accomplished by electing and appointing persons of greater sophistication and less cynicism to those posts that rely on intelligence. It is hard to escape feeling that many in the Bush administration thought intelligence didn't really matter, that it was, at the end of the day, only one more public relations tool: that reality would eventually conform to presentation.

Most importantly, for the first time we must undertake to educate the public so that they can be mature examiners of the arguments, based on intelligence sources, that will be adduced to support policy. The most important HUMINT, in a way, is the human judgment that must assess the information that has been collected.

VIII.

The notion of "intelligence failure" looks very different from the British perspective. It is no coincidence that the most influential novelists writing about clandestine intelligence activities—Erskine Childers, Graham Greene, Ian Fleming, and John le Carré—have been British, for the culture of U.K. intelligence is sharply circumscribed by the collection of secret materials. Whereas the Americans have, since the Second World War, defined the mission of intelligence very broadly to include not only collection but also analysis, integration, and interpretation, the British have maintained that of these activities only collection—and only the secret collection of secrets—is really intelligence. Sherman Kent's definition of intelligence was captured in his maxim, "Intelligence is knowledge." By contrast, the British maxim is "Intelligence is about secrets, not mysteries."

Michael Herman noted this distinction in his book, *Intelligence Power in Peace and War*.[140] Describing a spectrum of concepts of intelligence ranging from "all-source analysis" (typified by Kent's practice) to narrow interpretations that concentrate on clandestine collection, Herman noted that Americans tended toward the former view and the British toward the latter.

> In current usage, "intelligence" in US parlance tends to refer to "fin-ished" intelligence that has been put through the all-source analysis process and turned into a product that can provide advice and options for decision makers. . . . [I]n British practice, raw intelligence moves straight into policymaking circles without passing through a separate, intervening analytical stage. [A]ll-source analysis is subsumed by the civil service employees [in their various departments]. As a result intelligence as such tends to refer more narrowly to those kinds of information not available from the "normal product" of departmental activity . . . In British usage, then, "intelligence production" means raw intelligence collection.[141]

It was Philip Davies who used such distinctions with some virtuosity to pose these questions: "How do different countries and institutions define intelligence?" and "What are the consequences of those different definitions?" In an important article circulated mainly among American intelligence professionals, Davies noted that

> [s]ince the invasion of Iraq, the understated reaction in the UK to what one former British official has described as the "worst intelligence failure since 1945" has been the source of some surprise and curiosity amongst American observers of the intelligence process.[142]

Davies accounted for this by pointing to the fact that in British practice, assessment is viewed "as a *government* function and not specifically as an *intelligence* function."[143] This truth has many implications. For one, it draws attention to the monstrous injustice done by the media to the SIS officials in charge of collecting intelligence against Iraq. In contrast to the Americans, who had no current human sources in the regime, the British ran a stable of six, four of whom were described in the Butler Report as "main sources" who were considered reliable prior to the invasion and emerged after the war as generally validated.

For our current study, another implication of this distinction must be addressed. If the fault lines in the American intelligence process lie along the six antinomies described above, what was wrong with the British pro-cedures that also led the government into a damaging public reliance on insufficient evidence of Iraqi WMD? It can't be that producers were too separated from consumers; the producers of finished intelligence—the

Foreign Office, the Cabinet Office, the various departmental representatives on the Joint Intelligence Committee (JIC)—were the consumers, it appeared. For Davies, the problem lay in the weakening of the validating role once played by the Requirements Directorate that provided liaison to the various consumers of the SIS product. This was in part the result of organizational changes; and these in turn were driven by budget cuts as a result of the post–Cold War review of British intelligence that led to a 25 percent cut in SIS staffing and expenditure and a 40 percent decrease in senior staff. A significant factor, however, was that technology allowed the dissemination of reports without a person actually doing the briefing.

> "Modern communications technology and computers," observed one former officer, "have made it easier for everyone to know the same thing at the same time." . . . [T]he day had passed when disseminating intelligence involved officers carrying locked briefcases across St. James's Park. The increased centrality of tasking and dissemination dominated perceptions of this change. . . . *The quality control implications were completely overlooked.*[144]

The producers were not in fact merged with the consumers, as it happened, because the crucial liaison function of senior, experienced collectors who evaluated raw intelligence had been submerged in the steady downgrading of the Requirements Directorate personnel. This meant that the needs of consumers, though they appeared to be addressed by the JIC apparatus they dominated, were not being met. Interpretations were superimposed on what had been successfully collected, and the collectors found themselves powerless to prevent any exaggerated or unsophisticated interpretation of the product that they had collected but others were analyzing.

The British experience is thus quite different from the American, yet analogous in this way: another antinomy—the distinction between raw and finished intelligence—had to be bridged in an era in which governments took decisions based on an assessment of largely hypothetical risks. This could only be done by senior persons who knew intimately the varying quality of agent reports and could communicate this persuasively to the political personnel shaping the public presentation of evidence.

There is of course much, much more to these cultural distinctions. In the United States conventional legal practices tame the influence of politics on law. This is far from the British convention that attempts to isolate law from politics. The former always risks illegitimacy, which comes from law being reduced to no more than the decisions of those in power; the latter risks irrelevance or, more likely, hypocrisy. These differing attitudes played themselves out in the different approaches to intelligence. The

British sought a rigid isolation of the collectors of secrets, which in the end made those secrets vulnerable to public misunderstanding. The Americans tried to perfect conventional practices—the operation of the legalistic antinomies—that crippled the supple coordination required by twenty-first century threats.

There is much to be said for the British approach to intelligence. Giving responsibility to the departments of government for understanding today's torrent of overt information, rather than further burdening an agency that also must collect secret information, makes sense. The departments know what they are looking for. They can come to the intelligence services when there are otherwise insurmountable difficulties in obtaining what they want. But this view requires very sensitive liaison with the departments and, because analysis has now been ceded to them, it also requires a highly professional civil service.

IX.

With the end of the Long War,[145] a good deal of moral clarity was lost. Many persons involved in Cold War intelligence operations acted out of moral conviction and a particular sense of duty rather than solely out of an assertion of the national interest.[146] Basing security policy on essentially moral grounds is what Tony Blair has attempted; so has George Bush, with perhaps less success. The debacle around Iraqi WMD weakened both.

Yet such moral clarity is precisely what is required in confronting the problems posed for the legitimacy of government action in the face of the hypothetical. I have already stated my conviction that armed intervention should have occurred to prevent the Rwandan genocide. But suppose this had happened. Suppose 50,000 Rwandans and 3,000 American soldiers had been killed in the ensuing conflict. Imagine the outcry in America and around the world. Who would have believed that 800,000 deaths were prevented thereby?

If government is not trusted, its claims to the moral "high ground" will not be accepted. Without that moral high ground, the difficult problem of relying on secret intelligence as the basis for profound strategic choices becomes, for the states of consent, a virtually impossible challenge because the skeptical public—in the absence of an actual attack—cannot be brought to support the decisions of a government that it does not trust.

We should bear in mind that the system of nuclear deterrence, which was a decisive element in the Long War of the twentieth century, also depended upon assessing the hypothetical: thoughtfully considering a war that was never fought, with the objective that it should never be fought,* required intellectual tools we have yet to develop with regard to the Wars on Terror.

In the twentieth century, the fundamental dilemma for democracies coping with the national security threats of the Long War arose from our desire to defeat our enemies without taking on their characteristics. Could we preserve guarantees of free speech in the face of fascist propaganda like the *Protocols of the Elders of Zion;* could we assure freedom of association despite communist penetration of trade unions for the purpose of subversion; could we hold fast to civil liberties at home and respect for the choices made by other societies overseas while carrying out surveillance at home and covert action abroad? The key we found, an imperfect key wielded by imperfect human beings, was the interposition of law.

In the twenty-first century, the fundamental problem for states of consent that must confront the challenges of terror will be to achieve public endorsement and official accountability in the face of largely hypothetical threats that require anticipatory action based on secret intelligence. Can we take preemptive action based on information that can easily be manipulated and whose sources cannot be revealed? Can we legitimately prevent states from arming themselves with nuclear weapons when they vehemently deny that is their intention? Can we put measures in place to minimize the harm done by future catastrophes when so many present needs insistently claim our resources? The key again will be law, but not law that is interposed to block the demands of strategy, but rather law that is integrated with strategy. Whereas the nation state saw its role in opposition to the market, market states will want to use the market—including the markets in information—for their own purposes. Only this can possibly enable the intelligence community to cope with the dizzying increase in the number of targets and subjects that it must identify, develop, track, and analyze. As Treverton put it in the CIA paper quoted earlier, the "most powerful driver of both the international system and of intelligence's role . . . is the transition [to] the market state."

*In the Cold War, both sides held vast arsenals of nuclear weapons in reserve precisely so that they would not have to fight. The notorious ladder of escalation was summed up by one of its most reflective (and wittiest) analysts, Henry Kissinger, when he mordantly wrote: "First we lose the conventional war. Then we lose the tactical nuclear exchange. Then we blow up the world." Quoted in Robert Cooper, review of *The Utility of Force: The Art of War in the Modern World,* by General Sir Rupert Smith (September 2005), http://www.envirosecurity.org/ges/TheUtilityOfForceByGeneral SirRupertSmith.pdf (accessed November 17, 2006).

CHAPTER SEVEN

The Strategic Relationship
Between Ends and Means

"Who is this man?"

"M-major Danby, sir," Colonel Cathcart stammered. "My group operations officer."

"Take him out and shoot him," General Dreedle demanded.

"S-sir?"

"I said take him out and shoot him. Can't you hear?"

"Yes, sir!" Colonel Cathcart responded smartly, swallowing hard, and turned in a brisk manner to his chauffeur and his meteorologist. "Take Major Danby out and shoot him."

"S-sir?" his chauffeur and his meteorologist stammered.

"I said take Major Danby out and shoot him," Colonel Cathcart snapped. "Can't you hear?"

. . . "I think you'd better wait a minute, Dad," [Colonel Moodus, General Dreedle's son-in-law] suggested hesitantly. "I don't think you can shoot him."

General Dreedle was infuriated by this intervention. "Who the hell says I can't?" he thundered pugnaciously in a voice loud enough to rattle the whole building. . . . "Why the hell can't I? . . . You mean I can't shoot anyone I want to? . . . Is that a fact?" he inquired, his rage tamed by curiosity.

"Yes, Dad. I'm afraid it is."

"I guess you think you're pretty . . . smart, don't you?"

—Joseph Heller, *Catch-22*

I.

IN THE MIDST of the early period in the war against global terrorism, a conservative columnist for the *Washington Times* wrote, "We are in far more danger from the belief that the ends justify the means than we are from terrorists."[1] To this insipid cliché perhaps the most appropriate response belongs to the late Washington lawyer Paul Porter, who is said to have once remarked, "If the ends don't justify the means, I'd like to know what in the hell does." This acid response from a gentle and witty man prompts another question: Why do so many commentators share the assumption that ends and means must be disconnected in order for us to preserve our rights in the Wars against Terror? It is my view that this separation—the demand that terrorism be defined exclusively by attending to the means it employs—is symptomatic of a larger intellectual failure.

There are a number of fundamental and mistaken assumptions about the ends and means of terrorist violence that tend to disable us from even accurately defining terrorism.

- The belief that terrorism is necessarily and only about means and not ends, and therefore that one cannot, when discussing terrorism, discriminate between the use of violence to deter violence and the use of violence to deter lawful activity.
- The corollary of this belief, that "one man's terrorist is another man's freedom fighter" because, after all, terrorism is only a technique and not the necessary means of certain ideologies.
- The indifference to the fluidity between means and ends and thus the inability to imagine that theatrical violence in the hands of al Qaeda (or its twenty-first century successors) can be an end in itself.
- The conclusion that violence that inevitably harms civilians that the states of consent claim to seek to protect amounts to no more than terrorism in different hands.

Interestingly, those that share these assumptions include some persons who believe terrorism can and must be defeated and also those who believe that a war on terror is a futile misnomer. In both cases, it is their shared evaluation of the relationship between means and ends when confronting terrorism that causes a kind of paralysis, preventing us from achieving a consensus on the definition of terrorism and thus either disarming us or discrediting our efforts at arming ourselves. Moreover, this attitude toward ends and means also has the effect of blocking us from recognizing the state of terror, and thus results in a conceptual disconnect between terrorism and the Wars on Terror. Because we do not see that twenty-first century terrorism is crucially connected to the goals and objectives of the state of terror, we are handicapped in our appreciation of the goals and objectives of the Wars against Terror of which the struggle against terrorism is a part.

II.

Is terrorism always and only a means to an end? This is the common ground of each of these assumptions, namely, that terrorism is merely a technique of conflict. In this view, terrorism today is simply the warfare of the oppressed, or at least the relatively underfunded, when confronting the sophisticated war machines of the developed world. Thus terrorist acts need not be committed on behalf of any particular goal to be terrorism. After all, what causes do the PLO and the Jewish Underground,[2] the IRA and the Ulster Defense Association, the Red Brigades and the Black Shirts have in common? These groups share little except a hatred of each other and a habituation to violence against civilians or military persons who are noncombatants at the time of the attack. There are many persons who look at terrorism this way. Some of them would forge a worldwide coalition against this phenomenon, defined by the means—the techniques of violence—used by different groups, notably suicide bombing. Most of the questions of ends would be absorbed into the issue of means; law would collapse into strategy. At times, this seems to have been the approach of figures as disparate as George W. Bush, Vladimir Putin, and Ariel Sharon.

In past discussions of a definition of terrorism, there has been some general agreement that it is performed by non-state actors, that it involves the use of violence for political ends, and that it targets civilian populations. But this has proved insufficient, for we know that while terrorism often is used by non-state actors, states too use terror; and that the acts of terrorists—bombing for example, including even suicide bombing—are often indistinguishable from conventional warfare, which also uses violence in pursuit of political objectives; that civilians are often the targets of ordinary criminals as well as terrorists; and that terrorists do target military and official persons. There has been no consensus on whether the defining parameters should be the nature of the attack, the identity of the perpetrators, or the character of their targets.[3]

By contrast, consider the following definition: *Terrorism is the pursuit of political goals through the use of violence against noncombatants in order to dissuade them from doing what they have a lawful right to do.*[4] This definition puts the goals of terrorism back into the picture by linking strategic means (attacks on civilians) with legal ends (the deterrence of lawful action). Was it terrorism when the Allies bombed Berlin in 1944, knowing countless civilian deaths would occur? No, because the city was crucial to the political and economic pursuit of unlawful wars by the Nazis. What about the firebombing of Dresden, where the inhabitants had every right to do what they were doing as civilians? Perhaps it was an attack directed at the Nazi regime, whose aerial defense of Dresden crucially weakened its war effort,[5] and not an attack on civilians per se, or perhaps it was simply state terrorism and because it occurred in wartime, it was a war crime. To turn this around, one might say that a war crime—such as the taking of hostages, the murder of captives, the waging of wars of annexation and conquest, the singling out of racial or ethnic groups for attack, and so on—is an act of terrorism that occurs in a theater of war. Similarly, acts that in war would be classified as war crimes are acts of terrorism when they occur outside the conventional theaters of war.

Take again the case of Zacarias Moussaoui, who has admitted to being part of a conspiracy to attack U.S. civilians. If we assume that the attacks on September 11 were acts of war, as I have argued in chapter 3, then isn't Moussaoui a prisoner of war—whether or not he comes within the Geneva Conventions' definition—who can be tried for conspiring to commit war crimes? Terrorism, in the current context, is the very paradigm of a war crime.[6]

It is crucial that we agree on a definition of terrorism, even if we may disagree on some particular applications of that definition, because this agreement is the necessary foundation for collaboration. If there is a consensus on the basic definition, then we can isolate outlying cases and either resolve them politically or, failing that, at least be capable of identifying those elements that cannot serve as a basis for cooperation.

The U.S. Department of State defines terrorism as "premeditated, politically motivated violence perpetrated against noncombatant targets by subnational groups or clandestine agents."[7] To see how insufficient this is, we have only to consult a recent study of Arab public opinion on this subject. In 2004, a polling expert at the Center for Strategic Studies at the University of Jordan presented some striking findings from opinion polls he had conducted in five Arab countries on the question of what counts as "terrorism."[8] Respondents in Syria, Palestine, Jordan, Egypt, and Lebanon drew sharp distinctions between organizations like Hamas and Hezbollah, on the one hand, and al Qaeda on the other. About 90 percent of those polled saw the former as legitimate resistance organizations, but this number dropped considerably with respect to al Qaeda. Only 8 percent of Syrians, 18 percent of Lebanese, and 41 percent of the Egyptians polled thought al Qaeda was a legitimate organization, and even among those populations most sympathetic to al Qaeda—the Palestinians in both Palestine and Jordan—scarcely 60 percent refused to label al Qaeda a terrorist group. Yet all of these groups would be swept up within the U.S. definition of terrorism.

At the same time, the poll inquired as to what constitutes a terrorist act.

This table presents the percentage of respondents in national samples by country who labeled these acts and events "terrorist."

Event	Jordan	Syria	Lebanon	Palestine	Egypt
Killing by Israel of Palestinian civilians in West Bank and Gaza Strip	90	97	88	96	91
Bulldozing by Israel of agricultural land and crops in West Bank and Gaza Strip	88	96	83	94	90
U.S.-led Coalition operations in Iraq	86	94	64	89	87
Assassination by Israel of Palestinian political figures	84	93	80	94	87
Bombing of U.N. and Red Cross headquarters in Iraq	48	78	80	36	61
Bombing of housing compounds in Saudi Arabia	46	73	82	28	69
Bombing of hotel in Morocco	50	72	75	30	73
World Trade Center attacks 9/11	35	71	73	22	62
Attacks on Jewish synagogues in Turkey	21	54	59	13	44
Attacks on Israeli civilians inside Israel	24	22	55	17	33
Attacks on settlements in West Bank and Gaza Strip	17	16	42	3	17
Attacks on U.S. Coalition forces in Iraq	18	9	28	9	14
Attacks on Israeli military inside Israel	17	5	25	3	9
Hezbollah operations against Israel	10	3	16	2	7

The figures suggest that those societies rejecting the view of terrorism prevalent in the U.S. and U.K. governments actually disagree as to the underlying legitimacy of the presence of the targets attacked. The U.S. definition is of no help here because it provides no possible common ground: all acts of the State are excluded, and all acts of violence against the personnel of the State are included. Yet there is common ground to be had. Consider, finally, the polling data elicited by the question whether the respondent disapproved of the killing of foreign civilians (including women and children) where those foreign forces have occupied Muslim lands.

Samples	Lebanon	Syria	Egypt	Jordan	Palestine
Nationals	88	85	77	76	64
University Students	90	84	77	76	52
Business	93	86	87	85	69
Media	89	81	85	79	68

It is disturbing that the least disapproving respondents were Palestinian university students, but even here there are grounds for dialogue. These figures suggest that Palestinian respondents simply do not believe that Israeli civilians or Coalition contractors, for example, have any lawful right to be present in Arab lands such as the West Bank or Iraq.

An inquiry into lawfulness,[9] however, introduces the question of proportionality, which necessarily brings us back to the subject of ends. For it is to particular ends that the means must be proportionate. Without a principle of proportionality, the ends/means inquiry urged here would be pointless for then any means could be urged so long as it made some marginal contribution to achieving its goal whereas the point of the ends/means inquiry is to focus on the relationship between ends and means. It would do little good to reintroduce ends into our analysis only to then discard them because practically any means would serve, to some extent, its end. Is a Palestinian attack on Jewish civilians in the new settlements of the occupied territories an act of terrorism? Suppose we assume that the settlements are unlawful; the answer turns, as it would in wartime, on the necessary and proportionate use of violence. Even if we assume that the Israelis have no lawful right to occupy settlements, is killing them the only effective way to dislodge them?

What of the Iraqi insurgents, then? Can we say that they are not terrorists when they decapitate civilians because the occupation is illegal and there is no other realistic way to force an end to it? Even if we assume, *arguendo,* that the Coalition invasion of Iraq was illegal, subsequent U.N. Security Council action has nevertheless ratified the proposition that Coalition forces at present remain there legally. In a later chapter I will urge that U.S. and U.K. forces remain in Iraq as long as the duly constituted government asks them to, and not one moment longer. Indeed, because remaining in Iraq despite a request to withdraw by a duly constituted Iraqi regime could render the insurgency lawful, we have one more reason to comply with such a request.

The definition of terrorism offered above brings with it a nexus of inquiry, a basis for conversation. It may be that we will still disagree, but we will also know what we must change, in ourselves and in others, to bring about collaboration. These polls, and others, suggest that for most Arabs, as for most Muslims, what is objectionable about the U.S. and its allies is their policies. It is not, as is sometimes urged, that Arabs simply hate our way of life.[10] But there are Muslim groups, some of them Arab, who do hate our freedoms and hate the West for having them. It is precisely these groups that must be isolated, a process that can only begin with a perspicuous determination of what separates them from our potential collaborators. It is not that these potential collaborators simply accept terrorism as necessary to advance their political agenda—as does al Qaeda—but rather that they don't see these acts as terrorism in the first place. That fact is reflected in the failure of the international community, after several decades, to agree on a definition of terrorism.

Kenneth Roth, the executive director of Human Rights Watch, has cogently argued for "a counterterrorist strategy that scrupulously and transparently respects international standards . . . [and] a positive vision of societies built around democracy, human rights, and the rule of law— something that people can be *for*—to accompany the important but partial vision of being *against* terrorism."[11] This seems to me right, but I would go further. I would say that being opposed to terrorism is, in light of the definition I have proffered, already to be committed to the rule of law, which includes respect for systems of consent and human rights. What we lack is a set of international standards that expresses this understanding of terrorism.[12]

A war against terror is a war in support of law, and that implies, for those of us who wish to see states of consent prevail, that it is a war in support of consensual governance as the legitimating way to ground lawful behavior. In such a conflict, terrorism becomes something more than just a means. It becomes a kind of politics expressed through the use of violence against civilians. This occurs when the purpose of terrorism is to punish civilians and other noncombatants for their reliance on law and order. That is one more reason why it is important to define terrorism as having something crucial to do with the lawful behavior of its victims.*

This behavior is movingly captured in an essay by Jean Bethke Elshtain, written after September 11. She writes of the

> simple but profound good that is mothers and fathers raising their children, men and women going to work, citizens of a great city making their way on streets and subways, ordinary people buying airplane tickets in order to visit their grandchildren in California, business men and women en route to transact business with colleagues in other cities, the faithful attending their churches, synagogues, and mosques without fear. This quotidian idea, this basic civic peace, is a great good.[13]

This links the definition I here proposed[14] to acts of the state against its own people. Consider, for example, the French Revolution's Reign of Terror or the People's Republic of China's Cultural Revolution. The objective—the end sought—of these campaigns was to maintain a state of terror. Even if undertaken with the consent of the great mass of citizens, these campaigns can never be lawful because they arrogate to the State a sovereignty it cannot have. No consent can make unlawful the ordinary exercise of the inalienable rights of the victims of these mass atrocities. Not only, therefore, are these acts of terrorism, they are acts of states of terror that rule by sustaining terror as an ongoing state of affairs—that is, as an end.

Terror can be an end in itself[15] rather than just a means to some other political goal. In the case of al Qaeda, the goal of the terror network is the destruction of Western values in any area where these can have an impact on Muslims. Rendering persons too frightened to act lawfully on their basic values is both a means and an end, for such a situation of terror, of terrified people in a terrified society too fearful to freely choose their actions (and thus manifest their values) is an end roughly equivalent to the total destruction of Western values. This is what bin Laden really had in mind when, on October 7, 2001, he said, "America will never dream nor those who live in America will never taste security and safety unless we feel security and safety in our land and in Palestine."[16] This may also be said of *genocidaires* who seek a permanent state of terror in their victims

---

*Including their voting. The reason why bin Laden is wrong in saying that the citizens of states of consent are proper targets for al Qaeda attacks (because they are responsible for government policy) is not that such citizens are not morally responsible, but rather that they have a lawful right to vote and that making the exercise of this right the basis for violence against them is inconsistent with a system of consent.

to render them helpless and eventually to extinguish them and similarly of those states that seek nuclear and other weapons of mass destruction in order to create a permanent condition of terror in their neighbors who then dare not oppose the aggression of the compelling state.

In *The Quranic Concept of War* the Pakistani brigadier S. K. Malik puts it this way: "Terror struck into the hearts of the enemies is not only a means, it is the end in itself. Once a condition of terror into the opponent's heart is obtained, hardly anything is left to be achieved. It is the point where the means and the end meet and merge. Terror is not a means of imposing decision upon the enemy, it is *the decision* we wish to impose upon him."[17] From this perspective, terror itself becomes the objective of war.

Terrorism is the name of a means, the employment of violence against civilians whether in war or peace. But it is not only the name of a means. As we saw in part 1, terrorism can be classified according to the different objectives that have been sought by terrorists in different constitutional eras. The use of violence against civilian populations embraces a multitude of tactical contexts and political objectives. In the twentieth century, these included the bombing campaigns of World War II; the independent struggles of colonial states in the Third World; and Cold War violence sustained by third parties in Southeast Asia, the Caribbean, and elsewhere. Perhaps violence against noncombatants can never be legitimate.[18] But if such means are ever legitimate, it has to be a matter of the lawful context within which such violence takes place and of precisely what ends are sought.

Consider the case of insurgents opposing a highly organized and well-armed police state against which any attack on its armed forces by persons without heavy arms is useless. Must we say that in this case, no armed struggle against the regime—say the regime is Hitler's or Stalin's or Mao's—is legitimate because the insurgency will inevitably employ force that can result in killing and injuring innocent persons (if only through state reprisals)? No. "It is hard to think of any means, for example, that would have been unacceptable if used by the inhabitants of the Warsaw ghetto in 1943."[19] Surely the issue does not rest on tactics alone, but on the evil to be combatted and the effectiveness and availability of other means of doing so. The nature of the end does, thoroughly, affect our judgment of the means used to achieve it.

We can all agree that Mohandas Gandhi's "Quit India" movement was not a terrorist organization because it endeavored to act scrupulously within the laws of war even while violating certain other laws. What about the African National Congress (ANC), which refused to do so, which pursued goals that were really quite similar to those of the Quit India movement? Doesn't the key lie in the attitude of the government against which the insurgents fight? As Byford has pointed out, "passive resistance would not have impressed the Afrikaners."[20] Does that make the Mau Mau movement of the early 1950s unlawful terrorism—or the Stern Gang's attack on the King David Hotel, which killed twenty-eight British soldiers in 1946—but the Islamic resistance to the Soviets in the 1980s permissible? One's inclination is to say "yes" for as long as there are constitutional institutions in place that provide for the consent of the governed, and the protection of political and civil rights, including nonviolent protest, there is no right of extralegal violence.[21] In such a society, only the State may take up arms. But where such rights do not exist, proportionate violence against persons engaged in unlawful acts, including aid to the unlawful regime, is not terrorism. Proportionate violence can only amount to terrorism when it is waged against rights-respecting democracies. Thus when one writer concluded that "we will always be in the wrong so long as we imply the ends do not justify the means unless they are *our* ends"—he has it precisely backwards. We will never be in the right—never be able to establish a principled standard for identifying terrorism—unless we insist on assessing the ends sought, and we give reasons for doing so that apply to us (and that condemn us when our behavior does not correspond to the proportionate pursuit of lawful ends).

It is generally assumed that groups are driven to terrorism when they have no reasonable alternative to combat an overwhelming force. "Give us F-16s," a Palestinian terrorist is supposed to have said, "and we will stop employing suicide bombers." When terrorists attack civilians, it is assumed that although this is an illegitimate means, as Chris Brown put it, it may be in pursuit of a legitimate end.

> While some terrorists engage in terrorism in pursuit of the kind of freedoms and rights recognized by modern liberal-democratic and social-democratic polities, others reject these freedoms, and pursue goals antithetical to these freedoms and rights . . . The goals of the terrorist are crucial here, and sometimes these goals are themselves repressive, and, if achieved, would actually bring about, as opposed to lessening, oppression.[22]

This is in part—but only in part—the distinction between a terrorist attack on a marketplace in Sarajevo and the NATO bombing of Belgrade. The former is meant to bring about a state of affairs in which ordinary people will be compelled to surrender their lawful rights. Any civilian casualties attendant to the latter bombing, however, are a by-product that is contrary to the objective of the mission, though it may be unavoidable. Thus, once again, we are compelled to consider ends and to measure the justification of means in their light.

In order to appreciate this point, consider four hypotheticals.

First, suppose armed dissidents take a group of tourists hostage in an effort to force the local government to release political prisoners. Assume these are prisoners held entirely on account of their lawful, political activities. If we assume that there is no nonviolent means of redress, isn't this still terrorism? The tourists are being prevented by violence from doing what they would do lawfully. They are not an arm of the government. Here it is the *means* that condemns the terrorists.

Next, suppose a head of state is assassinated. Does it matter to us whether it's Adolf Hitler or John F. Kennedy? Whether the objective is to end a Nazi war of aggression and an unspeakable domestic policy of genocide or whether the goal is to impress your wife or satisfy a paranoid reaction to the indignities of the FBI, here it is the *ends* that seem to determine the answer.

Now suppose an animal rights activist hacks into the computer systems that control energy and water in an agricultural area, and as a consequence, hundreds of thousands of chickens, kept in cramped industrial pens, die. The means are nonviolent—at least to humans—and perhaps the ends are not inconsistent with our democratic system because the rights of animals may be said to be structurally underrepresented by legislatures, anthropocentric as they admittedly are. But aren't the means wildly disproportionate to the ends sought, and doesn't this relationship between means and ends create the ecoterrorist?

And finally, consider this hypothetical drawn from my family's history. My great-grandmother's earliest memory was of General Sherman's cavalry riding through her family's plantation and cutting off the heads of the geese with their sabers. Sherman's march to the sea during the American Civil War was clearly meant to terrorize the local population. He was trying to force that population to withdraw its material and political support for the Confederate regime. In this, it was no different from the bombing of Belgrade by a later American government. When the goals of these campaigns for human rights are considered—and I do not mean that these wars, or any wars, were fought solely to vindicate human rights but only that this was a genuine and significant objective—and when the unlawful behavior* of the civil regimes they opposed is also considered, can't we absolve their leaders of the charge of terrorism? Whichever way you decide, both ends and means have to be considered to provide an answer.

---

*Assuming *arguendo* that secession without the consent of Congress was unconstitutional and hence unlawful in the case of the Confederacy and that the government-sponsored massacres in Kosovo were unlawful under international law.

III.

Perhaps, however, this argument goes too far. If, for states of consent, terror can never be a lawful end in itself, and even if terrorism—by definition—is not the right term for violent action against the agents of a state of terror, does this imply that any proportionate methods, even torture and assassination, are available to the states of consent—or to democratic revolutionaries struggling against dictatorships—so long as they are necessary and effective?

Or does the approach taken above mean, instead, that states of consent forfeit that status when they adopt the means of terror to wage a war on terror? And if so, because terrorism is the use of violence to advance a political agenda by preventing persons from doing what they would otherwise lawfully do, is the appropriation of certain unsavory methods fatal to the claim by the state of consent that violent acts against it constitute terrorism? For in this situation, the agents of the state of consent are being attacked by terrorists to prevent those agents from doing *unlawful* things, such as torture or assassination (or aerial bombing, which is in some contexts both torture and assassination on a broad and indiscriminate scale)?

This brings us to the awful subject of torture. There are some rules to be derived from the ends-and-means approach proposed in this chapter, rules that might serve as the basis for the reform of law as it is applied to the interrogation of terrorists. In this preliminary section, I am anxious to make one overriding point: the moral rules that govern the official of a state of consent impose a "duty of consequentialism"[23]—that is, any contemplated course of action must be measured in terms of the foreseeable costs and benefits that are its result and not against any absolute or categorical rule, including those regarding intentions.[24] That is, what is achieved in such contexts is at least as important as how this is done.[25]

Let me deal at once with the notorious hypothetical of the "ticking bomb."[26] Those who would advocate a complete ban on the use of violence to interrogate terrorists must confront the provocative question posed by this hypothetical much as the proponents of the abolition of capital punishment had to confront the disconcerting question, "So, what would you do if you came home and surprised a man who had raped and killed your wife and daughters? Would you still reject the death penalty for such a creature?" The right answer to the "ticking bomb" hypothetical, like the right answer for the capital punishment question, does not lie in a regretful but sophisticated disquisition on the human rights of criminals.

The "ticking bomb" hypothetical is usually posed like this: Imagine that interrogators learn that a terrorist in custody knows where a bomb has been planted. In order "to overcome an obdurate will not to disclose [this] information and to overcome the fear of the person under interrogation that harm will befall him from his own organization, if he does reveal"[27] the location of the bomb, it is proposed that sufficient dissuasion be applied to prevent the terrorist from refusing to provide the needed information. Threats, harsh words, unpleasant behavior escalating to beatings and other violence, are suggested, and the question is asked: At which of these methods would one cavil?

The right answer—the only answer available to the official of the state of consent who has taken up the responsibility of protecting the safety of the public whose endorsement has put him in this position of authority—is that whatever methods are most effective must be employed. Indeed, Judge Richard Posner has argued, "If the stakes are high enough [even] torture is permissible. No one who doubts that should be in a position of responsibility."[28] It is an easy question.

But look closely at the assumptions the hypothetical enfolds. We are to assume (1) that we have a person in custody, (2) that the person is a terrorist who (3) actually knows the location of a bomb that (4) is about to go off, and that (5) under torture he will accurately disclose the location of the bomb, that (6) cannot be determined by any other means. In such a situation, only a self-absorbed monster would say, sweetly, "Oh no, I mustn't (even if I wish I could), sorry," thus deliberately sentencing unnumbered innocents to death and dismemberment in order to protect the manifestly guilty.

The real difficulty does not lie in such a situation, as we shall see, but rather with cases whose contours are not so carefully shaped so as to provide such perfect information.[29] Suppose the person we have in custody is a roommate—someone otherwise unimplicated who can lead us to the terrorist but who refuses to give this information. Suppose that person is suspected of terrorist activity, but there is substantial doubt about his involvement. Suppose his pleas that he really doesn't know the location of the bomb are plausible. Suppose there is no bomb—yet—but the person knows of plans to acquire such weapons. Suppose he is so averse to pain that he will say anything that he believes will appease his captors and in his fear provides the most plausible, but not the most accurate, information. Suppose an inhibition-reducing drug, coupled with a friendly and trusted interrogator, is a more effective means than violence, or that data cross-correlation, sensors that detect explosives, or other methods are more effective. Suppose that all these suppositions are in fact true or, more likely, suppose that we don't really know which ones are true.

This is not to assume that coercive interrogations and even torture are necessarily ineffective, a claim that will be discussed below. It is rather that their potential effectiveness depends upon a great many factors and that the "ticking bomb" hypothetical tends to focus our attention away from those contextual factors.

The preliminary claim I wish to make is simply that anyone with the responsibility for protecting others must discharge that responsibility with an eye firmly on the consequences—that is, the relationship between means and ends must govern the decision. If, for the public official whose role has been authorized by the consent of the governed,* anything else trumps this relationship, he or she should resign. A pacifist should not be asked (or allowed) to be a general.[30]

Machiavelli was among the first to appreciate this, and his argument that the moral imperatives for the official are different from those of the rest of us has earned him the condemnation of many successive generations. Yet it was a key insight at the birth of the modern state, and indeed one can account for the timing of this insight by correlating it with the emergence of the State. Whereas feudal princes fused the personal with the political, Machiavelli saw that the State was by no means synonymous with the person of the prince and concluded that the head of a princely state is obligated to govern in light of this distinction.

In his essay, "Political Action: The Problem of Dirty Hands,"[31] the American political philosopher Michael Walzer also calls attention to this distinction. Walzer is seeking an answer to a dilemma posed by a symposium on the rules of war: [32] Can a man ever face a situation where he must choose between two courses of action, both of which it would be wrong for him to undertake? The philosopher Thomas Nagel suggested[33] that this could occur when someone was compelled to choose between upholding an important moral absolute and avoiding an imminent human catastrophe. Walzer places this dilemma in the context of a government official and draws a conclusion that would have been most unwelcome to Machiavelli:

> I don't think I could govern innocently; nor do most of us believe that those who govern us are innocent . . . even the best of them. But this does not mean that it isn't possible to do the right thing while governing. It means that a particular act of government . . . may be exactly the right thing to do in utilitarian terms and yet leave the man who does it guilty of a moral wrong . . . If on the other hand he remains innocent, chooses, that is, the "absolutist" [position] . . . he may also fail to measure up to the duties of his office.[34]

---

*This consent I presume to include not only the laws validly adopted but also the constitution that provides for lawmaking on the basis of consent.

In Walzer's view, it is the official's duty of consequentialism[35] that requires him to do things the rest of us would regard as immoral—lying, deceiving, killing, even torturing. This in turn leads to the moral contempt in which the members of the public hold public officials.

> [A political leader] . . . is asked to authorize the torture of a captured rebel leader who knows or probably knows the location of a number of bombs hidden in apartment buildings around the city, set to go off within the next twenty-four hours. He orders the man tortured, convinced that he must do so for the sake of the people who might otherwise die in the explosions—even though he believes that torture is wrong, indeed abominable, not just sometimes, but always . . . [H]e is not too good for politics and [indeed] he is good enough. Here is the moral politician: it is by his dirty hands that we know him. If he were a moral man and nothing else, his hands would not be dirty; if he were a politician and nothing else, he would pretend that they were clean.[36]

One should dispute this conclusion, with all its negative implications for the governance of a democracy (for what sort of leaders would one choose, knowing they were being obligated to debase themselves, and what sort of men and women would aspire to such roles?). Far from having "dirtier hands," the officials of a democracy have hands at least as clean as those of the rest of us and possibly a good deal cleaner. Machiavelli's distinction absolves the official and leaves his personal morality uncompromised, whereas the citizen who authorizes the distinctive role of a governing official but disclaims any responsibility for the action of government is a hypocrite, or worse.*

The origin of the "duty of consequentialism" lies in the constitutional makeup of the state of consent. That is because the officials of a state of consent are bound to behave, in their official capacity, in a way that maximizes the "ends" or goals of the persons in whose name they govern.[37] It is this delegation that imposes the duty of evaluating means in terms of the ends they serve, and that displaces the deontological[38] or a priori moral rules that are so much a part of personal life. By contrast, the dictator or the ruler of a state of terror can say, "My religion imposes upon me a duty that I, in my governing role, will superimpose on the public." Damn the consequences for the public, and damn their wishes for themselves. The Ten Commandments might govern a state, but it is unlikely to be a state of consent because these rules are so categorical. And perhaps this is as it should be: we do not revere these rules because we think they would come tops in the polls.

*See the conclusion to chapter 12.

Of course, leaders in a democracy can persuade us to behave in a way that is in concord with our moral goals, even at the sacrifice of our temporary interests, but this too is a matter of ends—shaping the ends chosen by the public—rather than obeying a fixed, nonsituational rule.[39]

Why then shouldn't we feel morally superior to those who govern? Perhaps we're only luckier not to have had to make these decisions—the Sophie's choices[40] that daily order the public agenda (and not only in wartime)—but even so, aren't we better human beings for not having done so? Not at all, because the moral calculus *is* different for public officials. Within their separate spheres, government officials must obey a moral code just as rigorous as that we apply in our personal lives. It is simply not the same code because, for the officials of the state of consent, it is necessarily consequentialist. Because these men and women are not inferior to us—because, that is, their official duties are judged by a different moral rubric—we are not superior to them. Because they act in our name, doing things we have authorized them to do, it may well be that, as moral agents, they are *our* superiors, for they at least have the excuse that they are acting for us, as we have instructed them in law, whereas we can only say that we delegated our power to accomplish the distasteful. Nor are they subject to the substantial moral hazard[41] that confronts the person without responsibility for the safety of others. This has important implications, as we shall see, for practices such as extraordinary renditions in which the U.S. sends a terrorist abroad to be interrogated by foreign officials who are thought to be less squeamish than our own.

Machiavelli's insight—that officials must disregard their personal moral codes in carrying out the duties of the State[42]—is seldom assessed within the context of law (just as, for a long time, the fairness of negligence rules was seldom evaluated in the context of insurance), even though for the contemporary state it is law, and not the judgment of the prince, that guides those who govern. If the customary institutions of a state of consent have forbidden the torture and the cruel and degrading treatment of prisoners, then the conscientious official has little choice but to obey. He cannot substitute his personal moral imperatives as if he were acting as a nongovernmental agent. So what does he do when the "ticking bomb" case actually does arise? He disobeys the treaty, the statute, the regulation, and saves the city, of course. It is the right thing to do, not because of his private morality (which might in any case vary from official to official), but rather because the consequentialist calculus of obeying the law is so clear and so absolutely negative. This was, it will be recalled, Lincoln's position when he suspended habeas corpus during the American Civil War—in direct contradiction of a specific provision of the U.S. Constitution—in order to arrest some 13,000 persons under martial law. Defending his decision in a message to Congress on July 4, 1861, he wrote:

To state the question more directly, are all the laws, *but one,* to go unexecuted and the government itself go to pieces, lest that one be violated? Even in such a case, would not the official oath be broken, if the government should be overthrown, when it was believed that disregarding the single law, would tend to preserve it?[43]

This is plainly a consequentialist argument, but look carefully at how it sorts out ends and means. The objective sought (the end) that justifies the violation of law (the means) is in fact the *preservation* of the rule of law, which is shall we say "dented" by the very means that avoid a catastrophic collision.[44]

Could the laws of a state of consent actually authorize torture, for example, by statute? There will be an opportunity below to address, briefly, the most considered of such proposals by the civil liberties attorney and law professor Alan Dershowitz, but for the moment our concern is simply whether or not, as a constitutional matter, a legislature or Congress could validly pass such a statute.

Market states of consent ground their constitutional legitimacy in the delegation of power to government by the people who are governed. One important aspect of this delegation, as mentioned earlier, is the limitations it imposes. Limited government derives limits from the parameters of popular delegation. Yet there is a further limitation that is equally profound, viz, that there are limits to what the public may authorize. These are the "inalienable" powers discussed above. A citizen may not enslave himself, even if he wishes to; nor may he lawfully sell his vote (or give it away) to another; and so on with the entire list of human decisions as to whom to marry, or where to live, how many children to have.[45] Statutes that purported to authorize the government to make such decisions would be unconstitutional, and indeed there is some doubt as to whether even an amendment empowering the government to execute such laws would be compatible with the constitutive ideas of the market state of consent and its relationship to its people.[46]

This doesn't quite end the matter, however. Interstate relations—relations among governments[47]—are not solely a matter of the delegation of power to the State. Rather the powers to make war, to conduct foreign relations, and to be represented in international bodies can be inferred from the various means to pursue these objectives that are explicitly provided in the constitutional text. For example, there is no explicit power to make war, but there are provisions for raising, supporting, and regulating armies, declaring war, ratifying treaties, etc. Moreover, the text of the U.S. Constitution carefully distinguishes between laws "made in Pursuance" of the Constitution and treaties "under the Authority of the United States,"[48] a distinction Justice Holmes believed indicated a source of additional government power.[49] So it might be that if the international community or some group therein were to sanction torture or coercive interrogation, this would provide the basis on which a state like the U.S. could then adopt regulations governing such procedures so long as these regulations did not offend the human rights protected by the Constitution.[50]

On the other hand, however, this would ignore the universal international consensus banning torture and cruel and degrading treatment. As Henry Shue has put it: "Torture is . . . contrary to every relevant international law, including the laws of war. No other practice except slavery is so universally and unanimously condemned in law and human convention."[51]

But this, too, is not quite the end of the matter. States are not required to so conduct their affairs that they are extinguished. Just as Article 51 provides a self-defense exception to the U.N. Charter's requirement that the use of armed force must first be authorized by the U.N. Security Council pursuant to Article 2(4), so too a state that is under attack can, if its very existence is imperiled in an international armed conflict, resort to whatever methods are effective and proportionate to preserve itself. This suggests that a state might, either in accord with other states or in the context of a threat to its very existence, act lawfully when it tortured enemy captives or interrogated them using cruel and degrading methods.

In the past, this unsettling conclusion would have nevertheless been tempered by two immutable restraints: first, such horrific methods could only be used in warfare, and second, they could never be used against the citizens of one's own state. This is the import of the Supreme Court's limitation of the executive power in *Youngstown Sheet and Tube v. Sawyer* when the Court, having rejected the Truman administration's seizure of steel mills in order to prosecute the Korean War, nevertheless was careful to observe that its ruling only applied to noncombat theaters. But what if the struggle against al Qaeda is properly seen as warfare, and what if the homeland is as much a combat theater as any remote terrorist sanctuary?

Several conclusions, drawn from this preliminary overview, will structure the discussion to follow:

1. The current practice of extraordinary rendition, by which a non-U.S. national held in U.S. custody is handed over to the state of which he is a citizen in order that he can be coercively interrogated, may amount to just the sort of interstate compact mentioned above.

2. If interrogations of terrorists are a matter of intelligence collection in the midst of war, then there may be a way to regulate those interrogations based on the residual authority of a state at war to defend itself and its forces.

3. If authority over captured terrorists is a consequence of a state's war-making powers, then special care must be taken to avoid militarizing the domestic environment when that war is a war against terror.

4. One can more easily see what the Bush administration has been doing—fecklessly perhaps, and with little care for point 3 above—when it has attempted to supplant the usual processes of law with military tribunals, claims of executive authority to surveil in spite of statutory requirements to the contrary, and extraterritorial penal colonies.

5. Doubt is cast on any of the three popular proposals with regard to the practice of torture (an absolute ban enforced absolutely, an absolute ban with the possibility of prosecutorial nullification, and a partial ban subject to judicial oversight).

6. The "ticking bomb" is not simply a red herring, an attempt to distract our attention from the real questions surrounding policies of interrogation. Indeed, as I have suggested, the "ticking bomb" problem can illuminate many of the difficulties in coming to terms with the need for warning of terrorist atrocities. Most significantly, this problem steers us toward the "duty of consequentialism" that is imposed on any public servant of a state of consent. What then are the implications of this duty?

7. There is a reason why, in the very teeth of explicit and pervasive law to the contrary—domestic and international—states of consent like the U.S., the U.K., France, and Israel have repeatedly engaged in highly coercive techniques of interrogating terrorists. That reason has more to do with the moral imperatives of taking responsibility for others than it does with the depravity of officials. Only a consequentialist argument can ultimately alter these practices.

THE PREVAILING LAW

Both Machiavelli and Walzer observe that there are two different moral codes, one for the civilian and one for the government official. As a rule, the way that states of consent integrate these two otherwise alienated roles is through law. Law, because it represents the ethos of a society, is thus more than the obstacle course it often appears to be to the utilitarian.[52] It is rather a guide to action, because it embodies those moral principles that the society has deemed ends in themselves, ends against which the means chosen by the government official must be measured.

Following the exposure of German and Japanese practices in World War II, the U.N. General Assembly adopted in 1948 the Universal Declaration of Human Rights, which contains an absolute ban on torture in order to eliminate, according to the drafters, "methods of torture and cruel punishment which were practiced in the recent past by the Nazis and fascists." Article 5 of the declaration provides: "No one shall be subjected to torture or to cruel, inhuman or degrading treatment or punishment."

This ban has been incorporated into the International Covenant on Civil and Political Rights (ICCPR) and into the Convention Against Torture or Other Cruel, Inhuman or Degrading Treatment or Punishment (the Torture Convention), which provides in Article 2 that "No exceptional circumstances whatsoever, whether a state of war or a threat of war, internal political instability or any other public emergency, may be invoked as a justification of torture."

This language is also codified in the European Convention for the Protection of Human Rights and Fundamental Freedoms, the African Charter on Human and Peoples' Rights, and the American Convention on Human Rights.

In 1949, the Geneva Conventions were revised to forbid the "mutilation, cruel treatment and torture" of prisoners of war and detained civilians. It seems plain that detained al Qaeda forces do not fit within the convention's Article 4 definition of a prisoner of war, nor is al Qaeda itself a signatory to the convention. What is less clear is whether such forces come within the convention's Article 3 provisions banning "violence to life and person, in particular murder of all kinds, mutilation, cruel treatment and torture" as well as "outrages upon personal dignity, in particular, humiliating and degrading treatment" because these provisions apply only to conflicts "not of an international character." On the one hand, the history of the drafting and ratification of this article seems to contemplate application to internal insurgencies (and not international terrorism), and the influential U.S. Court of Appeals for the District of Columbia has taken this view. On the other hand, several important international tribunals have construed this provision more broadly by interpreting "international" to mean "inter–nation state," which would bring al Qaeda detainees within the convention (though not within its more protective provisions for valid POWs). This is the view taken by the U.S. Supreme Court. This is important for the prosecution by the U.S. of any person accused of torture, because the War Crimes Act (the federal statute governing such acts) implements the Geneva Conventions and not the Torture Convention or the ICCPR. Two important points highlighted by this legal ambiguity are, first, that it demonstrates yet again that the Geneva Conventions need reform to cope with twenty-first century global terrorism, and second, that the U.S. has rather foolishly thrown away the legitimating tool of the conventions by abandoning the practice of previous U.S. administrations that applied Article 3 as a matter of policy.

It may be, as Sanford Levinson has argued, that the very categorical nature of these prohibitions against torture* has tempted states—including the U.K. and the U.S.—to write definitions of torture that are rather narrow. Indeed, because the U.S. administration at one time appeared to have interpreted away the restraints created by conventions to which it is a signatory, partly on the basis of Senate reservations made at the time of U.S. consent to these conventions, the U.S. Congress in 2005 adopted the McCain amendment, which provides: "No individual in the custody or under the physical control of the United States Government, regardless of nationality or physical location, shall be subject to cruel, inhuman, or degrading treatment or punishment."[53]

This apparently categorical prohibition is nevertheless to be distinguished from the no less categorical prohibition against torture. To put it in the most summary terms possible, torture can be distinguished from cruel and degrading treatment. This distinction has been recognized by the European Court of Human Rights, the Israeli Supreme Court, and the U.S. Department of State. The importance of this distinction, since both are unlawful, is that the U.S. Supreme Court has recognized a "necessity" exception with respect to cruel and degrading treatment.[54] This takes us a long way toward the recognition of certain otherwise unlawful methods that was at the core of the Bush administration's efforts to legitimate coercive interrogation techniques. These efforts have led, if anything, to a delegitimation of the very institutions—the presidency and the U.S. Justice and Defense departments—that were thought to provide legal cover for these techniques.

ENDS AND MEANS

ENDS

There are three basic objectives (ends) sought by states when they employ torture. They can be categorized as evidentiary, political, and informational. These distinctions are intuitively obvious, but let me give brief historical examples of each category.

---

*The ICCPR and the Torture Convention are sufficient, in themselves, to establish the illegality of torture for all their signatories, including the U.S.

EVIDENTIARY

The U.K. has long prided itself on having early abandoned the use of torture for evidentiary purposes as, in the thirteenth century, trial by jury replaced trial by ordeal. Beccaria, among others, celebrated this fact and compared British practice favorably with that of governments on the continent. As John Langbein has convincingly shown, however, this is probably owing to the more primitive jury system adopted by the British that relied upon the knowledge of local veniremen to supplement whatever testimony was given at trial. The continental methods of evidentiary inquiry, being far more sophisticated, and relying on the collection of real evidence by magistrates, relied too on highly coercive interrogations.

The British did, however, retain until quite late torture when administered under the auspices of the executive, rather than the judiciary. By this means persons were occasionally tortured to extract confessions. Torture was notoriously employed in the numerous prosecutions arising from a terrorist plot to murder the king and the members of Parliament in 1605.

The British state of King James I, by uniting the kingdoms of Scotland and England, consolidated the transition from the princely states of the early Tudors to the kingly states of the Stuarts. Consistent with this transition, James VI of Scotland, on becoming king of England, intimated that he would pursue a more tolerant policy toward Catholics, moving away from the intense sectarianism in public policy that characterized the princely state. Nevertheless, believing this policy of toleration to have been abandoned by the king, a number of English Catholics plotted to blow up the Houses of Parliament during the State Opening, a plan roughly similar to an attack on the chamber of the House of Representatives during a State of the Union address by the president.

The plot was organized by a group of Catholic country squires. They enlisted the services of Guido Fawkes, an experienced soldier with training in demolition, and having leased space adjacent to the House of Lords in May of 1604 were eventually able to rent a cellar under the House. This they filled with 1,800 pounds of gunpowder that, it has been recently established, would have completely destroyed the House of Lords and killed instantly everyone on its premises. No one within 100 meters of the blast would have survived, and much of the Old Palace of Westminster, as well as part of Westminster Abbey, would have been reduced to rubble.

A letter from one of the conspirators to a Catholic peer, warning him away, was immediately disclosed to the king's chief advisor, Robert Cecil. A search of the vaults beneath the House of Lords early on the morning of November 5 disclosed the barrels of gunpowder hidden among the wood stored for fuel. Fawkes was discovered and arrested. He was brought into the king's bedchamber at 1 a.m. and interrogated. He was then taken to the

Tower of London and questioned under torture explicitly authorized by the king. In a letter dated November 6, King James wrote, "The gentler tortours are to be first used unto him, *et per sic gradus ad maiora tenditur*, and so God speed your good worke." After initial resistance, Fawkes broke on November 8 and on the 10th made a signed confession. Below are copies of his normal signature, his signature during his ordeal, and his signature after he had been on the rack.

The conspirators were tried on January 27, 1606. All pleaded guilty except one who defended himself on the grounds that the king had failed to carry out his promises of nonsectarian toleration. As prosecutor, Sir Edward Coke, known to many subsequent generations of law students as a defender of due process, used the confession extracted from Fawkes. The trial lasted only one day. Four of the plotters were executed in St. Paul's churchyard on January 30; Fawkes and the remaining conspirators were hanged, drawn, and quartered the next day.

The American Civil Liberties Union amicus brief in the Jose Padilla case relies heavily on Coke, so there is some irony in this link between the state's response to kingly state terrorism and the market state terrorism of al Qaeda. Padilla was held for a considerable period without charge and without trial or access to counsel—without, that is, what is commonly regarded as due process in a criminal matter—based on an executive finding that he was planning to explode a bomb laden with nuclear isotopes (a "dirty bomb") in the U.S. This finding in turn was based on statements by an al Qaeda leader (it is thought to have been Abu Zubaydah) who was subjected to highly coercive interrogation, and possibly torture, at a secret location outside the U.S. (possibly in Afghanistan or Pakistan). The quandary for the U.S. government was that any ordinary prosecution would have to rely on those statements, which would be inadmissible as hearsay, or if the deponent were produced in court, would doubtless have been rejected as having been made under duress.

At present, there is no move in either the American or British jurisdictions to use information gained by torture conducted by their officials as evidence in court,[55] and this in turn has led to rather absurd efforts to prosecute persons believed to be lethal terrorists on other, trivial grounds so as to continue their detention. One can imagine that there might be pressure to change these evidentiary rules, if no other way were available to detain persons whose incrimination was largely the product of such interrogations. It is inconceivable, however, that statements of self-incrimination could be introduced into testimony if these were the result of torture.

The persecuted Guido Fawkes became immortal: on November 5 each year, Guy Fawkes Day is celebrated by bonfires and street parties. Children make colorful effigies of Fawkes from old clothes stuffed with newspapers that are burned in commemoration. In the nineteeth century the word "guy" came into our language for a colorfully dressed person, and now means simply a "man." The children do not mention the torture that they would almost certainly be willing to inflict on their manikins.

POLITICAL

Torture is undertaken for political purposes when the object is less to coerce than to intimidate. This may be aimed at the victim himself, if he is subsequently released, or his family and associates, or even an entire society. Rather than hiding its hideous acts, if torture is employed for political ends, then it must be advertised. Although there is an ancient history of such practices, in the current day nothing is quite so exemplary as the practice of human beheadings by al Qaeda and its franchisees.

The Greeks and Romans used beheadings as an honorable means of execution; Roman citizens were killed by means of beheading while noncitizens were crucified. Beheading still takes place in Saudi Arabia, Qatar, Yemen, and Iran and was in use in France and Germany until 1938. These executions should not be confused with the methods of torture brought to prominence by al Qaeda. Official executions depend upon a rapid severance of the spinal column to minimize the suffering of the victim. Torture by beheading, by contrast, maximizes the terror and pain of the victim. The distribution of videotapes of these killings via the Internet underscores the political purpose that is their objective.

This can be illustrated by recent examples.

In May 2004, Nicholas Berg, a Philadelphia businessman working on reconstruction projects in Iraq, was kidnapped. A video of his murder, posted on May 12, 2004, became the single most popular search item on the Internet. It showed him in an orange jumpsuit—which doubtless resonated with a public that had seen the Abu Ghraib photographs of Iraqi prisoners that had recently hit the press[56]—with his arms bound behind his back, sitting in front of five men wearing black masks. One of them read a statement, and then the men pulled Berg onto his side, and one of them—possibly Abu Musab al Zarqawi—plunged a knife into his neck. Berg repeatedly screamed in agony as the men appeared to saw through his neck, shouting, "God is great!"[57]

On September 28, 2004, two Iraqis, Fadhel Ibrahim and Firas Imeil, were kidnapped in Baghdad. It was alleged that both were working for the Iraqi government. Two weeks later, a ten-minute videotape was posted on the Internet showing the two captives, who identified themselves. In a pattern often repeated, masked gunmen stood behind the prisoners and before a banner identifying their particular terrorist group; in this case it was the Brigades of Abu Bakr al-Sidiq. Ibrahim and Imeil were shown apologizing for their work with the government and advising fellow Iraqis to quit their jobs with the Iraqi state and "repent to God." Then two masked men gripped Ibrahim while a third cut his throat and then eventually severed his head completely. Imeil was killed in the same fashion.

The two points to be noted about these horrible events and the many others that follow their ritualistic pattern is that they are torture-murders, not simply executions, and that the video distribution and the choice of victims reflect the torturers' goal of inciting fear. In the case of Nicholas Berg, this terror was meant to dissuade contractors and their employees from going to Iraq; in the case of Fadhel Ibrahim and Firas Imeil, the objective was to terrorize persons who might seek employment with the new Iraqi government.

Sometimes, however, the political goal sought by torturers is more attenuated. In the case of Kenneth Bigley's captors, it was to bring pressure on the British government to remove its forces from Iraq. Bigley was a civil engineer from Liverpool who, on September 16, 2004, was kidnapped along with two Americans, Jack Hensley and Eugene Armstrong.

Armstrong was beheaded on September 20 and Hensley twenty-four hours later. Videos of their beheadings were posted on Islamicist websites. Bigley was temporarily spared, and the British media responded with extensive coverage of his life, friends, family, and so on. The British foreign secretary and the prime minister personally contacted the Bigley family on several occasions to reassure them of efforts being made on Bigley's behalf.

On September 22, a second video was released. This showed an exhausted and drained captive who spoke directly to the British prime minister: "I need you to help me now, Mr. Blair, because you are the only person on God's earth who can help me." This video was shown on al

Jazeera television and then picked up by British networks that displayed it frequently during the next weeks.

When it emerged that Bigley's eighty-six-year-old mother had been born in Dublin (making Bigley an Irish citizen), the Irish government issued him a passport in absentia, which was then shown on al Jazeera apparently with the notion that, because Ireland had not joined the Coalition in the second Gulf War, this change of identity would expunge any antipathy held by the kidnappers toward Bigley as a British person.

A third video was released on September 29. This showed the prisoner chained inside a small cage built out of chicken wire. He was wearing an orange jumpsuit, again to remind the viewer of the prisoners held by the Americans at Guantánamo and Abu Ghraib. On this video, Bigley begs for a change in British policy. "Tony Blair is lying. He doesn't care about me. I'm just one person."

Bigley was beheaded on October 7. A video made of his torture and killing seems contrived to blame the British government for his plight and records Bigley's last words as "Tony Blair has not done enough for me."

Later that month, the U.K. defense secretary announced that 500 Black Watch soldiers and 350 support personnel would be moving from Basra to the U.S. sector in central Baghdad. Shortly thereafter, on October 19, as she was leaving home for work at CARE, Margaret Hassan was seized by kidnappers. Within hours of her capture, the first in a series of increasingly harrowing videos was released. Al Jazeera broadcast a second video on October 22, 2004.

Hassan was shown crying and pleading: "Please, please help me. Please help me. . . . Please, the British people, ask Mr. Blair to take the troops out of Iraq and not to bring them here to Baghdad. That's why people like Mr. Bigley and myself are being caught. And maybe we will die like Mr. Bigley." At this point in the tape, she buried her head in her hands.

Margaret Hassan was CARE's director for Iraq. CARE International is the world's largest private humanitarian charity. It is also American. Hassan was appointed to the job of director in 1991 after the first Gulf War; previously, she had been director of the Baghdad office of the British Council. She was born Margaret Fitzsimmons in Dublin shortly before VE day in 1944. After moving to London in her teens, she began work with Catholic relief charities. She met her future husband, Thaseen Ali Hassan, while he was studying engineering in London. After their marriage in 1972, they moved to Iraq, where she began working for the British Council. By every account, she considered herself an Iraqi and stayed on during both Gulf wars to be of assistance to the Iraqi people. She opposed both wars and was a vocal critic of U.N. sanctions. This was apparently immaterial to her captors.

Now the initiative passed to al Jazeera, which appears to have carefully screened and edited the tapes to protect the deteriorating image of the Iraqi insurgency. On October 27, al Jazeera aired a third video, which showed Hassan in a dimly lit room. The audio portion of the tape was indistinct; after her asking for the release of women prisoners in Iraq, the remainder of her pleas could not be heard clearly. These were supplied by al Jazeera, who helpfully stated that "[s]he appealed to British Prime Minister Tony Blair to withdraw troops from Iraq and not deploy them in Baghdad." She was also reported by al Jazeera to have asked CARE to end its operations in Iraq.

Al Jazeera's editorial role was most pronounced in the release of the fourth video on November 2. The tape showed Hassan first making an emotional plea and then fainting and collapsing on the floor. While the tape continued to capture this image, water was then thrown on her in an attempt to revive her. She was then filmed, wet and helpless on the floor, before struggling to get up and crying. The video showed a masked gun-man speaking but no audio was broadcast. At first al Jazeera stated it would not broadcast the tape in full "due to editorial . . . reasons" and "because of the state in which the hostage appears." No doubt this reflected a hitherto undetected editorial delicacy, but it does also seem to have caught al Jazeera's concern at the heightening sense of revulsion in the global Muslim community. Finally, al Jazeera withdrew the tape completely (although previously it had repeatedly shown its torture videos).

Finally, al Jazeera simply announced on November 15 that it was in possession of a video showing Hassan being shot to death. It refused to broadcast this.

Perhaps the most interesting element in this abhorrent sequence was the changing role of the media as al Jazeera moved from being passive collaborators in achieving the political objectives of torture to acting as editorial advisors for the terrorists. This underscores not only the critical role of the global media[58] in a world of emerging market states[59] but also the political objectives of this sort of torture.

INFORMATIONAL

The infliction of pain and the fear of pain can also be used simply to extract information. It is in this context that the subject of torture was raised after 2001, when the urgency of preventing another 9/11 attack suggested to many that harsher methods of interrogation were necessary in order to thwart terrorist plots.

"Terrorists" was the term used by the Nazis in France for the Free French partisans known as the Resistance. Jean Moulin was called "the martyr of the Resistance" because following his capture by the Gestapo he was tortured so violently that he died on the way to a German prison.

Moulin, the son of a history professor, was a young political leader of the left in the south of France during the 1920s. He was an art lover and cartoonist, a passionate skier, and a political organizer of rare abilities. As head of the cabinet office of the Popular Front government in the mid-thirties he organized the French clandestine assistance to the Spanish Republicans during the Spanish Civil War. After Spain, Moulin returned to local politics and in 1938 became the youngest mayor in France.

When the Third Republic collapsed in 1940 following France's defeat by Germany, Moulin was the prefect for the Eure-et-Loire region. He refused to follow the Vichy regime's orders to cooperate with the Germans in unoccupied France. On June 17, 1940, he declined to sign a document, concocted by the Germans, that would have placed blame for recent civilian massacres on a unit of Senegalese French Army troops. A detachment of German soldiers came to his office and demanded he endorse the document. Moulin refused; he was repeatedly beaten but maintained his refusal, finally seizing a piece of broken glass and cutting his own throat. Though fortuitously saved, he was thereafter obliged to wear a scarf around his neck to hide his wounds. On November 2, 1940, the Vichy government removed him from all posts.

In October 1941, having contacted various Resistance groups, Moulin was smuggled out of France and taken to Britain. At this time, the Resistance was little more than an unstructured collection of disparate groups—some maintaining clandestine presses, some providing intelligence to their favorite sponsors, each claiming its legitimacy from the ally that armed and supported it. It was Moulin's opinion, however, that

> [i]t would be insane and criminal, in the event of Allied action on the continent, not to make use of troops prepared for the greatest sacrifices, scattered and unorganized today, but tomorrow capable of making up a united army of parachute troops already in place, familiar with the terrain and having already selected their enemy and determined their objective.[60]

Meeting Charles de Gaulle in London, he sought "moral support and frequent, rapid, secure links" with the Free French forces. Allying himself with de Gaulle, Moulin was ordered to France to create a united organization of resistance and an underground armed force. He carried, in the false bottom of a box of matches, a microfilm of this concise order from de Gaulle: "Mr. Moulin's task is to bring about, within the zone of metropolitan France not directly occupied, unity of action by all elements resisting the enemy and his collaborators."

Moulin parachuted into France on the night of January 2, 1942, bringing funds for the Resistance. When the Allied landings occurred in North Africa, it began to seem a real possibility that France would again become a theater of combat operations. The fractionated Resistance was unprepared to be of much assistance in this. As André Malraux has observed:

> The clandestine press and the intelligence service . . . were geared to the Occupation . . . and not to war. . . . Gradually the Resistance learned that, while it was relatively easy to blow up a bridge, it was no less easy to repair it; if, however, the Resistance could blow up two hundred bridges, it would be difficult for the Germans to repair them all at once. In short, the Resistance realized that if they were to provide effective aid to Allied armies on landing, they would have to have an overall plan . . . And such an overall plan could only be devised and executed by a united Resistance.

Using the code names Rex and Max, Moulin tirelessly went from one Resistance group to another with this message and was ultimately successful in welding together the fractious, disparate elements of the Resistance forces. In October 1942, de Gaulle named him president of the coordinating committee that would direct the Secret Army Organization (OAS) and would coordinate the other three larger Resistance groups. In January 1943, the steering committee of the united Resistance movements was set up under his chairmanship.

In February 1943, Moulin and Charles Delestraint, the head of the new Secret Army, traveled to London for meetings. As Moulin was preparing to return to France in March, de Gaulle directed him to create the National Council of the Resistance, on which Moulin sat as de Gaulle's sole representative, to maintain the political unity of the Resistance. This group was composed of the various Resistance movements, political parties, and union groups all over France. Moulin became chairman.

But now the enemy also began to change. The Resistance, which had faced the daily prospect of defeat or captivity, now confronted the world of the concentration camps and "the certainty of torture." On receiving a report about the concentration camps, Moulin told his liaison agent, Suzette Oliver, "I hope they shoot us first." This period became a "time of cellars, and the desperate cries of the torture victims, their voices like those of children. . . . The great battle in the darkness had begun."

On May 27, 1943, the first meeting of the National Council was held in Paris in the rue du Four. Moulin stated the war aims of Free France: "To prosecute the war [in order to] restore freedom of expression to the French people, re-establish republican freedoms in a state which incorporates social justice." In the next few months, many difficult tasks would be undertaken, but on June 9, Delestraint was betrayed and arrested by the Gestapo. He was brutally interrogated by the notorious Klaus Barbie and ultimately executed at Dachau.

Moulin went to Caluire, near Lyon, on June 12, 1943, to coordinate the choice of Delestraint's successor with the various movements in the south. He was, however, betrayed—perhaps by the same man or woman who had betrayed Delestraint—and was arrested by Barbie. He was taken to Barbie's torture chambers at the Hotel Terminus, where, after initial beatings by Gestapo agents, he was interrogated over a period of days by Barbie.

At one point in this appalling series of interrogations, Barbie handed Moulin a blank piece of paper on which Moulin was instructed to write the names of Resistance leaders; Moulin's torture had left him unable to speak. He asked for a pen and set to work; when Barbie was handed the paper, it contained only a caricature of the Gestapo agent himself (for Moulin was a gifted cartoonist). Barbie ordered that Moulin be further tortured, including attacks with knives, fire, and scalding water. For many days, Moulin alternated between torture at the Hotel Terminus and confinement at Montluc Prison. Both his arms and legs were broken, and most of his ribs. Still he refused to succumb to torture and maintained an effective control over his precious information. "Jeered at, savagely beaten, his head bleeding, his internal organs ruptured, he attained the limits of human suffering without betraying a single secret, he who knew everything."

An attempted escape was thwarted by his transfer to Paris. There, incredibly, Moulin continued to protect his secrets. When he was finally sent to Germany, his injuries were so severe that he died en route. His body was burned by the Nazis. In 1964, his ashes were transferred to the Pantheon, where an especially affecting speech was given by Malraux:

> [E]nter here [the Pantheon], Jean Moulin, with your terrible cortége. With all those who, like you, died in the cellars without breaking; or even, perhaps more atrocious still, those who did break; with all those in the striped garb and shaven heads of the concentration camps, with the last stumbling body from the monstrous lines of Night and Fog, falling prey at last to the rifle-butts; with the 8,000 French women that never returned from the prisons, with the last woman who died in Ravensbrück for having sheltered one of ours . . . Today, young people of France, may you think of this man as you would have reached out your hands to his poor, unrecognizable face on that last day, to those lips that never let fall a word of betrayal.

———————

This excursion through these terrible histories has not been a detour. On the contrary, it is my aim to suggest to the Reader by this means several complexities. First, there is an overlap among ends. James I wanted a confession, but he also wanted information, and he was eager to cow his

Catholic subjects. This last is the purpose of drawing and quartering. Second, the Reader will have seen that at least two of our subjects, Guido Fawkes and Jean Moulin, were regarded by their torturers as terrorists. This imposes on us the requirement of distinguishing between Nazis and resisters to Nazism. Similarly, the torturers of Margaret Hassan, Nicholas Berg, Kenneth Bigley, Firhas Imeil, Fadhel Ibrahim, and the others claim that they, too, are resisters to an unlawful occupation. These complexities demand that we be able to tell the difference, and explain the difference, between those who wish to impose terror through an occupation and those occupiers who come to dispel terror and are risking their lives to do so.

It is of course tempting to shun this difficult task and simply to say that the use of violence in interrogation, for any purpose, is always impermissible; that it is the means, and not the ends, that must guide our judgment. This move is made immeasurably easier by making the assumption that torture simply never works. Persons in pain and afraid are unlikely to give correct information in their eagerness to appease their tormenters. Consider then this account, however, told to Bruce Hoffman by a Sri Lankan army officer charged with fighting the Tamil Tigers:

> [His] unit had apprehended three terrorists who, it suspected, had recently planted somewhere in the city a bomb that was then ticking away, the minutes counting down to catastrophe. The three men were brought before [him]. He asked them where the bomb was. The terrorists—highly dedicated and steeled to resist interrogation—remained silent. [He] asked the question again, advising them that if they did not tell him what he wanted to know, he would kill them. They were unmoved. So [he] took his pistol from his gun belt, pointed it at the forehead of one of them, and shot him dead. The other two, he said, talked immediately; the bomb, which had been placed in a crowded railway station and set to explode during the evening rush hour, was found and defused, and countless lives were saved.[61]

If we put this in the context that the Tamil insurgency had already claimed the lives of more than 60,000 people and that it was arrayed against a democratically elected government whose president, candidate for president, and the Indian prime minister Rajiv Gandhi it had murdered, one is hard-pressed not to conclude that the putative victims of an atrocity deserve more care than the would-be perpetrators.

Ends do matter. As we shall see, however, only when they are related to means can we derive usable rules.

MEANS

The problem is made more realistic by assuming that, in some circumstances, torture and assassination are effective—an assumption as to which there is some debate. Nevertheless, it must be obvious that at least in some situations this will prove to be the case and that these are the situations for which we require an answer, not a blithe assuming away of the problem.[62] Because these activities are conducted in the dark, there is little adequate data to confirm an assumption either way. Occasionally, there are reports in open sources such as the case of an al Qaeda terrorist, Jamal Beghal. He was arrested in the Dubai airport in October 2001. His lawyer subsequently charged that he had been "tossed into a darkened cell, handcuffed to a chair, blindfolded and beaten and that his family was threatened." It is not unreasonable to conclude that these measures had some effect: after some weeks in captivity, he suddenly decided to cooperate and "out poured a wealth of information" that thwarted a planned bombing of the U.S. embassy in Paris and could have prevented the 2001 attacks on the World Trade Center in New York had it come earlier.[63]

I will discuss four alternatives prescribing what means of coercive interrogation are permissible. These are (1) an absolute ban; (2) a qualified ban, perhaps permitting some forms of cruel and degrading treatment but banning torture; (3) a ban with exceptions, perhaps permitting torture and any lesser means in certain certifiable circumstances; (4) rendition to a lawful authority, permitting some forms of coercive interrogation, including even torture, depending on the willingness of the State transparently to acknowledge its role.

ABSOLUTE BAN

The first thing to recognize about an absolute ban is that it will not prevent all torture any more than an absolute ban on smoking in elevators means that every cigar is extinguished by every solitary passenger. Even draconian penalties like stoning to death have not stopped adultery in Saudi Arabia; nor has capital punishment in America stopped capital crimes. Indeed, the most important moral lesson of the "ticking bomb" problem is that no rule can entirely govern our conscience. That is the lesson of free will, which makes the conscience and thus morality itself possible. Free will makes alternative worlds possible, and one of these must always be a future in which a crime is committed rather than a law obeyed.

This means that an "absolute ban" is actually more like a lottery: it leaves to chance *when* torture occurs by refusing to specify the precise exculpatory circumstances. On the other hand, an absolute ban can be enforced with greater consistency and, if the penalties are significant, can bring about the highest level of deterrence. Indeed, an absolute ban has to be tightly enforced, or it loses its point. As Kenneth Roth put it, " 'Never' cannot be redeemed if allowed to be read as 'sometimes.' "[64]

The difficulty is that an absolute ban gives a spurious clarity to what could be an ambiguous situation. "No torture" rules sound fine, but the world in which they are to be applied can present situations in which such rules should not be followed. Is the "absolute ban" the right rule for the real world? In such a world, an order by the president to torture a captive would be an unlawful order, regardless of even the most extreme circumstances, and therefore it is highly unpredictable whether it would be obeyed.

QUALIFIED BAN

This reflects an effort to capture in law and regulations those truly exceptional situations in which there is a political consensus that highly coercive methods, even torture, should be tried. Perhaps the most imaginative of these proposals is the suggestion by Alan Dershowitz, that courts— perhaps special courts—be authorized to issue "torture warrants." Studying practices in Israel—which is "the only country at the end of the twentieth century officially to sanction the intentional infliction of pain and suffering during interrogation"[65]—Dershowitz concluded that the "ticking bomb" scenario had led officials to an increasing use of torture and highly coercive means of interrogation in cases quite remote from the assumptions of the scenario.

> In 1987, the Landau Commission in Israel authorized the use of "moderate physical pressure" in ticking-bomb situations. A practice initially justified as rare and exceptional, taken only when necessary to save lives, gradually became standard procedure. Soon, some 80 to 90 percent of Palestinian security detainees were being tortured . . .[66]

Dershowitz argued that judicial oversight would curtail or eliminate these practices in a way that "don't ask, don't tell" rules and paper prohibitions had failed to do; he believed that requiring a warrant of some kind as "a precondition to the infliction of any type of torture under any circumstances"[67] would accomplish this. When torture was taken out of the clandestine area of government activity and exposed to visibility and accountability, Dershowitz held, torture would drastically decline. In such circumstances, the "ticking bomb" hypothetical might actually serve as a limiting, rather than expanding, engine because a judicial warrant could be granted in this, but in no other, situation.

Notable objections have been made to this proposal: that by limiting authorized torture to the "ticking bomb" scenario, it in fact does not bring transparency (and thus accountability) to other situations when officials may still use violence to get information;[68] that even with respect to warrants, the affidavits supporting them, the requests for them, and the judges' decisions granting them are all likely to be secret, which does little for transparency; that, because warrants are issued in ex parte proceedings before judges or magistrates chosen by the applicant, they are an ineffective check on executive discretion.[69] What makes them effective in the ordinary criminal context is the use of materials gained by warrant in subsequent trials. That presumably is unlikely to be a significant motivation in a war against terror, particularly if enemy agents can be indefinitely detained without the usual trial proceedings. Finally, if torture is written into law—even if only for extreme situations—its use is bound to become routine, as interrogators test the limits of the law.

BAN WITH EXCEPTIONS

This proposal probably comes closest to the customary way in which such matters are usually dealt with in the democracies. In *Leon v. Wainwright*[70] the Eleventh Circuit considered the following facts. Two kidnappers seized a taxi driver and held him for ransom. One of them was apprehended while collecting the ransom. The court found that

> [w]hen he refused to tell them the location, he was set upon by several of the officers . . . they threatened and physically abused him by twisting his arm and choking him until he revealed where [the cab driver] was being held . . . This was . . . a group of concerned officers acting in a reasonable manner to obtain information they needed in order to protect another individual from bodily harm or death. [The acts of torture] were motivated by the immediate necessity to find the victim and save his life.[71]

Sanford Levinson, who more than anyone courageously broke the silence of the academy on this subject, has concluded that such extraordinary methods must always be forbidden by law.[72] This view need not make terrorists of those who protect us in the most perilous cases, however, because the last word rests with the juries and publics that are unlikely to condemn those persons who have acted wisely out of pity and not irresponsibly out of cruelty. Levinson holds that it is better wholly to outlaw such activities by the military and the police knowing that, on occasion, they may breach the law out of necessity. This is an appealing approach because it attempts to preserve our values in the face of anguishing choices. And because torture is unlawful, it must not be practiced routinely, in defiance of the law, if we are to maintain the charge of terrorism against those who attack us. Terrorism only takes place, in our current circumstances, when violence is directed against persons who are behaving lawfully.

This approach relies upon a necessity defense to the purportedly "absolute" ban. Of course, the officers couldn't know for certain that the courts would exonerate them,[73] any more than the intelligence officers who torture a terrorist to locate a ticking bomb are certain they will not be prosecuted. But it can be assumed that no jury is likely to convict the men who saved their city, especially if the alleged offense is committed against a person attempting mass murder.

The principal virtues of such uncertainty are threefold. First, it allows us to state that we have an absolute ban on torture (in principle), not unlike the absolute prohibition against congressional action that abridges the freedom of speech, which in its application makes room for laws against disclosing classified documents, colluding to fix prices, and libel. Second, it depends upon the "bracketing"[74] of the calculus of necessity, forcing the agent who must decide whether to disobey the law, to determine if torture would really save sufficient lives to justify its terrible imposition. As Henry Shue put one variation on this:

> An act of torture ought to remain illegal so that anyone who sincerely believes such an act to be the least available evil is placed in the position of needing to justify his or her act morally in order to defend himself or herself legally . . . Anyone who thinks an act of torture is justified should have no alternative but to convince a group of peers in a public trial that all necessary conditions for a morally permissible act were indeed satisfied . . . If the situation approximates those in the imaginary examples in which torture seems possible to justify [such as the "ticking bomb" scenario], a judge can surely be expected to suspend the sentence.[75]

Third, it avoids the real cost of giving potential adversaries and terrorists extensive knowledge about what to expect when they are captured. As with nuclear deterrence,* governments have been unwilling to spell out exact limits to the action they would regard as tolerable in extremis.

This proposal has widespread support among civil libertarians, philosophers,[76] and jurists who "want nonlethal torture to be used if it could prevent thousands of deaths, but [do] not want torture to be officially recognized by our legal system."[77] "It is better," wrote Judge Richard Posner, "to stick with our perhaps overly strict rules, trusting executive officials to

---

*I am indebted to Sir Michael Quinlan for this analogy.

break them when the stakes are high enough to enable the officials to obtain political absolution for their illegal conduct."[78]

Nevertheless, this approach is not without its flaws. Far from prompting the rigorous analysis that its proponents imagine, because it is essentially a customary approach it relies upon our intuitive sense of our values, which is specific to every particular culture. The reason to debate an issue openly and write our conclusions into law is to overcome the many different attitudes that prevail in the military, among lawyers, in religious circles, and so on. "Don't ask, don't tell" may be a tolerant rule, but it gains this tolerance at the expense of achieving true consensus.

At what point does custom become law, whatever the actual provisions of the law? If the answer is "never," then those who attack the torturing state with violence are not terrorists, whatever they are (vigilantes?), because they are not trying to keep their victims from doing things they have a lawful right to do. If the answer is "always," then we have simply institutionalized hypocrisy, robbing it even of La Rochefoucauld's modest admiration. It is not even a vice anymore, but rather a gloss. If the answer is "sometimes," then how can we expect conscientious men and women to obey the law—whatever it may be—the law being so uncertain?*

EXTRAORDINARY RENDITION

A fourth approach could be caricatured as "outsourcing to the unregulated market." "Rendition" is the practice of removing a prisoner from the jurisdiction in which he is held and delivering him to another country, typically for the purpose of criminal prosecution. It is contrasted with "extradition" and "deportation," which are lengthier processes subject to judicial intervention. Renditions, however, usually involve a person being brought to the U.S. (sometimes by kidnapping or other extralegal procedures) in order that he can then be prosecuted, or the rendering of a person apprehended by the U.S. to another country for prosecution or interrogation. The latter has come to be known as "extraordinary rendition."[79]

Intelligence officials have acknowledged that terrorists captured by the U.S. have been sent to other countries where the security services are known to have engaged in torture, including Egypt, Jordan, the Philippines, Saudi Arabia, Syria, and Morocco. It is plainly in violation of the Torture Convention for the U.S. to send prisoners to countries with the expectation that they will be tortured, however, and the U.S. attorney general and the legal advisor to the U.S. Department of State have both categorically denied that this is in fact American practice. Officials have

---

*Excepting, of course, the most extreme examples when the moral imperative to protect others is overwhelming, e.g., the "ticking bomb" scenario described above.

386   TERROR AND CONSENT

sought and received diplomatic assurances that the persons rendered to
foreign countries will not be tortured. Whether the reality corresponds to
these assurances or whether highly coercive interrogation techniques by
other countries are believed not to rise to the level of torture,[80] it is hard to
say. The convention does not bar sending a prisoner to a state where he
will be subject to cruel and degrading treatment.[81]

A variant on the practice of extraordinary rendition is the practice of
holding detainees off the acknowledged registers in secret, non-U.S. locations. It has been reported that as many as a hundred "high-value"
detainees are being thus held under the control of the CIA, though at present it is only known that fourteen such "high value" detainees have been
moved to Guantánamo Bay. These persons were either captured by U.S.
forces or rendered to U.S. control by other countries. The U.S. administration has long taken the view that the International Covenant on Civil and
Political Rights, which bans torture and cruel and degrading treatment,
does not apply outside the U.S., nor does it apply to military operations
during an international armed conflict. This interpretation would permit
U.S. renditions both from one country to another, and to its own agencies
as these operated abroad, even where cruel and degrading treatment was
concomitant with interrogations.

Thus we live, today, in a world of casual deceit—strictly applying
insufficient laws in some jurisdictions because we are willing to dispense
with law altogether in others. One key to the important intelligence gained
after Afghanistan, which has saved so many innocent lives, undoubtedly
lies, in part, in the hands of those less squeamish governments to whom
captive terrorists were rendered for interrogation. Few officials wish to
discuss this, but ignoring it sacrifices the legitimacy that law can give to
desperate, if necessary, measures.

The obvious shortcoming of this approach is that it is entirely outside
the law. Richard Clarke, the former head of counterterrorism at the
National Security Council, has recorded this anecdote, which, unfortunately, drips with contempt for the lawyer's point of view:

> "Snatches," or more properly "extraordinary renditions," were opera-
> tions to apprehend terrorists abroad, usually without the knowledge of
> and almost always without public acknowledgement of the host gov-
> ernment . . . The first time I proposed a snatch, in 1993, the White
> House counsel, Lloyd Cutler, demanded a meeting with the President
> to explain how it violated international law. Clinton seemed to be sid-
> ing with Cutler until Al Gore belatedly joined the meeting, having just
> flown overnight from South Africa. Clinton recapped the arguments
> on both sides for Gore: Lloyd says this. Dick says that. Gore laughed
> and said, "That's a no-brainer. Of course it's a violation of interna-

tional law, that's why it's a covert action. The guy is a terrorist. Go
grab his ass."[82]

Perhaps Mr. Cutler was concerned with the following problem, which
is a considerable shortcoming of this approach: When democratic, rights-
respecting states violate international norms of humane conduct, as by torture or assassination, proportionate attacks upon the perpetrators—the
armed forces and security services of those states—are not terrorism;
rather, they become legitimate acts of war. Furthermore, violations alleged
to have been committed by such states are subject to prosecution as war
crimes by competent international tribunals that, if they condemn such
states, exculpate the terrorist.

One can go further. If such acts are condemned under the norms of
international law, and if they are nevertheless supported by civilians acting
democratically, then cannot the terrorist lawfully attack those civilians—
anyone, really, in the democracy—and be absolved of the charge of terrorism because he wishes to prevent them from supporting acts (torture,
assassination) that are unlawful to commit? This argument might also
apply to the citizens of states like the U.S. and the U.K. if these states were
held to have acted unlawfully by invading Iraq. It is what is meant by the
claim that "in a democracy, only the unenfranchised are innocent civilians."[83] With the market approach—rendition—one could get the worst of
both worlds: national responsibility for acts as to which the agents we have
empowered are unaccountable.

None of these approaches seems fully satisfactory. Absolute bans on torture, absolutely enforced, are essentially lotteries, and while they are
admirably conscientious about the rights of prisoners, they are studiedly
indifferent to the fate of the terrorist's victims. Qualified bans are legalistic, political attempts to manage torture. They are, nevertheless, inconsistent with international law, import a judicial process into warfare, and as
currently proposed, are probably unconstitutional on the grounds that they
authorize punishment without a jury's determination of guilt. Bans on torture that depend upon exceptional behavior can call on the legitimating
ethos of society because they are "customary" approaches. In the U.S. and
the U.K., we rarely depend on legal rules to compel the behavior of the
Good Samaritan,[84] or heroic intervention in an emergency, or the self-
sacrifice and deference that hold a society together. We depend instead on
custom. Yet for that very reason, such an approach can be highly unreli-
able, especially in a complex society that holds many cultures within it. An
approach that depends upon guessing how a court would calculate the
necessity of breaking the law is a pretty uncertain one. To save a mil-

lion lives, anyone ought to be willing to brutalize a terrorist in the midst of his fevered attempt to become a mass murderer. But what about five lives, when the person to be tortured may or may not have the crucial information—or may or may not be a terrorist? Holding that every life is priceless makes these calculations seem as paradoxical as those mathematical comparisons of infinite classes (is the class of all even numbers half the size of the class of all whole numbers?). Denying that every life is priceless might make the calculation more feasible, but it does not, in itself, supply the rule. Indeed, the whole point of the ban qualified by custom is to avoid stating a rule.

Finally, rendition—the market approach—outsources our crimes, which puts us at the mercy of anyone who can expose us, makes us dependent on some of the world's most unsavory actors, and abandons accountability. It is an approach we associate with crime families, not with great nations.

IMPLICATIONS OF AN ENDS AND MEANS ANALYSIS

Let us see if we can make any progress in considering this dreadful issue if, instead of separating ends from means, we carefully winnow out acceptable ends and see if these can guide our choice of means.

What is the overall objective of the state of consent in the Wars against Terror? It is to protect the lives and human rights of our own people or of others for whom we have accepted responsibility without becoming a state of terror, that is, while continuing to protect the rights of consent and conscience. From this premise alone we can infer that we can never torture persons for political ends. If the state of consent engages in acts that intimidate its own population it poisons any consent it may thereafter win, and thus sacrifices its legitimacy. Torture and coercive interrogation can never be used to achieve the "political" ends discussed above.

A similar rationale applies to the use of torture for evidentiary purposes. It is true that courts can compel testimony: A witness who has been given immunity from prosecution (and thus is not being compelled to give evidence that might incriminate her) can be held in prison until she relents. If the testimony is false, she can be prosecuted for perjury. It is also true that evidence gained by torture does not necessarily taint a prosecution. A tip provided by coercive interrogation in Afghanistan has probably already led to prosecutions in the U.S.

If we bear in mind, however, that it is warfare—not crime—that is the arena of the Wars against Terror, then we ought to conclude that (except possibly for war crimes) states of consent can never use torture to gain evidence for prosecution and trial. The aims of warfare are prospective, not retrospective. We are not engaged in a war in order to punish our enemies, but to prevent them from imposing on us a political end of their own. A state of consent cannot bring torture to bear in order to gather evidence for a prosecution without importing the means of warfare into its own, domestic institutions—without, that is, becoming a state of terror and losing the war itself.

There remains, then, the goal of getting information through violence. If we recognize that this "end" is also a "means" to another "end"—winning the Wars against Terror—then perhaps we can shape the proper means that serve those goals.

The use of violence in the Wars against Terror is justified by our claims of self-defense.[85] Having been attacked, we have the right to defend our societies. This basis, in self-defense, is different from the related claim of necessity. The U.N. Charter, for example, provides that states may take up arms in self-defense in the absence of an authorizing Security Council resolution but offers no similar exception for cases of necessity generally.

In the Wars against Terror, violence can be used when a state of consent is threatened with violence by the agents of states or inchoate would-be states of terror. In many circumstances, this threat consists of armed men assigned to commit violent acts. They may be hunted down and killed, unless they choose to surrender themselves and their arms. In the information age, however, the threats posed by hostile agents may not be confined to the conventional weapons they carry. They may also possess information that, if not disclosed to the authorities, helps perpetrate a terrorist atrocity. The terrorists' refusal to disclose information truthfully can deny the target state of consent the ability to prevent a civilian catastrophe, such that *but for* this refusal many innocent lives would have been saved. We have already seen in chapter 4 that such precautionary and anticipatory action is a principal means in the Wars against Terror.

So the state of consent, if it has been or is going to be attacked, can use violence against the agents of its attacker to coerce them to lay down their arms and to force them to disclose information in their possession that, if it went undisclosed, would capacitate and abet deadly attacks on civilians. This means that, unlike the soldier who is protected by those particular terms of the Geneva Conventions that determine him to be a valid prisoner of war, the terrorist[86] is not within his legal rights when he refuses to disclose more information than his name, rank, and the unit to which he is attached. The terrorist can be compelled further to provide such information as he has that is relevant to future attacks. "To refuse to comply with the further demand [for information] would then be to maintain a second line of defense. The victim would, in a sense, not have surrendered—at least not fully surrendered—but instead only retreated."[87]

The difficulty, of course, lies in determining that the detainee really is a terrorist, precisely because he is not wearing a uniform, and that he is not complying fully with requests for information. The interrogator cannot be permitted to be the sole judge of this because he will always be tempted to make those assumptions that would err on the side of maximizing his take of information. He will hold hundreds of men as detainees on the grounds that perhaps a few of them might have useful information, though he does not know which ones. He will resort to violence even after he has been given information or told that there is none to be had, on the grounds that if there is any further truth to be wrung from the prisoner, violence can do it.

This cannot be permitted because the rationale for permitting violence in this context cannot sustain such practices. It is perhaps true that such practices would be permitted, though doubtless impermissible on other grounds, if the rationale for them depended upon an argument from *necessity*. After all, it might be reasonable to torture even an innocent child if the stakes were high enough, repellent though that idea is. It is said that the family of at least one senior executive of al Qaeda (who is a captive) is being held, and we can infer that this is being done to bring pressure on him. The argument from *self-defense,* however, permits no such measures. Nor does it apply to the otherwise innocent bystander who may have crucial information but declines to give it up. Only the terrorists in the Wars on Terror can be analogized to the armed soldier; only men and women at war can be threatened with violence unless they put down the instruments of war (including information) they have taken up to do violence.

There must be some independent authority whose incentives are not so wholly driven by the desire to maximize the amount of information gathered, who is trustworthy enough not to disclose the secrets of operations and intelligence sources, and who is sophisticated enough to be able to accurately assess the claims of the interrogator. Moreover, such authority must be accorded legal status under international law.

What is needed is not a judge so much as a jury—that is, not an official who represents the government seeking information but a group of persons chosen from a pool of responsible people who represent, not the government, but the society in whose name the government is acting. Their identities can be secret in order to avoid reprisal, but they should be chosen randomly from the largest number that is practicable. Unless they can be persuaded that the detainee is in fact a terrorist with valuable information, he cannot be coercively interrogated. Unless they can be persuaded that he has lied—unless, that is, his claims cannot be persuasively disconfirmed— any coercive methods beyond the mildest cannot be used. Such procedures, it apparently needs to be added, must be created pursuant to statutory action by legislative bodies, and whatever they authorize must be clearly distinguished from the infliction of pain that is tantamount to torture under existing law. I have in mind coercive methods such as sleep deprivation, isolation, and the administration of drugs. Where there is no severe pain, there is no torture. The terrifying prospect of pain is a kind of terror itself, and thus once a state of consent is believed to practice torture as a matter of course, then—even if some progress is made in a War against Terror by such practices—that state will have suffered a considerable blow in the Wars against Terror. To reiterate: it is terror that we are fighting, not simply terrorists.

It is important that we create laws that provide a framework for our actions in war while at the same time avoiding the statement of a legal standard that might incorporate provisions for torture, and so this proposal is not meant to solve the "ticking bomb" problem, which, as I have indicated, more or less solves itself. In October 2002, police in Frankfurt, Germany, arrested Magnus Gafgen, the former tutor of an eleven-year-old boy who had been kidnapped. A ransom had been paid—a large sum of money was found at Gafgen's residence—but the child had not been released. Wolfgang Daschner, a police official, authorized that Gafgen be threatened with physical harm in the hope that he would then lead police to the boy. Gafgen then confessed that he had already killed the boy, and the threatened torture never occurred. Daschner was removed from his post and prosecuted; he was convicted by a trial before a judge but ultimately received a warning rather than a prison sentence. Thus, even here, the legal system showed compassion while upholding an absolute ban. Had Daschner been tried before a jury—whose rulings in common law jurisdictions have no precedential weight—it is even less likely that he would have been punished. But if an authoritative statement of the permissible context for torture were endorsed as law, it might well serve as a predicate for action against officials who refused to torture a detainee.[88]

The proposal I have diffidently put forward is addressed to a different problem. The proposed statutory authorization ought to confine these juries to the *operational* leadership of terrorist armies. We are not in the same situation as Israel, and we should not pretend to be and thus bring it about. Rather, this proposal addresses the osmotic outflow from that problem, which seeps into interrogation practices until torture has become the norm. "Once it is deemed legitimate to use physical coercion against a terrorist who may be planning an attack in an uncertain future, it becomes legitimate to use such methods against any person that could be the 'lead,' however remote, to that terrorist."[89] When that happens, the Wars against Terror are being lost by the state of consent owing to the acts of its own misguided defenders. At the same time, terrorists and their operational controllers must assume that once captured they will be forced to disclose their plans. Only this assumption will lead to the positive spillover in which the uncaptured terrorists abandon their schemes for fear these have been disclosed.

SUMMARY

There must be an absolute ban on torture and coercive interrogations of any kind for political or evidentiary purposes. There ought to be an absolute ban on torture or coercive interrogations for the purpose of collecting tactical information, with the acceptance that this ban will be violated in the "ticking bomb" circumstances: the prosecutions that must follow will allow juries to consider the mitigating question of whether a reasonable person, motivated by a sincere desire to protect others, would have violated the law. There cannot be a ban on the collection of strategic information—information from terrorist leaders and senior managers—by whatever means are absolutely necessary short of inflicting severe pain when that information is likely to preclude attacks, when it is disconfirmable by interrogators (and thus the means used are actually no more violent than is necessary), and when a nongovernmental jury has decided the government has met its burden of proof in establishing these matters. Such terrorists-at-war are in the same position as ordinary soldiers who can be compelled by violence to surrender their arms and cease hostile action. For the terrorist-at-war, in an information age, that means surrendering information.

The true "ticking bomb" detainee, one with knowledge of an atrocity about to be committed, is very rare; this is not the case with the operational commander who has knowledge of the logistics for (and financing of) many, many ticking bombs. The solution here proposed for this problem depends upon our understanding of the conflict from which it arises as a war: at the same time, as we have seen in chapter 3, the sort of warfare we are facing—networked, decentralized, outsourced—means that while the information any one person has is likely to be more limited than that possessed by commanders in the wars of nation states, it is information that provides the critical weapon for the wars of informational market states, just as industries provided weapons for the industrial nation states.

A number of thoughtful writers have addressed the limits of permissible action in war by the democracies.[90] Each recognizes, in a different way, that limited government cannot have unlimited means. At a minimum, we ought to conclude that a state of consent, which governs on the basis of powers delegated by the People, can never be lawfully empowered to subject them to cruel and degrading treatment, much less torture. Whether the People can empower the State to coercively interrogate an alien enemy is another matter, but this ought to be governed by an international compact. The terrorists-at-war of al Qaeda have sworn allegiance to a virtual state; they have alienated themselves from the states in which they are born or naturalized. If an internationally recognized process determines this, then they can be coercively interrogated should they refuse to surrender their most dangerous weapon, their deadly plans.

The inquiry—which law can structure—asks whether coercive violence is done to individuals whom we are entitled to harm. In a conventional war, it is permissible to kill a sentry in the course of an operation to get crucial information. In a war against terror, the terrorist, by his adamant refusal to provide information to which the interrogator is lawfully entitled, can by that act render himself liable to coercion short of severe pain. The scope of that coercion, however, must be determined by the imminence and gravity of harm to civilians that can thereby be avoided, and the fact that this avoidance is not otherwise achievable. This much is imposed by the duty of consequentialism.

Bruce Hoffman and others have argued that it was the use of terror against captives in Algiers in 1957 that outraged public opinion in France while alienating the Muslim community in North Africa, swelling the ranks of the FLN and increasing its popularity even while French forces relying on information gained from torture were breaking the back of the revolt. The French army's tactical success in the Battle of Algiers led, in other words,[91] to the strategic defeat of the overall endeavor. So it will be with the wars against global, networked terror if we do not openly and transparently confront these issues, writing laws that reflect a democratic debate, and applying those laws sensitively in those rare contexts when an heroic official risks prosecution to save the rest of us. Otherwise, when the dreadful truth emerges, domestic opinion will abandon its government's war efforts in disgust.

Such a debate might lead to the relaxation of some international norms—like the employment of chemical weapons when these could provide a nonlethal way of subduing terrorists and freeing hostages, or the development of safe and effective truth serums when used in conjunction with polygraphs—and the tightening of other rules, like those that forbid the use of family intimidation and group arrests to dishearten prisoners. This combination of accountability, transparency, and an unflinching appreciation of the challenges that market state terrorism poses can be seen in Stephen Grey's proposal about CIA renditions: "Instead of protesting about the existence of CIA detention centers in Europe, [European policy makers] should insist at the same time that those centers be acknowledged publicly, be subject to outside inspection and exist under the rule of law."[92]

Whatever the outcome of such a debate, we cannot lose sight of the distinction between our ends and those of terrorists, partly because to do so will disable us from using necessary violence to protect the innocent and partly because we might otherwise forget precisely what we are fighting for in the effort to ensure that we win. Sheikh Khalid Mohammed is not Jean Moulin.

IV.

Finally, let us consider a statement by another national columnist, this time a liberal who seems to me to have got it exactly wrong. This writer summed up his advice to the U.S. by saying: "We have to fight the terrorists as if there were no rules, and preserve our open society as if there were no terrorists."[93]

It should be evident that this book offers precisely the opposite counsel. The states of consent must develop rules that define what terrorism is, who is a terrorist, and what states can lawfully do to fight terrorists and terrorism. Unless we do this, we will bring our alliances to ruin as we appear to rampage around the world, declaring our enemies to be terrorists and ourselves to be above the law in retaliating against them. We will become, in the eyes of others, the supreme rogue states and will have no basis on which to justify our actions other than the simple assertion of our power.

At the same time, we must preserve our open society by careful appreciation of the threat that terror poses to it and not by trying to minimize that reality or to appease the sensibilities of people who would wish it away. We must jettison nonconstitutional rules like those against information acquisition from the private sector of data voluntarily provided, and also many rules against information sharing among agencies. We must develop new practices like the requirement of national identity cards, including biometrics when these become reliable; increased CCTV surveillance at transportation, energy, and communication hubs; sophisticated data mining as well as standards for the detention of terrorist combatants on a noncriminal basis. We must do this because an open society depends upon a government strong enough and foresighted enough to protect individual rights. If we fail to develop these legal standards, we will find we are progressively militarizing the domestic environment without having quite realized that we are at war. And, when a savage mass strike against us does come, we will react in a fury that ultimately does damage to our self-respect, our ideals, and our institutions.

Most urgently, the U.S. and the E.U. must build international monitoring and enforcement regimes that mandate the intrusive examination of state practices to ensure compliance. As we shall see in later chapters, a nonproliferation treaty (NPT) that is compulsory for all states and does not allow for withdrawal, as well as international consortia that locate, identify, monitor, regulate, and protect WMD facilities (including tagging all fissile material) everywhere in the world[94]—including in the U.S., the U.K., France, and other states of consent—will become a necessity.

Ultimately, the war against the terrorist network al Qaeda is, like all wars, a political struggle. Only political ends can justify the use of violent means. All politics pose an ethical question, but also a moral imperative. The question is: What are you willing to do to get what you want? The imperative is: You must do what has to be done in order to be able to answer that question freely and without coercion. The question and the imperative must not be separated if we are to preserve a role for conscience in a world of real threats and illusory promises.

It is the responsibility of parliamentary states, which won the Long War and largely dominate the international institutions created in the twentieth century, to ensure that their citizens are allowed to make ethical decisions free of coercion. That is why the al Qaeda bombing of the Madrid trains was such a disaster for a parliamentary state, rather than the triumph for democracy as it is often described. The Spanish citizenry was perfectly free to vote for a government that would withdraw its forces from the Coalition in Iraq. A vast majority of Spaniards opposed the intervention, but a clear majority nevertheless supported the party in power, presumably on other grounds. The government was unable to reassure the public, however, that a choice could be made without fear of al Qaeda retribution. Terrorism had become the extension of diplomacy by other means, and, regrettably, it had succeeded. None of the other political issues that Spanish voters had deemed salient before the bombing—the economy, education, health, etc.—could be allowed to be decisive after the bombing. It was a sickening day for democracy, made more so by the jubilation of those candidates who were unexpectedly lifted to victories they scarcely could have expected and had not earned.

The terrorists need not "win" simply because we take truly firm measures that nevertheless protect our societies' rights to judge such matters for themselves, even if this means that, someday, they are thereby rendered free to condemn us for this. We ought not pretend that the goals for which we fight deny us the means necessary to achieve them.

Our ends don't justify any means, but neither are they irrelevant to the legitimacy of what means we employ in their pursuit. We allow police officers to carry guns, and not criminals; we allow soldiers to kill enemy soldiers, but put them on trial when they intentionally kill civilians. In both instances, we are trying to enforce the rule of law. Ends do matter. In warfare, we do not seek a level playing field with those who would destroy our basic rights if only they could achieve victory. Without legal reform, however, we are in the paradoxical position of putting ourselves at a potentially fatal disadvantage: if we adhere to law as it stands, we disable effective action against terror; if we act lawlessly, we throw away the gains of effective action.

We need legal reform so that law reflects the new strategic context that we are entering. Although that was doubtless what the Bush administration may have intended with its reinterpretation of the various constraints on torture, in fact this accomplished the opposite. The U.S. administration understood—or at least some elements did—that twenty-first century market state terror had created a strategic context that amounted to war, and called on the practices of preemption and prevention associated with state practice in war (as opposed to law enforcement). What they did not seem to appreciate was the nature of this war—its very novelty—even as they struggled to create novel rules. The appropriate rules must take into account not only that we are conducting a war, but that it is a new kind of war. As David Luban observed,

> Thus, in a traditional war, captured enemy troops do not get federal hearings on whether they can be held captive; but . . . in a traditional war, there is seldom any question whether uniformed captives are actually enemy combatants and not cases of mistaken identity. Likewise, in a traditional war, captives can be held until hostilities end. Yet in the new kind of war, where no enemy commander has the authority to surrender, the internment of enemy combatants [amounts to] indefinite imprisonment.[95]

We are fighting for the rule of law. That end imposes certain means. We had better be sure that these means do not compromise our ability to resist those who, by definition, use violence to prevent persons from doing what they lawfully may.

> . . . Nothing has changed
> The body shudders as it shuddered
> before the founding of Rome and after,
> in the twentieth century before and after Christ.
> Tortures are as they were, it's just the earth that's grown smaller,
> and whatever happens seems right on the other side of the wall.

> —Wislawa Szymborska,
> "Tortures"

CHAPTER EIGHT

Terrorism: Supply and Demand

Our remedies oft in ourselves do lie.

—William Shakespeare,
All's Well That Ends Well, 1.1.231–32[1]

I.

THE DEBATE ON terrorism since 9/11 has mainly[2] focused on al Qaeda, and on terrorism refracted through that focus, not on human rights and the impact of terror on human rights. We have concentrated on the strategic and tactical threats that beset us rather than on how those threats may actually affect what we are trying to protect, defend, and preserve.

Indeed, up to now most analytical work on terrorism has focused on the *demand* side—that is, on the social conditions that are said to be the "root" causes of terror, on the political demands of terrorist groups, on the psychological and sociopathological aspects of terrorists themselves, and on their techniques and tactics. This is, of course, quite sensible. The first task in warfare is to determine the nature of the enemy. One must remember, however, the answer bin Laden gave as to why he began attacks on the U.S. He offered two reasons: one, because the U.S. stands in the way of the theocratic reform of Muslim political society through its support for local regimes (demand), and two, because he observed in Lebanon, and was confirmed in this observation by events in Somalia, that if attacked the U.S. would abandon the region (supply). In any case, the paramount reason why we must undertake a supply side analysis that focuses on our own exposure is that we are entering a world where it will be impossible to identify our attackers in a timely way. Indeed, there are few terrorist scenarios that inflict the magnitude of harm wrought by an earthquake in California or an epidemic of avian flu, catastrophes that have no "demand" side. These facts alone are sufficient reason to supplement our focus on the perpetrators of terror with insights into our own vulnerabilities.

Most countries, especially American allies, don't actually dwell on this, for a number of reasons. The U.S. General Accounting Office studied five key

countries—Canada, France, Germany, Israel, and the United Kingdom—
and found striking similarities in their approaches to terror.[3] Officials in all
these countries stated that they made funding decisions based on the likelihood of terrorist activity, not on their vulnerability to attack. Because these
states do not present global targets, most are less likely to be attacked than
the United States. Even so, the single parameter of the likelihood of an attack
ignores its consequences. Low-probability but high-impact catastrophes are
given short shrift in such assessments. Some officials stated that the effect
of salvos of WMD would so alienate the population from the political aims
of the terrorists that they viewed such events as highly unlikely and implied
that should they occur the cause for which the terrorists fight would be
ruined. It is a common error to focus on denying the enemy his objectives
rather than on achieving one's own, but it is the latter that determines victory. Only France has created new capabilities to respond to attacks by
WMD and even France has focused its attention principally on its own
indigenous Muslim population and its susceptibility to terrorist incitement.

Most of the common demand-side assumptions* about the causes of
terrorism are difficult to confirm, however. Karin von Hippel summed up
the consensus in the scholarly community, noting that although "[c]ommon
sense would dictate that there is a direct correlation between poverty and
terrorism, . . . the evidence gathered thus far does not lend credence to this
proposition, and if anything, supports the opposite."[4] In June 2003 the
Norwegian Institute of International Affairs convened a panel of international analysts to discuss the root causes of terrorism. There was, as one
might expect, some difference of opinion on the subject, but on four
propositions there was broad agreement:

(1) There is only a weak and indirect relationship between poverty and
terrorism. As individuals, terrorists do not usually come from poor
backgrounds. Indeed they are typically better educated and better off
than their contemporaries.[5] The levels of terrorism are not conspicuously high in the poorest countries; rather those with an average level
of development, often characterized by rapid modernization, tend to
spawn terrorist recruits.

(2) State sponsorship is not a principal cause of terrorism. Some states
do draw on preexisting groups, but as a rule they do not create them.
(Iran's relationship to Hezbollah is a notable exception.) By sheltering

*For the historical ache, the ache passed down / which finds its circumstance and becomes / the
present ache, I offer this poem . . . / Still, I must say to you / I hate your good reasons. / I hate the hate-
fulness that makes you fall / in love with death, your own included. / Perhaps you're hating me now, / I
who own my own house / and live in a country so muscular, / so smug, it thinks its terror is meant / only
to mean well, and to protect. —Stephen Dunn, "To a Terrorist"

terrorist organizations, states give them far greater capabilities than they would otherwise have, but state control over terrorists—as has existed in Iraq, Libya, or Pakistan, to take the most conspicuous examples—is rare.

(3) Suicide terrorism is not driven by religious fanaticism (or more specifically, by Islam). Many suicide terrorists are secular or belong to non-Islamic faiths. The Tamil Tigers, a conventional nation state terrorist group fighting against the Hindu majority in Sri Lanka, invented late twentieth century suicide bombing. Like members of other such groups, including Hamas, these terrorists are motivated mainly by political goals, usually to end foreign occupation or domestic domination by a different ethnic group, even if their deaths are glorified by the incorporation of religious themes.

(4) Terrorists are neither insane nor irrational actors. Symptoms of psychopathology, including the typical risk factors for suicide, are actually rather rare among terrorists as individuals.[6] There is apparently no common personality profile that distinguishes terrorists who are in fact likely to manifest relative normality.

To these conclusions about the "demand" side of terrorists—their characteristics and the causes that motivate them—we can add one more consideration. Even if poverty, psychopathology, state sponsorship, or religious fanaticism had motivated the terrorists of the nation state, the challenge posed by a global, market state terror network is quite different. While that network clearly outsources operations to preexisting, nation state terrorists, it is unlikely that their motivations are identical to those who direct the network. This makes demand side inferences even harder to draw.

There is a final, additional reason why we should not limit ourselves to studying the demand side of twenty-first century terrorism. The retaliatory requirements of a demand-side antiterrorism strategy present notable drawbacks. It is sometimes forgotten that al Qaeda initially denied any involvement in the 9/11 atrocities, a disclaimer widely credited in some circles. This tactic of disclaiming responsibility is yet another feature of market state terrorism that distinguishes it from nation state terrorism. It will increasingly be the case that we will not be able to assert with confidence or to persuade others that we know the identity of those who attack us. That fact weakens deterrence by casting doubt on the availability of retaliation as an option. Perhaps equally important, but usually overlooked, are the costs of maintaining deterrence. If the terms of trade, so to speak, between the State and the terrorists that besiege it mean that the

State is forced to spend tremendous funds to counter rather modest costs to the terrorists, then this is an incentive to mount terrorist threats and attacks.

Equally significant, but more neglected, is the supply side cost of demand-side deterrence: the fact that the centralization of authority and of the economy required by deterrence structures creates highly lucrative targets for terrorists. As Bruno Frey and Simon Luechinger observed: "A polity with many different centres of decision-making and implementation is difficult, if not impossible, to destabilize. If one of the centres is hit and destroyed by a terrorist attack, the other centres can take over."[7]

By contrast, deterrence strategies tend to increase political and economic centralization because this facilitates command and control, and because protection of the leadership is easier and cheaper in a concentrated area. Equally troubling, with respect to global, networked agents, is the fact that the effective deterrence policy of one target state simply diverts attacks to allied states. Finally, deterrence and demand side approaches often alienate dissident but nonviolent groups who may be the target of retaliation or the threat of retaliation by states. It is unlikely that many of the 1,200 persons detained in the American dragnet after 9/11 ultimately were released with a more positive view of the U.S. government.

An alternative perspective, or perhaps a supplementary view, is to reconceptualize terrorism as an epiphenomenon of our own economic and political development. It is because America is so very vulnerable and at the same time so ubiquitously and overwhelmingly powerful that twenty-first century global terrorism has arisen. In this sense, the U.S. is its principal root cause, and this would remain true even if American policies vis-à-vis Israel or Iraq or Iran changed.

> [T]he United States is projecting uncoordinated economic, social, and political power even more sweepingly than it is in military terms. Globalization, [the "gradually expanding process of interpenetration in the economic, political, social, and security realms, uncontrolled by . . . traditional notions of state sovereignty" and] in forms including Westernization, secularization, democratization, consumerism, and the growth of market capitalism, represents an onslaught to less privileged people . . . repelled by the fundamental changes that these forces are bringing—or angered by the distortions and uneven distributions of benefits that result.[8]

At the same time, it is we in the developed world who have built skyscrapers, invented jetliners, and caused flying schools to be created. It is we who have piled more and more chips onto the baize[9]—more people, more networks, more buildings in fewer places—as we found that creating wealth was accelerated by proximity to wealth, and by greater links among those who maintained such a system, including those informal links that can only be nurtured face-to-face.*

By increasing the investment of capital and the productivity of our workers through an unprecedented connectivity, the developed world has increased the satisfaction of individual wants through markets. As a consequence, we have also enlarged the potential losses we will suffer when these markets are disrupted. Linking the infrastructure that is critical to the operation of energy, financial, trading, transportation, and governmental systems by means of computers, we have vastly enriched our societies while at the same time rendering them much more susceptible to catastrophic attacks.† Moreover, by creating a global communications network, we have enabled the creation of a global terrorist network. It is we who, by our acquisition of nuclear weapons and armed forces of awesome lethality, have made futile any conventional military challenge to our political interests.

Appreciating this, the supply side of terrorism, can yield new perspectives on the strategies and tactics we need to adopt in the war on global, networked terror. Tactically, we must determine what assets of highest value are at risk; what can be done in advance to reduce the impact of their loss; and how to reconstitute these functions in the wake of a catastrophe. Strategically, we must so posture ourselves that the worst attacks have been precluded. This is especially true when we enter the next phase of this war, where we will not know—and cannot find out at an acceptable

---

*This applies also to market state agents like al Qaeda, which suggests that implementing a rigorous ID and transit screening system is an urgent matter. Global terrorist operations require face-to-face meetings, despite the sophisticated reliance by market state terrorists on the Internet, satellite communications, etc. See the discussion of the Connectivity Paradox in chapter 2.

†*Lately I was looking from a night mountain-top
On a wide city, the colored splendor, galaxies of light: how could
  I help but recall the seine-net
Gathering the luminous fish? . . .
I thought, We have geared the machines and locked all together
  into interdependence; we have built the great cities; now
There is no escape.*

*. . . The circle is closed, and the net
Is being hauled in. They hardly feel the cords drawing, yet they
  shine already. The inevitable mass-disasters
Will not come in our time nor in our children's, but we and our
  children
Must watch the net draw narrower, government take all powers
  —or revolution, and the new government
Take more than all, add to kept bodies kept souls—or anarchy,
  the mass-disasters . . .*
                              —Robinson Jeffers, "The Purse-Seine"

cost to our civil life and to the resources needed to wage war—precisely who or where the enemy is.

This proposal is controversial, and readers should not be misled into assuming otherwise. For example, John Gearson has warned us that we must not "divert [c]ounterterrorist thinking to some extent away from the core tasks of understanding the motives and likely objectives of terror organisations towards a preoccupation with technology, weapons systems and high end risks."[10] That is precisely what I am trying to do in this chapter.

II.

The same essential ambiguity that enshrouds cyberattacks* also cloaks biological warfare. A nuclear explosion is clearly not a natural event, but the spread of a communicable disease or sickness from a biotoxin is assumed to be so. When members of a religious cult in Oregon infected 750 persons with salmonella in 1984, it was more than a year before it was determined that the infection had been initiated by terrorists.

More than 140 million persons enter the U.S. by air every year; the flight time between their ports of departure and arrival is seldom more than twenty-four hours. Yet diseases such as plague and smallpox have incubation times ranging from three days to two weeks, respectively.

Writing in 2002, Christopher Chyba reminded us:

In 1972, a single religious pilgrim returned to Yugoslavia from Mecca via several days in Iraq, where he had contracted smallpox. Smallpox had spread to Iraq from Iran, where a family had introduced it after acquiring it while traveling through Afghanistan. The disease in Yugoslavia went undiagnosed while the original infected individual spread the disease to others, one of whom traveled 100 miles by bus.[11]

It is absurd that an airline passenger, who would never be allowed to board a plane with a revolver, is welcomed on board carrying typhus, or cholera, or drug-resistant tuberculosis.†

---

*Indeed, one case has already occured; see Mark Landler and John Markoff, "War Fears Turn to Cyberspace in Estonia," New York Times, 29 May 2007, reporting on cyberattacks thought to originate with the Russian government, but unconfirmed to be so. The Estonian defense minister was quoted as saying, "It can effectively be compared to when your ports are shut to the sea."

†Indeed, this too has already happened; see Lawrence K. Altman, "TB Patient Is Isolated After Taking Two Flights," New York Times, 30 May 2007; Lawrence K. Altman, "Agent at Border, Aware, Let in Man with TB," New York Times, 1 June 2007, reporting on the admission into the U.S. of a traveler with a dangerous strain of tuberculosis that is resistant to antibiotics.

If we are to address this vulnerability from the supply side, we must strengthen public health systems worldwide. Surveillance of outbreaks of disease will be crucial, as will the ability to alert centers for disease control. As Chyba notes, the "anthrax mail attacks [of 2001] tragically confirmed the importance of disease surveillance, since the speed with which doctors recognized the signs of anthrax infection determined whether patients were treated immediately or sent home, only to return later to die."[12] This means that our own security is only as strong as the weakest of the public health systems worldwide.

The vulnerability of our critical infrastructure, as well as our susceptibility to imported toxins, is the consequence of the same globalizing developments that have led to the West's unprecedented economic and strategic success. Indeed, it is one measure of our success that we have eradicated smallpox, thus ironically rendering our populations wholly vulnerable to the reintroduction of this disease. The Soviet Union once held the world's largest supply of smallpox virus. Co-opting the scientists and engineers who ran this program, as suggested by John Arquilla[13] in an analogy to the farsighted Nunn-Lugar legislation that finances cooperation with Russian nuclear personnel,[14] is one more example of a supply side approach to the Wars against Terror.

We have dominated the present era because we were best situated to benefit from a globalized market, and because we did not shrink from international leadership, even when we became vulnerable to weapons of mass destruction. Now we are learning that the same forces that brought globalization and universal vulnerability are bringing a new ubiquity of ambiguous threats. We must, therefore, supplement demand side thinking with attention to the supply side.[15]

Suppose we don't. Writing before 9/11, I posited the following hypothetical:

When a disguised attack with these new weapons [is suspected], and its author is not definitely identified, three deadly risks will arise: (1) a state that is unwilling or unable to suppress the elements believed to be responsible will forfeit its sovereignty and be subject to attack and even occupation; (2) a state that is the subject of an attack will sacrifice its constitutional institutions and turn on its own people—or a discrete minority within—with violence and despotic police methods; (3) a state, though disavowing responsibility, will be deemed the author of the attacks through unknown agents, and will become the target for retaliation. All three of these scenarios fall along the seam of sovereignty that separates law from strategy, and all three are laden with peril.[16]

That is why, in addition to stockpiling vaccines,* we need to stockpile rules, international as well as domestic, to anticipate such a crisis, for that step too is a way of decreasing our vulnerabilities. In a state of consent, that means a public debate leading to public laws.

Stephen Flynn[17] seems to have this right when he observes that "[t]he secretive, top-down, us-versus-them culture that is pervasive in government security circles must give way to more inclusive processes."[18]

"Rather than working assiduously to keep the details of terrorism and our vulnerabilities out of the public domain," according to Flynn, "the federal government should adopt a new imperative that recognizes that Americans have to be far better informed about the dangers that they face."[19]

In sum, "[w]e must continue to remind the world that it is not military might that is the source of our strength but our belief that mankind can govern itself in such a way as to secure the blessings of liberty."[20] This wise observation leads us directly to the subject of the "emergency constitution."

III.

One aspect of a "preclusive" strategy is stockpiling laws as well as vaccines. We want to preclude the loss of legitimacy that can flow from panic and doubt about the basis for legal authority, so that we can avoid becoming a state of terror. If we don't use the democratic process to put laws in place now, then in a way we become the unwitting ally of the terrorists: when a truly terrible series of mass atrocities does occur, we won't have a set of appropriate procedures to fall back on, and we will inevitably resort to martial law. That could presage a complete democratic collapse, and the State could become the source of terror itself. That would amount to losing a war against terror.

Consider four narratives of what might ensue if the domestic law of the U.S. as it is currently constituted is not reformed.

- On an evening in 2021 the new president has just entered the chamber of the House of Representatives to deliver his State of the Union address. All the members of his cabinet are present except one, who by custom stays away in case of an assassination attempt on the executive leadership, as are all the members of the U.S. Supreme Court, and all the membership of both houses of Con-

---

*And not just vaccines; Norway has begun a project—the Svalbard International Seed Vault—to hold in cold storage seed samples of nearly every food crop (some 3 million seeds) to reduce the vulnerability of agricultural production. "Building the Fort Knox of Seeds," *U.S. News & World Report,* 19 February 2007, 17.

gress (less a group of sixty Democrats who are boycotting the address to protest the president's new budget proposals).

A few minutes before, EgyptAir flight 900 is given clearance to depart Dulles Airport en route to Cairo. The cockpit is, according to U.S. regulations, sealed. That prevents the copilot of the Airbus 688—the largest passenger jet ever created—from receiving help when the strychnine-laced chewing gum given him by the pilot begins to take effect. No one comes to his aid as the plane lifts off, makes a lazy turn, and begins to climb. At only 5,000 feet, however, the pilot takes over manual control from the computer-governed takeoff and begins to streak toward Washington. He is 18 miles away, accelerating to over 600 miles per hour. Although air traffic controllers quickly react to this change of direction, and frantically try to reach the pilot by radio, there is not enough time to effect an interception. By the time a commander at Andrews Air Force Base has scrambled jets, the Airbus is only seconds away from the Capitol. At 8:15 p.m., it crashes into the House chamber, igniting more than twice the jet fuel carried by the airliners that attacked the World Trade Center. The Secret Service has managed to evacuate the president at the last minute, but suicide bombers in the tunnel to which he is rushed have set up an ambush. By the time emergency vehicles arrive, the president is dead, the vice president, and the Speaker of the House (all members of the Republican party), more than four hundred members of the Congress and the Senate, and most of the cabinet and Supreme Court are dead or dying either from burns or asphyxiation.

Within an hour, the absent cabinet member, the secretary of veterans' affairs, is sworn in as president by a state judge with whom he was watching the address on television. The Presidential Succession Act provides that, in the event of the death of the vice president, the Speaker of the House, and the president pro tempore of the Senate, of the living cabinet officers the person whose department was created prior shall be made president. The Department of Veterans Affairs is a recent addition to the cabinet, but its head appears to be the only cabinet official surviving and not disabled. The secretary of agriculture still lives, but is unconscious and not thought likely to survive. When he does pull through, the previous swearing-in of his colleague at Veterans Affairs will take precedence.

That does not end matters, however, because the office of the Senate president pro tem announces that he has also recovered, surprisingly (he is the oldest member of the Senate, chosen for this ceremonial office on the basis of his seniority), and that he now wishes to be sworn in as president himself. The new president resists this claim, on the grounds that although the statute does give the president pro tem the right to supersede any cabinet official, the elderly senator's incapacity to govern (he is still in intensive care) rules him out. When and if the president decides that his competitor for office is fully recovered, he will, he promises, relinquish the office.

His first act is to replace the fallen members of the Supreme Court, which he attempts to do expeditiously. A few senators have survived, and the governors of the various states are filling vacancies rapidly, but the president pro tem's Democratic allies in the Senate refuse to call confirmation hearings until it is clear that their colleague will not be president.

At this point the rump House—for there are only fifty or so surviving congressmen (plus the sixty Democrats who boycotted the address)—decides to elect a new Speaker. Though the House had been held by Republicans (and the Senate by Democrats), the majority of the survivors are Democrats. They elect a Speaker who now claims the statutory right, as provided by the Presidential Succession Act, to be sworn in as president. A judge duly does so, over the protests of the acting president that the House didn't have a quorum when it elected the new Speaker. The Speaker/President announces *his* choices for the U.S. Supreme Court, and, expecting trouble with Senate confirmation, names nine new justices to hold recess appointments (temporary roles until the end of the Congressional term). The Speaker/President petitions this court to affirm his authority and order the acting president to vacate the White House. When the latter refuses to obey this order, the Speaker/President orders troops to occupy the West Wing. Some of them refuse, on the grounds that it is an unlawful order.

Responsibility for the EgyptAir attack is claimed by several groups, although the FBI eventually determined that the pilot had simply suffered a breakdown brought on by an impending job loss, divorce, and other personal matters, and that the suicide bombing assassination had been entirely coincidental. This finding is greeted with universal skepticism.

• On April 1, 2020, the president returns to Cambridge, Massachusetts, to give the commencement address at Harvard, his alma mater. His itinerary includes an awards ceremony for local volunteer leaders, an appearance at a magnet school, and a visit to a Red Sox baseball game.

The FBI has information suggesting a possible threat to the

president's party from a terrorist group, but has no specific intelligence about the form of the attack. The group is suspected of having acquired biological pathogens, including anthrax, and of having procured aerosolization equipment. The FBI issues a general threat warning to local law enforcement agencies but does not deem the information serious enough to alert state or municipal health authorities.

One week later, FBI informants report rumors that something happened while the president was in Boston. The Secret Service issues a denial.

The next week a twenty-year-old student goes to the Harvard infirmary with respiratory distress and muscle aches. She is pale, has a temperature of 102º F and is slightly leukopenic but the physical exam and lab results are otherwise normal. She is diagnosed as having flu and is sent home with instructions to drink fluids and take ibuprofen. Later that day a forty-year-old electrician employed by the state arrives at the emergency room of the largest city hospital manifesting nausea, chest pains, and difficulty breathing. He appears pale and has a temperature of 102º F. As his breathing becomes more labored, he is put on a ventilator and removed to the intensive care unit; because he has recently returned from a holiday in Belize he is diagnosed as suffering dengue fever and put on the critical list. Over the course of the day, four more young adults come to the university infirmary with influenza-like symptoms.

Ten days after the president's visit, the female student returns to the infirmary after collapsing in class. Though her blood pressure is normal and her temperature has stabilized at 102º F, her breathing is strained. That same day another state employee comes to the municipal emergency room with similar symptoms. Massachusetts state law, however, forbids the sharing of information about an individual's health status without his express consent; as a result, neither physicians in the two hospitals nor public health authorities are made aware of these two simultaneous cases.

In Washington, a member of the president's Secret Service detail is admitted to George Washington University Hospital, where he is diagnosed as suffering from Spanish influenza, the strain of swine flu that raged during the First World War. He is treated with Tamiflu, a broad-spectrum antiviral.

As a result of the Washington diagnosis, the Centers for Disease Control (CDC) alert hospitals in all cities where the Secret Service agent had traveled in the period during which infection would have been contagious; Boston is among these cities. Five new cases present at Harvard University Health Services; two at other hospitals in the city. When both the university infirmary and the city hospitals report similar cases to the CDC, FBI personnel are dispatched in order to secure blood and other biological samples from the patients. A military aircraft flies these samples to the CDC's Biosafety Level 4 lab in Atlanta. The FBI requests that Cambridge police be called to help maintain order at the infirmary where rumors are circulating of a biological attack on campus. City police at first direct that no patients, staff, or visitors be allowed to leave the hospital until all occupants have been identified and their addresses recorded. More FBI agents and city police arrive on the infirmary grounds.

Hospital visitors are confused and angered by police refusal to allow anyone to leave the hospital. Ambulances are rerouted to other hospitals. The rumor that smallpox has broken out rapidly spreads through the campus, as do rumors that a terrorist wanted by the FBI is in the infirmary. When the FBI attempts to secure the records of the stricken students, city police and hospital officials resolve to prevent this, and a fight erupts. Three persons are injured and sent to the infirmary emergency room which has now been cordoned off by the FBI.

Local television stations report the scene on campus; the local CNN affiliate arrives and demands access to the hospital and the affected patients. Rumors about contagious diseases quickly spread, including claims that meningitis, Ebola virus, smallpox, or measles have hit the campus. The FBI is reluctant to let anyone leave the building, partly on the theory that some of the infected persons might be perpetrators who accidentally have infected themselves in the course of aerosolizing the influenza virus. After an acrimonious conversation between the Massachusetts attorney general and the United States attorney general, FBI agents are withdrawn and a cordon around the university infirmary is maintained by local police.

A melee ensues on the campus as anxious parents try to storm the infirmary to release their children, and as friends of the quarantined try to break in and join loved ones.

Over the next ten days, cases of Spanish flu are reported in a number of cities; there appears to be some link to each of the venues the president has visited since the beginning of the month. It is widely believed that the president and his family have been inoculated, but not the members of his Secret Service detail. A run on Ciproxin reduces commercially available stocks of this drug to negligible levels. The president goes on television to inform the nation of a bioterrorist attack by unknown parties, perhaps linked to remnants of the al Qaeda network. He vows that the assailants will be identified and brought to justice; he urges cooperation with health authorities; and he announces the promulgation of an executive order that puts into effect most provisions of a CDC-drafted Emergency Health Powers Act that had been rejected by the Congress the preceding year. This executive order purports to empower the executive to issue quarantine notices, despite opposition by state governments. When the National Guard is federalized by presidential order and directed to quarantine the entire Harvard campus, many commanders refuse, believing this to be an unlawful order.

"Credit" for the flu outbreak is claimed by several different groups (including an antitechnology network, and an animal rights terrorist movement, both citing research done at Harvard), which explain on various websites how the influenza was engineered.

- On a sunny spring day in 2019 an earthquake strikes northern California. It measures 6.5 on the Richter scale[21] and lasts about forty-five seconds, and is followed hours later by one measuring 7.8. About 1,400 persons die within twenty-four hours. There are more than 100,000 injured. Hospitals are quickly overwhelmed. More than a million structures are damaged and roughly 300,000 households are displaced.

Highways are obstructed by collapsed bridges, abandoned vehicles, and debris. Airports are closed for two weeks owing to soft-earth damage beneath runways. More than a million persons have no water; local reservoirs are quickly exhausted and more than 2,000 fires rage, depleting emergency cisterns.

Fifty levees in the southwestern region of the Sacramento delta collapse, causing waves of saltwater from San Pablo Bay to flood the delta. These levees were known to be poorly maintained. The earthquake—as predicted—causes the soil to liquefy, destroying levees that were built on sand and silty soil. Aqueducts carrying water to the Bay Area from the Sierra Nevada fail. Another 400,000 persons are displaced.

The Stafford Act empowers the U.S. president to declare an emergency upon the request of the state governor. The California governor, however, refuses to make the statutory request, on the grounds that the Federal Emergency Management Agency (FEMA) is so poorly staffed that a Stafford Act request would leave the afflicted area in worse hands. Recalling the experience of New

Orleans following Hurricane Katrina, the governor borrows funds from the private sector, pledging to secure these debts by federal funds once the crisis is over.

This move is deemed illegal by the U.S. attorney general in an opinion that causes the cost of funds to California to soar. Anxious to help the stricken area, the president next orders the U.S. Navy to provide emergency stores of water and medicines. Action by the U.S. armed forces in a civil capacity, however, is contrary to the provisions of the Posse Comitatus Act and can only be lawfully ordered following the declaration of an emergency, which the governor has refused to request. When rioting breaks out in San Francisco, army forces brought to the city refuse orders to police the riot-swept areas.

The expectation that San Francisco will be unpoliced for some time unexpectedly causes thousands of persons to flood the area, looting homes and businesses and taking over whole neighborhoods in a reign of terror. Refugees in Candlestick Park (a sports stadium) are robbed and beaten. Rapes make lavatory areas unsafe to use, and sanitation becomes precarious.

When the standoff between federal and state governments is finally ended, FEMA takes charge of evacuation efforts. FEMA seeks to place what now has swelled to over a million refugees in other communities. Some cities revolt and try to prevent the settlement of these displaced persons.

Rumors of a second series of quakes about to occur sweep Los Angeles and Southern California, where 18 million persons live in an area with indigenous water for 3 million. The resulting panic causes an exodus of almost 300,000 persons, including many police and government officials. Communications are swamped by overloading demand, and it becomes impossible to use telephones in the area. Only text messaging remains a reliable link.

Private areas in Los Angeles—affluent neighborhoods like Bel Air and Beverly Hills, for example—hire guards for protection. When criminals wearing police and army uniforms attempt to disarm these groups, small-scale warfare breaks out.

But the situation is worse in the poorest areas. Despite the fact that no new earthquake occurs, these persons are abandoned. No food flows into their communities, where stocks are depleted within hours. Looting keeps fresh commodities from coming in. Red Cross and local charities are attacked and a series of No-Go areas emerge, governed by local Latino gangs. For weeks, something like anarchy holds sway, made worse by an influx of illegal

Mexican immigrants taking advantage of the collapse of border control around Tijuana.

When order is eventually restored, the total economic loss is put at $500 billion. "Credit" for this catastrophe is assigned to a radical Mexican American terrorist group that claims to have planned for some time to exploit such an event.

• On September 11, 2021, U.S. space-based sensors detect a missile launch from what is believed to be a non-nuclear airbase in Russia. A single ICBM, targeted on a now-decommissioned field of American former missile silos, lands about thirty minutes later. Before it does the Washington-Moscow hotline is activated. It appears that the U.S. learned of the launch before the Russian leadership; if so, that would support the conclusion that the launch was probably accidental.

But that is by no means certain. Consider the choice of targets: because the targeting codes seem to have been left over from the Cold War, the actual death toll from a 20-kiloton, MIRVed ICBM was fewer than 800. Had the warheads struck New York, it might have been as many as 800,000. This could mean either an accident or a studied decision not to trigger retaliation (because of the minimal loss) or, it is suggested in some quarters, an effort to force retaliation against Russia (perhaps engineered by Chechens) without embittering the U.S. if the true hand of the conspiracy were disclosed. The stricken target is a group of empty underground installations that once held U.S. ICBMs. The MIRV pattern is one that would have been necessary to destroy the hardened silos when they contained American weapons and thus appears to conform to a preprogrammed, damage limitation attack. In any event, it helps account for the relatively few casualties.

Any nuclear arsenal is, of course, subject to the vagaries of unauthorized or accidental use. From 1975 to 1990, some 66,000 military personnel assigned to the U.S. nuclear forces were removed from their positions; of these 66,000, 41 percent were removed owing to alcohol or drug problems and another 20 percent were reassigned because of psychiatric problems.[22] In 1998 it was noted that

[s]ince the end of the Cold War, Russia's nuclear command system has steadily deteriorated. Aging nuclear communications and computer networks are malfunctioning more frequently, and deficient early-warning satellites and ground radar are more prone to reporting false alarms.[23]

It is widely known that Russian budget cuts have forced cut-backs in the training of nuclear commanders, and that low morale has plagued the Russian Strategic Rocket forces for some time. It has also been reported that suicide has become a serious problem in the forces. It may be, however, that Russian forces were reacting to a false alarm which the Russian leadership now denies: in January 1995, a warning triggered by a U.S. scientific rocket launched from Norway led to the activation of the "nuclear suitcases" carried by top Russian leaders. For almost eight minutes—with only four minutes remaining before a decision had to be made—the leaders deliberated before deciding the report was not a harbinger of a surprise U.S. attack.[24]

Several groups claim to be the authors of the launch, most of them adding that this attack is a warning and that further attacks would be forthcoming if the U.S. doesn't comply with the demands of the particular terrorists alleging they were responsible. This confusion, coupled with the awful speculation about what might have happened had other, more populated areas been targeted, fuels competing congressional inquiries in the House and Senate into the identity of the true attackers and what could be done to prevent future launches. Clearly, deterrence wasn't sufficient.

In the confusion following the detonation, there is strong pressure in some U.S. quarters to destroy the Russian nuclear systems completely, if only to prevent future accidents. This option gains some traction simply because there had been so little public discussion of what the U.S. would do in such unclear circumstances.

Back in 2006, Thomas Kean, former chairman of the 9/11 Commission, had complained that there was little progress being made at securing the nuclear weapons of the former Soviet Union. At the current pace, he said, securing the roughly one hundred sites worldwide would take fourteen years. Apparently even this relaxed tempo had not been kept up. In a crucial report in 2001, Howard Baker and Lloyd Cutler had concluded that, for less than 1 percent of the U.S. defense budget or up to a total cost of $30 billion over the next eight to ten years the world's supply of fissile material could be locked down.[25] This was not done.

These slender stories have been used to draw attention to what needs to be done in domestic law to preclude the catastrophes they describe. We cannot prevent earthquakes any more than we can with certainty prevent accidental launches or maniacal attacks, but we can prevent much of the damage these would do. Most important, we can minimize the damage to our institutions of consent and human rights.

The problem of the "emergency constitution" has usually been conceived as a problem of executive government. Not surprisingly, the proposals that address this problem fall therefore into two groups: those that use the legislative branch as a check on the executive, and those that rely on the judiciary to provide this check. These proposals are often insufficient, even on their own terms, in a parliamentary system like the U.K.'s where the legislature and the executive are combined but their most telling deficiency lies elsewhere. The villain in emergencies is not executive power per se, as much as it is the unpreparedness that leads to authoritarianism.

In the current debate,[26] however, the response to the challenge that emergencies pose to states of consent has nevertheless been largely structured in terms of restraining executive power. Some scholars and academic commentators, of whom Bruce Ackerman is the most prominent, urge the adoption of *ex ante* statutes, and in some cases constitutional amendments that would become operational only with the declaration of emergency and which are restrained by various provisions written into these laws. Such special powers are fixed—and limited—in advance of the emergency, and their duration is studiedly reserved to the legislature. William Scheuerman describes the fundamental premise of this approach:

[D]ecisions to institute as well as end emergency government never should be left in the hands of those who exercise emergency power, constitutional provisions must specify when and how it is to be put into effect and subsequently revoked, and no emergency action can be given a permanent legal character beyond the immediate crisis . . . [E]lected representative legislatures are seen as best suited to overseeing emergency power because of their superiority, *vis-à-vis* both the executive and judiciary, as formally organized sites for free-wheeling democratic deliberation and debate.[27]

The South African constitution appears to be based on this approach because it provides that emergency powers can only be invoked when exacting supermajoritarian requirements have been met, thus ensuring that the broadest popular democratic endorsement underpins government action. Reflecting the South African approach, Ackerman has proposed an "emergency constitution" that would impose strict limits on U.S. executive authority: (1) the president could not simply declare an emergency on his own, save for a limited period of a week or two while Congress debates the matter; (2) following this period, any emergency powers would lapse unless a majority of both houses voted to continue them—and even this endorsement would only be valid for two months; (3) for a reauthorization, a supermajority of 60 percent of both houses of Congress would be required; (4) after another two months, a supermajority of 70 percent would be needed to continue the emergency authorities; (5) after another two months, and for every two-month extension thereafter, an 80 percent vote of both the House and Senate would be necessary.

There are a number of virtues to this version of legislative oversight and restraint on the actions of the executive. As Ackerman argues, his proposal maximizes the need for collaboration across party lines. This makes it more useful than many alternatives as a check on the executive for parliamentary systems, like the U.K.'s, where the executive and legislative branches are combined. It also puts a restraint on the political temptation to exploit emergencies for partisan benefit. Few steps have cast more doubt on the sincerity of the U.S. government's oft-repeated claims that it is waging war against terror than the Bush administration's reflexive partisanship in appointments (and the aggressively partisan way its appointees have gone about their jobs). If a president truly believed he was conducting a global war, one might think he would surely have had a bipartisan war cabinet and that he would surely not have entrusted the leadership of the CIA to a Republican congressman, the Department of Homeland Security to a Republican governor, and the Department of Justice to a defeated Republican senator.

Ackerman's proposal also has the profound consequence of strengthening the rule of law by relying on the rule of law. A number of constitutional commentators have argued that liberal democracies—and perhaps states of consent generally—are not up to the task of anticipating emergencies because such states depend on laws, and emergencies are too unpredictable to be adequately governed by law. This was the position taken by the fascist political philosopher Carl Schmitt, for example, before World War II, and it finds echoes in a number of critical legal theorists at present. But Schmitt was reacting to a description of law such as that depicted by Hans Kelsen—rigid and formulaic as well as formalistic. Kelsen's view held that the legitimacy of a legal regime depended upon a certain formal character of the legal proposition; Schmitt's attack on this view in a way accepts Kelsen's positivism as a kind of baseline for the state of consent. Ackerman (and before him, Lon Fuller)[28] appears to believe that a legal system can retain its legitimacy even while compromising some of its precepts[29] if it maintains its "identity as a normatively defensible model of legality."[30] Whether he is right about this, Ackerman's approach—retaining the processes and procedures of lawmaking—is certainly the surest method of taming the threat posed by the fact that no legal code can effectively foresee all the measures that might be necessary in an emergency. In fact, if Schmitt is right that law unavoidably must sometimes be suspended in emergencies then this is merely a feature of law as it is, and the legitimacy of law is not thereby necessarily jeopardized. It is when we fail to take precautions such as Ackerman's that emergencies can destabilize the legitimacy of the state of consent by exacting lawless remedies in crisis, including of course dispensing with the ways by which law itself is enacted in a liberal democracy.

Nevertheless, some of the measures that Ackerman proposes seem to me to reflect the passing nation state, with its heavy reliance on legal regulation and its marked reliance on legal process. Some of the proposals share with the notorious War Powers Resolution the inevitable destiny of irrelevance, and in this context such an outcome is fraught with enormous risks (as it is not regarding war powers, where there are many precedents for executive action disregarding the statute). In the case of a truly horrific terrorist attack the executive's refusal to abide by the superescalator statute could persuade a disoriented public, in a crisis for which there are no precedents, that a coup d'état was under way. This in turn could lead some patriotic citizens to sympathize with or even aid terrorists.

Ackerman's supermajority escalator is just the type of very precise law that the future can make a mockery of. His president cannot declare an emergency for longer than two weeks without an endorsement by Congress. This is meant to cabin the president's powers, but any president who declared an emergency in the face of substantial congressional opposition—after only a week—is unlikely to be deterred by the prospect of further congressional defiance. Insofar as the supermajority requirement does not need the authorization of a constitutional amendment, as Ackerman claims, it may make matters worse: two months into a crisis a small minority of congressmen can stymie action by the president. The law professors might rally around such a minority, but the country would be outraged. Overriding the law—which would then ensue—does not mean that the momentum for lawless behavior would be decreased but rather, as we have seen in other cases of civil disorder and in warfare, the desire to disregard law would be whetted. Nor, if the superescalator provisions do not require entrenchment in the Constitution, is there any reason why a mere majority cannot repeal them, which would vitiate the entire enterprise and lead to even further confusion.

The automaticity that Ackerman builds into his Doomsday Machine is not its greatest virtue, allowing the Constitution to prevail despite panicky pressures to compromise it; rather, this is the greatest vice of the supermajoritarian escalator because it inflexibly assumes (and indeed relies entirely on this inflexibility) that the future will not confound us by frustrating a legislative quorum, by threats of extortion that prey on individual congressmen, by providing an excuse for a dictatorial president to dispense with legislative government altogether. Ackerman raises this objection perfectly when he writes: "There are two kinds of emergency. One kind is created by a terrorist attack . . . another when the government is paralyzed and can't respond in a credible fashion."[31]

The competing school that would institutionalize checking devices on executive action relies on ex post action by the judiciary. It implicitly recognizes that the sorts of novel powers the president might need in the aftermath of an attack are actually not likely to require sweeping suspension of law on emergency grounds.[32]

As David Dyzenhaus, like Scheuerman a distinguished scholar of Carl Schmitt, puts it, "the law that rules is not just positive law; the law includes values and principles to do with human dignity and freedom. It also presupposes that judges are the ultimate guardians of those values."[33] There is much to be said for this approach, and it has also been well said by another law professor, David Cole.[34] He offers several reasons why the case law of common law adjudication especially suits states of consent confronting the difficulties posed by governments acting in crises. Because courts assess situations after matters have cooled a bit,[35] because they must create as well as rely on precedent,[36] because their decisions must be supported by legal arguments rather than simply appeals to necessity,[37] because court decisions are available to scrutiny by the press and public,[38] and because the judiciary is relatively independent of politics—for all these reasons we can expect a more deliberate and dispassionate examination of the conflicts that arise when executive power tests its limits.

These are very sensible, even wholesome, observations—though, as indicated in the notes, the performance of the U.S. Supreme Court has not been entirely unsullied by departures from the stricter methods of what Henry Hart, one of the Court's keenest critics, called "the thrilling tradition of Anglo-American law." They address the important issue of how to legitimate executive practices by correcting or endorsing the actions of the president and his appointees and how to protect the values and provisions of the U.S. Constitution. But as with the "emergency constitution," these observations do not address whether law, as it is at present configured, actually is appropriate to a state besieged by terrorists.[39]

Here is a brief list of the sort of proposals I have in mind. Although these are ideas that are compatible with the newly emerging constitutional order of the market state and responsive to the threats that beset it, they are offered diffidently because the point is not that any particular policies are necessary but rather that we must urgently begin to consider them. As Ackerman wrote:

> We are in a race against time. It takes time to confront the grim constitutional future that lies ahead; and more time to separate good proposals from bad ones; and more time to engage in a broad-based public

discussion; and more time for farsighted politicians . . . to enact a constitutional framework into law.[40]

Nevertheless, it seems coy not to offer some substantive proposals. Here are a dozen:

1. Enact a federal isolation and quarantine* statute and regulations pursuant to that statute that rigorously spell out the authorities by which persons and designated areas can be sequestered. At present in the U.S. there is a complete hodgepodge of state and local rules. A good place to start would be the Emergency Health Powers Act (EHPA) proposed by the Centers for Disease Control for adoption by states. This would permit officials to compel a person to submit to a physical exam or a test without a court order. Physicians and other health workers could be directed to do this testing. While court orders would be required for quarantines, officials could quarantine first and go to court afterwards. Officials could compel persons to be vaccinated, isolated, and/or treated for infectious and noninfectious diseases. The EHPA could serve as a model for federal legislation. The U.S. government would have broad emergency powers temporarily to commandeer facilities, including subways, hospitals, and pharmaceutical laboratories.

2. Create national identification cards with clear and enforceable constraints on the use of the personal information to which the card can be linked. Students, whatever their political leanings, hate this idea. They believe they have an inalienable right to be anonymous when they are properly questioned by a police officer, or seek access to an airplane (though they are quite resourceful when it comes to acquiring identification that would pass a bartender's scrutiny). As Martha Minow has pointed out, however, the U.S. government is in the process of creating a national ID by withholding federal highway funds unless states issue driver's licenses in the same format, although enforcement of the Real ID Act of 2005 has been put off until at least 2009. Doing it that way avoids addressing the issues of privacy that could be thrashed out in a forthright ID plan, which could also adopt the most advanced biometrics. Similar biometric IDs should also be required in Iraq or any urban theater of terrorist operations.[41]

---

*Isolation involves the separation of persons who have a specific infectious illness from those who are healthy; quarantine refers to the separation and restriction of movement of persons who, while not yet ill, have been exposed to an infectious agent.

3. Repeal the Posse Comitatus Act and pass new legislation to permit the president to federalize National Guard troops in a natural disaster. The Posse Comitatus Act is a law[42] passed at the end of the Reconstruction period following the American Civil War. The original purpose of the statute was to prevent U.S. marshals from calling on federal troops to supervise elections in the formerly secessionist states of the South, intimidating voters in order to increase the Republican vote. It prohibits federal military personnel and units of the National Guard under federal authority from acting in a law enforcement role within the United States.[43] There are exceptions to this prohibition: the Insurrection Act[44] has been held to authorize the use of federal troops to suppress riots; the Stafford Act[45] grants the president powers that may be invoked when he has declared an emergency; a recent congressional gloss[46] on Posse Comitatus appears to authorize the domestic use of the armed forces in the aftermath of a nuclear or radiological attack. Despite these exceptions, and much recent precedent, the Posse Comitatus Act is still "viewed as a major barrier to the use of U.S. military forces in planning for homeland defense, [and] many in uniform believe that the act precludes the use of U.S. military assets in domestic security operations in any but the most extraordinary situations."[47] The inept handling of the humanitarian crisis caused by Hurricane Katrina is evidence that the U.S. Department of Defense is not well integrated into American disaster relief.

Although the president already has the authority to call up reserves in case of a terrorist attack overseas or domestically in case of an attack using WMD, that power does not at present extend to natural or other man-made disasters.

4. Amend the Stafford Act. The Robert T. Stafford Disaster Relief and Emergency Assistance Act (1988) created the mechanism by which the president declares a national emergency, triggering assistance through the Federal Emergency Management Agency. It establishes the process by which a state governor, through a request, can obtain a presidential declaration so that emergency assistance can begin to flow. There must be a request by a governor for the declaration to be made unless it can be shown that the subject of the emergency declaration is the exclusive or preeminent responsibility of the federal government. This mechanism, as we saw during the New Orleans debacle, can pit the White House against a state governor in a test of wills by which either side can withhold consent while the victims of a catastrophe suffer. When FEMA is in the hands of manifest incompetents, there is an incentive on the part of the state to negotiate over the terms of assistance as the price for making the request for a declaration of

emergency; when the state is governed by reckless men, the statute provides a handy means of laying blame on the federal government. It should also be noted that, at present, federal authority to override state laws governing quarantines rests on the slender reed of the Stafford Act, which—in an anthrax attack, for example, because anthrax is not communicable—might be held to impose legal requirements some fact patterns would not meet. Finally, the act does not recognize the extra local costs imposed by a terrorist attack, apart from the damage already done; though New York was obliged to suspend travel into Manhattan and heighten security around the U.N. and elsewhere after the 9/11 attacks, the Stafford Act did not cover expenses that were not at the site of the actual "disaster."

5. Reform FISA to recognize data mining. As I have argued in chapter 5, the Foreign Intelligence Surveillance Act does not contemplate the change from a communications paradigm that is circuit-based and point-to-point to a new paradigm of packet-based information. Nor does its national/international criteria fit the globalization of the communications infrastructure (so that a telephone call originating abroad can appear to be a national call). Most importantly, however, the act does not contemplate the advances made in automated monitoring techniques. The U.S. executive doesn't believe it needs new legal authorities to cross-correlate information and analyze traffic flows when that analysis does not depend on the substantive content of an intercepted conversation or the particular identity of its participants, while civil liberties groups and the public at large are concerned that this eavesdropping is done entirely without regulation.

A better solution would provide "program" authorization—by judges—augmented by regulations limiting the use of intercepted communications, recording the names of persons whose communications are intercepted, and setting up various checks on how this information is used including after-action review by judges.

After disclosing the program of National Security Agency (NSA) intercepts in December 2005, the *New York Times* also reported that the agency had cooperated with a number of private telecommunications companies, notably including AT&T. While this is precisely the sort of market state, public/private coordination that is needed, the result was a series of lawsuits against AT&T and the gleeful announcement by some of its competitors that they would decline to cooperate if approached by the U.S. government. What is needed is a statutory basis for these partnerships that will protect private companies from liability and make clear what statutory and regulatory protections are in place for the privacy of their customers. As an additional measure,

NSA analysts should be provided with personal security, anonymity where requested, and various home security technologies.

6. Implement statutory rules for preventive detention. Because Congress has not written laws governing the novel problem of terrorists at war with the United States, the U.S. has attempted to cope with this problem by detaining those believed to be non-POW combatants in accordance with the laws of war. This has led to the absurd conclusion that some persons may be held without charge, indefinitely, even though they have been captured without weapons and dispute the claim that they are combatants. Congress should instead amend Title 18 of the U.S. Code to provide for (a) the power to hold a person suspected of terrorist activity for twenty-eight days without charges (U.S. law generally requires that a suspect be charged or released within forty-eight hours), thus conforming U.S. practice to that of the U.K.; and (b) the detention of any non-U.S. citizen arrested within the U.S. on proof of a reasonable suspicion that he is planning or assisting or has executed an act of terrorism. Upon a showing to a court that an immediate trial would be impractical owing to evidence that cannot be publicly revealed or admitted consistent with the rules of evidence, and upon a further showing of reasonable grounds that release of the detainee would significantly endanger the lives of others, any date for the trial of such a crime can be delayed for a period of six months. During this period the government may seek orders extending pretrial detention for further periods of six months, not to exceed two years in toto. Every such order should be subject to appeal. Habeas corpus must be available, consistent with the protection of classified sources and methods. Counsel of the detainee's own choosing must be provided. Any person so detained who is not thereafter brought to trial and convicted shall be entitled to fair compensation from the U.S. for the period of detention. Detention should be separate from that of persons convicted of crimes or awaiting ordinary criminal trials. The U.S. Supreme Court has approved preventive detention for persons deemed a threat to society—the insane, pedophiles, persons with infectious diseases—who are not guilty of having committed crimes.

7. Amend the U.S. Constitution to provide for the immediate replacement of dead or disabled members of the House of Representatives. The Constitution provides that all members of the House must be elected, in contrast to the members of the Senate who, on the death or resignation of a senator, can be appointed by the state governor to serve until a new election is held. The Constitution also provides that, in order to conduct any official action, the House must have a quorum

of half its membership (at present, this number is 218). A dubious nineteenth century ruling of the Speaker holds that this requirement can be adjusted to only half the living members. If this questionable interpretation were correct, then in the event of a catastrophic attack on the membership of the House, the remaining membership would act—no matter how small the number—for the many months before new members could be seated, if it could even be determined precisely how many members were able to function. If the president and vice president were killed or disabled, such a rump House would choose the new president. If the Speaker's ruling is incorrect, the U.S. would be without a lower chamber for quite a while, unable to act lawfully, unable even to declare war on its attackers; the entire bicameral legislative process would be paralyzed. In either case, prudence requires that some mechanism be established to replace dead or incapacitated congressmen until new elections are held. There have been several proposals for the appointment of interim members of the House, including alternates who are elected along with the serving member, appointments by the state governors, and other schemes.[48] The best proposal is simply an amendment authorizing the Congress to create its own plan.

8. Rewrite the Presidential Succession Act of 1947. It was President Harry Truman who insisted that the Speaker of the House and the president pro tempore of the Senate be inserted into the line of succession to the presidency; he believed, quite wisely, that someone who had actually run for office could better govern than those cabinet members who, in many cases, have never been elected to anything other than the Council on Foreign Relations and a few clubs. The Constitution, however, limits those eligible to succeed to the office of president to "officers of the United States," a phrase that has repeatedly been held to mean only officials of the executive branch. Moreover, the current statute is fraught with practical and political pitfalls. The president pro tem (an honorary position usually given to the longest-serving senator of the majority party) is likely to be an elderly, sometimes very elderly, man unused to the rigors of the modern presidency; a Speaker chosen by the majority party in the House is as likely as not in the current era to be of the opposite party to that of the president, a wrenching change following an assassination. These two officials should be removed from the line of presidential succession.

9. Adopt a statute providing for emergency succession to the U.S. Supreme Court. The appointment of Supreme Court justices has become the most contested front on the political landscape, coincident

with the increasing reliance on the Court for the legitimating of government action. Its most grotesque follies—*Bush v. Gore* and *Clinton v. Jones* come to mind—have demonstrated that the American people defer to its judgments and accord it a respect that no other branch holds, regardless of the wisdom or even coherence of its worst opinions. Yet at that time when the Court's legitimating influence will be most needed, the confirmation of a large number of new justices appointed by a single president could well be very difficult to achieve. Congress should create an emergency Court consisting of the chief judges of the thirteen circuit courts (the courts of appeal directly below the Supreme Court). This court would be on the shelf, as it were, and would only decide cases when the number of surviving Supreme Court justices dropped to four or fewer members (who would themselves join this emergency court).

10. Authorize the National Academy of Sciences to study and report on the problem of restricting information about dangerous diseases and biotoxins. This is an especially tricky issue because the distribution of such information facilitates the development of vaccines and antidotes as well as terrorist attacks. It is alarming that the genetic codes for smallpox and polio have been posted on the Web. At the same time, it is idle to assume (and probably idiotic to expect) that the rapid dissemination of scientific information and technology will abate. DNA starter kits can be purchased by any person with access to the Internet. Armed with the growth media thus delivered and with a first-year graduate student's knowledge of molecular biology, a terrorist group could engineer a deadly virus. Imagine a suicide bomber whose bomb consisted of microscopic viral cells and who simply shook hands with passersby in an international airport or distributed free cups of coffee from a pot into which she had spat. This is a problem of such complexity, and one that requires a consensus in the scientific community that is not currently present, that an NAS study should be authorized and funded by Congress.

11. Create an Article III frederal court with special jurisdiction over terrorism cases (we already have specialized courts to deal with patents, tax cases, and bankruptcies). This court would have special rules for the introduction of evidence and the conduct of hearings and trials. With respect to evidentiary matters, statutory provisions would permit the use of hearsay evidence, anonymous witnesses, testimony by affidavit, and self-incriminatory statements offered without coercion but also without the usual warnings; with regard to procedures, judges would have the discretion to seal and redact records and to

close hearings, subject to the normal appellate review and habeas corpus proceedings in ordinary federal courts. The principal work of these courts would be to implement a comprehensive system of preventive detention; except for detentions arising from overseas combat, its jurisdiction would be exclusive—it would thus confine military tribunals. By contrast, the jurisdiction of ordinary state and federal courts would still be available for ordinary criminal prosecutions.

12. Adopt information security statutes that require a certain level of protection for those privately held assets that are crucial to the public good, and underwrite insurance programs that indemnify the owners of these assets. By so doing, the market will be brought into play so that companies desiring insurance will be monitored not only by government agencies but by private insurance investigators, without whose imprimatur neither insurance nor, more crucially, significant credit will be forthcoming from the private sector. This program can serve as the basis for an internationalized solution to the problem of critical infrastructure that can be implemented more quickly and far more effectively than an international convention or series of bilateral treaties.

These brief, summary recommendations are hardly the fount of all wisdom. On the contrary, they are meant chiefly to stimulate others to make their own suggestions. There is, moreover, a superb report written by Philip Heymann and Juliette Kayyem[49] that makes detailed and carefully reasoned proposals on a number of matters (coercive interrogations, indefinite detention, military commissions, targeted killing, the interception and collection of information, surveillance) that might serve as the starting point for congressional action. Furthermore, I am keenly aware that these specific proposals address only the U.S. response. It seemed officious to me to propose reforms for Britain, and in any case, I am not well informed enough regarding British statutes and practices to do so. But we must begin, and that beginning starts with a public debate on specific proposals.

A focus on the "supply side" of terrorism—that is, on our vulnerabilities—may seem an obvious complement to "demand-side" efforts, but it is in fact rather controversial. A recent essay concluded:

The only strategy that is likely to be effective in securing the homeland is one that emphasizes offensive action . . . It must involve a political strategy to win friends, cow enemies and delegitimize terror as an instrument of policy or a means of warfare . . . [T]errorists must be hunted down and destroyed by the most lethal covert operations since World War II. For the most part, defensive measures . . . are likely to consume vast amounts of resources for little if any additional security.[50]

While offering a partial answer, such an approach if pursued exclusively puts at risk the very things we are fighting to protect. Even the most aggressive, offensive demand side measures are unlikely to wholly prevent the many operations that are relatively easy for the terrorists to execute. More importantly, assassinations, restaurant bombings, and hostage takings, though they are horrifying and can temporarily rivet the attention of the society that is attacked, do not translate into terror on a nationwide scale. Bearing in mind what our ultimate goal is—to protect consent by protecting civilians—we should not neglect those unlikely but enormously consequential attacks that may or may not arise from human agency.[51] We should, as observed earlier, remember that we are fighting a war against terror, not just against terrorists.

The most catastrophic acts—attacks with WMD, for example—are also those that lend themselves best to a supply side approach: it is more difficult to acquire such weapons than those required by the small-scale acts of terror that are more probable but of less consequence.

As I emphasized in the introduction to this work, there is no reason to be terribly alarmed at present about acts of terrorism, or even the proliferation of WMD or the inevitable mass suffering brought on by catastrophe. Terrorism today does not pose a significant threat to the existence of states of consent; states that acquire WMD in the future can be deterred; suffering from catastrophes can be alleviated, as it has been in the past. It is when these three threats intersect that we confront novel and very difficult problems. When terrorists possess nuclear or biological weapons of mass destruction, for example, they can bring about civilian suffering on a scale that can destabilize the most mature democracy.

Nor should we focus our supply side efforts solely on those catastrophes that cause tens of thousands of deaths. As argued in chapter 2, the last decades have brought a complete transformation of the infrastructures in banking and finance, energy, telecommunications, transportation, and government services. These all depend now on complex computer and electronic links. The nodes that connect these infrastructures present tempting targets because their failure to function would cascade across many different sectors of the economy and geographic regions. Although we have long known that these vulnerabilities were mounting, a Government Accountability Office (GAO) report in late 2005 found that the

Department of Homeland Security has yet to develop assessments of the threat of an attack on major computer links, nor has it created plans for recovering key Internet functions in the wake of an attack. "[A] national plan to secure our cybernetworks is virtually nonexistent,"[52] commented an American congresswoman who had requested the GAO report, despite the fact that Presidential Decision Directive 63, adopted in 1998, mandated such a plan.

It is imperative that we anticipate these eventualities and act to preclude them from happening. Other chapters have discussed various means of attacking terrorism and preempting proliferation. Later ones will take up the subject of intervening to prevent gross abuses of human rights and civilian catastrophes. This chapter has dealt with situations that may arise if we fail to avert such an intersection of threats.

As societies, we must come to some understanding of what we're facing, and in these times of relative tranquillity organize ourselves and debate what we will do if a catastrophe should come to pass. We will have to develop habits of greater vigilance, including especially the inspection of travelers for disease and of cargo for pests, weapons, and viruses. The acquisition of such "supply side" habits is not unprecedented; our watchfulness crossing the street, which we take for granted, was generally unnecessary before the eighteenth century.[53] As I urged at the beginning of this chapter, we should store up laws for such an eventuality, just as we lay away vaccines and antibiotics. Then we will have an excellent chance of getting through attacks with systems of consent in place. If we don't do this, if we are lulled into complacency by the observation that the Wars against Terror are not another Second World War; if we lapse into cynicism, responding to the warnings of our leaders with the reaction that they are exaggerating the threat for political gain; if we don't use the democratic process to put laws in place now, then in a way we become the ally of the terrorists because when a truly terrible series of mass atrocities or catastrophes really does occur we will be propelled into an indefinite period of martial law. We will have brought into being a system in which democracy has collapsed, and the State has become the source of terror itself; it will have become the disease of which it purports to be the cure (in Karl Kraus's famous phrase). No, bin Laden isn't going to invade the U.K. and occupy Westminster. We are unlikely to see Ayman al Zawahiri in the House of Lords. If Britain becomes a state of terror it will be because we did not prepare when we had the time and the peace to do so by law and by consensual processes.

The United States could do the same thing. If we are busy casting aside laws, the one steady craft we have to get through this period, Washington will turn America into a state of terror. When we are hit with terrible attacks, perhaps repeatedly over some time, we will complete the task of this transformation ourselves. We will confront this fate with repugnance at first, of course, and then with reluctance, then with desperation, and finally with resignation.

> *The hundreds of windows filling with faces*
> *Because of something that happened on the street,*
> *Something no one is able to explain,*
> *Because there was no fire engine, no scream, no gunshot,*
> *And yet here they all are assembled,*
> *Some with hands over their children's eyes,*
> *Others leaning out and shouting*
> *To people walking the streets far below*
> *With the same composure and serene appearance*
> *Of those going for a Sunday stroll*
> *In some other century, less violent than ours.*

—Charles Simic, "The Alarm"

PART III

STRATEGY AND LAW IN THE INTERNATIONAL THEATER OF TERROR

There is nothing more difficult to carry out, nor more doubtful of success, nor more dangerous to handle, than to initiate a new order of things.

—Niccolò Machiavelli

CHAPTER NINE

The Illusion of an
American Strategic Doctrine

Nothing can come of nothing.

—William Shakespeare, *King Lear*, 1.192

IN 1821, Czar Alexander I declared that all coastal land bordering on the Pacific Ocean from the Bering Strait to 51° north latitude henceforth belonged to Russia, a claim that cut deeply into the Oregon Territory of the United States. At the same time, the czar forbade all foreign shipping within 100 miles of the coastline. The American secretary of state, John Quincy Adams, replied to the Russian declaration with a diplomatic note refusing to recognize the Russian claims. Adams had taken the position in President James Monroe's cabinet that the U.S. "should contest the right of Russia to *any* territorial establishment on [our] continent," adding that "we should assume distinctly the principle that the American continents are no longer subjects for *any* new European colonial establishments."[1] The means of enforcing such a principle, however, lay well beyond the American state when events far from Alaska took an unexpected turn.

On August 16, 1823, Richard Rush, the U.S. ambassador to the Court of St. James's, was summoned to Whitehall for an urgent meeting with George Canning, the British foreign secretary. They met against the background of still-breaking events on the continent of Europe. Spanish revolutionaries had recently arrested King Ferdinand VII and proclaimed a constitutional monarchy. This revolution followed uprisings in Latin America that had deprived Spain of most of her American colonies, and established new republics. Now, in response to events in Spain, the three reactionary members of the Holy Alliance—Russia, Prussia, and Austria—were trying to persuade France to mount an invasion of Spain in order to rescue Ferdinand. If this happened, President Monroe believed that the alliance would then attempt to regain lost Spanish colonies in Latin America, requiring the U.S. either to abandon these fledgling republics to conquest and subjugation or to intervene militarily on their behalf.

Rush probed British intentions by observing that "should France ultimately effect her purposes in Spain, there was at least the consolation left that Great Britain would not allow her to go further and lay her hands upon the Spanish colonies."[2] To which Canning unexpectedly replied by asking "what I thought [the U.S.] Government would say to going hand in hand with his, in the same sentiment."[3] This took Rush by surprise; after all the U.S. had less than half the merchant tonnage of Britain and a navy with only one-sixteenth as many guns. Why would Britain, with which the U.S. had fought a war that ended only eight years before, seek to ally itself with such an insignificant maritime partner?

On August 22 Rush received a letter from Canning. It contained a five-point reformulation of British policy on the issue of European interests in the Americas: that Britain did not herself desire new colonies in the Americas; that Britain believed that Spain could never recover its colonies on its own; that Britain nevertheless would wait before recognizing the new governments in Latin America; that Britain would not act to prevent an amicable reunion between Spain and the former colonies, in the unlikely event this could be negotiated; and most importantly that Britain would not see any portion of these colonies transferred to any other power with indifference. The letter then asked what the United States would do?

Rush replied that nonentanglement in European affairs had been American policy since President Washington's administration. Indeed President Monroe regarded the Europeans as uniquely fated for violent state quarrels, from which the U.S. should stay resolutely apart.

To this Canning, on September 18 in another face-to-face encounter, replied that

> however just such a policy might have been formerly, or might continue to be as a general policy, he appreciated that powerful and controuling circumstances made it [inappropriate] on the present occasion. . . . [The United States] were the first power established on that continent, and now confessedly the leading power. . . . Were the great political and commercial interests which hung upon the destinies of the new Continent, to be canvassed and adjusted in this hemisphere without the co-operation or even knowledge of the United States? . . . He hoped not . . .[4]

Rush sent Canning's invitation to collaboration to Washington, D.C. Monroe considered accepting it outright, but was dissuaded by Adams. Instead the two men crafted a statement of U.S. policy asserting two basic tenets: the first, based on Adams's negotiations with Baron Tuyl, the Russian ambassador, declared that the U.S. would oppose any new colonization by European imperial states in the Americas; the second, drawing on

Rush's conversations with Canning, announced that the U.S. would "view any interposition" in the affairs of the nations of the Western Hemisphere "for the purpose of oppressing them, or controlling in any other manner their destiny, . . . as the manifestation of an unfriendly disposition toward the United States."[5] By December 2, these ideas had become the center-piece of President Monroe's annual message to Congress. The president reemphasized that the U.S. would not take part in European wars, but expressed alarm that the Holy Alliance might impose its political system in the Western Hemisphere. The United States would regard such an attempt, he said, as "dangerous to our peace and safety."[6] The message picked up Canning's words and said that the American government could not "behold such interposition in any form with indifference."[7]

Thus was born the most famous of American foreign policy pronounce-ments, the Monroe Doctrine. It was not approved by Congress; it was not an American idea; and it was not enforceable by American means. Yet it had the effect of cooling the ambitions of European states to reverse the trend toward republicanism in the American hemisphere. It was breathtak-ingly anti-imperial,[8] in the very teeth of the advance of the imperial state nation, for it did not claim Latin America as a locus for new U.S. or British colonies but rather offered protection for the newly liberated states.

Since that time the United States has rarely offered such statements. Subsequent presidential doctrines number fewer than ten. These doctrines do not say when the U.S. will actually intervene, but rather when it will regard itself as rightfully contemplating intervention. Some are proscrip-tive, declaring the parameters of forbidden acts (like the Monroe or Stim-son doctrines). Some are prescriptive, announcing the intention to pursue specific geopolitical aspirations (like the Truman or Johnson doctrines). All reflect the evolving interface between a great state's strategic rules for itself and the rules of international law.

The earliest of the twentieth century doctrines of this kind was announced by Theodore Roosevelt as no more than an adumbration to the Monroe Doctrine. The Roosevelt Corollary, as it is known, asserts the right of the United States to intervene in Central America if instability is severely threatened from within or from abroad.

The Stimson Doctrine, promulgated in a note of January 7, 1932, addressed to Japan and China, stated that the United States would not rec-ognize any arrangements in China that might violate the Open Door Pol-icy[9] or subvert the Kellogg-Briand Pact against war.[10] As such, it was an attempt to prevent depredations against the weakened Chinese state. When Japan invaded China in 1931 and created the puppet state of Manchukuo, however, there was little the United States could do.

The Truman Doctrine was a direct response to communist insurgencies in Turkey and Greece. On March 12, 1947, President Truman spoke to a special session of Congress, saying that the "seeds of totalitarian regimes are nurtured by misery and want" and that unless the U.S. offered help, its own security would be imperiled. "[I]t must be the policy of the United States to support free peoples who are resisting attempted subjugation by armed minorities or outside pressures." This puts the Truman Doctrine in the category of the prescriptive—promising support for embattled democratic regimes—in contrast to the Stimson Doctrine, which simply declined to acquiesce in, and thus legitimate, what it deemed to be an unlawful or unfriendly act by a foreign state. The Truman Doctrine announced the policy of containment toward communist expansion and thus was a foundational element in the foreign policy of eight subsequent presidents.

This was followed ten years later by the Eisenhower Doctrine, which stated that the United States would intervene in the Middle East if any government threatened by a communist takeover requested aid.

Having witnessed firsthand the 1962 Cuban Missile Crisis, and thus the potential consequences of a Soviet client state in the hemisphere, in 1965 President Lyndon B. Johnson announced that the United States would henceforth prevent by force "a communist dictatorship" from coming to power in the Americas. That year he sent 24,000 troops to the Dominican Republic to accomplish this task in the political chaos that followed the assassination of the dictator Rafael Trujillo. Elections were successfully held and U.S. forces withdrawn. These three doctrines—Truman, Eisenhower, and Johnson—all proclaimed the bases for U.S. intervention.

The Nixon Doctrine asserted that the United States would in the future rely on local allies to handle the hot flare-ups of the Cold War. The U.S. would furnish military and economic assistance but would expect the country directly threatened to assume the primary responsibility of providing troops for its defense. This doctrine led to the policy of Vietnamization—turning over to the South Vietnamese an increasing role in their own defense while American forces were drawn down. Prescriptive in nature, it failed when the U.S. Congress refused to continue material assistance to its ally in Saigon even though the North Vietnamese had openly violated the Geneva Accords of 1973 by invading the south with overwhelming force.[11]

By contrast the proscriptive Carter Doctrine harkened back to the Monroe and Stimson precedents. Reacting to a perception of looming crisis in the Persian Gulf arising from the Soviet invasion of Afghanistan and the Iranian revolution, President Carter announced that the United States would regard any attempt by any outside force to gain control of the Persian Gulf region as an assault on the vital interests of the U.S. Such an attempt would be repelled "by use of any means necessary"—which implied a possible resort to nuclear weapons. Then the Reagan Doctrine swung back to the prescriptive pole, asserting a commitment to low-intensity military action by supporting local anticommunist guerrillas in their struggles with Soviet clients in Afghanistan, Nicaragua, Angola, Ethiopia, and elsewhere in the Third World.

Now we have the Bush Doctrine, which resonates a bit with both traditions. Proscriptively, it claims that certain states, owing to their unlawful character, do not have the sovereign right to arm themselves (or their terrorist surrogates) with weapons of mass destruction or to support terrorists; that the U.S. has the lawful right to act preemptively to prevent such threatening proliferation and to destroy terrorists wherever they may be found; and that if international organizations do not act to prevent such threats from coming into being, the U.S. will do so unilaterally.

> [W]e will not hesitate to act alone, if necessary, to exercise our right of self-defense by acting preemptively against . . . terrorists, to prevent them from doing harm against our people and our country . . . We must be prepared to stop rogue states and their terrorist clients before they are able to threaten or use weapons of mass destruction against the United States and our allies and friends. . . . The greater the threat, the greater is the risk of inaction—and the more compelling the case for taking anticipatory action to defend ourselves, even if uncertainty remains as to the time and place of the enemy's attack.[12]

There is a good deal of sense in the proscriptive, anticipatory elements of this doctrine, though they are wildly controversial at present. In retrospect, passively awaiting the fruition of al Qaeda's programs in Afghanistan was an unsustainable policy; only the timing of al Qaeda's premature strikes on 9/11 prevented that policy from being a truly historic blunder. Imagine the situation if al Qaeda had waited, secure in a sovereign state, until Afghanistan had acquired WMD from allies in Pakistan.

Prescriptively, the Bush Doctrine asserts the need to reform the political societies of the world by introducing democracy and the recognition of human rights where these are currently suppressed, especially in the Middle East. By contrast, there is a good deal of support for the proposition that, as the president said, for "[s]ixty years . . . Western nations [have been] excusing and accommodating the lack of freedom in the Middle East"[13] while proclaiming their commitment to democracy, limits on the absolute power of the State, and human rights.

The difficulty with the Bush Doctrine is that the prescription (advance democracy in the world and notably in the Middle East) and the proscription (states that threaten the U.S. either directly via WMD or indirectly through terrorists render themselves vulnerable to American intervention) are not entirely in synch with each other. It's not just that in many, and perhaps the most important, theaters of conflict the pursuit of one element of the Bush Doctrine does not advance the other; it is rather that in country after country, and *especially* in the Middle East, the imposition of democracy will decrease American safety from WMD proliferation and global terrorism, while the pursuit of unilateral preventive intervention will isolate the U.S. and provoke antidemocratic coalitions.

There is a cure for this, as the administration is well aware. The U.S. can separate the two elements of the doctrine, intervening for well-recognized security reasons and then imposing democracy as the only acceptable postwar alternative (after all, the U.S. did not fight Japan and Germany in order to impose parliamentary democracies so much as to protect the democracy it had) on the one hand and proposing democratic reforms ad hoc where these seem pragmatic (that is, when U.S. security interests are served—in Myanmar, not China; in Zimbabwe, not Bosnia) on the other. The difficulty with this move is that it converts a strategic and legal doctrine into a tactical and lawless jumble of policies. They may be the right policies—perhaps a jumble is appropriate to our chaotic times—but if these are U.S. policies, then there is no Bush Doctrine.

Consider each of the two elements. First, let us examine the bases for the claim that the U.S. ought to be able to preempt certain states seeking WMD. Strategically, once a hostile state has achieved a significant WMD capability, there is little effective action that can be taken against it, and in the case of regional predations that do not threaten the vital interests of the U.S., containment of such a state is highly difficult. If Saddam Hussein had only waited eighteen months to complete his nuclear program before annexing Kuwait it is doubtful a 500,000-person force could have been safely assembled to dislodge him. In the case of a WMD threat developing against an American or British city, simply waiting for the attack in the sure confidence that it will be deterred can be a costly policy. Before 9/11 the U.S. waited to confront al Qaeda; it waited too long. Such developments must be anticipated and met before they mature into an actual threat.[14] Deterrence is unlikely to succeed, in any case, where it depends upon targeting for retaliation a terrorist network that is global and decentralized and presents no appropriate targets. Even when deterrence is relied upon to impede a conventional state, when the politics of that state are bent towards compulsion by terror—against its own people, and against its perceived enemies—it is scarcely inconceivable that an errant weapon will be diverted to an extremist group that has lost patience with the more cautious state administration, or will be unsheathed in a quest for martyrdom.[15]

As a legal matter, international law has long recognized a right of self-defense against imminent attack. The criteria are expressed in the famous *Caroline* case.

In 1837 Canadian rebels, operating out of a base on Navy Island in Lake Ontario, were receiving arms and men transported from Buffalo on the *Caroline,* a private schooner. On December 29, a party of British marines crossed into American waters, set the *Caroline* on fire, and cut her adrift to be carried across Niagara Falls by the current. Several of her crew were killed though she ran aground before actually going over the falls. The British ambassador, Henry Fox, justified the attack on the ground of preemptive self-defense. In reply, the American secretary of state, Daniel Webster, wrote that a state has a right of preemptive self-defense only where the "necessity of that self-defense is instant, overwhelming, and leaving no choice of means, and no moment for deliberation."[16]

As a matter of law, it is certainly true that any right of self-defense implies a right to act while action is still possible. The test for imminence is applied to the harm, not to the overt act sought to be prevented. As one commentator has observed, "if waiting for 'imminence' implies waiting until it is no longer possible to act effectively such a right would be illusory."[17]

In 2004, the U.N. secretary general convened the High-level Panel on Threats, Challenges and Change. The conclusions of this panel state clearly that "any group seeking to attack civilians is guilty of terrorism; that the right of self-defense includes thwarting an imminent attack, without waiting for the actual dire event . . . ; and that reckless regimes should not be entitled to acquire weapons of mass destruction."[18]

"Whatever one calls it," concluded a prominent international lawyer, "the doctrine that states sponsoring terror groups should not be permitted to develop weapons of mass destruction is inherent in the current security environment."[19]

Thus there are both strategic and legal grounds for this element of the Bush Doctrine. That is also true for the claim that the U.S. ought to support the development of democracy, respect for human rights, and the rule of law. From a strategic point of view, states that adhere to these principles are more difficult to rouse to aggression and more respectful of their treaty commitments. From a legal stance, many international treaties and institutions recognize the desirability of "democracy plus"—the set of practices that goes much further than mere popular representation and includes also free markets, rights of conscience, the recognition of minorities, equal legal status for women, and so on—in other words, the contemporary state of consent.

The difficulties with the Bush Doctrine arise when one tries to reconcile its two elements. The invasion of Iraq is instructive. It is true that the Coalition invaded Iraq in order to preempt its acquisition of WMD and that in the aftermath the Coalition imposed a democracy that is broadly supported by the Iraqi people, the United Nations, and the international community. But that backing does not validate the invasion in either law or strategy, and in any case it is doubtful that the invasion was undertaken in order to bring democracy to the Middle East, whatever the post hoc justifications. Indeed, in terms of promoting the rule of law and democracy plus, whatever the merits of the invasion—which was undertaken according to the first, preemptive rule of the doctrine, thus bypassing multilateral institutions and employing a force that was pathetically inadequate for the purposes of pacification and democratization—the occupation has been a disaster precisely because it aroused an implacable and bloody resistance that has crippled economic development and has presented the elected government with insurmountable security challenges. The rule of law has more or less completely broken down in the wake of the sectarian killings that followed the collapse of the Baathist government.

As Paul Berman concluded in a symposium addressing the Bush Doctrine:

> There is an obvious way to go about launching military actions that deploy large numbers of troops and observe liberal principles and encourage a new political culture, and this obvious way is to make use of the elephantine mechanisms of law and multilateral institutions. The first strand of the Bush Doctrine emphasizes the military value of being sleek, agile, and indifferent to world opinion, but the second emphasizes the military value of actions that are plodding, punctilious and popular.[20]

Equally disturbing, the attempt to promote democracy plus has undermined—and if pursued convincingly will radically erode—the West's strategic position in the Middle East.

Polling in many countries allied with the U.S. in the Middle East, and also in Pakistan, indicates that free and fair elections would bring the most violent anti-Western elements to power. As Josef Joffe wrote, "[R]emoving the Abdullahs and Hosnis will bring on a new tyranny under the green flag of the Prophet."[21] We have already seen this in the popular uprising in Iran in 1978, in the aborted Algerian election in 1991, and in the 2006 elections in Gaza that gave Hamas power and ended the truce with Israel. Popular attitudes toward the West are most hostile, according to recent polling, in Jordan, America's closest Arab ally and a state with which the U.S. has a free trade union; in Egypt, the recipient of almost $3 billion in U.S. aid annually; and in Pakistan, which has a long-standing security relationship with the U.S.[22]

There is nothing wrong with the Bush administration's emphasis on promoting democracy. Indeed, the U.S. has been a decisive force in the transition from dictatorship to democracy in Nicaragua, El Salvador,

Guatemala, Haiti, Chile, Panama, the Philippines, South Korea, Lebanon, Georgia, and Ukraine. None of these states, however, posed the threat of acquiring WMD, and none provided any significant support for international terrorists.

The incompatibility of these two elements of the Bush Doctrine is made even more apparent if we attempt to generalize it to theaters outside the Middle East. Are the U.S. and its allies prepared to impose economic sanctions (to say nothing of an ad hoc coalition invasion) on China, whose political system has little role for democratic practices and for the rule of law and in many respects holds these ideals in contempt? What of North Korea, whose internal political system is even more vile than that of Saddam Hussein, if such things can be measured? The Bush Doctrine would use unilaterally organized violence to prevent rogue states—states outside the democratic pale—from acquiring WMD. Yet both China and North Korea are at present in the process of adding to their arsenals of WMD as rapidly as possible. What deference is the U.S. prepared to grant Hugo Chávez of Venezuela or his new ally, Evo Morales of Bolivia, because they came to power through democratic elections, if either is found to be pursuing WMD or supporting terrorists?

Even if the Bush Doctrine is confined to the Middle East, the most telling case that reveals its incoherence—owing to the inconsistency of its two strands—is that of Iran, where, far from providing guidance, it has paralyzed U.S. policy. Iran's president, Mahmoud Ahmadinejad, enjoys widespread popular support; indeed, his public popularity had sharply increased precisely because he has believed to be pursuing nuclear weapons. A preemptive invasion would deny the Iranian people's right to choose their own leader; deference to Iranian popular sovereignty would empower a radical state that is committed to the absolute destruction of its neighbor and has a long history of supporting terrorism. The Bush Doctrine is simply irrelevant to the only realistic course available: market state bribery (including a security guarantee from intervention, as well as access to nuclear energy), multilateral economic sanctions, and an aggressive, long-term campaign to expand the opportunities (political as well as economic) of Iran's citizens and denuclearization of the register.

Is President Bush's announcement really the statement of a presidential doctrine, or is it merely the statement of something far less overarching—a tactical policy?[23] To answer this we should examine the purpose of presidential doctrines of foreign policy.

We announce rules for ourselves in order to influence others, to provide guidance to our own officials, and to inform the public. Yet a national security doctrine does something more than this because any official white paper would also fulfill these functions.

Doctrines like the Monroe Doctrine are supposed to establish neutral,

general principles. By "doctrine" I mean a statement of official government policy in foreign affairs and military strategy. "Neutral" describes a
proposition that will guide behavior in the future, regardless of who is
president or what party is in power. "General" denotes a rule that applies to
more than one situation and is conceived to govern a whole class of cases.
The Convention on International Civil Aviation, for example, sets forth
rules governing the regulation of international air travel. The United States
is a party to the convention and therefore applies its rules whenever confronted with an issue related to international air travel. It does not invent
new criteria when American administrations change (therefore it embodies
neutral principles); it does not change depending on the nationality of an
aircraft (therefore it is general in application).[24] The U.S. is a party to the
Montevideo Convention, which determines the criteria for the recognition
of states.[25] When a new regime comes to power and meets these criteria for
international recognition (a permanent population; a defined territory; a
functioning government; the capacity to enter into relations with other
states), the U.S. is obliged to accept that government as a state (though not
necessarily to have diplomatic relations with it). It does not matter whether
the U.S. president, who is the "sole organ of American foreign affairs,"* is
a Democrat or a Republican; it does not matter whether the state in question is pro- or anti-American. In rendering the decision to treat the state as
a legal entity under international law, the president is obliged to do so on
the basis of the principles laid down in the convention (e.g., "the political
existence of the state is independent of recognition by the other states").

The idea of neutral, general principles is usually associated with the
rule of law,[26] not with strategy. Like the rule of law, however, strategic
needs can also be served by the creation and application of neutral, general
principles. Doctrine is where law and strategy meet. Whether proscriptive
or prescriptive (and all presidential doctrines are something of both, being
categorized by their predominant character), a doctrine like the Monroe or
Johnson doctrines should tell us not simply what, but why. It does not
merely announce a shift in tactics—how we will accomplish our goals—
but also on what basis we will act in the first place.

Contrast such presidential doctrines with a well-known tactical policy,
the Weinberger-Powell Doctrine, named for Casper Weinberger, the secretary of defense under President Reagan, and Colin Powell, the chairman
of the Joint Chiefs of Staff under President George H. W. Bush (and later
secretary of state under President George W. Bush).

---

*This familiar but often misunderstood phrase from *United States v. Curtiss-Wright*, 299 U.S. 304
(1936) has recently been reaffirmed by the U.S. Supreme Court in *Pasquantino v. United States*, 125 S.
Ct. 1766 (2005). It comes from a speech by then congressman John Marshall in 1800. See H. Jefferson
Powell, *The President's Authority over Foreign Affairs: An Essay in Constitutional Interpretation*
(Carolina Academic Press, 2002).

This doctrine sets six criteria for U.S. armed intervention: vital American interests must be at stake; there must be a clear intention to seek military victory; goals must be clearly defined; support by Congress and the public must be assured; a continual reassessment of the forces employed and their objectives must take place; and force must be a last resort. These rules are clear, but they do not specify on what basis force should be used. Though the rules provide neutral, general principles, they do not constitute a doctrine in the same sense as the presidential doctrines discussed earlier. The principles themselves are procedural, not substantive.

For many reasons the Weinberger-Powell Doctrine is at present inoperable. These criteria would not have prevented U.S. intervention in Vietnam, as is sometimes advertised, but would have stopped action in Bosnia and Kosovo and quite possibly the second invasion of Iraq.

Because the Bush Doctrine—to be fair, it should be noted that President Bush has never called it such—fails to provide neutral, general principles for action, it is not a doctrine at all. It tells us what we might do (use preemptive action, act unilaterally) but not when we should do these things—not, that is, on what basis we will act. It tells us what we are seeking (democratic reform) but not what we plan to do to bring this about. When we try to square the circle by connecting the means offered by the doctrine (unilateral action, preemption of the acquisition of WMD, counterterrorism) to its ends (promoting democracy), the doctrine falls apart. It is highly implausible that the president intended to suggest that the U.S. would, or should, use preemptive military strikes to impose democracy, or that democracy, whether imposed or not, supplies a check on proliferation, terrorism, or ethnic cleansing. By assuming that (1) a rogue state is an undemocratic one, (2) that the terrorists who threaten the U.S. and its allies are clients of such states, and finally that (3) the failure to win multilateral endorsement, rather than the imminence of peril, triggers a legal right of U.S. intervention, the advocates of the Bush Doctrine vitiated the legal and strategic strengths of both democracy promotion and counterproliferation, and invited a charge of empire seeking.

But does the U.S. need such a doctrine at all? Why can't the sole remaining superpower do pretty much what it wants, when it wants? Why can't the U.S. act as it thinks best, according to the situation? After all, announcing a doctrine, particularly in a period of great uncertainty, runs the risk that the U.S. will find itself compelled to violate that doctrine when circumstances unpredictably change.

The U.S. needs a strategic doctrine *because* it must confront a period of such uncertainty, a period not only of unpredictability but also of importance and, as we shall see, of opportunity. For without a doctrine, it is almost impossible to marshal the legitimacy abroad and domestically to sustain a course of action that contemplates the use of force. Paradoxically, it is in periods of transition that transparent rules are most useful: they may fail, but they will fail publicly, and the new rules that emerge will have a foundation of understanding to support them. If our publics, and those of our allies, are aware of what rules we are trying to enforce—for ourselves as well as others—then debate and persuasion are possible. But if there are no rules or principles, then positions harden and exchanges degenerate into soliloquies—gestural,[27] emotive, irreconcilable.

The president of the Council on Foreign Relations, Richard Haass, observed in an essay:

> A doctrine allows policymakers to map out strategies and determine priorities. Those strategies and priorities in turn guide decisions of long-term importance, like where to invest the country's intelligence and diplomatic assets, as well as how to deploy its military forces and channel its assistance programs. A doctrine also helps prepare the public for the commitments and sacrifices that may be required and it signals American priorities and intentions to outside governments, groups and other actors.[28]

We are entering an era of turbulent and even dangerous change, such as has occurred less than half a dozen times in the last five centuries. The dominance of the nation state, codified in the practices and constitutions of the last 130 years, will give way. It is our task to manage this kind of transition, which in the past has been accompanied by the state-rending violence of epochal wars. Modestly different decisions today will take us to very different futures decades hence, including future wars. It is in periods such as these that new rules are laid down.

When the U.S. absents itself from international affairs, it makes conflicts *within* regions more likely, as we saw on the Asian subcontinent and most disturbingly in the Middle East. When the U.S. acts unilaterally, as with the denunciation of the Kyoto Protocol or the steel tariff announcement, it runs the risk of alienating allies and creating conflicts *among* regions. Only by managing coalition efforts can these two pitfalls be avoided. The U.S. should be the world's greatest producer, marketer, and distributor of collective goods such as multilateral coalition building, extending deterrence in order to prevent nuclear proliferation, and devising regimes that protect the environment.

Containment was a useful doctrine for the U.S. during the Cold War, but as we learned with Saddam Hussein, containment abandoned the civil population to an apparently endless period of degradation whose effects are still being felt. The purpose of a new presidential doctrine ought to be to prevent the emerging market states of the world from becoming states of terror. This purpose recognizes the deep changes that are under way in the nature of the State, changes that will engulf every country. The most recent political leader who seemed to best understand this was Tony Blair.

Blair has for several years attempted to put into place the foundation for a new legal and strategic doctrine for the democracies. This is evident, for example, in his 1999 addresses in Chicago and to the North Atlantic Council, in which he described a future where NATO could be adapted to become the military arm of the world order of states of consent rather than a strictly defensive alliance confined to the European theater. Blair consistently campaigned for a foreign policy doctrine that would link military action in Kosovo, Sierra Leone, Afghanistan, and Iraq, on the one hand, with diplomatic action on climate change, world trade, aid to Africa, and progress between Israel and Palestine, on the other, by stressing the common challenge to the values of states of consent that all these issues raise.

> The basic thesis is that the defining characteristic of today's world is its interdependence; that whereas the economics of globalisation are well matured, the politics of globalisation are not; and that unless we articulate a common global policy based on common values, we risk chaos threatening our stability, economic and political . . . "We" is not the West. . . . "We" are those who believe in religious tolerance, openness to others, to democracy, liberty and human rights administered by secular courts. . . . We can no more opt out of this struggle than we can opt out of the climate changing around us.[29]

This awareness of the interconnectedness of the various elements of the new strategic environment was a constant theme in Blair's speeches. In a series of addresses, for example, Blair developed the theme of "global interdependency," which is a counterweight to regionalism.

> The critics will say: but how can the world be a community? Nations act in their own self-interest. Of course they do. But what is the lesson of the financial markets, climate change, international terrorism, nuclear proliferation or world trade? It is that our self-interest and our mutual interests are today inextricably woven together.[30]

> We are all internationalists now whether we like it or not. We cannot refuse to participate in global markets if we want to prosper. We cannot ignore new political ideas in other countries if we want to innovate. We cannot turn our backs on conflicts and the violation of human rights within other countries if we want still to be secure.[31]

This is a moment of great opportunity for the United States, for the United Kingdom, and for the European Union. There are important precedents for this undertaking. In the nineteenth century Great Britain abolished the slave trade, established the principle of the freedom of the seas, and built lighthouses and ports available to all. In the twentieth century, American presidential administrations established global institutions that brought together the capital markets and ingenuity of North America, Western Europe, and Japan. These administrations took care of American interests by taking care of the interests of others, principally by maintaining an open trading system and relatively stable prices. Above all they created, funded, and maintained international institutions, including NATO, the World Bank, the U.N., the International Monetary Fund, and GATT (the General Agreement on Trade and Tariffs), "that embedded America's welfare in the well-being of the rest of the world."[32] These were appropriate institutions of, and for, a society of nation states. They emphasized legal regulation, the equality of states, and collective security. Market states have yet to develop appropriate institutions on this scale.

What is lacking in order to respond to the remaking of the global strategic environment that is under way and the emergence of market states is far more than a declaratory policy of preemption. We need a systematic renovation of our thinking, roughly like that which occurred during the First World War when the U.S. emerged from isolation to become a great power.[33] Then, as now, states were called upon to find new bases for legitimacy, both internationally and domestically. Legitimacy makes possible the production of collective goods internationally. Legitimacy will also make possible the production of public goods at home, often by private actors, that can mitigate the negative domestic effects of the transition to market states.

Similarly, after the Second World War was terminated by the use of atomic bombs, there appeared a group of intellectuals who, in a remarkably short period of time, developed the concepts of nuclear deterrence to reform the theory of strategic bombing that had dominated the prenuclear era.[34]

Now we desperately need a body of theory to understand the Wars on Terror. It is shocking that, years after 9/11, the U.S. government has generated no consensus on the general nature of the struggle we face.[35] The core of the struggle has to do with the threats to the legitimacy of the market state of consent, brought about by the destruction of civilian life on a mass scale, and the efforts by our adversaries to place blame for this destruction on the states of consent.

How is it that so-called rogue states (states that are non-democratic, do not respect human rights, prey upon their neighbors, etc.) or terrorists or human catastrophes like the tsunami or a hurricane delegitimate the state of consent? There are the obvious ways: if governments are unable to protect the well-being of civilians, then it is possible that their publics will turn to more authoritarian constitutional regimes. This could occur in the wake of a threatening regional lunge (in Japan, for example, if North Korea is able to co-opt South Korea through nuclear threats; in Israel, if Iran acquires nuclear weapons and continues its rhetoric of extermination), or as the result of a terrorist attack with WMD, or even in the aftermath of a terrible epidemic, perhaps especially one whose causes are unclear. These are the obvious ways.

There is another, more insidious path, however, by which states of consent are delegitimated. It comes about through the very practices by which consent is assured, that is, through the press and public debate. It is the result of the charge, repeated in a thousand ways, that we—the states of consent—are responsible for the terrorist attacks against us and our forces. Although, as previously argued, this struggle will by no means be limited to attacks by radical Islamists, their war with the West and her allies gives a good example of how the stakes I have described are in play.

With respect to that war, the delegitimating argument I have in mind runs this way: (1) On the basis of the principles of sovereignty, what happens internally in other states is a matter that cannot legitimately lead to Western military intervention so long as we in the West are not directly and immediately threatened; (2) having rejected this premise regarding sovereignty, and having injected ourselves into the affairs of other countries by force, we have caused a counterreaction leading to armed resistance to our interventions and the recruitment of terrorists to strike at our societies; (3) thus every new beheading or attack on Coalition troops in Iraq or NATO forces in Afghanistan is fresh proof that it was a mistake to put our soldiers in these theaters in the first place; (4) and every terrorist attack on our own countries is no more than a reasonable reaction to the depredations we have visited on others.

This argument has the most profound consequences for democracy. This is obvious with respect to Afghanistan or Iraq, where democracy is fighting for its life and where the implications of this approach—a rapid withdrawal of NATO and Coalition forces—would abandon the nascent democratic regimes in these countries to their ruthless enemies. It is less obvious, but also true, that this is the case with regard to established democracies. That is because this argument legitimates the attack on these societies by terrorists, and withdraws legitimacy from those democratically elected regimes that continue to sustain their interventions despite widespread public protests. One hears all of these elements in the videotaped statement of Mohammed Sidique Khan, released by al Qaeda with a

commentary by al Zawahiri, two months after Khan and a group of terrorists he led attacked civilians in London, causing fifty-six deaths and
wounding more than seven hundred.

1. Until we feel security, you will be our target. Until you stop the
bombing, gassing, imprisonment and torture of my people, we will not
stop this fight.

2. This is how our ethical stances are dictated. Your democratically
elected governments continuously perpetrate atrocities against my
people and your support of them makes you directly responsible, just
as I am directly responsible for protecting and avenging my Muslim
brothers and sisters.

3. [O]ur words have no impact upon you therefore I'm going to talk to
you in a language that you understand. Our words are dead until we
give them life with our blood.[36]

Khan was born in Leeds, and spent most of his life in and around that
English city. He studied at Leeds Metropolitan University. His wife, whom
he met there, worked in the schools assisting pupils with disabilities. He
was employed in the state schools, too, helping immigrant children adapt
to a new educational environment once they arrived in Britain. In the
videotape he announces:

4. We are at war and I am a soldier. Now you too will taste the reality
of this situation.[37]

Only this last remark sets this mild-mannered teacher's assistant apart
from the editorialists at some leading British newspapers and television
channels, or, for that matter, from many American and British academics.
A great many of these persons believe that it is the United States and her
principal allies who are responsible for the violence in Iraq[38] and Afghanistan (point 1), that the terrorist attacks on the democracies that refuse to
withdraw from these countries are to that extent justified and in that way
explicable (point 2), and that these governments, out of stupidity and
relentless folly, refuse to listen to them and must someday relent in the
face of even further violence (point 3).

Hatred of American policy (or, in some cases, simply hatred of the
U.S.) is at the center of this reaction, and so, in the end, only the United
States can answer the charges that George Bush, rather than Osama bin
Laden or Saddam Hussein, is the greatest threat to peace in the world, or
that the U.S. is the most dangerous rogue state. The U.S. must have a

strategic doctrine that persuasively explains why it is intervening in the affairs of other states that do not appear to threaten us, and this must be matched (as will be discussed in the next chapter) by legal doctrines that set the parameters for such interventions.

The best reasons to develop doctrine have to do with legitimacy and how strategy can contribute, or detract, from that legitimacy. In a representative democracy, an explicit doctrine tells the people what to expect from its leaders. It requires something like consensus between the political parties if it is going to last beyond the next election. It brings coherence to the bureaucracy. It tells allies what we intend to do in future cases. It states or implies the moral basis for the war aim that strategy is devised to pursue. Legitimacy is not sufficient for confidence, but without such a foundation, long-term confidence will be hard to come by.

In devising such a strategy we will want to generalize to the global theater of operations those tactics that are appropriate to particular battlegrounds where warfare must be fought "amongst the people" and where the preservation of civil society is an important element in victory. Those tactics, in turn, must reflect our global war aim. The political context of the Wars against Terror requires that the purpose and practice of American and British forces must be governed by humane values.

As suggested in chapter 3, an antiterror regimen for Coalition forces in Iraq would concentrate our arms in those areas we had sufficient troops to fully protect, rather than trying to pacify the entire country.[39] Within that secure area economic and legal resources should be poured in, to create an example of what a rights-respecting society might look like. Gradually, this zone would expand, shrinking the area of operations of the terrorists who opposed it. If we generalize this approach to the global struggle, it implies that while it will be imperative to integrate those parts of the world that have not benefited from globalization,[40] and steadily improve their lot our first objective must be the consolidation of decent health, physical security, free trade, free movement, and the rule of law within states of consent. Any presidential doctrine addressing global strategy in the twenty-first century should be crafted with these objectives in mind.

This is what a new presidential doctrine might look like, whether to combat terrorism or to treat human rights crises or to preempt the proliferation of weapons of mass destruction, for they are all intertwined.

An alliance of democracies* that includes the United States and Great Britain will intervene[41] in three circumstances: when substantial strate-

*An alliance of democracies is discussed in chapters 10 and 12 and in Ivo Daalder and James Lindsay, "An Alliance of Democracies," *Washington Post*, 23 May 2004, 137. The suggested doctrine is mine. I unsuccessfully proposed a similar doctrine while serving in the Clinton adminstration in 1999.

gic interests and substantial humanitarian concerns intersect; or when, absent a vital strategic interest, humanitarian concerns are extremely high owing to an acute crisis—famine, civil war, disease, genocide—and risks are apparently low; or when truly vital strategic interests are in truly imminent danger.

The rationale for intervention lies in the fact that unconventional threats—like the development of WMD for purposes of compellance, extraordinary terrorist threats against civilians, and human catastrophes, whatever their origin—threaten the ability of states to preserve, protect, and defend systems of consent that are manifested in the rights to conscience, political representation, and the protection of human rights. Rather than passively await the fruition of these threats, this alliance must anticipate it, prevent it where possible, and where this proves impossible, mitigate its effects.

Such a doctrine would justify intervention in Haiti (where the U.S. did act) and Rwanda (where it regrettably did not) on the basis of humanitarian concerns, and in Bosnia and Afghanistan, where it had both strategic and humanitarian reasons for action. In Iraq application of this doctrine would have turned on two questions: (1) Would significant Western strategic interests in the region be so imperiled by the acquisition of WMD by Iraq—which would enable it to deter any state that opposed its regional ambitions—that anticipatory action was necessary before these weapons were actually deployed? (2) Could the U.S. and its allies assure the Iraqi people a more prosperous and freer future after such intervention, knowing that war would kill innocent persons and might cause the society to unravel? That is, the issue would have turned on the intersection of strategic and humanitarian issues.

These are difficult questions and we may differ among ourselves as to the right answers. But they are at least some of the right questions. If this proposed doctrine is unacceptable, others need to offer alternatives that would deal with WMD proliferation to such a state, or the maintenance of terror camps by states like the one described here:

> Let us picture a small, comparatively weak nation, governed by someone who commits any number of atrocious crimes to stay in power. Let us assume that the citizens are incapable of overthrowing her by themselves. Let us assume too that all non-violent means have been exhausted, that the dictator shows every sign of living for another 30 years, and has children to succeed her. What, if anything, should the people of more powerful nations call on their governments to do?[42]

A doctrine like the one proposed here structures an answer to this question.

It also suggests how states might collaborate in enforcing such a doctrine. There are immense military resources available to the United States, and we should not underestimate the potential defense capabilities of the European Union. At present, the U.S. share of the NATO budget is greater than that of the E.U. members of the alliance by about 30 percent.[43] Even so, the E.U. countries' combined defense outlays substantially exceed those of Russia and China, as well as every other state save the U.S. The combined armed forces of the E.U. member states are greater than that of the U.S. (about 1.8 million to about 1.5 million);[44] their shortfall is in terms of equipment, training, and air- and sealift capacity. Operating with American resources, however, European manpower can go anywhere, quickly and in force. What these forces do not have is adequate training for combat and the high technology that modern combat involves.

As we saw in chapter 3, however, that sort of combat is only one element in contemporary warfare. At least as important is the role of constabulary forces to protect civilians and maintain order in the aftermath of combat. In 2000 and 2001, about seven times more troops from E.U. countries undertook U.N. peacekeeping missions than did U.S. troops.[45]

To put it the other way around, American units do not have the equipment (including intangibles like foreign languages) and training for effective peacekeeping. Moreover, the American public has little taste for the prolonged exposure of its troops to the hazards of constabulary duties: suicide bombers at checkpoints, snipers firing from apartment houses, improvised explosive devices aimed at convoys.

> The obvious solution, short of a substantial expansion of the U.S. Army, is to continue the now well-established practice of sharing the burdens of peacekeeping with . . . America's European allies, with their relatively generous aid budgets and their [abundant manpower]. If they are not used for peacekeeping, it is hard to see what these soldiers are for, in a Europe that has declared perpetual peace within its own borders and is no longer menaced by Russia.[46]

This cannot be done in the absence of a strategic consensus, which itself can only be forged around a coherent, consistent strategic doctrine.

There are many objections that may be made to this doctrine. It will be said that it blurs the distinction between preemptive and preventive war.

> In a *preemptive* war, you know the enemy is planning to attack you . . .
> A preventative war is fought to prevent a shift in the balance of power,

448 TERROR AND CONSENT

i.e., to prevent an enemy from increasing its capabilities, whether that
enemy has any intention of attacking any time soon or not. . . . It's a
decision for war based on a guess about the future [that] . . . we've all
regarded as illegitimate . . .[47]

Although I am inclined to the view that the various developments in the
threats facing the U.S. and its allies make this distinction invalid, even as it
is posed, the doctrine I propose is scarcely unprecedented. U.S. entry into
World War I was taken to prevent a shift in the balance of power and not
because America feared imminent attack;[48] the Cuban Missile Crisis was
brought to an overt confrontation in order to prevent an enemy from
increasing its capabilities. In a sense, all wars are wars of prevention.
Aggressors do not seek war. They seek victories and are willing to risk war
to gain those victories, should this prove necessary. Wars usually begin
when a state resists aggression. A state whose strategic position is deteriorating will join battle—for it takes two to make war—in order to prevent a
further worsening of its situation.

Then it will be objected that such a doctrine places heavy demands on
accurate intelligence.

Preventive war is always based upon some assumptions about the
future, but the future is always inherently unknowable. . . . [Further-
more,] our leaders won't be able to make all the information at their
disposal public without compromising sources and methods. So the
decision to wage preventive war will always be hotly debated.[49]

Of course this is true. Indeed, it is so true that it proves too much: all
policy decisions are about the future. We cannot evade decisions because
our intelligence agencies are inadequate; we simply try to improve them
and do the best we can with the knowledge that we possess, limited as it is.
There are costs to warfare, and there are costs to doing nothing. The public
will be skeptical of a president who relies on evidence he cannot disclose,
and they should be, but the public is not naïve. As this period wears on, the
citizenry will become more mature consumers of the ambiguities and partial truths of the intelligence product. The debacle of Iraqi WMD will cast
a shadow, but it would be a mistake to think that the opposition to the war
in Iraq—in Europe, in America, in Iraq itself—would be any less determined had a hundred gallons of chemical and biological weapons been
found.

It will also be objected that this doctrine will only entice states to
acquire WMD. If the U.S. and its allies are on the march to preempt the
acquisition of WMD, perhaps the safest route is to acquire these weapons
quickly.

[A] doctrine of preventive war encourages others to start looking for strategies that can check American power . . . How will they do that? By trying to acquire weapons of mass destruction, of course, which will enable them to deter American military intervention.[50]

But this objection assumes that U.S. *doctrine* is the driver behind those states of terror—for they are the only ones to which intervention applies—that seek WMD. Surely that was not the case with either North Korea or Iran, both of which began their nuclear weapons projects many years before the Bush Doctrine was announced. It is implausible that U.S. policy was behind proliferation to Pakistan or India or Israel. What is far more likely is that regional insecurity drives these decisions, and that insecurity is accelerated by American lack of interest. Of course the Iraqi intervention has made an impression—not least on Libya, which has now abandoned its nuclear weapons program—but the sequence of events simply doesn't support the idea that acquiring WMD had never occurred to our enemies (including al Qaeda) before the invasion of Iraq in 2003. Nor does it follow that the surest route to nonintervention lies in a race to acquire weapons of mass destruction, the acquisition of which is the cause of intervention in the first place. The safest, surest, and cheapest route to avoid intervention is a transparent disclosure to the world that a state has no such weapons nor any intention of getting them. If Saddam Hussein had done this, even he—with all his squalid history—would have doubtless avoided intervention by the Coalition.

And, observing the difficulties we face in Iraq, it will be objected that anticipatory war almost necessarily means regime change and occupation in order to prevent a recurrence of the behavior sought to be avoided in the first instance. "The problem, of course . . . is that once you remove the regime, you end up being responsible for running the whole country. . . . [F]oreign occupiers are rarely popular. . . . It didn't work for the Israelis in Lebanon, it didn't work for the Soviets in Afghanistan, and it's not working for us in Iraq."[51]

The evidence for this point is both overwhelming, it seems, and yet rather narrowly tailored. Putting aside the successful regime changes and occupations that have followed many wars of the twentieth century, the invasion of Afghanistan was an anticipatory war and the removal of the Taliban and their replacement by an elected government appears, so far, to have been a success, even if a difficult one. Four million Afghans have returned to their country,[52] which suggests that they at least seem to prefer things as they are now rather than as they were.

Despite many well-known and serious errors, it is simply too soon to conclude that the removal of Saddam Hussein by the Coalition invasion will prove to be a mistake. What is happening in Iraq and in Afghanistan is an experiment to which most precedents (including the occupation of Japan and Germany) are largely irrelevant. Iraq and Afghanistan, along with Turkey, are the most democratic Muslim states in the region. In the last election, more than 8 million Iraqis voted in very dangerous circumstances, a turnout that was higher, proportionately, than that of the last U.S. presidential or British parliamentary elections. It all may be futile. A new despot may arise who seeks WMD just as Saddam Hussein sought them and would have eventually obtained them had he survived in power. But all life is an experiment. Every important decision is taken with inadequate knowledge by imperfect men and women whom the future will confound. Yet we act nevertheless.

That brings us to the final and most troubling objection to be discussed. Doesn't the doctrine I have proposed commit the U.S. to an "endless series of wars and interventions, whenever some problem or whenever some dangerous state emerges"?[53] Two initial points must be borne in mind: first, the doctrine that the U.S. will have the capability and the intention to intervene under certain circumstances does not commit the state to *military* action when it is inappropriate; second, while intervention is a factor in the genocides, the clandestine WMD markets, or the global terrorism it seeks to quell, it is idle to suppose that without the possibility of intervention these events would not occur. The doctrine, on the contrary, is an attempt to prepare the country when these events occur in any case.

Finally, however, it must be acknowledged that such a doctrine accepts that there will always be wars and that some of them will be ones in which we will want to be prepared to participate on the basis of commitments we make reflectively in relative tranquillity rather than in desperate reprisal, having waited too long to act.

———————

Although it is largely forgotten now, the issue of European reconquest of the Latin American independent republics was not the only foreign policy crisis confronting James Monroe. In the spring of 1821, fighting had begun between Greeks and the Ottoman Empire. Because Russia was thought to be behind this insurrection, it was assumed the Czar would intervene and, equally, that if he did not, the Turks would quickly crush the revolt. Neither happened. In early 1822, the Greeks issued a declaration of independence modeled on Thomas Jefferson's, and proclaimed a republican form of government. They appealed to Washington and to the capitals of Europe for help.

Newspapers reported Turkish atrocities. In October 1822 the *National Intelligencer,* Washington's chief broadsheet, declared that nothing occupied the public mind so much as Greece. There were large public rallies in various states on behalf of the Greek revolution. Public addresses and editorials called for American financial and military aid.

In the event, these pleas were not answered. Though Monroe had taken note of the Greek crisis in his message to Congress in December 1822, by the next year, when the Monroe Doctrine was announced, active assistance was out of the question. U.S. intervention in the Balkans on humanitarian grounds would wait for 175 years.

We should fight to protect democracies, not to impose them. Where countries are struggling to become states of consent, we ought to defend them. Wherever people live in fear, we should be found on their side—in Sudan, Zimbabwe, Myanmar, North Korea, Iran—but also in London, New York, Madrid, and even in New Orleans and Dili—bringing the appropriate means at hand to serve the ends of civilian protection and freedom of conscience. These means need not necessarily or even primarily be military, but they must be limited only by our capabilities and our foresight.

Finally, U.S., U.K., and NATO strategic doctrine should be lucid and comprehensive so that all states, regardless of their international allegiances, will know under what circumstances they will *not* be the subject of intervention. As we will see in the next chapter, such a strategic doctrine can then be reflected in a reformed international law.

CHAPTER TEN

Mise-en-Scène:
The Properties of Sovereignty

The law hath not been dead, though it hath slept.

—William Shakespeare, *Measure for Measure*, 2.2.112

EVEN IF AN alliance of the democracies were formed, and even if a strategic doctrine of the kind envisaged in the last chapter were promulgated by that alliance and endorsed by its members, by what right would they act? Would such a doctrine infringe on the rights of those states that rebuffed an invitation to join a transparent alliance (or, more likely, that were not invited in the first place)? These are questions about the most fundamental element of statehood: sovereignty.

I.

At present, the rule of law is eroding because the prevailing doctrines of international law are radically insufficient to regulate the efforts of states that must cope with global, networked terrorism, and with the related threats of weapons of mass destruction, genocide, and overwhelming civilian catastrophes. Mass murder, it has been remarked, has gone "mass market," making anticipatory acts by states an imperative, but the rules of international law have not changed accordingly.

Article 2(4) of the United Nations Charter operates in tandem with Article 51 to establish the code of *jus ad bellum* for the society of nation states (that is, the basis on which a state may lawfully go to war). The former provides the general rule and the latter the exception. The background rule is simply that states may not use violence against other states. Article 2(4): "All members shall refrain in their international relations from the threat* or use of force against the territorial integrity or political indepen-

---

*There is some opinion that Iran's repeated threats against Israel—"to wipe Israel off the map," as Iran's president put it—may have violated this proscription. See David B. Rivkin, Jr., and Lee A. Casey, "A Legal Case Against Iran," *Washington Post*, 6 June 2006, A15.

dence of any state . . ."[1] The foreground exception is to be found in Article 51, the guarantee of a residual right of self-defense. "Nothing in the present Charter shall impair the inherent right of individual or collective self-defense if an armed attack occurs against a Member of the United Nations, until the Security Council has taken measures necessary to maintain international peace and security."[2] Thus Articles 2(4) and 51 not only act together but in concert.

The original understanding of the U.N. Charter was structured by the legal concepts of a society of nation states with *opaque* sovereignty. Each state stands in relation to the society of states as a rights-bearing citizen stands in relation to his individual state. The equal sovereignty of each U.N. member permits it to choose to develop whatever weapons it judges to be necessary for its own defense, and no state may use violence or the threat of violence to prevent this.[3] Similarly, opaque sovereignty assures to every state the supreme authority to govern matters within its domestic jurisdiction, including the exercise of police powers, which are typically involved in incidents of genocide and ethnic cleansing as well as in health crises and other catastrophes.

Yet precautionary threats that anticipate the acquisition by a hostile state of nuclear or biological weapons can come, of necessity, far in advance of the sort of imminent attack that might trigger Article 51. Truly preventative attacks (if not preemptive attacks) appear to be in violation of the charter. Indeed, in the debate at the Security Council over an attack on Iraq, it was never forthrightly urged that the Council should authorize U.N. member states to change the regime by force in order to prevent future weapons proliferation to Iraq. The most recent example of a preventive attack—Israel's destruction of the Iraqi nuclear reactor at Osirak in 1981—was roundly condemned by all members of the Security Council, including the U.S. and the U.K.[4] Many of those who opposed U.S.-U.K. intervention in Iraq argue that the failure to find WMD in that country after the invasion shows that the U.N. sanctions alone were working. On the contrary, it demonstrates that U.S. threats of force compelled Saddam Hussein to accommodate the new inspections regime, yet just such threats of force appear to violate the charter's provisions in Article 2(4).

Humanitarian intervention would also appear to be a violation of the text of the charter and its notions of opaque sovereignty. Indeed, some commentators think that the Universal Declaration of Human Rights is fundamentally at odds with state sovereignty. In 2005,

[t]he U.N. Commission on Human Rights had before it a report on torture in the Sudan [torture is forbidden by Article 5 of the Declaration] from its own special investigator. It described the penalty of "cross amputation"—the right hand and the left foot—[for various crimes

and] noted cases where Sudanese women had been stoned to death for
adultery after trial in a language they did not understand and without
legal representation. A draft resolution condemning this sort of treatment was opposed by Pakistan on behalf of the Organization of the
Islamic Conference. . . . The resolution was defeated. And for good
measure, the investigator's position was shut down.[5]

Nevertheless, humanitarian intervention has been endorsed by the
Security Council. This brings intervention on humanitarian grounds
within the custom and practice of the charter, which has recently come to
reflect ideas of *translucent* sovereignty. On this view, anticipatory intervention can be lawfully undertaken, but only with the Council's blessing.
On the basis of the doctrine of translucent sovereignty, presumably, Iraq
was denied the right to exercise its otherwise sovereign decision to seek
WMD. Such U.N. endorsement is rarely forthcoming, however, because
the Security Council's unanimity requirement tends to block action against
even the most unsavory states when they have the sponsorship of a permanent member. Indian intervention in Bangladesh, NATO intervention in
Kosovo, Vietnamese intervention in Cambodia, all occurred without the
authorization of the Security Council.[6] It has been argued that, as noted
above, the authorizing resolution adopted by the Council following the
Kosovo intervention implies that the initial action has been sanctified *nunc
pro tunc,* but even if this is so, it does not mean that, absent Council action,
states are lawfully empowered to use armed force to achieve humanitarian
objectives in other countries in anticipation of later Council approval. No
one is arguing, I believe, that subsequent U.N. resolutions affirming support for Iraqi reconstruction can be taken as ratifications of the Coalition
invasion. The Kosovo example may mean, however, that the absolute
requirement of U.N. authorization in the absence of an imminent threat to
the intervenor is becoming, as a matter of customary international law, a
nullity.

Chapter 7 of the charter authorizes the Security Council to take appropriate measures to restore international peace and security. It provides no
such authority to interfere in the domestic life of a state, for even the most
horrific internal practices—like North Korea's policy of state-compelled
starvation—do not necessarily spill over, creating regional or multistate
chaos. If these rules are changing, it is because they are inadequate to cope
with the new threats confronting societies and the new sensitivities highly
developed societies have come to share regarding the fate of other peoples.

Perhaps most conspicuous is the current system's inability to deal with
global, international terrorism. We have already seen this in the lack of an
international warrant system, a lack that enables terrorists to move from
one national jurisdiction to another whenever they feel the press of surveil-

lance or fear arrest. Foreign intelligence collection is illegal under domestic laws, which are supposed to be given recognition under current international law. As we saw in chapter 6, the clandestine practice of foreign intelligence operations is essentially outside international law, and in defiance of the state laws within whose jurisdiction it transpires. Since intelligence collection operations are reciprocally tolerated by states nevertheless, this casts doubt on the vitality of the legal rules that are defied. Indeed, the entire system of the laws of war, which is predicated on definitions of warfare, on distinctions between the public and the private, on wars that have a beginning and an end, that are conducted on battlefields, that pit states against other states, is coming unraveled.

> Shifts in the nature of security threats have broken down once clear distinctions between armed conflict and "internal disturbances" that do not rise to the level of armed conflict between states and non-state actors, between combatants and noncombatants, between spatial zones in which conflict is occurring and zones in which conflict is not occurring, between temporal moments in which there is no conflict and temporal moments in which there is conflict and between matters that clearly affect the security of the nation and matters that clearly do not.[7]

On November 4, 2002, an American armed surveillance drone flying in Yemeni airspace launched a missile activated by remote control. The target it struck was an automobile carrying six al Qaeda suspects, one of them an American. All were killed. How is current international law applied to this? If the attack was part of an international armed conflict, then the law of war applies, and the persons believed to be al Qaeda militants were lawfully subject to attack. The government of Yemen appears to have given its consent to the missile launch. But if the attack took place outside a theater of warfare, then ordinary human rights law would apply, and Yemeni consent would be immaterial: the victims should have been tried according to ordinary criminal processes—arrest, indictment, trial, conviction, appeal—before they could have been lawfully executed. It is simply unclear at present what law applies,[8] or indeed whether the "spatial" notion of a zone outside the theater of warfare makes any sense in a global war against terror.

Other instances abound. The system of global terrorist financing depends upon the inability of states to compel other states to disclose financial holdings and transfers. Bulwarks of international law like the Geneva Conventions[9] do not really contemplate the treatment of terrorist organizations that may fight on a battlefield but are not bona fide soldiers of a state, and who may commit murderous crimes but are not, usually, common criminals; who attack the State but are not parties to civil war. If detained, they are often not amenable to conventional prosecutions.[10] The nauseating spectacle of a German court twice releasing co-conspirators in the 9/11 massacres on the grounds that the right of confrontation—the right of an accused to confront his accuser—would be compromised if senior al Qaeda persons held for interrogation were not produced for cross-examination is based not on any extraordinary rationale but one that is routine.[11] Nor is it by any means clear that a tribunal, like the International Criminal Court (ICC), would have the power to try such figures successfully or that such a court would not actually be used to prevent the "snatches" or renditions, interrogations, and uses of lethal force that are important elements in the Wars against Terror. It is just this fear, and the concern about irresponsible and politicized investigations,[12] that has kept the U.S.—under both the Clinton and Bush presidencies—out of the ICC. Yet rather than seeking legal reform, the U.S. has used the inadequacy of the currently prevailing law as a basis for avoiding legal restrictions on government entirely.

> The breakdown of these once reasonably straightforward distinctions gave the U.S. government an opening to argue, among other things, that noncitizen detainees held at Guantanamo Bay, Cuba may be detained indefinitely without charge; that U.S. citizens (including those detained inside the U.S.) may be designated "unlawful combatants" by executive fiat and held indefinitely without charge or access to attorneys; and that the U.S. may kill any suspected terrorist in any state in the world at any time.[13]

Sometimes the elements in international law that would frustrate preemption, humanitarian intervention, and counterterrorism reinforce one another. Thus, before September 11, it was widely held as a matter of international law that U.S. attacks on the training camps in Afghanistan were barred on the grounds that they were preventative in nature and violated the national sovereignty of the Taliban state. As a consequence, as many as sixty thousand jihadists from some fifty-six countries were given terrorist training in Afghan camps during the 1990s and then sent back to their native societies as agents of al Qaeda, while within Afghanistan the Taliban ruled a long-suffering people with sadistic rigor.

These difficulties are systemic and cannot be made good by piecemeal repair—enlargement of the U.N. Security Council, U.S. ratification of the ICC treaty, E.U. adoption of a central intelligence clearing house, to take three of the most widely touted proposals. This does not mean, however, that states are faced with the stark choice of supporting law to the exclusion of strategic concerns (the European Way, one might say) or ignoring law altogether on allegedly strategic grounds (the American Way, at least as of late). On the contrary, the same developments that now demand a union of strategy and law in our thinking are bringing into being a constitutional order that will reflect such a union in its international law. As the fundamental nature of the State itself changes, the leading members of the society of states are moving away from nation state models, including the global system of rules created by and for a society of nation states.

For the law of nations has not been static in the past—it has evolved along with the constitutional order of states—and the remedies for the problems we now face need not be confined to the methods on which we currently rely. Even the briefest glance backward at earlier eras of international law will reveal dramatic, if episodic, evolution. We are now entering a new period of transition in international law.

II.

The international law of the nineteenth century, after the Congress of Vienna and in many respects up until the Peace Conference at Versailles after World War I, constituted a unique period in the development of the international system, just as the international law of earlier constitutional eras was unique to its constitutional orders. Harold Koh has aptly noted that this period saw

> intergovernmental and nongovernmental organizations playing relatively minor roles on the global stage. Custom and state practice formed the primary sources of international law, which served a largely interstitial, laissez-faire function, reflecting vested national interests and leaving large realms of unregulated state activity.[14]

This was the international law of the great imperial state nations.[15] It was superseded by a legal environment—that of the nation state—that was more regulatory and less customary in nature. Francis Lieber drafted a codification of the laws of war, which were promulgated by President Lincoln as General Orders No. 100 during the American Civil War; Jean Henri Dunant began the movement, at almost precisely the same time, that culminated in the Geneva Conventions.[16]

> The [twentieth century] introduced a new era, which has been characterized as that of international *institutions* rather than international *law*. The customary practices of the great state nations gave way to the codifications of the nation state, which created the League of Nations and the Permanent International Court of Justice. These products of

Versailles reflected the nation state's characteristic reliance on law. . . .
The San Francisco replay of Versailles had intensified the move
toward institutionalizing international law, with not much better
results.[17]

At some point in the twenty-first century a new constitution for the
society of states will come into being that reflects the emerging constitutional order of the market state. By varying the degree of sovereignty
retained by the people—an idea that is itself incompatible with the conventional conception of sovereignty as equal, indivisible, and complete—
states will develop different forms of the market state, resulting in a
pluralism that the constitution of the society of market states will necessarily reflect. This new international law will be built out of radical devolutionary ideas of sovereignty, including markets in sovereignty (such as
the E.U.).

This evolution will be driven by the same forces that are changing the
constitutional order. In security matters, these forces include new nuclear
and other threats from weapons of mass destruction; global, networked
terrorism; potential attacks on the global critical infrastructure; and the
threat that links all of these, the threat that terror, rather than consent, will
be the basis of the new market state.

Consider the problem of nuclear materials. The states of the twenty-
first century will face nuclear threats that are as novel and as market-driven
and decentralized as the states themselves are. Nuclear vandalism—both
on a large scale, involving threats against nuclear reactors, and on a
smaller level, using the nuclear materials commonly found in hospitals,
universities, and laboratories—is more likely than an attack using a
nuclear warhead. Still, the international trade in weapons delivery systems
and even fissile material will experience the same heady change in the
scope of its markets, the speed of its transactions, and the astounding
return on investment that the international market has provided other commodities, especially illicit ones. At some point it will simply be impossible
to keep up with the nuclear weapons trade, which is at once lucrative and
easily concealed. We missed a chance to slow this down when the United
States failed to take up the suggestion that Soviet missiles simply be
bought intact and destroyed rather than dismantled. This failure led to new
opportunities for the diversion of nuclear fissile material, but some diffusion would have taken place in any case. Twenty-first century proliferation
will be of a different kind, less statist and all the more difficult to manage
for that reason. The society of market states will find it difficult to police
such proliferation because intelligence sharing is as politically and strategically fraught for market states at peace with one another as it was for
allied nation states waging war.

Deterrence and reassurance (through the "extension" of deterrence to provide security guarantees[18]) are the keys to the prevention of nuclear proliferation to states, but they offer little in the way of help vis-à-vis transnational, non-territorial aggressors. This is the most troubling part of a nonproliferation agenda. Still, if such organizations can be denied a state sanctuary, it will be difficult for them to assemble and deploy nuclear weapons on any scale that might disturb the system of stable deterrence, though they may be able to wreak a terrible destruction nevertheless.

There may be a useful analogy: if the contribution of deterrence to non-proliferation is primarily that of reassurance,[19] then the entire battery of market state mechanisms for reassurance—surveillance, missile defense, redundancy of critical infrastructure, transparency, even market programs as mundane as insurance—should prove helpful. Ultimately, only a global coalition that shares intelligence and information can hope to forestall terrorist attacks using nuclear weapons. We are in something of a race against time:[20] can the new society of market states develop technologies of information collection—like nanosensors, for example, that detect nuclear traces—and can that society develop habits of cooperation and mutual disclosure before terrorists deploy nuclear devices in an attack? And can these practices be written into law?

III.

Candidates for the reform of international law range from renovations to the Geneva Conventions, to amendments to the U.N. Charter that would embed certain treaty violations as threats to international peace and security, to changes in *jus in bello* and *jus ad bellum*, even to redefinitions of sovereignty itself. I am braced for the outraged reactions of my colleagues who think that international law has already been traduced by the barbarians of the Bush administration ("men without the law" as the ancient phrase has it) and who may see these arguments as further assaults upon the citadel they are charged with defending. "Just Say No" might with more justice be their motto than that of other missionaries.

The reform of law is always a fraught enterprise for lawyers, jurists, and law professors because we must criticize the very edifice upon which we stand, the structure on the basis of which we claim authority. There are law commissions that are dedicated to such efforts just as there are chaperoned dances but these usually aren't where the action is; such groups perform the important function of ratifying change, but usually they don't initiate it. There are political philosophers who demand that the law correspond to their ideas of propriety and scorn the harassed officials who must daily deal with the complex exigencies of affairs. As long as they can stock the seminar room, or dominate respectable faculties and journals, they can perhaps persuade themselves that theirs is the driving force of change. Perhaps they see themselves as unacknowledged legislators; it's always pretty to think so.

Change in the law most often comes about through argument, when that argument is picked up to serve as a weapon for other, non-jurisprudential interests. Rarely is change the result of a coherent, consistent, and comprehensive program. Arguments such as those in this chapter for the influence of strategy on law can be picked up in order to support political views with which I may have little affinity. That, however, is how change has always come about. That is one reason why the current American administration's indifference, even hostility, to legal reform has been so costly. Failing to press for changes in the law despite an overwhelming need to do so has frozen the evolutionary process. Professor S. F. C. Milsom once put it this way:

> How can a system of law, a system of ideas whose hypothesis it is that rules are constant, adapt itself to a changing world? It has not been the ordered development of the jurist or the legislator, of men thinking about law for its own sake. It has been the rough free enterprise in argument of practitioners thinking about nothing beyond the immediate interest of each client; and the strength of the system has been in the doggedness, always insensitive and often unscrupulous, with which ideas have been used as weapons.[21]

This tension—between incremental reform driven by changes in context and resistance to change supported by the need for predictability and skepticism about the plans and motives of reformers—seems to lie in the very nature of a constitutional system (including an international one) governed by law. The pendulum of change in Anglo-American law forever oscillates between two iconic figures, Mansfield and Blackstone. Perhaps, in the heart of every Anglo-American lawyer, whether he knows it or not, a metronome keeps beating between the jurisprudence of these two men.

Sir William Blackstone in 1758 became the first person to lecture on English law at an English university, ultimately becoming the professor of common law at Oxford. His *Commentaries* have gone through countless ponderous editions, and were considered authoritative by the young lawyers who founded the American state. In these volumes, Blackstone purported to trace English common law back to King Alfred, who, it was claimed, had established a medieval system of law based on Holy Scripture. As this law was conscientiously applied to particular cases, it further developed in succeeding centuries. This notion of inherited legitimacy is so powerful that when the American revolutionaries sought to justify their rebellion, they accused the king of having violated the common law as described by Blackstone. For Blackstone, the common law was the result of indwelling fundamental legal principles found in the life of the English people, "the custom of the realm from time immemorial." One might sum up Blackstone's position and that of the countless Blackstonians who are his heirs in this way:

> Let us preserve, unchanged, the estate which we have been lucky enough to inherit. Let us avoid any attempt at reform—either legislative or judicial—since the attempt to make incidental changes in an already perfect system can lead only to harm in ways which will be beyond the comprehension of even the most well-meaning and far-sighted innovators.[22]

Though they might be horrified to hear it, most professors of public international law[23] are likely to be firmly in Blackstone's camp and to see their roles as defending the tradition that, as Blackstone himself saw it, put the king (and the State) under God and pitted the law against the "newer ideas of statecraft, absolutism and a supreme royal equity."[24]

Against this view are ranged the legatees of Mansfield. William Murray, first Earl of Mansfield, came from an aristocratic background, was educated at Christ Church, Oxford, and became a trial judge after having been an MP and leader of the House of Commons. Though he had a reputation for impartiality, his opinions were not popular and during the Gordon riots of 1780 his house was burned down. He was, in the eyes of his contemporaries as in those of his successors, the greatest judge of his period.[25] Mansfield believed that commercial law—of which he is generally regarded as the modern founder[26]—had to be sensitive to the realities and practices of the marketplace. He often empaneled special juries composed of merchants to inform him on questions of commercial custom and usage;[27] he walked along the docks talking to shipping merchants and examining bills of lading. "His opinions are notable for their salty wit, their almost complete irreverence for the past, and their extraordinary sensitivity to the actual practices of the mercantile community."[28]

Mansfield's cases are relevant to our inquiry in two ways. First, they offer good examples of how actual practice can be brought to bear on particular doctrines of law. If the Justice Department lawyers who created the "wall" between law enforcement and intelligence[29] had consulted intelligence collectors on a routine basis, only the most formalistic could have devised the ludicrous doctrine that the U.S. Department of Justice applied to prevent the sharing of information. Second, Mansfield's cases offer good examples of "double standards."[30] For example, under the general common law rule of derivative title, the transferee receives no more rights than the transferor has to grant. But under the commercial doctrine of bona fide purchase, a transferee who takes title in good faith and without notice of infirmities in the transferor's title may take free of those flaws. Without this distinction, the modern development of negotiable instruments—bills and notes that evidence an obligation to pay money—could hardly have gotten off the ground.[31] Finally, these cases from commercial law reflect the international, cosmopolitan character of the mercantile community. Common law rules may be as quirky as a local community wishes; tradition is enough to confer legitimacy. But international rules must bear a closer resemblance to the actual practices of international actors or these rules will be ignored and a separate set of customs will take the place of law. As one recent commentator put it, "The UN system's dysfunctionality was not, at bottom, a legal problem. It was a geopolitical one."[32]

Bringing international law into line with the changed strategic environment is apostasy to the Blackstone in so many international lawyers. They resent and fear any derogation from the true faith.* It is one reason there are almost no books on the history of international law. For it is heresy in some quarters to suggest that international law has developed because that implies yet further developments to come. But Mansfield's heirs will be heard or, as has already begun to happen, law will simply be ignored in favor of custom. Customary international law is a staple of that field and has long provided a mechanism by which the realities of the strategic environment are brought to bear on doctrine, but it does not favor the weak or the needy or the victims of predation, and it is seldom animated by a concern for world order or indeed for any subject of long-term consequence. Moreover, with respect to states of consent, it is hard to account for the constitutionality of binding rules to which no elected representatives have given their official approval.

We are told, by those who would separate strategy and law, that we must choose between Machiavelli and Thucydides on the one hand, and Grotius and Vattel on the other. It is a false and absurd choice. The real decision, which must be made in each generation and in every application of the law, is between Mansfield and Blackstone.

The international law of the twentieth century reflected the priorities and agendas of nation states. If the international law of state nations was frankly imperial and used to promote the geostrategic interests of the metropolitan powers, the international law of nation states was regulatory: it attempted to direct the activities of states in some desired direction. The

---

*As John Witt has observed, "Not only did Blackstone value the common law because of its historical pedigree, he invested in it a natural order that purported to be based in reason and the heavens rather than in history and human polities." See S. F. C. Milson, "The Nature of Blackstone's Achievement," *Oxford Legal Studies* 1 (1981): 1.

international law of market states will focus on enhancing the rights of conscience of the individual, on protecting the diversity of the environment, on maximizing global opportunity. To ignore the changed strategic context in which such international law must operate, however, would cripple it.

A good example of how this happens is provided by the debate over Common Article 3 of the Geneva Conventions. Common Article 3 was intended to supplement the protections for combatants[33] contained in Articles 1 and 2, which were designed for warfare among nation states. Common Article 3 attempts to provide protections—at a lower level than those for regular forces*—for irregulars in civil wars. By its terms it applies only to "non-international conflicts." It would apply to nation state terrorists like the IRA, ETA, and others, but it pretty clearly does not apply to al Qaeda. How, then, did the various communities vested with responsibility for human rights in warfare respond to this situation? One commentator announced that the war with al Qaeda was an "unprecedented" example of a "non-international conflict fought on a global battlefield."[34] The U.S. government recognized that Article 3 did not apply by its terms, but acknowledged that it had always applied the article's rules nevertheless as a matter of policy, and thus over a period of half a century, the U.S. had helped create a rule of customary international law. Now, it announced, it would discontinue this policy. The president directed the U.S. armed forces to treat prisoners in a manner consistent with Article 3 "to the extent appropriate and consistent with military necessity."[35] This provided no legal guidance to forces in the field. The International Committee of the Red Cross (ICRC) and Human Rights Watch, on the other hand, opined that if al Qaeda terrorists—global, networked terrorists—came neither within Article 2 (which applies to armed conflict between state parties to the convention) nor Article 3 (because the conflict was very plainly international in scope), they must be civilians and thus could not be detained except as a part of the criminal process.[36] Commenting on this opinion, William Lietzau wryly observed that

> [w]e must remember that the law of war [follows, not precedes, war itself]. A claim that the law's failure to recognize war's various manifestations effectively negates a particular war's existence must be acknowledged as ludicrous. Similarly, a failure of a body of law that attends war to address all its possible circumstances is hardly an argument that an entirely different body of law applies.[37]

---

*Common Article 3 protects prisoners from torture or "outrages upon personal dignity, in particular, humiliating and degrading treatment."

When presented with this confusion in *Hamdan v. Rumsfeld*,[38] the U.S. Supreme Court decided that, purely as a textual matter, when applied to conflicts the words "not of an international character" plainly meant any conflict that was not between states. Although I welcome the holding that Common Article 3 applies to combatants in the Wars against Terror as a provisional matter until the convention can be amended, as a matter of textual argument I confess I find this a good deal less than compelling. As Kenneth Anderson has pointed out, the Court seems not to have appreciated that Common Article 3 applies to all parties to a conflict. If a global conflict waged by a network of loose affiliates is not "international" in nature—that is, is not fought among many different nations—then the entire nature of al Qaeda has not been grasped.[39]

This is a difficult problem, and these are tense times, but it is still hard to excuse such performances. Why didn't the U.S. government simply decide what sort of rules it thought appropriate, propose these as amendments to the Geneva Conventions, and obey them in the meantime? This is how customary international law is changed: by how states behave. Why didn't the human rights community acknowledge that the old rules are not really meant for the present situation (as at least some courts have recognized) and propose new rules? The result instead has been a continued derogation of the rule of law, in which both the U.S. government and its erstwhile opponents in the human rights community have had a hand.

IV.

At present, three dogmas of sovereignty dominate our thinking.

Sovereignty, it is said, *must be fully vested*. It is the right to command without legitimate interference. Just as a bachelor cannot be, so the saying goes, "only a bit married," so a state, if sovereign, must be wholly so. It must be able to determine those issues appurtenant to sovereignty without direction from any other source than itself and its will must be accepted accordingly. Sovereignty is the right to be obeyed without legitimate objection.

> [A] holder of sovereignty possesses authority. That is to say, the person or entity does not merely wield coercive power, defined as A's ability to cause B to do what he would otherwise not do. Authority is rather what philosopher R. P. Wolff proposed: "the right to command and correlatively the right to be obeyed."[40]

If there were an unresolvable conflict as to governing authority, there would be no sovereign, for the sovereign is he who—or that which—finally resolves conflicts of law.

Sovereignty, it is also thought, *is necessarily territorial*. The writ of the sovereign must run somewhere, and that domain must have defined boundaries that determine jurisdiction.

> The borders of a sovereign state may not at all circumscribe a "people" or a "nation," and may in fact encompass several of these identities, as national self-determination and irredentist movements make evident. It is rather by simple virtue of their location within geographic borders that people belong to a state and fall under the authority of its ruler. It is within a geographic territory that modern sovereigns are supremely authoritative.[41]

Otherwise, where conflicts as to authority arose there would be uncertainty as to what law was to govern. That would violate the third dogma, that sovereignty *cannot be shared*.

> But if sovereignty is a matter of authority, it is not a matter of mere authority, but of supreme authority. Supremacy is what makes . . . any holder of sovereignty different from a police chief or corporate executive. The holder of sovereignty is superior to all authorities under its purview.[42]

From these three principles, several corollaries may be drawn. It follows from this conception that because there can be only one supreme state authority, and no more than one set of laws can emerge supreme in any state jurisdiction. This role for the sovereign is so important that, under international law, statehood itself is judged by it. A state cannot claim recognition from other states when there are competing laws with no rule for priority among them because there is no effective sovereign to declare definitively what the governing law is (as in disputed territorial areas or during civil wars).

It also follows from this idea of sovereignty that statehood is continuous until the complete destruction of a state; statehood cannot "spring"—that is, the same state cannot reemerge once it has been dissolved. A state may subdivide or enlarge, may confederate or even be conquered and extinguished, but the same state cannot inherit a sovereignty it once enjoyed if its statehood has ceased. Resurrection is not an idea that applies to states.

Finally, it follows from this notion of sovereignty that international law never contravenes the sovereignty of a state, because the society of states that is the source of international law admits its members solely on the grounds of equal sovereignty. Thus the lawmaking authority of that society depends upon the sovereignty of its members; to diminish that sovereignty by law would undermine the basis for international law.

Now it happens that all of these principles are about to be abandoned. That should not be too disturbing to Americans, for the United States has, from its inception, flourished under an idea of sovereignty that is perhaps unique within the society of states and has never accepted the dogmas listed above. The American theory of limited government is founded on the notion that the People possess rights that can't be alienated by delegation to the government. That theory is enshrined in the text of a constitution that provides that "[t]he powers not delegated to the United States by the Constitution . . . are reserved . . . to the people." Sovereignty is not fully vested in the American state. This way of declaring human rights as retained stands in contrast to declarations of human rights like Magna Carta or the Universal Declaration of Human Rights that purport to grant rights to the People.

In the view of some eighteenth century European political theorists this was incomprehensible: how could a state be less than fully sovereign? In Europe, ideas of popular sovereignty had also been taken up, but there it was held that the People, having taken sovereignty from dynastic rulers, had wholly vested their governments with sovereignty. Indeed, this was thought to be the indispensable basis for interstate relations. The American view of sovereignty was not accepted by other states when the constitutional order of state nations swept Europe. It was Napoleon, not Madison, whose concepts of sovereignty (and of the imperial state nation) were adopted. A similar preference for European ideas of statehood was manifested in the late nineteenth century. When the multinational American nation state came into being, once again, the European variant of the nation state was copied around the globe while the American version remained almost singular. This time it was Bismarck, and not Lincoln, whose ideas about the definition of "nation" prevailed, with many terrible consequences, including the emergence of fascism.

Nor is sovereignty necessarily territorial, as shown by the relationship of the United States to its aboriginal population. The U.S. government makes treaties with the Indian tribes although these tribes reside entirely within U.S. territory. Indian tribes control their own membership, determine who can run for office and who can receive tribal benefits. It has long been held by the U.S. Supreme Court that Indian tribes exercise sovereignty that predates the Constitution, and that they are therefore not bound by the Constitution's Bill of Rights, whereas the government is bound to accord them the human rights guarantees of the Bill of Rights in its relations with them.[43] At the same time, the U.S. government controls immigration to tribal lands and has opened reservation land to purchase and residence by non-Indians on almost every reservation. An Indian tribe's jurisdiction over tribal members is personal rather than territorial.[44]

Finally, U.S. sovereignty is shared. The full text of the constitutional amendment quoted above reads: "The powers not delegated to the United States by the Constitution, nor prohibited by it to the States, are reserved to the States respectively, or to the people." There are a number of constitutional subjects at which the state governments in the U.S. are exclusively competent, including aspects of real property, inheritance, and domestic relations, as well as various spheres such as the possession of alcohol and the qualifications for holding state office or indeed what offices are held by elected officials.

This peculiar American constitutional position sits uneasily within international law, which is based on European ideas of sovereignty. Usually this awkward fit can be disguised, but there remain trace elements of conflict. Perhaps the most irritating to other states is the American "last in time" rule by which Congress can, by subsequently adopting a statute, override or qualify any treaty. This follows directly from the legal incompetence of the U.S. partial sovereign to bind the electorate. The British Parliament, for example, could withdraw from the European Union altogether by renouncing the treaties of Rome and Maastricht, but if Parliament passed a statute that contravened these treaties, or if Whitehall instituted a practice that was inconsistent with E.U. regulations, the courts would declare these acts incompatible with the union and therefore unenforceable so long as the U.K. was a member of the E.U.[45] The American constitutional rule is to the contrary. If Congress passed a civil detention statute that contravened a preexisting international treaty—for example, denying an arrested and indicted alien the right to meet with a diplomatic official—the statute would prevail. The residual right of the People to change their minds would be superior to any commitment by their representatives.

Developments at the end of the twentieth century, however, have moved European states closer to abandoning the three dogmas of sovereignty. The most important of these is European integration, which began in 1950 as a postwar, nation state exercise urged by the U.S., when six states formed the European Coal and Steel Community via the Treaty of Paris. The treaty established joint international authority over the coal and steel industries of these six countries, with executive control exercised through a permanent bureaucracy and a Council of Ministers composed of the foreign ministers of each state. This nation state form, similar to other international institutions like NATO and the U.N., was expanded to embrace a number of subjects related to trade in the Treaty of Rome in 1957. The creation of a judicial body, the European Court of Justice, and a legislature, the European Parliament, did not derogate from the essential dogmas of state sovereignty. This changed with the 1991 Maastricht Treaty, which expanded the community's powers and reconfigured it as the European Union. The European Union is not a superstate (which would be a comfortable[46] extension of the nation state form); rather it "pools" important aspects of the sovereignty of member states into a supranational institution in which the freedom of individual state action is constrained. This development, because it relies on a set of supranational legal institutions including courts, a bureaucracy, and a parliament, has moved European states toward *translucent* sovereignty, that is, the assessment of the legality of the acts of sovereign states by an international legal body whose purview penetrates the veil of sovereignty. Advocates of translucent sovereignty hold the state accountable when it violates its obligations to other states. Some potential examples are cheating on treaty undertakings with respect to WMD, defying U.N. Security Council resolutions regarding a cease-fire (either international, as in Iraq, or national, as in Darfur), or refusing to allow an epidemic to be checked by permitting World Health Organization (WHO) surveillance and inoculation. This view is based on the notion that sovereignty depends upon an implicit compact with the society of states.

A similar transition can be seen in the second great revolution in sovereignty, that occasioned by armed interventions to vindicate human rights. In 1948 the majority of states signed the Universal Declaration of Human Rights, committing themselves to respect a list of rights for all persons. This declaration was not legally binding and contained no enforcement mechanisms. Similarly the Genocide Convention signed the same year committed states to refrain from genocide but contained no provisions that might have qualified the sovereignty of the signatory states. In the mid-1960s, two further conventions—the Covenant on Civil and Political Rights and the Covenant on Economic, Social and Cultural Rights—bound states to respect the human rights of their own people, but both conventions carefully protected traditional conceptions of sovereignty. Subsequent human rights covenants, also signed by the vast majority of states, contained similar reservations. They reflected *opaque* sovereignty, that is, the cloaking of internal acts by state sovereignty that bars external interference with those acts.

The change away from such vacuous nation state undertakings came at the end of the century when violations of human rights by states began to be challenged by armed interventions. In a series of incidents starting in 1990, the U.N. Security Council or various regional organizations contemplated by the U.N. Charter have endorsed interventions that previously would have been regarded as illegitimate violations of state sovereignty. Unlike peacekeeping operations during the Cold War, these interventions have often lacked the consent of the government of the state against which the intervention was directed. These have occurred in Iraq, the former state of Yugoslavia, Bosnia, Kosovo, Somalia, Rwanda, Haiti, Sierra Leone, Cambodia, Liberia, and elsewhere. These actions also are consistent with a translucent view of state sovereignty.[47] Only the 2003 Coalition intervention in Iraq is inconsistent with this view, owing to the fact that endorsement of the original invasion by the Security Council or by NATO[48] was withheld (although the Security Council has endorsed the occupation of Iraq and NATO has participated in various missions in support of that occupation[49]).

In Kosovo the intervention by NATO was not approved initially but was later ratified by U.N. Security Council resolutions.[50] Because intervention in Kosovo was not initially approved by the Security Council, however, it may be that, like the Coalition invasion of Iraq, Kosovo reflected a different concept of sovereignty, which one might call *transparent*. This doctrine holds that a state's acts toward the state's own citizens, within its own territory, can be judged by other states and serve as a predicate for armed intervention even in the absence of an endorsement by the appropriate international institutions. This fully fits the American concept of sovereignty, for when a state violates the compact of human rights it implicitly holds with its people, it forfeits or at least sharply compromises its sovereignty, because popular consent is the source of state sovereignty. The People cannot consent to violation of their own rights. As Richard Haass put it:

> Sovereignty entails obligations. One is not to massacre your own people. Another is not to support terrorism in any way. If a government fails to meet these obligations, then it forfeits some of the normal advantages of sovereignty, including the right to be left alone inside your own terrritory. Other governments, including the US, gain the right to intervene. In the case of terrorism, this can even lead to a right of preventive, or peremptory, self-defense.[51]

On this view,[52] the support of terror arrogates to the State powers it cannot have (to say nothing of its violations of international obligations) because the People cannot authorize their state to take away another people's right of consent (the same way that voters in Texas cannot levy taxes against the citizens of California).

To summarize: roughly speaking, there are three current views of state sovereignty that contend within the society of states: *opaque* sovereignty, a traditional concept that holds that events within a state's borders are entirely internal matters, beyond the judgment of other states; *translucent* sovereignty, an outgrowth of European integration and the campaign for human rights, which holds that authoritative agencies like the U.N. Security Council can declare a state in violation of fundamental international norms—against genocide, for example—and forfeit or compromise the perpetrator's sovereignty; and, a more recent result of the human rights movement, *transparent* sovereignty, which holds that because a regime's sovereignty arises from its compact with its people as well as with the society of states, sovereignty can be penetrated when a state commits widespread acts of violence against its own people, or acquires weapons of mass destruction in violation of its international agreements, or supports global terrorists who threaten the civilians of other states. At present, critical states holding some version of these paradigmatic positions are, for example, China and Israel (opaque), France and Germany (translucent), and the U.S. (transparent).[53]

The opaque sovereignty of the nation state that is enshrined in the institutions and rules of the society of nation states does not admit of any internal, domestic acts that empower the U.N. or any other body to strip a state of its sovereignty, thereby making it legally vulnerable to legitimate intervention. Neither genocide, nor ethnic cleansing, nor human experimentation, nor slavery, nor religious persecution, nor even the calculated starvation of one's own population necessarily renders a state, in the system of nation states, liable to intervention by other states. This is to be contrasted with the view "that the word 'sovereignty' can no longer be used to shield the actual suppression of popular sovereignty from external rebuke and remedy."[54] For example, when the results of free elections are

> ignored by a local caudillo who either takes power himself or assigns it to a subordinate he controls, a jurist rooted in the late twentieth century can hardly say that an invasion by outside forces to remove the caudillo and install the elected government is a violation of national sovereignty. . . . [If outside intervention] displace[s] the usurper and emplace[s] the people who were freely elected, [it] can [scarcely] be characterized . . . [as a] violation of some mystical survival of a monarchical right that supposedly devolves *jure gentium* on whichever warlord seizes and holds the presidential palace or . . . the term [be] used in the jurisprudentially bizarre sense to mean that inanimate territory has political rights that preempt those of its inhabitants.[55]

This emphasis on the popular sources of sovereignty is the basis of a transparent perspective. A translucent view stresses the common duties that states have toward each other and toward the society of states of which they are a part; for this reason, this perspective confines intervention to that which is authorized by duly constituted international organizations. These conflicting views of sovereignty are obviously fraught with potential for conflict among states. Yet they might also point the way to assure legitimacy to the novel kinds of state action that will be undertaken in the Wars against Terror.

V.

States of consent face threats that are coalescing in the Wars against Terror and that have a number of things in common. First, these threats were spawned by the parliamentary nation states that won the Long War and that have created, nemesis-like, each of their besetting problems. That war was ultimately won not simply on the battlefield but by the discrediting of European fascism through the exposure of its human rights abuses; the discrediting of Japanese militarism by the American use of nuclear weapons; and by the evolution of a global, networked economy that led to the repudiation of communism. Each of these successful means to a more humane world order in the twentieth century was essential to the birth of the menacing developments of the early twenty-first century.

Second, these threats are all linked to the emergence of the market state. Market states rely on concepts of qualified sovereignty that permit and perhaps invite humanitarian intervention when the popular basis for state sovereignty has been compromised. The publics of market states are acutely aware of the sufferings of other peoples, and press their leaders to act to relieve that suffering. The influential political role of the media in a market state reinforces this agitation. More ominously, the same privatizing influences that are evident in other aspects of the market state are bringing about the commodification of weapons of mass destruction,[56] which makes proliferation so much more dangerous by enlarging the number of states and non-state entities that can acquire such weapons as well as shortening the time necessary to deploy them.

Third, all these threats challenge the prevailing doctrines of current international law. Humanitarian intervention, for example, is not recognized by the U.N. Charter, even though human rights guarantees, validated in treaties and by international institutions, are rapidly proliferating.

As a legal response to these threats, Lee Feinstein and Anne-Marie Slaughter have proposed changing international law to recognize a "duty to prevent"—that is, to create a legal obligation for outside intervention when a state commits crimes against humanity, develops weapons of mass destruction, or shelters terrorists.[57] This was offered as a corollary to the doctrine known as the "responsibility to protect," a far-reaching principle that holds that states have a responsibility to protect the lives, liberty, and basic human rights of their citizens and that if they fail or are unable to carry this out, the international community has a responsibility to step in. That principle was elucidated by an international commission of lawyers and scholars, the Evans-Sahnoun Commission,[58] responding to a call by the secretary-general of the U.N. in 1999 and repeated in 2003 to find "the best way to respond to threats of genocide or other comparable massive violations of human rights."[59] It was proposed by the High-level Panel on Threats, Challenges, and Change[60] created by the secretary-general, and ratified in the "outcome document" on U.N. reform adopted by the General Assembly in September 2005, which endorsed "collective action . . . through the Security Council . . . should peaceful means be inadequate and national authorities are manifestly failing to protect their populations from genocide, war crimes, ethnic cleansing and crimes against humanity."[61]

The "duty to prevent" goes beyond the "responsibility to protect." It is a provocative doctrine that recognizes that in some instances preventative action—though not necessarily military action—must take place before a famine or an epidemic rages out of control, before nuclear weapons are actually deployed, and before a terrorist training camp has indoctrinated, trained, and dispersed the fighters who attack civilians. If the doctrine of a "responsibility to protect" is a step toward translucent sovereignty, the doctrine of a "duty to prevent" takes us to (and perhaps across) the threshold of transparent sovereignty.

Feinstein and Slaughter suggest criteria that would determine which regimes should be subjected to strict scrutiny. These criteria include adherence to human rights and the rule of law; protecting rights of association, freedom of belief and expression; and securing property rights, economic rights, and personal autonomy. Regimes that categorically and unequivocally violate all these guarantees have compromised their right to govern. Similarly, the Evans-Sahnoun Commission concluded that "[w]here a population is suffering serious harm, as a result of internal war, insurgency, repression or state failure, and the state in question is unwilling or unable to halt or avert it, the principle of nonintervention yields to the international responsibility to protect."[62] The difficulty is that, having accepted this conclusion, it does not follow that the acquisition of WMD, or the training of paramilitary forces for terrorist attacks, or even policies like ethnic cleansing are in fact analogous to the Evans-Sahnoun conditions, or, more significantly, that any body other than the regime responsible for governing is entitled to make such a judgment, much less another hostile regime whose intervention is bound to cause great suffering to the people it claims to be "protecting."

Is it obvious that the North Korean people are less safe from harm because their odious government is now thought to possess a small number of nuclear weapons? Feinstein and Slaughter write that

> [a]fter all, the danger posed by WMD in the hands of governments with no internal checks on their power is the prospect of mass, indiscriminate murder. Whether individuals are targeted for execution over time or vaporized in a single instant, the result is the same: a massive and senseless loss of life. We argue, therefore, that a new international

obligation arises to address the unique dangers of proliferation that have grown in parallel with the humanitarian catastrophes of the 1990s.[63]

But isn't the chance of being "vaporized" rather less for the citizens of states that possess nuclear weapons, for example? Would Japan have been attacked at Hiroshima and Nagasaki if it could have replied in kind against Los Angeles and San Francisco?

The reason Feinstein and Slaughter give for any insistence on internal constitutional checks and balances and other hallmarks of liberal democracy is not, they emphatically state, that they wish to choose between "good" and "bad" governments, "much less democracies from nondemocracies."[64] That is to say, their rationale is not based on a constitutional, legal motive. Rather, it reflects a strategic preference based on the observation that the behavior of "open societies" is subject to various countervailing pressures, internal and external, and thus that the adoption of certain constitutional forms has important strategic consequences. This important insight, however, is undercut by the authors' agnosticism about constitutional norms, which reflects a separation of law and strategy.

Consider the formidable problem posed by China—not a regime notable for its adherence to human rights—and its nuclear arsenal that is, unlike that of other great powers, still growing. The authors dispose of this by saying that "the duty to prevent cannot apply to all closed societies with WMD programs. To be practical, the duty has to be limited and applied to cases when it can produce beneficial results. It applies to Kim Jong Il's North Korea, but not to Hu Jintao's (or even Mao's) China."[65]

This is no doubt sensible, but what precisely is the legal rule then? For if it is that Mao's China was simply too powerful—too dangerous—to confront successfully, then that undercuts the argument against proliferation in the first place, as Mao himself recognized when he broke with the Soviet Union over its unwillingness to assist in China's development of a nuclear arsenal.

Once Feinstein and Slaughter refuse to judge regimes as "good" or "bad," they have moved from trying to base a right of intervention on a loss of sovereignty (forfeited by a regime owing to its own behavior toward its people) to an attempt to preserve such a right in the face of the practical exigencies of getting authoritarian regimes to change their policies. The pragmatism of this move is understandable enough, but when we abandon the democratic litmus test (or some other qualitative criteria), it is far from obvious why the people of the United States or even the members of the Security Council are a better judge of the welfare of another society than its own rulers (who presumably would also be vaporized in warfare).

Feinstein and Slaughter argue that in closed societies it is far more difficult to find out what governments are doing and take effective measures to stop them, and this is doubtless true, but there was no lack of information about the terrorist training camps in Afghanistan; Pakistan was still a functioning parliamentary system when it developed nuclear weapons and began selling its technology to others; and Serbia conducted massacres in Kosovo under the aegis of an elected and media-hungry president.

There *is* a link between crimes against humanity, WMD, and terrorism but it is not simply that those states that treat their own peoples' rights with disdain are more likely to be dismissive of the rights of other states (though this is also doubtless true). The link must be both strategic (the practical elements to which Feinstein and Slaughter wish to be sensitive) as well as legal (the effort to ground intervention in a principle), and in their analysis the two elements are at war with one another. Their strategic considerations utterly vitiate the legal rule, as in the case of China; and the legal rule that results has little to offer in the way of practical, strategic guidance, as in the case of North Korea.

VI.

For Feinstein and Slaughter, the key actor that triggers a "duty to prevent" is the State. This might appear to be obvious. The principal driver in scenarios that depict a humanitarian crisis is the failed or failing state. Whether it is the arena for civil war, sickness, or famine (which are often linked as one group in power tries to destroy another by driving it away from its villages and into camps vulnerable to starvation and disease), the weak, contested state is a conduit for human suffering and a leaky valve for the aid that might alleviate suffering. And, too, many failing states, from Afghanistan in central Asia, through Somalia on the east coast of Africa, to Liberia on the west coast, offer bases, recruits, banking facilities, and arms to terrorists. These failing states are what Cooper calls "premodern," which is to say that while they may shelter virtual market states like al Qaeda, they do not contain them or bring them into being. Draining the swamp is certainly worth doing, as has been noted; denying sanctuary to terrorists is a positive step. But "swamp management"—a phrase never heard in Washington—is costly and difficult, so costly as to call into question the strategy and so difficult as to suggest that it may actually foment local terrorism in some theaters such as Somalia.

Similarly, the main driver behind the proliferation of weapons of mass destruction seems to be states. By far the most important nuclear weapons treaty regime is the Nuclear Nonproliferation Treaty (NPT) pressed for and negotiated by President Johnson over the forceful objection of his advisors.[66] At its center is a bargain: in exchange for forswearing nuclear weapons development, powers without nuclear weapons will have access to nuclear technology for energy. This has been a very successful treaty. International law interacts with a dynamic strategic environment, however, and the NPT has suffered from two increasingly alarming defects. Because strategy is shaped by law, those states that refuse to participate in the legal regime have become prime candidates for marketing their weapons development programs. Like a river flowing around an obstacle, the strategy of Pakistan, which refused to sign the NPT, has broadened its channel to include trade with other states in nuclear weapons technology and design. Because law is shaped by strategy, signatory states have found ways to comply with the letter of the treaty while evading its intent. Like a river sharply confined within a ravine, the legal tactics of Iran, an NPT signatory, have been to cut deeper and deeper into clandestine development under the superficial cover of energy development. In the case of North Korea both dimensions are at work at once: though a signatory of the NPT and a party that has frequently relied on the excuse of its energy needs to explain the operation of its nuclear reactors, North Korea has also been a marketer of nuclear weapons technology; when caught, it simply renounced participation in the treaty regime altogether. At present we are very close to a breakdown in the nonproliferation system. If Iran—a state with legitimate security concerns—were to resume its pursuit of nuclear weapons, there seems little question that these weapons will proliferate in the region.

But if states are the source of the problem, then fundamental changes in international law are unlikely to be the solution because these changes—as international institutions are presently constituted—must come from a consensus of states. This can happen. It has happened in previous eras—but only when decades-long warfare eventually compelled consensus. If we are to wring modification from the legal structure of the society of states without the benefit of the exhaustion and devastation that accompanies epochal wars, then we must look for a different link between WMD, crimes against humanity, and global, networked terrorism than that provided by the legal relationship of states to each other.

That linkage is the states' strategic relationship to terror. It is the awful prospect of unprecedented civilian suffering that can unite the states of the world once the conjunction of WMD, global terrorism, and humanitarian crises is confronted. What leader can contemplate the immediate deaths of more than 200,000[67]—one hundred World Trade Center attacks—in one morning, knowing that no city, not Madrid, not Washington, not Nairobi, not Dar es Salaam, not Riyadh, not even once tranquil Denpasar, is immune?

In the past century, states knew who their enemies were, and because these were other nation states, each knew against whom to retaliate for an attack. In the past there was little point in worrying about the ability of terrorists to gain weapons of mass destruction. No state would provide WMD to its covert, terrorist allies. Nor did terrorists possess the sophisticated expertise that could gain access to computer networks in order to disable the infrastructure from remote, untraceable terminals. Moreover, there was a natural check on weapons deployed by terrorists that arose from the relationship between nation state terrorists and the nation they sought to represent. Even if it were technically feasible for the IRA to use WMD against London, it would have been politically suicidal; even if it were politically feasible for Hamas to use WMD against Israel, it would have been technically suicidal, for as many Arabs would have been irradiated or infected as Jews.

With the awful conjunction of the creation of a market in nuclear weapons technology, the development of a virtual state like al Qaeda, and the emergence of a political goal like creating a perpetual state of terror, however, these checks vanish. As discussed in chapter 2, the Libyan renunciation of nuclear weapons development has exposed the trade in WMD technology by giving us the first public airing of this covert market. Blueprints for a proven warhead design (originally from China); machinery (largely from European companies); nuclear materials[68] from several sources, including North Korea; sophisticated centrifuges (from a firm in Malaysia with a free-trade zone in Dubai as the main shipping point); and missile technology (from North Korea) have all been for sale. There is ample evidence that al Qaeda has sought nuclear technology,[69] and we must presume that this was done with the intent to use it.

Similarly, the burgeoning market in biotechnology information will create a non-state source for pathogens that can be weaponized. It is already the case, as we also saw in chapter 2, that smallpox DNA can be ordered through the mail, sequenced with publicly available technology, and weaponized simply by infecting a willing squad of suicide bombers. "One study estimated that because most people on the planet have no resistance to the extinct virus, an initial release which infected just 10 people would spread to 2.2 million people in 180 days."[70]

We must also presume that, sooner or later, some non-state actor within the global network will acquire sufficient fissile material, the most difficult element in the chain of nuclear weapons development. How do we think about an event that today seems at once highly unlikely and yet ultimately inevitable? How do healthy persons think about their deaths, at once so remote and yet so finally unavoidable?

Some commentators suggest that we must act as if the worst cases were a given fact simply because the devastation attendant on ignoring such cases would be so great. This view is sometimes phrased as the "precautionary principle." The U.S. vice president, Dick Cheney, is said to hold the view that "[i]f there's a one percent chance that Pakistani scientists are helping al Qaeda build or develop a nuclear weapon, we have to treat it as a certainty in terms of our response."[71] The difficulty, as Cass Sunstein has persuasively shown, is that the Precautionary Principle gives no guidance as to what steps should be taken to be "safe rather than sorry."[72] Applied generally, it would paralyze policy because any action invariably brings risks, and because some risks are worth bearing.* For example, assume that we accept that an engineered smallpox virus could cause hundreds of thousands of deaths, perhaps more, and that the only remaining live viruses are in the possession of U.S. and Russian laboratories. Do we destroy these viruses because if they were somehow captured by terrorists the resulting epidemic would be catastrophic? Or do we make certain they are not destroyed because, by retaining the cultures, we have a head start on a vaccine should it become necessary? The vice president is quoted as saying that it's not about "our analysis," it's about "our response."[73] But the Precautionary Principle *must* be about analysis—the comparative likelihoods, costs, and benefits of a particular course of action—in order to yield a prudent response. Standing alone it trumps itself in an infinite series of contradictory precautions.

The use of biological and nuclear weapons by virtual states and global networks presents a problem we really haven't thought through. A similar situation arose in the early 1950s when the U.S. and the Soviet Union deployed nuclear weapons against each other. At that time the problem was not well understood; in many quarters these weapons were thought simply to be larger, more effective bombs that didn't present any new strategic difficulties. In response to this situation intellectuals, scientists, and military and other government officials painstakingly created a new theoretical apparatus for understanding the use of nuclear weapons.[74] Ironically it is this system of deterrence—a brilliant *intellectual* achievement—that is now failing us because it depends upon a retaliation that must be considered ineffective against a dispersed, networked, and global attacker whose objective is to create a global state of terror.[75]

In Russia and the other former Soviet states, there are large quantities of weapon materials—enough to make thousands of weapons—that are widely held to be insufficiently protected.[76] "In 40 countries there are more than 100 research reactors that use highly enriched uranium . . ."[77] A recent interview with a "diplomat in Vienna"—presumably accredited to the UN/IAEA—reported that "[t]here is a nuclear network of black market centrifuges and weapons design that the world has yet to discover."[78] Whereas it has been assumed that some states would cheat on their NPT obligations in order to produce and sell their own nuclear material,

*It may be, for example, that we must bear the risks of sharing information about pathogens in order to create effective treatments.

[w]hat we have instead is a black-market network capable of producing usable nuclear materials and nuclear devices that is not limited to any one nation. We have nuclear dealers operating outside our front door, and we have no control over them—no matter how good we are in terms of verification.[79]

New initiatives in international law must take cognizance of this problem. Only an international plan can possibly cope with this problem, one using legal institutions like the U.N., as well as voluntary coalitions like the G8.[80] What legal rules will such a plan embody? If not the duty to prevent or the precautionary principle, then what?

There are at present a number of antiterrorism conventions, both global and regional. However useful they may be, they can have little broad, practical impact on the Wars against Terror because they are constructed on the basis of a law enforcement paradigm rather than with an eye to organizing and legitimizing warfare. International terrorism has

been treated primarily as a criminal law matter, with emphasis on preventing the commission of the crime through intelligence or law enforcement means or, if prevention failed, on the apprehension, prosecution and punishment of the perpetrators . . . [T]he law of armed conflict has hardly occupied the field.[81]

Moreover, none of these conventions deal with the vulnerability of critical infrastructure, and most importantly, they are designed to change neither *jus ad bellum*—the international law of what legitimates the use of force in the wars against global, networked terrorism—nor *jus in bello,* which determines what methods can be undertaken to prosecute such a war on terror. Nevertheless, there are some measures that our current international institutions could undertake that are not incompatible with existing conventions.

A reformed international law could comprise these legal initiatives:

(1) The promulgation of an international convention that makes it a crime against humanity, subject to enforcement in any jurisdiction, including a reformed International Criminal Court,* to trade in biological or fissile stocks for weapons; and that also makes it a crime to aid in such sales by financing, transport, or any other material facilitation; and that provides for recognition by the Security Council that state participation in this trade is a valid ground for sanctions, including, as a last resort, the use of armed force.

*See p. 497 discussing the proposal to make the ICC answerable to the U.N. Security Council.

(2) The negotiation of an amendment to the NPT flatly prohibiting the creation of highly enriched uranium or weapons-grade plutonium by any state that cannot prove it already has such a program as of the date of the adoption of the ban; a prohibition on the traffic across borders in fuel-cycle technology; and the mandating of an international obligation of states to prove periodically, after the ban on new stocks takes effect, that they do not have such materials or programs except as licensed by an international energy consortium administered by the G8.

(3) The application of rigorous verification rules (like the Additional Protocol of the IAEA[82]) to those states that do register their preexisting programs under the NPT (at present only declared sites can be inspected by the IAEA) and the recognition by the Security Council that states cannot unilaterally withdraw from the NPT, as well as the adoption by the Council of a requirement that all member states cease nuclear cooperation with any country not in compliance with IAEA safeguards.

(4) The informal recognition of trading rights by which states can sell their rights to develop fuel-cycle technology and biological and nuclear weapons before the date the ban takes effect to a consortium of states organized by the G8 in exchange for aid, subject to even more intrusive verification.

(5) A Security Council resolution finding that the development of weapons-grade fissile material or biological stocks for weapons constitutes an ongoing threat to international security under Chapter 7 of the U.N. Charter and a resolution providing for the physical interdiction of nuclear-related products going to countries that fail the IAEA's standards of transparency, cooperation, and verification.

(6) The monitoring of nuclear reactors, nuclear weapons stocks, and biological laboratories by intrusive no-notice inspections subject to a warrant requirement, using specially created regional tribunals pursuant to Security Council authorization.

(7) The offer of international bounties for fissile material and toxins by the G8 consortium.

(8) Additional funding by the E.U., to supplement that of the U.S., for the Cooperative Threat Reduction program with Russia, and for the Nuclear Threat Initiative, an NGO that promotes prophylactic

measures to protect the nuclear stockpile from theft, trading, and negligent management.[83]

(9) The inclusion of Russia and China in the Proliferation Security Initiative, a voluntary consortium of states that is committed to interdicting traffic in weapons of mass destruction.

(10) The recognition in customary international law that surveillance and the use of sensor technology to detect weapons of mass destruction are not a violation of a state's sovereignty.

(11) The creation of a standing international Terror Court to which prosecutions of terrorists could be referred by the U.N. Security Council. This court would have a permanent seat, a sufficient staff, and an accredited bar. It could try terrorists in absentia and would generally be governed by rules of procedure developed by the court set up in the aftermath of the genocide in Rwanda and the Yugoslav tribunal created following the collapse of the state of Yugoslavia.

(12) Finally, remembering always the mutually affecting dimensions of law and strategy, the most significant event toward keeping weapons of mass destruction out of the hands of al Qaeda would be the denuclearization of the Middle East. The first step has already been taken in Iraq: it is inconceivable that Israel or Iran would ever give up its nuclear programs if Saddam Hussein were still in power.[84] If a demilitarized Iraq emerges, and if Iran can be kept non-nuclear through a combination of security guarantees and access to nuclear energy, it is not impossible to hope that Israel will voluntarily renounce its nuclear weapons program in exchange for theater-missile defenses and a security guarantee from the U.S. With access to U.S. precision-guided munitions, Israel has little use for nuclear weapons if no other states in the region possess them. These are essentially strategic matters that can be enforced by law but do not fit within the current institutional system of international law that has, for example, actually protected proliferation to Iran.

These suggestions,[85] which are bound to strike many in international law as both officious and destructive, do not go nearly far enough. They do not sufficiently address the role of warfare in confrontation with global terrorism. They rely on international institutions whose makeup holds them hostage to the vagaries of the nation state when it is the globalized, terrorist market state that poses the threat. Nation states are in principle equal sovereigns whereas what our current environment demands is the legitimation of the authority of democratic, human rights–respecting states—states of consent—and legal recognition of the strategic importance of G8 members, some of which are well on the way to being market states. The U.N. has both of these drawbacks—it privileges states of terror and it makes consensus both necessary and very difficult to achieve. As the former secretary-general of the United Nations Kofi Annan has said, we should not have a world in which either a single state controls all affairs or a single state can block action.[86] "The Security Council," in his view, "is not just another stage on which to act out national interests."[87]

This is not welcome advice to the leaders of nation states. It was Hubert Vedrine, the French foreign minister, who said, "We have to keep defending our vital interests just as before; we can say no, alone, to anything that may be unacceptable,"[88] and Gerhard Schroeder, the German chancellor, who said frankly, "I do not feel obliged to other governments."[89]

> For France, Russia, and China, one of [their] tools is the Security Council and the veto that the charter affords them. It was therefore entirely predictable that these three countries would wield their veto to snub the United States and advance the project that they had undertaken: to return the world to a multipolar system.[90]

And no less predictable that the U.S. administration would refuse to capitulate in order to advance its project of a unipolar world. Not surprisingly, the members of international, nation state organizations behave as nation states. If it was absurd to expect the Mafia "Commission" to succeed in allocating spheres of control to the various American crime families because, after all, they were *criminals,* it is equally absurd to expect an institution of nation states to put aside narrow national interests. This was especially evident when some Security Council members claimed that it was their aim to enhance the role of the Council by blocking action to enforce its own resolutions.

> During the Security Council debate on Iraq, the French were candid about their objective. The goal was never to disarm Iraq. Instead, "the main and constant objective for France throughout the negotiations," according to its UN ambassador, was to "strengthen the role and authority of the Security Council" [meaning actually the role of France vis-à-vis the United States].[91]

Bearing these attitudes in mind, I offer this provocative proposed rule: a state of terror can never be sovereign. The "right to prevent" should in fact be very much a matter of the state's constitutional valence (whether it denies human rights on a crippling scale, attempts to annex its neighbors, refuses to govern by consent, rejects the rule of law, etc.) whether the subject state to which the doctrine applies is the intervenor or the target of intervention. Persons within a state of terror may prosecute armed struggles against the State and not be subject to lawful sanction or extradition; they are not terrorists unless they attack civilians with no connection to the state depredations they are resisting. Other states may lawfully intervene against such a state to halt the proliferation of weapons of mass destruction, genocide, or international terrorism, or to forestall mass human catastrophes ignored by the regime—all indicia of states of terror. To be assured of sovereignty, and of the protection of the international community, both domestically and among states, a state need only become transparently a state of consent.* International law should be reformed to recognize this rule as a fundamental element in the constitution of the society of states. Without this reform, it is idle to expect that either law will be strengthened (by insisting on its present composition) or that interventions will be eschewed.[92] Moreover, without such a distinction, grounded in the constitutional valence of the state, a right to prevent becomes an invitation to predation by states of terror seeking pretexts for their aggression.

This rule depends upon the broader doctrine of transparent sovereignty. It addresses the issue of double standards—and perhaps manifests such standards—by discriminating between states of consent and states of terror. Only states of consent can invoke this rule as a basis of intervention, and it can only be invoked against states of terror. Otherwise, either the Security Council or a regional security organization recognized by the Security Council must authorize the intervention. Such a rule would be brought into being by the concerted action of the leading states of consent that formed themselves into an alliance.

This might begin with a joint declaration of doctrine by the United States, the one state that is already a global power, and the European Union, the one umbrella state that has a functioning market in sovereignty. It is crucial that these emerging market states cooperate in tackling transnational issues and the pursuit of humane policies, in order that a decent example be given of governance by market states. Because the international order derives from the constitutional order of states, an exemplary relationship between U.S. and E.U.—a kind of G2,[93] as it were, that permitted overlapping memberships—would, in itself, be a positive step toward the way the world should be governed.

Zbigniew Brzezinski has observed that

---

*This would legitimate the Indian intervention in East Pakistan in 1971, but not the Argentine seizure of the Falklands in 1982; it would legitimate the intervention by Vietnam in 1979 against the Khmer Rouge, but not North Vietnam's invasion of South Vietnam in 1975; it would legitimate the U.S. intervention in Panama in 1989 but not the American efforts to overthrow the Sandinistas in the 1980s.

[t]he economic and military strength of the Atlantic community makes it the gravitational center of world affairs. While only 13% of the world's people are in NATO and/or EU nations, together they account for 63% of the world's GDP, producing over $27 trillion worth of goods and services in 2005, and over 77% of the world's military spending, allocating over $780 billion to their militaries in 2005 alone.[94]

A G2 would not be a formal body but rather the energizing force in creating a global alliance of democracies and in animating joint action by the G8. This proposal is worthy of consideration for two overriding reasons: first, it is the sort of informal, market-based grouping that could facilitate the birth of market state, global governance. The U.S. and the E.U. are the world's dominant economic superpowers, Japan having faded slightly, and China remaining still a relatively poor country. Second, a G2 would help correct for the United States' "tendency to unilateralism and the European tendency towards introversion and fragmentation."[95] If it is true, as my late father remarked, that to make a man trustworthy you first have to trust him, then a G2 could provide both emerging market states, the U.S. and the E.U., with partners each could rely upon to complement its strengths. Both are democracies, both have convertible currencies, both are market economies, and above all, both face the perils of the Wars against Terror (though Europeans may have to suffer a significant attack, on the scale of 9/11, before they are willing to confront this fact).

Though it is generally unappreciated, the G8 already has an impressive record in international security. It has, for example, integrated Japan and, later, Russia into Western security discussions. More importantly, it avoids the legal structure of the Versailles peace treaty, the nation state international constitution reflected in the U.N. Security Council. There is no veto. All states are not equal. There is no voting. All of which is to say that its acts at present are not transparent, lack some traditional sources of international legitimacy, but yet have been remarkably effective—itself a ground of legitimacy.[96] It is something to build on, though it is plainly insufficient as it stands. The absence of India, Brazil, Indonesia, and South Africa must be remedied. If Russia is acceptable despite its increasing authoritarianism then perhaps including China might be acceptable, too.

CHAPTER ELEVEN

_____

Danse Macabre:
Global Governance and Legitimacy

*. . . but I tell you . . . out of this Nettle, Danger, we pluck this flower,
Safety.*

—William Shakespeare,
King Henry the Fourth, Part I, 2.3.9–10

HOW COULD GLOBAL LEGITIMACY be achieved for the doctrine of
transparent sovereignty in international law? How indeed is legitimacy
achieved for any doctrine in a society of states?

It depends on what sort of states they are. For the society of twentieth
century parliamentary nation states, legitimacy was achieved by the parliamentary ratification of legal rules by the various national governments.
This practice has led theorists of global governance to two very different
proposals for the governance of the twenty-first century.

The first of these is by the writer and noted antiglobalization cam-
paigner George Monbiot. He suggests a global democracy of the following
form: a parliament of 600 representing the world's population of 6 billion,
to be elected on the basis of one person, one vote.[1] This parliament would
have no taxing authority, no power over police or any armed forces, no
power to establish courts or any organs of governing, but would, by virtue
of its democratic origins, possess "moral authority." This authority would
be deployed to hold the various states to public account when they trans-
gressed its edicts. Perhaps if such a world parliament were to promulgate a
doctrine of transparent sovereignty, then, whatever the objections of the
various states, this would grant such a doctrine legitimacy.

Such a proposal reflects a mechanical view of how communities of
consent operate. It simply inflates the model of the democratic nation
state, as if it were a balloon that, when filled, retains the relative positions
of any point on its surface. Legitimacy, however, does not come from the
correspondence between formal institutions and the practices of the most
rudimentary concept of democracy, but from the correspondence of democratic practices with the consent of a community. Democracies don't cre-

ate communities, and neither do social theorists; rather, communities create democracies.

That recognition is behind a second proposal to assure legitimacy to global governance. Anne-Marie Slaughter has observed that "networks of national government officials" are everywhere emerging as central bankers, finance regulators, police investigators, judges, health officials, and others create communities of consultation in order to address problems that are transnational.[2] Such networks could create a genuine global rule of law without centralized global institutions. This is an ingenious yet realistic idea because it tracks the way globalization is in fact transforming government-to-government consultation, and because it uses this development to leverage the legitimacy conveyed to officials by the democratic processes that appointed them.

These communities won't be much help in legitimating a doctrine of transparent sovereignty, however, because they ignore the fundamental principle upon which such a doctrine is based, the limitations on government that derive from popular sovereignty and retained rights. The law that binds U.S. officials, for example, must either be the consequence of power directly authorized by the Constitution (like the commander in chief's power or the original jurisdiction of the Supreme Court, for example), or that arising from legislation passed by Congress, or in the treaties consented to by the Senate. There is no American constitutional authority for law made any other way, either by decree or by repeated practice—which is, unfortunately, the basis for customary international law as well as for the social habits of informal "communities of consultation."

Translucent sovereignty rests on different assumptions. As Jed Rubenfeld has powerfully articulated it, this perspective relies on

[a] universal authority, residing in a normative domain above politics and nation states . . . [that allows] international organizations and courts to frame constitutions, establish international human-rights laws, interpret these constitutions and laws, and, in general, create a system of international law to govern nation states. . . . From this viewpoint, it's not particularly important for a constitution to be the product of a national participatory political process. What matters is that the constitution recognize human rights, protect minorities, establish the role of law, and set up stable, democratic political institutions . . .[3]

So we have this dilemma: a doctrine of translucent sovereignty is limited by the very international nation state institutions on which it depends for its legitimacy; a doctrine of transparent sovereignty cannot be legitimated by the acts of international institutions alone. Legitimacy can only come from a new set of treaty regimes, consented to and ratified by states.

States, on the other hand, are the last institutions likely to urge that their own sovereignty be qualified by transparency.

Or are they? For what is true of nation states (and international institutions built out of nation states[4]) may not be true of market states. The society of market states, unlike that of nation states, is not a field of zero-sum conflict. For market states, the wealth and security of each really depends upon the wealth and security of all. The health of American citizens is only as safe as the weakest health care system in the poorest country can make it, because the avian flu that begins in Yangon can be in Los Angeles within days. Insecure WMD in Russia is as much a threat to the U.S. from al Qaeda as they are to Russia from those Chechen separatists with whom al Qaeda is affiliated. North Korean fissile material is as threatening to the U.S., once that material enters a clandestine market, as it is to Japan when it is placed within a warhead atop a medium-range ballistic missile. Indeed, it was this recognition that has undermined the nation state and is bringing the market state into being.

Similarly, the wealth of rich states cannot depend upon extracting wealth from poorer states; if that were its source, it would not last long. Only by creating wealthier states in what were some of the poorest countries—India and China—can the wealth of the rich states continue to grow.

The nation state depended upon its complete freedom in its internal affairs, and its complete legal equality externally. These two conditions defined its sovereignty. It is hardly surprising that the intellectual dogma in international relations known as "Realism" arose in the twentieth century, that is, in the period of the dominance of nation states.[5] Realism could ignore the individual constitutional variations among states by an analysis that was determined entirely by the trait they shared: a will to power. The Molotov-Ribbentrop Pact between a communist and a fascist state is perhaps the most notable historical exemplar that can be used as evidence for this perspective, although many other acts (notably de Gaulle's veto of British membership in the European Community) can be found in late-nineteenth and throughout twentieth century diplomacy.

Now, however, these two foundations of the state, inner and outer, have undergone a dramatic transition. Internally, the state must compete with global, private actors for authority and influence (principally the media, but also transnational financial markets, NGOs, and multinational corporations) and for legitimacy (owing to the growing body of human rights law, among other developments). Externally, the power and presence of the U.S. effectively removes the option of alliance as a practical matter—as we have seen in the repeated but fruitless attempts to organize the "balancing" groups of states (Russia and China, for example) that Realist theory would predict. Above all, the threat from global, networked terrorism[6] has blurred the traditional division between the foreign (the realm of strategy) and the domestic (the realm of law) that has transformed the rules of engagement that hitherto allowed nation states to achieve internal peace and external stability.[7]

Realism, it seems, is increasingly unrealistic. We must look at the internal constitutional life of states to understand their external imperatives.[8] States of terror are driven by a different compulsion—to increase certain opportunities of their citizens (cultural and religious, for example) by weakening those of others—than states of consent, that seek to maximize the opportunities of their citizens by empowering the citizens of other states. In both cases, however, the focus has shifted away from the State to the individual citizen, either as a target or as the locus of concern.

> Treating states as equals prevents treating individuals as equals: if Yugoslavia truly enjoyed a right to nonintervention equal to that of every other state, its citizens would have been denied human rights equal to those of individuals in other states, because their human rights could be vindicated only by intervention.[9]

Chirac's France will lose influence in such a new system, but the France of the European Union will gain. Bush's United States may also find its freedom of action constrained but the U.S. will continue to be the only state that matters everywhere; a later section of this chapter will suggest why this might be an attractive development for the U.S., regardless of the attitude of its current administration. For now, let us simply note that a global order based on transparent sovereignty need not displace the U.S. as a hegemon* so much as adapt that role from the world of bipolarity to the new world we are entering. In the new context, the U.S. would be more claviger and steward—protector and conservator—than hegemon. But in either case why would the states of consent want the U.S. as a leader?

I.

Only the United States has the resources to maintain its defense forces globally and to address the proliferation of WMD, networked transnational terrorism, crimes against humanity, and catastrophes for humane civilian conditions with the deployment of intelligence, military, humanitarian, and diplomatic assets worldwide. It cannot do so successfully alone, yet none of these issues can be satisfactorily resolved without the U.S. Every other power is essentially regional.[10]

*Of course I am using Thucydides' understanding of this term, not Gramsci's.

The equality of states presumed by international law as that law is currently written and understood—the institutionalized rejection of "double standards," as it were—does not reflect this singular strategic role. In time, of course, rules of behavior will ultimately follow strategy whether or not these are rules of law (just as strategy will eventually conform to certain rule-bound constraints if it is to be successful), but it is not clear just how much time we have. The threat posed by global, networked terrorism may be sufficiently menacing that it might provide the impetus for new rules of international law or it may be that support for these reforms will have to await some new, cataclysmic attack. What is needed is an international law that induces and enables the U.S. and its allies to undertake action in the wars on terror; that sets parameters for this action and thereby legitimizes it; and thus sustains it. On all of these fronts—capability, legitimacy, and sustainability—hostile objections to U.S. leadership have been mounted by much of the civilized world.

Considerable effort is currently being expended, much of it by American allies, to construct an international system that will prevent rather than enable the use of U.S. power. It's not that most states want France or Germany or Russia to be the "unipolar" power charged with maintaining a system of world order. If it has to be one state, then the U.S. is probably as good as any, better than most, and likeliest to shoulder such a responsibility.[11] But many states want a countervailing power to the U.S.[12]

The European Union would become, it is hoped in some quarters, a more powerful nation state rather than the umbrella market state I have discussed in earlier chapters. France* and others have pursued the nation state model enshrined in the U.N. and the North Atlantic Council, for these institutions also act as a check on U.S. action so long as unanimity is required before any action can be authorized. The difficulty is that if this check is deployed to frustrate measures necessary to prevent the acquisition of nuclear or biological weapons by a global terrorist movement then the check becomes a lightning rod for terrorist diplomacy. Suppose al Qaeda, or its successors, could threaten European or east Asian cities with nuclear attacks. This would paralyze the permanent members of the Security Council upon which international law today depends. As Michael Reisman has observed, "No leader of a democratic government would be able to undertake elective military action in defense of regional or world order, if a probable cost of victory were the nuclear destruction of one of the country's own major cities."[13] The same paralysis holds for humanitarian intervention. In Somalia, for example, al Qaeda was instrumental in compelling the U.S. to abandon its mission by threatening U.S. forces there. In Iraq, troops from the Philippines were withdrawn to prevent the

*But this was the France of Chirac, not Sarkozy, and the Germany of Schroeder, not Merkel.

beheading of a Filipino whose pleas were broadcast on national television. After the Madrid bombings and the Spanish election, this precedent for accommodation, as Lawrence Wright put it,[14] was quickly followed by the Dominican Republic, Honduras, and Nicaragua.

Perhaps the U.S. would act despite such institutional obstacles.[15] It was not, after all, G. W. Bush's administration but the second Clinton administration that declared it would be "multilateral when we can, unilateral when we must."[16] The issue then becomes one of legitimacy. In the absence of a new international law that legitimates action by a U.S.-led coalition that does not have the consent of all the permanent members of the Security Council—or even the less legitimating consent of all the members of the North Atlantic Council—there is no process generally accepted by the international community to authorize the lawfulness of the use of force. That matters a good deal in the case of discretionary action, like that to avert crimes against humanity, or to preempt the acquisition of WMD, or to deter and detain terrorists, all of which depend on speculative judgments about the future. The publics of democracies are loath to take such actions in any case, and to do so unlawfully makes them even more reluctant. Without the imprimatur of law and legitimacy it is much more difficult to win the cooperation of the public, without which the Wars against Terror cannot successfully be prosecuted.

Or perhaps it's just as well that the U.S. doesn't act. After all, it hasn't done such a great job in Iraq, we are often told. The military campaign against Saddam Hussein was a dazzling success: swiftly accomplished with remarkably low casualties on both sides, without the humanitarian and environmental crises that were predicted.[17] What then went wrong in Iraq was directly attributable to the lack of legitimacy for the U.S.-led Coalition. Practically from the start it was taken to be an occupying force, animated by pro-Israeli, anti-Muslim American policies aided almost solely by the former imperial master of Iraq, Great Britain. Had there been a broader coalition, with experienced troops from many countries (including Muslim and Arab states), there would have been no need for American reservists to run prisons, or for lightly armed Coalition troops to act as police without interpreters, and there might have been the 500,000 troops the task of pacification required. At the very least the problems faced would have been mitigated. If U.S. allies like France and Germany had wished the Iraqi project to succeed, there is much they could have done to legitimate the occupation and marginalize the insurgency without suggesting they had been wrong to oppose an authorizing U.N. resolution. That instead every step was taken to delegitimate the Coalition presence implies that some states, at least, do not wish to encourage American leadership and are willing to sacrifice human rights, antiproliferation, and democratization projects like Iraq in order to frustrate the U.S.

Suppose that a broad coalition is impossible with the Americans; what about one without them? Why must it always—in Panama, in Haiti, in Bosnia, in Kosovo, in Liberia, in Iraq—be the Americans? Why not build up the Article 43 forces called for in the U.N. Charter that have never materialized, or strengthen a European detachment? Or why not write a new U.N. Charter that authorizes humanitarian intervention and that forbids the U.S. from even participating, as was proposed in a remarkably fatuous essay in the *Guardian:* "Only [if the U.S. is excluded] then will international law be able to distinguish an act of aggression from an act of compassion. Only then can humanitarianism be divorced from imperialism."[18] Everyone agrees that regional forces, like ECOWAS in west Africa or NATO in Bosnia, are preferable to outsiders. Why must intervention so often depend on the hegemonic, globe-straddling U.S.? The answer is that intervention, whether for humanitarian reasons or on behalf of world order, is not sustainable without a strategic interest to accompany the legal rationale, and only the U.S. has truly global *strategic* interests.* Thus necessity requires us to confront the problem of how to distinguish between aggression and compassion. This is unavoidable if we seek sustainable effective intervention on humanitarian grounds, and cannot be resolved simply by excluding the despised Americans.

This conclusion flies directly in the face of the usual left-wing criticism of U.S.-led intervention that has been helpfully summarized as asserting three basic arguments: first, it is impossible to send in American forces anywhere, no matter how ghastly the crisis, without affecting the global balance of power elsewhere, thus violating Noam Chomsky's principle that it is better to do nothing than to do something that is accompanied by great harm (i.e., a shift in favor of American interests or power); second, that humanitarian intervention is never against the strong—Russians in Chechnya, Chinese in Tibet—but only against the weak and that this too is illicit (even though presumably the persons on whose behalf humanitarian intervention is taken are weaker still); and finally, that by accepting the possibility of a lawful humanitarian intervention we will be forced to endure innumerable acts of conquest masquerading as humanitarian action.

> As Chomsky points out, Japan claimed that it was invading Manchuria to rescue it from "Chinese bandits"; Mussolini attacked Abyssinia to "liberate slaves"; Hitler said he was protecting the peoples he invaded from ethnic conflict. It is hard to think of any colonial adventure for which the salvation of the bodies or souls of the natives was not advanced as justification. . . . To accept that force can sometimes be

---

*Although the economic interests of all market states are increasingly global in nature.

a just means of relieving the suffering of an oppressed people is to hand a ready-made excuse to every powerful nation that fancies an empire.[19]

Put aside the logic of the argument that because imperialist aggressors have customarily cloaked their depredations in assertions to help the oppressed, any intervening state that claims to be liberating oppressed peoples is an imperialist aggressor. Any act by the U.S. is apparently to be deemed odious. It is hard to conceive that such critics are champions of the dispossessed so much as deeply stained antagonists of the U.S. Whatever their motivation, however, their conclusion is the same for Japanese fascists, Italian fascists, German fascists, and the Bush and Clinton administrations, and it is based on a widely shared assumption that when a state has an obvious interest in the outcome of intervening, it is necessarily intervening improperly and hypocritically.[20]

In fact, it is only when great powers can find an intersection between their own strategic interests—which rightly include their economic interests and the material well-being of their peoples—and humanitarian and human rights concerns, that these states will act with any consistent chance of success in addressing those concerns. Consider these cases.

Perhaps the most selfless international intervention by a major power in the twentieth century was the U.S. entry into World War I. The *Kaiserreich* did not realistically threaten American interests, and there were no markets to be gained, material resources to be commandeered, or territory to be seized and annexed by the U.S. President Wilson had just been reelected on the campaign slogan "He kept us out of war," and the American public was strongly against intervention. Instead of pursuing this popular course, Wilson and his aide, Colonel House, studiedly moved the United States into war to achieve the benign objectives of the famous Fourteen Points, which specifically forbade cessions to the victors (much to the dismay of their allies). The ultimate consequence of all this high-mindedness, however, was the scuttling of the Fourteen Points by the victorious European states at Versailles, the rejection of American participation in the League of Nations by the U.S. Senate, the defeat of the Democratic Party in the 1920 elections, and the American isolationism of the ensuing decades. Wilson's magnanimous instincts could not underpin a long-term policy in the absence of a well-defined strategic imperative and of allies who were willing to run risks in order to distribute burdens.

To many persons in Europe, doubtless an American withdrawal from the world seems as attractive as it does unlikely. They have already forgotten George Bush's 2000 campaign for the presidency, which promised to reject "nation-building" and to walk away from the Framework Agreement with North Korea, and the Middle East peace process—departures that struck a responsive chord with many American voters. It took September 11 to apply a reality check to these temptations, but they are never far below the surface in American politics. Those who favor humanitarian interventions must bear this in mind: without mixed motives, and without American participation, such interventions will bear the stamp of Srebrenica and Ituri, not Kabul or Pristina. The best way of persuading governments to risk the lives of their armed forces for humanitarian goals is to establish a strategic nexus. Partly this will mean redefining what constitutes a strategic interest in order to encompass the collective good of world order; partly it will mean not giving in to the ridiculous game of pretense that a state, or its leaders, can have one and only one value in mind when contemplating intervention.

On May 30, 2003, the U.N. Security Council authorized France to lead a 1,400-man armed force to the Congo, where local militias backed by six different African countries had been at war for more than four years.[21] During this period over 1 million lives had been lost. But the great powers had done virtually nothing save to dispatch 712 soldiers, lightly armed, in 1999 to guard U.N. property and escort humanitarian aid. Even the new French mandate only ran until September, when the French-led force was to be replaced by a weaker Bangladeshi contingent. The humanitarian concerns are overwhelming; the armed opposition slight. Why has nothing, even now, been done? It is because states are unwilling to send their young men and women to be killed without a strategic as well as a humanitarian rationale.

In 1995, 400 lightly armed Dutch peacekeepers stood by while more than 7,000 Muslim men and boys, seized from a U.N.-denominated "safe area," were massacred at Srebrenica which the troops were meant to be protecting.[22] Intervention by the Dutch government at the highest levels, which it went to great lengths to conceal, had compelled the U.N. secretary-general to refuse air strikes to relieve the besieged Muslims. Only after this atrocity, with all that it revealed about the United Nations as a security instrument, did NATO step in and bring about an end to the conflict. The case was finally made in Washington that the U.S. could not claim leadership in the North Atlantic Council while using deference to its European allies as an excuse for nonintervention in a war in Europe; that is, a strategic rationale was provided by the magnitude of the humanitarian crisis.

It is a familiar charge that, because WMD have not been found in Iraq and thus Saddam Hussein never really posed the imminent security threat that might otherwise have justified the Coalition attack, the alleged U.S.-U.K. interest in the welfare of Iraqis has been invented as an alternative justification for intervention. In fact, charges of hypocrisy plagued the Coalition from the outset because it was plain that the West's interest in prising Iraq's oil out of Saddam's hands was at least as important a motivation to the U.S. and the U.K. as making the benefits of that oil pay for ordinary Iraqis. It was Saddam's great wealth, derived from oil revenues, and put in service of his pursuit of WMD,[23] that made his removal so imperative. He was rich, aggressive, and repressive to a degree remarkable even for the Middle East. Other states are just as rich, but have benign geopolitical agendas; Saddam had the unique distinction of organizing the first seizure and annexation of a member state of the U.N. since the organization's founding. Other states are just as vicious and intoxicated with dreams of regional domination, but they are not as rich; even under sanctions, Saddam was able to skim perhaps as much as $12 billion[24] in illicit revenue—with the complicity of elements of the U.N. bureaucracy and various member states, it now seems clear. This is of paramount relevance in an era in which it is no longer necessary for a state that seeks nuclear weapons to develop them on its own, an era that will be notable for black-market trading in WMD technologies. Finally, other states do cruelly repress their own citizens, but few have the wealth to create a state apparatus that can systematically wreak human rights violations on the scale of Saddam's regime and not risk revolution.

And so Iraq's oil wealth cannot have been irrelevant. Why would critics of the war demand that it be so? Why do we expect states never to have multiple, mixed motives when most of us wouldn't choose a university—wouldn't even buy a car—without a complicated calculus of many values, sometimes in conflict?

This demand—that a state's motives must be purely self-sacrificing if they are not to be judged discreditable—reflects expectations about states that are so unrealistic as to be counterproductive to those very goals that human rights advocates wish to promote. Instead of concluding that states with geopolitical interests should be barred from interventions, we should instead be devising doctrines, like the one proposed in the previous chapter, that clearly state how strategic interests, measured on a global scale, intersect with humanitarian interests in order to move states in the direction of protecting civilians. Surely the defeat of global terrorism, which in practice targets the weak and innocent, and the restraint of weapons proliferation, which in principle does not discriminate between the innocent and the guilty, must be humanitarian objectives.

That proposed doctrine, it will be recalled, had three elements. Voluntary coalitions of states led by an alliance of democracies, at best, or a transatlantic alliance at least[25] would intervene when the threat to vital strategic interests was overwhelming and imminent; or when significant strategic interests and humanitarian concerns coincided; or when absent a significant strategic interest, humanitarian concerns were high and strategic risks were low.

If such a doctrine amounted to no more than carte blanche for the use of force whenever it struck the fancy of an American administration or a British government, then it could not provide a basis for legitimacy, to say nothing of predictability, two qualities international law and American policy are much in need of just now. But if, on the other hand, such a doctrine served as the occasion for defining "strategic interests" in terms of collective goods—goods such as building coalitions for humanitarian intervention, extending deterrence and defensive systems in order to prevent nuclear proliferation, and devising global regimes against networked terrorism and for the protection of critical infrastructure and the environment—then the resulting precedents might lay the basis for the new international law that the post–Long War strategic environment requires. That basis would be transparent sovereignty.

If the political left has a negative view of U.S. intervention, so does the right wing. It is captured in the line that "[i]t should occur more naturally to a conservative than a progressive that even a despot is permitted his sovereignty, so long as he does not threaten us."[26] This statement touches on the relationship between an important element remaining to be discussed in this chapter, the relation of the nature of the threat to the status of state sovereignty.

For it is the change in the nature of the threats we are facing that must prompt a change in the international law governing the use of force. Both the rules that determine when it is lawful to go to war and the rules that govern the conduct of warfare will be affected because as presently construed they reflect the passing strategic context of the twentieth century nation state.

The law setting the conditions under which states may resort to military force, the *jus ad bellum,* was shaped in the early part of the twentieth century and largely codified in the United Nations Charter. The unilateral and discretionary use of proactive military force, until then lawful, was henceforth prohibited; reactive military force was to be limited to self-defense and then only insofar as, and until, the international community could come to the assistance of a victim of unlawful military force. . . . [T]ime was less of the essence then than now, given [that] the arsenals of adversaries . . . consisted essentially of kinetic weapons of relatively limited range, often requiring significant time for pre-positioning before activation. . . . Most important, critical weapons were likely to be available in militarily significant quanta only to other states . . . Each [state's] own territorial base made it at once member and beneficiary of, as well as hostage to, the system, susceptible to the ongoing dynamic of reciprocity and retaliation that generates the effectiveness of international law.[27]

The emergence of a territory-less, virtual state and weapons of mass destruction that can be acquired and deployed clandestinely has changed this picture. The *jus ad bellum* of the U.N. Charter simply does not contemplate a strategic context in which the anticipatory use of force is a necessity for a state's survival because the threat, if permitted to mature, can only be suppressed—if it can be suppressed—by running unacceptable risks.

This scarcely ought to be a contested legal issue with respect to al Qaeda. Because a state of war exists between it and other states, parties to that warfare are not required to wait on Security Council authorization in order to respond with force. The state that is under attack is entitled to determine the moment of its response. Indeed, "[s]ince the relation between Al Qaeda and the United States can generally be characterized as a state of war, it would be inappropriate to characterize unilateral United States actions after September 11 as falling in the area of preemptive self-defense."[28] Rather the more contestable point has to do with future networked, non-territorial terrorist states. Their potential victims must be free to use force in order to keep their attackers from gaining WMD without the requirement that these target states must suffer an attack, or be able to prove that an attack is imminent, in order to use force lawfully, for once a terrorist state gains WMD it will be too late to disarm it. Like the context for humanitarian intervention, anticipatory self-defense need not be preceded by an "armed attack" within the meaning of the charter; if this were a prerequisite, the opportunity for meaningful self-defense, which must include the right to be free of political coercion, would be lost, perhaps irretrievably. No one can restore the status quo ante in Rwanda, Cambodia, or Bosnia.

The difficulty, of course, is that such claims on the part of many states would risk international anarchy, for the right to be free of political coercion is an attribute of sovereignty and therefore is available to all states. Does not North Korea have the right of preemption against the U.S. owing to the threats made by Washington against it for its exercise of its sovereign right to acquire nuclear weapons and owing to the fact that the U.S. itself has such weapons, possibly poised for attack on Pyongyang? If we restrict the principle to operation against territory-less states, we avoid such a conclusion and we can rely on deterrence to prevent state aggression, but if we take this route we sacrifice anticipatory action against conventional states that clandestinely assist global terrorism. What then of humanitarian intervention, and precautionary threats to prevent weapons proliferation, actions that will usually take place against conventional states?

A better course is to incorporate the doctrines proposed in this chapter and in chapter 11 into the body of international law as an exception, as was done with the Monroe Doctrine in the days of the League of Nations. This would prevent the anarchic spread of violence among states by confining the use of anticipatory force to states of consent. It would raise, however, the danger of abuse by the U.S., the U.K., and their allies as well as the charge that such a legal rule "would place a particular group of states in a privileged position and would open the possibility that such states may impose on the majority of other states a value system not acceptable to them. This is hardly reconcilable with the principles governing the international community at present."[29]

Well, of course; we are looking to reform the present rules. We need, however, a neutral, general principle of law that would legitimate this departure from present practice. Otherwise it will be a matter of the U.S. and the U.K. acting ad hoc, increasingly hated and distrusted, and eventually finding that the very necessity that compelled their acts has, owing to their illegitimacy, overwhelmed them because that perception of illegitimacy cost them the allies and allegiance they had to have for their strategies to succeed.

That much-needed principle is the rule of transparent sovereignty. The rule for *jus ad bellum* should be that henceforth when a state develops and trades in weapons of mass destruction, or makes alliances with or intentionally harbors global terrorists, or commits large-scale human rights abuses against its own people (including the refusal to treat epidemics, or admit World Health Organization officials to mitigate natural catastrophes*), it compromises that state's sovereignty and becomes a subject for lawful intervention. The determination that it has done so can be made by a global institution of law like the U.N.; or by a regional group, like NATO; or by a concert of states whose members' sovereignty, held to the same standards by the groups of which it is a member, is intact and uncompromised. The sovereignty permitted any particular despot would be no less, but also no more, than that permitted any other despot.

The rules for *jus in bello* must be different, however, because the sovereignty of a state, however rights-respecting, does not accord it the authority to be the sole judge of its behavior in warfare. Indeed, the idea of transparent sovereignty is abhorrent to this practice. Transparent sovereignty is limited sovereignty because the people necessarily retain certain powers, that is, rights they cannot delegate to others, including their governments. That means that reform of the laws of war, including the Geneva Conventions, is an urgent matter—especially for those who wish to prevent the U.S. and its allies from being judges in their own case with respect

*It has been reported that officials in Vietnam lied about the outbreak of SARS cases out of concern for the possible impact on the tourist economy, and there have been persistent reports of WHO apprehensions about being excluded from Myanmar, which has, up to now, cooperated with avian flu investigations.

to their behavior in armed conflicts. Such new rules should be enforced by an international criminal court that, unlike the ICC at present, answers to the U.N. Security Council.

Why then do we want the U.S. to undertake the role of claviger and steward? First, because of all states, it is most able to organize an alliance of democracies owing to its global interests and global power. Second, because American constitutional arrangements are consistent with the doctrine of transparent sovereignty. Third, because we do not believe that any other great power would be markedly less arrogant, less self-interested, less obsessed with increasing its power at the expense of its allies.

Why do we want a claviger or a steward at all? Because such roles are antithetical to the pursuit of empire and provide our best means of avoiding regionalism, which has the potential for global violence previously associated with nationalism. To reemphasize the point: nationalism does not simply go away in market states. In some respects, it is more powerful than ever, as can be seen in the successful campaigns for Catalonian nationalism among others that the market state of Europe—the E.U.—has made possible.* Nationalism in the market state simply has a different relationship to the state than it has with respect to nation states. Because the U.S. is not organized as the representative of a particular region and because its interests span many regions; because it seeks overlapping memberships (such as that enjoyed at present by the U.K., which has allied itself militarily with the world's strongest military power, and economically with the world's largest market) rather than exclusive ones, it remains our best hope for avoiding regional rivalry.

While the emergence of market states has empowered global, networked terrorism, Wars against Terror are not the only or even the most threatening strategic contexts for such states. Far worse would be a regional competition overlaid on the struggle against terrorism. In such a competition great powers would be ranged against one another; some would clandestinely employ terrorist groups against their competitors; others would exploit the Wars against Terror as a means of delegitimating their regional adversaries or even as a pretext for an attack on them, and for violently suppressing the devolution that the structure of market states invites. If the protection of civilians is the overarching goal of states of consent, nothing—and certainly nothing mounted by terrorists—would be as perilous to that goal as a reappearance of great power conflict.

*Connectivity may globalize commercial markets, but it actually localizes political ones. Once we see that "nationalism" is not confined to the particular nations that dominated states—the English, the Han, the Castilians—we see that nationalism actually flourishes in market states once it has freed itself from the nation state. Thus Lombards, Catalans, and Flemings are more vigorously assertive than before. Connectivity also allows immigrants to stay in touch with the societies from which they came, which helps them resist assimilation to the new state and bolsters their nationalism.

There is one especially perilous link between state-to-state conflict and the threat posed by a global network of terror, and this link has important consequences for one current crisis in foreign affairs. As much of the political society of Iran struggles to become a state of consent while the country is in thrall to a theocratic state of terror that has sought nuclear weapons, the members of that society must ask themselves whether acquiring a nuclear arsenal is really in their interest. For if Iran becomes a nuclear weapons state, and the U.S. or Russia are hit with nuclear weapons smuggled into its country and detonated by terrorists, against whom will the stricken state retaliate? There are ample motives for al Qaeda to wish to provoke a war between the U.S. or Russia against Iran. As if to foreshadow such tactics, in Iraq Zarqawi carried out a campaign of slaughter against Shia civilians in order to consolidate Sunni militancy arising from fear of Shia retaliation. This incitement to civil war in Iraq is a minor reflection of what would be a far more ambitious al Qaeda strategic objective. In the event of a WMD attack on the U.S. or Russia, accurate forensics may take many, many months during which new threats may be made to a society already shaken by an unprecedented atrocity.[30] Nor is it impossible that some elements in either the U.S. or Russia might blame the other country.

II.

Why would the U.S. take up the role of claviger and steward?

I have urged that American power be used to build and strengthen a global alliance of the states of consent. The development of new legal rules is crucial to that effort because only adherence to international rules can deliver legitimacy to such an enterprise. Yet there are many who are skeptical about the very notion of an international community whose sense of legitimacy is actually important. They see international rules as obstacles to protecting the American national interest. They hold that legitimacy begins and ends at home. It is sufficient for the U.S. that its constitutional rules are followed. In other words, they reject the fundamental premises of this book: that terrorism has changed from the twentieth century nation state terrorism epitomized by the IRA, ETA, and the PLO to twenty-first century market state terrorism of which the leading exemplar is al Qaeda; that warfare has changed from the large platforms that won World War II and the first Gulf War to the information-driven, light-arms combat and constabulary tasks of Baghdad in 2006, and that the war aim has changed from seizing capitals and deposing leaders to protecting civilians. Rejecting these premises, what have they brought us? While the al Qaeda leadership continues to broadcast its propaganda from a hidden redoubt, we await what seem to be inevitable, escalating attacks; having proclaimed the second Gulf War over in 2003, more Coalition troops have died and are dying in Iraq at present than were killed in the "war" as it was understood by planners; the U.S. is seen in Europe and throughout the Muslim world as a threat to world peace—indeed, as a threat greater than that posed by the acquisition of nuclear weapons by Iran. The survey by the Pew Research Center that collected these dismal figures[31] also found that little remained of the goodwill the U.S. had earned for its aid to victims of the 2004 tsunami in the Indian Ocean. The number and lethality of international terrorist attacks against U.S. and allied targets has steadily increased since 1995 as terrorist networks have acquired a more global character.

Surely such a comprehensive record of failure suggests that the source of our failures is a profound misunderstanding of the situation, and not simply mismanagement or unwise decisions.* Suppose, then, if only for the sake of argument, that the analysis put forward in this book is correct. Why would the U.S. want to strengthen the grip of international law through reform, endorsement, and adherence at a time when we will need the maximum freedom of action to protect ourselves?

The answer runs like this: the problem the U.S., the U.K., and their allies face is not that there is too much international law, but rather that, for two principal reasons, there is not enough. These reasons are first, that as we have seen, international law has not kept up with the changed external, strategic context just as, for example, copyright law has not kept up with the changed informational environment brought on by the Internet; and second, that, as will be seen, actual adherence to (rather than mere endorsement of) the rules of international law is bedeviled by insufficient adherence to the rule of law domestically, that is, within states. To achieve a higher rate of compliance with international law, we must first secure greater observation of the rule of law, which can come only with the acknowledgment of transparent sovereignty (one more example of the mutually affecting nature of inner and outer). This transparent sovereignty can only be underwritten by a cohesive and forward-looking alliance of the states of consent. Such an alliance can only be organized and led by the U.S. This alliance and this concept of sovereignty offer the best way to ensure the safety of the U.S. and its ability to prevail in the Wars against Terror. A system of neutral, general principles is the only means by which the U.S. can protect itself while avoiding the charge of imperialism and the charge that it, and not its enemies, is the real threat to world peace.

The U.S. needs a strong international law to provide the basis for rules

*Nor do I confine these charges of misapprehension to the Bush administration. The Democratic Party, of which I am a member, is overwhelmingly in favor of abandoning Iraq at a crucial moment when the elected Iraqi leaders—Sunni, Shia, and Kurd—have insisted they need American forces to enable their government to organize its own defense. If I am correct in my assessment of the intellectual underpinnings of these false impressions, I must nevertheless concede that they are widely shared.

that will protect it and its allies. Weak laws—either domestically, owing to lax enforcement, or internationally, owing to desuetude and anachronism—favor the states of terror. They can induce states of consent to become states of terror because, in the absence of legal rules, force is the only option remaining that offers safety. Just as we saw in chapter 5[32] that sometimes enhancing the power of states enhances our rights by giving states the means to protect those rights, sometimes increasing the potency of international law increases the powers of states to protect themselves. This apparent paradox recognizes that we must ever compare future states of affairs with other, alternative futures, not with the present or the past. Qualifying sovereignty will mean states have less autonomy than in the past; we will be more constrained than we are at present, but we will be better able to cope in the future with the challenge terror poses to consent because systems of consent depend, in the end, on the rule of law. If this seems like a radical proposal, we should keep in mind the current realities, in which American and Europeans can utterly frustrate one another. Without European endorsement, U.S. initiatives are widely perceived as illegitimate *even in the U.S.* Without American endorsement, European diplomacy is largely irrelevant. And analogous points can be made about Russia (for example, with respect to Iranian nuclear programs) and China (for example, with regard to the North Korean arsenal). We are already in the position where even the greatest powers cannot realize their policies without buy-in from others.

In this chapter, we have already gone through much of this argument: the need for international law reform, the desirability of an alliance of democracies, the indispensability of American leadership, the attractiveness of transparent sovereignty, the undesirability of empire, the paradox of rights and powers. What remains to be shown is how the rule of international law is related to the rule of law within a state and why it is in the interest of the U.S. to join with others in writing rules that in some instances will constrain it.

In a series of important essays,[33] Oona Hathaway addressed the following puzzle: Why is it that international law routinely compels the most powerful states to obey its rules (pointing, for example, to the U.S. decision to rescind steel tariffs that the World Trade Organization found to be illegal under the General Agreement on Tariffs and Trade) and yet has been hopelessly unable to enforce other rules on even the weakest state-parties to treaties and conventions (noting, for example, the dismal fact that 100 of the 140 signatories to the Convention Against Torture have engaged in proscribed practices, including some states—Egypt, Jordan, and Mexico are cited—that use torture just as aggressively at present as they did before the treaty entered into effect)?[34]

To this paradox, Hathaway added various theoretical anomalies:

"interests-based" theories—which hold that states only agree to those commitments whose costs are outweighed by their benefits—couldn't seem to account for the fact that many countries sign on to, and enforce, human rights agreements that effectively constrain their power or that many agreements, like human rights treaties, have little or no binding power on states that choose not to live up to their commitments (and thus cannot deliver reciprocal benefits); "norms-based" theories—which hold that states make agreements that are consistent with their values and aspirations—couldn't account for the fact that autocratic states sign on to human rights agreements at a far greater rate than democracies, or explain why ratification of such treaties seems to bear little relation to their actual enforcement.

Hathaway proposed an analysis that, to put it in the terms of this book, integrated the inner and outer dimensions of the State by looking at the domestic enforcement of international law, and she urged policy proposals to strengthen that enforcement that relied on a decidedly market state approach: using incentives to effect compliance (for example, offering ongoing benefits such as trade, aid, and other tangible inducements to states agreeing to, and complying with, otherwise unrelated international agreements), and enhancing the role of private actors (who, among other tactics, use the legal institutions of the state to wring compliance from it).

Drawing on a large amount of empirical data from a wide variety of treaties, Hathaway argued that rather than relying exclusively on international enforcement of international treaties, it was domestic enforcement that often proved crucial. States where the rule of law was strong, and thus where treaty commitments could be enforced domestically, were less likely to commit to treaties but more likely to comply with those they agreed to. In the absence of transnational enforcement, authoritarian states with a weak commitment to the rule of law were happy to sign on to human rights and environmental treaties with which they had no intention of complying.

Therefore, if the states of consent wish to promote the rule of law domestically, they must strengthen the transnational enforcement of international law or otherwise there will remain a disincentive for states to empower private actors through their own domestic law. In those situations, it is the weak domestic law that, in tandem with weak international law, allows the authoritarian state a way out. By contrast, where there is strong transnational enforcement there is both a bargaining incentive (to participate in a reciprocal regime with other states) to strengthen the rule of law domestically and no longer a reason[35] to maintain a weak commitment to the rule of law. Thus, for example, China's wish to join the WTO—which has a potent transnational enforcement mechanism—has moved it to adopt rule-of-law reforms that were hitherto unthinkable.[36]

Transparent sovereignty strengthens the rule of international law; strength-ening international law helps achieve the objective of states of consent to strengthen the rule of law within states; and strengthening the rule of law domestically further strengthens the enforcement of international law.

Hathaway writes:

> Far from weakening states, international law strengthens those states that choose to use it. It offers them a tool that they otherwise would not have. And in doing so, it allows states to accomplish goals that might otherwise be out of reach. Hence international law empowers even the most powerful of states.[37]

One could go further. The most powerful states are the ones most empowered by law because they have the most influence to write rules favorable to their circumstances and values; because they have the most to lose when law breaks down, even in remote parts of the world where a global power will have interests other states do not; because they cannot ally with each other without coming to an agreement on common rules; and because when they fall out, the most powerful states are the ones that can do each other the most damage.

Furthermore, at present international law, in the words of Jed Ruben-feld, is "often perceived as a vehicle for anti-American resentments."

> A case in point is the position taken by the "international community" with respect to the continuing use of capital punishment in some American jurisdictions . . . [There is a] concerted effort to condemn the United States as a human-rights violator because of the death penalty and to expel the United States from international organizations on that ground. When the international community throws down the gauntlet over the death penalty in America while merely clearing its throat about the slaughter in Yugoslavia, [Americans] see a sign that an anti-American agenda can be expected to find expression in interna-tional law.[38]

I am afraid that there are countless other examples. But we need not assume that "the international community"—an amorphous group of unaccountable and often entirely self-appointed organizations and per-sons—is the principal entity deploying international law. Precisely because international law is being used as a weapon with which to attack the U.S., it must be wrested from the hands of those who at present domi-nate it by default.[39] Disdain for law simply plays into their hands.

A March 2005 National Defense Strategy memorandum by the Penta-gon warned that "[o]ur strength as a nation state will continue to be challenged by those who employ a strategy of the weak using international fora, judicial processes, and terrorism."

A peculiar juxtaposition—courts and terrorists—but one that raises this insistent rejoinder: Isn't the strategy of the strong to resist terrorism and to promote the rule of law, judicial processes and all? It can be better, even from the perspective of our power—in the long run—to write the rules with others, though these rules may sometimes be applied against our wishes, than to abandon rule-following in favor of policies that have no more general appeal than that we want them followed, at least for the time being.

The world is moving from an international order that for a century has been heavily dominated by law and by legal institutions towards an order that relies more on the market and informal, consensual institutions. United Nations peacekeeping forces will be supplemented by coalitions of peacemaking forces and by private military companies; complex arms-control regimes will be replaced by more flexible agreements requiring greater mutual transparency and based on ongoing, mutual incentives for restraint; once-repressive states will adopt more humane practices in order to get access to markets. The emerging market state of which these developments are harbingers is not simply a market, however. The state's essential and unique role lies in its creation and adherence to law.

The current attitude of the U.S. government has been manifested in the studied disdain for the prevailing elements of the international legal order. This distrust of the legal order has unfortunately masked the fact that its destruction would have occurred anyway as we move from the era of one constitutional order to another, from nation state to market state. Instead, the president of the United States has become the person most publicly identified with contempt for international law. The law, it seems, is merely a set of irksome rules to be ignored, or to be evaded, but not to be reformed. Yet, none of the central problems that he faces—terrorism, WMD, the vulnerability of the global infrastructure, precarious financial systems, stolen intellectual property rights, escalating trade barriers—can be solved without law.

It is the element missing in all of the U.S. president's post–September 11 international initiatives. There is no doctrine in the National Security Strategy similar to the doctrine of containment expressed in a legal document, NSC 68,* that governed U.S. policy for four decades. There are no efforts made to write new rules for international law that would give a greater role to the G8 in security matters and global governance, or that

---

*Which includes, by the way, a quotation from *The Federalist* (no. 28). See NSC 68, "United States Objctives and Programs for National Security," 7 April 1950, in vol. 1 of Department of State, *Foreign Relations of the United States:* 1950 (Washington: GPO, 1976), 244.

would reconcile the U.N. Charter with interventions like those in Kosovo and Iraq, or indeed that would set any limits on or standards for humanitarian intervention or WMD preemption or the prevention of terrorist attacks. The U.S. administration offers techniques, like preemption, but refrains from giving guidelines for their use, thus robbing them of any chance to win enduring legitimacy. As Raymond Aron once argued, "The national interest of the United States . . . will not win over any state or arouse any sentiment of loyalty unless it appears jointly liable for an international order, an order of power as well as law."[40]

The U.S. can extend its influence beyond its temporary preeminence if it joins with others in crafting a system of rules to govern state responsibility for civilian well-being, preventing the proliferation of WMD, combating terrorism, and underwriting the creation of institutions that preserve civil society. To fail to do so risks more than the present mood of widespread anti-Americanism: it risks the unity of the states of consent, and all the good they can do together for the world.

III.

The world ought to be governed in new ways, ways that realistically reflect the emerging constitutional order of market states that is replacing the order of nation states. For the nation states of the world—precisely because they are organized around nations—cannot solve global problems. Those states that attempt to do so will be tarred as imperial; those states that fail to even make an attempt will always find national interests to justify their failure. Yet, driven largely by global as well as national devolving forces, deep changes in the governance of nation states are already and irreversibly under way.

It was a fundamental principle of the global governance sought by the nation states of the twentieth century that law and strategy should be separated. Parliamentary nation states sought the primacy of law. As Woodrow Wilson put it at the time of the Versailles Conference in 1919, "What we seek is the reign of law, based upon the consent of the governed, and sustained by the organized opinion of mankind." By contrast, communist and fascist nation states held that law should be rejected in favor of strategy.

The peace conference at Versailles sought a constitution for the new society of nation states that was superseding the society of imperial state nations destroyed by World War I. The constitution for global governance that emerged basically replicated at the global level the system of law that had governed the domestic jurisdictions of parliamentary nation states. Under such a constitution each state stood in relation to the society of states as individual citizens stood in relation to individual states. Each had the same sovereign rights; each was equal before the law; each was represented in a broad-based legislature—the League of Nations—and could appeal to a judicial system, the Permanent Court of International Justice; all states looked to an executive body, the Council, which was supposed to assure security. Although this attempt at global governance failed to arrest the Long War of the twentieth century, which began again in earnest in the 1930s, it was essentially reproduced in the U.N. Charter, which modified but did not fundamentally change the system of global governance introduced at Versailles. The end of the Long War in 1990 and the triumph of the parliamentary nation states left the charter as the basic constitutional framework for the society of nation states as a whole.

This constitution, having achieved so much—decolonization, great power consensus, the imposition of the rule of law in the aftermath of genocide and ethnic cleansing—is now coming unraveled as ad hoc arrangements like those that fought the war in Kosovo and the recent coalition that invaded Iraq marginalize the role of the international institutions of the society of nation states. Some blame the United States for this, as the world's most powerful state that seems to have turned its back on the very institutions for which it fought; some blame other states that have paralyzed the Security Council in Yugoslavia, in Rwanda, in Sudan, in Iraq, and rendered its resolutions practically unenforceable save by unilateral action. But the real fault is simply that organizations made out of nation states are now vulnerable to a new set of challenges that face those states. Insofar as these are fatal to the order of the nation state, they will of course infect the global institutions that nation states dominate and it doesn't much matter which nation states are playing leading roles.

The challenges that nation states are unable to cope with are precisely those that global institutions might resolve but because these institutions create global governance of, by, and for nation states they are disabled almost by definition from adopting the global perspectives such challenges require. As the distinguished diplomat Sir Jeremy Greenstock has observed, the last decades have witnessed a "polarization of globalization": there has yet to be a political globalization, decision-making structures remain national, and the U.N. (to which he was the British ambassador) has failed to manage the political effects of the other globalizations (economic, cultural, technological). The very tactics, technologies, and strategies that brought parliamentary nation states success in the twentieth century have now brought challenges that cannot be met by the currently prevailing international order created by those states.

The transition to a new constitutional order will occur over many decades, and there are many varying forms that the new market state might take. From the perspective of nation states to which we are accustomed, market states seem a disavowal of much we have been taught to expect from the State. With regard to global governance, the preferences of market states for informal incentives, deregulation, and voluntary association may seem like a renunciation of the rule of law itself. Many members of the fraternity of international lawyers have set themselves the task of defending our current arrangements as if this—rather than solving the problems our institutions were set up to treat—were the duty of those who want to preserve the rule of law in a period of fundamental change.

This is complicated by the fact that some political leaders seem to want to dispense with the tedious process of creating new laws and new legal institutions to reflect the changed strategic environment. It is a mystery why the United States has decided to ignore legal reform in favor of a purely strategic approach to the problems confronting the society of states. Here, too, it may be the hangover of long habits of separating law and strategy that is to blame. In much of Europe, American action against Iraq is deplored, but no one tells us exactly how Saddam Hussein was to be brought into compliance with the norms of human rights and international undertakings. In America, we are told that force must be used to preempt potentially mortal threats, but we are not informed as to what standards permit U.S. action against Iraq but do not favor Indian action against Pakistan, North Korean action against South Korea, or Iranian action against Israel (or vice versa for that matter).

Market states, by contrast, will unite law and strategy because they face threats that cannot be met without a broad-based sense among the world's publics that the use of force is legitimate. At the same time, states will encounter strategic threats that require action that is incompatible with the current system of international rules that would protect the acts of predator states by assertions of sovereignty, and international institutions that require unanimity among nation states that purely national interests almost invariably do not permit. But just because market states will be more adept at maintaining their legitimacy than nation states when faced with the novel challenges of the twenty-first century, it scarcely follows that they will develop global institutions that are superior to the ones we have. Indeed, there is every reason to think that because the market itself is global, market states will shun the responsibilities of global governance in favor of a regime that is both far more centralized around one great power and at the same time far more laissez-faire. That suggests that the crucial issue facing us today is how to incentivize market states to take up the responsibilities of statecraft to address issues that will otherwise be shunned.

For example, what states are to be permitted to develop nuclear weapons? When does one state's refusal to protect the global environment by changing its domestic policies—including everything from adopting stronger security standards at nuclear power plants, to inoculating its citizens against epidemics, to moderating its creation of greenhouse gases—call forth sanctions? When can one state intervene in the affairs of another to prevent genocide? To seize terrorists? What universally acceptable norm can serve as the unifying purpose for rules that resolve these questions?

Sir Lawrence Freedman suggests that there is already emerging "a shared norm that organized violence should not be used against civilians."[41] This norm is more novel than it might seem to those who recognize the risks contemporary soldiers run to avoid civilian casualties, and who have no memory of the strategic bombing theories of the twentieth century. Recognizing this norm in law would bring jurisprudence into harmony with the strategic war aim described in chapter 4, namely, that victory consists in minimizing the harm suffered by civilians. Such a norm would also undergird the doctrine urged in the previous chapter, which unites humanitarian intervention, antiterrorism, and counterproliferation. It would also reflect the market state's sensitivity to civilian casualties, which can be seen in the fact that, as Freedman writes, "the trend in Western military thinking is . . . to stress the importance of restraint in situations where innocent civilians may get harmed."[42]

If new rules evolve from market states that reject the nation state's one state, one vote rule for the U.N. General Assembly, and its one permanent member, one veto rule for the U.N. Security Council, what will make these rules legitimate in the eyes of the world? Legitimacy will come from the success of the market states themselves in establishing new rules that are responsive to our changed strategic circumstances. We sometimes forget that institutions whose legitimacy we take for granted—like the U.N. with its basis in the legitimacy of nation states—would not have been perceived as legitimate in earlier eras dominated by other constitutional orders.

It may be that the market state's unique ability to partner with non-state organizations, as well as its global perspectives, offer one avenue to international legitimacy. Some institutions, like the G8, that require neither unanimity nor equality among all states, will play crucial roles. Achieving legitimacy for such a manifestly elite group to take up these roles will not be easy. If, however, nongovernmental organizations can barter legitimacy for adherence to new rules by states, for example by certifying so-called best state practices,[43] this might offer a way forward.

The market state shifts the domestic focus from groups to the individual. A related objective must prevail in the international arena: the structures of global governance for the twenty-first century must be based on the primacy of individuals as members of self-chosen and overlapping groups rather than on the primacy of nations. We must move from state sovereignty based on the role of state citizenship in the global institutions of governance, to a sovereignty based on respect for human rights; from the right of states to develop weapons of their own choosing to the right of societies to be free of predation, including the threat of nuclear annihilation that inevitably accompanies nuclear proliferation; from the rights of states simply to determine the application of their own criminal laws and leave it at that, to the responsibility not to harbor and facilitate the activities of terrorists who target innocent persons abroad.

The inalienable rights of individual persons provide the constitutional basis for limited sovereignty. Limited sovereignty provides the basis in international law for the strategic initiatives of humanitarian intervention, counterterrorism, and limits on the diffusion of WMD, that is, the means by which the state of consent seeks to protect civilians. Limited sovereignty is what makes a state of consent (as opposed to simply a democracy, as Abu Musab al Zarqawi, no less than James Madison, recognized). Therefore one of our first tasks is to develop international legal standards that determine what is comprised by the idea of inalienable rights in the current era.

This move to the primacy of persons as individuals and as members of self-chosen groups rather than only as nationals has several other implications for global governance. Foremost, considerations of history, culture, and geography that were suppressed or highly structured by nation states will be more keenly felt (and expressed). As a corollary, it ought to be possible for individuals to be citizens of more than one state and for their states to be members of more than one regional group. Another implication suggests that wiring the global population to enable access to a universal communications architecture is an important benchmark for global governance. As Betty Sue Flowers has put it:

> The technology that helped to create [the crisis of the nation state] also has the potential to help resolve it. For the first time in human history, a significant fraction of people can interact with each other directly— actively through the Internet and passively through the mass media— rather than through the mediated power structures of their national governments. At this point, the technology outstrips our imaginations: we can use the Internet and mobile phones to organize resistance to global organizations and to make certain national abuses of power better known. But we're only just beginning to imagine how this ad hoc power can be used to help with the challenge of governance. Even so, inherent in this technology is a revolutionary possibility: the organization of global complexity that reaches down to the level of the individual.[44]

Dr. Flowers is right that we don't quite know how to mobilize ourselves to bring a new global governance into being. Having said that, the global governance that emerges from a decentralized, outsourcing, market-oriented network of states will naturally allow for a number of different non-state institutions to work together for the global good. Several institutions can provide models for this.

There are the U.N. agencies, whose record of responsible oversight and transparency has often been inspiring.

> [A]gencies like the High Commissioner for Refugees, the United Nations Development Program and the World Food Program [whether] coordinating the global relief effort in the aftermath of the tsunami [or] providing shelter for refugees from southern Sudan [or] shepherding East Timor to independence . . . have brought meaningful, measurable progress to millions around the world. . . . Taking one step further toward the model of, say, the World Health Organization (which operates independent of United Nations governing structures, though it is part of the United Nations family) [would neither] disrupt its operations nor damage its finances. To the contrary: freed from the management rules and practices still imposed by the General Assembly, the Development Program would be even more able to attract the [most capable] people and improve the lives of the poor.[45]

These agencies are already beginning to outsource operations and to cooperate with NGOs on problems such as public health and rural development. Royal Dutch Shell has a joint partnership with the U.N. to address AIDS in Africa; there is no reason why Archer Daniels Midland could not similarly activate the U.N. agricultural agencies to prevent famine and malnourishment. Because, as earlier observed, the health of any society is only as secure as the medical conditions of the worst-off society, whose infections can circle the globe in hours, there must be ample reason for GlaxoSmithKline or Pfizer to join with the World Health Organization to improve preventive care and early warning systems in the poorest countries.

International NGOs do not have that basis in legitimacy that is provided by democratic processes. What is needed is greater transparency in the operations and funding of NGOs. Among the most important NGOs, although we don't think of them this way, are multinational corporations. Just as governments in the era of the market state will have to learn the business methods of wealth creation, so businessmen—however much they may dislike it—will have to learn the methods of winning public consent, for they have truly global interests. Demonstrating that these interests coincide with the interests of the peoples of the world will also require greater transparency. Instead of harassing corporations, at least some activists should be working for them and moving them towards trans-

parency and the furtherance of the public interest.* A really successful
African venture capital fund would do far more to end poverty, on a sustained basis, than the charitable support from businesses and governments
that is, rather pathetically, in vogue.

Every society has a constitution, and the society of states is no different. Therefore global governance does not require a global government.
It is absurd to say that for global governance to exist we must write a constitution or that the forms of representation individual cultures rely on are
the only ways of assuring legitimacy to global institutions. When a new
society of states emerges, we will find that it, too, has a constitution. Our
duty is to see that it is a humane one, that it gives primacy to the health,
safety, and opportunity of the people of the earth and not to states that,
generally, do not have the self-interest sufficient in the matter to address
global problems.

We must bear in mind that even long-running wars against terror, with
all their risks, are not the worst fate for the U.S., the E.U., or mankind. Far
worse would be armed conflicts among great powers. "Symmetric warfare," to coin a phrase, would be infinitely more malignant than anything a
terrorist network or "rogue state" could mount. In such wars the cost in
lives would be measured in the hundreds of millions. Because law and
strategy exist in this mutually affecting relationship, developing legal
practices and institutions now can steer our fate away from such terrible
conflicts.

As the Summary Report of the Grand Strategy Working Group concluded,

> doctrines of active counterproliferation, the preemption of terrorist
> attacks, and an agreed-upon basis for humanitation intervention all
> await international legal recognition. Without both legal reform to
> bring international and domestic law into accord with strategic con-
> text, and a thorough re-thinking of doctrines of warfare to integrate
> regard for law into our strategic missions, the war against terror cannot
> be won.[46]

The Wars against Terror offer opportunities for collaboration among
the great powers, incentives to attend to otherwise neglected political conflicts, and enormous penalties for the single-minded pursuit of the nationalist, nation state agenda. For the states of consent the imperative is
"cooperate or die."

---

*Official government aid to developing countries is at present only a small fraction of that sup-
plied by private capital, a dramatic change from the recent past. From 1983 to 1988, the ratio of public
to private flows of capital to the poorer countries averaged just under 2:1; from 1989 to 1995, the ratio
switched to 1:5; by 1997 it was 1:10. See Treverton, "Intelligence and the Market State."

CHAPTER TWELVE

The Triage of Terror

I have heard that voice many a time when asleep
And, what is strange, I understood more or less
An order or an appeal in an unearthly tongue:

Day draw near
Another one
Do what you can.

—Czeslaw Milosz, "On Angels"

THE REMAINING TASK is to infer a new kind of decision making from the historical, comprehensive coup d'oeil that comprehended the Wars against Terror as composed of its three elements. We must take anticipatory action in each arena—through military preemption, diplomatic preclusion, or taking preparations to mitigate—because once a truly horrific catastrophe occurs the strategic result follows ineluctably. That is because the result is terror itself, which alters the political ecology of consent. From that requirement we can infer this *coup de raison:* a changed way of making decisions that focuses on the hypothetical state of affairs sought to be prevented. This puts greater burdens on intelligence, consistently avoids Parmenides' Fallacy, prefers scenario planning to strategic estimates, and requires greater trust and transparency in the relationship between governments and their peoples.

Once we have accomplished this integration, however, we are made aware of a very difficult problem. It is this: we cannot pursue an agenda in the Wars against Terror that will positively affect all three theaters of concern (global, networked terrorism; WMD proliferation; and human catastrophe) at the same time. In fact, often the most successful pursuit of any one of these objectives operates negatively with respect to the others.

If we pursue market state terrorists ruthlessly to their harbors, we will frighten their hosts (who may then seek protection by acquiring WMD) and destroy many innocent lives in the process of twenty-first century warfighting (as we have done in Iraq). If, on the other hand, we give security guarantees and share technology as the surest way to prevent proliferation, we take on board partners whose commitment to human rights may be highly questionable (Russia, for example, or China) and whose campaign against terror is largely confined to the national liberation groups that bedevil them, leading in the end to new alliances for our terrorist adversaries. We have seen this in Chechnya, in Palestine, and elsewhere. If we focus principally on human rights, we sacrifice necessary allies in the war on terror—where would we be in Afghanistan without the collaboration of Pakistan?—and give incentives to states to arm themselves to avoid humanitarian intervention. Finally, to complete the "triage" we know that a secret military mission in early 2005 to capture Zawahiri and other senior al Qaeda figures was aborted at the last minute by the U.S. owing to fears that the operation might destabilize the Pakistani government, conceivably even to the extent of allowing an anti-Western regime to come to power and with that to come into possession of nuclear weapons.[1] This union linking the comprehensive view of the conflict as an epochal war with possible-worlds analytics* is not contrived. Recall the disturbing case of Dr. A. Q. Khan, an early innovator in the commodification of nuclear weapons discussed in chapter 2.

We do not know the extent of the client base Khan's network developed. It is believed that the list included not only Iran and North Korea but also Egypt, Saudi Arabia, Algeria, Kuwait, the United Arab Emirates, Malaysia, Indonesia, Afghanistan, and Myanmar. Khan was arrested in 2004 but it is assumed that the network is still functioning; the failure to roll up this enterprise is the direct result of the triage of terror.

That is because Khan occupies an important role in Pakistani public life—he is widely revered as the father of Pakistan's nuclear program—and Pakistan's president, Pervez Musharraf, is a crucial ally in the struggle against al Qaeda. Musharraf has not permitted any interrogation of Khan. Pakistan continues to maintain that neither its military nor its intelligence services were aware of Khan's activities.

To this of course must be added the compromise of human rights and the restriction on democratic processes that have characterized Pakistan since the military took over the government in 1999. This completes the triage: of the three elements of the Wars against Terror, only one—the fight against global terrorism—has been served by U.S. policy. Were the others pursued as ardently, and Pakistan lost as an ally owing to the weakening of President Musharraf's position, it is widely believed that the creators of the Taliban and allies of al Qaeda might now have a nuclear weapons arsenal and control of a state whose human rights record would grow dramatically worse.

---

*For various reasons, it has been decided to publish separately a short volume illustrating these possible words. See *Global Scenarios for the Wars on Terror* (forthcoming, 2008).

Thus it may be that Coalition operations in Iraq have made matters better than they otherwise would have been in the Wars against Terror by removing Saddam Hussein, but they have made things clearly worse with respect to terrorism. Not only has Iraq become a rallying cry for militant Muslims around the world, the Iraqi theater of combat operations itself has replaced the camps in Afghanistan as a training ground for jihadists. The skills learned there—surveillance and tracking, the use of safe houses and concealed weapons caches, bomb-making and ambush—are, in the words of a former senior intelligence analyst at the U.S. State Department, "more relevant terrorist skills . . . to Europe than [those learned in] Afghanistan."[2]

Militants in Iraq are turning out instructional videos and electronic newsletters on the Internet that lay out their playbook for a startling array of techniques, from encryption to booby-trapped bombs to surface-to-air missiles, and those manuals are circulating freely in cyberspace. [T]actics common in Iraq are showing up in other parts of the world. . . . "[I]n the future the jihad will be fueled from the battle-field in Iraq . . . [m]ore so than the battlefield in Afghanistan."[3]

A similar triage occurs with respect to biological weapons. If we attempt to prevent their development, we infringe the rights of inquiry on which scientists rely as well as the well-being of those persons who might have received effective treatment had the research that was restricted actually been carried out and borne fruit. "Even generalized restriction within fields with greatest application towards bioterrorism or [biological weapons] could greatly hinder biodefense research efforts to develop medical countermeasures, including new vaccines and therapeutics." And when we attempt to thwart a terrorist attack using such weapons by developing vaccines or treatments we inevitably make proliferation possible. Consider these cases:

In 2000, Australian researchers genetically engineered a strain of mousepox virus in a way that inadvertently increased its virulence. [Their technique is openly available; it would allow mousepox to be used against humans.] . . . In July 2002, researchers at the State University of New York at Stony Brook revealed that they had successfully created infectious poliovirus from artificially engineered DNA sequences. Some observers saw open publication of their achievement in the journal *Science* as enabling the proliferation of a methodology with high BW [biological weapons] potential. Researchers at the University of Pittsburgh identified key proteins in *variola* (smallpox) that contribute to the virus' virulence and demonstrated how to synthesize the virulence gene via genetic modification of smallpox's less deadly cousin *vaccinia*. . . . Researchers at the University of Pennsylvania successfully developed a hybrid virus composed of an HIV core surrounded by the surface proteins of *ebola*. This new virus was capable of infecting lung tissue, potentially enabling aerosol delivery, and could facilitate the expression of foreign genes in infected cells. . . . Researchers in Germany reported the creation of a DNA-based system for performing reverse genetics studies on the *ebola* virus. This system introduced the possibility of reconstituting live *ebola* virus from DNA in the absence of a viral sample.[4]

The triage with respect to the life sciences can be especially cruel because the research needed to fight disease—and bioterrorism—cannot be separated from the knowledge it yields.

We can observe this triage of terror in a range of scenarios for the next three decades. One such scenario leads to empire, which is relatively effective in supporting humanitarian interventions, less so with regard to proliferation, and would be a disaster at fighting global terrorism, which it actually tends to excite. In another we achieve multipolarity, which is a catastrophe for proliferation even if it is rather better at suffocating terrorism and has little effect on humanitarian crises. In yet another scenario we find that regimes of martial law become inevitable; these, though they can be effective against terrorism (torture, perhaps, can work in such an environment, in part because it is hidden), do nothing to inhibit proliferation and provoke humanitarian crises brought about by crimes against humanity—including the crimes of which state torture is an example.

There are more positive scenarios that can make terrorism, proliferation, and humanitarian assistance much more manageable—the doctrine proposed in chapter 9 and the legal reforms of chapter 10 make their appearance in these possible worlds—but they are realized only by a constant shifting of priorities in order to accommodate the aspects of triage that characterize the Wars on Terror. Such regimes demand by far the most of leaders and also of their publics. Vis-à-vis Americans and Europeans, they require, among other sacrifices, that we contemplate the disagreeable assumption that our difficult friends may, after all, have a point. Because market state terrorism is most lethal when it acquires WMD, it is reasonable to give the pursuit of nonproliferation a priority, if only temporarily so. For the foreseeable future, we must reenergize our nonproliferation efforts, beginning with an active but sober approach to denuclearization in the most politically fraught regions. The role such weapons play in the warfare of market states is far different from the role they played in the Long War of nation states.

First, the crucial function of certain retaliation has no saliency against a terrorist enemy who is hidden among civilians. Second, the advancing technology of the most developed states has created weapons that are equally effective at destroying armies and infrastructure because these weapons are so accurate, and are far more effective in achieving the war aim because they are more discriminating and less colossally destructive. Third, it is not credible that states will forswear the development of nuclear weapons so long as these are held by their neighbors.

The most important step thus far taken against proliferation was that of President Johnson in the 1960s with the ratification of the NPT. Much has changed since then. The central though tacit element in Johnson's policy was the maintenance of extended deterrence—the threat to use weapons to protect allies that otherwise might acquire their own nuclear weapons. No realistic policy of denuclearization can take place unless a market state replacement for extended deterrence—through defensive systems, security guarantees, redundant infrastructure, shared intelligence and warning—is found.

I have earlier discussed how denuclearization might come to the Middle East through such a combination of market state incentives. We sometimes forget that while South Africa is the only state thus far to have created a nuclear weapons capability and then destroyed it, many states have abandoned advanced nuclear weapons research programs, among them Australia, Argentina, Brazil, South Korea, Sweden, and Taiwan. Moreover, at least three states—Belarus, Kazakhstan, and Ukraine—had large numbers of deployed nuclear weapons that were voluntarily relinquished. The key element in these decisions, as it was also the key to keeping Japan and Germany nonnuclear, was providing credible security guarantees.

Paul Stares, vice president for conflict analysis and prevention at the U.S. Institute for Peace, has proposed a similar approach to the problem of North Korean proliferation.[5] Guaranteeing security to Kim Jong Il might well, along with other steps, move him to credibly abandon his modest but nonetheless deeply troubling nuclear program. This would be a notable achievement, but it would also be a disaster for human rights on the peninsula and would do nothing to improve the malignant relationship between the North Korean regime and terrorism. This, again, is the triage that the problem of dealing with terror in this century can impose.

On January 4, 2007, four respected figures in U.S. national security—I am inclined to say the four most respected figures*—authored an essay in an American newspaper. It urged this program:

---

*Henry Kissinger, Sam Nunn, William Perry, and George Shultz. See "A World Free of Nuclear Weapons," *Wall Street Journal*, 4 January 2007, A15. But see also Michael Quinlan, "Abolishing Nuclear Armouries: Policy or Pipe-Dream?" *Survival* 49, no. 4 (Winter 2007–2008) (forthcoming), and Michael Quinlan, "The Abolition of Nuclear Weapons: Time for Serious Examination?" on file with author.

First and foremost is intensive work with leaders of the countries in possession of nuclear weapons to turn the goal of a world without nuclear weapons into a joint enterprise. Such a joint enterprise, by involving changes in the disposition of the states possessing nuclear weapons, would lend additional weight to efforts already under way to avoid the emergence of a nuclear-armed North Korea and Iran. The program on which agreements should be sought would constitute a series of agreed and urgent steps that would lay the groundwork for a world free of the nuclear threat. Steps would include:

- Changing the Cold War posture of deployed nuclear weapons to increase warning time and thereby reduce the danger of an accidental or unauthorized use of a nuclear weapon.
- Continuing to reduce substantially the size of nuclear forces in all states that possess them.
- Eliminating short-range nuclear weapons designed to be forward-deployed.
- Initiating a bipartisan process with the Senate, including understandings to increase confidence and provide for periodic review, to achieve ratification of the Comprehensive Test Ban Treaty, taking advantage of recent technical advances, and working to secure ratification by other key states.

A world free of nuclear weapons would be, I fear, only a temporary one. But a world in which U.S. nuclear guarantees underpinned regional denuclearization is possible. The way to achieve this is connected to the phenomenon of market state terrorism.

This link arises from the problem of nuclear attribution. If a target state is struck by terrorists using nuclear weapons, how does its leadership know against whom to retaliate? After the October 2006 detonation by North Korea, President Bush issued an explicit warning that the "transfer of nuclear weapons or material" to terrorists would be "considered a grave threat to the United States," and that North Korea would be held "fully accountable."

Such a warning is possible because the IAEA has a library of nuclear samples taken from North Korean reactors before the agency's inspectors were ejected in 2002. If the device were derived from North Korean plutonium materials, it ought to be forensically feasible to determine its origin. But that would work only if such a database were available for every nuclear source, worldwide, and that can happen only when the states of the world agree to nuclear transparency.

Moreover, such a global approach would also help with the problem of the security of nuclear materials. As Robert Litwak has pointed out,[6] there is an important distinction between the "leakage problem," which implies an inadvertent loss of control, and the "provider problem," which arises from an intentional act, to which I would add the "insubordination problem," which occurs when some element of the nuclear weapons state acts in defiance of the leadership and intentionally leaks nuclear material to terrorists.

So long as states face the possibility of savage retaliation should attacks be conducted with nuclear materials whose DNA, as it were, can be traced to their arsenals, these states will want to enforce the strictest security for these arsenals and will be presented with an important incentive to denuclearize themselves. The accuracy and therefore the lethality of weapons in the U.S. armory will soon mean that such retaliation need not be nuclear to be assuredly convincing. This means that the U.S. need only retain a modest nuclear force to deter a surprise breakout.

When confronting the argument that the Wars against Terror link market state terrorism, WMD, and human rights, some commentators may at first be inclined to conclude that this is merely a matter of maniacally expanding the scope of the threat[7] (perhaps in order to justify ever-expanding state authority), but in fact, this approach produces a constraint on our methods. We cannot indulge in "homeland security" because our vulnerabilities are international. We must have international support to undertake interventions like Iraq successfully; this gives American allies a more effective voice than any veto in a multilateral forum because an unsuccessful intervention collapses the triage, making all aspects worse. As observed in the previous chapter, if the United States is unable to persuade its European allies to join in concert with regard to any proposed action, that action loses legitimacy: if Europe cannot persuade the U.S. to participate in joint action, that action is unlikely to succeed.

We are required to merge counterinsurgency and counterterrorism, which hitherto we separated as war and crime. This will mean a very much larger defense establishment at the time when the armed forces are becoming more expensive to recruit and retain. This linkage also means that humiliations like Abu Ghraib are more costly than battlefield defeats but more difficult to avoid; that practices like the Guantánamo interrogations cannot be conducted outside of the law but are counterproductive within the law as it is currently written. All of our failures thus far reflect, then, a lack of appreciation for this linkage, not an oversensitivity to it.

We must remember that the future is something that we create—that is, that the constraints within which we operate are not so strong as to determine the outcome of our endeavors independently of our decisions. Therefore the future is, in the vivid phrase, something to be achieved, not predicted.[8]

We are entering an era of turbulent and even dangerous constitutional change among and within states. The dominance of the nation state, codified in the practices and constitutions of the last 130 years, will slowly ebb until, at an unpredictable moment, its legitimacy collapses. It is our task to manage this transition, knowing that in the past such transitions have been accompanied by the great violence of epochal wars, often begun by civil wars such as the civil war now raging within Islam.

In the United States we may well face a constitutional crisis within the next three decades. One can already see harbingers of the market state and of the changes terrorism will wring from our constitutional processes as those processes become "de-massified,"[9] with more differentiation, more customization, a higher demand for information by the public, greater complexity for decision makers, and a greater diversity of public policy and public choice. To take but two recent examples, California has now trumped the Bush administration's plan to restrict stem-cell-research funding by offering a $3 billion bounty program to stimulate this research (a market state evasion of the federal commerce power's constitutional limitation on state regulation when it conflicts with the federal government's power); and the State Department has put a commercial broadcasting station on its list of terrorist organizations, with all the implications for First Amendment jurisprudence that a globally connected communications structure implies.

Such domestic confusion reflects, perhaps unexpectedly, a moment of great international opportunity for the United States and the E.U. There is a better alternative than either submitting to an international legal regime that does not recognize America's unique global responsibilities or disdaining the rule of law in favor of the ad hoc. Rather we should be writing those rules and learning how to achieve consensus for them.

We need a thorough and methodical reformation of our habits of thinking about the world, roughly like the one that occurred during the First World War when the U.S. emerged from isolation to become a great power. At that time E. M. House,[10] Woodrow Wilson's national security advisor, convened the Inquiry. This group, composed of lawyers, journalists, educators, diplomats, and civil servants, conducted in secret a far-ranging exploration of America's role in what was hoped would become the postwar world. We need a new Inquiry composed of fewer lawyers and more businessmen, fewer academics and more journalists, fewer diplomats and more scientists, and especially persons from other important countries. The work of such a body can guide us in writing the rules for the international society of states.

We sometimes forget that the Wars against Terror are by no means the worst eventuality in a world moving from nation states to market states. That status would have to be reserved for high-intensity wars among the most highly developed states. This frightening possibility has many implications for defense budgets, for example: it suggests, paradoxically, that we will have to maintain expensive conventional armaments, as well as nuclear ones, in order to force conflict into those asymmetric channels within which those armaments are not useful. It implies that the force structure of our alliance will have to specialize rather than create expensive and diminutive national duplicates of the U.S. force structure. It also suggests that an international legal consensus is more than just a necessity for winning the Wars on Terror (which it is).

Just as the parliamentary nation state emerged from three contending possibilities for that constitutional order, so too will the market state offer several variations. One possibility is an *entrepreneurial market state*. Applying this model, deregulation and privatization are key features of government. These go hand in hand with other policies, which include reduced rates of taxation, lower welfare benefits coupled with greater opportunity for labor retraining, free trade, and relaxed immigration rules. Security issues are likely to be a paramount concern. Life in such a society might be best characterized as a permanent condition of impermanence when it comes to questions of government policy, as improvisational decision making supplements long-range policy planning. It is a good environment for market states of terror because it sacrifices legal rules, preferring instead to rely on the market supplemented by ad hoc legal action.

States following the model of the *mercantile market state* are more concerned with supporting commerce and preserving national and cultural identity. Here, strong alliances are forged between government and industry; capital rather than labor is the focus of domestic fiscal policy. Protectionism has a place as well. In matters of culture, ethnic homogeneity and continuity are core values. These policies are likely to lead to less international cooperation between states on matters of security and, alarmingly, the proliferation of nuclear and other forms of weaponry. Here, too, market states of terror can flourish, in this instance behind a façade of nationalism.

Yet another form of the constitutional order might be called the *managerial market state*. Life in these societies is a high-maintenance affair, akin to contemporary life in the Federal Republic of Germany. The economy will be slow to innovate and grow: economic efficiency will be sacrificed in favor of social cohesion and equality. Aggravating this situation will be continuing resistance to the liberalization of labor markets in order to protect high-wage jobs. Managerial market states are more concerned with the quality of life than with growth (entrepreneurial) or market share (mercantile).[11] Such comfortable societies are reluctant to campaign against massive human rights violations, even on their own doorsteps. This model poses the special risks attendant to exalting regionalism and antiglobalization. I am inclined to believe that different approaches to statehood, more than the mishandling of affairs, are responsible for the current differences manifest in the Atlantic Alliance.

It is by no means impossible that these different constitutional forms might find themselves in conflict—perhaps provoked by the internal collapse of the formerly Second World states of Russia or China, for example, as these states struggle against the devolutionary pressures attendant to becoming a market state; or by disagreements regarding counterterrorist interventions in the former Third World; or when regionalism presents the same sort of destructive threat to the state system in the twenty-first century that nationalism did in the twentieth, with all its propensity for conflict and the proliferation of WMD. But wars between the market states of the future can be avoided if we cultivate the habits of cooperation learned in the coalitions needed to prosecute the Wars against Terror successfully. In acquiring such habits, with others, the United States and the E.U. should have a decisive role, if we are only aware of what is required of us and can persuade others to see what is required of them.

This era will not see the end of war; but it need not fall victim to cataclysmic wars either. The United States is a key driver in this future: it is because the U.S. maintains such a high level of conventional preparedness that warfare has moved into the asymmetric dimension. By attending to that high level—which is expensive—the U.S. can force conflict into a lower zone of intensity. In the end the Wars against Terror may prove our best hope for a relatively better future than we would otherwise have. "It is mournful work," wrote St. Augustine, "sustaining relative good in the face of greater evil."

> what is our innocence,
> what is our guilt? All are
>   naked, none is safe. And
>   whence is courage: the unanswered question,
> the resolute doubt,—
> dumbly calling, deafly listening—that
> in misfortune, even death,
>   encourages others
>   and in its defeat, stirs
>
> the soul to be strong?
>
> —Marianne Moore, "What Are Years?"

CONCLUSION

A Plague Treatise for
the Twenty-first Century

It is not the function of the poet to relate what has happened, but what may happen that is possible according to the law of probability or necessity. The poet and the historian differ not by writing in verse or in prose. . . . The true difference is that one relates what has happened, the other what may happen.

—Aristotle, *Poetics,* IX

PLAGUE TREATISES were books written in the fourteenth, fifteenth, and sixteenth centuries by physicians and clerics trying to explain to their contemporaries what had caused the plagues that attacked Europe and how to cope with them. Some blamed the sinfulness of the victims. Others blamed infidels like Muslims and Jews, or heretics like certain Christian radical sects we might nowadays call "fundamentalists." One author, John of Paris, wrote at the beginning of the fourteenth century that we might never know what truly caused the plague. Today, at the beginning of the twenty-first century, global, networked market state terrorism is not much better understood than the plague was then.

WE MUST REFORM OUR IDEAS ABOUT TERRORISM,
WAR, AND THE WAR AIM IF WE ARE TO WIN THE WARS
OF THE TWENTY-FIRST CENTURY IN ORDER TO PRESERVE
STATES OF CONSENT AND PREVENT THE TRIUMPH
OF STATES OF TERROR.

The problem of terrorism is similar in some ways to that of an epidemic. Like new antibiotic-resistant strains of tuberculosis, market state terrorism is a function of what we have done to eradicate old threats. That is, its principal causes are the liberalization of the global economy, the internationalization of the electronic media, and the military-technological revolution—all ardently sought innovations that won the Long War of the twentieth century. New, mutated strains of tuberculosis are resistant to antibiotics for similar reasons, that is, they are the direct result of the successful attack on earlier forms of the virus, remnants of which have mutated in order to survive. In the twentieth century we managed to tame an acute problem—the industrial wars of the nation state that claimed tens of millions of lives. In the process we have created a chronic problem. That chronic problem will be the destabilizing, delegitimating, demoralizing terror that arises from the intersection of market state terrorism, the market state's commodification of WMD, and the increasing vulnerability of market states to catastrophic events.

We have had states of terror before, though perhaps we didn't call them that. For Saddam Hussein no less than for Philip II and the Inquisition, terror was an important technique of governance. And, too, states of consent have long been menaced by groups for whom terrorism was an effective method of disruption. Ebola and Marburg viruses, too, have long existed in remote parts of the world. The difference is that now the connectivity of all parts of the world means once deadly epidemics that burned themselves out in the obscure corners of a continent now spread quickly across the globe.

Similarly, states of consent face a much greater threat from terror than ever before. That is because twentieth century market state terrorists will seek terror as an end as well as a means, promising a perpetual and global threat owing to their non-national goals as well as to the virtual proximity that allows them to pursue these goals globally.[1] States of terror, too, pose a new kind of threat: by using WMD to prevent humanitarian and defensive interventions, they will achieve lateral deterrence. WMD will become a tool of compellance in international affairs, making the human rights regimes states of consent extraordinarily difficult to sustain.

Like the authors of the plague treatises, who did not know the true etiology of the plague because they did not have the germ theory of infection, we may not know the true etiology of market state terrorism simply because we do not have the conceptual tools that enable us to analyze this new and complex phenomenon. We must confront the possibility that we will not extinguish global terrorism because we and the rest of the international community will be unable to transform our ideas rapidly enough. Much important work remains to be done on the conceptual side of this war. We do not, as of yet, have the intellectual movement of which Jacob Viner, Bernard Brodie, and Thomas Schelling were leaders, and the RAND Corporation and the International Institute for Strategic Studies were centers, that provided a framework with which to analyze nuclear strategies during the Cold War.

What we do know is that terror is the enemy of conscience and therefore it is the enemy of consent. One who can't say "No" cannot truly say "Yes."[2] That places terrorism along with crimes against humanity and compellance by WMD at the center of the threats to our survival as states of consent. Others know this, too. On December 28, 2004, on the eve of the Iraqi elections, Osama bin Laden released an audiotape. "Everyone who participates in these elections will be considered infidels," he said, and as such subject to attack. The true image of al Qaeda and the Sunni cells with which it has linked up in Iraq is not merely that of a stately bin Laden draped in the robes of an emir, announcing diplomatic initiatives on al Jazeera, but rather also a grainy telephoto of a gunman standing over a kneeling, unarmed election official whom he is about to murder in a street while passersby do nothing.* That is an image from a state of terror.

We must also be clear, however, about what constitutes a state of consent. A state of consent need not be a Western-style democracy.[3] Furthermore, as states evolve, the precise indices that identify the state of consent change. We have had states of consent in the past—the Florentine republic or Hanoverian Britain, for example—that were far from democracies. James Madison and the framers of the American constitution were at pains to stress that they were creating a state of consent but not a democracy. Indeed, as I have suggested, one terrible possibility is that the Wars against Terror will be lost and that our democracies will become states of terror, as eventually happened to Rome. Today, a market state of consent is one in which all persons can exercise the rights of conscience and in the politics of which the individual conscience plays the decisive role by means of a consensual, constitutional system of laws.

We will not win the Wars against Terror if we do not understand the novelty of the problem we face. By assimilating this struggle into the Long War against twentieth century fascism and communism, we mistake what is unique to the Wars against Terror—the import into our societies of psychological states that render free consent impossible and the export into states of terror of global effects that jeopardize traditional means of coercion. Terrorism is changing, as it has in the past, with the emergence of a new constitutional order. Warfare, too, is changing, and our attempts to assimilate it into the patterns we grew accustomed to in the twentieth century have proved very costly indeed. Finally, our war aims are changing, and an appreciation of this will be necessary before we know precisely of what true victory consists. Here again our confusion has already been manifest as we have repeatedly sacrificed the legitimacy of our efforts in a vain attempt at "victory" misconceived.

The reason why the United States is not itself a terrorist state even though its warfare brings suffering and destruction to many innocent persons, including civilians, is that it acts within the law. When it ceases to do so—because, for example, the law itself has not kept up with changes in

*See the frontispiece to this book.

the strategic context—the U.S. runs the risk of becoming, in the eyes of many, simply another state of terror.

For some persons, this seems already to be the case. They see air strikes against Fallujah or Belgrade or Mazar-e-Sharif, and they conclude that they are witnessing the acts of a terrorist state. Perhaps they have fewer objections to the regimes of Saddam Hussein, Slobodan Milosevic, and the Taliban because these were, they presumably believe, lawful regimes. That such a conclusion could be drawn, one so costly to unity among the states of consent, only emphasizes how important it is that law be sharply and thoroughly reformed so that we can determine precisely when a state is using force legitimately in this new context. As Sir Michael Quinlan has urged,

> Especially today, legitimacy has an important bearing on efficacy and therefore on credibility. Partly for reasons of economic globalization and interdependence, and partly for reasons of the worldwide transparency that modern communications bring, it will be increasingly hard to bring to bear against the dangers of bad behavior the threat of serious penalties unless the pressures thus to be exerted are plainly in conformity with international law. . . .[4]

A vivid example of this occurred in November 2001, when authorities in Spain refused to extradite eight terrorism suspects to the U.S. citing the U.S. administration's executive order creating military commissions in place of civilian courts.[5]

THE CHANGES IN WARFARE AND TERRORISM ARE BOTH A CONSEQUENCE AND A DRIVER OF THE CHANGE IN THE CONSTITUTIONAL ORDER.

Wars are acts of State, and therefore there has never until now been a war on terror. Of course states have fought terrorism, in many guises, for centuries. But a war on terror had to await the development of states—including virtual states like al Qaeda's global *ummah*—whose constitutional order was not confined to a particular territory or national group and for which terror could be a permanent state of affairs. Such a condition would either be sought by groups like the Taliban in order to prevent persons within a state's control from resisting oppression by accessing global, empowering resources and networks, or suffered because terrorist states wished to press such a condition on us and because our global vulnerabilities could not be detached from our prosperity and freedom.

This book has been therefore not so much about al Qaeda as about the larger phenomenon of twenty-first century terrorism of which al Qaeda is only a herald. Just as terrorists in earlier centuries mimicked the states they were struggling against, so terrorists in the twenty-first century will not be like the national liberation groups of the twentieth century that fought nation states but will instead copy the decentralized, devolved, outsourcing, and privatized market state of the twenty-first century.

While many recognize the revolution in military affairs that is under way, and some comprehend the revolution in constitutional affairs that is partly its result, very few seem aware that the revolution in constitutional affairs is, in turn, driving the revolution in military affairs. The overwhelming military power of the U.S. is a direct consequence of its continuing emergence as an entrepreneurial market state. This will force other states and non-state competitors to adopt asymmetric tactics, and both these developments—U.S. military dominance and its reciprocal, the asymmetric, outsourced tactics of its competitors—will accelerate the further emergence of market states. At the same time the market state, with its all-volunteer military forces, decentralized command, networked communities, and so forth, will determine the conditions of warfare. The ever-accelerating trend toward individual empowerment, to which the market state is a contributor, will inevitably, if paradoxically, imperil democratic systems that depend upon the individual conscience by empowering those who would destroy individual rights and powers.

It is the U.S., our global presence, our overwhelming armed power, and our example as one of the first emerging market states, that is the principal driver behind this new form of terrorism. Those who oppose the United States, for many different reasons, confront an adversary they cannot attack by traditional military means, but whose organization for war—the market state—they must copy in order to challenge it. Market state terrorism will not be limited to Muslims or persons from the Middle East; indeed, in its most troubling form we may never know the true identity of those who attack us. But these attacks will come because the U.S. is too powerful to challenge in any conventional way, too vulnerable to be free from assault, and too ever-present either to avoid hostility or to be secluded from harm.

After the September 11 attacks it became fashionable to ask whether those atrocities were perpetrated by persons who hated the U.S. for what it does (aid to Israel, for example) or because of who we are (freedom-loving and materialistic, perhaps*). Each of these answers is a kind of half-truth because by the things we do, so are we known, and we are, to a large extent, what we do. The agenda of human rights protection is the central

---

*. . . and all this while I have been shopping, I have
been let us say free
and do they hate me for it
do they hate me
     —Alicia Ostriker,
      "the window, at the moment of flame"

political idea of the West today, and it is an idea that, on the one hand, so reflects our identity and our aspirations that to abandon that idea is unthinkable, while on the other hand, it is a profoundly disturbing idea to those who believe we will not permit them—or perhaps owing to globalization, cannot coexist with others who want—to live as they wish, in defiance of global human rights guarantees.

To say that the U.S. presence is the principal driver of market state terrorism is not to blame the U.S. any more than fourteenth century urbanization can be blamed for the plague. The resentment this presence fosters cannot simply be laid to American interventions. U.S.-led intervention has been undertaken on behalf of Muslims in Bosnia, Kosovo, Kuwait, and Somalia. Even during the pitiless reign of the Taliban, the principal donor of aid to Afghanistan was the U.S. Moreover, in many places, the U.S. was the target of anger when it failed to intervene.[6]

If the source of Islamic terrorism lay in Western intervention in the conflicts of the Middle East, one strategic response would recommend itself strongly: abandon Afghanistan and Iraq, vacate U.S. bases in the region, and disavow the state of Israel. Whatever the other consequences of such a response, however, it is certain that Islamic terrorism would continue; indeed, it would become far more confident and virulent. That is because the cause of this plague does not lie in the Middle East at all.

Of course al Qaeda relentlessly raises the issue of the oppression of Muslims in Palestine, Iraq, and Afghanistan as a way of gaining adherents and legitimacy, but events in these theaters cannot be said to be the motivating cause of a global jihad.[7] As has been often pointed out, the invasions of Afghanistan and Iraq came after 9/11 and well before bin Laden (or Mohammed Atta) showed any interest in Palestine, whose national liberation struggle he and other al Qaeda figures disparaged. And although bin Laden complained of the proximity of U.S. bases to the holy Muslim shrines in Saudi Arabia following the first Gulf War, this came some time after his conversion to global jihad, and in any case, the bases have been closed and yet the jihad continues.

As Olivier Roy has observed, if Afghanistan, Iraq, and Palestine were the proximate cause of al Qaeda, why do we find almost no Afghans, Iraqis, or Palestinians among those jihadists who attack the West? "Why would a [British citizen of] Pakistani [descent] or a Spaniard [of Moroccan ancestry] be more angry than an Afghan about American troops in Afghanistan? It is precisely because they do not care about Afghanistan as such, but see the United States' involvement there as part of a global phenomenon of cultural domination. . . . Their vision of a global ummah is both a mirror of and a form of revenge against the globalization that has made them what they are."[8]

As we have seen in earlier chapters, the emergence of the market state is transforming warfare, evoking a new form of terrorism, and changing the war aim. These phenomena have precedents in past transformations of the constitutional order. They reflect the symbiosis between strategy and law that is manifested in the revolutions in military and constitutional affairs that are under way and the transformation of the State that is both a cause and a consequence of those revolutions. Owing to this two-way relationship, terrorism is one of the principal forces destroying the legitimacy of the nation state and leading to the market state, and the market state is a principal force in transforming twentieth century, nationalistic terrorism into twenty-first century global, networked terrorism. Ignoring this relationship will delegitimate our standing in international and constitutional law and forfeit the fruits of our strategic advantages, including that predominance that assures deterrence.

> [E]ven the exceptional weight and diversity of U.S. power will need in most fields to have the political support and often the active participation of other states. That is plainly so in the area of economic sanctions, but I suspect that it may increasingly apply even to the military field. [Moreover] in open democracies like ours, people will be less and less willing to take the actions of governments on trust without asking questions, including questions about legitimacy. . . . And this too will be evident to external observers, which is what counts for deterrence.[9]

THE WARS AGAINST TERROR ARE SIMILAR TO
EARLIER EPOCHAL WARS, LIKE THE LONG WAR OF
THE TWENTIETH CENTURY, BUT ARE ALSO RADICALLY
DIFFERENT, AND THE TWENTIETH CENTURY TRIAD OF
DETERRENCE, CONTAINMENT, AND ARMS CONTROL
REGIMES MUST NOW GIVE WAY TO TWENTY-FIRST
CENTURY STRATEGIES OF PRECLUSION.

An "epochal war" is one that challenges and ultimately changes the basic constitutional structure of states by linking strategic and constitutional innovations, leading to a change in the international order. It is animated by a single constitutional question that links the several conflicts that are known as separate wars to their contemporaries. For us, that question is: Can a market state make terror the basis of its claim to legitimacy, or must it win legitimacy by seeking the consent of the people it would govern?

Bin Laden and his as-yet-inchoate successors understand that states that govern by consent cannot do so in conditions of terror. They also realize that their own prescriptive role for the state demands that it create a condition of terror for its citizens. Achieving states of terror is their objective. This constitutional question is a common feature that ties together terrorism, the acquisition of weapons of mass destruction for compellance (rather than deterrence), and the terrorizing of domestic populations through genocide and catastrophe.

In the twentieth century, the constitutional issue that united World War I and World War II, the Bolshevik Revolution, the Spanish Civil War, the wars in Korea and Vietnam, and the Cold War was: What sort of industrial nation state—a constitutional order that arose in the late nineteenth century superseding the imperial order of state nations that had dominated that century—would succeed to the legitimacy of that earlier order? Would it be a communist, fascist, or parliamentary nation state?

The twentieth century had barely ended, and its Long War been resolved in favor of the parliamentary state, when a new war, the First Terrorist War began. This war, like the First World War that began the Long War or the Bohemian Revolt in 1618 that sparked the Thirty Years' War, started for local reasons, in this case arising from the ambitions of Salafist fundamentalism and the transnational civil war it sought within Islam. But the First Terrorist War is only a part of the Wars against Terror. That larger war will continue until the fundamental issue about the legitimacy of a new constitutional order is resolved. The constitutional question this larger war poses is: Will the legitimate form of the market state be a state of consent or a state of terror? That is why historians may one day see the Wars against Terror as an epochal war, an historical and constitutional characterization that can only be made retrospectively.

As Clausewitz observed,[10] wars do not begin with an aggression but rather with the resistance to aggression. It is only when the state that is attacked decides to resist by resorting to war that a belligerency then ensues. "To prevent [the aggressor achieving his goals unopposed] one must be willing to make war."*

The wars against twenty-first century terror did not begin when Osama bin Laden declared war against the United States on August 23, 1996, or when al Qaeda terrorist forces attacked two American embassies in Africa on August 7, 1998, and a U.S. naval vessel on October 12, 2000, or even when the Pentagon and the World Trade Center were struck by hijacked commercial airliners on September 11, 2001. Rather, they commenced when the United States determined by means of warfare to prevent further attacks. Bin Laden's 1996 "Declaration of Jihad Against the Americans" was an act of diplomacy, an ultimatum, for which there are many precedents.[11] It was only when the U.S. decided to treat the attacks as acts of war, however, that the Wars against Terror commenced.

The wars against twenty-first century terror are preclusive in nature;

---

*I am indebted to Sir Michael Howard for this reference.

that is, they seek to head off a state of affairs that has the potential to disable consensual governance well in advance of imminent aggression. That is because once these states of affairs come about they bring with them a condition of terror that is almost impossible to reverse. Once Kim Jong Il actually deploys nuclear weapons, or once a million refugees have been driven from their ruined villages in Darfur, or once a terrorist mass atrocity is actually executed in Manhattan, only tragedy and terror will follow. If unchecked, the ensuing loss will eventually include the conditions of consent that govern civilized societies or, for nascent market states, preclude those conditions from ever coming into being.

Paradoxically, realizing that the problem is amorphous and universal gives us a precise locus for the solution. We must heal ourselves and strengthen our alliances if we are to bear the burden of warring against terror. There is really no alternative to this struggle. Even though American power is the main element inspiring a new form of terrorism, reducing or hobbling that power will not make the terrorists go away even while it cripples the one state capable of leading coalitions to defend us. Indeed, that power must be employed preclusively rather than waiting for an acute crisis to set in that irrevocably puts us at a disadvantage. Preemption of terrorist attacks, active counterproliferation, and preventive intervention to forestall human rights abuses like genocide or other gross violations of human rights all have roles to play. The use of scenario planning, as opposed to strategic planning, is an appropriate but at present underused means of anticipating future crises and coping with or even preventing them. Finally, greater inclusiveness in the societies of the democracies can inoculate those persons who might otherwise be drawn into terrorist activities. This, too, is an important element in a preclusive strategy.

THE STATES OF CONSENT MUST CONFORM THEIR STRATEGIC BEHAVIOR TO THE RULE OF LAW; AND THE LAW TO WHICH THEY CONFORM MUST BE REFORMED TO TAKE INTO ACCOUNT CHANGES IN THE STRATEGIC CONTEXT.

We must urgently develop legal and strategic parameters for state action in the Wars against Terror. Ultimately, this will be a matter of drawing the links between successfully warring on terror and evolving legal concepts of sovereignty and its relationship to lawful, legitimate governance. As Sir Michael Howard has wisely put it:

[A]n explicit American hegemony may appear preferable to the messy compromises of the existing order, but if it is nakedly based on com-

mercial interests and military power it will lose all legitimacy. Terror
will continue and, worse, widespread sympathy with terror. But American power placed at the service of an international community legit-
imized by representative institutions and the rule of law, accepting its
constraints and inadequacies but continually working to improve
them: that is a very different matter. It is by doing this that the US has
earned admiration, respect, and indeed affection throughout the world
over the past half century.[12]

There is, at present, no more important question before the world
because failure to resolve the issue of legitimate action to preclude terror
will frustrate not only our efforts against global terrorism but also success
in avoiding regional and global epidemics, and great power confrontation.

We might start with the definition of what constitutes terrorism offered
in chapter 7: *Terrorism is the use of violence in order to advance a political
agenda by preventing persons from doing what they would otherwise lawfully do.* Beginning with such a definition, we can then work out what a
state is permitted to do in its search for terrorists and its efforts to suppress
them. With such a definition we could seek an international convention
universally outlawing terrorism as we outlaw piracy. With such a definition we could determine when a group are terrorists or "freedom fighters,"
and when other states may intervene to stop them and what other states are
empowered to act. I have suggested that only states of consent are, prima
facie, the victims of terrorism.

We might then be able to address the U.S. National Security Strategy
and its call for preemption in light of its obvious conflict with Article 2(4)
of the U.N. Charter, which prohibits the use of force outside the charter's
carefully circumscribed limits. These limits provide that it is unlawful for
a state to use force in the absence of an actual or imminent attack except on
the basis of a Security Council authorization. This suggests that it is also
unlawful, in the absence of a Security Council resolution, for one state to
preempt another's war-making capabilities before these are about to be
used. Yet in the era we are entering of disguised attack using terrorist networks, the proliferation of WMD can make preemption an absolute necessity. For once any state, no matter how repugnant, acquires nuclear
weapons—a moment that no monitoring seems capable of predicting with
precision—it is too late to compel deproliferation. Once summoned, the
genie must do the bidding of its new master.

Nor should a search for new parameters exclude the consideration of
charges of American state terrorism. If assassinations and torture by allied
states are countenanced, indeed financed, by the United States, then, it is
argued, the U.S. is rightly subject to the same accusations of terrorism it
would hurl at any other state that employed such methods. It may be that

the United States will persuade its citizens and its allies that the tactics of terror are the only effective means of protecting a society at war with those who can easily infiltrate it, and whose operations prefigure the tactics we will ourselves be forced to adopt. Given the theatrical nature of twenty-first century terrorism, we cannot exclude the possibility that it will inevitably escalate in violence, as terrorists and states of terror vie with their own past atrocities to capture the horrified attention of a busy and easily distracted people. If such events compel the U.S. and its allies to adopt what are at present unlawful methods such as the use of nonlethal chemical weapons or strategies such as anticipatory interventions, we must develop new standards to determine whether they are essentially counterforce measures, like the air campaigns of World War II that attacked V-2 sites, or whether they are countervalue strikes that seek instead an *in terrorem* effect in the targeted civilian population. If it is the latter, then we have become an enemy to our state, having lost sight of the conditions for victory of a state of consent. Our means must be guided by our ends. It has been widely reported, and not denied, that President Bush discussed the possibility of painting a U.S. surveillance plane in the colors of the United Nations in the hope of drawing fire from Iraqi anti-aircraft batteries, thus providing a casus belli for an American invasion.[13] If this was ever seriously considered, it reflects more than an amateurish approach where international security issues are concerned; rather, it would amount to a complete misunderstanding of the bases for legitimate intervention and how to secure those bases.

We must develop new rules of international law that incorporate these parameters. These rules would be used to determine when it is permissible for one state to intervene in another's affairs in order to protect itself or its allies from terrorism or to protect civilians from catastrophic events or pre-clude the proliferation of WMD *(jus ad bellum)*. Similarly, they would govern the ways states may lawfully treat prisoners during warfare and the actions of the defense forces *(jus in bello)*. Obviously the Geneva Conventions apply in some fashion to all prisoners taken in the Wars against Terror. This is one consequence of designating this conflict as a war. But just as obviously we need to amend the Geneva Conventions to deal with the question posed at Guantánamo: What treatment is to be accorded terrorist prisoners of the Wars against Terror? They are not combatants in uniform, with a publicly acknowledged chain of command, to whom the status of POW is accorded. But they are not spies or partisans either. As soldiers, even if unlawful ones, who are captured on the field of battle they can be held in prisons until the end of the conflict without trial or arraignment. This scarcely makes sense, however, when there is no nation state with which to agree to end the conflict, or to make arrangements for prisoner exchanges—when, that is, these prisoners may be held for decades because the field of battle is everywhere and the conflict may last indefinitely. Finally, we must also develop rules for the collection of intelligence—what methods are permissible—and to what uses the materials collected can be lawfully put.

Because current international law has not caught up with the changes in the global strategic context, it seems to present states with an intolerable choice: either follow the rule of law and sacrifice one war aim (the protection of civilians) or dispense with law and sacrifice the legitimacy of the war effort (which is, after all, another war aim, namely the legitimation of market states as states of consent). The answer to this dilemma is to reject it: law must be reformed.

Michael Reisman has observed[14] that international lawyers feel they must rally around existing international rules in order to protect the overall influence of international law. This is precisely what is vitiating that influence. A similar remark might be made of civil libertarians. Consider, for example, the report of the commission on the use of data mining, in which the majority took the view that even more restrictive policies regarding the sharing of information should be now put in place than those required by U.S. Supreme Court precedent[15] when it is evident that our current policies were too restrictive to head off the attacks of September 11.

WITH RESPECT TO DOMESTIC LAW, THE U.S. MUST
SO CONSTRUE ITS CONSTITUTIONAL LAW THAT IT
PROTECTS HUMAN RIGHTS, AND THIS WILL OFTEN MEAN
STRENGTHENING THE POWERS OF GOVERNMENT.

In every era of the State, throughout the evolution of its constitutional orders, societies have confronted the problem of determining the proper relationship between strategy and law. Outside its domain, the State seeks to be free of external coercion; this is strategy. Inside its jurisdiction, the State tries to monopolize legitimate violence; this is law. But what measures are appropriate to prosecute the war outside when inside and outside have lost their clear boundaries—when terrorist warfare occurs within national peoples, like the civil wars of the past, and when hitherto domestic events in faraway societies have a destructive effect on our own states?

With the coming of the latest constitutional order, the market state, governments will be compelled to explore these changing relationships: between the intelligence agencies (as their work is relied on more heavily by the public as providing the basis for crucial anticipatory decisions) and the media (as they become more powerful purveyors and validators of secrets); between exclusive executive power, and ordinary empowering statutes and laws that might be necessary in a time of emergency; between federal unions and their constituent parts (both in the U.S. and the E.U.), where intelligence, in the case of the U.S., is not shared by the central union and, in the case of the E.U., not shared with the central union. Governments will have to learn how to select and work with private sector collaborators, partly because the latter own most of the critical infrastructure that we must make less vulnerable, and partly because they are market-oriented and global and thus arc some of the gaps between the nation state and the market state. Governments must rethink ideas like "Homeland Security" when the threats to security cannot be neatly cabined as in or out of the homeland, just as the American and British governments must revisit the issues of cooperation between the CIA and the FBI and between MI5 and MI6—issues that arise owing to jurisdictional divisions between domestic and international operations—because these agencies are so completely defined by the Long War and its basis in the nation state.

States must measure their tactical and strategic policies against the impact these policies are likely to have on their legitimacy. If the United States were to abandon its executive order prohibiting assassinations and targeted killings, what is the cost to its legitimacy as a State that follows the rule of law, one principle of which is that no criminal penalty can be levied without a fair and open trial? On the other hand, if the U.S. is at war, is the executive order even relevant? By such means, the domestic environment of states will be steadily militarized. Similarly, does it matter what we are fighting for or is "one man's terrorist another man's freedom fighter"? We do not apply murder statutes to soldiers in battle, even enemy soldiers. Soldiers are permitted to maim and kill civilians (so long as this is not their aim). By such means, the foreign environment can be degraded into a sea of "collateral damage." Put the two together and the Wars on Terror can make our soldiers into organized vigilantes, using the methods of warfare against civilians, domestic and foreign.

When our governments engage in torture or degrading behavior, perhaps by turning over prisoners to less squeamish national intelligence services, they substantiate the charges made against them by those who say ours are the true rogue states,[16] and that the state terror of the U.S. and its allies is as much a threat to mankind as the terrorism of al Qaeda. These are essentially constitutional issues, but they are not so much matters of civil liberties as they are profound questions of the self-definition societies achieve through their constitutional processes in time of war. They are matters of constitutional legitimacy because they are matters of self-respect. States must have clear answers to these questions because if their legitimacy is compromised they will seed new terrorists of their own who will take up arms against the State in revulsion. There must be a bright-line rule against the intentional infliction of pain on any person detained by government. Torture must be forbidden anywhere even if, in the rarest and most extreme circumstance, this rule is broken by decent men willing to risk the legal penalties for their acts. Rules governing coercive inter-rogation must be crafted in a way that gives clear guidance so that these methods do not approach torture, and that allocates a decisive role to non-governmental oversight by juries whose role is recognized by international covenants.

If the U.S. and the U.K. ally themselves with autocracies that show contempt for human rights but who share our fear of al Qaeda, we are bor-rowing against a future in which those peoples we have helped later rise up and blame us—much as we are blamed for collaborating with dictators in the Third World to fight communism (though we are seldom blamed for the no less dreadful collaboration with communism to defeat fascism). Yet if it is true that full and fair elections in a dozen Islamic states would bring bin Laden to power in every one of them, the international community of states of consent dare not press for such elections. Taking these two propo-sitions together, does this make us hypocrites to claim that the sovereignty of other states, like Saddam Hussein's Iraq, is forfeited owing to their undemocratic practices and then turn a blind eye toward the legitimacy of regimes that are allied to ours but which deny their citizens basic human rights? Not necessarily. Our commitment to globalize the systems of human rights and government by consent is no less sincere because it must be measured in terms that capture the strategic interests of the states of consent to enlarge their number in relative safety.

Thus, answering urgent strategic questions about terror will also require us to give some thought to larger constitutional questions about sovereignty, democracy, and the laws of war because if we ignore these issues we will find in times of crisis that we have decided them inadver-tently. As argued in the preceding pages, the key concept we must care-fully define is not democracy per se but the inalienable rights the protection of which is the purpose of government. Respect for these rights assures a state of inviolable sovereignty, and that sovereignty is a fortiori a limited one. It is limited sovereignty, not simply majority voting, that cre-ates a state of consent. Therefore one of our most urgent tasks is to develop legal standards, in constitutional law and in international law, that help us determine what is comprised by the idea of inalienable human rights. When this limited sovereignty is forfeited by acts of a state—against its own citizens, or its neighbors, or against the system of world order that underpins the recognition of sovereignty itself—then the state can be sub-ject to sanction by the international community and attack by the domestic polity. Whether that state is subject to intervention, however, ought to be measured by the relationship between the strategic interests of the states of consent and the severity of the deprivations of human rights. To separate the two is clarifying for a seminar but can be fatal for the world of states of consent.

THE WARS AGAINST TERROR CANNOT BE WON BY THE STATES OF CONSENT WITHOUT ALLIANCES; INDEED, ALLIANCES CAN BE ONE OF OUR CHIEF ADVANTAGES OVER STATES OF TERROR.

All technologically advanced countries will ultimately be threatened by twenty-first century terrorism. It is clear, however, that the al Qaeda terrorists believe they can win this war because they perceive that many states, including some American allies, entertain doubts about collaborating with the U.S. It is understandable if regrettable that some of these states would want to protect their publics by dissociating themselves from the United States because it is the most prominent terrorist target in the West.

Some British commentators have struggled with the question, What does the U.K. get for its American alliance? It's not a new question. In 1974, shortly after he became prime minister, Edward Heath questioned civil servants about the close intelligence relationship that existed between the U.S.'s National Security Agency (NSA) and the U.K.'s Government Communications Headquarters (GCHQ), both of which intercept electronic communications. What do we get for all the material we give the Americans? he asked. His intelligence chiefs explained that, actually, they would be hard-pressed to do modern communications collection without U.S. cooperation. The U.K. gained far more from the Americans than it gave to them. To this Heath replied, If that is so, why do they do it?

Why indeed? Why did the U.S. enter World War I? Why didn't the U.S. first fight the Pacific war, where we had been attacked, rather than rushing to Europe in World War II? Why did the U.S. for more than forty years guarantee the security of Central Europe in the Cold War by making itself a target for tens of thousands of Soviet nuclear weapons? National interest, of course, has a lot to do with this; it ought to. Democratic leaders are chosen to pursue the interests of their peoples, not to ride some hobbyhorse of their own devising, however noble. The key, however, is that the Americans defined their national interest in a way that included protection of and prosperity for their allies.

Does Britain define its interests in a similar way? Or do the British feel their interests are actually put at risk by an alliance with the U.S.? In the last five years terrorists linked by the al Qaeda network have mounted ambitious attacks in Spain, Indonesia, India, Jordan, Nigeria, Algeria, Egypt, Russia, Turkey, France, Italy, Kenya, Somalia, Morocco, and Britain. Some of these states supported U.S. interventions in Afghanistan and Iraq; most did not. Some have a larger percentage of Muslims in their populations than the U.K.; some do not. It requires a kind of self-absorption bordering on solipsism to think that the political issues that perturb one (for example, intervention in Iraq) exhaust the list of those that perturb others, including terrorists. The issue isn't really why British citizens with ties to al Qaeda are attempting terror attacks on Britain—it would be surprising if they did not—but why worse things haven't happened.

The principal reason the U.K. has not been hurt far worse than it has is because it is now more difficult for al Qaeda to mount spectacular operations, and much of the reason for this has to do with intelligence cooperation among the states of the Atlantic Alliance and among their allies. Would it be wise for us to trade this sort of protection for the chance that, without it, no one would wish to harm us? States whose politicians delight in bedeviling the U.S. nevertheless insist on the closest cooperation at the working level of intelligence operations. This is in part owing to a perception of a common danger, but it also seems to reflect the shared sense that it would be folly to forgo the help of one's friends in the hope of propitiating one's enemies. As Shakespeare puts it in *King Lear*, "He's mad that trusts in the tameness of a wolf . . . "[17] If there is one lesson of the Long War of the twentieth century, it is that standing together the democracies are practically invincible, but that standing apart they can be picked off, one by one.

There is something slightly contemptible about the wish to detach one's country from any member of the alliance that has been threatened or stricken in order to conciliate Islamist terrorists.

What some seek is isolation—for the United States, whose foreign adventures are thought to have spread the infection of terrorism, and from the United States, so that its allies will no longer be the subject of attacks. Is this really a moral or even mature way to conceive of the historic cooperation between America and Europe, which has been of such benefit to the world in the twentieth century?

The post–Cold War age is not the postwar age. Indeed, the dangers to civilians steadily mount each year, and that is the case without terrorists having yet acquired biological or nuclear weapons and will certainly be the case when they do.

But hasn't the U.S.-U.K. alliance made Britain less safe by agitating the hornet's nest? Global, networked terrorism and biological and nuclear proliferation to predator states like Saddam Hussein's Iraq—to say nothing of the combination of these threats—are best dealt with as soon as possible. That necessarily means we will be less safe, in the near term, than we would have been if we just ignored these issues. Only a person paralyzed by fear, however, closes the door to the room that's on fire and sits and waits in another part of the house.

The U.S. and the U.K. have taken the lead, and have been joined by many states, including Japan and all the members of NATO, in challenging a danger that will mount inexorably if it is not checked. Yes, we might be safe for a while, if we repudiated Blair's policy of close cooperation with the U.S. or Bush's promise to provide armed resources to the government of Iraq as long as they request them in their struggle against terror. Such repudiations would bring satisfaction, even joy, in some quarters, I suppose. A recent film depicts a British prime minister rhetorically cuffing a boorish American president, and doubtless Hollywood does not have its stars play unpopular roles.

But when the U.K. is struck again, as it will be someday, and we have hidden as far away as possible from our unpopular ally, where would we hide then? When Iraq collapsed into a full-scale civil war, and Iran invaded with an army of Shia "volunteers" bringing images of civilian deaths in the tens of thousands, not the dozens, would we simply change the television channel?

While the United States and the United Kingdom must play leading roles in winning the Wars against Terror, those wars can only be won with the collaboration of many states. I and others have proposed an alliance of democracies. I have suggested that the U.S. change its role as hegemon in NATO to "claviger and steward" in such an alliance. Is this role for America a good idea for the states of consent (including the U.S. itself)?

The risks of U.S. leadership are twofold: if the U.S. is out in front, it becomes the target for every terrorist group that simply wants a free hand for its local predations while, at the same time, America becomes the focal point of charges by other states that it is seeking an empire, charges that alienate allied publics. There are indeed many who see the war on terrorism as a kind of stalking horse for the creation of an American empire.[18] Some of those who make this charge believe simply that overwhelming power necessarily leads to empire—that this is the very definition of empire.

The United States is very powerful, economically and militarily. It has the world's largest economy, greater than that of all the other members of the G8 combined, and it is growing at a faster rate than they are. The U.S. is the only state that can settle its debts in its own currency. It is, militarily, the one remaining superpower owing to the collapse of the Soviet Union and U.S. defense budgets that approach half a trillion dollars. Yet we should not be misled by these figures; like the much-cited rise in the gap between high- and low-income earners, these statistics conceal an equally important truth—that the development gap between high and low is closing. This means that while the U.S. has a large army equipped with infinitely superior weaponry and communications, the harm that can be done to the American nation is growing more quickly (as technology disperses and becomes cheaper) than its lead is increasing. In other words, poor states—or rich terrorist groups—who could not begin to mount a challenge by invading across a contested plain can hope to do enough damage to persuade the U.S. or any other powerful state to change its policies. This paradox—the simultaneously increasing greater power and greater vulnerability of the U.S.—means that America is the indispensable leader of the wars on terror (because it alone has the resources) and that it has a vital interest in being such a leader (because it is also very vulnerable).

Yet American leadership actually tempts disarray and noncooperation. The former French foreign minister Hubert Vedrine spoke for many when he said, "We cannot accept a politically unipolar world."[19] One must shudder at the consequences for the world, to say nothing of the Wars against Terror, of striking such poses and the attitudes they reflect for they invite an anti-American multipolarity with which the worst and most retrograde forces can tacitly combine. Multipolarity is not simply a condition of mutually affecting forces but of mutually opposed forces. How many persons who have called for a European army in order to "balance" the Americans have actually thought through what such an army would do to achieve the objective of thwarting U.S. unilateralism? If that army were to join American expeditions then it might well have influence on allied policy, but this is not what the opponents of U.S. leadership have in mind. Indeed, they have frantically (and successfully) tried to keep NATO forces out of Iraq. If, however, the objective is to prevent U.S. forces from intervening in Serbia or Afghanistan or Iraq or Sudan, then such an army must be used to threaten the use of force. What other role could it possibly play in achieving such an objective? That was how multipolarity checked U.S. policies before 1989 when the Soviet army stood ready to oppose any allied attempts to liberate Eastern Europe. Is it possible that any sane person would want to re-create the conditions for such an armed confrontation in the twenty-first century?

There is one scenario for which the world is not prepared. A catastrophic series of strikes against the American and British homelands using nuclear or biological weapons could remove from the world's affairs the two states willing and, with others, able to organize the defense of the society of states of consent. Like the collapse of the Soviet Union, this is the one contingency no one has planned for. I implore the Reader to contemplate how terrible a fate this would be for human rights, for the economic development of all states, and for the security of those societies that wish to live in tranquillity. We may think that it is the United States that today disturbs that tranquillity because we measure our anxiety against the most peaceful recent past. We should instead measure our states against the alternative future of a world without the global but benign ambitions of America.

WE ARE NOT WINNING THE WARS AGAINST TERROR BECAUSE WE DON'T UNDERSTAND THEIR DEEP CONNECTIONS TO HISTORIC CHANGES IN THE NATURE OF THE STATE.

As a consequence of the transition from nation state to market state, terrorism will become the continuation of diplomacy by other means. It will be waged by state proxies and by entities that are not controlled by conventional states and that seek to influence the politics of states by theatrical killings and atrocities. It may seem odd, at first, that market states could ever be states of terror; after all, free enterprise, open borders, and enhanced role of the individual are all exalted by market states. Yet some market states will become states of terror precisely because they are convinced that only authoritarian governments can protect the individual and his opportunities in the face of terrorist violence, catastrophic events, and threatening WMD. Others will be born as states of terror, for the choices they wish to maximize are choices that states of consent disparage though some societies appear to crave them. These societies abhor the protection of the rights of conscience for those persons the state would call "infidels," the rights of women, the rights of economic development, the rights of representation itself. Al Qaeda's caliphate is only one imagined market state of terror. So are the states that ecoterrorists or antiglobalization terrorists would impose. They are market states because they are decentralized, devolved, outsourcing, global, networked political entities declaring law and enforcing it by violence. They are not nation states because their claim to legitimacy is not based on bettering the welfare of a national group. They cannot accept the existence of states of consent because by their assertion of regimes of human rights these pose a perpetual threat.

The first step toward winning this struggle is simply to face the challenges it poses.[20] We must shatter the complacency that reassures itself that nothing has really changed, that is persuaded that any imposition is too irksome to be justified, that protests that any concern is trumped-up in order to exploit fear for political purposes, whose most powerful argument is the observation that nothing so awful has happened yet. This must be done without at the same time using the new threats as a Trojan horse for government policies that were ardently pressed in the absence of such threats, or as a way of discrediting the arguments of adversaries by impugning their motives or patriotism.

In the current political climate my arguments and conclusions are apt to be assimilated into one or another of the standard positions. That would mistake my perspective. To quote a letter from a friend who read a portion of this book in manuscript:

If I understand . . . correctly, (1) you are arguing against the likes
of Bruce Ackerman and other liberals, that we truly do now have a
"war" . . . (2) And you are arguing against [John] Yoo and [the] unitary
executive people that it is war that must be subject to law. (3) And you
are arguing against certain neo-conservatives that we can only win this
war through alliance. (4) And you are arguing against certain civil liberty types, that this war must change our notions of civil liberties [to
allow for an effective war on terror].[21]

There is in my book, it seems, something to offend everyone. The flip
side of being adverse to all the conventional positions on these matters is
being assimilated into postures taken that appear, if only tangentially, to
intersect with one's own. I do not believe that Americans live in an oppressive state, or that the Bush administration has dramatically curtailed the
constitutional rights of Americans, but I do think that the U.S. government
has been unmindful of what precisely we wish to achieve in the Wars on
Terror and this has led to a series of mistakes in policy.

What is at stake in these wars, at least as far as the U.S. and the U.K. are
concerned, are the practices and ethos of consent. We need not be concerned that our adversaries will defeat and occupy us, interning our civilians and executing our officials. What is threatened is threatened by our
own actions when we are persuaded that compromises with our constitutional traditions of consent are necessary to protect us.[22]

That might sound as if I can be counted among those who believe
that the only thing we have to fear is fear itself, the blind unreason-
ing panic that comes from politicians hyping the scale of the threat
we face. But that is not quite what I believe. The situation that concerns me
is one that comes about when our fears are justified, when it is quite
rational to become convinced that only dramatic change in our constitutional ethos can provide safety because we have neglected to protect
ourselves—including protecting ourselves psychologically—by denying
the existence of the threat or pretending it is insubstantial and thus failing
to take consensual measures before that threat manifested itself in acute
catastrophes.

On this score, the Bush administration has a mixed record for it has
rather consistently chosen what one might call "the path of least consent."[23] When it wanted to expand electronic surveillance it did so in a
secret executive order; when it wished to avoid habeas corpus petitions
from its detainees it put them in an offshore penal colony rather than risking judicial oversight; when it wanted to change the interrogation procedures with respect to captives, it altered the Army Field Manual rather than
seeking fresh legislative authority from Congress.

The consensual practices of states like the U.S. and the U.K. are time-consuming, often frustrating, and usually suffused with compromise and half-measures. That is why we rely on professional, experienced persons to undertake them; it is too difficult for amateurs to manage these practices. This is especially true in a time, like our own, when politics is so partisan, and the media so bitterly opportunistic. Yet we really have no choice in the matter: the surest way to lose our way, to take on the characteristics of a state of terror, is by failing to rely on our conventions and processes of consent when as now we are in a period of relative tranquillity. Otherwise, when catastrophe does strike we will eagerly cast aside the ways of consent because they will appear—as they in fact will be—too cumbersome and ineffectual to provide security.

Let me summarize: We need not sacrifice our constitutional freedoms to win the Wars against Terror. Indeed, the principal point of this book is to draw attention to the fact that twenty-first century terrorism poses a dangerous threat to those freedoms. Claims that the U.S. Constitution doesn't apply abroad, or that habeas corpus is a quaint irrelevance, or that persons can be held incommunicado indefinitely, are ones with which I have little sympathy. But neither do I believe that there is a God-given right to not be burdened with carrying an identity card, or to not disclose to the government information we have gladly given to private corporations[24] or that they have collected with our consent. The wars of the twentieth century have given us the conviction that the threat to our liberties would come from a totalitarian state; now we are locked into this way of thinking heedless of the fact that in the twenty-first century such threats can come from relatively small groups that are not associated with a state. Looking around for a threatening state, we end up indicting our own.

We should not abandon the constitutional restraints on the executive that distinguish states of consent. Indeed, this book is aimed at forestalling a situation in which we might be forced to declare martial law because we refused to debate openly and to act through our customary representative processes to write laws that would anticipate such a crisis. But neither do I believe that all the post-Watergate reforms in the U.S. have the sanctity of the structures of government that are constitutional in nature.

The principal recommendation of my Plague Treatise is that we pay more attention to our vulnerabilities. We need to build up our immune systems, which include our alliances, and our laws. Right now we are focused on a particular virus—call it the Islamist flu—and we are tempted to imagine that future conflicts will be, like this one, a clash of cultures. In fact this is unlikely. We must continue our fight against the flu; where possible we need to get flu shots and treatment, like progress toward resolving the Israeli-Palestinian conflict that might lower the temperature of the patient. But in the long run, we have to prepare for sicknesses from many other quarters, including those of which we have as yet no knowledge.

Abandoning law, constitutional or international, is strongly contraindi-
cated for the states of consent in the Wars against Terror because law
directs our "immune system" by identifying what must be rejected; but
law must be reformed to reflect the changed "epidemiologic" environment
in which we find ourselves, where "infections" must be combated even
when we cannot identify their source, and treated though we cannot
eradicate them, and, above all, prevented before they damage our systems
irrevocably.

We must not fret about making conditions worse in one of the three theaters of the Wars against Terror by pursuing action in the other theaters.
This is unavoidable. Rather we must cultivate a leadership in whom we
trust, an educated populace of mature citizens well aware of the trade-offs
implicit in the human condition, and institutions that can adjust to the
changes that protecting our rights—under the conditions imposed by
reality—will require. States of consent must be able to move nimbly
between each of the three areas of conflict, shoring up one at the expense
of the others, then shifting to another theater without the loss of confidence
that can come from pursuing incompatible tactical objectives on behalf of
misapprehended strategic goals.

It is terror we are fighting, not just terrorists. That will require energy
and resolution in all three dimensions of this struggle, knowing that there
is no equilibrium, no one tactical policy, that will provide a successful
alternative to the need to choose among dreadful options over time as
things deteriorate owing to our own decisions in the theaters we are forced
to subordinate temporarily. This need for maturity, trust, and agility will
help us avoid the worst. That worst is a great power conflict, where casualties are measured in the tens of millions, not wars against terror that, if
dealt with, do not approach such devastation. Every step in the Wars
against Terror should be taken with this awful possibility in mind. That is
yet one more reason why maintaining legitimacy—the union of law and
strategy—must be foremost in our minds as we fight.

In the autumn of 2007, the *New York Times* published an essay lament-
ing the lack of "big ideas" in the area of international security. I am
inclined to think that we have had a good many big ideas in the last twenty
years, and that the problem wasn't their scope or their wisdom. After the
fall of the Berlin Wall and the end of the Cold War a great many persons
were impressed with the notion that the dialectic of history had also ended.
This was given memorable expression by Francis Fukuyama, who was
unfairly accused of concluding that history itself had come to an end.
What Fukuyama actually argued was that the international community had
come to a consensus on the desirability and legitimacy of parliamentary
systems with free markets and human rights guarantees. He was right to

argue this, and his title—*The End of History*—was well chosen, for it comes from Hegel, who thought much the same thing after the Battle of Jena, when it became apparent that a new constitutional order had emerged that would dominate Europe. The idea of a global consensus found its greatest champion in the administration of George H. W. Bush, and was reflected in the grand coalition that, under U.N. auspices, successfully fought the First Gulf War. But as a structuring idea, "the new world order" collapsed when confronted by the conflicts in the Balkans, a region that produces more history than can be locally consumed.

The next big idea was that globalization would bring harmony. "The Virtuous Circle" of globalization had no more prominent advocate than Thomas Friedman, who argued in books and in columns for the *New York Times* that freer markets would lead to greater prosperity; greater prosperity would bring greater respect for human rights, which would bring more rights for women; more rights for women would bring them into the labor force, bringing greater prosperity; greater prosperity would promote peace; peaceful relations would foster even freer trade, and so on. This notion, which is largely correct, permeated the administration of Bill Clinton. But this idea, too, crashed when the dark side of globalization turned its face to the World Trade Center Towers on September 11.

Then came the overarching scheme that new conflicts would be fought not along the ideological borders of the First and Second Worlds but rather along the ancient fault lines of culture. This idea—powerfully rendered in an essay by Samuel Huntington for *Foreign Affairs* and then in a book by the same title, *The Clash of Civilizations*—seemed to many to have been vindicated by al Qaeda's attacks on the U.S. It has been thoroughly adopted by George W. Bush's administration and is reflected in many U.S. policies. Again, this idea embodies an important insight but it, too, however, has been rebuffed by events, viz, the agonizing struggle in Iraq, which, whatever else it may be, pits Shia against Sunni in an internecine bloodbath that looks, at least to Western eyes, as being pretty firmly within a single, Huntingtonian civilization. (And much the same can be said for the al Qaeda–led civil war within Islam, the Pakistani-Indian conflict that almost came to war in 1992, the awful bloodlettings in Central Africa, and other conflicts.)

What is wrong with all these big ideas is that they were in fact not big enough. They all capture something: the Long War over the ideological valence of the nation state did end, and there is consensus among the great powers on the constitutional issues over which that war was fought. Globalization does bring both freer markets and freer societies, and the two are linked. Culture, including especially religion and ethnicity, does become more fraught with conflict as the world grows smaller; others are harder to get away from. But all these perceptions are only part of the picture. They are facets, and that is why as a basis for public policy they were quickly repudiated by reality.

A more fundamental portrait of the international developments of the last two decades would show that these developments are elements of an impending change in the constitutonal order of states. One consequence of this change is the struggle against twenty-first century terror. The emergence of a new constitutional order is difficult to contemplate for persons who cannot imagine any other order than the nation state.

The twentieth century, industrial regulatory nation state is unable to cope with a number of challenges to its claim to legitimate power, challenges that include the proliferation of WMD, transnational threats like twenty-first century terrorism, AIDS, SARS, climate change, immigration, a global system of human rights that supersedes national law, a global system of financial markets that removes the power of states to control the value of their own currency, an international system of communications and a global culture irresistibly spread by those communications. These challenges are delegitimating the constitutional order whose history did indeed end in 1990. They are both driving globalization (in both its vicious and virtuous circles), which depends upon global communications and markets, and are being intensified by globalization. And, too, these developments are responsible for the emergence of a global terror network, which, in turn, is undermining the clumsy national efforts of states to eradicate it.

That will not mean the end of the State; far from it. But it will engage the dynamic of state evolution that has been ongoing since the Renaissance. Of the many arguments presented in *The Shield of Achilles,* none seems to have been more elusive to a certain sort of reader than the idea that the historic dynamic it describes is not unidirectional, as is typical of a trajectory, but is mutually affecting, as is characteristic of field relations. Strategic innovations do lead to constitutional transformations, but constitutional transformations breed strategic transformations. Their causal relationship is that of a circuit, not an arrow. And thus, where the historian steps into the Heraclitan stream is entirely a matter of sensibility, even perhaps chance, because these two dynamics are mutually related. The historian does not discover propositions so much as create them by his own choiccs, and these propositions may be true or false depending on how helpful his overlays are in making sense of the terrain.

As this book goes to press, a presidential election campaign is under way in the United States. There is no one big idea that could possibly prepare the victor in that contest for the transformations in strategy and law that will occur during her (or his) term of office. But there is this: that on the horizon there is something—possibly inimical to our system of governance—

that we have never encountered before and that, without those who came before us, we could never have imagined. That is the growing union of strategy and law that will emerge as the legitimating basis of the State itself as it undergoes fundamental change.

THE PLAGUE TREATISE CONCLUDED

Much of this book has been devoted to the future. The magnetic power of Parmenides' Fallacy, perhaps paradoxically, requires we achieve a greater facility in dealing with possible futures. The preemption of terrorism, the preclusion of humanitarian crises brought on by genocide or ethnic cleansing and natural catastrophe, the prevention of the proliferation of weapons of mass destruction for compellance, all require this. But the greatest of these trials of the imagination will be the Wars against Terror themselves. For we can only know an epochal war for certain when it is past, and that past is, for the present, deep in our future.

It has been said that all history is contemporary history. One might say the same sort of thing about the study of the future, for we cannot escape the impress of current preoccupations and dispositions whether we look backward or forward. This book is about the nature of the twenty-first century Wars against Terror, their antecedents and their prospects. But the future is a land no one has visited. Like the appointment with Major Major in the satirical novel *Catch-22,* as soon as one steps into the office of the future, it is gone. Our appointments are scheduled that way.

The past, too, has its iron imperative. We can visit but only as tourists, never as natives. No matter how ingenious or frantic our evasions of the present, we cannot stay in an unchanging world. This book puts the Wars against Terror in a strategic and legal context, and though it therefore has had many things to say about the past and about our common future, about law and about war, it is ultimately about our unfinished present. It is about how we shall decide.

WHEN the clouds' swoln bosoms echo back the shouts of the many and strong
That things are all as they best may be, save a few to be right ere long,
And my eyes have not the vision in them to discern what to these is so clear,
The blot seems straightway in me alone; one better he were not here.
The stout upstanders say, All's well with us; ruers have nought to rue!
And what the potent say so oft, can it fail to be somewhat true?
Breezily go they, breezily come; their dust smokes around their career,
Till I think I am one born out of due time, who has no calling here.
Their dawns bring lusty joys, it seems; their evenings all that is sweet;

Our times are blessed times, they cry: Life shapes it as is most meet,
And nothing is much the matter; there are many smiles to a tear;
Then what is the matter is I, I say. Why should such a one be here? . . .
Let him in whose ears the low-voiced Best is killed by the clash of the First,
Who holds that if way to the Better there be, it exacts a full look at the Worst,
Who feels that delight is a delicate growth cramped by crookedness, custom
    and fear,
Get him up and be gone as one shaped awry; he disturbs the order here.

—Thomas Hardy, "In Tenebris II"

CODA

In this book I have often emphasized the theatrical nature of terror,[1] and how a global stage has been seized by terrorists in the twenty-first century through the use of the Internet, satellite television, cable channels, videocassettes, and the globalization of media.

For sectarian terrorists, this is how the drama is cast: God is the prompter whispering lines to the actors, who are the political leaders inciting violence, while the world's peoples are the audience. But this stage setting arrogates to those leaders a certain knowledge of God's politics that no religious text can provide; it is, in its way, quite secular because it removes God from the scene and keeps him in the wings. This is the theater of states of terror.

Imagine instead this arrangement: It is the political leader who prompts the people, and it is they who are the actors onstage. This is the world of states of consent. God is present as the audience, and He is everywhere and at all times.[2]

Therefore I wish to associate this book's message, even with its terrors, with that which is hopeful in mankind and gallant in mankind's adversity, which is indomitable and gives life, and leads our sympathy away in recoil from that which acclaims fear, and exalts death.[3]

We have time.[4] The deaths and destruction caused by twenty-first century terrorism have thus far been negligible compared to those of twentieth century conventional wars. We must, however, prepare our defenses, chief of which is our ingenuity and adaptability. When we finally determine to take up the Wars against Terror in earnest, we will face a threat to mankind that is unprecedented and is potentially measureless in its tragedy. Having prepared, however, we will act to preclude such tragedies; having acted in time, we will have preserved our liberties despite the historic suffering we could not in the end prevent; having protected our liberties while enduring such awful pain, we will have prevailed. We must each play our part as though the entire plot depended upon it, because it just might.

Every constitutional order evokes a unique form of terrorism. In Heaven, there will be no terror, and the lion will lie down with the lamb.[5] In Hell, there will be nothing but terror, and every generation unto the last will proffer its lambs.

Philip Bobbitt
October 19, 2007

ACKNOWLEDGMENTS

The last five years—the years I have spent writing this book—have mingled exhilarating achievement and tarnished hopes for America, Britain, and the world. The moral authority forged by the U.S. as leader of a global coalition that enforced the U.N. resolution restoring Kuwait and stopped ethnic cleansing in Europe was perhaps never higher than in those days following the September 11 attacks, which were directed against the U.S. precisely because of its leadership. The liberation of the Afghan people from the Taliban and its ally, al Qaeda; the daring valor with which Saddam Hussein's dynasty was removed; the Libyan cancellation of plans to nuclearize their weapons stocks; the secret Iranian suspension of their nuclear weapons program; the forging of an anti-terrorist alliance with Pakistan and other states—all promised greater security for the world's peoples. Yet despite this, U.S. stature and respect have sharply declined. A bewildering incompetence has characterized many of Washington's actions in Iraq, before international organizations, and in the U.S. itself, most notably during the relief efforts following Hurricane Katrina. This, and an evident willingness to cut corners where matters of consent and law are concerned, has led to a loss of esteem at the very time when trust and cooperation have been most needed for the success of the initiatives of the Alliance that the U.S. leads. At least some Alliance leaders, and many in their publics, welcomed this and felt a thrilling schadenfreude at the vertiginous decline of the once dazzling American fortunes.

During this same period, numerous theories were crafted to explain the history and the future of American national security. None of these addressed the fundamental question of what national security now meant and what armed forces are for in an age of postindustrial war.

> Nothing was done, in any radical sense, to reassess the nature of the threat and match capabilities to challenges. In fact the first Gulf War simply re-enforced core aspects of industrial war and our belief in large-scale fire and maneuver warfare.*

Yet also during this period I encountered many persons in the U.S., in the U.K., and elsewhere who were anxious to examine the strategies of the West—including American strategic failures—from a nonpartisan, dispassionate, and rigorous intellectual perspective, and who saw that law reform was indispensable for a return to respect for the rule of law. At the working level of professionals and operatives, one rarely encounters the hostility toward the U.S. that is such a prominent feature of European political life. These encoun-

---

*Sebestyen L. V. Gorka, *Al Qaeda and von Clausewitz: Rediscovering the Art of War.* Paper delivered to the U.S. Joint Special Operations University (JSOU) Symposium: "Countering Global Insurgency," Hurlburt Field, Florida, 2–5 May 2006.

ters have given me hope and this hope has been further strengthened by those who have selflessly read and commented on my work in progress.

Once again I wish to thank a circle of Austin friends—Paul Woodruff, Lawrence Wright, and most of all, Betty Sue Flowers—for their careful and thoughtful comments on what must have seemed an endless series of drafts. And, too, I wish to thank a group of London friends—Professor Sir Lawrence Freedman, Philip Ziegler, Simon Jenkins, and Sir Michael Quinlan, and most of all Sir Michael Howard—who have also responded generously and cogently to my manuscripts.

Beyond this cast of estimable players there was a chorus of supportive friends and colleagues on both sides of the Atlantic. From a series of remarkable research assistants I must single out Suzi Sosa, Krista Nelson, Erin Kerbow, Marc Matthews, Marissa Troiano, Noel Pacheco, Eric Harrington, Ryan Newman, and especially Brian Stolz and Nathan Bruggeman. Their efforts to set me straight on factual and reference matters were added to those of friends—Mark Sagoff, Ed Binkowski, Finlay Lewis—and academic colleagues Sanford Levinson, Robert Post, Harold Edgar, John Witt, Sarah Cleveland, and Jack Goldsmith, without whose reflections this would be a much poorer book.

I can scarcely praise Ashbel Green, in the U.S., and Stuart Proffitt, in the U.K., sufficiently. I know of no editors in their respective communities who are held in higher regard. I have my own theories about where inspiration comes from, but it would not be wrong to say that these two men, so different in many superficial ways, were much alike in possessing the gift of inspiring the writer who can, working in this doleful field, sometimes be dispirited. My agent, Andrew Wylie, was unfailingly responsive and encouraging.

My miraculous secretary, Ms. Jennifer Lamar, has once again pulled me through a long struggle with her flawless competence, her good humor, and her much-needed patience. Her colleague, Terri Germany, has provided unfailing and timely aid.

Excepting the presidencies of Richard Nixon and George W. Bush, I have worked in some capacity in the federal government for every administration from President Johnson's to the present. I realize how easy it is to criticize public officials when one does not bear any operational responsibility, how facile one's prescriptions become, and how one superimposes one's own experience onto the very different problems of one's successors. I have tried to correct for these temptations but I fear I may have not altogether succeeded.

Instead of the stimulus of government these last five years, I have been engaged by my students. It is always hard to say just what role these young people play in one's work. On the one hand, I am grateful to Deans William Powers and Lawrence Sager of the University of Texas and Dean David Schizer of Columbia University for generously arranging leaves from my teaching so that I might complete this work. On the other hand, I know that I am here engaged in the kind of dialogue that characterizes my classes, and that there lies behind my arguments a thousand, ten thousand, promptings and interventions and improvisations that arose in my classes.

Nor would this work have been possible without the steadfast support of Ms. Barbara James and the profound perspectives she brings to the questions of the future.

My editors, students, colleagues, and friends have greatly changed this book. Originally it was to be called "Plagues in the Time of Feast"; originally it had excerpts from plays at the beginning of each chapter; originally the superstructure of the narrative was drawn from drama. Above all, the book was considerably longer. For all of these changes, I surmise that readers will be grateful.

Many persons have contributed to this reworking. Audrey Kurth Cronin, George Fletcher, John Gray, Loretta Napoleoni, Peter Neumann, David Phillips, Steven Simon, Jessica Stern, Karin von Hippel, and Lawrence Wright were especially helpful on the subject of terrorism. Craig Drill, Sir Lawrence Freedman, Sir Max Hastings, and General Sir

Rupert Smith were helpful in many ways and most especially with respect to contemporary warfare. James Billington, Roger Louis, and Sir Michael Howard abundantly shared their superb historians' perspectives and encouraged an approach that is, in the main, more historical and philosophical than anything else. Regarding the subject of intelligence, I had enormous assistance from Sir Mark Allen, Robert Hutchings, Admiral Bob Inman, Sir Michael Quinlan, Charles S. Robb, James Woolsey, and my old friend Gregory Treverton. With respect to the subject of what I have called the supply side of terrorism, I benefited from the reactions and commentary of Bruce Ackerman, Richard Danzig, Philip Heymann, Norman Ornstein, and Tara O'Toole. It is difficult to advise a professor of constitutional law on constitutional matters, but somehow a number of my colleagues in this field managed this: Akhil Amar, Judge Michael Boudin, Judge Guido Calabresi, Richard Fallon, Anthony Lewis, Judge Debra Livingston, and the fine journalists Sidney Blumenthal, Jeff Rosen, and Stuart Taylor. The international law chapters were greatly enriched by Kenneth Anderson, Sarah Cleveland, Michael Reisman, Sir Adam Roberts, and Ruth Wedgwood. The difficult questions of ends and means were made less impossible and more tractable for me by Dennis Patterson, Kim Lane Scheppele, and my colleague and friend of three decades, Sanford Levinson. In questions of diplomacy and diplomatic history I consulted Robert Cooper, Rolf Ekeus, Niall Ferguson, Sir Jeremy Greenstock, Lord Hannay, and Henry Kissinger. The international relations scholars Timothy Garton Ash, Ivo Daalder, Frank Gavin, Charles Kupchan, Michael Lind, and James Steinberg were generous in giving me advice and counsel. My literary friends—Robert Pinsky, Henry Reath, and Isabella Thomas—have tried to make of this work something that will last. The playwrights and filmmakers Mirra Bank, Richard Brockman, and Frederick Wiseman have tutored and nurtured me.

I will always be grateful to the late Arthur Schlesinger for his friendship and encouragement, despite the fact that he would have disagreed with practically everything in this book.

Despite all this wonderful collaboration, I must bear responsibility for the arguments, the assessments, and the judgments of this book. I hope that readers who are inclined to disagree with my analyses will suspend the temptation to reject my book entirely when they encounter a conclusion so antithetical to their expectations that, like the thirteenth stroke of a clock, it seems to discredit all that has gone before. I am attempting to provide a fundamental rethinking of this subject, and I am well aware that the odds are against me.

In a fascinating paper entitled *Plutarch, Machiavelli, and Montaigne,* Travis Pantin asks the question why these cultivated figures should admire Sparta, an anti-intellectual and anti-aesthetic state if there ever was one. He answers that each was interested in political philosophy expressed in action, and that the law-giving of Lycurgus, to say nothing of the rigorous exercise of his philosophical ideas over several centuries by a small city-state beset by threats, captivated these readers. In that sense, this book is a work of political philosophy and not simply of law or strategy.

About Troy

1.

Troy O Troy
an archeologist
will sift your ashes through his fingers
yet a fire occurred greater than that of
the Iliad
for seven strings—

too few strings
one needs a chorus
a sea of laments
and thunder of mountains
rain of stone
—how to lead
people away from the ruins
how to lead
the chorus from poems. . . .

2.

They walked along ravines of former streets
as if on a red sea of cinders

and wind lifted the red dust
faithfully painted the sunset of the city

They walked along ravines of former streets
they breathed on the frozen dawn in vain

they said: long years will pass
before the first house stands here

they walked along ravines of former streets
they thought they would find some traces

a cripple plays
on a harmonica
about the braids of a willow
about a girl

the poet is silent
rain falls

—Zbigniew Herbert

NOTES

1. Czeslaw Milosz, "A Poem for the End of the Century," in *Provinces: Poems 1987–1991,* trans. Czeslaw Milosz and Robert Hass (New York: Ecco Press, 1991), 42.

INTRODUCTION: Plagues in the Time of Feast

1. See Philip Bobbitt, *The Shield of Achilles: War, Peace, and the Course of History* (New York: Knopf, 2002), and see also Bruce Ackerman, *Before the Next Attack: Preserving Civil Liberties in an Age of Terrorism* (New Haven, Conn.: Yale University Press, 2006).
2. Compare Brian M. Jenkins, "True Grit: To Counter Terror, We Must Conquer Our Own Fear," *RAND Review* 30, no. 2 (Summer 2006): 10: "Such an approach, if adopted, would attack the terror, not just the terrorists. It would see the White House working closely with the legislative and judicial branches to increase security without trespassing on liberty. It would aim at preserving national unity. In sum, it would be a strategy that seeks lasting strength."
3. Audrey Kurth Cronin, "Sources of Contemporary Terrorism," in *Attacking Terrorism: Elements of a Grand Strategy,* ed. Audrey Kurth Cronin and James M. Lundes (Washington, D.C.: Georgetown University Press, 2004), 33.
4. See Winning and Losing, p. 13. Lawrence Wright reports that "[a]lthough bin Laden and his chief lieutenants escaped death or capture, nearly eighty per cent of al Qaeda's members in Afghanistan were killed." Lawrence Wright, "The Master Plan," *The New Yorker*, 11 September 2006, 48. "One by one, the masterminds and operatives behind Al Qaeda's spectacular attacks . . . were killed or arrested, along with bin Laden's regional coordinators in Southeast Asia, Europe, and the Middle East." Corine Hegland, "Global Jihad," *National Journal* 36 (2004), 1397.
5. Simon Jenkins, "Him and Us," review of *The Politics of Good Intention: History, Fear and Hypocrisy in the New World Order,* by David Runciman, *Times Literary Supplement,* 24 February 2006, 11. Nor are these views confined to Europeans; see George Soros, *The Age of Infallibility: Consequences of the War on Terror* (New York: Public Affairs, 2006). See also Javier Marias, "How to Remember, How to Forget," *New York Times,* 11 September 2004, A15: "Here in Spain, we don't feel as if we are at war, because we aren't. And neither are the inhabitants of the United States, however vociferously many Americans may insist that they are. War is something else entirely. No semi-normal life can be led while a war is going on. The Madrilenians who lived through the siege of their city from 1936 to 1939 know that very well. The survivors of the daily bombardments of London during the Second World War know it, too.

And those Americans who participated in that war know it also. But there is no war against terrorism. There can be no such thing against an enemy that remains dormant most of the time and is almost never visible. It's simply another of life's inevitable troubles, and all we can do as we continue to combat it is repeat Cervantes's famous phrase, '*Paciencia y barajar*': 'Have patience, and keep shuffling the cards.' "

6. Daniel Benjamin and Steven Simon, "Zarqawi's Life After Death," *New York Times,* 9 June 2006, A27.

7. John Mueller, "Why Isn't There More Violence?" *Security Studies* 13, no. 3 (Spring 2004): 196; see also John Mueller, "Is There Still a Terrorist Threat? The Myth of the Omnipresent Enemy," *Foreign Affairs* 85, no. 5 (September/October 2006): 2.

8. See Bethany Lacina and Nils Petter Gleditsch, "Monitoring Trends in Global Combat: A New Dataset of Battle Deaths," *European Journal of Population* 21 (June 2005), and the corresponding online Battle Deaths Dataset, which features updated data, at http://www.prio.no/page/Project_detail/Publication_detail_channel/9244/45656.html. See also Monty Marshall and Ted Gurr's studies, titled *Peace and Conflict,* which are published as the 2001, 2003, and 2005 reports of the Center for International Development and Conflict Management.

9. A good many experts date the onset of contemporary international terrorism to the construction of a terrorist infrastructure by the East Germans in 1968. Reports published yearly by the U.S. State Department appear to adopt this premise. For example, the 1981 State Department report notes that "[b]etween 1968 and 1981, 189 American citizens were killed in international terrorist attacks." State Department, *Patterns of International Terrorism: 1981* (Washington, D.C.: July 1982), 5. The more recent reports, *Patterns of Global Terrorism* (1995–2003) and *Country Reports on Terrorism* (2004–2005), are available at http://www.state.gov/s/ct/rls/crt/.

10. About one in 80,000. Mueller, "Is There Still a Terrorist Threat?," 8.

11. Mueller, "Why Isn't There More Violence?," 195.

12. Christopher Hitchens, *Love, Poverty, and War: Journeys and Essays* (New York: Nation Books, 2004) (quoting Nat Hentoff), 324.

13. Which perhaps is the source of the notion that Bush and Blair have contrived the war on terror to stay in power. See Simon Jenkins, "Him and Us," review of *The Politics of Good Intention: History, Fear and Hypocrisy in the New World Order,* by David Runciman, *Times Literary Supplement,* 24 February 2006, 11.

14. "For fifteen years—or since the end of the first Gulf War—Iran has been busy building a secret global army of highly trained personnel and the necessary financial and technological capabilities to carry out any kind of mission. . . . Iran has identified American . . . targets around the world." Wright, "The Master Plan," 56 (quoting Fouad Hussein in *Al-Zarqawi: The Second Generation of Al Qaeda*).

15. Compare Thomas C. Schelling's description of a similar scenario with respect to nuclear weapons, in *The Strategy of Conflict* (Cambridge, Mass.: Harvard University Press, 1960), 207. In the succeeding pages I will argue that we must urgently develop doctrines, much as we did in the Cold War with respect to nuclear weapons, to cope with the dangerous cycle such scenarios present.

16. Cf. Edward Tenner, *Why Things Bite Back: Technology and the Revenge of Unintended Consequences* (New York: Knopf, 1997), 74.

17. *Shell Global Scenarios to 2025: The Future Business Environment Trends, Trade-Offs, and Choices* (London: Shell International Limited, 2005), 18, 161.

18. Quoted in Alfred Rolington, "Objective Intelligence or Plausible Denial: An Open Source Review of Intelligence Method and Process Since 9/11," *Intelligence and National Security* 21, no. 5 (October 2006): 745.

19. State of terror: both a political state whose legitimacy is underpinned by a relationship to its people maintained through terror (the fear of imminent violence against persons), and also a state of affairs in which people are kept in terrifying circumstances.

20. See chapters 10 and 11.

21. See, e.g., Laura K. Donohue, *Counter-Terrorist Law and Emergency Powers in the United Kingdom, 1922–2000* (Dublin: Irish Academic Press, 2001).

22. For a thoughtful analysis of the different ways in which legitimacy is grounded, see Richard H. Fallon, Jr., "Legitimacy and the Constitution," *Harvard Law Review* 118 (2005).

23. Thom Shanker, "A Nation Challenged: The Allies," *New York Times,* 19 December 2001, B1.

24. Corine Hegland, "Global Jihad," *National Journal* 36 (2004): 1396.

25. Bruce Riedel, "Al Qaeda Strikes Back," *Foreign Affairs* 86, no. 3 (May/June 2007).

26. Richard Fallon, letter to the author, 8 December 2006.

27. Just before the manuscript of this book was sent to its publisher in 2006 I decided to include a record of a single week's events in these wars. Arbitrarily, I picked the week of my birthday, July 22. *Excluding* the ongoing warfare in Iraq, Afghanistan, and Israel, this is a sampling of the reported incidents of that week:

Somalia: The transitional government sought troops from Ethiopia to deter Islamist militia encircling the provisional capital, Baidoa. Ethiopia sent hundreds of armored carriers 100 miles into Somalia. In Mogadishu, Islamists in a machine-gun-mounted pickup arrested 20 men watching an allegedly pornographic video.

Iran: A U.S. official told Congress that Iranians may have paid for and observed North Korea's seven long-range and medium-range missile test launches on July 4 and 5.

U.S.: The Homeland Security Department is investigating a pipe bomb found in Lake Pontchartrain, La. Officials fear it could be part of a practice run for a future attack that could shut down commerce on a critical U.S. waterway. Meanwhile, two students in Georgia with terror contacts in Canada were indicted for allegedly plotting a jihadist attack after undergoing paramilitary training in north Georgia.

Separately, customs officials said religious visas were being abused by radical clerics from Syria, Algeria, Pakistan, and Egypt.

In addition, experts said an analysis of the suicide plot that was revealed on July 7 to blow up the PATH trains of lower Manhattan and flood the financial district had a good chance of success.

Romania: Prosecutors prepared a case against Florian Lesch, 29, a convert to militant Islam, who was arrested after trying to detonate two gas cylinders in Timisoara to punish Romania for its good relations with the U.S. Police connected him to the Muslim Brotherhood.

Syria: Iranian president Mahmoud Ahmadinejad met with Hezbollah leaders in Damascus, prompting fears of more coordinated terrorist attacks [which subsequently came to pass, prompting Israeli reprisals and a full-scale attack on Lebanon].

United Kingdom: Two more Islamist organizations, Al-Ghurabaa and the Saved Sect, were banned as terrorist groups. They split off from the group founded by ter-

ror cleric Omar Bakri Mohammed, now in Lebanon. Meanwhile, militants on paltalk.com called for the destruction of Israel and all Jews worldwide.

India: Three men affiliated with the terrorist group Lashkar-e-Tayyaba were apprehended in a string of bombings on Bombay's transit system July 11 that killed 208 and injured 800. India's army reported new al-Qaida terror camps on the Pakistani border specializing in unconventional training, including the use of female recruits.

Thailand: Six people were killed by Islamist militants in drive-by motorcycle shootings around Pattani. Victims included an assistant village chief. Police reported growing numbers of terror suspects with such pervasive links to Indonesian terror group Barisan Revolusi Nasional that it is now suspected that BRN and Thailand's own RKK terrorists may be the same organization.

Bosnia: Three men accused of plotting a terror attack on Sarajevo or another European capital went to trial.

Canada: The Canadian Council on American Islamic Relations urged Muslims not to apologize for the activities of terrorists nor cooperate with the Canadian security forces in terrorist investigations.

Kashmir: Six Lashkar-e-Tayyaba terrorists were killed in two gunbattles with security forces that came looking for them and were ambushed. In a third village, a twenty-six-year-old woman's throat was slit by terrorists who accused her of collaborating with police.

Indonesia: A total of 217 jihadists—72 Indonesians, 57 Filipinos, 36 Malaysians, 45 Thais, 3 Bengals, 3 Bruneians, and 1 Singaporean—embarked to fight Israel in south Lebanon, according to an Islamic Youth Movement leader. Meanwhile, 90 militants from Aceh province's Islamist separatist movement also declared their intent to fight in south Lebanon.

Argentina: Known Hezbollah operatives in Iran remained at large despite their 1994 terrorist attack on a Jewish center in Buenos Aires. Jewish groups protested its twelfth anniversary, pointing out that it was Hezbollah's first attack on foreign soil and "a forerunner of all other attacks," one Jewish leader said.

Sweden: A top-secret trial of three terror suspects continued in Malmö. British intelligence reportedly supplied the information that led to arrests.

Russia: Chechen terrorists put new threats of attacks on their website. Two other websites published hagiographic videos extolling the life of the terrorist mastermind of the Beslan massacre, Shamil Basayev, who was killed July 10 by Russian troops.

And that was a quiet week. See Editorial, *Investor's Business Daily*, 24 July 2006, A18.

28. Partly this vertiginous rise reflected a redefinition of what counted; in 2003 the Department was forced to withdraw its reported data on the grounds that it was grossly understated. Even conservative estimates, however, seem to agree that the civilian fatalities from terrorism had doubled. Tom Baldwin, "US Admits Iraq Is Terror 'Cause,' " *Times* (London), 29 April 2006, 46.

29. Which is criticized in chapter 2 on the grounds that it surrenders strategic initiative to the enemy. This approach renders the civilian environment chronically insecure as terrorist forces continually reemerge among the civilian population that has been periodically abandoned to the terrorists when search-and-destroy missions are concluded. Instead of killing terrorists, the more important objective, I will argue in this book, is to protect civilians (which can only be partly accomplished by killing terrorists).

30. Quoted in Douglas Jehl, "The New Magic Bullet: Bureaucratic Imagination," *New York Times*, 25 July 2004, section 4, 1.

31. See Schelling, *Strategy of Conflict*.

32. Conversation with the author, 6 March 2007.

33. This joint resolution by Congress was passed unanimously in the Senate, and with one dissenting vote in the House. Jane Perlez, "U.S. Demand Arab Countries 'Choose Sides,' " *New York Times*, 15 September 2001, A1. A separate joint resolution adopted by Congress in October 2002 authorized the president as commander in chief to wage war against Iraq. See "Authorization for Use of Military Force Against Iraq Resolution of 2002," Pub. L. No. 107–243, 116 Stat. 1498.

34. "Neither Hitler's Germany nor the Stalinist Soviet Union was recognized as a democracy in the conventional liberal sense. Yet both assumed that they had a democratic complexion, indeed, that their form of democracy was identifiably superior to the western model. . . . The problem with conventional parliamentary democracy was the existence of parties or factions, whose purpose in Soviet eyes could only be to undermine the revolutionary state and divide popular opinion, or, in the German case, to splinter and weaken the nation in the throes of its rebirth. The Soviet people, Stalin [said when he announced the new Soviet constitution on November 1936] only needed one party because there was no longer division between capitalists and workers, landlords and peasants. A few months later, in April 1937, Hitler gave a long speech on the nature of democracy to local party leaders in which he, too, explained that only one party was needed in a society united with one will: 'But we cannot tolerate an opposition above all, for it would certainly always result again in decomposition.' " Richard Overy, *The Dictators* (London, Penguin, 2004), 58.

PART I

1. Thucydides, *History of the Peloponnesian War* (New York: Penguin Books, 1972), Book II, paragraph 43, 149–50; paragraph 40, 147.

CHAPTER ONE: The New Masque of Terrorism

1. John Gay, *Polly: An Opera. Being the Second Part of the Beggar's Opera* (London: Tho. Anstley, 1729), 2.5.17–23.

2. See Philip Bobbitt, *The Shield of Achilles: War, Peace, and the Course of History* (New York: Knopf, 2002), 5–17.

3. Though the British army countered the IRA for decades.

4. Indeed, the killings that day dwarf earlier terrorist incidents. Prior to September 11, the deadliest attacks were the bombings of commercial aircraft such as the 1988 explosion of Pan Am flight 103 over Lockerbie, Scotland, or the 1985 bombing of an Air India airliner. Two hundred and seventy people died in the Pan Am attack; the Air India attack killed more than 300. The August 1988 al Qaeda bombings of U.S.

embassies in Kenya and Tanzania killed 224. The 1983 Islamist attack on a U.S. Marine barracks in Beirut killed 241 Americans.

5. Because this is not only the date, rendered in the American style of month/day, of the atrocity but also the telephone number for calls to the emergency services throughout the United States; for the origin of this service see Bobbitt, *Shield of Achilles*, 411–13.

6. John Gearson, "The Nature of Modern Terrorism," in *Superterrorism: Policy Responses*, ed. Lawrence Freedman (Oxford: Blackwell Publishing, 2002), 14.

7. See Martin Goodman, *Rome and Jerusalem: The Clash of Ancient Civilizations* (London: Allen Lane, 2007), 407.

8. Gearson, "Nature of Modern Terrorism," 14.

9. Ibid.

10. Apparently falsely; see Louise Richardson, *What Terrorists Want: Understanding the Enemy, Containing the Threat* (New York: Random House, 2006), 27.

11. Jonathan Riley-Smith, "Religious Warriors," *Economist*, 23 December 1995, 67.

12. Ibid.

13. Ibid. The terms in brackets are mine; see Bobbitt, *Shield of Achilles*. As Sir Michael Howard has written, "Knighthood was a way of life, sanctioned and civilized by the ceremonies of the Church until it was almost indistinguishable from the ecclesiastical orders of the monasteries. . . . [Priests and knights were] equally dedicated, equally holy, the ideal to which medieval Christendom aspired. This remarkable blend of Germanic warrior and Latin *sacerdos* lay at the root of all medieval culture." Michael Howard, *War in European History* (Oxford: Oxford University Press, 1976), 4–5. See also Jonathan Riley-Smith, "Rethinking the Crusades," *First Things*, no. 101 (March 2000).

14. Roman Curia, Swiss Guard History, "The Sack of Rome," http://www.vatican.va/roman_curia/swiss_guard/swissguard/storia_en.htm (accessed October 9, 2006).

15. John C. Rao, "The Sack of Rome: 1527, 1776," *Seattle Catholic*, 27 April 2004; see also Luigi Guicciardini, *The Sack of Rome*, trans. and ed. James H. McGregor (New York: Ithaca Press, 1993). Luigi Guicciardini was the brother of the historian Francesco Guicciardini.

16. F. X. Kiiads, "Medicean Rome," available at http://www.uni-mannheim.de/mateo/camenaref/cmh/cmh201.html (accessed October 13, 2006).

17. Rudi Bosschaerts, "What Happened in Flanders," *Bosschaerts–Persyn Genealogical Research*, http://users.pandora.be/bosschaerts/EN/08en_geschiedenis_main.html (accessed February 14, 2007).

18. Geoffrey Parker, *The Military Revolution: Military Innovation and the Rise of the West, 1500–1800* (Cambridge: Cambridge University Press, 1996), 59.

19. Frederic Harrison, *William the Silent* (London: Macmillan and Co., 1897), 115.

20. Compare Rapoport, who argues that the terror practiced by the radical Christian groups of the princely state "was a sort of state terror; the sects organized their communities openly, taking full control of a territory, instituting gruesome purges to obliterate all traces of the old order, and organizing large armies, which waged holy wars periodically sweeping over the countryside and devastating, burning, and massacring everything and everyone in their paths." David C. Rapoport, "Fear and Trembling: Terrorism in Three Religious Traditions," *American Political Science Review* 78 (1984): 660 n. 4.

21. Bobbitt, *Shield of Achilles*, 97, 102.

22. "Pirate and Piracy," *Encyclopaedia Britannica*, 11th ed., vol. 21 (New York: Encyclopaedia Britannica, 1911), 640: "Some trace of these [men] may be found in the

Letter Books of the Old Providence Company, a puritan society formed in the reign of Charles I, of which Pym and the earl of Warwick, afterward the Parliamentary admiral of the Civil War, were governors. It was founded to colonize Old Providence on the coast of Honduras . . . [but] took to plain piracy and was suppressed by the Spaniards in 1638. Warwick made . . . large profits by fitting out privateers, which were in fact pirates on the 'Spanish main.' . . ."

23. Russ Campbell, "The Buccaneers," http://www.it4biz.com/omnibus/PortOfCall/ buccaneer.htm (accessed October 9, 2006).

24. "Pirate Utopias: Under the Banner of King Death," *Do or Die* 8 (1999): 66.

25. Thomas Hobbes, *Behemoth; or, The Long Parliament*, ed. Ferdinand Tönnies (London: Simpkin, Marshall, and Co., 1889), 4.

26. One can hear echoes of this constitutional order and its pirates in Kipling's story, "The Man Who Would Be King": "We will . . . go away to some other place where a man isn't crowded and can come into his own . . . in any place where they fight. . . . Then we will subvert that King and seize his throne and establish a Dy-nasty." Rudyard Kipling, "The Man Who Would Be King," in *The Man Who Would Be King and Other Stories* (Oxford: Oxford University Press, 1999), 252–53.

27. "Pirate Utopias," 71.

28. Marcus Rediker, *Between the Devil and the Deep Blue Sea: Merchant Seamen, Pirates and the Anglo-American Maritime World, 1700–1750* (Cambridge: Cambridge University Press, 1987), 270.

29. "Pirate Utopias," 66.

30. Ibid.

31. This is from the charter governing Bartholomew Roberts's company; a similar provision governed George Lowther's crew: "He that shall have the Misfortune to lose a Limb, in Time of Engagement, shall have the Sum of one hundred and fifty pounds Sterling, and remain with the Company as long as he shall think fit." Quoted in ibid., 67.

32. Matthew Teorey, "Pirates and State-Sponsored Terrorism in Eighteenth Century England," *Perspectives on Evil and Human Wickedness* 1, no. 2 (2003): 57.

33. See B. R. Burg, *Sodomy and the Pirate Tradition: English Sea Rovers in the Seventeenth-Century Caribbean* (New York: New York University Press, 1995). According to Burg, "The best that can be had from surviving evidence, at least that available on relationships between pirates and females, is some indication that the proportion of homosexuals among pirate crews was higher than among convict populations studied." Ibid., 111.

34. Teorey, "Pirates and State-Sponsored Terrorism," 56 (citing Lee Wallace, "Too Darn Hot: Sexual Contact in the Sandwich Islands on Cook's Third Voyage," *Eighteenth Century Life* 18, no. 3 [1994]: 232–42; Hans Turley, "Piracy, Identity, and Desire in *Captain Singleton*," *Eighteenth-Century Studies* 31 [1998]: 199).

35. "Pirate Utopias," 72.

36. Teorey, "Pirates and State-Sponsored Terrorism," 60.

37. "Piracy in the Caribbean," quoted from http://en.wikipedia.org/wiki/Piracy_in_the_ Caribbean.

38. "Pirate Utopias," 76.

39. Bobbitt, *Shield of Achilles*, 120–21.

40. "Pirate Utopias," 66. "During wartime, due to the demands of the navy, there was a great shortage of skilled maritime labour and seamen could command relatively high wages. The end of war, especially Queen Anne's War, which ended in 1713, cast vast numbers of naval seamen into unemployment and caused a huge slump in wages.

40,000 men found themselves without work at the end of the war—roaming the streets of ports like Bristol, Portsmouth and New York. In wartime privateering provided the opportunity for a relative degree of freedom and a chance at wealth. The end of war meant the end of privateering too, and these unemployed ex-privateers only added to the huge labour surplus. Queen Anne's War had lasted 11 years and in 1713 many sailors must have known little else but warfare and the plundering of ships. It was commonly observed that on the cessation of war privateers turned pirate. The combination of thousands of men trained and experienced in the capture and plundering of ships suddenly finding themselves unemployed and having to compete harder and harder for less and less wages was explosive—for many piracy must have been one of the few alternatives to starvation." Ibid.

41. For a description of these and related events, see Edward Channing, *The Jeffersonian System, 1801–1811* (New York: Harper & Row, 1968), 36–46.

42. Richard Leiby, "Terrorists by Another Name: The Barbary Pirates," *Washington Post*, 15 October 2001, C1.

43. Thomas Jewett, "Terrorism in Early America," *Early America Review* 4, no. 1 (2002).

44. See Thomas Jewett's riveting essay, "Terrorism in Early America," which contains a dramatic account of Stephen Decatur's heroics in the struggle to free American hostages and chasten the dey.

45. Ibid.

46. This is the characterization of Jefferson's position by Brent Stuart Goodwin in "On War in the 21st Century," an op-ed available at http://www.brown.edu/ Administration/News_Bureau/2001–02/01–023.html.

47. Jewett, "Terrorism in Early America." But see Leiby, in "Terrorists by Another Name," who calculates payments of $990,000 (perhaps excluding direct ransoms, but in any case a significant sum).

48. Leiby, "Terrorists by Another Name."

49. There are some interesting constitutional lessons to be drawn from this history regarding the question of war powers and the declaration of war clause—principally that this is one more piece of evidence (along with the wars against France during John Adams's administration)—that the framers and ratifiers did not consider the declaration of war to be a condition precedent to war-making. See Philip Bobbitt, "War Powers: An Essay on John Hart Ely's *War and Responsibility: Constitutional Lessons of Vietnam and Its Aftermath*," *Michigan Law Review* 92 (May 1994).

50. Jewett, "Terrorism in Early America."

51. Notably in Robespierre's speech to the French National Convention in 1794.

52. Quoted in Bruce Hoffman, *Inside Terrorism* (New York: Columbia University Press, 1998), 16.

53. The territorial state flourished in eighteenth century Europe, achieving dominance at the time of the Treaty of Utrecht (1713). These states are often called *anciens régimes* to distinguish them from the imperial state nations that emerged in the aftermath of the French Revolution.

54. Quoted in Paul Halsall, "Maximilien Robespierre: Justification of the Use of Terror," in *Internet Modern History Sourcebook* (August 1997), http://www.fordham.edu/ halsall/mod/robespierre-terror.html (accessed October 13, 2006).

55. Audrey Kurth Cronin, "Behind the Curve: Globalization and International Terrorism," *International Security* 27, no. 13 (Winter 2002/03): 34.

56. Mark Burgess, "A Brief History of Terrorism," Center for Defense Information, 2 July 2003, http://www.cdi.org/friendlyversion/printversion.cfm?documentID=1502 (accessed October 13, 2006).

57. Which could hardly have been vindicated without the development of the telegraph and the reform of open criminal trials. These allowed a mass propaganda effect to be given to terrorists' deeds. I am indebted to James Billington for this observation.

58. Burgess, "A Brief History of Terrorism."

59. David C. Rapoport, "The Four Waves of Rebel Terror and September 11," *Anthropoetics* 8, no. 1 (Spring/Summer 2002).

60. See Sergius Stepniak, *Underground Russia: Revolutionary Profiles and Sketches from Life* (London: Smith, Elder, & Co., 1883), 39–40.

61. Bobbitt, *Shield of Achilles*, 146, 178.

62. "Why the Black Flag?," in *Reinventing Anarchy, Again*, ed. Howard J. Ehrlich (San Francisco: AK Press, 1996), 31. "The earliest definite report of a black flag being flown by anarchists or used in working class revolt is of the famous anarchist Louise Michel leading a crowd of rioting unemployed to ransack bakers' shops with a black flag on March 9th 1883. However there are reports that she had flown a skull and cross-bones flag 12 years earlier in 1871 while leading the women's battalions of the insurrectionary Paris Commune. The Paris Commune even had a daily paper called *Le Pirate*." "Pirate Utopias," 72; see also George Woodcock, *Anarchism: A History of Libertarian Ideas and Movements* (New York: Meridian Books, 1962), 284; Jason Wehling, "History of the Black Flag: Why Anarchists Fly It; What Are Its Origins?," *Fifth Estate* 31, no. 1 (Summer 1997). This suggests that terrorists can be sensitive to their antecedents, perhaps more so than historians of the phenomenon of terror.

63. Rapoport, "Four Waves of Rebel Terror."

64. "He preached that the revolutionary was someone who had 'broken every tie with the civil order . . . and with the ethics of this world,' and he put his concept into practice. He set up a secret society, persuading its members that it was but one cell of a vast network, whose sole representative among them was himself. [O]n the strength of his fabrications, he persuaded Bakunin to part with a good deal of money. . . . Back in Russia he alleged to his followers that one of their number was a police spy and that they must murder him. They did so, and after a police investigation Nechaev was brought to trial in 1872—a trial which the authorities decided to hold openly, in the expectation that the evidence presented would awaken public repugnance toward the revolutionaries. In fact . . . the newspaper reports inspired many young people with admiration for Nechaev . . . and . . . for his break with conventional morality."

65. See Bobbitt, *Shield of Achilles*, chapter 8 ("From State-Nations to Nation-States: 1776–1914").

66. Carl Savich, "Gavrilo Princip and Patrick Pearse: Nationalism, Patriotism, and Rebellion: A Comparison," *Serbianna*, 24 May 2002, http://www.serbianna.com/columns/savich/028.shtml (accessed October 13, 2006). Both the Young Bosnia movement, of which Gavrilo Princip was a member, and the Black Hand, which is believed to have supplied the assassins of the Archduke Franz Ferdinand with weapons, were anarchist groups.

67. Ibid. Like other nationalist movements, the Young Bosnia movement was influenced by the anarchist writings of Pyotr Kropotkin and the actions of Narodnaya Volya.

68. "Locked-up Lori," *Economist*, 11 December 2004, 37.

69. See Walter Laqueur, *The New Terrorism: Fanaticism and the Arms of Mass Destruction* (New York: Oxford University Press, 1999), 39.

70. Christian Rousseau, "Military Power in the Post-Modern State," Canadian Forces College, available at http://198.231.69.12/papers/nssc5/rousseau.doc (accessed October 9, 2006).

71. David Greenberg, "Is Terrorism New?," *History News Network*, 21 September

2001, http://historynewsnetwork.org/articles/article.html?id=289 (accessed October 9, 2006).

72. See Rapoport, "Four Waves of Rebel Terror": "If the process of atrocities and counter-atrocities was well planned, it worked nearly always to favor those perceived to be weak and without alternatives."

73. See discussion in the introduction.

74. Bobbitt, *Shield of Achilles*, 229. The deregulation of industry as well as the deregulation of women's reproductive choice, the replacement of conscription by all-volunteer forces, welfare reform that attempts to replace unemployment allowances with education and training to help the unemployed enter the labor market, and the use of NGOs and private companies as outsourced adjuncts to traditional government operations—all reflect the emerging market state. See also *Shell Global Scenarios to 2025: The Future Business Environment Trends, Trade-Offs, and Choices* (London: Shell International Limited, 2005).

75. Cf. Martha Crenshaw, "Innovation: Decision Points in the Trajectory of Terrorism," paper prepared for the Minda de Gunzburg Center for European Studies Conference on Trajectories of Terrorist Violence in Europe, 9–11 March 2001.

76. Audrey Kurth Cronin, "Rethinking Sovereignty: American Strategy in the Age of Terrorism," *Survival* 44, no. 2 (Summer 2002): 135. See also Steve Simon and David Benjamin, "The Terror," *Survival* 43, no. 4 (Winter 2001).

77. Anna Reid, "Introduction," in *Taming Terrorism: It's Been Done Before*, ed. Anna Reid (London: Policy Exchange, 2004), 17.

78. Steve Simon and Daniel Benjamin, "America and the New Terrorism," *Survival* 42, no. 1 (Spring 2000): 59.

79. Paul Wilkinson, *Terrorism Versus Democracy: The Liberal State Response* (London: Frank Cass, 2001), 49–50; see also Bruce Hoffman, "Terrorism Trends and Prospects," in *Countering the New Terrorism* (Santa Monica, Calif.: RAND, 1999).

80. Brent Ellis, "Countering Complexity: An Analytical Framework to Guide Counter-Terrorism Policy-Making," *Journal of Military and Strategic Studies* 6, no. 1 (Spring/Summer 2003): 3 (emphasis in original omitted).

81. Anna M. Pluta and Peter D. Zimmerman, "Nuclear Terrorism: A Disheartening Dissent," *Survival* 48, no. 2 (Summer 2006): 55.

82. See Brian Michael Jenkins, "The Future Course of International Terrorism," *Futurist*, July/August 1987.

83. See David Tucker, "What Is New About the New Terrorism and How Dangerous Is It?," *Terrorism and Political Violence* 13, no. 3 (Autumn 2001): 7; see also Brian Michael Jenkins, "Terrorism: Current and Long Term Threats," statement to the Senate Armed Services Subcommittee on Emerging Threats, 15 November 2001, available at http://www.rand.org/pubs/testimonies/2005/CT187.pdf (accessed October 13, 2006): "Wanton violence could jeopardize group cohesion, alienate perceived constituents, and provoke ferocious government crackdowns. . . . I still believe this to be true of most of the groups that have resorted to terrorism. . . ."

84. Bruce Hoffman, *Inside Terrorism* (New York: Columbia University Press, 1988), 162.

85. Alan Cowell, "Two Faces of Terrorism: Is One More Evil Than the Other?," *New York Times*, 31 July 2005, section 4, 4.

86. National Commission on Terrorism, *Countering the Changing Threat of International Terrorism*, report submitted June 7, 2000, pp. 1, 2, iv. A similar conclusion was reached by Audrey Kurth Cronin, who wrote that "[c]areful analysis of terrorism data compiled by the U.S. Department of State reveals other important trends regarding the frequency and lethality of terrorist attacks. [Although] there were fewer such

attacks in the 1990s than in the 1980s . . . even before September 11, the absolute number of casualties of international terrorism had increased, from a low of 344 in 1991 to a high of 6,693 in 1998. . . . More worrisome, the number of people killed per incident rose significantly. . . . Thus, even though the number of terrorist attacks declined in the 1990s, the number of people killed in each one increased." Cronin, "Behind the Curve," 43. This data has been disputed as understating the actual number of attacks; see Alan B. Krueger and David D. Laitin, "Misunderestimating Terrorism," *Foreign Affairs* 85, no. 5 (September/October 2004), and in any case we have more recent data. I am indebted to Jessica Stern for the graphs in the text.

87. Brian M. Jenkins, "Combating Global War on Terrorism," in *Countering Terrorism and WMD*, ed. Peter Katona et al. (New York: Routledge, 2006), 182.

88. Cronin, "Behind the Curve," 49.

89. See Loretta Napoleoni, *Terror Incorporated: Tracing the Money Behind Global Terrorism* (New York: Penguin Books, 2003). Wright, however, indicates that al Qaeda was not as well funded as many had assumed, and in fact was often nearly insolvent. See Lawrence Wright, *The Looming Tower: Al Qaeda and the Road to 9/11* (New York: Knopf, 2006), 248, 270.

90. See Napoleoni, *Terror Incorporated*, 214–20. But, according to Wright, bin Laden's companies do not seem to have ever made a good deal of money. Wright, *Looming Tower*, 196–97.

91. Cronin, "Behind the Curve," 49–50 (citing Roger G. Weiner, "The Financing of International Terrorism," Terrorism and Violence Crime Section, Criminal Division, U.S. Department of Justice, October 2001, p. 3). Cronin further notes that "[i]n addition to gold, money was transferred into other commodities—such as diamonds in Sierra Leone and the Democratic Republic of Congo, and tanzanite from Tanzania—all while hiding the assets and often making a profit, and all without interference from the sovereign governments that at the time were at war with al-Qaeda and the Taliban" (Ibid., 50).

92. National Commission on Terrorism, *Countering the Changing Threat*, iv: "They are less dependent on state sponsorship and are, instead, forming loose, transnational affiliations based on . . . a common hatred of the United States."

93. Peter R. Neumann, "Europe's Jihadist Dilemma," *Survival* 48, no. 2 (Summer 2006): 77.

94. Neumann, "Europe's Jihadist Dilemma," 83–84 (citing Emerson Vermatt, "Bin Laden's Terror Networks in Europe," Mackenzie Occasional Paper, May 2002, available at http://www.mackenzieinstitute.com/2002/2002_Bin_Ladens_Networks.html [accessed October 13, 2006]).

95. See Marc Sageman, *Understanding Terror Networks* (Philadelphia: University of Pennsylvania Press, 2004).

96. See John Horgan and Max Taylor, "The Provisional Irish Republican Army: Command and Functional Structure," *Terrorism and Political Violence* 9, no. 3 (Autumn 1997): 3.

97. Canadian Security Intelligence Service, Backgrounder No. 8, "Counter-Terrorism" (revised August 2002), http://www.csis-scrs.gc.ca/en/newsroom/backgrounders/backgrounder08.asp (accessed February 10, 2005).

98. John Arquilla, David Ronfeldt, and Michele Zanini, "Networks, Netwar, and Information-Age Terrorism," in *Countering the New Terrorism*, 45, 56.

99. See Bruce Berkowitz, *The New Face of War: How War Will Be Fought in the 21st Century* (New York: Free Press, 2003), 22.

100. Ibid, 15–16.

101. Corine Hegland, "Global Jihad," *National Journal* 36 (2004): 1399.
102. Quoted in ibid., 1399, 1402.
103. Quoted in ibid., 1400.
104. Ibid., 1397.
105. Cf. Martha Crenshaw, "The United States as Target of Terrorism," in *Global Terrorism After the Iraq War*, United States Institute of Peace, Special Report 111 (October 2003): 6–9, available at http://www.usip.org/pubs/specialreports/sr111.pdf (accessed October 13, 2006). Professor Crenshaw is notable for the insight that "terrorism is best understood in terms of its strategic function."
106. Kurt M. Campbell and Michèle A. Flournoy, *To Prevail: An American Strategy for the Campaign Against Terrorism* (Washington, D.C.: CSIS Press, 2006), 42.
107. Neumann, "Europe's Jihadist Dilemma," 72.
108. Riedel, "Al Qaeda Strikes Back," 30.
109. Letter from Robert Earle to author. In November 2006, Eliza Manningham-Buller, the director general of the British Security Service, known as MI5, said that some two hundred networks of Muslims of South Asian descent were being monitored in the United Kingdom. At the "extreme end of this spectrum," Manningham-Buller said, "are resilient networks directed from al Qaeda in Pakistan," and terrorist plots in the United Kingdom "often have links back to al Qaeda in Pakistan, and through those links al Qaeda gives guidance and training to its largely British foot soldiers here on an extensive scale." Riedel, "Al Qaeda Strikes Back," 31. Since 2001, these foot soldiers are suspected of having plotted thirty or so attacks on targets in the United Kingdom or aircraft leaving for the United States. (All but one of them were disrupted.) These networks' most notable success was the July 7, 2005, attacks on the London public transport system. Videos later released by Zawahiri left no question that al Qaeda had sponsored the attacks.
    The *New York Times* published this chart:

TERROR PLOTS IN EUROPE

Major Terrorist attacks or plots uncovered by authorities in Europe:

2004	2005	2006	2007
Spain On March 11, four bombs placed on commuter trains in Madrid killed 191 people. Twenty-nine men [are on trial].	**Britain** Four suicide bombers killed at least 52 people on the London transit system on July 7. On July 21, another group tried to detonate their backpacks with explosives on three subway trains and a bus, but the explosives failed to detonate. Four men were convicted in July 2007 and sentenced to life in prison. . . .	**Germany** In July, two homemade bombs carried on to commuter trains in Cologne in suitcases [by] Lebanese men failed to explode. Officials later said the plot was fuelled in part by anger over the publication of satirical cartoons about the Prophet Muhammad in a Danish newspaper.	**Britain** In June, two car bombs were found in London and two men rammed a Jeep Cherokee into an entrance at Glasgow Airport. . . . Three doctors have been charged, and fourth suspect died of burns sustained in the Jeep crash.
Britain On March 30, British authorities said they had foiled a plot to set off fertilizer bombs around London . . . [F]ive men were convicted . . . and jailed for life. . . .			**Denmark** Eight men were arrested this month on suspicion of plotting a bombing.

2004	2005	2006	2007
		Britain In August, authorities said there was a plot to blow up as many as 10 passenger jets bound for the United States and began raids across Britain to break up the plot. They said 24 suspects were planning to carry liquid explosives onto the airliners. . . .	Investigators described the threat as imminent and said the arrests grew out of an international investigation that had lasted several months. . . . Some of the suspects had connections to "high-ranking members of Al Qaeda." . . .
		Denmark In September, nine men were arrested on suspicion of preparing explosives for a terror attack. . . .	

New York Times, 11 September 2007, A6.

110. Abraham R. Wagner, "Terrorist Use of New Technologies," in *Countering Terrorism and WMD*, ed. Katona et al., 109.

111. Gabriel Weimann, *www.terror.net: How Modern Terrorism Uses the Internet*, United States Institute of Peace, Special Report 116 (March 2004): 2, available at http://www.usip.org/pubs/specialreports/sr116.pdf (accessed October 13, 2005).

112. Cronin, "Behind the Curve," 47. See also Dorothy Denning, "Cyberwarriors: Activists and Terrorists Turn to Cyberspace," *Harvard International Review* 23, no. 2 (Summer 2001).

113. Luis Miguel Ariza, "Virtual Jihad: The Internet as the Ideal Terrorism Recruiting Tool," 26 December 2005, http://www.sciam.com/article.cfm?articleID=000B5155–2077–13A8–9E4D83414B7F0101&sc=I100322 (accessed October 13, 2005).

114. Quoted in Hegland, "Global Jihad," 1402.

115. Cronin, "Behind the Curve," 47. See also Paul R. Pillar, *Terrorism and U.S. Foreign Policy* (Washington, D.C.: Brookings Institute, 2001).

116. This technology reinforces the less hierarchical nature of market state terrorism. Whereas nation state terrorists depended on broadcasts—top-down, centralized communications—jihadists often thrash out strategy online and have adapted the user-driven techniques of the Internet to enhance the growth of terrorist networks, even to creating self-organizing units. *Asharq al-Awsat* (2 May 2007), cited in *Terrorism Focus* 4, no. 13 (8 May 2007).

117. Quoted in Hegland, "Global Jihad," 1402.

118. Cronin, "Behind the Curve," 48.

119. Robert F. Worth, "Iraqi Insurgents Put the Web in Their Arsenal," *International Herald Tribune*, 12 March 2005, 1. Worth noted that one writer, reflecting on the increased political pressure on the Italian government to withdraw its troops from

Iraq following the kidnapping and murder of an Italian national, proposed taking another Italian hostage "to add fuel to the fire while it is hot." This post drew a response from Abu Maysar al-Iraqi, the nom de guerre of Zarqawi's press spokesman, who promised to "repeat the nightmare, again and again."

120. Quoted in Gordon Corera, "A Web Wise Terror Network," *BBC News*, 10 October 2004, http://news.bbc.co.uk/2/hi/in_depth/3716908.stm (accessed October 13, 2005). See also Scott Shane, "The Grisly Jihadist Network That He Inspired Is Busy Promoting Zarqawi's Militant Views," *New York Times*, 9 June 2006, A1: "While other militants . . . had built Web sites to spread their message, Mr. Zarqawi and his aides were the first to take full advantage of the technology. . . . [I]t also helped secure the Internet as a center of terrorist recruitment and instruction, partly supplanting the role of old Qaeda training camps in Afghanistan. . . . In recent months, his video images and vivid images of violence have been posted on multiple computer servers to avoid downloading delays, with one version designed for viewing on cellphones."

121. Corera, "A Web Wise Terror Network."

122. Quoted in Shane, "Grisly Jihadist Network."

123. See Joseph S. Nye, Jr., "How to Counter Terrorism's Online Generation," *Financial Times*, 13 October 2005, 19; see also Susan B. Glassert and Steve Coll, "The Web as Weapon: Zarqawi Intertwines Acts on Ground in Iraq with Propaganda Campaign on the Internet," *Washington Post,* 9 August 2005, A1. David Talbot reported in early 2005 that the Berg video has been downloaded 15 million times from one server alone. David Talbot, "Terror's Server," *Technology Review* 108, no. 2 (February 2005): 48.

124. Joseph S. Nye, Jr., "Terrorism and the Internet," Op-Ed, 2005 (on file with author).

125. Benedict Anderson, *Imagined Communities: Reflections on the Origin and Spread of Nationalism* (Thetford, Norfolk, U.K.: Thetford Press, 1983).

126. Conversation with Steven Simon, Cambridge, Massachusetts.

127. Pew Global Attitudes Project, *Views of a Changing World* (Washington, D.C.: Pew Research Center, 2003), 46.

128. There is evidence that al Qaeda did acquire what it believed to be fissile material but was apparently duped.

129. See testimony by former FBI director Louis Freeh before the Senate Committee on Appropriations, Subcommittee for the Departments of Commerce, Justice, and State, the Judiciary, and Related Agencies on Feb. 4, 1999, available at http://www.fas.org/irp/congress/1999_hr/990204-freehct2.htm (accessed October 13, 2006).

130. James K. Campbell, "Excerpts from Research Study 'Weapons of Mass Destruction and Terrorism: Proliferation by Non-State Actors,'" *Terrorism and Political Violence* 9, no. 2 (Summer 1997): 25.

131. National Commission on Terrorism, *Countering the Changing Threat*, 4.

132. In the previous era, practitioners of counterterrorism were mainly concerned with small arms, explosives, and other conventional munitions. Today, there is increasing concern about the possible use by terrorists of nuclear, radiological, chemical, and biological weapons.

133. And quite possibly other nuclear states, such as the U.S. At Los Alamos National Laboratory, the largest nuclear weapons laboratory in the U.S., recent security lapses have been serious and widely reported. Classified information has been improperly downloaded and removed from the laboratory, security measures have dramatically failed in Red Team/Blue Team security drills, and a computer hard drive containing volumes of information on weapons designs has disappeared, only to turn up behind

a copier machine during the subsequent FBI investigation. Perhaps most seriously, Los Alamos personnel have lost two keys to Technical Area 18, where highly enriched uranium and plutonium are stored. See "Los Alamos to Remove Nukes," *Wired News*, http://www.wired.com/news/privacy/0,1848,65012,00.html?tw=wn_top head_6 (accessed March 25, 2007).

134. Scott Shane, "Zarqawi Built Global Jihadist Network on Internet," *New York Times*, 9 June 2006.

135. In Iraq, the "videos made by the killers have been distributed across the Arab world and North Africa as recruitment tools. They are also intended to terrorize, if not coalition soldiers, at least the foreign civilian workers who are essential to the construction of the new state. Thus a group of Nepalese cooks were captured and murdered [on film]. It is hard to imagine anyone more innocent." William Shawcross, *Allies: The U.S., Britain, Europe, and the War in Iraq* (New York: Public Affairs, 2005), 262.

136. "[T]errorism as something separate from globalization is misleading and potentially dangerous. Indeed, globalization and terrorism are intricately intertwined forces characterizing international security in the twenty-first century." Cronin, "Behind the Curve," 52.

137. For more on this point, see Christopher Coker's superb "Globalisation and Insecurity in the Twenty-first Century: NATO and the Management of Risk," Adelphi paper no. 345 (London: International Institute for Strategic Studies, 2002), 40.

138. "One recent document purporting to come from bin Laden berates the United States for failing to ratify the Kyoto agreement on climate change. . . . Zawahiri has decried multinational companies as a major evil. Mohammed Atta . . . once told a friend how angered he was by a world economic system that meant Egyptian farmers grew cash crops such as strawberries for the West while the country's own people could barely afford bread." Jason Burke, "Al Qaeda," *Foreign Policy* no. 142 (May/June 2004): 20.

139. Sir Lawrence Freedman, "Globalization and the Wars against Terrorism."

140. Of course I do not wish to imply that simply because Islam is a global religion that it should be particularly threatening. I mean simply that al Qaeda was able to exploit a global network.

141. See John Gray, *Al Qaeda and What It Means to Be Modern* (London: Faber and Faber, 2003). Peter Bergen, who interviewed bin Laden in 1997, views the terrorist, and by extension the al Qaeda network, as "at once a product of globalization and a response to it." Foreign Policy Association, Recently in Focus: al-Qaeda, http://www.fpa.org/newsletter_info2478/newsletter_info_sub_list.htm?section=Al-Qaeda (accessed October 13, 2006). See also Peter L. Bergen, *Holy War, Inc.: Inside the Secret World of Osama bin Laden* (New York: Free Press, 2001).

142. Hegland, "Global Jihad," 1402.

143. Pew Global Attitudes Project, *Views of a Changing World*, 46.

144. Olivier Roy, Social Science Research Council, "Neo-Fundamentalism," http://www.ssrc.org/sept11/essays/roy_text_only.htm (accessed October 13, 2006).

145. See Daniel Benjamin and Steve Simon, *The Age of Sacred Terror* (New York: Random House, 2002), and *The Next Attack: The Failure of the War on Terror and a Strategy for Getting It Right* (New York: Times Books, 2005) by the same authors; Peter Bergen, *Holy War, Inc.*; Steve Coll, *Ghost Wars: The Secret History of the CIA, Afghanistan, and Bin Laden* (New York: Penguin Books, 2004); Lawrence Wright, *The Looming Tower* (New York: Knopf, 2006).

146. See Jessica Stern, "The Protean Enemy," *Foreign Affairs* 82, no. 4 (July/August 2003): 27–40.

568 — Notes to Pages 64–74

147. "Terrorism: An Interdisciplinary Perspective," http://www.wadsworth.com/shared_features/popups/terrorism/booklet.html (accessed October 13, 2006).

148. Olivier Roy, "The Political Imagination of Islam," interview by Harry Kreisler, April 16, 2002, http://globetrotter.berkeley.edu/people2/Roy/roy-con4.html (accessed October 13, 2006).

149. Anthony Cordesman, *Terrorism, Asymmetric Warfare, and Weapons of Mass Destruction: Defending the U.S. Homeland* (Westport, Conn.: Praeger, 2002), 308.

150. Burke, "Think Again! Al Qaeda," 18.

151. "The Power of Nightmares: Baby It's Cold Outside," *BBC News*, 14 January 2005, http://news.bbc.co.uk/1/hi/programmes/3755686.stm (accessed October 13, 2006).

152. Ibid.

153. Andy Beckett, "The Making of the Terror Myth," *Guardian*, 15 October 2005, 2.

154. See Michael Elliot, "The Shoe Bomber's World," *Time*, 16 February 2002, http://www.time.com/time/world/article/0,8599,203478,00.html (accessed February 23, 2007). See also the government's sentencing memorandum filed in U.S. District Court during the sentencing phase of Reid's trial, which is available online at http://fl1.findlaw.com/news.findlaw.com/hdocs/docs/reid/usreid11703gsentm.pdf.

155. This is according to an affidavit by bomb technician Gregory Carl, submitted to the U.S. District Court. Sebestyén Gorka, "Islamist Radicalism in the UK—A Case Study from 2001," *Jane's Terrorism and Security Monitor*, 6 September 2005.

156. "Richard Reid," *NNDB*, http://www.nndb.com/people/828/000058654/ (accessed February 23, 2007).

157. Gorka, "Islamist Radicalism in the UK."

158. Though it is not clear that even this would have shaken their convictions: several national media rushed to insist that the London bombers were not connected to al Qaeda, even after al Qaeda released the first video statement of the leader of the attacks. This view has now been further discredited by the release of a second video by al Qaeda, along with a message of condolence from bin Laden, that features a tape of a second terrorist explaining his motives. On July 7, 2006, the anniversary of the London bombings, Zawahiri stated in the videotape released by al Qaeda that two of the bombers had been trained in al Qaeda camps.

159. But see Jason Bennetto and Ian Herbert, in "London Bombings: The Truth Emerges," *Independent*, 13 August 2005, who reported that some elements of the government had concluded that there was no link between the attacks and al Qaeda, and that the two groups of bombers had acted independently of any outside assistance. This conclusion was immediately picked up by the worldwide press, especially in the Middle East.

160. Lawrence Wright, "The Man Behind bin Laden," *The New Yorker*, 16 September 2002, 78.

161. Ibid., 76.

162. "Bin Laden's Fatwa," *Online NewsHour* (PBS), http://www.pbs.org/newshour/terrorism/international/fatwa_1996.html (accessed October 13, 2006).

163. Wright, "The Man Behind bin Laden," 81.

164. See Andrew Bolt, "Terror Wins a Victory," *Herald Sun*, 26 November 2003, section 1, 19; Youssef H. Aboul-Enein, "Ayman Al-Zawahiri's *Knights Under the Prophet's Banner*: The al-Qaeda Manifesto," *Military Review* 85, no. 1 (January–February 2005): 84. The list of targets is taken from Ayman Al Zawahiri's *Knights Under the Prophet's Banner*, which was serialized in *al-Sharq al-Awsat*, a London-based Saudi newspaper, in December 2001.

165. Sebestyén L. V. Gorka, "Al Qaeda's Rhetoric and Its Implications," *Jane's Terrorism*

and Security Monitor, 16 February 2005, available at http://www.itdis.org/portals/11/TSMalQrhetoric.pdf (accessed October 13, 2006).

166. According to the Australian Federal Police, 202 people were killed in the 2002 Bali bombing. See also "Bali Death Toll Set at 202," *BBC News*, 19 February 2003, 168.

167. See chapter 3, pages 144–145.

168. Riedel, "Al Qaeda Strikes Back," 40.

169. In July 2005 the Egyptian chief of mission was kidnapped and killed in Baghdad. Later that month, on the twenty-sixth, two kidnapped Algerian envoys were filmed and murdered. The organization "al Qaeda in Iraq" broadcast a statement on a website confirming these murders.

170. "Full Text: Bin Laden Tape," *BBC News*, 15 April 2004, http://news.bbc.co.uk/2/hi/middle_east/3628069.stm (accessed October 13, 2006).

171. "Text of al-Zawahri Statement," *BBC News*, 4 August 2005, http://news.bbc.co.uk/2/hi/world/middle_east/4746157.stm (accessed October 13, 2006).

172. See, e.g., Chris Blackhurst, "Afraid and Angry, We Ask: 'Why Us?,' " *Evening Standard*, 11 August 2006, 13: "I found myself thinking: why us? What have we done to deserve this hatred? Why are we bearing the brunt when other countries escape relatively lightly? Why can't we be left alone to get on with our lives? . . . Lining up with the [U.S.] is fine—but not, surely if [it] is universally loathed. . . . [T]he government pushes for national identity cards. . . . They press for community leaders to educate and integrate. . . . No, what would have an impact would be if we loosened ourselves from our unpopular pal [the U.S.]. . . . Try as I might, however, I can't think what, in this post-Cold War age, this partnership is actually bringing us. . . . What the alliance is giving us, in abundance, is hatred, death and destruction."

173. According to Saudi journalist Jamal Khashoggi, bin Laden "was not the one who originated the radical thinking that came to characterize Al Qaeda. He joined these men, rather than the other way around. His organization became the vehicle for their thinking." Quoted in Wright, "The Master Plan," 50.

174. See the Internet work attributed to Naji, "The Management of Savagery." William McCants's translated version is available at http://www.ctc.usma.edu/Management_of_Savagery.pdf (accessed December 15, 2006).

175. See Lawrence Wright's superb *New Yorker* article, "The Master Plan," published September 11, 2006.

176. Just as the war aim for the market states of consent is to protect civilians; see chapter 4.

177. This 1,600-page essay was published on the Internet in December 2004. Wright, "The Master Plan."

178. Quoted in ibid., 50.

179. Ibid., 56.

180. Quoted in ibid.

181. Christopher M. Blanchard, *Al Qaeda: Statements and Evolving Ideology*, report of the Congressional Research Service, 4 February 2005, 8–9.

182. Various partial translations are available online, as well as in Gilles Kepel, *The War for Muslim Minds: Islam and the West* (Cambridge, Mass.: Belknap, 2004), and *Anti-American Terrorism and the Middle East*, ed. Barry Rubin and Judith Colp Rubin (Oxford: Oxford University Press, 2002). Laura Mansfield has also published a translation in *His Own Words: Translation and Analysis of the Writings of Dr. Ayman Al Zawahiri* (U.S.A.: TLG Publications, 2006).

183. For Zawahiri, Napoleon's invasion of Egypt and his invitation to the Jews to return to the Near East are another example.

184. "Full Text: bin Laden's 'Letter to America,' " *Observer Worldview*, 24 November 2002, http://observer.guardian.co.uk/worldview/story/0,11581,845725,00.html (accessed October 13, 2006).

185. Ibid.

186. "Full transcript of bin Laden's speech," Al Jazeera, 2 November 2004, http://english .aljazeera.net/English/archive/archive?ArchiveId=7403 (accessed March 26, 2007).

187. "Full Text: bin Laden's 'Letter to America.' "

188. "Transcript of President Bush's Address," *CNN.com*, 20 September 2001, http:// archives.cnn.com/2001/US/09/20/gen.bush.transcript/ (accessed October 13, 2006).

189. Correlli Barnett, "Why al-Qa'eda is Winning," *Spectator*, 13 December 2003, 26.

190. Although therefore wrong when he later sometimes tended to equate all forms of terrorism. Indeed, lumping all terrorists together not only ignores the distinctions between nation state and market state terrorism, it risks augmenting the assets of the latter with those of the former, for example, adding the likes of the PLO and Hamas to the number of groups available for al Qaeda outsourcing.

191. Daniel Benjamin and Steven Simon, "Zarqawi's Life After Death," *New York Times*, 9 June 2006, A27.

192. See Peter Bergen's comments in note 141 above.

193. On November 9, 2005, a Belgian convert to Islam conducted a suicide bombing in Iraq, becoming Europe's first female suicide bomber (outside of Russia). See Craig S. Smith, "Raised Catholic in Belgium, She Died a Muslim Bomber," *New York Times*, 6 December 2005, A10.

194. Richard K. Betts, "How to Think About Terrorism," *Wilson Quarterly* 30, no. 1 (Winter 2006): 46. Professor Betts was a member of the National Commission on Terrorism.

195. Cronin, "Behind the Curve," 53–54.

196. See, for example, the August 4, 2005, televised statement by Zawahiri in which he demanded "security for Palestine," the termination of Western support and recognition for "infidel leaders," and the withdrawal of all foreign forces "from the land of Muhammad" as the conditions that must be met in order to prevent further bombings in London.

197. Cf. Philip H. Gordon, who writes that "the potential combination of terrorism and weapons of mass destruction does require a fundamental rethinking of the conventional wisdom in foreign policy." "American Choices in the 'War on Terror,' " *Survival* 46, no. 1 (Summer 2004): 152.

CHAPTER TWO: The Market State: Arming Terror

1. The two public figures who seem to have the greatest grasp of this development are the Archbishop of Canterbury, Rowan Williams, and the former British prime minister Tony Blair. Both have said in various ways that the emergence of the market state is a *fact*, but that what values will govern it are a matter of *choice*. See, for example, the Dimbleby Lecture given by Rowan Williams on December 19, 2002, a transcript of which is available at http://www.archbishopofcanterbury.org/sermons_speeches/2002/021219.html (accessed October 20, 2006).

2. Bruce Ackerman, "Before the Next Attack," *New Statesman*, 3 July 2006.

3. This summarizes arguments first laid out in Bobbitt, *Shield of Achilles*.

4. Cf. Mark Tushnet, "The Supreme Court, 1998 Term Foreword: The New Constitutional Order and the Chastening of Constitutional Aspiration," *Harvard Law Review* 113 (1999): 29.

5. "At the Twenty-second Party Congress in 1961, Soviet premier Nikita Khrushchev pledged that within 20 years his country would be outproducing the United States in all the traditional sectors of industrial might: coal, steel, cement, fertilizer, tractors, and metal-cutting lathes. The pledge was fulfilled: in 1981, the Soviet Union out-did America in every one of those industries; it had successfully reproduced a mid-twentieth century industrial economy. But the West by then was inventing a different kind of economy altogether, one based on plastic and silicon, on the new service sector. . . ." Martin Walker, "America's Romance with the Future," *Wilson Quarterly* 30, no. 1 (Winter 2006): 24.

6. See Bobbitt, *Shield of Achilles*; Robert Cooper, *The Breaking of Nations: Order and Chaos in the Twenty-first Century* (London: Atlantic Books, 2003).

7. Diane Coyle, "Getting the Measure of Knowledge" (paper presented to the 3rd Social Study of IT Workshop, London School of Economics Department of Information Systems, April 24, 2003), 14, available at http://www.csrc.lse.ac.uk/Events/SSIT3/coyle2.pdf (accessed October 13, 2006).

8. See "The Avuncular State—The New Paternalism," *Economist*, 8 April 2006, 75–76.

9. Ibid. (emphasis supplied).

10. See Jonah Levy, ed., *The State After Statism* (Cambridge, Mass.: Harvard University Press, 2006).

11. Providing access to improvements in the quality of goods and enhanced technology for all, for example, even when wages for the bottom quartile stagnate.

12. For a rather dramatic proposal along these lines, see Eric Werker, "KPMG for Mayor!," *Forbes*, 26 March 2007, 40, which, instead of privatization, suggests that private entities actually run for office.

13. In part this is because representative institutions represent, they do not reflect. Indeed, the monologue of officials is largely a matter of top-down "broadcasts" to the public with the occasional reply in the form of an election. The contrast between nation state and market state can be seen any evening when one can watch congressmen and parliamentarians speaking to practically empty chambers while the Internet is rich with debate and dialogue. I am indebted to Tim Gardam for this evocative image.

14. Raina Kelley, "Dollars for Scholars," *Newsweek*, 3 September 2007, 39.

15. Williams, Dimbleby Lecture.

16. Paul Woodruff, *Reverence: Renewing a Forgotten Virtue* (New York: Oxford University Press, 2001).

17. "If you cannot ask for sacrifice, then you cannot run risks." Henry Kissinger, conversation with author.

18. Stephen Goldsmith and William D. Eggers, "Government for Hire," *New York Times*, 21 February 2005, A19.

19. Ted Koppel, "These Guns for Hire," *New York Times*, 22 May 2006, A21. "Since the late 1990s, the conduct of war and the consequences of its aftermath have been transformed. On battlefields, in conflict zones and in areas being rebuilt after war, private actors are playing a progressively more important role. While private companies have often been present on twentieth century battlefields, notably to provide logistical assistance, their role today is increasingly pivotal. Private companies now provide military and security services ranging from translation to interrogation, from land-mine clearing to close protection for national leaders, and from guarding oil installations to security work for non-governmental organizations (NGOs). Taken together, private security companies (PSCs) provided the second-largest contingent in the US-led 'coalition of the willing' during and after the invasion of Iraq in 2003. There are currently at least 20,000 PSC employees working in

Iraq. The scale of private involvement on today's battlefields has not been seen since mercenaries disappeared from state armies in the nineteenth century." Sarah Percy, *Regulating the Private Security Industry*, Adelphi paper no. 384 (London: IISS, 2006), 7.

20. Allison Stanger, "Foreign Policy, Privatized," *New York Times,* 5 October 2007 (http://www.nytimes.com/2007/10/05/opinion/05stanger.html).

21. "The New Market State and Corporate Social Responsibility," *Strategic Chronicle* no. 10 (Spring 2004): 3.

22. McKinsey Quarterly Survey, December 2006, reported in *The Public Strategies Report,* Public Strategies, Inc., July 2007.

23. Medard Gabel and Henry Bruner, *Global Inc.: An Atlas of the Multinational Corporation* (New York: New Press, 2003), 2.

24. Ibid.

25. Jiang Jingjing, "Wal-Mart's China Inventory to Hit US $18b This Year," *China Daily*, 29 November 2004, http://www.chinadaily.com.cn/english/doc/2004-11/29/content_395728.htm (accessed March 25, 2007).

26. "It is a symptom as well as a cause of a culture in which the spirit of consumerism is more prevalent than ever before. The postwar ethos of queuing and rationing is almost dead, its last institutional home being the [National Health Service] where the overwhelming support for the principle of equity which the health service enshrines still outweighs patients' grievances." Matthew d'Ancona, *Confessions of a Hawkish Hack: The Media and the War on Terror* (London: Policy Exchange, 2006), 30.

27. Larry Elliott, "It's the Tories Who Will Gain from Labour's Market State," *Guardian*, 9 June 2006, 35.

28. The philosopher Mark Sagoff has observed that it is a mistake to suppose that the market state has no compelling morality, or that that morality amounts to no more than the claim that where there is no want there is no injustice. Sagoff argues that the moral mission of the market state is to make possible the freedom of the individual to find one's own path and to recognize this in law. Interestingly, the most important demand of al Qaeda—far more significant to that group than any of its forays into international affairs—is the assertion that sharia governs societies.

29. As Cronin concluded, "The current wave of international terrorism, characterized by unpredictable and unprecedented threats from non-state actors, not only is a reaction to globalization but is facilitated by it. . . ." Audrey Kurth Cronin, "Behind the Curve: Globalization and International Terrorism," *International Security* 27, no. 13 (Winter 2002/03): 30.

30. The most insightful commentary on this development comes from the theologian Rowan Williams; see his Dimbleby Lecture.

31. "The New Market State and Corporate Social Responsibility," 4.

32. Ibid. According to the Organisation for Economic Cooperation and Development *Observer*, Switzerland was the largest OECD economy in terms of GDP output per head in 1970, at $5,149. This figure increased sixfold to more than $30,000 in 2000, but in the meantime the United States had increased its per capita GDP to more than $35,000, from a figure in the $4,000–$5,000 range in 1970. "Wealth of OECD Nations," *OECD Observer* no. 235 (December 2002).

33. "Europe & America: An Economic Union," *EUFocus*, July 2005, 1, 8.

34. John Witt, letter to author, 24 September 2007.

35. "The group of Internet activists, who call themselves Electronic Disturbance Theater, support the Zapatista rebels in Chiapas, fighting against the Mexican government. To draw attention to this cause, they attempted to temporarily disable certain

websites by asking demonstrators to load a hostile Web-based program called Flood-Net. [A FloodNet attack] attempts to overwhelm Web servers by requesting multiple pages simultaneously. . . . The Defense Department hinted that electronic counter-measures fended off the protesters." Niall McKay, "Pentagon Deflects Web Assault," *Wired News*, 10 September 1998, http://www.wired.com/news/politics/0,1283,14931,00.html (accessed March 25, 2007).

36. After 9/11, a group of scientists called for a project, modeled on the Manhattan Project, "to prevent, detect, and respond to potential [cyber]attacks"; four years later the *New York Times* lamented that "disturbingly little has been done" in the interim to decrease the nation's vulnerability to cyberattacks. Editorial, "Virtually Unprotected," *New York Times*, 2 July 2005, A24.

37. One survey found 50 percent of engineering graduate students in America to be foreign-born, while 41 percent of math and physical sciences graduate students were. Alan Finder, "Unclear on American Campus: What the Foreign Teacher Said," *New York Times*, A1.

38. Wright, "The Master Plan," 58.

39. "If the influenza strain the world saw in 1918 appeared today, it would be even more devastating. . . . Yes, we have better medical facilities, Yes, we have better plans for isolating victims. But did we have air travel back then? Did we have mass transit? Did we have today's population densities?" Dr. Charles Bailey, quoted in Mark Williams, "The Looming Threat," *Acumen Journal of Life Sciences* 1, no. 4 (January 2004): 47.

40. Thomas Homer-Dixon, "Two Years After the Lights Went Out," *New York Times*, 13 August 2005, A11.

41. Neumann, "Europe's Jihadist Dilemma," 80. See the excellent report by Susan Ginsburg, Independent Task Force on Immigration and America's Future, *Countering Terrorist Mobility: Shaping an Operational Strategy* (Washington, D.C.: Migration Policy Institute, February 2006).

42. Gordon McGranahan and David Satterthwaite, "Urban Centers: An Assessment of Sustainability," *Annual Review of Environment and Resources* 28 (2003): 248.

43. Global Insight, *The Role of Metro Areas in the U.S. Economy* (report prepared for the United States Conference of Mayors, January 13, 2006), 6.

44. City Mayors estimated London's GDP to be $452 billion, while the World Bank estimated the GDPs of Sweden, Belgium, and Switzerland to be $354, $364, and $365 billion, respectively. See City Mayors, "The 105 Richest Cities in the World by GDP in 2005," http://www.citymayors.com/statistics/richest-cities-2005.html; World Bank, Total GDP 2005, http://siteresources.worldbank.org/DATASTATISTICS/Resources/GDP.pdf (both accessed March 25, 2007).

45. " 'We work in tall buildings, we live in dangerous places, we fly in monster airplanes. We concentrate ourselves in places that make for targets, or that make us more vulnerable when a worst case scenario comes our way. Eighty percent of Florida's population lives within 20 miles of coastline. Over half of America's population now lives close to the coast.' The Pacific Rim's 'ring of fire' is dotted with volcanoes—and major cities." Lydialyle Gibson, "The Big One," *University of Chicago Magazine* 98, no. 5 (June 2006): 32 (quoting Rutgers sociologist Lee Clarke, author of *Worst Cases: Terror and Catastrophe in the Popular Imagination* [Chicago: University of Chicago Press, 2005]).

46. Robert Wright, "Will Globalization Make Hatred More Lethal?," *Wilson Quarterly* 30, no. 1 (Winter 2006): 35.

47. Michael D. Intriligator and Abdullah Toukan, "Terrorism and Weapons of Mass Destruction," in *Countering Terrorism and WMD: Creating a Global Counter-*

Terrorism Network, ed. Peter Katona, Michael D. Intriligator, and John Sullivan (New York: Routledge, 2006), 75.

48. An August 2003 report by the General Accounting Office found that sources of radioactive material are widespread throughout the world in industry, medicine, and research. Of the approximately 2 million sources of radioactive material in the U.S., the report stated that many are poorly tracked and protected, and that in the five years from 1998 to 2002, 1,300 sealed radiation sources were stolen or lost. U.S. General Accounting Office, *Nuclear Security: Federal and State Action Needed to Improve Security of Sealed Radioactive Sources*, report to the Ranking Minority Member, Senate Subcommittee on Financial Management, the Budget, and International Security, September 2003, 4.

49. Richard L. Garwin and Georges Charpak, *Megawatts and Megatons: The Future of Nuclear Power and Nuclear Weapons* (Chicago: University of Chicago Press, 2001), 341.

50. Arnaud de Borchgrave, "Commentary: Al-Qaida's Nuclear Option," *SpaceWar*, 22 March 2006, http://www.spacewar.com/reports/Commentary_Al_Qaidas_Nuclear_Option.html (accessed October 13, 2006) (quoting Sam Nunn).

51. Although the U.S. government may have inadvertently released some of this information when it set up a website containing an archive of Iraqi documents that included detailed accounts of Iraq's secret nuclear research. After complaints from IAEA officials, public access to the sensitive material was suspended. William J. Broad, "U.S. Web Archive Is Said to Reveal Nuclear Primer," *New York Times*, 3 November 2006, A6.

52. But see Anna M. Pluta and Peter D. Zimmerman, "Nuclear Terrorism: A Disheartening Dissent," *Survival* 48, no. 2 (Summer 2006): 55.

53. See William C. Potter, Charles D. Ferguson, and Leonard S. Spector, "The Four Faces of Nuclear Terror," *Foreign Affairs* 83, no. 3 (May/June 2004): 130–32.

54. Central Intelligence Agency, *Acquisition of Technology Relating to Weapons of Mass Destruction and Advanced Conventional Munitions, 1 July Through 31 December 2003*, Report to Congress, November 2004, 8 (Washington, D.C.).

55. De Borchgrave, "Al-Qaida's Nuclear Option" (quoting Sam Nunn).

56. According to Rolf Ekeus, the former head of the U.N. weapons inspection team in Iraq, Saddam Hussein had a program to experiment with camel pox, a virus similar to smallpox.

57. The FBI claimed, after the 2001 attacks, that a "lone individual" could have weaponized anthrax spores using a makeshift basement laboratory at a cost of no more than $2,500. Eric Lichtblau and Megan Garvey, "Response to Terror, the Anthrax Threat: Loner Likely Sent Anthrax, FBI Says," *Los Angeles Times*, 10 November 2001, A1. This conclusion probably applies to some, but not all, of the anthrax letters.

58. Gigi Kwik, Joe Fitzgerald, Thomas V. Inglesby, and Tara O'Toole, "Biosecurity: Responsible Stewardship of Bioscience in an Age of Catastrophic Terrorism," *Biosecurity and Bioterrorism: Biodefense Strategy, Practice and Science* 1, no. 1 (2003): 30.

59. Jeronimo Cello, Aniko V. Paul, and Eckard Wimmer, "Chemical Synthesis of Poliovirus cDNA: Generation of Infectious Virus in the Absence of Natural Template," *Science* 297 (2002): 1016.

60. See "Life from Scratch," *New Atlantis*, no. 5 (Spring 2004): 102; Ray Kurzweil and Bill Joy, "Recipe for Destruction," *New York Times*, 17 October 2005, A19.

61. James Randerson, "Revealed: The Lax Laws That Could Allow Assembly of Deadly

Virus DNA," *Guardian*, 14 June 2006, 1. Randerson further explained: "The potential to manufacture viruses from scratch first came to light in 2002 when U.S. researchers pieced together the genome of the polio virus using short sequences of DNA around 70 letters long. And last year, another team recreated the 1918 flu virus, a devastating and now extinct strain that killed an estimated 50 million people, more people than the first world war. Building smallpox using the same technique as scientists used to make polio and 1918 influenza would be technically difficult because the virus is larger. . . . But as techniques improve there is no theoretical reason why it could not be done."

62. Robert Carlson, "The Pace and Proliferation of Biological Technologies," *Biosecurity and Bioterrorism: Biodefense Strategy, Practice and Science* 1, no. 3 (2003): 1.

63. Ibid.

64. Richard Danzig, "Proliferation of Biological Weapons into Terrorist Hands," in *The Challenge of Proliferation: A Report of the Aspen Strategy Group*, ed. Kurt M. Campbell (Washington, D.C.: Aspen Institute, 2005), 70.

65. Ibid.

66. Quoted in John Mintz, "Technical Hurdles Separate Terrorists from Biowarfare," *Washington Post*, 30 December 2004, A1.

67. Richard Danzig, *Catastrophic Bioterrorism—What Is to Be Done?* (Washington, D.C.: National Defense University, 2003), 1.

68. "Unfortunately, the potential threat presented by proliferation of biotechnology information cannot be contained as easily as that presented by research in nuclear fission; unlike much of the fission research, which has few applications except development of nuclear weapons, all biotechnology research builds on previous findings across a variety of disciplines." James B. Petro, Theodore R. Plasse, and Jake A. McNulty, "Biotechnology: Impact on Biological Warfare and Biodefense," *Biosecurity and Bioterrorism: Biodefense Strategy, Practice and Science* 1, no. 3 (2003): 165.

69. Kwik et al., "Biosecurity: Responsible Stewardship," 29.

70. Paul Valéry, *History and Politics,* trans. Denise Folliot and Jackson Matthews (New York: Pantheon, 1962), 71.

71. Robin M. Frost, *Nuclear Terrorism After 9/11*, Adelphi Paper no. 378 (London: International Institute for Strategic Studies, 2005).

72. Christopher O. Clary, "The A. Q. Khan Network: Causes and Implications" (thesis, Naval Postgraduate School, Monterey, Calif., December 2005), 87, 1, available at http://www.fas.org/irp/eprint/clary.pdf (accessed October 13, 2006).

73. Quoted in Gordon Corera, *Shopping for Bombs: Nuclear Proliferation, Global Insecurity, and the Rise and Fall of the A. Q. Khan Network* (New York: Oxford University Press, 2006), 4.

74. Ibid., 6.

75. Ibid., 14.

76. Ibid., 15.

77. The number reflecting the number of neutrons in the nucleus of the uranium atom. As stability is a function of the strong nuclear force (which has a short range and binds the nucleus of protons and neutrons, as neutrons attract protons) versus the electro-weak force (a longer range electromagnetic force that causes protons to repel each other), the more neutrons there are, the more stable the particular isotope.

78. Clary, "A. Q. Khan Network," 24.

79. Ibid.

80. Ibid.; see also Steve Weissman and Herbert Krosney, *The Islamic Bomb: The*

Nuclear Threat to Israel and the Middle East (New York: Times Books, 1981), 199–206.

81. This was in fact Khan's observation. See Corera, *Shopping for Bombs*, 22.

82. Clary, "A. Q. Khan Network," 82.

83. Pierre Goldschmidt, Statement to the IAEA Board of Governors, March 1, 2005, available at http://www.iranwatch.org/international/IAEA/iaea-goldschmidt-statement -030105.htm (accessed March 25, 2007).

84. Tim Reid, "Blueprints 'Prove Iran Is Pursuing Nuclear Weapons,'" *Times* (London), 13 February 2004, 22.

85. David Albright and Corey Hinderstein, "Documents Indicate A. Q. Khan Offered Nuclear Weapon Designs to Iraq in 1990," *Institute for Science and International Security*, 4 February 2004; quoted in Corera, *Shopping for Bombs*, 103. A translation of the memo can be found at http://www.isisonline.org/publications/southasia/ khan_memo_scan.pdf (accessed October 13, 2006).

86. Corera, *Shopping for Bombs*, 104.

87. Clary, "A. Q. Khan Network," 55.

88. "It was a cash transaction, no exchange of nuclear technology. Exchanging nuclear technology for missiles was never even discussed during my visit." Quoted in Corera, *Shopping for Bombs*, 89 (citing Peter Roff, "Bhutto Missile Story Raised Hill Hackles," United Press International, 7 March 2005).

89. So named for the twelfth-century Muslim commander Mohammed Shahabudin Ghauri, whose invasions of the Hindu kingdoms of South Asia inaugurated Muslim rule that continued until the British infiltrations of the eighteenth century.

90. "It has been estimated the Nodongs would have cost at least three billion dollars. But by 1997, cash was getting harder to come by for the Pakistani government with foreign reserves nosediving to critically low levels. Could they have looked for an alternative form of payment? The circumstantial evidence points to a deal in which Khan provided enrichment technology in return for missile assistance." Corera, *Shopping for Bombs*, 90. Corera also notes that Hwang Jang-ypo, a North Korean defector who had been an aide to Kim Il-Sung, has testified that there was a deal to trade long-range North Korean missiles for Pakistani enrichment technology. Ibid., 92 (citing Larry A. Nilksch, "North Korea's Nuclear Weapons Program," Congressional Research Service, 25 March 2005).

91. Clary, "A. Q. Khan Network," 64–66. Clary has an excellent discussion of this debate; see pp. 62–66.

92. "Pakistan Tests Ghauri Missile, Offers Olive Branch to India," text of report by Pakistan TV on 6 April 1998, *BBC Worldwide Monitoring*, 6 April 1998, quoted in Clary, "A. Q. Khan Network," 61–62.

93. Corera, *Shopping for Bombs*, 97–98.

94. Clary, "A. Q. Khan Network," 77.

95. Arnaud de Borchgrave, "A $1.5 Trillion Mistake," *Washington Times*, 6 May 2007.

96. Clary, "A. Q. Khan Network," 78.

97. Corera, *Shopping for Bombs*, 108.

98. Ibid., 108–9.

99. Ibid., 120.

100. The Commission on the Intelligence Capabilities of the United States Regarding Weapons of Mass Destruction, *Report to the President of the United States*, 31 March 2005 (Washington, D.C.: GPO, 2005) (hereinafter Robb-Silberman Report), 257.

101. House of Commons, Report of a Committee of Privy Counsellors, *Review of Intelli-*

gence on Weapons of Mass Destruction (London: Stationery Office, 2004) (here-inafter Butler Report), 18.

102. Corera, *Shopping for Bombs*, 35. Indeed, the U.S. reaction to its discovery of North Korea's illicit uranium enrichment program may have backfired. Once North Korea was publicly exposed, it demanded the withdrawal of the inspectors who had sur-veilled the North Korea plutonium project, and it was a *plutonium* weapon that North Korea exploded in 2006.

103. Butler Report, 18.

104. Robb-Silberman Report, 252.

105. "Nuclear Scientist Apologises—Text," *BBC News*, 4 February 2004, http://news.bbc.co.uk/2/hi/south_asia/3459149.stm (accessed October 13, 2005).

106. The lack of effective export controls meant that ambitious proliferators were not deterred from their activities. One key member of the network was convicted in 1985 of selling a prohibited oscilloscope to Pakistan; he never served any time. In 1998 he was caught again when five illegal shipments were intercepted. Two important fig-ures in the Khan enterprise were investigated in the 1980s but not prosecuted; another was reported to have been investigated by the Swiss government for illegal shipments to Pakistan but was found not to have broken any law. Perhaps the worst example occurred in Britain, where a partner of Khan's was convicted of knowingly violating the export control laws over the period of a decade but was nevertheless given a suspended sentence. Corera, *Shopping for Bombs*, 111–12.

107. "The European end was also tricky for the United States. American diplomats occa-sionally got into rows with allies when they discovered that the United States had been spying on European citizens or businesses involved in proliferation in the 1990s." Ibid., 111.

108. "Rather than try to provide security guarantees to countries like India and Pakistan to reduce their desire for nuclear weapons, the existing weapons states decided to try to deal with supply rather than demand by restricting the export of equipment." Ibid., 20. This led to the creation of the London Club (later the Nuclear Suppliers Group).

109. Jason Epstein, "Hurry Up Please It's Time," *New York Review of Books*, 15 March 2007, 28.

110. In Clary's mind, determining the extent of the Pakistani leadership's knowledge of Khan's activities is "[o]ne of the most challenging questions" raised by the entire affair; Clary suggests that certain Pakistani leaders may have initially been predis-posed toward nuclear cooperation with other states, but that Khan "likely exceeded whatever mandate he received from Pakistani leadership." Clary, "A. Q. Khan Net-work," 89.

111. See Mike Harding, "Russian Jailed for Trying to Sell Weapons-Grade Uranium for $1m," *Guardian*, 26 January 2007, 22. Furthermore, the requirements of terrorists are more modest than those for professional armies; a "fizzle" is a failure for a state but can be a success for terrorists.

112. Osama bin Laden, "Conversation with Terror," interview by Rahimulla Yusufzai, *Time*, 11 January 1999, 39.

113. Michael Scheuer, interview by Steve Kroft, 60 *Minutes*, CBS, 14 November 2004.

114. Some of the hadith (prophetic traditional proverbs and narratives) of the Prophet Mohammed forbid killing women, children, and the elderly. For example, in the compilation of hadith by Ahmad ibn Hanbal, the Prophet says, "Do not kill the chil-dren [of the polytheists]." In the Hadith compiled by Abu Daoud, the Prophet tells Khald ibn al-Walid during one of the Islamic raids, "Do not kill a woman or an oppressed person."

115. Further arguments claim that it is permissible to kill women, children, and the elderly if this is not done with premeditation (the collateral damage argument), if they are aiding the war effort, or if a general attack on the resources of the enemy—for example, on his fortifications or fields—is thought necessary. A writer whose pen name is Salah al-Din made these arguments in a September 2001 essay, "The Truth of the New Crusader War." See Middle East Media Research Institute, "Contemporary Islamist Ideology Authorizing Genocidal Murder," Special Report 25, 27 January 2004, available at http://www.memri.org/bin/articles.cgi?ID=SR2504#_ednref40 (accessed October 13, 2006).

116. Abu Gheith continues by asserting that "it is our right to fight them with chemical and biological weapons, so as to afflict them with the fatal maladies that have afflicted the Muslims because of the [Americans'] chemical and biological weapons." Quoted in Intriligator and Toukan, "Terrorism and Weapons of Mass Destruction," 58.

117. Kamran Khan and Molly Moore, "2 Nuclear Experts Briefed Bin Laden, Pakistanis Say," *Washington Post*, 12 December 2001, A1. See also David Albright and Holly Higgins, "A Bomb for the Ummah," *Bulletin of the Atomic Scientists* 59, no. 2 (March/April 2003). The accounts on which I rely are Gordon Corera's in *Shopping for Bombs* and Ron Suskind's in *The One Percent Doctrine: Deep Inside America's Pursuit of Its Enemies Since 9/11* (New York: Simon & Schuster, 2006).

118. Peter Baker, "Pakistani Scientist Who Met Bin Laden Failed Polygraphs, Renewing Suspicions," *Washington Post*, 3 March 2002, A1; Oliver Burkman, "Bin Laden Asked Scientist to Build N-Bomb," *Guardian*, 30 December 2002, 2.

119. "[I]ndependent specialists cast doubt on whether Mahmood . . . could have given bin Laden enough help to build a bomb. '[He] didn't deal with the weapons program, [he] had nothing to do with the designing of nuclear devices,' said Zahid Malik, a biographer and friend of Abdul Qadeer Khan. . . ." Baker, "Pakistani Scientist."

120. Ibid.

121. Which the U.S. government apparently does not think implausible. In October 2001, a Nuclear Emergency Support Team was dispatched to New York City on information from a CIA agent code-named Dragonfire. Dragonfire had reported that al Qaeda had procured a Soviet nuclear weapon and had smuggled it into Manhattan.

122. Danzig, *Catastrophic Bioterrorism*, 2.

123. For Iranian presence at North Korean launches, see Deborah Tate, "US Official Says Iranians Witnessed North Korean Missile Tests," *Voice of America*, 20 July 2006, http://www.voanews.com/english/archive/2006-07/2006-07-20-voa46.cfm?CFID=1111683&CFTOKEN=57764512 (accessed October 13, 2006) (reporting testimony of Assistant Secretary of State Chris Hill before Senate Foreign Relations Committee). For North Korean presence at Syrian facility, see Mark Mazzetti and Helen Cooper, "An Israeli Strike on Syria Kindles Debate in the U.S.," *New York Times*, 10 October 2007.

124. Petro et al., "Biotechnology," 165–66, 163, 162.

125. See Brian Rappert, "Biological Weapons, Genetics and Social Analysis: Emerging Responses, Emerging Issues—I," *New Genetics and Society* 22 (2003): 169–81.

126. Noah Shachtman, "Hi-Tech vs. Low-Tech Threats," GlobalSecurity.org, 12 December 2002, http://www.globalsecurity.org/org/news/2002/021212-terror01.htm (accessed October 13, 2006).

127. See chapter 8, pp. 404–12.

128. As Secretary of Defense Donald Rumsfeld advised the president and NSC in January 2001, "[T]he post–Cold War liberalization of trade in advanced technology goods

and services has made it possible for the poorest nations on earth to rapidly acquire the most destructive military technology ever devised, including nuclear, chemical and biological weapons and their means of delivery. We cannot prevent them from doing so." Quoted in Suskind, *One Percent Doctrine*, 212.

129. And is the best explanation extant for why Saddam Hussein refused to demonstrate to the U.N. inspectors that he had in fact destroyed his stocks of WMD.

CHAPTER THREE: Warfare Against Civilians

1. See John B. Stubbs, "Superterrorism and the Military Instrument of Power," research report, Air Command and Staff College, Air University, Maxwell Air Force Base, Alabama, April 1998, 28: "[S]uperterrorism represents an RMA [revolution in military affairs] and must be countered with fundamental changes in doctrine and operational concept rather than just relying on technology improvements. . . . ." The full text of this report is available at http://www.fas.org/irp/threat/98–274.pdf.

2. Published in *Al-Quds Al-Arabi*, an Arabic newspaper in London, the declaration was titled "Declaration of War Against the Americans Occupying the Land of the Two Holy Mosques." It explained, in pertinent part, "Today your brothers and sons, the sons of the two Holy Places, have started their Jihad in the cause of Allah, to expel the occupying enemy from the country of the two Holy Places. And there is no doubt you would like to carry out this mission too, in order to re-establish the greatness of this Ummah and to liberate [its] occupied sanctities. Nevertheless, it must be obvious to you that, due to the imbalance of power between our armed forces and the enemy forces, a suitable means of fighting must be adopted, i.e., using fast moving light forces that work under complete secrecy. In other words to initiate a guerrilla warfare, where the sons of the nation, and not the military forces, take part in it. And as you know, it is wise, in the present circumstances, for the armed military forces not to be engaged in a conventional fighting with the forces of the crusader enemy (the exceptions are the bold and the forceful operations carried out by the members of the armed forces individually, that is without the movement of the formal forces in its conventional shape and hence the responses will not be directed, strongly, against the army) unless a big advantage is likely to be achieved; and great losses induced on the enemy side (that would shake and destroy its foundations and infrastructures) that will help to expel the defeated enemy from the country. The Mujahideen, your brothers and sons, request that you support them in every possible way by supplying them with the necessary information, materials and arms. Security men are especially asked to cover up for the Mujahideen and to assist them as much as possible against the occupying enemy; and to spread rumours, fear and discouragement among the members of the enemy forces. . . . My Muslim Brothers of The World: Your brothers in Palestine and in the land of the two Holy Places are calling upon your help and asking you to take part in fighting against the enemy—your enemy and their enemy—the Americans and the Israelis. [T]hey are asking you to do whatever you can, with [one's] own means and ability, to expel the enemy, humiliated and defeated, out of the sanctities of Islam." "Bin Laden's Fatwa," *Online News-Hour* (PBS), http://www.pbs.org/newshour/terrorism/international/fatwa_1996.html (accessed March 22, 2007).

3. Whose valence is submission: ". . . submission to sharia, submission to fatwas, submission to the requirement of active jihad, submission ultimately to what they believe is the will of Muhammad and of God . . . (as interpreted by men like bin Laden, et al.)." Audrey Kurth Cronin, letter to the author, 24 December 2006.

4. Michael Howard, "What's in a Name?: How to Fight Terrorism," *Foreign Affairs* 81, no.1 (January/February 2002): 8. See also Frédéric Mégret, " 'War'? Legal Semantics and the Move to Violence," *European Journal of International Law* 13 (2002): 361–99.

5. Failing to make these distinctions leads us toward the policy cliché that we must win "hearts and minds" in order to defeat al Qaeda. This strategy may have been indispensable when confronting the nation state terrorists of the 20th century, but it has little to offer policymakers fighting al Qaeda. This is one more reason why we ought to think of this conflict as warfare. But the tactics of nation state warfare are not appropriate either. Brian Jenkins captures this distinction well when he writes, "We must therefore wage political warfare, which is notably different from advertising American values or winning hearts and minds—efforts aimed at the broader population. Political warfare comprises aggressive tactics aimed largely at the *fringes* of the population, where personal discontent and spiritual devotion turn to violent expression. Political warfare targets those on their way into enemy ranks, those among the ranks who might be persuaded to quit, and those in custody. It sees enemy combatants as constantly recalibrating their commitments. It accepts no foe as having irrevocably crossed the line. It sees every prisoner not merely as a source of intelligence, but as a potential convert. It accepts local accommodations to avoid violence, offers amnesties to induce divisions and defections, and cuts deals to co-opt enemies." Brian M. Jenkins, "True Grit: To Counter Terror, We Must Conquer Our Own Fear," *RAND Review* 30, no. 2 (Summer 2006): 12.

6. That world, the most hopeful dream of the society of nation states, is from our past and we are moving away from it at warp speed.

7. Robert Cooper, "The Way We Fight Now," review of *The Utility of Force: The Art of War in the Modern World*, by Rupert Smith, *Sunday Times* (London), 18 September 2005, 43.

8. See Henry Kissinger, *Diplomacy* (New York: Simon & Schuster, 1994), 697–98.

9. Kaija Virta, "The Way We War," *Helsingin Sanomat*, 15 September 1999, available at http://www2.hs.fi/english/archive/thisweek/38031999.html (accessed October 13, 2006). See also Mary Kaldor, *New and Old Wars: Organized Violence in a Global Era* (Stanford, Calif.: Stanford University Press, 1999).

10. See Michael R. Gordon, "Military Hones a New Strategy on Insurgency," *New York Times*, 5 October 2006, A1; see also George Packer, "Knowing the Enemy: Can Social Scientists Redefine the 'War on Terror'?," *The New Yorker*, 16 December 2006, 60.

11. Thom Shanker and Eric Schmitt, "Pentagon Weighs Strategy Change to Deter Terror," *New York Times*, 5 July 2005, A1.

12. Howard, "What's in a Name?"

13. See chapter 1.

14. "Report: Al Qaeda 18,000 Strong," *CBS News*, 25 May 2004, http://www.cbsnews.com/stories/2004/05/25/terror/main619467.shtml (accessed March 4, 2007).

15. Riedel, "Al Qaeda Strikes Back," 25.

16. Bruce Ackerman, *Before the Next Attack: Preserving Civil Liberties in an Age of Terrorism* (New Haven, Conn.: Yale University Press, 2006), 14.

17. Jeffrey Record, "The Creeping Irrelevance of U.S. Force Planning," monograph presented to the U.S. Army War College's Annual Strategy Conference, 31 March–2 April 1998, 4, available at http://www.strategicstudiesinstitute.army.mil/pdffiles/PUB311.pdf (accessed October 13, 2006).

18. See pages 4–5.

19. And, of course, France. The view that the U.K. wasn't really a beneficiary of the victory of the Long War because it ended the Second World War exhausted, soon lost its empire, and by the time of victory over communism had become a middle-ranking power, is itself an example of Parmenides' Fallacy. For Britain, the alternative to such developments was not that time should stand still at 1910 but that Britain would have been defeated by the dynamic aggressors that wished to crush her (and almost succeeded).

20. See "Key Facts and Figures About Europe and the Europeans in 2006," *Europa*, http://europa.eu/abc/keyfigures/tradeandeconomy/production/index_en.htm (accessed February 23, 2007).

21. Central Intelligence Agency, *World Factbook*, https://www.cia.gov/cia/publications/factbook/geos/uk.html; see also Burkard Schmitt, Institute for Security Studies, "Defence Expenditure," February 2005, http://www.iss-eu.org/esdp/11-bsdef.pdf (listing the U.K. defense budgets as percentage of GDP from 2001 to 2003 as 2.5%, 2.4%, and 2.4% respectively).

22. Bush's introduction to *The National Security Strategy of the United States of America* (2002).

23. Ibid., 14, 15.

24. Donald K. Ulrich, "A Moral Argument on Preventive War," paper submitted in pursuit of Master of Strategic Studies Degree, U.S. Army War College, Carlisle Barracks, Pennsylvania, 18 March 2005, 1.

25. Quoted in Michael Walzer, *Just and Unjust Wars: A Moral Argument with Historical Illustrations* (New York: HarperCollins, 1977), 77.

26. Schelling, *Strategy of Conflict*, 207.

27. Cf. Michael Walzer, "No Strikes," *New Republic*, 23 September 2002.

28. Though some recent analysis has suggested that the Osirak raid actually gave the Iraqi nuclear program more impetus and drove it underground, such that its eventual discovery alarmed the international community. See Sammy Salama and Karen Ruster, "A Preemptive Attack on Iran's Nuclear Facilities: Possible Consequences," *Center for Nonproliferation Studies*, 9 September 2004, http://cns.miis.edu/pubs/week/040812.htm (accessed April 11, 2007).

29. Jonathan R. White, *Terrorism: An Introduction* (Belmont, Calif.: Wadsworth, 2002), 19.

30. Lawrence Freedman, "The Coming War on Terrorism," in *Superterrorism*, 45.

31. White, *Terrorism: An Introduction*, 166–67.

32. Neumann, "Europe's Jihadist Dilemma," 80. Motassadeq was a member of the Hamburg cell who assisted in the planning of the September 11 attacks. His conviction on 3,000 counts of accessory to murder was overturned on appeal (it is discussed in chapter 5), and he finally received a seven-year sentence for being a member of a terrorist organization. The Madrid trial of twenty-four alleged conspirators resulted in the conviction of eighteen on various terrorism related charges. Al Goodman, "Terror Trial Begins in Spain," *CNN.com*, 30 October 2006, http://www.cnn.com/2006/WORLD/europe/10/30/spain.trial/index.html (accessed November 20, 2006).

33. *The Federalist Papers*, particularly nos. 47, 48, and 51, show us that such a construction was certainly not the intent of either the framers or the ratifiers of the U.S. Constitution. For a concise discussion of how the authors of *The Federalist Papers* viewed the dependent relationship between the branches of the federal government, see Philip Bobbitt, "The Constitutional Canon," in *Legal Canons*, ed. J. M. Balkin and Sanford Levinson (New York: New York University Press, 2000), 338–40.

34. See Eliot A. Cohen, *Supreme Command: Soldiers, Statesmen, and Leadership in*

Wartime (New York: Free Press, 2002), chapter 2 ("Lincoln Sends a Letter") and appendix ("The Theory of Civilian Control").

35. All bitterly resented by their militaries; see Lothar Gall, *Bismarck: The White Revolutionary, Volume I: 1851–1871,* trans. J. A. Underwood (London: Allen & Unwin, 1986), 154; David Parrott, *Richelieu's Army: War, Government and Society in France,* 1624–1642 (Cambridge: Cambridge University Press, 2001), 491–504 ("Management by Intimidation: The Attempt to Control the High Command After 1635").

36. I ask my constitutional law students: what was the most important constitutional decision made in the U.S. in 1803? Hint: It wasn't *Marbury v. Madison.*

37. Isaiah Wilson III, "The Beyond War Project: In Search of a Theory and Method of War for the Postmodern Age," project proposal, 15 March 2005, 3 (on file with author).

38. But see John Yoo and John Delahunty, "Application of Treaties and Laws to Al Qaeda and Taliban Detainees," Memo for the Department of Defense, 9 January 2002, available at http://lawofwar.org/Yoo_Delahunty_Memo.htm (accessed February 12, 2005).

39. Robert Perito, "Where Is the Lone Ranger When We Need Him? America's Search for a Post-Conflict Stability Force," remarks to the Carnegie Council, 10 March 2004, available at http://www.cceia.org/resources/transcripts/4427.html (accessed October 13, 2006).

40. Ibid.

41. Ibid.

42. Ibid.

43. Royal United Services Institute for Defence Studies, *Transformation of Military Operations on the Cusp,* conference report, 14–15 March 2005, A(1), available at http://www.rusi.org/downloads/assets/Conference_Report.doc (accessed October 13, 2006).

44. "Terror Charges Dropped Against 5 in Italy," *New York Times,* 26 January 2005, A9.

45. *The Brig Amy Warwick.; The Schooner Crenshaw.; The Barque Hiawatha.; The Schooner Brilliante,* 67 U.S. 635, 666 (1863).

46. Christopher Coker, "Cultural Ruthlessness and the War Against Terror," *Australian Army Journal* 3, no. 1 (Summer 2005–2006): 150.

47. Sometimes indiscriminately; see David Anderson, *Histories of the Hanged: Testimonies from the Mau Mau Rebellion in Kenya* (London: Weidenfeld and Nicolson, 2005).

48. "Full Transcript of Bin Laden Video," *ABC News,* 1 November 2004, http://abcnews.go.com/International/story?id=215913&page=1 (accessed October 13, 2006).

49. Quoted in Elena Lappin, "The Enemy Within," *New York Times,* 23 May 2004, section 7, 15 (book review).

50. Quoted in Steven Erlanger, "Turmoil in the Mideast: Casualty Figures," *New York Times,* 19 July 2006, A1.

51. Etgar Keret, "The Way We War," *New York Times,* 18 July 2006, A21.

52. Cordesman, *Terrorism, Asymmetric Warfare, and Weapons of Mass Destruction,* 1.

53. See, e.g., Rupert Smith, "Reflections on Conducting Operations in Support of the Law," keynote address delivered to the Bruges Colloquium, College of Europe, 26–27 October 2001, available at http://www.coleurop.be/content/publications/pdf/Collegium25.pdf (accessed October 13, 2006); Rupert Smith, "What Is War?," discussion given at the Leverhulme Programme on the Changing Character of War, University of Oxford, Department of Politics and International Relations, 3 Febru-

ary 2004, synopsis available at http://ccw.politics.ox.ac.uk/events/archives/ht04_smith.pdf (accessed October 13, 2006).

54. Rupert Smith, *The Utility of Force: The Art of War in the Modern World* (London: Allen Lane, 2005).

55. Ibid., 26.

56. I have selected Smith as exemplary, and wish to recommend his book, *The Utility of Force*, but there are many military writers who are expressing similar views. See, e.g., John B. Alexander, "The Evolution of Conflict Through 2020: Demands on Personnel, Machines, and Missions"; Arthur K. Cebrowski, "Transforming Transformation—Will It Change the Character of War"; Daniel Marston, "Force Structure for High- and Low-Intensity: The Anglo-American Experience and Lessons for the Future"; Robert Scales, "Fighting on the Edges: The Nature of War in 2020." All of these are papers submitted to a workshop on the "Changing Nature of Warfare" sponsored by the National Intelligence Council 2020 Project, and are available at http://www.dni.gov/nic/NIC_2020_2004_05_25_intro.html (accessed October 13, 2006).

57. The exact number of civilian casualties is impossible to determine, but a study conducted by Johns Hopkins University and published October 12, 2006, in the British medical journal *Lancet* estimated that more than 600,000 Iraqis had died on account of the war; however, this estimate has been sharply disputed by other groups, some of whom claim that the true number is less than a tenth of the *Lancet*'s figure. See Anne Badkhen, "Critics Say 600,000 Iraqi Dead Doesn't Tally," *San Francisco Chronicle*, 12 October 2006, A9.

58. Christopher Coker, *Waging War Without Warriors?* (Boulder, Colo.: Lynne Rienner, 2002); see also Christopher Coker, *Human Warfare* (London: Routledge, 2001), and Christopher Coker, *The Future of War: The Re-enchantment of War in the Twenty-first Century* (Oxford: Blackwell, 2004).

59. Mary Kaldor, "Iraq: The Wrong War," openDemocracy, 9 June 2005, http://www.opendemocracy.net/conflict-iraq/wrong_war_2591.jsp (accessed October 13, 2006).

60. Ibid.

61. Smith, *Utility of Force*, 17.

62. Audrey Kurth Cronin, "Cyber-Mobilization: The New *Levée en Masse*," *Parameters* (Summer 2006), 85.

63. Ariana Eunjung Cha, "From a Virtual Shadow, Messages of Terror," *Washington Post*, 2 October 2004, A1.

64. Michael Ignatieff, "The Terrorist as Auteur," *New York Times Magazine*, 14 November 2004, 50.

65. Robert Leitch, "Not My Father's War: Future Warfare and Military Medical Readiness," *U.S. Medicine*, November 2001, http://www.usmedicine.com/column.cfm?columnID=63&issueID=32 (accessed October 13, 2006).

66. Smith, *Utility of Force*, 17.

67. Ibid.

68. Leitch, "Not My Father's War."

69. Ibid.

70. "Private military companies or firms are increasingly important players in international security and conflict. . . . This is especially visible in Iraq where profit-making organizations account for one out of every ten American 'soldiers' involved in the conflict. . . . [P]rivate security firms provide services to both states and non-state actors, including businesses and non-governmental organizations (NGOs) engaged in humanitarian aid. The role of PMCs [private military companies] will likely influ-

ence the disposition of civil peace, global security and the rule of law during the market state transition. In essence, the PMC is civil society's counterpart to criminal private armies such as Al Qaeda and its network of market state forces." John P. Sullivan, "Terrorism, Crime and Private Armies," *Low Intensity Conflict & Law Enforcement* 11, nos. 2–3 (Winter 2002): 246.

71. Henry Adams, " 'Civilian Contractors' on Front Lines in Era of Market State," United for Peace of Pierce County, 18 March 2005, http://www.ufppc.org/content/view/2463/2 (accessed October 13, 2006), quoting Gregory Alderete in the *Army Logistician*, March–April 2005.

72. See Robert D. Kaplan, "Send in the State Department," *New York Times*, 21 February 2006, A19.

73. Alex Tewes, "National Security or Just Defence? The Next White Paper," research note no. 45 2004–05, prepared for the Australian Parliament, 10 May 2005, available at http://www.aph.gov.au/library/pubs/rn/2004–05/05rn45.pdf (accessed October 13, 2006).

74. Ibid.

75. Smith, *Utility of Force*, 17.

76. See Michael Roberts, "The Military Revolution, 1560–1660," in *Essays in Swedish History* (London: Weidenfeld and Nicolson, 1967), 195–225; see also Bobbitt, *Shield of Achilles*, part 2 ("The Brief History of the Modern State and Its Constitutional Orders").

77. GPS is a satellite-based navigation system that was originally intended for the sole use of the military, but was made available for civilian use in the 1980s. See "What is GPS?," *Garmin*, http://www.garmin.com/aboutGPS/ (accessed March 25, 2007).

78. Leitch, "Not My Father's War."

79. See Ray Kurzweil, "The Law of Accelerating Returns," 7 March 2001, available at http://www.kurzweilai.net/articles/art0134.html?printable=1 (accessed March 25, 2007).

80. Smith, *Utility of Force*, 1.

81. Even the 1868 St. Petersburg Declaration (which banned certain types of projectiles) spoke of disabling "the greatest possible number of men."

82. See Burrus M. Carnahan, "Unnecessary Suffering, the Red Cross, and Tactical Laser Weapons," *Loyola of L.A. International and Comparative Law Journal* 18 (1996) for one proposal. Others might include the use of gases and toxins that temporarily incapacitate without causing permanent injury. See Robert J. Bunker, ed., "Nonlethal Weapons: Terms and References," Institute for National Security Studies Occasional Paper no. 15, U.S. Air Force Academy, Colorado, July 1997, available at http://www.usafa.af.mil/df/inss/OCP/ocp15.pdf (accessed October 13, 2006).

83. Quoted in Andy Salmon and Mary Kaldor, "Principles for the Use of the Military in Support of Law Enforcement Operations," available at http://www.lse.ac.uk/depts/global/publications/humansecurityreport/principlessalmonkaldor.pdf (accessed September 30, 2007).

84. Smith, *Utility of Force*, 378–79.

85. William S. Lind, et al., "The Changing Face of War: Into the Fourth Generation," *Marine Corps Gazette*, October 1989, 22.

86. Here, too, Mary Kaldor proved prescient: see Andy Salmon and Mary Kaldor, "Principles for the Use of the Military in Support of Law Enforcement Operations," draft paper presented at Berlin Conference, Centre for the Study of Global Governance, 18–19 May 2004, available at http://www.lse.ac.uk/Depts/global/Publications/HumanSecurityReport/PrinciplesSalmonKaldor.pdf (accessed October 13, 2006).

87. Perito, "Lone Ranger" remarks.

88. According to the Independent Inquiry Committee into the United Nations Oil-for-Food Program, these are the main estimates of the *total* illicit Iraqi income (both smuggling- and program-related): Coalition for International Justice (September 2002): $9.583 billion; GAO (June 16, 2004): $10.1 billion; ISG Report (30 September 2004): $10.946 billion. See Independent Inquiry Committee into the United Nations Oil-for-Food Programme, *Comparison of Estimates of Illicit Income During United States Sanctions*, 1, available at http://www.iic-offp.org/documents/ComparisonofEstimates.pdf (accessed February 23, 2007). For helpful graphs, see also http://www.oilforfoodfacts.org.

89. Michael J. Dziedzic, "Introduction," in *Policing the New World Disorder: Peace Operations and Public Security*, ed. Robert B. Oakley, Michael J. Dziedzic, and Eliot M. Goldberg (Washington, D.C.: National Defense University Press, 1998), 8.

90. David T. Armitage, Jr., and Anne M. Moisan, "Constabulary Forces and Postconflict Transition: The Euro-Atlantic Dimension," *Strategic Forum*, no. 218 (November 2005): 2.

91. Perito, "Lone Ranger" remarks.

92. See Rachel Bronson, "When Soldiers Become Cops," *Foreign Affairs* 81, no. 6 (November/December 2002).

93. Armitage and Moisan, "Constabulary Forces," 3.

94. See, for example, Boutros Boutros-Ghali's Agenda for Peace, which reflects this picture.

95. Armitage and Moisan, "Constabulary Forces," 3.

96. Erwin A. Schmidl, "Police Functions in Peace Operations: A Historical Overview," in *Policing the New World Disorder*, 22.

97. Armitage and Moisan, "Constabulary Forces," 2–3.

98. Quoted in Michael R. Gordon and Steve Erlanger, "Troops Say Kosovo Duty Sharpens Their Skills," *New York Times*, 18 January 2001, A8.

99. Defense Science Board, "Transition to and from Hostilities," report of the Office of the Undersecretary of Defense for Acquisition, Technology, and Logistics, Washington, D.C., December 2004.

100. François Heisbourg, director of the Strategic Research Foundation in Paris: "It is simply not imaginable to have the Germans or the French acting as auxiliaries to the American occupation troops [in Iraq]. We don't want body bags any more than the Americans do. The Americans chose to go into this mess. We have not chosen to go into the mess of occupation duty." *Morning Edition*, National Public Radio, 22 July 2003.

101. There are precedents for using U.S. forces in this way. Before World War II, the American armed forces were assigned to map and explore uncharted territories, construct roads and canals, and police Indian reservations and the defeated Confederate states. See Record, "Creeping Irrelevance," 28.

102. Thom Shanker and David S. Cloud, "Pentagon to Raise Importance of 'Stability' Efforts in War," *New York Times*, 19 November 2005, section 1, 14.

103. Armitage and Moisan, "Constabulary Forces," 6.

104. Smith, *Utility of Force*, 371. "The inability to pass responsibility from elite combat forces to paramilitary or constabulary units . . . saddles elite American troops with the full spectrum of tasks. This overcommitment has been running U.S. forces ragged. . . . Bosnia provides an example of how this problem can develop. . . . [B]ecause Bosnia still has no way to provide a minimal level of security for itself, crack American combat forces remain stationed there today. The same is true in Kosovo, where U.S. troops have become a 'sort of Serbian school bus.' Years after its initial deployment in the

Balkans, the U.S. military still operates jails in the region, goes on patrol, plows snow, and guards religious sites." Bronson, "When Soldiers Become Cops."

105. Ackerman, *Before the Next Attack*, 6.

106. Chris Brown, "Reflections on the War on Terror Two Years On," *International Politics* 41 (2004): 52–53.

107. John Witt, letter to the author, 24 September 2007.

108. This chronology is taken from a PBS *Frontline* documentary, *Operation Iraqi Freedom*, and its related website, http://www.pbs.org/wgbh/pages/frontline/shows/invasion/cron/ (accessed October 13, 2006), as well as from Michael R. Gordon and Bernard E. Trainor, *Cobra II: The Inside Story of the Invasion and Occupation of Iraq* (New York: Pantheon Books, 2006).

109. According to the *Guardian*, the full coalition included forty-five states: thirty states allowed the U.S. to publicly name them, while fifteen others requested anonymity. Ewen MacAskill, "US Claims 45 Nations in 'Coalition of Willing,'" *Guardian Unlimited*, 19 March 2003, http://www.guardian.co.uk/Iraq/Story/0,2763,917268,00.html (accessed February 23, 2007). That tally is supported by Sarah Anderson et al., "Coalition of the Willing or Coalition of the Coerced?, Part II," Institute for Policy Studies (Washington, D.C., 23 March 2003): 1, available at http://www.ips-dc.org/COERCED2.pdf (stating that the final coalition number was forty-five), and by the Center for Media and Democracy, "Coalition of the Willing," *SourceWatch.org*, 26 May 2005, http://www.sourcewatch.org/index.php?title=Coalition_of_the_willing (accessed February 25, 2007): "U.S. Secretary of State Colin L. Powell stated on March 18, 2003, 'We now have a coalition of the willing that includes some 30 nations who have publicly said they could be included in such a listing. . . . And there are 15 other nations, who, for one reason or another do not wish to be publicly named but will be supporting the coalition.' " The Council on Foreign Relations, however, provided the *New York Times* with a list of forty states participating in the coalition, but did note that there were a few more unnamed states. "Q&A: What Is the 'Coalition of the Willing,' " *New York Times*, 28 March 2003, http://www.nytimes.com/cfr/international/slot1_032803.html (accessed February 25, 2007).

110. *Frontline, Operation Iraqi Freedom.*

111. James Fallows, transcript of interview for PBS documentary, 21 November 2006, http://www.pbs.org/wgbh/pages/frontline/shows/invasion/interviews/fallows/html.

112. It certainly was not foreordained that the intervention in Iraq would fail in the ways that it has. See, for example, "Guiding Principles for U.S. Post-Conflict Policy in Iraq" (report cosponsored by the Council on Foreign Relations and the James A. Baker III Institute for Public Policy, 2003). This report, published some months before the invasion of Iraq, addresses some of the matters that have turned out to be so difficult for the occupation forces, including providing adequate postinvasion security. It counseled against disbanding the Iraqi army, among other useful proposals.

113. Isaiah Wilson III, "Thinking Beyond War: Why America Fails to 'Win the Peace,' " 50, available at http://thinkbeyondwar.com/Documents/A_Study_of_Politics_and_War.pdf.

114. Ibid.

115. Gordon and Trainor, *Cobra II*, 467–68.

116. Ibid., 468–69.

117. Ibid., 501.

118. Michael Moss and David Rohde, "Misjudgments Marred U.S. Plan for Iraqi Police," *New York Times*, 21 May 2006, section 1, 1.

119. Perito, "Lone Ranger" remarks.

120. Thomas E. Ricks, "Army Historian Cites Lack of Postwar Plan: Major Calls Effort in Iraq 'Mediocre,' " *Washington Post*, 25 December 2004, A1.

121. See discussion of the ABC problem in Bobbitt, *Shield of Achilles,* 299.

122. See the excellent treatment of this issue in Bruce Berkowitz, "The Numbers Racket," *The American Interest* 2, no. 1 (September/October 2006): 139. See also a RAND study later published as James Dobbins et al., *America's Role in Nation-Building: From Germany to Iraq* (Santa Monica, Calif.: RAND, 2003). In testimony before a House Armed Services subcommittee, William L. Nash called attention to this book and its lesson that the "highest levels of casualties have occurred in the operations with the lowest level of U.S. troops, suggesting an inverse ratio between force levels and the level of risk." William L. Nash, "U.S. Post-Conflict Operations: Preparing Our Military for the Future," statement to the House Armed Services Subcommittee Defense Review, 9 November 2005, available at http://www.cfr.org/publication/9210/us_postconflict_operations.html (accessed October 13, 2006).

123. Ricks, "Army Historian."

124. Peter Ross Range, "Worst Laid Plans," *Blueprint: Ideas for a New Century*, 17 May 2006.

125. Gordon and Trainor, *Cobra II*, 494, quoting Brigadier General John Kelly, assistant division commander of the Marine division in Iraq.

126. Kenneth Pollack, "Insurgent Dilemma: Finding the Right Strategies in Iraq," *Berlin Journal*, no. 11 (Fall 2005): 6.

127. Ibid.

128. Ibid.

129. This accords with the RAND estimates prepared by James Dobbins's study group, as well as a study for the NSC attributed by Gordon and Trainor to a Marine major on the NSC staff. See Gordon and Trainor, *Cobra II*, 477–78.

130. With approximately 130,000 U.S. troops deployed to Iraq with its population of 25 million, this works out to roughly 5 U.S. soldiers per 1,000 Iraqis. This is significantly smaller than such operations as Germany, Bosnia, and Kosovo, which had 100, 20, and 18.6 soldiers per 1,000 inhabitants respectively. The Iraq troop level is on par with such failed U.S. efforts as Somalia and Haiti. Using the Bosnia and Kosovo ratios, between 450,000 and 500,000 total forces would be necessary in Iraq. Seth G. Jones, "Leaving Iraq Too Soon Leads to Failure," *Newsday*, 10 December 2003, http://www.rand.org/commentary/121003ND.html.

131. Gordon and Trainor, *Cobra II*, 484; see also Michael R. Gordon, "Debate Lingering on Decision to Dissolve the Iraqi Military," *New York Times*, 21 October 2004, A1.

132. David Kilcullen, interview with Charlie Rose, *Charlie Rose Show* (PBS), 5 October 2007, transcript at http://www.iht.com/articles/2007/10/08/america/08rose-kilcullen.php (accessed October 24, 2007).

133. David S. Cloud, "Gates Says Military Faces More Unconventional Wars," *New York Times,* 11 October 2007, http://www.nytimes.com/2007/10/11/Washington/11gates.html (accessed October 25, 2007).

134. See, e.g., Nicholas D. Kristof, "Saving the Iraqi Children," *New York Times*, 27 November 2004, A15. Kristof labeled as "delusional" the following policies of the administration: "we would be welcomed with flowers, we should disband the army, security is fine . . ."

135. Gordon and Trainor, *Cobra II*, 485.

136. Ibid., 499.

137. Coker, "Cultural Ruthlessness," 149.

138. As recorded in the now-famous photograph of an American officer on horseback with Afghan forces calling in an air strike.

139. The criticism by Major General John Batiste, the commander of the 1st Infantry Division in Iraq, was typical: "We need leadership . . . that respects the military. . . . And that leadership needs to understand teamwork." Quoted in Thomas E. Ricks, "Rumsfeld Rebuked by Retired Generals: Ex-Iraq Commander Calls for Resignation," *Washington Post*, 13 April 2006, A1.

140. Gordon and Trainor, *Cobra II*, 497, 500.

141. See discussion on pages 480 and 516.

142. See "Hezbollah," *Council of Foreign Relations*, 17 July 2006, http://www.cfr.org/publication/9155/ (accessed October 13, 2006).

143. From the Hamas charter; see Charles Krauthammer, "Actually, the Middle East Is Our Crisis Too," *Time*, 7 August 2006.

144. Paul Pillar, former deputy chief of the CIA's Counterterrorism Center, reflected this attitude when he concluded that the fight against terrorism "is not accurately represented by the metaphor of *a* war. Unlike most wars, it has neither a fixed set of enemies nor the prospect of coming to closure. . . ." Pillar, *Terrorism and U.S. Foreign Policy*, 217.

145. Simon Jenkins, "They Opted to Bomb, It Had Better Work," *Times* (London), 10 October 2001, 22.

146. Compare Truman's decision to call the Korean War a "police action." Or President Ford's direction to his chairman of the Council of Economic Advisors not to use the "I" word.

147. James Fallows, "Declaring Victory," *Atlantic Monthly*, September 2006, 71. Compare Ackerman, who argues that the rhetoric of war makes it easier for the executive to take unilateral military action without the consent of Congress, and provides the opportunity to invoke the precedents of Lincoln and Roosevelt set during more perilous times. Ackerman, *Before the Next Attack*, 16, 21.

148. Isaiah Wilson III, "Thinking Beyond War: Civil–Military Operational Planning in Northern Iraq," paper prepared for the Peace Studies Program, Cornell University, 14 October 2004, 8, available at http://www.einaudi.cornell.edu/files/calendar/3989/BEYOND_WAR.wilson_(PSP_10.14.04).pdf.

149. Brian Jenkins makes a similar point, referring to the "needless bravado, the arrogant attitude toward essential allies, . . . the exaggerated claims of progress, the persistence of a wanted-poster approach while the broader ideological struggle is ignored, . . . the failure to deploy sufficient troops, . . . the cavalier dismissal of treaties governing the conduct of war, the mistreatment of prisoners, . . . the use of homeland security funding for political pork barrel spending, and the failure to educate and involve citizens." Jenkins, "True Grit," 11.

150. See the Kilcullen interview, n. 132, above.

151. "FFI Explains al-Qaida Document," *Forsvarets forskningsinstitutt*, 19 March 2003, http://www.mil.no/felles/ffi/start/article.jhtml?articleID=71589 (accessed October 13, 2006).

152. Ibid.

153. Stephen Ulph, "Latest Video from Zawahiri an Exercise in Band-Wagoning," *Terrorism Focus* 2, no. 15 (August 5, 2005): 1–2.

154. Neumann, "Europe's Jihadist Dilemma," 79.

155. *A v. Secretary of State*, [2004] UKHL 56, [96].

156. Lawrence Freedman, "The Transformation of Strategic Affairs," Adelphi Paper no. 379 (London: IISS, 2006).

157. Daniel Benjamin and Steven Simon, "A War the Pentagon Can't Win," *New York Times*, 24 July 2007, http://www.nytimes.com/2007/07/24/opinion/24benjamin.html (accessed October 25, 2007).

158. David Petraeus and James Amos, *Counterinsurgency* (Dept. of the Army, 2006), ix; quoted in LaRue Robinson, "A New Age of Warfare," 19 February 2007, 2 (paper on file with author).

159. Adam Liptak, "The Line Between Civilian and Soldier," *New York Times,* 13 June 2007, http://www.nytimes.com/2007/06/13/washington/13combatant.html (accessed October 25, 2007).

160. Quoted in Bronson, "When Soldiers Become Cops," 132.

CHAPTER FOUR: Victory Without Parades

1. *Our Dumb Century:* The Onion *Presents* 100 *Years of Headlines from America's Finest News Source* (New York: Three Rivers Press, 1999), 163. The actual headline reads "Drugs Win Drug War."

2. See Thucydides, *Peloponnesian War*, book 1, paragraph 19, p. 46; book 2, paragraph 37, p. 145; see also Thucydides, *On Justice, Power, and Human Nature: Selections from* The History of the Peloponnesian War, ed. and trans. Paul Woodruff (Indianapolis: Hackett, 1993); Paul Woodruff, *First Democracy: The Challenge of an Ancient Idea* (New York: Oxford University Press, 2005), 10–11.

3. Cronin, "Rethinking Sovereignty," 134, 119.

4. I am indebted to Adriana T. Luciano for presenting an interesting psychological variant of this argument in "Crises of Self and State: The Paradox of Choice, Fundamentalism, and Individualized Terror," and for bringing *The Paradox of Choice* to my attention. See Barry Schwartz, *The Paradox of Choice: Why More Is Less* (New York: HarperCollins, 2004).

5. Wright, "The Master Plan," 53.

6. Ibid.

7. Riedel, "Al Qaeda Strikes Back," 28.

8. Quoted in James Hider, "Hatred, Bombs, Hope and Confusion Mark a Desperate Country's Trial of Democracy," *Times* (London), 24 January 2005, 9.

9. William Hawking, "Anti-Democratic Forces . . . Starring Iran," *Washington Times*, 4 December 2005, B4.

10. Paul Newell, "Voters Are Infidels, Say Iraq Rebels," *Birmingham Post*, 24 January 2005, 9.

11. Quoted in "Purported al-Zarqawi Tape: Democracy a Lie," *CNN*, 24 January 2005, http://www.cnn.com/2005/WORLD/meast/01/24/iraq.zarqawi/index.html (accessed October 13, 2006).

12. Quoted in John F. Burns, "The Conflict in Iraq: Threats to Voters," *New York Times*, 24 January 2005, A10.

13. Quoted in Hawking, "Anti-Democratic Forces."

14. Quoted in Alan Cowell, "Al Jazeera Video Links London Bombings to Al Qaeda," *New York Times*, 2 September 2005, A3.

15. Kaija Virta, "The Way We War," *Helsingin Sanomat*, 15 September 1999, available at http://www2.hs.fi/english/archive/thisweek/38031999.html (accessed October 13, 2006).

16. Ronald Dworkin, "Do Not Sacrifice Principle to the New Tyrannies," *Financial Times*, 9 October 2006, 15.

17. Quoted in William Shawcross, "Iraq's Liberators Should Be Proud," *Australian*, edition 1, 8 October 2004.

18. Frederick Lewis Allen, *Only Yesterday: An Informal History of the Nineteen-Twenties* (New York: Harper & Row, 1957), 16–17.

19. Angus Calder, *The People's War: Britain 1939–45* (London: Jonathan Cape, 1969), 567.

20. Of course, earlier elements of what amounts to victory persist in the state system from era to era in the history of the State and even from periods that antedate the modern State itself. Neither the State nor its war aims are wholly reinvented and redefined with each new constitutional order. Similarly, elements of the constitutional order reappear in successive periods as new orders replace old ones. What is distinctive in each period, however, is what is distinguishing. Thus, for example, the kingly state that dominated the seventeenth century carried forward notions of dynastic rights and a permanent bureaucracy from the princely states it superseded; what marked it as a separate constitutional era was the introduction of state sovereignty and the abandonment of sectarianism as core principles of statehood. The nation state that dominated the twentieth century inherited ideas of state supremacy, sovereignty, territoriality, and nationalism from earlier forms; what made it distinctive was the introduction of the welfare state as a key basis for its legitimacy. A change in a state's constitutional order is not a wholesale rejection of what came before; frequently, transformed states carry forward facets of the previous constitutional order. What changes is the basis of legitimacy of the state's power, not necessarily the instruments of exercising that power. Thus, when the United States underwent a transformation from state nation to nation state, the structure of the government remained largely the same. Presidents were still elected, the courts still interpreted law, and Congress was not disbanded. So too is it with the definitions of victory.

21. The descriptions in this chapter are taken directly from *The Shield of Achilles*.

22. Consider the experience of Carl von Clausewitz. As a young man he served in a Prussian army led by officers "defined by class rather than capability" and "filled with deserters from foreign armies, prisoners of war, criminals and vagabonds." The reforms prompted by the defeat of this army by the French at Jena in 1806 (a battle at which Clausewitz himself was captured) led to the creation of a new type of force defined by ability and professionalism. This was the model that "came to be emulated by many of the leading militaries in the world." See Smith, *Utility of Force*, 45–50.

23. Carl von Clausewitz, *On War*, trans. J. J. Graham (London: Penguin, 1982), 408–9. I am indebted to Paul Monk, who called this passage to my attention.

24. See Harold Macmillan, *Winds of Change, 1914–1939* (New York: Harper & Row, 1966), 503.

25. Mary Kaldor, "Iraq: The Wrong War," openDemocracy, 9 June 2005, http://www.opendemocracy.net/conflict-iraq/wrong_war_2591.jsp (accessed October 13, 2006).

26. George F. Kennan, *Memoirs: 1925–1950* (New York: Little, Brown, 1967), 309.

27. Gregory Scoblete, "The Market State President," *TCS Daily*, 8 September 2004, http://www.tcsdaily.com/article.aspx?id=090804C (accessed March 22, 2007).

28. See, for example, the David Nicholls Memorial Lecture given by Rowan Williams, "Law, Power, and Peace: Christian Perspectives on Sovereignty," on 29 September 2005, a transcript of which is available at http://www.archbishopofcanterbury.org/sermons_speeches/2005/050929.htm (accessed October 13, 2006).

29. Cronin, "Rethinking Sovereignty," 127.

30. North Korea is, I believe, the only state to have been caught and censured for using its diplomatic pouches to smuggle illicit animal pelts.

31. The Montevideo Convention on the Rights and Duties of States, signed on Decem-

ber 26, 1933, sets out only four requirements for the legal recognition of statehood: (1) a permanent population, (2) a defined territory, (3) a government, and (4) capacity to enter into relations with other states.

32. Ruth Leger Sivard, *World Military and Social Expenditures 1996* (Washington, D.C.: World Priorities, 1996), 7, 17.

33. Ibid.

34. Freedman, "The Coming War on Terrorism," in *Superterrorism*, 48, 43.

35. See Campbell and Flournoy, *To Prevail*, 51–64 ("Building and Sustaining a Coalition of Coalitions").

36. The term comes from Thomas Schelling's *The Strategy of Conflict*; see also the discussion in Philip Bobbitt, *Democracy and Deterrence: The History and Future of Nuclear Strategy* (New York: St. Martin's Press, 1988), chapter 6.

37. "To compel is to punish until the target takes the desired action. This is different than deterrence, where punishment is applied only if the target takes a certain action." Mark Smith, "Corcyraean Interventions: Internal War and External Involvement," paper prepared for the University of Chicago Comparative Politics Workshop, 4 February 2002, 12.

38. See al-Zarqawi's letter to the al Qaeda leadership, which was released by the Coalition Provisional Authority. The text of the letter is available online at http://www.globalsecurity.org/wmd/library/news/iraq/2004/02/040212-al-zarqawi.htm (accessed March 26, 2007).

39. Andrew F. Krepinevich, Jr., "How to Win in Iraq," *Foreign Affairs* 84, no. 5 (September/October 2005); see also David Brooks, "Winning in Iraq," *New York Times*, 28 August 2005, section 6, 11.

40. Freedman, "Transformation of Strategic Affairs," 82.

41. Cronin, "Rethinking Sovereignty," 131.

42. Gordon and Trainor, *Cobra II*, 517.

43. See Margaret-Anne Coppernoll, "The Nonlethal Weapons Debate," *Naval War College Review* 52, no. 2 (Spring 1999). See also David Koplow's thoughtful essay, "Tangled Up in Khaki and Blue: Lethal and Non-lethal Weapons in Recent Confrontations," *Georgetown Journal of International Law* 36 (Spring 2005): 703 (analyzing the use of force in the Waco, Moscow, and Basra confrontations).

44. Defense Department, *Policy for Non-Lethal Weapons*, directive no. 3000.3, 9 July 1996, 2.

45. Erik L. Nutley, "Non-Lethal Weapons: Setting Our Phasers on Stun?" (Center for Strategy and Technology Occasional Paper no. 34, Air University, Maxwell Air Force Base, Alabama, August 2003), 14, available at http://www.au.af.mil/au/awc/awcgate/cst/csat34.pdf (accessed October 13, 2006).

46. National Research Council of the National Academies, *An Assessment of Non-Lethal Weapons Science and Technology* (Washington, D.C.: National Academies Press, 2001), 59–60. There is a burgeoning literature on this subject; see Koplow, "Tangled up in Khaki and Blue," 713 nn. 20–25.

47. Eric M. Koscove, "The Taser® Weapon: A New Emergency Medicine Problem," *Annals of Emergency Medicine* 14 (1985): 1206.

48. Koplow, "Tangled up in Khaki and Blue," 727.

49. Rick Atkinson, "Lean, Not-So-Mean Marines Set for Somalia," *Washington Post*, 25 February 1995, A22.

50. See Amy Chua, *World on Fire: How Exporting Free Market Democracy Breeds Ethnic Hatred and Global Instability* (New York: Doubleday, 2002).

51. See Bronson, "When Soldiers Become Cops"; Perito, "Lone Ranger" remarks.

52. Quoted in Thomas L. Friedman, "The Chant Not Heard," *New York Times*, 30 November 2003, section 4, 9.

53. "Aftereffects: Transcript of President Bush's Remarks on the End of Major Combat in Iraq," *New York Times*, 2 May 2003, A16.

54. As attested to by the enormous number of returning refugees; it is estimated that some 4.7 million have returned since the fall of the Taliban in late 2001. Carlotta Gall, "Afghans, Returning Home, Set Off a Building Boom," *New York Times*, 30 October 2006, A10.

55. Sometimes called the "Parmenidean Fallacy," after the Greek philosopher who held that all change was illusion. This fallacy occurs when one tries to assess a future state of affairs by measuring it against the present, as opposed to comparing it to other possible futures. Let me give a famous example of Parmenides' Fallacy in operation. The turning point in the 1980 presidential race came in a debate when Ronald Reagan criticized President Jimmy Carter's record by asking the American people, "Are you better off today than you were four years ago?" While rhetorically devastating, this question is hardly the way to evaluate a presidency. After all, the state of the nation will never stay the same for four years, regardless of who is in office. A more relevant question to have asked would have been, "Are you better off now than you would have been if Gerald Ford had continued as president—and if he had had to cope with rising oil prices, a revolution in Iran, a Russian invasion of Afghanistan, and soaring interest rates?" Parmenides' Fallacy can also occur prospectively: Will we be better off in five years if we adopt policy X than we are now should be rephrased as "Will we be better off in five years if we adopt policy X than we will be in five years if we do not?" See Philip Bobbitt, "Today's War Is Against Tomorrow's Iraq," *New York Times*, 10 March 2003, A19.

56. Amelia Gentleman, "India Finds Ex-Official Guilty in Oil Scandal," *New York Times*, 5 August 2006, A8.

57. See Brian Urquhart, "The UN Oil-for-Food Program: Who Is Guilty?," *New York Review of Books*, 9 February 2006. See also "The Management of the United Nations Oil-for-Food Programme," a report by the Independent Inquiry Committee into the United Nations Oil-for-Food Program, the press release accompanying which noted that "[i]t is important to note that the regime derived far more revenues from smuggling oil outside the Programme than from its demands for surcharges and kickbacks from companies that contracted within the Programme. . . . The value of oil smuggled outside of the Programme is estimated by the Committee to be USD 10.99 billion as opposed to an estimated USD 1.8 billion of illicit revenue from Saddam Hussein's manipulation of the Programme."

58. See in particular the "IAEC Modernization" section in vol. 2 of *Comprehensive Report of the Special Advisor to the DCI on Iraq's WMD with Addendums*, 30 September 2004, 66–69. One scientist said that the Iraq Atomic Energy Commission's budget increased sharply beginning in 2000, while another recalled that Saddam himself overruled the finance minister's opposition to a budget increase in 2001/2002. Ibid., 67. Others described special classified projects, conducted outside of the normal nuclear export controls, that were undertaken beginning in 2001 with the aim of modernizing IAEC's machining capabilities. Ibid.

59. Mahdi Obeidi, "Saddam, the Bomb, and Me," *New York Times*, 26 September 2004, section 4, 11. See also Mahdi Obeidi and Kurt Pitzer, *The Bomb in My Garden: The Secrets of Saddam's Nuclear Mastermind* (Hoboken, N.J.: John Wiley & Sons, 2004).

60. See Kamal Ahmed, "Revealed: How Kelly Article Set Out the Case for War in Iraq,"

Guardian, 31 August 2003, 1; and David Kelly, "Only Regime Change Will Avert the Threat," *Guardian*, 31 August 2003, 8.

61. Paul Rogers, " 'War on Terror': A Balance Sheet," *openDemocracy*, 29 December 2003, http://www.opendemocracy.net/articles/ViewPopUpArticle.jsp?id=2&articleId=1662 (accessed October 13, 2006).

62. Quoted in David Ignatius, "Beirut's Berlin Wall," *Washington Post*, 23 February 2005, A19.

63. Antulio J. Echevarria II, "Globalization and the Nature of War" (Strategic Studies Institute, March 2003), 12, available at http://www.au.af.mil/au/awc/awcgate/ssi/globalization.pdf (accessed March 26, 2007).

64. See Joseph Cirincione, *Bomb Scare: The History and Future of Nuclear Weapons* (New York: Columbia University Press, 2007); and see also an essay reviewing such a proposal in Jason Epstein, "Hurry Up Please It's Time," *New York Review of Books*, 15 March 2007, 28.

65. "One of the most interesting things about the September 11 attack by al Qaeda and the operations of U.S. military forces in Afghanistan was how the two sides used essentially the same tactics. . . . Both were connected to their fighters by an encrypted, secure global communications system using a variety of modes—cellular, satellite, fiberoptic, voice, fax and Internet. Both used small teams of special forces covertly deployed deep in enemy territory to assist in terminal guidance. . . . Both directed their military operation from headquarters located halfway around the world. . . . Both used large fuel-air bombs to level high profile targets and command centers. . . . In Afghanistan, both adversaries were foreigners relying on local allies for ground operations. . . ." Bruce Berkowitz, *The New Face of War: How War Will Be Fought in the 21st Century* (New York: Free Press, 2003), 15–16.

66. Editorial, "Death of an American City," *New York Times*, 11 December 2005, section 4, 11.

67. Quoted in Jim VandeHei and Josh White, "Bush Urges Shift in Relief Responsibilities," *Washington Post*, 26 September 2005, A12; see also Eric Schmitt and Thom Shanker, "Military May Propose an Active-Duty Force for Relief Efforts," *New York Times*, 11 October 2005, A15.

68. The American experience in the aftermath of the intervention in Bosnia is illustrative. See Robert M. Perito, *Where Is the Lone Ranger When We Need Him? America's Search for a Postconflict Stability Force* (Washington, D.C.: U.S. Institute of Peace Press, 2004), chapter 1 ("Brcko: SFOR vs. the 'Rent-a-Mob' ").

69. See ibid., 30–32.

70. Lydialyle Gibson, "The Big One," *University of Chicago Magazine* 98, no. 5 (June 2006): 37.

71. Robert D. Kaplan, "A Force for Good," *New York Times*, 3 March 2005, A31. Kaplan recounts that "[a] decade ago, [U.S.] carrier battle groups mainly did planned, six-month-long 'pulse' deployments. Since 9/11, the Navy has put increasing emphasis on emergency 'surge' deployments, in which carriers, cruisers and destroyers have to be ready to go anywhere, anytime, to deal with a security threat. The new strategy explains why, in late December, the *Abraham Lincoln* strike force was able to so quickly leave Hong Kong for Indonesia at a best speed of 27 knots. . . . [T]he Navy has also instituted sea swaps, in which crews are rotated in the middle of a deployment, without the battle group having to return to port, [allowing] the ships to remain on call in unstable areas of the globe. . . ." Ibid.

72. Robert D. Kaplan, "Next: A War Against Nature," *New York Times*, 12 October 2005, A23.

73. Jenkins, "True Grit," 16.
74. Gibson, "The Big One," 30.
75. Kaplan, "Next: A War Against Nature."
76. In Scandinavia, defense departments are given disaster responsibilities.
77. The militia that has been conducting attacks against civilian settlements in Sudan.
78. Kaplan, "Next: A War Against Nature."
79. Ibid.
80. Where "Phase III" denotes armed combat.
81. This was the carrier on which President George W. Bush proclaimed that "major combat operations have ceased," though the U.S. has suffered more casualties in the so-called postcombat phase than before this ill-timed remark.
82. Kaplan, "Next: A War Against Nature."
83. Boutros Boutros-Ghali, "An Agenda for Peace," report of the Secretary–General, 17 June 1992, available at http://www.un.org/Docs/SG/agpeace.html (accessed October 13, 2006). Ghali also lists another stage: "preventative diplomacy."
84. See Nina M. Serafino, *Peacekeeping and Related Stability Operations: Issues of U.S. Military Involvement*, report of the Congressional Research Service, 13 July 2006, 2–7, available at http://www.usis.it/pdf/other/RL33557.pdf (accessed March 28, 2007).
85. Perito, "Lone Ranger" remarks.
86. Afghanistan before the Taliban might more properly be called a failed state where chaos and anarchy reigned.
87. Quoted in Perito, "Lone Ranger" remarks.
88. Ibid.
89. Lawrence J. Korb, "Over Here," *New York Times*, 27 May 2007.
90. Human Security Centre, *Human Security Report 2005: War and Peace in the 21st Century* (Oxford: Oxford University Press, 2005), 31.
91. A tsunami is a wave train, or series of waves, generated in a body of water by an impulsive disturbance that vertically displaces the water column. Earthquakes, landslides, volcanic eruptions, explosions, and even the impact of cosmic bodies, such as meteorites, can generate tsunamis. They can exceed 400 miles per hour in the deep ocean. In deep water a tsunami may only be inches, or a few feet, high. But when it reaches a shoreline it becomes a wall of water that can be a mile high. According to researchers, there has been a significant rise both in numbers of waves and in death tolls over the past century. The higher death rate is partly due to increases in coastal populations. See International Institute for Geo-Information Science and Earth Observation, "Characteristics of Tsunamis" (2005), available at http://www.itc.nl/library/Papers_2005/tsunami/Tsunami.pdf (accessed February 14, 2007).
92. According to the U.S. Defense Department, this was "the largest relief operation since the Berlin airlift," which lasted from June 1948 until September 1949. See "DoD Briefing on Operation Unified Assistance," 9 January 2005, available at http://www.pacom.mil/speeches/sst2005/050109presstranscript.shtml (accessed March 26, 2007).
93. Hurricanes are categorized according to intensity using the Saffir-Simpson Hurricane Scale. No storm combines duration, scope, and wind speed more destructively than a hurricane. These storms are called typhoons in the western Pacific, and cyclones in the Indian Ocean.
94. See Nicholas D. Kristof, "Scandal Below the Surface," *New York Times*, 31 October 2006, A25.
95. Jim Dwyer and Christopher Drew, in "Fear Exceeded Crime's Reality in New Orleans," *New York Times*, 29 September 2005, A1, report thirty-four deaths at or around the Superdome and convention center.

96. FEMA director Michael Brown, for one, failed to grasp the magnitude of the situation after the initial breach of two levees. "I don't want to alarm anyone that New Orleans is filling up like a bowl," he said. "That isn't happening." Quoted in Joseph B. Treaster and N. R. Kleinfield, "New Orleans Is Inundated as 2 Levees Fail," *New York Times*, 31 August 2005, A1. Brown later admitted on live television that the federal government did not learn that thousands of people were stranded in the New Orleans convention center until Thursday, September 1, several days after the hurricane. See Eric Lipton and Scott Shane, "Leader of Federal Effort Feels the Heat," *New York Times*, 3 September 2005, A17.

97. Brown's predecessor as FEMA director, Joe Allbaugh, told Congress, "Many are concerned that Federal disaster assistance may have evolved into both an oversized entitlement program and a disincentive to effective State and local risk management. Expectations of when the Federal Government should be involved and the degree of involvement may have ballooned beyond what is an appropriate level. We must restore the predominant role of State and local response to most disasters. Federal assistance needs to supplement, not supplant, State and local efforts." Joe Allbaugh, Testimony Before the Veterans Affairs, Housing and Urban Development and Independent Agencies Subcommittee of the Senate Appropriations Committee, 16 May 2001, available at http://www.tulsapartners.org/archive/pi87.htm (accessed February 14, 2007).

98. Lipton and Shane, "Leader of Federal Effort Feels the Heat."

99. Along with a few absurdities: thus FEMA must now follow post-9/11 security procedures, including holding up evacuation flights until air marshals (which had to be recruited and deployed to New Orleans) could be found. Because electric power was insufficient to permit X-ray machines to survey luggage, or metal detectors to function, matters were also held up.

100. Eric Lipton et al., "Breakdowns Marked Path from Hurricane to Anarchy," *New York Times*, 11 September 2005, A1.

101. In a letter to Congress, David Liebersbach, the head of the National Emergency Management Association (an association of state emergency managers), observed that "[t]he proposed reorganization increases the separation between preparedness, response and recovery functions . . . [which] will result in disjointed response and adversely impact the effectiveness of departmental operations." Liebersbach warned that the plan would have "an extremely negative impact on the people of the nation." See Robert Block et al., "Power Failure: Behind Poor Katrina Response, A Long Chain of Weak Links," *Wall Street Journal*, 6 September 2005, A1.

102. I haven't dwelt on the ineptitude of state and local agencies during the New Orleans nightmare because treating the problem as one appropriate for the defense agencies, as I argue, would take the matter entirely out of the hands of local authorities excepting insofar as these have been subordinated to federal authority in a time of mass emergency.

103. Such vessels can produce 100,000 gallons of fresh water per day.

104. According to a later interview with the *New York Times*, FEMA director Mike Brown states that on return to Baton Rouge from New Orleans, he became concerned about the lack of coordinated response from Louisiana officials. "What do you need? Help me help you," Brown said he asked them. "The response was like, 'Let us find out,' and then I never received specific requests for specific things that needed doing." The Louisiana governor's communications director has asserted, however, that during this period, state officials became frustrated with Brown and FEMA for expecting itemized requests before they would do anything. According to him, "It was like walking into an emergency room bleeding profusely and being expected to instruct

the doctors how to treat you." Quoted in David D. Kirkpatrick and Scott Shane, "Ex-FEMA Chief Tells of Frustration and Chaos," *New York Times*, 15 September 2005, A1.

105. Five hundred private boats headed for New Orleans to conduct rescue operations, trucks sent by Wal-Mart with food and water, shipments of diesel fuel, firefighters from Texas and Maryland, mobile medical labs from Mississippi, airboaters from Florida, even trains diverted by Amtrak were all turned back by FEMA. In a press release on August 29, 2005, FEMA urged all fire and emergency services departments not to respond to counties and states affected by Hurricane Katrina without being requested and lawfully dispatched by state and local authorities under mutual aid agreements and the Emergency Management Assistance Compact.

106. The director of FEMA "came to the agency with political connections but little emergency management experience. That's also true of . . . the chief of staff at FEMA, who was deputy director of advance operations for the Bush campaign. . . . [The] deputy chief of staff at FEMA had worked . . . as a media strategist for the Bush for President primary campaign and the Bush-Cheney 2000 campaign. . . . [The former] Republican lieutenant governor of Nebraska . . . became . . . a senior official at the agency's headquarters. The American Federation of Government Employees, which represents FEMA employees, wrote to Congress in June 2004, complaining, 'Seasoned staff members are being pushed aside to make room for inexperienced novices and contractors.' " Lipton et al., "Breakdowns Marked Path from Hurricane to Anarchy."

107. President George W. Bush asked Congress in September 2005 to consider a larger role for U.S. armed forces in responding to natural disasters. See Bill Glauber et al., "Response to Storm Not Perfect, but Better," *Chicago Tribune*, 26 September 2005, 1.

108. United Nations undersecretary for humanitarian affairs.

109. Quoted in "Earthquake Worse than Tsunami, says UN," *Guardian*, 21 October 2005, 24.

110. Gerry J. Gilmore, "Wolfowitz Salutes Armed Forces for Humanitarian, War Efforts," *American Forces Information Service*, 14 April 2005, http://www.defenselink.mil/news/Apr2005/20050414_605.html (accessed October 13, 2006).

111. Both sides' populations are dark-skinned and both are African in the sense that Sudan lies in Africa; neither are Arabs in the sense of a Semitic heritage. "[E]thnic differences do exist—the use of Arabic as a first language, agricultural practices, and a variety of more subtle cultural differences—and identification by ethnicity comes easily to Darfuris, even in matters such as gait and attire." Eric Reeves, "Genocide in Darfur—How the Horror Began," *Sudan Tribune*, 2 September 2005, available at http://www.sudantribune.com/article.php3?id_article=11445 (accessed October 13, 2006).

112. Ibid.

113. Ibid.

114. See Article II of the 1948 U.N. Convention on the Prevention and Punishment of the Crime of Genocide, which provides that genocide includes not only the killing of members of a "national, ethnical, racial or religious group, as such," but also "[d]eliberately inflicting on the group conditions of life calculated to bring about its physical destruction in whole or in part." The full text of this convention is available on the website of the U.N. High Commissioner for Human Rights, at http://www.ohchr.org/english/law/genocide.htm (accessed October 13, 2006).

115. "Debate over Darfur Death Toll Intensifies," *USA Today*, 29 November 2006, http://www.usatoday.com/news/world/2006-11-29-darfur_x.htm (accessed February 14, 2007).

116. As one European statesman put it, "[I]ntervention would only mean killing a different group of Sudanese." Conversation with author.

117. Tewes, "Just Defence."

118. See Tim Flannery, *The Weather Makers* (New York: Atlantic Monthly Press, 2005), 123–34.

119. William Falk, "While You Were Sleeping," *New York Times*, 30 December 2005, A27.

120. " 'The scary thing about SARS [according to Lee Clarke] was not its mortality rate but how quickly it traversed the globe.' . . . Ancient and medieval plagues, and 16th- and 17th-century syphilis epidemics, had to travel by foot or by coach. 'Nowadays if you introduce a pathogen even in a remote place in the world, its spread is almost ensured. The idea that it will infect large numbers of people is by now a fact.' " Gibson, "The Big One," 36, 33.

121. Craig A. Drill, "Avian Flu and Chicken Little," 8 December 2005 (on file with author).

122. David A. Relman, "Bioterrorism—Preparing to Fight the Next War," *New England Journal of Medicine* 354 (2006): 113.

123. Ibid., 113, 114.

124. Ibid., 113.

125. See Donald F. Thompson et al., *The Bug Stops Here: Force Protection and Emerging Infectious Diseases* (Washington, D.C.: NDU, 2005), available at http://www.unm .edu/~cstp/articles/DTP%2021%20Bug%20Stops%20Here.pdf.

126. See Food and Agriculture Organization of the United Nations, "UN Agency Says Risk of Bird Flu Spreading to Middle East, Africa Rises Markedly," 19 October 2005, available at http://www.fao.org/world/regional/rne/news/news359_en.htm (accessed February 14, 2007).

127. See Marie Breaux, "Lingua Calamitatis," *University of Chicago Magazine* 98, no. 5 (June 2006).

128. Paul Krugman, "A Can't-Do Government," *New York Times*, 2 September 2005, A23. I should note that things are rather different in the U.K., where the expertise of civil servants is not so little regarded.

129. Ibid.

130. Quoted in David Irvine, "A Free Pass on War Crimes?," *Salt Lake Tribune*, 19 August 2006.

131. Thom Shanker, "Pentagon Hones Its Strategy on Terrorism," *New York Times*, 5 February 2006, section 1, 16.

132. Ibid.

133. Quoted in Bruce Hoffman, "Plan of Attack," *Atlantic Monthly*, July/August 2004, 2.

134. Smith, *Utility of Force*, 379.

CHAPTER FIVE: The Constitutional
Relationship Between Rights and Powers

1. Oliver Wendell Holmes, Jr., *The Common Law and Other Writings* (Birmingham, Ala.: Gryphon Editions, 1982), 292.

2. Florida International University College of Law and Jack D. Gordon Institute for Public Policy and Citizenship Studies, "Conference Overview," in *At War with Civil Rights and Civil Liberties: A Constitutional Symposium* (October 17, 2003), available at http://www.fiu.edu/~ippcs/oct17_fo3_confoverview.html (accessed October 12, 2006).

3. Jon Wiener, "CIA-FBI Cooperation: The Case of John Lennon," *Huffington Post*, 27 September 2006, http://www.huffingtonpost.com/jon-wiener/ciafbi-cooperation-the-_b_30421.html (accessed November 25, 2006).

4. *New York Times Co. v. United States*, 403 U.S. 713 (1971).

5. *Ex parte Endo*, 323 U.S. 283 (1944).

6. In *Rasul v. Bush*, 542 U.S. 466 (2004), the U.S. Supreme Court held that United States courts do have jurisdiction to consider habeas corpus petitions brought by noncitizens detained at Guantánamo Bay. The Court rejected the spurious argument that because Guantánamo Bay lies outside U.S. territorial sovereignty, foreign nationals held there by U.S. forces acting under color of U.S. law could not challenge their detentions in a U.S. court.

7. In *Hamdi v. Rumsfeld*, 542 U.S. 507 (2004), which concerned the detention of an American citizen captured on the battlefield in Afghanistan, the U.S. Supreme Court held that the U.S. government must permit the person detained access to a neutral decision-maker to challenge his detention, a right that also includes notice of the factual allegations against him, the right to counsel, and the opportunity to rebut those allegations in court.

8. In *Hamdan v. Rumsfeld*, 126 S. Ct. 2749 (2006), the U.S. Supreme Court rejected the Bush administration's plan to try a detainee captured in Afghanistan before a military commission. The Court concluded that the commission was not expressly authorized by Congress, and that the structures and procedures of the commission violated both the Uniform Code of Military Justice and the Geneva Conventions.

9. This is also known as a *modality* of constitutional argument. See Philip Bobbitt, *Constitutional Interpretation* (Cambridge, Mass.: Blackwell, 1991), 11–22.

10. These papers were authored by Alexander Hamilton, James Madison, and John Jay.

11. Niccolò Machiavelli, *The Prince*, trans. George Bull (London: Penguin, 2003), 40.

12. Alexander Hamilton, "Federalist No. 1," in *The Federalist Papers*, ed. Clinton Rossiter (New York: Mentor, 1961), 35. "In a liberal republic, liberty presupposes security; the point of security is liberty." Thomas F. Powers, "Can We Be Secure and Free?," *The Public Interest* 151 (Spring 2003): 5.

13. See Lloyd Cutler and Alan Simpson, *Preserving Our Institutions—The First Report of the Continuity of Government Commission* (May 2003), available at http://continuityofgovernment.tamagazine.com/report/FirstReport.pdf. Also known as the Cutler-Simpson Commission (after its co-chairs Lloyd Cutler and former senator Alan Simpson), "[t]he Continuity of Government Commission is deeply dedicated to ensuring that our three branches of government would be able to function after a catastrophic attack that killed or incapacitated large numbers of our legislators, executive branch officials, or judges." Ibid., ii. The first report addresses the continuity of Congress, with subsequent reports on the presidency and judiciary to follow.

14. Nor is such a catastrophe far-fetched: it is now generally thought that the fourth plane seized by al Qaeda on September 11 was bound for an attack on the U.S. Capitol, where, as it happened, a roll call vote was under way in the House.

15. Michael Lind, "They Will Change Us," *Prospect*, 28 July 2005, 13; see also Michael Lind, *The American Way of Strategy* (New York: Oxford University Press, 2006), 15.

16. See Stuart Taylor, Jr., "The Bill to Combat Terrorism Doesn't Go Far Enough," *National Journal* 33 (2001): 3319.

17. 531 U.S. 32 (2000) (invalidating the city's program of suspicionless drug interdiction vehicle checkpoints).

18. I am indebted to Professors Carol Steiker and Harold Edgar, as well as Stuart Taylor, for help on these matters (correspondence on file with author).

19. Moussaoui was alleged to be, but is unlikely to have been, the "twentieth hijacker" who was detained prior to the attacks of September because of his suspicious activities at a Minnesota flight school. It now appears he was in flight training for other terrorist attacks.

20. See *Michigan v. Tucker*, 417 U.S. 433 (1974) (noting that "the Court in *Miranda*, for the first time, expressly declared that . . . a defendant's statements might be excluded at trial despite their voluntary character under traditional principles").

21. John Pike, quoted in James Kitfield, "Anti-Terror Alliance," *Government Executive* 33, no. 2 (2001): 51.

22. "31 Indicted in Italian Rendition Case," *International Herald Tribune*, 16 February 2007; "Factbox: Italy's CIA Kidnap Case," Reuters, 16 February 2007.

23. Judge Klaus Ruhle, quoted in Desmond Butler, "German Judge Frees Qaeda Suspect; Cites U.S. Secrecy," *New York Times*, 12 December 2003, A3.

24. Mark Landler, "Germany Frees Man in Qaeda Cell Linked to 9/11 Terrorists," *New York Times*, 8 February 2006, A8.

25. See, e.g., Proclamation No. 7463, 66 Fed. Reg. 48,199 (Sept. 14, 2001).

26. Authorization for Use of Military Force, Pub. L. No. 107–40, 115 Stat. 224 (2001).

27. See Philip Bobbitt, "War Powers: An Essay on John Hart Ely's *War and Responsibility: Constitutional Lessons of Vietnam and Its Aftermath*," *Michigan Law Review* 92 (1994): 1364–1400.

28. See chapter 12: the sanctions episode is an example of how action in one of these virtual theaters of operations in the Wars against Terror—antiproliferation—was sacrificed to counterterrorism; the case of the invasion of Iraq is an example of sacrificing counterterrorism to antiproliferation.

29. By the time this book is published, the statute, by its own terms, will have expired or been modified and superseded.

30. Though even ordinary warrant procedures do allow for sealed warrants under special circumstances.

31. One exception was where the evidence sought to be introduced could be shown to be the "by-product" of the search for foreign intelligence, e.g., where a valid search for intelligence materials turned up narcotics. It was rare for courts to admit such evidence.

32. This was the position taken by the Department of Justice; see Susan Schmidt, "Recognition of Patriot Act Urged," *Washington Post*, 24 August 2002, A6.

33. *In re All Matters Submitted to the Foreign Intelligence Surveillance Court*, 218 F. Supp. 2d 611, 623 (FISA Ct. 2002). A copy of this opinion is available online at http://www.fas.org/irp/agency/doj/fisa/fisc051702.html.

34. Ibid., 625.

35. Jack Goldsmith, *The Terror Presidency* (New York: Norton, 2007), 181. Controversy arose in 2006, discussed on 305–13 in the present work, when it was disclosed that intercepts of conversations with Americans had been conducted in the absence of warrants.

36. National Security; Prevention of Acts of Violence and Terrorism, 66 Fed. Reg. 55,066 (October 31, 2001).

37. "Well, let me first just mention [the detainees are] not being held incommunicado. The Red Cross visits them regularly. And insofar as any are dual nationals they have allowed consul or visits, the government has." Interview by Ruth Wedgwood, Yale Law School, with Margaret Warner, *NewsHour with Jim Lehrer*, 1 May 2002, available at http://www.pbs.org/newshour/bb/terrorism/jan-june02/tribunals_5–1 .html (accessed December 4, 2006).

38. Some civil rights groups, however, have complained that many detainees were not

allowed to contact family members or lawyers after their arrests. See Danny Hakim and Susan Sachs, "Judge Rules the Hearing for a Detainee Must Be Open," *New York Times*, 4 April 2002, A20. This seems to me clearly unlawful.

39. Ibid.

40. This training manual was seized by the Manchester Metropolitan Police (U.K.) during a search on May 10, 2000. It was contained on a computer file related to "Declaration of Jihad Against the Country's Tyrants," translated and entered into evidence in the New York trial of four persons accused of the 1998 bombings of the U.S. embassies in Kenya and Tanzania. It was later heavily redacted and posted on a U.S. Department of Justice website.

41. Interestingly, this was bin Laden's defense of Moussaoui against the charge that he was the twentieth 9/11 hijacker. Because Moussaoui had been arrested just prior to the attacks, bin Laden said, he could not have been a party to the conspiracy. Had he been, bin Laden would have called off the assault for fear that mission security had been compromised and a trap had been laid. It might also be noted that on this tape bin Laden states that he personally assigned the various tasks to the nineteen hijackers who staged the September 11 attacks. "Bin Laden Tape: No Moussaoui–9/11 Link," *CBS News*, 23 May 2006, available at http://www.cbsnews.com/stories/2006/05/23/terror/main1648914.shtml (accessed March 28, 2007).

42. For example, the various U.K. bombers in 2005 and 2006 were British citizens.

43. See Helen Fenwick, "Responding to 11 September: Detention Without Trial Under the Anti-Terrorism, Crime and Security Act 2001," in *Superterrorism: Policy Responses*, ed. Lawrence Freedman (Malden, Mass.: Blackwell Publishing, 2002), 80–104.

44. Sympathetic to the suggestion made above that aliens and citizens should face similar laws.

45. Comment, "Anti-Terrorism: But Does It Work?," *Guardian*, 23 December 2003, 19.

46. Philip B. Heymann and Juliette N. Kayyem, *Protecting Liberty in an Age of Terror* (Cambridge, Mass.: The MIT Press, 2005), 14–18, 41–52.

47. See Bruce Ackerman's proposal for statutory action governing a state of emergency in *Before the Next Attack: Preserving Civil Liberties in an Age of Terrorism* (New Haven, Conn.: Yale University Press, 2006), 106.

48. Ibid.

49. See *Wilson v. Arkansas*, 514 U.S. 927, 931–32 (1995).

50. Ibid., 934.

51. In 2002, British home secretary David Blunkett endorsed the notion of an "entitlement card"—a market state version of an identity card. The card would "contain data on an individual's entitlement to state health treatment, education and benefits to combat illegal immigration, the black economy and benefit fraud. However, police officers would not be given powers to demand to see the card and failure to carry one would not be an offence. Its production would be compulsory to claim benefits or to work." Philip Johnston and George Jones, "Blunkett Plans ID Card," *Daily Telegraph*, 6 February 2002, 1. About a hundred countries have compulsory ID cards, including Germany and Spain.

52. See Laura K. Donohue, "Fear Itself: Counterterrorism, Individual Rights, and U.S. Foreign Relations Post 9–11," in *Terrorism and Counterterrorism*, ed. Russell D. Howard and Reid L. Sawyer (Guilford, Conn.: McGraw-Hill Companies, 2003), 281.

53. The White House, Office of the Press Secretary, "Homeland Security Advisory System," press release, 12 March 2002, available at http://www.fas.org/irp/news/2002/03/hs031202.html (accessed October 31, 2006).

54. Sara Kehaulani Goo and Dan Eggen, "Security Threat Level Lowered to Yellow," *Washington Post*, 11 January 2004, A14.
55. I am indebted to Sir David Manning for these lucid and helpful distinctions.
56. See Douglas Barnes, "Total Information Awareness" (on file with the author).
57. Siobhan Gorman, "Adm. Poindexter's Total Awareness," *National Journal* 36, no. 19 (2004): 1430–32.
58. Ibid.
59. Heather MacDonald, "The 'Privacy' Jihad," *Wall Street Journal*, 1 April 2004, A14.
60. "How do you get the right people sharing all this information with each other? The answer [Poindexter believes] relies on a 'virtual organization' that would link people, in this case within the national security community, based on the kind of information they need to know. Networked properly, they could share that information with their bosses as well as with field agents who might be working on related issues in their own agencies and in others." Gorman, "Adm. Poindexter's Total Awareness," 1432.
61. Ibid.
62. Ibid., 1431–32.
63. On approximately December 12, 2002, the pyramid and eye disappeared from the TIA official webpage. The program's name, Total Information Awareness, with its Orwellian overtones, was changed to "Terrorism Information Awareness," presumably to conserve acronyms and delight satirists.
64. In 1987, I served as the legal counsel to the Senate Select Committee on Secret Military Assistance to Iran and the Nicaraguan Opposition (the Iran-Contra Committee) and, while taking a very dim view of the administration's actions in the affair, concluded that the former national security advisor should not have faced criminal charges.
65. See, e.g., "Curbing Pentagon Snoopers," editorial, *New York Times*, 25 January 2003, A18.
66. Gorman, "Adm. Poindexter's Total Awareness," 1431.
67. Jacob Goodwin, "Did DoD Lawyers Blow the Chance to Nab Atta," *Government Security News*, 1 August 2005, http://www.gsmagazine.com/aug_05/dod_lawyers.html (accessed November 26, 2006); see also Philip Shenon and Douglas Jehl, "9/11 Panel Members Ask Congress to Learn if Pentagon Withheld Files on Hijackers in 2000," *New York Times*, 10 August 2005, A14.
68. In the U.K., this separation between foreign and domestic intelligence collection, which is mirrored in the jurisdictions of MI6 and MI5, is to some extent ameliorated by the analytical products of the Joint Intelligence Committee.
69. See above, note 6 this chapter.
70. *Johnson v. Eisentrager*, 339 U.S. 763 (1950), in which the Supreme Court denied access to the courts to Germans seeking habeas corpus after a military commission convicted them for engaging in military activity after the German surrender, is not to the contrary. This can be seen from the Court's concluding remarks in that case: "We hold that the Constitution does not confer a right of personal security or an immunity from military trial or punishment upon an alien enemy engaged in the hostile service of a *government* at war with the United States." Ibid., 785 (emphasis supplied). In any case, my argument is that in the absence of a congressional exception, the U.S. government may not exempt itself from judicial oversight by choosing to act in one place rather than another.
71. The conventions, via Common Article III, apply certain basic minimums of protection to all persons detained, whether deserving of prisoner-of-war status or not.

72. Mark Denbeaux and Joshua Denbeaux, *Report on Guantanamo Detainees: A Profile of 517 Detainees Through Analysis of Department of Defense Data* (2006), 2–16, available at http://law.shu.edu/aaafinal.pdf (accessed March 28, 2007).

73. Interview by Donald Rumsfeld, secretary of defense, with Jerry Agar, KMBZ News Radio 980 (June 27, 2005), http://www.defenselink.mil/transcripts/2005/tr20050627-secdef3181.html (accessed October 31, 2006).

74. See above, note 7 this chapter.

75. *Miranda v. Arizona*, 384 U.S. 436 (1966). *Miranda* is the celebrated case in which the Supreme Court articulated the requirement that criminal suspects be informed of their rights (e.g., to remain silent, to the presence of an attorney, etc.) prior to questioning by the police.

76. See *Rasul v. Bush*, above note 6; *Hamdi v. Rumsfeld*, above note 7; and, *Hamdan v. Rumsfeld*, above note 8.

77. Military Commissions Act of 2006, Pub. L. No. 109–366, 120 Stat. 2600.

78. *Al-Marri et al. v. Wright*, no. 06–7427 (4th Cir. 2007), http://pacer.ca4.uscourts.gov/opinion.pdf/067427.P.pdf.

79. Attorney General John Ashcroft, quoted in Robin Toner and Neil A. Lewis, "A Nation Challenged: Civil Liberties; White House Push on Security Steps Bypasses Congress," *New York Times*, 15 November 2001, A1.

80. Eric Lichtblau, "Officials Want to Expand Review of Domestic Spying," *New York Times*, 25 December 2005, A28.

81. See the report transmitted to Congress at the end of February 2000 as required by the FY 2000 Intelligence Authorization Act. National Security Agency, "Legal Standards for the Intelligence Community in Conducting Electronic Surveillance" (2000), http://www.fas.org/irp/nsa/standards.html (accessed November 2, 2006).

82. See Philip Bobbitt, "*Youngstown*: Pages from the Book of Disquietude," *Constitutional Commentary* 19 (2002): 3–34.

83. This is, by the way, one of the criticisms frequently made of Marshall's famous opinion in *Marbury v. Madison*—an unwarranted criticism, I should add. Marshall was compelled to consider a highly dubious reading of the Judiciary Act, which resulted in its being struck down on constitutional grounds because the U.S. government failed to appear and the plaintiff-in-error's unchallenged construction was the only reading before the Court.

84. See the thoughtful piece by David Barron, "Constitutionalism in the Shadow of Doctrine: The President's Non-Enforcement Power," *Law & Contemporary Problems* 63 (Winter–Spring 2000): 61–106.

85. See Philip Bobbitt, *Constitutional Fate* (Oxford, 1982).

86. See my discussion of the Iran-Contra affair in *Constitutional Interpretation*, 74–75.

87. President George W. Bush, "Information Sharing, Patriot Act Vital to Homeland Security," remarks by the president in a conversation on the USA Patriot Act, 20 April 2004, http://www.whitehouse.gov/news/releases/2004/04/20040420-2.html (accessed November 2, 2006).

88. Jack Balkin, "Shorter Attorney General Gonzales," *Balkinization* (7 February 2006), http://balkin.blogspot.com/2006/02/shorter-attorney-general-gonzales.html (accessed November 2, 2006).

89. See 18 U.S.C. §§ 2340 et seq., implementing the U.N. Convention Against Torture.

90. The U.K. has renounced the use of the "five techniques"—wall-standing, hooding, noise, sleep deprivation, and reduced diet—on the grounds that they constitute cruel, inhumane, and degrading treatment.

91. Senate Executive Report No. 101–30, quoted in Memorandum for James B. Comey,

Deputy Attorney General (December 30, 2004), http://www.usdoj.gov/olc/dagmemo
.pdf (accessed November 2, 2006).

92. Headquarters, Department of the Army, *FM* 2–22.3 *(FM 34–52): Human Intelligence Collector Operations* (Washington, D.C.: Department of the Army, 6 September 2006), paragraphs 5–75, 5–76. A copy of this manual is available at http://www
.fas.org/irp/doddir/army/fm2–22–3.pdf.

93. U.S. Constitution, Article I, Section 8.

94. President George W. Bush, President's Statement on Signing of H.R. 2863,
the "Department of Defense, Emergency Supplemental Appropriations to Address
Hurricanes in the Gulf of Mexico, and Pandemic Influenza Act, 2006" (30 December 2005), available at http://www.whitehouse.gov/news/releases/2005/12/
20051230–8.html (accessed November 2, 2006).

95. See Memorandum for the Honorable Abner J. Mikva, Counsel to the President,
"Presidential Authority to Decline to Execute Unconstitutional Statutes," 2 November 1994, available at http://www.fas.org/irp/agency/doj/olc110294.html (accessed
November 2, 2006), which concludes that "if the President believes that the Court
would sustain a particular provision as constitutional, the President should execute
the statute," but if he determines that the statute is unconstitutional and has good
grounds to believe that the Court would agree, he has the constitutional authority to
decline to enforce the unconstitutional law.

96. The president should generally enforce statutes he takes to be unconstitutional, however, if this is the only way to trigger judicial review. See ibid.: "Also relevant [to the
decision whether to enforce an unconstitutional statute] is the likelihood that compliance or non-compliance will permit judicial resolution of the issue. That is, the President may base his decision to comply (or decline to comply) in part on a desire to
afford the Supreme Court an opportunity to review the constitutional judgment of the
legislative branch."

97. Thomas Jefferson, *The Writings of Thomas Jefferson*, vol. 8, ed. Paul Leicester Ford
(New York: G.P. Putnam's Sons, 1897), 311; see also Peter M. Shane and Harold H.
Bruff, *The Law of Presidential Power: Cases and Materials* (Durham, N.C.: Car-
olina Academic Press, 1988), 396.

98. *Marbury v. Madison*, 5 U.S. (1 Cranch) 137, 177 (1803).

99. See Scott Shane, David Johnston, and James Risen, "Secret U.S. Endorsement of
Severe Interrogations," *New York Times*, 4 October 2007, http://www.nytimes.com/
2007/10/04/washington/04interrogate.html (accessed October 25, 2007).

100. And thus the Military Commissions Act of 2006 (enacted at chapter 47A of Title 10
of the United States Code), which deprives the federal courts of habeas corpus
jurisdiction over suits challenging the lawfulness of military commissions, is self-
defeating, indeed reckless legislation. In an effort to give the government a free
hand, it has removed from that hand the most important tool it could be given, the
validating review of an independent court.

101. Department of the Army, *Human Intelligence Collector Operations*, paragraph
5–89.

102. These facts are taken from the government pleadings and news reports thereof. They
are at this stage merely allegations and have yet to be proved in a court.

103. In that brig, he was joined by Yasser Esam Hamdi, another U.S. citizen who had been
classified an enemy combatant after surrendering to Northern Alliance forces in
Afghanistan, where he had been serving as a fighter with Taliban forces. He was held
for two years without charges and, until December 2003, without access to a lawyer.
Clearly Hamdi is a prisoner of war, and does not need to be charged as such, but since

the Taliban have been defeated mustn't he either be released or tried for treason? In either case, it must be obvious that, absent congressional action to the contrary, Hamdi is entitled to habeas corpus, forcing the U.S. to make this choice. The government took the position that Hamdi could simply be held indefinitely, incommunicado, and surprisingly it found support for that position in a federal appeals court. That court held that Hamdi's confinement was within the president's authority as commander in chief. The Supreme Court, of course, has now overruled that decision. Hamdi has been released under an agreement that effectively expatriates him from the U.S.

104. Authorization for Use of Military Force, Pub. L. No. 107–40, 115 Stat. 224 (2001).

105. *Padilla v. Rumsfeld*, 352 F.3d 695, 722 (2nd Cir. 2003) (quoting the Authorization for Use of Military Force) (internal quotation marks omitted).

106. Defense counsel charged that the FBI had searched al-Marri's apartment without a warrant and had interrogated him without proper warnings.

107. That is, the same charges cannot be brought against al-Marri a second time.

108. Richard A. Serrano, "Showdown Nears over Terrorism Detentions," *Los Angeles Times*, 16 July 2003, part 1, 1.

109. Ibid.

110. Michael B. Mukasey, "Jose Padilla Makes Bad Law," 22 August 2007, available at http://www.opinionjournal.com/extra/?id=110010505 (accessed October 25, 2007).

111. 18 U.S.C. § 4001 (a).

112. Following the Supreme Court's decision in *Hamdi v. Rumsfeld*, 542 U.S. 507 (2004), the U.S. government and Hamdi reached an agreement under which Hamdi renounced his American citizenship and was sent to Saudi Arabia. See Eric Lichtblau, "U.S., Bowing to Court Ruling, Will Free 'Enemy Combatant,' " *New York Times*, 23 September 2004, A1.

113. See Henry J. Friendly, "Some Kind of Hearing," *University of Pennsylvania Law Review* 123 (1975), 1267–1317.

114. See, e.g., Richard M. Rorty, ed., *The Linguistic Turn: Essays in Philosophical Method* (Chicago: University of Chicago Press, 1992).

115. See Sanford Levinson, ed., *Torture: A Collection* (New York: Oxford University Press, 2004).

116. See Ackerman, *Before the Next Attack*.

117. See Akhil Reed Amar, *America's Constitution: A Biography* (New York: Random House, 2005).

118. See Jack M. Balkin and Sanford V. Levinson, "The Processes of Constitutional Change: From Partisan Entrenchment to the National Surveillance State," *Fordham Law Review* 75 (2006): 489–535.

119. See Jack L. Goldsmith and Eric A. Posner, *The Limits of International Law* (New York: Oxford University Press, 2005).

120. See Martha L. Minow, "Outsourcing Power: How Privatizing Military Efforts Challenges Accountability, Professionalism, and Democracy," *Boston College Law Review* 46 (2005): 989.

121. See Jed Rubenfeld, "The Two World Orders," *Wilson Quarterly* 27 (Autumn 2003): 22–36.

122. See Philip B. Heymann, *Terrorism, Freedom, and Security: Winning Without War* (Cambridge, Mass.: MIT Press, 2003); Philip B. Heymann and Juliette N. Kayyem, *Protecting Liberty in an Age of Terror* (Cambridge, Mass.: MIT Press, 2005).

123. See Stephen Holmes, "Al-Qaeda, September 11, 2001," in *Making Sense of Suicide Missions*, ed. Diego Gambetta (New York: Oxford University Press, 2005).

124. See Thomas E. Mann and Norman J. Ornstein, *The Broken Branch: How Congress Is*

Failing America and How to Get It Back on Track (New York: Oxford University Press, 2006).

125. See Samuel Issacharoff and Richard H. Pildes, "Emergency Contexts Without Emergency Powers: The United States' Constitutional Approach to Rights During Wartime," *International Journal of Constitutional Law* 2 (2004): 296; Samuel Issacharoff and Richard H. Pildes, "Between Civil Libertarianism and Executive Unilateralism: An Institutional Process Approach to Rights During Wartime," *Theoretical Inquiries in Law* 5 (2004): 1.

126. See David Golove, "Military Tribunals, International Law, and the Constitution: A Franckian-Madisonian Approach," *New York University Journal of International Law and Politics* 35 (2003): 363.

127. See Noah Feldman, *After Jihad: America and the Struggle for Islamic Democracy* (New York: Farrar, Straus and Giroux, 2003).

128. Kenneth Roth, "Counterterrorism and Human Rights: An Essential Alliance," in *The Nexus of Terrorism and WMDs: Developing a Consensus* (Princeton University, 2004), available at http://www.l20.org/publications/9_iY_wmd_roth.pdf (accessed November 3, 2006).

CHAPTER SIX: Intelligence, Information, and Knowledge

1. T. S. Eliot, "Choruses from 'The Rock,' " in *The Complete Poems and Plays: 1909–1950* (Orlando, Fla.: Harcourt Brace & Company, 1980), 96.

2. "It is possible that 'Intelligence Failure' may be a useful phrase when the whole system of tasking, collection, assessment and policy use fails." Memorandum from Sir Mark Allen to author.

3. Len Scott and R. Gerald Hughes, "Intelligence, Crises and Security: Lessons from History?," *Intelligence and National Security* 21, no. 5 (October 2006): 654.

4. For this prediction, see Russ Travers, "A Blueprint for Survival: The Coming Intelligence Failure," *Studies in Intelligence*, no. 1 (1997), available at https://cia.gov/csi/studies/97unclass/failure.html (accessed November 8, 2006).

5. Nowadays, we think of an *antinomy* in light of Kant's use of the term to describe the conflicts between paired, equally rational but contradictory conclusions derived from rationalism and empiricism, respectively. For example, time and space have a beginning, versus time and space are infinite. Kant, however, derived his notion of this term from its use in jurisprudence (from the Greek, *anti,* against, and *nomos,* law) where it referred to two different legal rules that applied to the same situation, depending on how that situation was characterized. For example, is a federal law banning headscarves in the public schools a violation of the free exercise clause or an example of Congress's power to enforce the First Amendment's ban on the establishment of religion? Is an unfulfilled promise to make a charitable contribution a problem of contract law (which might have required some exchange of promises) or of tort law (which might assess liability on the basis of a good faith reliance)? As I use the term "antinomy," I have in mind two opposing identities that apparently cannot be combined without contradiction (public/private, national/international, etc.) and which are used to allocate responsibility.

6. "In the current climate the familiar distinctions between foreign and domestic, national and international, intelligence gathering and criminal prosecution, the military and the police, and the public and the private are increasingly blurred. With increased internationalization and globalization . . . the meaning of national borders and foreign and domestic actions is less clear. . . . The emphasis on prevention blurs

the line between intelligence and crime-fighting activities and weakens the tradition of a predicate before invasive surveillance is undertaken. Government intelligence and security contracting with the private sector and greater government access to what had been private and private sector data (for example, communications, credit card transactions, library usage) muddies the line between the public and the private." Gary T. Marx, "Some Concepts That May Be Useful in Understanding the Myriad Forms and Contexts of Surveillance," in *Understanding Intelligence in the Twenty-first Century: Journeys in Shadows*, ed. L.V. Scott and Peter Jackson (New York: Routledge, 2004), 95.

7. Michael Quinlan, "Just Intelligence: Prolegomena to an Ethical Theory" (paper on file with the author).

8. Armstrong, Leonhart, McCaffrey, and Rothenberg, "The Hazards of Single-Outcome Forecasting," quoted in Woodrow J. Kuhns, "Intelligence Failures: Forecasting and the Lessons of Epistemology," in *Paradoxes of Strategic Intelligence: Essays in Honor of Michael I. Handel*, ed. Richard K. Betts and Thomas G. Mahnken (Portland, Ore.: Frank Cass Publishers, 2003), 90. See also the discussion in part 4 regarding straight-line forecasting.

9. See infra notes 104–5.

10. Desmond Ball, "Desperately Seeking Bin Laden: The Intelligence Dimension of the War Against Terrorism," in *Worlds in Collision: Terror and the Future of Global Order*, ed. Ken Booth and Tim Dunne (New York: Palgrave Macmillan, 2002), 60.

11. The British experience has been markedly different; it will be briefly discussed at the end of this chapter.

12. See Tracy Goss, *The Last Word on Power* (New York: Currency Doubleday, 1996), 1–2; Tenner, *Why Things Bite Back*, 24, 62.

13. This invariably gives rise to various conspiracy theories: if there was information in the system, it must have been ignored on someone's orders (FDR's at Pearl Harbor, Truman's in Korea, Bush's on September 11, etc.).

14. This was the thesis of Roberta Wohlstetter's influential study of Pearl Harbor that concluded the U.S. did not lack information about Japanese intentions but rather the intelligence it did have was misperceived or dismissed because its significance was masked by mistaken expectations. Roberta Wohlstetter, *Pearl Harbor: Warning and Decision* (Stanford, Calif.: Stanford University Press, 1962), 392–93.

15. At least if reports of the rendition of prisoners to be tortured as well as the kidnappings of a German citizen in Macedonia and a Milan-based imam in Italy, all allegedly done without the cooperation of the states of which the victims were citizens, prove accurate. Khaled al-Masri, a Lebanese-born forty-two-year-old German citizen, was allegedly abducted by CIA operatives while he was vacationing in Macedonia. Masri claims that he was taken to a secret CIA-run prison in Afghanistan, where he was drugged and beaten. Masri was released when it was realized that his identity had been confused with that of another man. Daniele Ganser, "The CIA in Western Europe and the Abuse of Human Rights," *Intelligence & National Security* 21, no. 5 (October 2006), 765.

16. See Dick Marty, Committee on Legal Affairs and Human Rights, *Alleged Secret Detentions and Unlawful Inter-state Transfers of Detainees Involving Council of Europe Member States* (Council of Europe, 2006), http://assembly.coe.int/Documents/WorkingDocs/doc06/edoc10957.pdf (accessed November 5, 2006).

17. A seventh important antinomy (the separation of police and military functions) is discussed in chapter 3 on the new warfare. This set of opposing rules arose for the same reasons as the six discussed here—that is, to protect constitutional liberties—

and became contradictory only with the emergence of new constitutional contexts. Because it has less to do with intelligence than with the use of armed force (even if a lightly armed constabulary force), the discussion appeared in the earlier chapter.

18. See Gregory F. Treverton, *Reshaping National Intelligence in an Age of Information* (New York: Cambridge University Press, 2001).

19. Unlike Italy, Spain, and France, for example, which for various reasons have inherited the *carabinieri,* the *guardia civil,* and the *gendarmerie.*

20. Richard Clarke was quoted as saying he was sure that bin Laden and his men stayed awake at night "around the campfire" in Afghanistan, "worried stiff about who we're going to get next." Reuel Marc Gerecht, "The Counterterrorist Myth: A Former CIA Operative Explains Why the Terrorist Usama bin Ladin Has Little to Fear from American Intelligence," *Atlantic Monthly,* 1 July 2001, 38.

21. This plot sought simultaneous attacks in Jordan, Yemen, and the U.S. on the occasion of the widely perceived turn of the century in January 2000. Two of the attacks were stopped by alert law enforcement and a third was aborted.

22. But see the disruption of a plot to use terrorists from Southeast Asia, recruited by Khalid Sheikh Mohammed—the operational mastermind of the 9/11 atrocities—to use bombs hidden in shoes to breach the cockpit of an airplane and fly it into the tallest building in Los Angeles, the Library Tower. This operation apparently relied on breaching the rules restraining the NSA.

23. See Michael Elliott, "They Had a Plan," *Time,* 12 August 2002, 28.

24. Elisabeth Frater, "FBI Must Switch Gears to Prevent Terrorism, Experts Say," GovExec.com, 9 October 2001, http://www.govexec.com/dailyfed/1001/100901nj1 .htm (accessed November 5, 2006).

25. Gregory F. Treverton, "President Obscured the Case for Spying," 5 February 2006, http://www.rand.org/commentary/020506SFC.html (accessed November 5, 2006).

26. It has been reported that the FBI had an informant who was al Mihdhar's and al Hazmi's landlord.

27. Michael Isikoff and Daniel Klaidman, "The Hijackers We Let Escape," *Newsweek,* 10 June 2002, 22.

28. See Executive Order No. 12,333, section 2.4, 46 Fed. Reg. 59,941, 59,950 (4 December 1981).

29. See Isikoff and Klaidman, "The Hijackers We Let Escape."

30. Quoted by Bob Drogin et al., "CIA, FBI Disagree on Urgency of Warning," *Los Angeles Times,* 18 October 2001, A1.

31. Joe Klein, "Closework: Why We Couldn't See What Was Right in Front of Us," *The New Yorker,* 1 October 2001, 48.

32. Quoted by Drogin et al., "CIA, FBI Disagree on Urgency of Warning."

33. For a good discussion of MI5 that draws on these distinctions, see Gregory Treverton and Jeremy Wilson, "The Global Challenge of Operational Intelligence," in *Countering Terrorism and WMD: Creating a Global Counter-Terrorism Network,* ed. Peter Katona et al. (New York: Routledge, 2006), 257–59.

34. See the withering analysis of FBI counterterrorism in Daniel Benjamin and Steven Simon, *The Age of Sacred Terror* (New York: Random House, 2002). To be fair, this fine book was written before the creation and maturing of the National Security Branch at the FBI in 2005.

35. Charles Cogan, "Hunters Not Gatherers: Intelligence in the Twenty-first Century," in Scott and Jackson, *Understanding Intelligence,* 152.

36. Ibid., 153.

37. Quoted in Gregory F. Treverton, "Intelligence, Law Enforcement, and Homeland

Security" (Century Foundation Homeland Security Project, 2002), 3, http://www
.tcf.org/Publications/HomelandSecurity/treverton-intelligence.pdf (accessed November 5, 2006).

38. Prior to the Patriot Act, the person applying for the warrant had to specify the location and nature of the facilities from which the communication was being made and to show that there was probable cause to believe that the facilities were being used, or were about to be used, in the commission of an offense or were owned by or leased to the target of the investigation. The Patriot Act removes these requirements so long as the warrant was being sought by or upon the authorization of the Department of Justice and there is a showing of probable cause that the target's actions could thwart interception from a specified facility. See USA Patriot Act, Pub. L. No. 107–56, 115 Stat. 272 (2001).

39. William C. Banks, "How We Uncover Their Plots," *Legal Times*, 17 September 2001, 44. See also the discussion in chapter 5.

40. Interview with Jeffrey Smith, former general counsel of the Central Intelligence Agency, by PBS *Frontline* (September 2001), http://www.pbs.org/wgbh/pages/frontline/shows/terrorism/interviews/smith.html (accessed November 5, 2006).

41. FBI personnel will disparage this, saying that if the CIA tells them what they're interested in, the FBI will attempt to find a way to inform them, but this is clearly insufficient. As has been notably remarked in another context, "There are things we know that we know. There are known unknowns. That is to say there are things that we now know we don't know. But there are also unknown unknowns. There are things we don't know we don't know." Press conference by Donald Rumsfeld, secretary of defense, at NATO Headquarters (June 6, 2002), http://usinfo.org/wf-archive/2002/020607/epf511.htm (accessed November 5, 2006).

42. Brian Friel, "Visa System in Need of Upgrades to Trap Terrorists," *GovExec.com*, 9 October 2001, http://www.govexec.com/dailyfed/1001/100901b1.htm (accessed November 5, 2006).

43. Indeed, at least one commentator has expressed doubt about whether bin Laden could be convicted *after* 9/11: "[O]n the December 2001 video bin Laden comes very close indeed to admitting the planning of the operation; the key moment is when he says 'They were overjoyed when the first plane hit the building, so I said to them: be patient.' [B]in Laden also spoke in this video of the calculations he had made of the effect of the jet fuel in melting the iron structure of the World Trade Center, causing the collapse of the floors above where the planes hit. But even these statements legally denote nothing more than that he knew about the operation in detail, and . . . I doubt a court or an international tribunal could find him guilty of ordering or planning the attacks." Steve Smith, "Unanswered Questions," in Booth and Dunne, *Worlds in Collision*, 50.

44. David Kahn, "Back When Spies Played by the Rules," *New York Times*, 13 January 2006, A21; see also David Kahn, *The Codebreakers: The Story of Secret Writing* (New York: Macmillan, 1967).

45. Quoted in Kahn, "Back When Spies Played by the Rules."

46. General Michael V. Hayden, "What American Intelligence and Especially the NSA Have Been Doing to Defend the Nation," address to the National Press Club, 13 January 2006, http://www.fas.org/irp/news/2006/01/hayden012306.html (accessed November 5, 2006).

47. James Bamford, "The Agency That Could Be Big Brother," *New York Times*, 25 December 2005, section 4, 1; see also James Bamford, *Body of Secrets: Anatomy of the Ultra-Secret National Security Agency from the Cold War Through the Dawn of a*

New Century (New York: Doubleday, 2001); James Bamford, *The Puzzle Palace: A Report on America's Most Secret Agency* (Boston: Houghton Mifflin, 1982).

48. Hayden, "What American Intelligence and Especially the NSA Have Been Doing to Defend the Nation."

49. See Newton N. Minow, "Seven Clicks Away," *Wall Street Journal*, 3 June 2004, A14; M. Mitchell Waldrop, "Can Sense-Making Keep Us Safe?" *Technology Review* 106, no. 3 (March 2003), 43.

50. Ball, "Desperately Seeking Bin Laden: The Intelligence Dimension of the War Against Terrorism," 70.

51. Richard A. Posner, "Wire Trap: What If Wiretapping Works?" *New Republic*, 6 February 2006, 15.

52. K. A. Taipale, "The Ear of Dionysus: Rethinking Foreign Intelligence Surveillance," *Yale Journal of Law and Technology* 9 (Spring 2007): 128.

53. Dan Eggen and Walter Pincus, "Spy Chief Gets More Authority over FBI," *Washington Post,* 30 June 2005, A1 (emphasis supplied).

54. See Shane Harris, "Intelligence, Inc.," *GovExec.com*, 15 May 2005, http://www.govexec.com/features/0505-15/0505-15s1.htm (accessed November 5, 2006) (describing how U.S. intelligence agencies are increasingly relying on outside help).

55. Commission on the Roles and Capabilities of the United States Intelligence Community, *Preparing for the 21st Century: An Appraisal of US Intelligence* (1996), 88–89 (hereinafter *Preparing for the 21st Century*), http://www.access.gpo.gov/intelligence/int/pdf/into12.pdf (accessed November 5, 2006).

56. The effort to get secret information invariably draws resources away from reliance on open sources. What might those open sources have told us before September 11? In 1986, Hezbollah terrorists were thwarted in a plan to explode a hijacked Pan Am flight over the city of Tel Aviv. In December 1994, French paratroopers stormed a hijacked Air France airliner after learning that an Algerian group planned to crash it fully fueled into the Eiffel Tower. In 1995, Abdul Hakim Murad told police in the Philippines of his intentions to hijack a commercial airliner and crash it into CIA headquarters; he had trained at four U.S. flight schools. In the summer of 1998, Sheikh Omar Bakri Mohammad, an associate of bin Laden's, described bin Laden's objectives as to "bring down [American] airliners." Seven weeks before the World Trade Center and Pentagon attacks, bin Laden and his aides briefed the pan-Arab channel MBC about an impending "big surprise" in the form of "a hard hit against [the] United States." He also told the London-based editor of the *Al-Quds Al-Arabi* newspaper to watch for a "huge and unprecedented attack." All interesting facts, but hardly enough in themselves to alert anyone to the atrocities of September 11.

57. Memorandum from Sir Mark Allen to the author.

58. Dan Pulcrano, "The Case for Smart Intelligence," *AlterNet*, 23 October 2001, http://www.alternet.org/911oneyearlater/11781/ (accessed November 6, 2006).

59. All charges against the scientist, Dr. Wen Ho Lee, were eventually dropped. In a written opinion dismissing the charges, the judge issued a stinging rebuke of the government's handling of the case.

60. Or like some scientists' ideas of a scientist.

61. See Lord Butler of Brockwell, *Review of Intelligence on Weapons of Mass Destruction* (London: Stationery Office, 2004) (hereinafter Butler Report), http://www.archive2.official-documents.co.uk/document/deps/hc/hc898/898.pdf (accessed November 6, 2006).

62. National Commission on Terrorist Attacks upon the United States, *The 9/11 Commission Report: Final Report of the National Commission on Terrorist Attacks upon*

the United States (Official Government Edition) (Washington, D.C.: Government Printing Office, 2004), 127 (hereinafter *9/11 Commission Report*), http://www .gpoaccess.gov/911/pdf/fullreport.pdf (accessed November 8, 2006).

63. This is the text of an item from the Presidential Daily Brief received by President Bill Clinton on December 4, 1998. Redacted material is indicated in brackets. The brief is reproduced in the *9/11 Commission Report*, 128–29.

64. Alfred Rolington, "Objective Intelligence or Plausible Denial: An Open Source Review of Intelligence Method and Process Since 9/11," *Intelligence and National Security* 21 (October 2006): 753.

65. Ibid., 757 n. 22.

66. Robb-Silberman Report, 14.

67. This is the text of an item from the Presidential Daily Brief received by President George W. Bush on August 6, 2001. Redacted material is indicated by brackets. Presidential Daily Briefing, "Bin Ladin Determined to Strike in US," 6 August 2001, http://news.findlaw.com/hdocs/docs/terrorism/80601pdb.html (accessed November 7, 2006).

68. Even the attorney general, the FBI director, and the NSC coordinator for counterterrorism did not routinely receive the PDB, although items might be forwarded to them.

69. See Markle Foundation Task Force, *Creating a Trusted Network for Homeland Security: Second Report of the Markle Foundation Task Force* (2003), 18, http://www .markletaskforce.org/Report2_Full_Report.pdf (accessed December 1, 2006).

70. Following the arrests of a terrorist cell in Jordan near the end of 1999, U.S. officials became aware of plans to carry out a terrorist attack inside the U.S. to coincide with the new millennium. Referred to as the Millennium Plot, the plan to explode a bomb at Los Angeles airport was prevented when alert border guards in Washington State discovered the explosives in the car trunk of Ahmed Ressam, who was trying to cross into the U.S. from Canada. *9/11 Commission Report*, 174–82. "According to [one official], the millennium crisis was the only time that the FBI effectively shared information with the NSC. Before that, White House officials complained, they got nothing from the FBI—and were told that they were being deliberately kept out of the loop on grounds of propriety. . . . In fact, it was completely appropriate for the NSC to be briefed by the FBI on its national security investigations. Moreover, the legal bar to sharing information was often exaggerated. Only information actually presented to the grand jury could not be disclosed. See Rule 6(e) of the Federal Rules of Criminal Procedure, which establishes rules for grand jury secrecy." Ibid., 502 n. 40.

71. Travers, "A Blueprint for Survival: The Coming Intelligence Failure."

72. Scott and Hughes, "Intelligence, Crises and Security," 670 (citing Michael Herman, *Problems for Western Intelligence in the New Century* [Oslo: Norwegian Institute for Defence Studies, 2005], 10).

73. Ibid.

74. See also Alexander L. George, "Strategies for Preventive Diplomacy and Conflict Resolution: Scholarship for Policymaking," *PS: Political Science and Politics* 33 (2000): 15–19.

75. *9/11 Commission Report*, 403.

76. This is the conclusion of the Robb-Silberman Commission. See Robb-Silberman Report, 6.

77. The U.S. government alone has "created nineteen different committees and panels to study intelligence reform since the end of the Second World War." Rolington, "Objective Intelligence or Plausible Denial," 750.

78. See *Preparing for the 21st Century*.
79. See U.S. Commission on National Security/21st Century, *Road Map for National Security: Imperative for Change* (15 February 2001), http://govinfo.library.unt.edu/nssg/PhaseIIIFR.pdf (accessed November 8, 2006).
80. See Lord Hutton, *Report of the Inquiry into the Circumstances Surrounding the Death of Dr David Kelly C.M.G.* (London: Stationery Office, 2004), http://image.guardian.co.uk/sys-files/Politics/documents/2004/01/28/huttonreport.pdf (accessed November 8, 2006).
81. See *9/11 Commission Report*.
82. See Butler Report.
83. "Indeed, commission after commission has identified some of the same fundamental failings we see in the Intelligence Community, usually to little effect. The Intelligence Community is a closed world, and many insiders admitted to us that *it has an almost perfect record of resisting external recommendations*." Robb-Silberman Report, 6.
84. Intelligence Reform and Terrorism Prevention Act of 2004, Pub. L. No. 108–458, 118 Stat. 3638.
85. Carmen Medina, unpublished manuscript (on file with author).
86. Anne Joseph O'Connell, "The Architecture of Smart Intelligence: Structuring and Overseeing Agencies in the Post-9/11 World," *California Law Review* 94 (2006): 1655, 1657, 1676–78.
87. Rolington, "Objective Analysis or Plausible Denials," 749.
88. See Robb-Silberman Report, 4: "For almost 50 years after the passage of the National Security Act of 1947, the Intelligence Community's resources were overwhelmingly trained on a single threat—the Soviet Union, its nuclear arsenal, its massive conventional forces, and its activities around the world."
89. Rolington, "Objective Analysis or Plausible Denials," 740.
90. Robb-Silberman Report, 16.
91. Much the same criticism can be made of U.S. and U.K. diplomacy. How many politically experienced officers were sent to help manage outreach to the public in Iraq? How many young diplomats are trained in dealing with the media as part of their efforts against terrorism?
92. Robb-Silberman Report, 4.
93. The U.S. Quadrennial Defense Review identified these as including "developments in low-observable technologies, nanotechnologies, robotics and biometrics [that] will enable people to be identified instantaneously by their facial features or the way they walk; reconnaissance systems mounted on platforms the size of mosquitoes [that can] track U.S. adversaries or penetrate their remote facilities." Desmond Ball, "Desperately Seeking Bin Laden: The Intelligence Dimension of the War Against Terrorism," in Booth and Dunne, *Worlds in Collision*, 67–68.
94. Gregory F. Treverton and Jeremy M. Wilson, "The Global Challenge of Operational Intelligence for Counter-Terrorism," in the *Introduction* to *Countering Terrorism and WMD*, ed. Katona et al., 10.
95. Carmen Medina, unpublished manuscript (on file with author).
96. Woodrow J. Kuhns, "Intelligence Failures: Forecasting and the Lessons of Epistemology," in *Paradoxes of Strategic Intelligence*, ed. Betts and Mahnken, 93–94.
97. Carmen Medina, unpublished manuscript (on file with author).
98. Robb-Silberman Report, 3.
99. "In October 2002, at the request of members of Congress, the National Intelligence Council produced a National Intelligence Estimate (NIE)—the most authoritative

intelligence assessment produced by the Intelligence Community—which concluded that Iraq was reconstituting its nuclear weapons program. . . . According to the exhaustive study of the Iraq Survey Group, this assessment was almost completely wrong. The NIE said that Iraq's biological weapons capability was larger and more advanced than before the Gulf War and that Iraq possessed mobile biological weapons production facilities. This was wrong. The NIE further stated that Iraq had renewed production of chemical weapons, including mustard, sarin, GF, and VX, and that it had accumulated chemical stockpiles of between 100 and 500 metric tons. All of this was also wrong. Finally, the NIE concluded that Iraq had unmanned aerial vehicles that were probably intended for the delivery of biological weapons. . . . In truth, the aerial vehicles were not for biological weapons. . . . The Intelligence Community's Iraq assessments were, in short, riddled with errors." Ibid., 8–9.

100. Members of this commission included the late Lloyd Cutler, the presidents of Yale and MIT, two federal appeals court judges, Senator John McCain and former senator Charles Robb, the former president of RAND, a former undersecretary of defense, and a former deputy director of central intelligence. Like its predecessor, the *9/11 Commission Report*, the Robb-Silberman Report is an excellent and readable analysis sorting out a complicated problem.

101. Robb-Silberman Report, 4.

102. Ibid., 14.

103. Ibid., 24.

104. Ibid., 88.

105. Ibid., 179. The NIC has since reformed this process. DO and Defense HUMINT personnel are to be early participants in the NIE production process, which ought to provide collectors with a more informed view of the weight being given to particular sources. A new post of NIO (national intelligence officer) for "intelligence assurance" has been created.

106. Ibid., 95. This was also the assumption of the head of the DO. Ibid., 220 n. 315.

107. Ibid., 178–79.

108. Kuhns, "Intelligence Failures: Forecasting and the Lessons of Epistemology," in *Paradoxes of Strategic Intelligence*, ed. Betts and Mahnken, 84.

109. Sherman Kent, quoted in Richard K. Betts, "Politicization of Intelligence: Costs and Benefits," in *Paradoxes of Strategic Intelligence*, ed. Betts and Mahnken, 63.

110. Sherman Kent, *Strategic Intelligence for American World Policy* (Princeton, N.J.: Princeton University Press, 1949), 195.

111. Robb-Silberman Report, 46.

112. Quoted in ibid., 176.

113. Richard K. Betts, "Politicization of Intelligence: Costs and Benefits," in *Paradoxes of Strategic Intelligence*, ed. Betts and Mahnken, 59.

114. "I have often thought that if there had been something like co-ordination of information in the government it would have been more difficult, if not impossible, for the Japanese to succeed in the sneak attack at Pearl Harbor." Harry S. Truman, *Memoirs: Years of Trial and Hope*, vol. 2 (Garden City, N.Y.: Doubleday & Company, 1956), 56.

115. Harry S. Truman, "Limit CIA Role to Intelligence," *Washington Post*, 22 December 1963, A11.

116. Letter from Robert Earle to author.

117. Robb-Silberman Report, 13.

118. Cf. U.S. Senate Select Committee on Secret Military Assistance to Iran and the Nicaraguan Opposition and U.S. House of Representatives Select Committee to

Investigate Covert Arms Transactions with Iran, *Report of the Congressional Committees Investigating the Iran-Contra Affair*, Senate Report No. 100–216 and House Report No. 100–433 (Washington, D.C.: Government Printing Office, 1987), 375–86.

119. Compare Sherman Kent's three categories of statements contained in an NIE: (1) statements of indisputable fact; (2) statements about things that are knowable but are not known by us; and (3) statements about things that are not known to anyone at all. Sherman Kent, "A Crucial Estimate Relived," in *Sherman Kent and the Board of National Estimates: Collected Essays* (Center for the Study of Intelligence, 1994), https://www.cia.gov/csi/books/shermankent/9crucial.html (accessed November 17, 2004).

120. "The Legacy of Hans Blix," editorial, *New York Times*, 30 June 2003, A20.

121. Philip Bobbitt, "Spooks and Spin Doctors: The Secret Services and the Media Are Mutating, with Each Becoming More like the Other," *Guardian*, 2 July 2003, 19.

122. See United Nations, "UNSCOM Debriefing of General Hussein Kamel," 22 August 1995, http://www.un.org/Depts/unmovic/new/documents/hk.pdf (accessed November 10, 2006).

123. The declarations by Iraq admitted that it had produced and weaponized biological agents. Iraq had, before the Gulf War, produced anthrax, botulinum toxin, and aflatoxin; produced 30,165 liters of BW agent; and deployed some of its 157 bombs and twenty-five missile warheads with BW agents. Iraq claimed that Saddam Hussein had been unaware of these activities.

124. "Similarly, in the 1950s the U.S. intelligence community first underestimated the testing of Soviet atomic and thermo-nuclear weapons, then overestimated the development of strategic bombers and missiles from the mid-1950s to the early 1960s, and then (at least within CIA) underestimated Soviet Inter Continental Ballistic Missile (ICBM) development in the 1960s." Scott and Hughes, "Intelligence, Crises, and Security," 669. Each time the agency overreacted to the mistaken estimate, creating a new one.

125. Robb-Silberman Report, 169 (emphasis in original).

126. Ibid.

127. But see the DNI's Open Source Center, formerly CIA's Foreign Broadcast Information Service (FBIS). It describes its mission as providing "foreign media reporting and analysis to policymakers, government institutions and strategic partners. We deliver targeted, timely and authoritative open source intelligence for analysis, operations, and policymaking." See Open Source Center, http://www.opensource.gov (accessed September 30, 2007). OSC functions could be broadened to include some of the tasks suggested by the Robb-Silberman Commission report, including strong Internet content. See also Bill Gertz, "CIA Mines 'Rich' Content from Blogs: Policymakers Turn to Internet, Other Open Sources for Intelligence," *Washington Times*, 19 April 2006.

128. Robb-Silverman Report, 23.

129. Zefram Cochran (pseudonym), "When Jack Welch Was Deputy Director for Intelligence," *Studies in Intelligence* 48, no. 3 (2004), https://cia.gov/csi/studies/vol48no3/article04.html (accessed November 10, 2006).

130. Robb-Silberman Report, 32.

131. There is no evidence that he was supplied by the Iraqi National Congress, an exile group eager for regime change in Baghdad. Like the claim that Zacarias Moussaoui sought flight training for takeoffs only, this is a widespread opinion without foundation.

132. Robb-Silberman Report, 171. "[O]ne can see how hard it is for the intelligence com-

munity to assemble enough of the puzzle pieces gathered by different agencies to make some sense of them and then develop a fully informed joint plan." *9/11 Commission Report*, 355.

133. INR at the State Department, the Department of Energy, and the Air Force all expressed varying degrees of skepticism.

134. We should bear in mind, however, that the "conclusion that there were no Iraqi WMD remains an assessment. . . . [I]t has been suggested that the amount of chemical (or biological) weapons in question are so limited in scale that they could fit into large trucks. Some, such as former Mossad Director Ephraim Halevy, have argued that [these] do exist and remain either concealed in the Iraqi desert or somewhere in Ba'athist Syria." Scott and Hughes, "Intelligence, Crises and Security," 661 (citing Philip H. J. Davies, "Discredited or Betrayed? British Intelligence, Iraq and Weapons of Mass Destruction," in *The Search for WMD: Non-Proliferation, Intelligence and Pre-emption in the New Security Environment*, ed. Graham F. Walker [Halifax, Nova Scotia: Dalhousie University Centre for Foreign Policy Studies, 2006], 152).

135. Robb-Silberman Report, 4.

136. Ball, "Desperately Seeking Bin Laden," 72–73.

137. Richard K. Betts, "Analysis, War, and Decision: Why Intelligence Failures Are Inevitable," *World Politics* 31 (1978): 61–89.

138. See Stephen Marrin, "Preventing Intelligence Failures by Learning from the Past," *International Journal of Intelligence and Counterintelligence* 17 (2004): 655–72.

139. Memorandum from Sir Mark Allen to the author.

140. Michael Herman, *Intelligence Power in Peace and War* (New York: Cambridge University Press, 1996).

141. Philip H. J. Davies, "Ideas of Intelligence: Divergent National Concepts and Institutions," *Harvard International Review* 24 (Fall 2002): 62–64.

142. Philip H. J. Davies, "A Critical Look at Britain's Spy Machinery," *Studies in Intelligence* 49, no. 4 (2005), https://www.cia.gov/csi/studies/vol49no4/Spy_Machinery_4.htm (accessed November 17, 2006).

143. Ibid.

144. Ibid.

145. This term has now been appropriated by the George W. Bush administration as applying to the War on Terror. See Bradley Graham and Josh White, "Abizaid Credited with Popularizing the Term 'Long War,' " *Washington Post*, 3 February 2006, A8.

146. Scott and Hughes, "Intelligence, Crisis, and Security," 644, referring to a similar observation made by Daniele Ganser.

CHAPTER SEVEN: The Strategic
Relationship Between Ends and Means

1. Paul Craig Roberts, "War on Terrorism a Threat to Liberty?" *Washington Times*, 21 March 2002, A16.

2. Jeffrey Goldberg, "Among the Settlers: Will They Destroy Israel?" *The New Yorker*, 31 May 2004, 48.

3. See Omar Malik, "Enough of the Definition of Terrorism," Royal Institute of International Affairs (2001). In 1977, Walter Laqueur wrote that "disputes about a comprehensive, detailed definition [of terrorism] will . . . make no notable contribution toward the understanding of terrorism." Walter Laqueur, *Terrorism* (London: Wei-

denfeld and Nicholson, 1977), 79 n., quoted in Alex P. Schmid, *Political Terrorism: A Research Guide to Concepts, Theories, Data Bases and Literature* (New Brunswick, N.J.: Transaction Books, 1984), 8.

4. Cf. John Locke contrasts illegitimate and legitimate insurgents (whom we might call terrorists and freedom fighters, respectively) in this way: the latter resist tyranny by force when resort to law is impossible, whereas the former resort to force when legal remedies are available. Michael Freeman, "Order, Right, and Threats: Terrorism and Global Justice," in *Human Rights in the "War on Terror,"* ed. Richard Ashby Wilson (New York: Cambridge University Press, 2005).

5. See Air Force Historical Studies Office, "Historical Analysis of the 14–15 February 1945 Bombings of Dresden," prepared by USAF Historical Division, Research Studies Institute, Air University, paragraph 17, 40, available at https://www.airforce history.hq.af.mil/PopTopics/dresden.htm (accessed March 29, 2007). The Allies were particularly concerned that Dresden could be used as a transfer point to move German soldiers to the Eastern front, where Russian armies were in a vulnerable position.

6. I have earlier indicated that I think Moussaoui's case should be referred to the International Criminal Court. His own trial in the U.S.—in which he pleaded guilty to crimes he patently did not commit—was exemplary of the difficulties of such prosecutions.

7. 22 U.S.C. § 2656f (d)(2). Compare the section on defining terrorism in the report of the high-level panel convened by Secretary-General Kofi Annan. The crucial part of their suggested definition is:

"[D]escription of terrorism as any action, in addition to actions already specified by the existing conventions on aspects of terrorism, the Geneva Conventions and Security Council resolution 1566 (2004), that is intended to cause death or serious bodily harm to civilians or non-combatants, when the purpose of such an act, by its nature or context, is to intimidate a population, or to compel a Government or an international organization to do or to abstain from doing any act."

Secretary-General's High-Level Panel on Threats, Challenges and Change, *A More Secure World: Our Shared Responsibility* (2004), 52, available at http://www .un.org/secureworld. This definition would appear to include strategic bombing campaigns like the nuclear doctrine of assured destruction. Or see the definition of terrorism from the U.S. Code, which appears to exclude the attacks on the Pentagon and World Trade Center:

As used in this chapter [18 USCS §§ 2331 et seq.]—
(1) the term "international terrorism" means activities that—
   (A) involve violent acts or acts dangerous to human life that are a violation of the criminal laws of the United States or of any State, or that would be a criminal violation if committed within the jurisdiction of the United States or of any State;
   (B) appear to be intended—
      (i) to intimidate or coerce a civilian population;
      (ii) to influence the policy of a government by intimidation or coercion; or
      (iii) to affect the conduct of a government by mass destruction, assassination or kidnapping; and
   (C) occur primarily outside the territorial jurisdiction of the United States, or transcend national boundaries in terms of the means by which

they are accomplished, the persons they appear intended to intimidate or coerce, or the locale in which their perpetrators operate or seek asylum. . . .

The former definition thus equates terrorism with warfare, which is not appropriate for most nation state terrorism, and the latter equates terrorism with crime, which is not sufficient for most market state terror.

8. Fares A. Braizat, "What Counts as Terrorism? The View on the Arab Street," Open-Democracy, 1 June 2005, http://www.opendemocracy.net/debates/article-2-103 -2298.jsp (accessed November 21, 2006).

9. Kim Scheppele raises this penetrating question: "Lawful in which system? It is lawful for adults to drink alcohol in the U.S., but not in Saudi Arabia. It is lawful for women to wear a wider variety of clothes in Western Europe than in much of the Islamic middle east. If women are attacked in Western Europe for failing to wear the hijab or modest dress—or Muslim men are attacked in the U.S. for drinking alcohol, then is this terrorism? Then reverse it—Western European women wearing immodest dress in the conservative parts of Afghanistan where Shari'a has been brought back, or American men drinking in Saudi Arabia." By "lawful" I have in mind the law of the local jurisdiction (so no one can lawfully attack a woman in the Netherlands for failing to wear a headscarf whether or not she is a Muslim), which incorporates international human rights guarantees (so no one may attack a man for attending a church, whatever the local law may provide).

10. Although undoubtedly some do; see the account of Sayyid Qutb's travels through America in the first chapter of Wright's excellent book *The Looming Tower*.

11. Kenneth Roth, "Counterterrorism and Human Rights: An Essential Alliance," conference paper presented at The Nexus of Terrorism and WMDs: Developing a Consensus, Princeton University, 12–14 December 2004, available at http://www .120.org/publications/9_iY_wmd_roth.pdf (accessed November 3, 2006).

12. This is the subject of chapter 12.

13. Jean Bethke Elshtain, "Luther's Lamb: When and How to Fight a Just War," *Common Knowledge* 8 (2002): 306.

14. "Terrorism is the pursuit of political goals through the use of violence against noncombatants in order to dissuade them from doing what they have a lawful right to do."

15. Indeed, this is when it is hardest to define because terror that seeks to establish a permanent state of fear is, in Audrey Kurth Cronin's apt phrase, "subjective and . . . is *intended* to be a matter of perception." Audrey Kurth Cronin, "Rethinking Sovereignty: American Strategy in the Age of Terrorism," *Survival* 44 (Summer 2002): 121. If market state terrorists seek a perpetual state of terror—if terror has become an end in itself—this is one more distinguishing feature from ordinary crime.

16. "Bin Laden: America 'Filled with Fear,' " *CNN.com*, 7 October 2001, http:// archives.cnn.com/2001/WORLD/asiapcf/central/10/07/ret.binladen.transcript/index .html (accessed November 26, 2006).

17. Brigadier S. K. Malik, *The Quranic Concept of War* (Karachi, Pakistan: Wajidalis, 1979), 59.

18. In the context of the operations of states, by *legitimate* I mean state practices that are generally accepted as being lawful. This excludes laws that are on the books but not accepted and includes practices that, while not codified, are generally believed to be appropriate to the operation of law. A more general treatment of this subject can be found in Richard H. Fallon, Jr., "Legitimacy and the Constitution," *Harvard Law*

Review 118 (2005): 1787–1853, where he distinguishes among legal, sociological, and moral legitimacy.

19. Grenville Byford, "The Wrong War," *Foreign Affairs* 81 (July/August 2002): 38.

20. Ibid.

21. But see Catherine Elkins, *Imperial Reckoning: The Untold Story of Britain's Gulag in Kenya* (New York: Henry Holt, 2005), and David Anderson, *Histories of the Hanged: The Dirty War in Kenya and the End of Empire* (New York: W. W. Norton & Co., 2005), which suggest that the Kikuyu rebels who launched the Mau Mau killings did not have peaceful access to legal redress of their grievances.

22. Chris Brown, "Reflections on the 'War on Terror,' 2 Years On," *International Politics* 41 (2004): 54. "Nasra Hassan, a United Nations relief worker in Gaza, interviewed 250 aspiring suicide bombers and their recruiters. She found that none were uneducated, desperately poor, simple-minded, suicidal or depressed." Riaz Hassan, "Terrorists and Their Tools—Part I," *YaleGlobal Online*, 23 April 2004, http://yale global.yale.edu/display.article?id=3749 (accessed November 26, 2006). See also Robert A. Pape, *Dying to Win: The Strategic Logic of Suicide Terrorism* (New York: Random House, 2005), 8–24.

23. "The denial of any distinction between foreseen and intended consequences, as far as responsibility is concerned, . . . explains the difference between old-fashioned Utilitarianism and that consequentialism, as I name it, which marks . . . every English academic moral philosopher since [Sidgwick]." G. E. M. Anscombe, "Modern Moral Philosophy," *Philosophy* 33 (January 1958): 12 (emphasis omitted).

24. Thus the rule for public servants I am proposing is in contrast to a *deontological* rule (such as Kant's categorical imperative, which holds that certain acts are wrong because they are inconsistent with the status of a person as a free and rational being, regardless of their consequences—slavery, for example) or to *aretaic* theories, which hold that neither the consequences of an action nor the absolute duties of the decider should be the basis for ethical behavior, but rather the pursuit of virtue.

25. That suggests one reason why I wish to distinguish "consequentialism" from "utilitarianism." Unlike at least some utilitarians I see no reason why governments should confine their calculus of costs and benefits to the satisfaction of wants and desires. I prefer to think that in addition to individual satisfaction, government may include other features of the consequences of its actions, including those interpersonal relationships that are the basis for respect, including respect for the rule of law, human rights, and humane conditions. As James Griffin put it, "Consequentialists hold that agents should seek to promote goods, including such moral goods, by bringing about their respect in people's actions generally, while non-consequentialists hold that agents should seek to respect goods by not damaging them themselves in their own action." "Consequentialism," in *The Oxford Companion to Philosophy*, ed. Ted Honderich (Oxford: Oxford University Press, 1995), 154. Some nonconsequentialists hold that killing is always wrong, apart from any good that might be the result. Some utilitarians hold that one killing can be justified on the grounds that two lives would be saved. The consequentialist position I believe is incumbent on officials of the states of consent holds that killing may be justified if it prevents more killing.

26. On the "ticking bomb" hypothetical, compare Kenneth Roth, "Justifying Torture," in *Torture*, ed. Kenneth Roth and Minky Worden (New York: New Press, 2005), 197–99, with Elaine Scarry, "Five Errors in the Reasoning of Alan Dershowitz," in *Torture: A Collection*, ed. Sanford Levinson (New York: Oxford University Press, 2004), 283–84. Perhaps the most interesting of the many essays on this subject is Kim Lane Scheppele, "Hypothetical Torture in the 'War on Terrorism,' " *Journal of*

National Security Law and Policy 1 (2005): 285–340, which takes a practical, "soci-ological" view of how the "ticking bomb" scenario might work out "on the ground."

27. "Experts of the Report of the Commission of Inquiry into the Methods of Investiga-tion of the General Security Service Regarding Hostile Terrorist Activity," *Israel Law Review* 23 (1989): 184, quoted in Miriam Gur-Arye, "Can the War Against Ter-ror Justify the Use of Force in Interrogations?," in *Torture*, Levinson, 184.

28. Richard A. Posner, "Torture, Terrorism, and Interrogation," in *Torture*, Levin-son, 295.

29. Noting this, Elaine Scarry wittily asks if "in a world where knowledge is ordinarily so imperfect, we are suddenly granted the omniscience to know that the person in front of us holds this crucial information about the bomb's whereabouts[, why] not just grant us the omniscience to know where the bomb is?" Elaine Scarry, "Five Errors in the Reasoning of Alan Dershowitz," in *Torture*, Levinson, 284.

30. See note 25 above and the accompanying text.

31. Michael Walzer, "Political Action: The Problem of Dirty Hands," *Philosophy & Public Affairs* 2 (1973): 160–80.

32. See Thomas Nagel, "War and Massacre"; R. B. Brandt, "Utilitarianism and the Rules of War"; and R. M. Hare "Rules of War and Moral Reasoning" in *Philosophy & Public Affairs* 1 (1972): 123–81.

33. Nagel, "War and Massacre," 1 123–44.

34. Michael Walzer, "Political Action: The Problem of Dirty Hands," in *Torture*, Levin-son, 61–62.

35. This is my phrase, not Walzer's. By "consequentialism" I mean those assessments that focus on the consequences (including those foreseen but unintended) of any par-ticular act as the basis for judging the act. Consequentialism is usually contrasted with deontology, which emphasizes the nature of the act, and with virtue ethics, which relies on the moral qualities of the actor in determining whether an action is morally right. I also distinguish consequentialism from utilitarianism; see note 24 above.

36. Walzer, "Political Action," in *Torture*, Levinson, 64–65.

37. Compare Richard Posner: "Suppose a terrorist is known to be at large with a suitcase full of aerosolizers filled with smallpox virus; his confederate is caught and refuses to answer any questions. . . . [W]hat is required is a balance between the costs and the benefits of particular methods of interrogation. . . . In so extreme a case, it seems to me, torture must be allowed. . . . [I]f the stakes are high enough torture is permissi-ble. No one who doubts that should be in a position of responsibility." Richard A. Posner, "Torture, Terrorism, and Interrogation," in *Torture*, Levinson, 293–95.

38. See note 24 above.

39. See ibid.

40. This refers to the dilemma presented to a Jewish mother during the Holocaust when she was forced to designate which of her children would be murdered in order to spare another of her children; if she refused to choose, all the children would be killed. The name "Sophie's Choice" refers, of course, to the novel by the American artist William Styron. I use this term to refer to moral dilemmas in which a person is required to choose between two courses of action, either of which it would be wrong for him to undertake. It should be clear that I do not think that the government offi-cial of the state of consent faces, in his or her official capacity, such choices. He or she does, of course, face what Calabresi and I have called "tragic choices," but that is another matter entirely.

41. The term "moral hazard" refers to the risk of immoral behavior that attends a per-

son's actions when there is an incentive to such behavior owing to the fact that he is not subject to the actual consequences of his own acts. Fire insurance, for example, may pose a moral hazard for someone whose insured property is more valuable if burned. In the U.S., federal insurance of home loan deposits may tempt investors to purchase certificates of deposit at a premium from a failing firm, knowing they will ultimately be redeemed by the government. Homeowners may be tempted to build houses in a floodplain knowing that disaster relief will prevent them from suffering loss if a hurricane destroys their house. Here, the opponent of torture may wish to adopt the attractive posture of a human rights advocate in a safe country who does not bear the costs of the consequences of a failure to thwart a terrorist act in an unsafe one.

42. See Niccolò Machiavelli, "The Discourses," in *The Prince and the Discourses* (New York: Modern Library, 1950), 139.

43. President Abraham Lincoln, quoted in Mark E. Neely, Jr., *The Fate of Liberty: Abraham Lincoln and Civil Liberties* (New York: Oxford University Press, 1991), 12. Compare similar situations in which the letter of the law is neglected in order to avoid undermining the purposes of the law: A statute that makes it a crime to "knowingly and willfully, obstruct the passage of the mail" ought not to be applied to "a police officer who arrests a homicidal postal carrier in the midst of his rounds," nor an ordinance providing that "whoever [draws] blood in the streets should be punished with utmost severity," be used "to condemn a doctor for performing emergency surgery on a person felled by a seizure in public." John F. Manning, "The Absurdity Doctrine," *Harvard Law Review* 116 (2003): 2402. The sign that says "Keep off the grass" cannot be realistically applied to the groundskeeper whose efforts keep the turf alive.

44. When a leader consciously violates the law—Jefferson, purchasing Louisiana without Congressional authorization; Roosevelt aiding Britain despite the Neutrality Act—he is not in quite the same position as the citizen who commits an act of civil disobedience. Like ordinary citizens, the representative of a state of consent must be bound to accept whatever punishment is appropriate for his act in violation of law, but unlike those persons he may not act (officially) in conflict with their interests because his official authority derives solely from their empowering him to act in their interests.

45. We don't allow the marriage of children, living on other people's property, or infanticide—that is, we may regulate decisions as to whom to marry, where to live, how many children to have—but we do not allow government to decide whom we marry, where we live, or how many children we have. Coercing a woman's decision to carry a child is one constitutional flaw in the statutes that would criminalize contraception and abortion.

46. Compare Michael Ignatieff, "Moral Prohibition at a Price," in *Torture*, Roth and Worden, 26–27: "The best I can do is to relate the ban on torture to the political identity of the democracies we are trying to defend, i.e., by claiming that democracies limit the powers that governments can justly exercise over the human beings under their power, and these limits include an absolute ban on subjecting individuals to forms of pain that strip them of their dignity, identity, and even sanity."

47. A concept that is itself undergoing change. See chapter 10.

48. U.S. Constitution, Article VI, Clause 2.

49. *Missouri v. Holland*, 252 U.S. 416 (1920).

50. *Reid v. Covert*, 354 U.S. 1 (1957).

51. Henry Shue, "Torture," in *Torture*, Levinson, 47.

52. See Anscombe's discussion of utilitarianism distinguished from consequentialism in "Modern Moral Philosophy," note 23, above, this chapter.

53. Department of Defense Appropriations Act, 2006, Pub. L. No. 109–148, sec. 1003, 119 Stat. 2680, 2739 (2005).

54. The McCain amendment specifies that "cruel, inhuman, and degrading treatment" is to be defined in terms of the Due Process Clause "shocks the conscience" test, which was developed in *Rochin v. California*, 342 U.S. 165 (1952). See also *Chavez v. Martinez*, 538 U.S. 760 (2003); *County of Sacramento v. Lewis*, 523 U.S. 833 (1998). The "shocks the conscience" test operates essentially as a balancing test, taking account of the governmental purpose in the challenged action. Some have argued that, in cases of extreme necessity, little would shock the conscience; thus, the test might operate to create a necessity exception. For background discussion, see generally Seth Kreimer, " 'Torture Lite,' 'Full Bodied' Torture, and the Insulation of Legal Conscience," *Journal of National Security Law & Policy* 1 (2005): 187; Seth Kreimer, "Too Close to the Rack and the Screw: Constitutional Constraints on Torture in the War on Terror," *University of Pennsylvania Journal of Constitutional Law* 6 (2003): 278; Sanford Levinson, "In Quest of a Common 'Conscience': Reflections on the Current Debate About Torture," *Journal of National Security Law & Policy* 1 (2005): 231.

55. But see Kim Lane Scheppele: "[C]ourts in at least three countries have caved in on the issue. In the U.S., the Moussaoui trial has proceeded with summarized, edited and redacted transcripts of interrogations of the highest-level detainees being introduced to an American criminal jury. Not only was the jury not advised that the statements obtained might have been the product of torture, but the jury was advised just the opposite: that the circumstances in which this evidence was obtained were designed specifically to produce reliable information. In Germany and the U.K., courts reiterated their principled objections to torture—before setting standards for proof that torture had in fact occurred so high that it is highly unlikely, given the impenetrable U.S. secrecy about the interrogations of specific detainees, that any information that comes out of the U.S. archipelago of detention centers will ever be regarded as the product of torture." "The Metastasis of Torture: Circulating Coerced Knowledge in the Anti-Terror Campaign," paper presented at Jurisprudence and the War on Terror, Columbia Law School (April 2006): 80, available at http://www.law.columbia.edu/jurisprudence (accessed March 29, 2007).

56. Interestingly, however, this may not have been the only resonance, at least for Islamic cultures. I am indebted to Kim Lane Scheppele for pointing out that in such cultures orange is the color of the condemned and that for this reason prisoners taken by the Coalition were terrified to be dressed in orange jumpsuits. That would suggest that Zarqawi employed a kind of double entendre when he displayed Berg to the world in one of these suits.

57. See Ronald H. Jones, "Terrorist Beheadings: Cultural and Strategic Implications" (Strategic Studies Institute, 2005), http://www.strategicstudiesinstitute.army.mil/ pdffiles/pub608.pdf (accessed November 28, 2006).

58. A particularly nauseating example of which can be found in a dispatch that, after accurately depicting Hassan as an heroic humanitarian, as she doubtless was, concluded with the sort of diction that might serve as the definition of innuendo: "Other abducted women were freed when their captors recognised their innocence. But not Margaret Hassan, even though she spoke fluent Arabic and could explain her work to her captors in their own language. If anyone doubted the murderous nature of the

insurgents, what better way to prove their viciousness than to produce evidence of Margaret Hassan's murder? What more ruthless way could there be of demonstrating to the world that the U.S. and Interim Prime Minister Iyad Alawi's tinpot army were fighting 'evil' in Fallujah and the other Iraqi cities?" The report ends with this innuendo, implying that the Coalition was behind the kidnapping and killing but not actually saying so, or giving any facts to support such an odious accusation. "What Price Is Innocence Now Worth?," *CounterPunch,* 18 November 2004 (accessed November 28, 2006).

59. See the discussion of the emergence of the market state in Bobbitt, *Shield of Achilles,* 228–42.

60. Jean Moulin, quoted by André Malraux, Remarks at the Transfer of Jean Moulin's Ashes to the Pantheon (December 19, 1964). The following facts and quotations recounting Jean Moulin's exploits were taken from this speech.

61. Bruce Hoffman, "A Nasty Business," *Atlantic Monthly,* January 2002, 52.

62. As Hand described Cardozo: "He never disguised the difficulties, as lazy judges do who win the game by sweeping all the chessmen off the table: like John Stuart Mill, he would often begin by stating the other side better than its advocate had stated it himself." Learned Hand, "Mr. Justice Cardozo," *Harvard Law Review* 52 (1939): 362.

63. Jerome H. Skolnick, "American Interrogation: From Torture to Trickery," in *Torture,* Levinson, 111. See also the reporting on the torture of Abdul Hakim Murad, whose interrogation disclosed details of phase 2 of Operation Bojinka, a plot to crash a commercial aircraft into CIA headquarters. CRA, Inc., Terrorism Assessment Center, "Operation Bojinka Foiled," 21–22 January 1995, http://www.cra-usa.net/ IR-US-950121.htm (accessed November 29, 2006).

64. Kenneth Roth, "Justifying Torture," in *Torture,* Roth and Worden, 198.

65. Eitan Felner, "Torture and Terrorism: Painful Lessons from Israel," in *Torture,* Roth and Worden, 32.

66. Kenneth Roth, "Justifying Torture," in *Torture,* Roth and Worden, 198.

67. Alan Dershowitz, "Tortured Reasoning," in *Torture,* Levinson, 257.

68. See Elaine Scarry, "Five Errors in the Reasoning of Alan Dershowitz," in *Torture,* Levinson, 286–87.

69. See Richard A. Posner, "Torture, Terrorism, and Interrogation," in *Torture,* Levinson, 296.

70. 734 F. 2d 770 (1984).

71. Ibid., 771–73.

72. See Sanford Levinson, "Contemplating Torture: An Introduction," in *Torture,* Levinson, 23–39, and Sanford Levinson, "Torture in Iraq & the Rule of Law in America," *Daedalus* 133 (Summer 2004): 5–9.

73. And *Leon* did not involve charges brought against the policemen who tortured the kidnapper.

74. Husserl called this bracketing the "epoché" by means of which a systematic exploration of one's assumptions are made. This is not only a method in phenomenology, but also in science. See Piet Hut, "The Role of Husserl's Epoche for Science: A View from a Physicist," paper presented at the 31st Husserl Circle Conference (February 2001), http://www.ids.ias.edu/~piet/publ/other/husserlcircle.html (accessed November 29, 2006).

75. Henry Shue, "Torture," *Philosophy & Public Affairs* 7 (1978): 143.

76. See the eloquent essay by Jean Bethke Elshtain, "Reflection on the Problem of 'Dirty Hands,' " in *Torture,* Levinson, 77.

77. Alan Dershowitz, "Tortured Reasoning," in *Torture*, Levinson, 272.

78. Richard A. Posner, "Torture, Terrorism, and Interrogation," in *Torture*, Levinson, 297–98.

79. See John T. Parry, "The Shape of Modern Torture: Extraordinary Rendition and Ghost Detainees," *Melbourne Journal of International Law* 6 (2005): 516–33.

80. Note that Article 3 of the Convention Against Torture provides: "No State Party shall expel, return ('refouler') or extradite a person to another State where there are substantial grounds for believing that he would be in danger of being subjected to torture." This appears to leave open the possibility of rendering to states that engage in coercive practices short of torture. The full text of the convention is available at http://www.ohchr.org/english/law/cat.htm (accessed March 29, 2007).

81. Though it does bar cruel, inhuman, and degrading treatment, see ibid. Article 16.

82. Richard Clarke, *Against All Enemies: Inside America's War on Terror* (New York: Free Press, 2004), 143–44. Covert action is not necessarily or even usually unlawful (unlike most intelligence collection or other clandestine activities). It is any "activity or activities of the United States Government to influence political, economic, or military conditions abroad, where it is intended that the role of the United States Government will not be apparent or acknowledged publicly," 50 U.S.C. § 413b(e). Covert actions are deniable activities, not merely secret activities; indeed most such actions are not themselves secret; only the hand of the U.S. is not disclosed.

83. Cf. Barry Buzan, "Who May We Bomb," in *Worlds in Collision: Terror and the Future of Global Order*, ed. Ken Booth and Tim Dunne (New York: Palgrave Macmillan, 2002), 85–94.

84. Though this is sometimes done in European civil law systems—one more confirmation, however, of the cultural, customary source of such rules.

85. Compare the argument by Miriam Gur-Arye, which relies on the "defenseless" nature of the torture victim to draw a distinction between the terrorist, whose defense consists in his ability to disclose life-saving information, and other potential victims of torture. See Miriam Gur-Arye, "Can the War Against Terror Justify the Use of Force in Interrogations?" in *Torture*, Levinson, 192–95.

86. The terrorist, after all, does not come within the conventions' indicia that designate a prisoner of war. Indeed, he quite calculatedly avoids complying with these standards so that he can wage a terrorist campaign.

87. Henry Shue, "Torture," in *Torture*, Levinson, 52.

88. I am indebted to Professor James Griffin for this point.

89. Eitan Felner, "Torture and Terrorism: Painful Lessons from Israel," in *Torture*, Roth and Worden, 34–35.

90. See, for example, Andrew Sullivan, "The Abolition of Torture," *New Republic Online*, 7 December 2005, http://www.tnr.com/doc.mhtml?i=20051219&s=sullivan 121905 (accessed November 30, 2006), and Michael Ignatieff, "Moral Prohibition at a Price," in *Torture*, Roth and Worden, 26–27.

91. Hoffman, "A Nasty Business," 50–51.

92. Stephen Grey, *Ghost Plane: The True Story of the CIA's Secret Rendition Programme* (New York: St. Martin's Press, 2005). See also Sanford Levinson, ed., *Torture: A Collection* (New York: Oxford University Press, 2006); and Karen Greenberg, *The Torture Debate* (New York: Cambridge University Press, 2005).

93. Thomas L. Friedman, "World War III," *New York Times*, 13 September 2001, A27.

94. See chapters 10 and 11, addressing the need to reform state sovereignty and international law respectively, and pp. 474–75 specifically, which discusses challenges facing the NPT. For general discussion of the threat currently presented by the

intersection of terrorism and the availability of nuclear weapons and material, see Matthew Bunn and Anthony Wier, *Securing the Bomb 2006* (Cambridge, Mass., and Washington, D.C.: Project on Managing the Atom, Harvard University, and Nuclear Threat Initiative, July 2006), www.nti.org/securingthebomb.

95. David Luban, "The Defense of Torture," *New York Review of Books*, 15 March 2007, 38.

CHAPTER EIGHT: Terrorism: Supply and Demand

1. William Shakespeare, *All's Well That Ends Well*, in *The Complete Works* (New York: Barnes & Noble Books, 1994), 755.

2. There are some exceptions. See, e.g., Michael Ignatieff, *Lesser Evil: Political Ethics in an Age of Terror* (Princeton, N.J.: Princeton University Press, 2004).

3. See United States General Accounting Office, *Combating Terrorism: How Five Foreign Countries Are Organized to Combat Terrorism* (2000), http://www.gao.gov/archive/2000/ns00085.pdf (accessed December 1, 2006).

4. Karin von Hippel, "The Roots of Terrorism: Probing the Myths," *Political Quarterly* 73, Supplement 1 (August 2002): 26.

5. See Alan B. Krueger and Jitka Maleckova, "Education, Poverty and Terrorism: Is There a Causal Connection?" *Journal of Economic Perspectives* 17 (Fall 2003): 119–44. See also Alan Dershowitz, "Does Oppression Cause Homicide Bombings?" *Jewish World Review*, 24 May 2004, http://www.jewishworldreview.com/0504/dershowitz_oppression_causes_suicide_bombings.php3 (accessed December 1, 2006).

6. See Robert A. Pape, *Dying to Win: The Strategic Logic of Suicide Terrorism* (New York: Random House, 2005), 17, 210–11.

7. Bruno S. Frey and Simon Luechinger, "Decentralization as a Disincentive for Terror," *European Journal of Political Economy* 20 (2004): 512–13. That this is indeed possible has been demonstrated by a recent incident in Switzerland. In September 2001, a man ran amok (he was not a terrorist) in the parliamentary building of the Swiss canton Zug and shot dead no fewer than three of the seven members of the government council (Regierungsrat), as well as eleven members of parliament. He also injured a significant number of other members of the government and parliament. Nevertheless, within a very short period of time (something like half an hour), the government was functional again, not least because the heads of the partly autonomous communes took over. Ibid., 513. A similar incident in Armenia plunged the country into a political crisis. In October 1999, five gunmen burst into Armenia's parliament and assassinated the prime minister, the parliamentary speaker, and seven other government officials. Armenia's defense minister stated that the situation that had been created was fraught with uncertainty; the internal and external security of the state were in danger. Because of the centralized nature of Armenia, the killings left a power vacuum, and lesser federal levels were not able to take over.

8. Audrey Kurth Cronin, "Behind the Curve: Globalization and International Terrorism," *International Security* 27 (Winter 2002/03): 45.

9. "The September 11 attacks were so devastating in part because modern societies are so highly tuned and depend so much on the smooth functioning of many separate parts. It is not just that we are dependent on technologies that most of us do not understand, but we are dependent on their working almost optimally. . . . 'We [also must recognize that we] are creating systems and structures that are vulnerable to fairly simple acts,' said Lord Wilson, now Master of Emmanuel College at Cambridge University." Stephen Fidler, "Catastrophic Terrorism," report of the meeting

organized by the Centre of International Studies, University of Cambridge, 18–19 November 2002, http://www.cambridgesecurity.net/pdf/catastrophic_terrorism.pdf.

10. John Gearson, "The Nature of Modern Terrorism," in *Superterrorism: Policy Responses*, ed. Lawrence Freedman (Malden, Mass.: Blackwell Publishing, 2002), 8.

11. Christopher F. Chyba, "Toward Biological Security," *Foreign Affairs* 81 (May/June 2002): 134.

12. Ibid., 131.

13. Philip Ross, "Terror and Its Antidote," *Acumen Journal of Life Sciences* 1 (2003): 61, 65.

14. Graham T. Allison et al., *Avoiding Nuclear Anarchy: Containing the Threat of Loose Russian Nuclear Weapons and Fissile Material* (Cambridge, Mass.: Center for Science and International Affairs, 1996), 20–48.

15. See Anthony H. Cordesman, "The Changing Face of Terrorism and Technology, and the Challenge of Asymmetric Warfare," testimony to the Senate Judiciary Subcommittee on Technology, Terrorism, and Government Information (27 March 2001), http://judiciary.senate.gov/oldsite/te032701ac.htm (accessed December 1, 2006).

16. Bobbitt, *Shield of Achilles*, 812. See also Kingsley Amis, "The Last War," in *The Oxford Book of Contemporary Verse 1945–1980*, ed. D. J. Enright (Oxford: Oxford University Press, 1980), 138–39.

17. Stephen Flynn, "The Best Defense," interview, *Conference Board Review* (May–June 2007): 43.

18. Stephen Flynn, *America the Vulnerable: How Our Government Is Failing to Protect Us from Terrorism* (New York: HarperCollins, 2004), 166; see also Center for Strategic and International Studies, Global Organized Crime Project, *Cybercrime, Cyberterrorism, Cyberwarfare: Averting an Electronic Waterloo* (Washington, D.C.: CSIS Press, 1998), 48–62.

19. Flynn, *America the Vulnerable*, 160. See also Brian Jenkins, "True Grit," 16: "Public education is the first step toward strengthening ourselves. We need to aggressively educate the public through all media. . . . This means more than speeches in front of the American flag. The basic course should include how to deal with the spectrum of threats we face, from 'dirty bombs' to natural epidemics. . . . [K]nowing what to do and having an assigned task in preparation, planning, and response not only increases preparedness but also reduces stress" (including the stress on the body politic).

20. Flynn, *America the Vulnerable*, 170.

21. The magnitude of an earthquake is expressed by a logarithmic scale that measures the amplitude of the seismic waves. A recording of 7 thus indicates a jolt with ground motion ten times as large as a recording of 6. Earthquakes that measure between 6 and 8 on the Richter scale are considered "major" quakes; magnitudes of 8 or greater are "great" earthquakes. The 1906 earthquake that devastated San Francisco measured 8.25 on the Richter scale.

22. Lachlan Forrow et al., "Accidental Nuclear War—A Post–Cold War Assessment," *The New England Journal of Medicine* 338 (1998), 1326–32.

23. Ibid.

24. Ibid.

25. Secretary of Energy Advisory Board, Russia Task Force, *A Report Card on the Department of Energy's Nonproliferation Programs with Russia* (10 January 2001), iv; http://www.seab.energy.gov/publications/rusrpt.pdf (accessed December 1, 2006).

26. See the excellent essay by the Carl Schmitt scholar William E. Scheuerman, "Emergency Powers and the Rule of Law After 9/11," *Journal of Political Philosophy* 14 (2006), 61–84.

27. Ibid., 75–76 (citing Clinton L. Rossiter, "Constitutional Dictatorship in the Atomic Age," *The Review of Politics* 11 [1949]: 395–418).

28. See Lon L. Fuller, *The Morality of Law* (New Haven, Conn.: Yale University Press, 1964).

29. For example, Ackerman proposes short-term detentions without trial or arrest warrants based on probable cause.

30. This insightful phrase is Scheuerman's. See Scheuerman, "Emergency Powers and the Rule of Law After 9/11," 65. See also Fallon, "Legitimacy and the Constitution," *Harvard Law Review* 118 (2005).

31. Bruce Ackerman, *Before the Next Attack: Preserving Civil Liberties in an Age of Terrorism* (New Haven, Conn.: Yale University Press, 2006), 167.

32. "Only where elected political institutions (e.g., the executive and legislature) can act flexibly in response to a crisis but are subsequently reined in by case-oriented judicial decision makers, serving as the chief defenders of fundamental liberal legal values, can we achieve both effective emergency action and sufficient protections against its potential excesses." Scheuerman, "Emergency Powers and the Rule of Law After 9/11," 77–78. See also Laurence H. Tribe and Patrick O. Gudridge, "The Anti-Emergency Constitution," *Yale Law Journal* 113 (2004): 1801–70.

33. David Dyzenhaus, "Humpty Dumpty Rules or the Rule of Law: Legal Theory and the Adjudication of National Security," *Australian Journal of Legal Philosophy* 28 (2003): 13. See also David Dyzenhaus, "The Permanence of the Temporary: Can Emergency Powers Be Normalized?" in *The Security of Freedom: Essays on Canada's Anti-Terrorism Bill*, ed. Ronald Daniels et al. (Toronto: University of Toronto Press, 2001).

34. See David Cole, "The Priority of Morality: The Emergency Constitution's Blind Spot," *Yale Law Journal* 113 (2004): 1753–1800. See also David Cole, "Judging the Next Emergency: Judicial Review and Individual Rights in Times of Crisis," *Michigan Law Review* 101 (2003): 2565–95.

35. But see *Ex parte Quirin*, 317 U.S. 1 (1942), in which the Supreme Court, on expedited review, validated the trial by military commission of eight recently captured Nazi saboteurs, and *Youngstown Sheet & Tube Co. v. Sawyer*, 343 U.S. 579 (1952), in which the Court granted review as early as the preliminary injunction stage and held that President Truman's executive order seizing private steel mills for the Korean War effort was unconstitutional.

36. But see *Bush v. Gore*, 531 U.S. 98 (2000), in which the Supreme Court held that the manual recount of votes ordered by the Florida Supreme Court did not satisfy equal protection requirements, but indicated rather shamelessly that its rationale applied to that case only and would not be used as precedent in the future.

37. But see *Home Building & Loan Association v. Blaisdell*, 290 U.S. 398 (1934), in which the Court held that Minnesota's mortgage moratorium law did not violate the Contract Clause in light of the economic crisis caused by the Great Depression.

38. With the exception of classified FISA court orders and opinions. The court has indicated a willingness to publish unclassified decisions, although it has done so only on a few occasions. See Letter from Judge Colleen Kollar-Kotelly to Senators Leahy, Specter, and Grassley, 20 August 2002, available at http://www.fas.org/irp/agency/doj/fisa/fisco82002.html (accessed March 30, 2007).

39. As Scheuerman concluded after a survey of the literature on the emergency constitution, "few bother to ask whether executive power, in its present form, is sufficiently attuned to emergency management." Scheuerman, "Emergency Powers and the Rule of Law After 9/11," 79.

40. Bruce Ackerman, "Terrorism and Civil Liberties," *Yale Alumni Magazine* (March–April 2006), http://www.yalealumnimagazine.com/issues/2006_03/forum .html (accessed December 1, 2006).

41. See the recommendations in Susan Ginsburg, Independent Task Force on Immigration and America's Future, *Countering Terrorist Mobility: Shaping an Operational Strategy* (Washington, D.C.: Migration Policy Institute, 2006).

42. 18 U.S.C. § 1385.

43. "Whoever, except in cases and under circumstances expressly authorized by the Constitution or Act of Congress, willfully uses any part of the Army or the Air Force as a posse comitatus or otherwise to execute the laws shall be fined under this title or imprisoned not more than two years, or both." Ibid.

44. See 10 U.S.C. §§ 331–335.

45. See Robert T. Stafford Disaster Relief and Emergency Assistance Act, 42 U.S.C. § 5121 et seq., as amended by Pub. L. No. 106–390, 114 Stat. 1552 (2000).

46. See 6 U.S.C. § 466.

47. Craig T. Trebilcock, "The Myth of Posse Comitatus," *Journal of Homeland Security* (October 2000), http://www.homelandsecurity.org/journal/articles/Trebilcock.htm (accessed December 1, 2006).

48. The Continuity of Government Commission has suggested these alternatives: (1) When one-fourth of the members of Congress are killed or incapacitated, governors of each state would make temporary appointments to fill vacancies until special elections are held, or in the case of incapacitation until the member recovers or the term of office ends. (2) Each member of Congress should pick three to seven successors who would serve as temporary appointments after a catastrophic attack. If one-third of the members were killed or incapacitated, the first living person on the list of successors would serve as a temporary appointment until special elections could be held or in the case of incapacitation until the member recovers or the term of office ends. (3) Each member of Congress would name three to seven successors who could serve as temporary appointments after a catastrophic attack. If 40 percent of the states had lost at least one-third of their congressional delegations, then the governors of those states would select a temporary successor from each deceased or disabled congressman's list.

49. See Philip B. Heymann and Juliette N. Kayyem, *Protecting Liberty in an Age of Terror* (Cambridge, Mass.: MIT Press, 2005).

50. Daniel Gouré, "Homeland Security," in *Attacking Terrorism: Elements of a Grand Strategy*, ed. Audrey Kurth Cronin and James M. Ludes (Washington, D.C.: Georgetown University Press, 2004), 278–80.

51. "In general, terrorist acts that can cause the greatest potential damage should be the first priority for preventive efforts, even if the probability of such acts is low." Richard K. Betts, "How to Think About Terrorism," *Wilson Quarterly* 30 (Winter 2006): 47.

52. Representative Zoe Lofgren, quoted in Editorial, "Virtually Unprotected," *New York Times*, 2 June 2005, A24.

53. Tenner, *Why Things Bite Back*, 277.

CHAPTER NINE: The Illusion
of an American Strategic Doctrine

1. John Quincy Adams, *Memoirs of John Quincy Adams: Comprising Portions of His Diary from 1795 to 1848*, vol. 6, ed. Charles Francis Adams (Philadelphia: J. B. Lippincott & Co., 1874), 163.

2. Richard Rush to John Quincy Adams, 19 August 1823, in vol. 6 of *A Digest of International Law*, ed. John Bassett Moore (Washington, D.C.: Government Printing Office, 1906), 386.

3. Ibid.

4. Richard Rush to John Quincy Adams, 19 September 1823, in vol. 6 of *The Writings of James Monroe*, ed. Stanislaus Murray Hamilton (New York: G. P. Putnam's Sons, 1902), 379.

5. James Monroe, "Seventh Annual Message," in vol. 2 of *A Compilation of the Messages and Papers of the Presidents 1789–1897*, ed. James. D. Richardson (Washington, D.C.: Government Printing Office, 1896), 218.

6. Ibid.

7. Ibid.

8. Contrast this doctrine, for example, with the sentiments Adams expressed in a letter to his father a decade before: "The whole continent of North America appears to be destined by Divine Providence to be peopled by one *nation*, speaking one language, professing one general system of religious and political principles, and accustomed to one general tenor of social usages and customs. For the common happiness of them all, for their peace and prosperity, I believe it is indispensable that they should be associated in one federal union."

   But see Walter McDougall, *Promised Land, Crusader State: The American Encounter with the World Since 1776* (New York: Houghton Mifflin, 1997), 73–74, 78, which quotes this passage in support of the conclusion that the frankly imperial doctrine of "manifest destiny" was a corollary of the Monroe Doctrine because the latter required the former (i.e., the U.S. had to occupy the North American continent to prevent European powers from doing so). See also Albert K. Weinberg, *Manifest Destiny: A Study of Nationalist Expansionism in American History* (Baltimore: Johns Hopkins University Press, 1935), 109. It should be noted, however, that Adams's letter (and many other similar expressions among the founders) comes quite a bit ahead of the Monroe Doctrine, and, also, that the word "nation" in the quoted passage refers not to the State, but to an ethno-linguistic group.

9. In 1899, U.S. Secretary of State John Hay addressed diplomatic notes to several great powers (the U.K., France, Germany, Russia, Italy, and Japan) that enjoyed commercial privileges with China and controlled various spheres of interest there. These notes asked the powers formally to guarantee Chinese territorial integrity and to declare that each would keep open to all states the trading ports they possessed by virtue of treaties with China. Although no country agreed to offer such assurances, replying only that each one would have to wait upon the agreement of the others, in March 1900 Hay announced that the U.S. request had been agreed to. This program regarding China and its international trade was known as the Open Door Policy.

10. Also known as the Pact of Paris, this treaty provided for "the renunciation of war as an instrument of national policy." It was the consequence of a French proposal by the French foreign minister, Aristide Briand, of a bilateral Franco-American treaty renouncing war between the two states. The U.S. secretary of state, Frank Kellogg, responded with a proposal for a multilateral treaty. On August 27, 1928, the treaty was signed by eleven states. Eventually sixty-two countries signed the pact.

11. Melvin R. Laird, "Iraq: Learning the Lessons of Vietnam," *Foreign Affairs* 84, no. 6 (November/December 2005): 25–26.

12. *The National Security Strategy of the United States of America* (2002), 6, 14, 15.

13. George W. Bush, "Remarks by the President at the 20th Anniversary of the National Endowment for Democracy," United States Chamber of Commerce, Washington,

D.C., 6 November 2003. The full text of the speech is available at http://www.white house.gov/news/releases/2003/11/20031106–2.html.

14. Adam Roberts, "Law and the Use of Force After Iraq," *Survival* 45, no. 2 (Summer 2003): 46.

15. Francis Fukuyama, however, has argued that "it was never clear that a rogue state— which (unlike stateless terrorists) has a return address—would go to all the trouble of developing nuclear weapons only to give them to a terrorist organization." Francis Fukuyama in "Defending and Advancing Freedom: A Symposium," *Commentary* 120, no. 4 (November 2005): 29. The A. Q. Khan network, which apparently included nuclear technology developed by North Korea, China, and Pakistan, may cast some doubt on this assertion, as discussed in chapter 2.

16. Daniel Webster to Lord Ashburton, 6 August 1842, in vol. 2 of *A Digest of International Law*, ed. John Bassett Moore (Washington, D.C., 1906), 409 (quoting a letter of 24 April 1841 from Daniel Webster to Henry Fox). But see Timothy Kearley, "Raising the Caroline," *Wisconsin International Law Journal* 17 (Summer 1999).

17. Hugh Beach, "The Concept of 'Preventative War'—Old Wine in a New Wineskin," *Contemporary Essays*, Occasional Paper no. 47 (Camberley, U.K.: Strategic and Combat Studies Institute, 2004): 65.

18. Ruth Wedgewood in "Defending and Advancing Freedom: A Symposium," *Commentary* 120, no. 4 (November 2005): 40.

19. Ibid.

20. Paul Berman in "Defending and Advancing Freedom: A Symposium," *Commentary* 120, no. 4 (November 2005): 22.

21. Josef Joffe in "Defending and Advancing Freedom: A Symposium," *Commentary* 120, no. 4 (November 2005): 64. "Abdullahs" refers to the king of Jordan; "Hosnis" to the president of Egypt.

22. See Pew Global Attitudes Project, *American Character Gets Mixed Reviews: U.S. Image Up Slightly, but Still Negative* (Washington, D.C.: Pew Research Center, 2005). The full text of the Pew Report is available at http://pewglobal.org/reports/pdf/ 247.pdf. In a recent election in Lebanon where candidates identified with the U.S. encountered unexpected difficulties, "voters joined the Palestinians who voted for Hamas; the Iraqis who voted for a government sympathetic to Iran; and the Egyptians who have voted in growing numbers for the Islamist Muslim Brotherhood. 'No politician can afford to identify with the West because poll after poll shows people don't believe in the U.S. agenda.' " Hassan M. Fattah, "U.S. Backs Free Elections, Only to See Allies Lose," *New York Times*, 10 August 2007, http://www.nytimes.com/2007/08/ 10/world/middleeast/10arab.html (accessed October 31, 2007).

23. "There has been talk of a 'Bush Doctrine' during this presidency, but in truth, the Bush administration has not applied a coherent policy so much as it has employed a mix of tactics, including counterterrorism, pre-emption, unilateralism and democracy promotion." Richard Haass, "Is There a Doctrine in the House?" *New York Times*, 8 November 2005, A27.

24. "Convention on International Civil Aviation," 7 December 1944, *United Nations Treaty Series* 15, no. 102 (1948).

25. "Convention on Rights and Duties of States," 26 December 1933, *League of Nations Treaty Series* 165, no. 3802 (1936), art. 1, p. 25.

26. See, e.g., Herbert Wechsler, "Toward Neutral Principles of Constitutional Law," *Harvard Law Review* 73 (November 1959). In the present context, see Curtis A. Bradley and Jack L. Goldsmith, "Congressional Authorization and the War on Terrorism," *Harvard Law Review* 118 (2005); Ryan Goodman and Derek Jinks, "Inter-

national Law, U.S. War Powers, and the Global War on Terrorism," *Harvard Law Review* 118 (2005); Cass R. Sunstein, "Administrative Law Goes to War," *Harvard Law Review* 118 (2005); Mark Tushnet, "Controlling Executive Power in the War on Terrorism," *Harvard Law Review* 118 (2005); and see Bradley and Goldsmith's rejoinder, "The War on Terrorism: International Law, Clear Statement Requirements, and Constitutional Design," *Harvard Law Review* 118 (2005).

27. On "gesture politics," see Christopher Caldwell, "The Triumph of Gesture Politics," *New York Times Magazine*, 23 January 2005, 11, and Richard Sennett, *The Fall of Public Man* (New York: Knopf, 1977). Caldwell points out that, when Tony Blair did not cut short his vacation at the time of the tsunami, the *Independent* in a self-revealing lead editorial wrote that "Blair has failed to grasp the essence of leadership." Caldwell, "Triumph of Gesture Politics," 11.

28. Haass, "Is There a Doctrine in the House?" A27. For the current period, Haass has proposed a new doctrine, "Integration": "Based on a shared approach to common challenges, [integration] means that we cooperate with other world powers to build effective international arrangements and to take collective actions. And those relationships would be expanded to include other countries, organizations and peoples, so that they too can come to enjoy the benefits of physical security, economic opportunity and political freedom. [W]e should offer rogue states the advantages of integration into the global economy in exchange for fundamentally changing their ways."

The problem with Haass's proposal, despite the fact that it enfolds many of the policies endorsed in the present work—organizing global efforts to defeat AIDS, preparing for an epidemic of avian flu, offering a realistic alternative to the Kyoto Treaty to combat climate change, and leading a diplomatic and legal offensive in support of the principle that governments that support genocide or terrorism forfeit their sovereignty—is that it has no teleology. What is the animating purpose of such a doctrine? Containment was meant to defeat communism. It resembles the proposals for a "liberal European empire" associated with the admirable diplomat Robert Cooper, and like them Haass's offer to include other states in a system that their publics deplore is a self-limiting one. The purpose—to increase European influence, or to sustain American hegemony—is not synchronized with the means that will be required for achievement of that purpose, namely, the allegiance of the world community.

29. Tony Blair, "Clash About Civilisations," London, 21 March 2006. The full speech is available at http://www.pm.gov.uk/output/Page9224.asp.

30. Tony Blair, Speech at the Labour Party Conference, 2 October 2001. The full text of the speech is available at http://politics.guardian.co.uk/labourconference2001/story/0,1220,561985,00.html.

31. Tony Blair, "Doctrine of the International Community," Economic Club, Chicago, 24 April 1999. The full text of the speech is available at http://www.pm.gov.uk/output/Page1297.asp.

32. "The United States has built institutions, which is another word for 'public goods.'... The genius of American diplomacy in the second half of this century was building institutions that would advance American interests by serving others. Who can count the acronyms made in the U.S.A.—from NATO to GATT, from the OECD to the PFP?" Josef Joffe, "How America Does It," *Foreign Affairs* 76, no. 5 (September/October 1997): 26–27.

33. See Bobbitt, "Colonel House and a World Made of Law," chapter 14 of *Shield of Achilles*, 367–410.

34. Fred N. Kaplan, *Wizards of Armageddon* (New York: Simon & Schuster, 1983). See

also Philip Bobbitt et al., ed., *US Nuclear Strategy: A Reader* (New York: New York University Press, 1989).

35. Berman, "Defending and Advancing Freedom," 23.

36. "London Bomber Video: Full Statement," *Times Online* (London), 2 September 2005, http://www.timesonline.co.uk/article/0,,22989–1762124,00.html. The video, which was first aired by al Jazeera, is a recording of Mohammed Sidique Khan's explanation of the motivation for the 7 July 2005 London bombings.

37. Ibid.

38. Indeed, many persons in Iraq believe that the U.S. has covertly incited the sectarian killings and insurgent bombings as a way of dividing Iraqi national sentiment.

39. General Petraeus's plan to "surge" forces into designated areas such as Baghdad is an example of such a plan.

40. See also Daniel Cohen, *Globalization and Its Enemies* (Cambridge, Mass.: MIT Press, 2006), arguing that poorer "countries have been hurt far more by exclusion than by exploitation," and critic Edward Binkowski's "Knowing I Loved My Books," vol. 18, nos. 1 & 2, 27 December 2006 (e-mail newsletter on file with author).

41. Bearing in mind of course that interventions are not necessarily military, or if military in nature, are not confined to the use of force.

42. George Monbiot, "A Charter to Intervene," *Guardian*, 23 March 2004, 21.

43. Niall Ferguson, *Colossus: The Rise and Fall of the American Empire* (New York: Penguin Books, 2004), 237.

44. Ibid., 238.

45. Ibid.

46. Ibid., 297; see also Andrew Moravcsik, "Repairing the Western Alliance," *Foreign Affairs* 82 (July/August 2003); Robert Hunter, "America Needs Europe, to Win Peace in Iraq," *Financial Times*, 21 July 2003, 17.

47. Stephen Walt, quoted in "Panel 2: The Strategic Environment," *Fletcher Forum of World Affairs* 29, no. 3 (Special Edition 2005): 58–59. I have selected these comments by Stephen Walt because they are especially lucid presentations of widely held views.

48. Nor was the entry into the war justifiable as a reprisal for U-boat attacks on U.S. shipping. If anything, the attacks on U.S. and U.K. aircraft by Iraq were a more familiar cause of war.

49. Walt, quoted in "Panel 2: The Strategic Environment," 61.

50. Ibid., 60.

51. Ibid., 61.

52. See United Nations High Commissioner for Refugees, "Afghan Repatriation from Pakistan tops 50,000 for 2006," UNHCR Briefing Notes, 16 May 2006, http://www.unhcr.org/news/NEWS/4469a3474.html.

53. Walt, quoted in "Panel 2: The Strategic Environment," 63.

CHAPTER TEN: *Mise-en-Scène:* The Properties of Sovereignty

1. Department of State, "Charter of the United Nations," 26 June 1945, *Treaties and Other International Agreements of the United States of America, 1776–1949*, vol. 3, pt. 1 (1969), art. 2(4), p. 1155.

2. Ibid., art. 51, p. 1165.

3. Of course, a state may limit its behavior in this respect by joining an arms control convention or treaty regime, but its sovereignty will still permit it to withdraw from such restraints should it choose to do so. Similarly, a state may lawfully train soldiers

who subsequently plan to take up arms under another state's flag and fear no lawful intervention so long as it is not launching attacks from its own soil. Finally, a state may decide what constitutional rights to accord to its citizens.

4. The United Nations Security Council unanimously passed a resolution following the Osirak attack that "[s]trongly condemn[ed] the military attack by Israel [as being] in clear violation of the Charter of the United Nations and the norms of international conduct." The resolution also "[f]ully recognize[d] the inalienable sovereign right of Iraq, and all other States, especially the developing countries, to establish programmes of technological and nuclear development to develop their economy and industry for peaceful purposes in accordance with their present and future needs and consistent with the internationally accepted objectives of preventing nuclear weapons proliferation." United Nations Security Council Resolution 487, 19 June 1981 (2288th meeting).

5. AtlanticBlog, 21 February 2004, http://www.atlanticblog.com/archives/2004_02.html (accessed June 24, 2007).

6. Compare French intervention in Chad and the Comoros, British intervention in Sierra Leone, U.S. intervention in Liberia, and African Union intervention in Burundi, which took place with and without specific authorizing resolutions.

7. Rosa Ehrenreich Brooks, "War Everywhere: Rights, National Security Law, and the Law of Armed Conflict in the Age of Terror," *University of Pennsylvania Law Review* 153 (December 2004): 677.

8. See generally David Wippman and Matthew Evangelista, ed., *New Wars, New Laws?: Applying the Laws of War in 21st Century Conflicts* (Ardsley, N.Y.: Transnational, 2005).

9. "The paradigmatic 'conflict' envisioned by the drafters of the Hague and Geneva Conventions was a war between sovereign nation states, in which well-organized regular armies fought each other on reasonably clearly defined battlefields. . . . Al Qaeda knows no borders, and its operatives wear no uniforms, operating by stealth more often than they operate openly." Brooks, "War Everywhere," 706, 710.

10. Owing to inappropriate evidentiary rules, the need to protect the sources and methods of intelligence collection, lack of jurisdiction over crimes committed in other states, and the requirement that a crime actually be committed or be about to be committed before detention and prosecution can take place.

11. Richard Bernstein, "Germans Free Moroccan Convicted of a 9/11 Role," *New York Times*, 8 April 2004, A18; Desmond Butler, "German Judge Frees Qaeda Suspect; Cites U.S. Secrecy," *New York Times*, 12 December 2003, A3.

12. William K. Lietzau, "International Criminal Law After Rome: Concerns from a U.S. Military Perspective," *Law & Contemporary Problems* 64, no. 1 (Winter 2001): 126–27. See, for example, the investigation conducted by Swiss senator Dick Marty into alleged secret CIA prisons in Europe. Dick Marty, Committee on Legal Affairs and Human Rights, *Alleged Secret Detentions and Unlawful Inter-state Transfers of Detainees Involving Council of Europe Member States* (Council of Europe, 2006), http://assembly.coe.int/Documents/WorkingDocs/doc06/edoc10957.pdf (accessed November 5, 2006).

13. Brooks, "War Everywhere," 677–78.

14. Harold H. Koh, "A World Transformed," *Yale Journal of International Law* 20, no. 2 (Summer 1995): x.

15. For an account of the development of international law through the periods of the modern state (princely, kingly, territorial, imperial, nation state), see Bobbitt, "States of Peace," book 2 in *Shield of Achilles*.

16. I am indebted to my colleague John Witt for this observation.
17. Harold Koh puts it well: "Following World War II, the architects of the postwar . . .
    system posited [a] complex positive law framework of charters, treaties, and formal
    agreements, [an] intensely regulatory, global framework. . . ." Quoted in Bobbitt,
    Shield of Achilles, 640.
18. Bobbitt, *Democracy and Deterrence*, 9–13.
19. See ibid. The connection, once rarely made but now widely accepted, is that by provid-
    ing nuclear deterrents for nonnuclear states, the substantial incentive for these states—
    for example, Germany and Japan—to acquire their own nuclear weapons is reduced.
20. See generally Graham Allison, *Nuclear Terrorism: The Ultimate Preventable Cata-
    strophe* (New York: Times Books, 2004).
21. S. F. C. Milsom, *Historical Foundations of the Common Law* (London: Butter-
    worths, 1969), xi.
22. Grant Gilmore, *The Ages of American Law* (New Haven, Conn.: Yale University
    Press, 1977), 5.
23. Compare Anthony Dworkin, "Revising the Laws of War to Account for Terrorism:
    The Case Against Updating the Geneva Conventions, on the Ground That Changes
    Are Likely Only to Damage Human Rights," *Findlaw's Writ*, 4 February 2003,
    http://writ.news.findlaw.com/commentary/20030204_dworkin.html (accessed
    November 3, 2006).
24. Theodore F. T. Plucknett, *A Concise History of the Common Law*, 5th ed. (Boston:
    Little, Brown, 1956), 283.
25. Zipporah Wiseman, "The Limits of Vision: Karl Llewellyn and the Merchant Rules,"
    Harvard Law Review 100 (January 1987): 513 n. 218; see also C. H. S. Fifoot, *Lord
    Mansfield* (Oxford: Clarendon Press, 1936), 115–17.
26. Two examples will partly explain why.

    In *Miller v. Race*, 97 Eng. Rep. 398 (K.B. 1758), a man had sent via the post a
    banknote that, along with other mail, was stolen in a robbery. The banknote subse-
    quently came by innocent means into the hands of the plaintiff, who sued the hapless
    victim for the value of the note. The defendant argued that the plaintiff may have had
    a right to the note—he had paid for it—but he had no right to the money, which had
    in effect been stolen. If it had been a stolen watch or a work of art, the true owner
    could have recovered it. Mansfield promptly decided in favor of the plaintiff (the
    judge "had no sort of doubt") on the ground that the consequences to trade and com-
    merce would "be much incommoded by a contrary determination." To see Mans-
    field's point, suppose that the dollars or pound notes in your purse suddenly became
    valueless because, at one time, they had passed through the hands of a thief.

    In *Pillans and Rose v. Van Mierop and Hopkins*, 97 Eng. Rep. 1035 (K.B. 1765),
    a London bank agreed to honor a draft for an Irish client, drawn on a Rotterdam
    bank. Before the draft was presented, the Irish merchant became insolvent. The Lon-
    don bank refused to pay. These facts implicated the common law doctrine of "con-
    sideration," the idea that a promise is only binding when it is given for something.
    This doctrine, which had been in English case law for more than two centuries, was
    abruptly dismissed by Mansfield, at least "in commercial cases among merchants"
    where the promise had been made in writing. His rationale was entirely pragmatic:
    bankers knew what they were getting into when they wrote letters to each other
    promising to honor drafts, and the system of which they were the beneficiaries could
    scarcely function without the enforcement of such commitments. One of Mansfield's
    colleagues on the bench concurred, observing that "[m]any of the old cases are
    strange and absurd: so also are some of the modern ones." This led Grant Gilmore to

note dryly that "[i]n Lord Mansfield's court the judges were not true Blackstone believers." Gilmore, *Ages of American Law*, 7.

27. Wiseman, "The Limits of Vision," 513 n. 218.

28. Gilmore, *Ages of American Law*, 114.

29. See chapters 5 and 6.

30. See Robert Cooper's excellent discussion of this inflammatory term in *The Breaking of Nations*.

31. Ronald J. Mann, "Searching for Negotiability in Payment and Credit Systems," *UCLA Law Review* 44 (April 1997): 956–62.

32. Michael J. Glennon, "Why the Security Council Failed," *Foreign Affairs* 82, no. 3 (May/June 2003): 31.

33. As previously noted, combatants qualify for the protections accorded prisoners of war only if they are commanded by someone who is responsible for their acts; bear distinctive insignia; openly carry arms; and follow the "laws and customs of war." "Geneva Convention Relative to the Treatment of Prisoners of War," 12 August 1949, *United Nations Treaty Series* 75, no. 972 (1950), art. 4, p. 138.

34. Anthony Dworkin, "Military Necessity and Due Process: The Place of Human Rights in the War on Terror," in Wippman and Evangelista, *New Wars, New Laws?*, 55.

35. See Donald Rumsfeld, "Status of Taliban and al Qaida," Memorandum for Chairman of the Joint Chiefs of Staff, 19 January 2002. The full text of the memorandum is available at http://www.defenselink.mil/news/Jun2004/d20040622doc1.pdf.

36. Though not all ICRC officials took such an absurd position: Paul Grossreider, the director general of the ICRC, acknowledged that "with the September 11 terrorist attacks, the nature of war is changing. . . . With al Qaeda, we face an emerging new type of belligerent, which are the transnational networks. To cope with this change, [international law] must adapt itself for fear of being marginalized." Interview with Paul Grossreider, *Le Temps* (Geneva), 29 January 2002; but see the official position of the ICRC, *International Humanitarian Law and the Challenges of Contemporary Armed Conflicts*, report prepared by the International Conference of the Red Cross and Red Crescent, September 2003.

37. William K. Lietzau, "Combating Terrorism: The Consequences of Moving from Law Enforcement to War," in Wippman and Evangelista, *New Wars, New Laws?*, 43–44.

38. 126 S. Ct. 2749 (2006).

39. Kenneth Anderson, "Hamdan and Common Article Three's Obligations upon Non-state Actors," *Kenneth Anderson's Law of War and Just War Theory Blog*, 13 July 2006, http://kennethandersonlawofwar.blogspot.com/2006/07/hamdan-and-common-article-threes.html.

40. Dan Philpott, "Sovereignty," *Stanford Encyclopedia of Philosophy*, ed. Edward N. Zalta (Summer 2003), http://plato.stanford.edu/archives/sum2003/entries/sovereignty/ (quoting R. P. Wolff, *The Conflict Between Authority and Autonomy* [Oxford: Basil Blackwell, 1990], 20).

41. Ibid.

42. Ibid.

43. See the discussion of the Cherokee cases in Bobbitt, *Constitutional Fate*, 108–19.

44. These observations are drawn from the work of David C. Williams, including "Legitimation and Statutory Interpretation: Conquest, Consent, and Community in Federal Indian Law," *Virginia Law Review* 80 (1994): 403; and "The Borders of the Equal Protection Clause: Indians as Peoples," *UCLA Law Review* 38 (1991): 759.

45. See, e.g., *R v. Secretary of State for Transport ex parte Factortame* (No. 2), [1991] 1

AC 603, I ALL E.R. 70. See generally Neil MacCormick, "Beyond the Sovereign State," Chorley Lecture, no. 21, London School of Economics, 3 June 1992.

46. Comfortable, that is, jurisprudentially.

47. Intervention in Kosovo was subsequently accepted by the U.N. and thus may be an example of translucent rather than transparent sovereignty.

48. That had ratified the Kosovo intervention when the U.N. Security Council did not act.

49. See, e.g., United Nations Security Council Resolution 1483, 22 May 2003 (4761st meeting); United Nations Security Council Resolution 1511, 16 October 2003 (4844th meeting); United Nations Security Council Resolution 1546, 8 June 2004 (4987th meeting); see also Mahmoud Hmoud, "The Use of Force Against Iraq: Occupation and Security Council Resolution 1483," *Cornell International Law Journal* 36, no. 3 (2004): 448 ("Resolution 1483 gave the Coalition the mandate to occupy Iraq and recognize the occupant's authority as provided for in the Resolution. It transformed the occupation from a belligerent one to a legal one, and created a special occupation regime that is controlled by the occupying power"); David J. Scheffer, "Agora (Continued): Future Implications of the Iraq Conflict," *American Journal of International Law* 97 (October 2003): 844–47 ("But Resolution 1483 established an unprecedented basis for American and British occupation of Iraq. . . . The two occupying powers were thus designated to shoulder primary responsibility").

50. United Nations Security Council Resolution 1244, 10 June 1999 (4011th meeting).

51. Richard Haass quoted in Nicholas Lemann, "The Next World Order," *The New Yorker*, 1 April 2002, 42.

52. Compare James Turner Johnson's explanation of the classical Christian understanding where "the rights of sovereignty are linked to its obligations" and, therefore, sovereignty "was an essentially moral construct." *The War to Oust Saddam Hussein: Just War and the New Face of Conflict* (Lanham, Md.: Rowman & Littlefield, 2005), 62.

53. The former British prime minister Tony Blair would, I think, also hold a transparent view of sovereignty, even if the British Foreign Office inclines toward a translucent approach.

54. W. Michael Reisman, "Sovereignty and Human Rights in Contemporary International Law," *American Journal of International Law* 84 (October 1990): 872.

55. Ibid., 871.

56. See chapter 2.

57. Lee Feinstein and Anne-Marie Slaughter, "A Duty to Prevent," *Foreign Affairs* 83 (January/February 2004). Note that this essay did not discuss the vulnerability of critical infrastructure.

58. See Gareth Evans and Mohamed Sahnoun, "The Responsibility to Protect," *Foreign Affairs* 81 (November/December 2002).

59. Kofi Annan, "Secretary-General's Address to the General Assembly," United Nations, New York, 23 September 2003. The full text of the speech is available at http://www.un.org/webcast/ga/58/statements/sg2eng030923.

60. Secretary-General's High-Level Panel on Threats, Challenges and Change, *A More Secure World: Our Shared Responsibility*, UN Doc. A/59/565, December 2004. The full text of the report is available at http://www.un.org/secureworld/ (accessed November 4, 2006).

61. United Nations General Assembly, "2005 World Summit Outcome," UN Doc. A/Res/60/1, 16 September 2005, paragraph 139, p. 30. The full text of the resolution is available at http://www.un.org/Depts/dpa/prev_genocide/outcome.pdf?OpenElement.

62. Gareth Evans and Mohamed Sahnoun, International Commission on Intervention

and State Sovereignty, *The Responsibility to Protect* (Ottawa: International Development Research Centre, 2001), xi. The full text of the report is available at http://www.iciss.ca/pdf/Commission-Report.pdf.

63. Feinstein and Slaughter, "Duty to Prevent," 141–42.

64. Ibid., 142.

65. Ibid., 143.

66. For a brilliant analysis of this history, see Francis J. Gavin, "Blasts from the Past: Proliferation Lessons from the 1960s," *International Security* (Winter 2004/05).

67. This figure is postulated by Richard Garwin as an estimate of the number killed in a single attack by terrorists using weapons of mass destruction. Andrew Hendel, "Scientist Claims Arms Reduction Is Best Defense," *Stanford Daily*, 10 March 2004.

68. For example, after Libya agreed to suspend its WMD program, it was discovered that Libya had purchased or received a large quantity of uranium hexafluoride. Initial reports point to North Korea as the likely source, although the A. Q. Khan network may also have been involved. See David E. Sanger and William J. Broad, "Using Clues from Libya to Study a Nuclear Mystery," *New York Times*, 31 March 2005, A12.

69. Osama bin Laden has stated that acquiring nuclear weapons is a "religious duty." David Stout, "Bin Laden Denies Role in Embassy Bombings," *New York Times*, 25 December 1998, A7. The International Atomic Energy Agency has concluded that al Qaeda is "actively seeking" an atomic bomb. Testimony by Jamal Ahmad al-Fadl, a former bin Laden associate, in the trial of those convicted in the 1993 World Trade Center bombing, recounted his extensive but unsuccessful efforts to acquire enriched uranium for al Qaeda. Dennis Overbye and James Glanz, "A Nation Challenged: Nuclear Fears; Pakistani Atomic Expert, Arrested Last Week, Had Strong Pro-Taliban Views," *New York Times*, 2 November 2001, B4.

70. James Randerson, "Revealed: The Lax Laws That Could Allow Assembly of Deadly Virus DNA: Urgent Calls for Regulation After Guardian Buys Part of Smallpox Genome Through Mail Order," *Guardian*, 14 June 2006, 1.

71. Ron Suskind, *The One Percent Doctrine: Deep Inside America's Pursuit of Its Enemies Since 9/11* (New York: Simon & Schuster, 2006), 62.

72. Cass R. Sunstein, *Laws of Fear: Beyond the Precautionary Principle* (The Seeley Lectures) (Cambridge: Cambridge University Press, 2005), 26–34; see also Robert W. Hahn and Cass R. Sunstein, "The Precautionary Principle as a Basis for Decision Making," *Economists' Voice* 2 (January 2005). One hears arguments of this kind often in the environmental context when demands are made for regulation to prevent undesirable consequences even where there is some scientific uncertainty regarding the potential damage and even when the costs of preventing a speculative effect are high: we should assume that the cause of species loss is carbon-based (even if this is at present uncertain), for example, because if we fail to halt this development, we will have forfeited the opportunity to forestall a truly terrible event.

73. Suskind, *One Percent Doctrine*, 62.

74. See Fred M. Kaplan, *The Wizards of Armageddon* (New York: Simon & Schuster, 1983).

75. It is hoped that the present work will be a step, even if a small one, toward a new theory analogous to the theories of strategic bombing and of nuclear deterrence that were themselves responses to the static warfare of World War I and the development of nuclear weapons in World War II.

76. Around the world, including the United States, laboratories working with deadly biological materials have insufficient security. For example, in 2002 researchers at the State University of New York made polio virus with pieces of DNA purchased

636   *Notes to Pages 477–480*

through the mail. See Rick Weiss, "Mail-Order Molecules Brew a Terrorism Debate; Virus Created in Lab Raises Questions of Scrutiny for DNA Suppliers," *Washington Post*, 17 July 2002, A1.

77. Sam Nunn, "Evian and Beyond: Priorities for the Global Partnership," speech launching the "Joint Declaration Strengthening the Global Partnership," Paris, 28 May 2003.

78. Seymour M. Hersh, "The Deal," *The New Yorker*, 8 March 2004, 36.

79. Ibid.

80. The G8 leaders seemed to understand these threats and committed $20 billion over ten years to establish the G8 Global Partnership Against the Spread of Weapons of Mass Destruction. James Gerstenzang, "Aid Promised for Nuclear Security," *Los Angeles Times*, 28 June 2002, A3. Risto Pentilla has written persuasively about this in an Adelphi Paper for the International Institute for Strategic Studies, *The Role of the G8 in International Peace and Security,* Adelphi Paper no. 355 (Oxford: Routledge, 2003). See also Bobbitt, *The Shield of Achilles,* 473–74.

81. John Murphy, "International Law and the War on Terrorism: The Road Ahead," in *International Law and the War on Terror*, vol. 79 of *International Legal Studies*, ed. Fred L. Borch and Paul S. Wilson (2003): 395–96.

82. "The Additional Protocol is a legal document granting the IAEA complementary inspection authority to that provided in underlying safeguards agreements. A principal aim is to enable the IAEA inspectorate to provide assurance about both declared and possible undeclared activities. Under the Protocol, the IAEA is granted expanded rights of access to information and sites, as well as additional authority to use the most advanced technologies during the verification process." International Atomic Energy Agency, "IAEA Safeguards Overview: Comprehensive Safeguards Agreements and Additional Protocols," http://www.iaea.org/Publications/Factsheets/English/sg_overview.html (accessed November 4, 2006).

83. Following a scenario exercise in Brussels that postulated an al Qaeda attack on NATO headquarters with a nuclear weapon, the Nuclear Threat Initiative proposed these measures (available at http://www.nti.org/c_press/release_nunnbrussels_050404.pdf):

• Launch a "Global Cleanout" of highly enriched uranium (HEU) at research facilities worldwide.
• Accelerate efforts to consolidate, secure, and eliminate the most dangerous materials, such as HEU and plutonium.
• Accelerate the consolidation of Russia's nuclear weapons stockpile.
• Expand efforts to employ former weapons scientists and personnel.
• Increase transparency and accelerate destruction of tactical nuclear weapons.
• Drastically increase and accelerate funding for chemical weapons destruction.
• Establish a truly global partnership to reduce the risk of weapons of mass destruction, specifically bioterrorism.
• Engage in biosafety/biosecurity confidence-building measures with Russia.
• Strengthen international nonproliferation regimes and work toward their universal implementation.
• Enhance and expand export controls.
• Build national and international capabilities for detecting and interdicting weapons of mass destruction.
• Establish international mechanisms for information sharing and crisis management.
• Improve counterterrorism measures, specifically by adding all countries to the inter-

national passport control database and beginning a regular pattern of antiterrorism exercises focused on missing material or missing weapons.

84. Indeed the Iraq Survey Group (ISG) concluded, after interviews with Iraqi scientists, that "senior Iraqis—several of them from the Regime's inner circle—told ISG they assumed Saddam would restart a nuclear program once UN sanctions ended." "Nuclear," in vol. 2 of *Comprehensive Report of the Special Advisor to the DCI on Iraq's WMD with Addendums*, 30 September 2004, 1. Also: "ISG judges that Iraq's actions between 1991 and 1996 demonstrate that the state intended to preserve its biological weapons capability and return to a steady, methodical progress toward a mature [biological weapons] program when and if the opportunity arose." "Biological Warfare," in vol. 3 of *Comprehensive Report of the Special Advisor*, 1.

85. The reader will immediately see that these proposals for the world community are meant to be parallel to the suggestions in chapter 9 that refer to the United States and its allies. It must be jarring to read such policy proposals in the midst of an essay that is supposed to be written as an effort in analysis. One way to justify this is to say that these programmatic suggestions act as a reality check on the analysis itself, but this is misleading because there will be many readers who accept the analysis but have no difficulty resisting my proposals. As with my earlier work, I want to make plain my own policy preferences and predispositions without claiming that my inferences as to the policies that flow from my analysis are dispositive. Rather, it is my objective to provide a realistic analytical framework that will inform my readers and critics even when we disagree as to the appropriate policies.

86. "But it is not enough to denounce unilateralism, unless we also face up squarely to the concerns that make some States feel uniquely vulnerable, since it is those concerns that drive them to take unilateral action. We must show that those concerns can, and will, be addressed effectively through collective action. [W]e have come to a fork in the road. This may be a moment no less decisive than 1945 itself, when the United Nations was founded. . . . Among those instruments, none is more important than the Security Council itself. In my recent report on the implementation of the Millennium Declaration, I drew attention to the urgent need for the Council to regain the confidence of States, and of world public opinion—both by demonstrating its ability to deal effectively with the most difficult issues, and by becoming more broadly representative of the international community as a whole, as well as the geopolitical realities of today." Kofi Annan, "The Secretary-General's Address to the General Assembly," United Nations, New York, 23 September 2003. The full text of the speech is available at http://www.un.org/webcast/ga/58/statements/sg2eng030923.

87. Kofi Annan, "As Secretary-General Prepares to Step Down, Five Lessons Learnt During Difficult but Exhilarating Decade," Truman Library, Independence, Mo., 11 December 2006. The full text of the speech is available at http://www.un.org/News/ossg/sg/stories/statments_full.asp?statID=40. "Against [the panoply of modern threats], no nation can make itself secure by seeking supremacy over all others. We all share responsibility for each other's security, and only by working to make each other secure can we hope to achieve lasting security for ourselves. . . . [A]ll Council members, and especially the major powers who are permanent members, must accept the special responsibility that comes with their privilege. The Security Council is not just another stage on which to act out national interests. It is the management committee, if you will, of our fledgling collective security system." Ibid.

88. Glennon, "Why the Security Council Failed," 25.

89. Ibid.

90. Ibid.

91. Ibid.

92. This is the opening of scene 5 in David Hare's *Stuff Happens*, a play about the American and British decisions to intervene in Iraq in 2003:

> An angry British journalist appears.
>
>   Journalist: Saddam Hussein attacked every one of his neighbours except Jordan. Imagine, if you will, if you are able, a dictator in Europe, murdering his own people, attacking his neighbours, killing half a million people for no other offence but proximity. Do you really then imagine, hand on heart, that the finer feelings of the international community, the exact procedures of the United Nations would need to be tested, would the finer point of sovereignty detain us, before we rose, as a single force, to overthrow the offender? Would we ask, faced with the bodies, faced with the gas, faced with the ditches and the murders, would we really stop to say, "Can we do this?"

93. I have chosen the name because C. Fred Bergsten and Caio Koch-Weser put it that way, and because it is suggested by the preexisting group, the G8. See C. Fred Bergsten and Caio Koch-Weser, "The G-2: A New Conceptual Basis and Operating Modality for Transatlantic Economic Relations," in *From Alliance to Coalitions: The Future of Transatlantic Relations*, ed. Werner Weidenfeld et al. (Bertelsmann Foundation, 2004), 237–49; C. Fred Bergsten and Caio Koch-Weser, "Restoring the Transatlantic Alliance," *Financial Times*, 6 October 2003, 19. Its purpose would be simply, in Bergsten and Koch-Weser's words, "to energize" broader groups in which the E.U. and the U.S. would consult with the varying countries that are most relevant to any particular issue in order to ensure that their views were fully taken into account in the G2's own decision making, and to give momentum to action. Although Bergsten and Koch-Weser are interested in a G2 for trade and economic leadership, its real contribution would be to galvanize the G8 in its new role as a supplementary forum for international peace and security.

94. Zbigniew Brzezinski, *Second Chance: Three Presidents and the Crisis of American Superpower* (New York: Basic Books, 2007), 188.

95. Bergsten and Koch-Weser, "The G-2," 238–39.

96. But see Richard H. Fallon, Jr., "Legitimacy and the Constitution," *Harvard Law Review* 118 (April 2005) and David Strauss, "Reply: Legitimacy and Obedience," *Harvard Law Review* 118 (April 2005), which seem to ignore sheer effectiveness as a ground for legitimacy (e.g., the discussion of the legitimacy of the Articles of Confederation).

CHAPTER ELEVEN: *Danse Macabre:*
Global Governance and Legitimacy

1. See George Monbiot, *The Age of Consent* (London: Flamingo, 2003).

2. See Anne-Marie Slaughter, *A New World Order* (Princeton, N.J.: Princeton University Press, 2004).

3. Rubenfeld, "Two World Orders," 26–27.

4. Michael Glennon makes this point well: "[T]he irrationality of treating states as equals was brought home as never before when it emerged that the will of the Secu-

rity Council could be determined by Angola, Guinea, or Cameroon—[states] whose representatives sat side by side and exercised an equal voice and vote with those of Spain, Pakistan, and Germany. . . . The upshot was a Security Council that reflected the real world's power structure with the accuracy of a fun-house mirror—and performed accordingly. Hence the . . . lesson of last winter: institutions cannot be expected to correct distortions that are embedded in their own structures." Glennon, "Why the Security Council Failed," 33.

5. See, e.g., Henry Kissinger, *Diplomacy* (New York: Simon & Schuster, 1994); John J. Mearsheimer, *The Tragedy of Great Power Politics* (New York: Norton, 2001); Hans J. Morgenthau, *Politics Among Nations*, 6th ed. (New York: Knopf, 1985); Stephen M. Walt, *The Origins of Alliances* (Ithaca, N.Y.: Cornell University Press, 1987). I am aware that some realists claim Thucydides and Machiavelli as forebears. This is not the place to dispute this claim, except possibly to note that it has always struck me as resembling the spurious "von" of the arriviste, or the portraits of someone else's ancestors on the walls of a recently purchased château.

6. "Although states have long been supportive of terrorist activity, we are now seeing an evolution from state sponsors with leverage over their terrorist 'clients' to international terrorist networks with increasing leverage over the associated states." See Audrey Kurth Cronin, "Is State Sponsorship an Outdated Concept?" unpublished paper cited in Audrey Kurth Cronin, "Rethinking Sovereignty: American Strategy in the Age of Terrorism," *Survival* 44, no. 2 (Summer 2002): 135; see also Steven Simon and Daniel Benjamin, "The Terror," *Survival* 43 (Winter 2001).

7. Bobbitt, "Postscript: The Indian Summer," in *Shield of Achilles*, 819–23; see also Peter Neumann, "Europe's Jihadist Dilemma," *Survival* 48 (Summer 2006).

8. Interestingly, perhaps the two most prominent realists authored a controversial paper arguing that the Israeli lobby had skewed U.S. foreign policy through the adroit manipulation of the domestic American political process, which would appear to accept this anti-realist conclusion. See John Mearsheimer and Steven Walt, "The Israeli Lobby," *London Review of Books* 28, no. 6 (23 March 2006). Their full paper is available at http://papers.ssrn.com/abstract=891198.

9. Glennon, "Why the Security Council Failed," 33.

10. See Brzezinski, *Second Chance*.

11. As Sir Michael Howard wrote, "An explicit American hegemony may appear preferable to the messy compromises of the existing order, but if it is nakedly based on commercial interests and military power it will lack all legitimacy. Terror will continue and, worse, widespread sympathy with terror. But American power placed at the service of an international community legitimised by representative institutions and the rule of law, accepting its constraints and inadequacies but continually working to improve them: that is a very different matter. It is by doing this that the U.S. has earned admiration, respect, and indeed affection throughout the world over the past half century. But if that relationship is to continue, and respect is to overcome hate, the U.S. must cease to think of itself as a heroic lone protagonist in a cosmic war against 'evil,' and reconcile itself to a less spectacular and more humdrum role: that of the leading participant in a flawed but still indispensable system of cooperative global governance." Michael Howard, "Smoke on the Horizon," *Financial Times*, 7–8 September 2002, 1.

12. As the distinguished historian Antony Beevor put it, "The new Constitution [for the European Union] also calls for a European foreign minister to direct a joint European foreign policy, and it wants to establish a common defense policy. This is a direct challenge to the primacy of NATO. It reflects the mainly French desire to re-

create Europe as a counterbalancing force to the United States, as opposed to the role of traditional ally." Antony Beevor, "Britain vs. the Eurocrats," *New York Times*, 10 May 2004, A21.

13. Michael Reisman, "Assessing Claims to Revise the Laws of War," *American Journal of International Law* 97 (January 2003): 85–86.

14. Lawrence Wright, "The Terror Web," *The New Yorker*, 2 August 2004, 53.

15. Although it is not clear why the U.S. would be any less deterred by the prospect of losing some of its cities than would France or the U.K.

16. Stephen Rosenfeld, "Going It Alone," *Washington Post*, 6 March 1998, A25. Although it might be said with some justice that the Bush administration in the early twenty-first century took as its motto "Unilateral when we can, multilateral when we must."

17. See the discussion above of the invasion in chapter 3, part 7. See generally Gordon and Trainor, *Cobra II*.

18. George Monbiot, "A Charter to Intervene," *Guardian*, 23 March 2004, 21. I put to one side the anti-American assumption that participation by a U.S. government can never be taken as anything other than an act of imperialist aggression, and the remarkably naïve assumption that if only the Americans were excluded, by law, then the acts of other states would be seen as purely humanitarian and compassionate. But I do wish to argue, as I have in the text, that the separation of high and low motives is a recipe for catastrophe for the persons one wishes to help. See also Philip Bobbitt, "What's in It for US?," *Guardian*, 7 June 2003, 21.

19. Monbiot, "Charter to Intervene," 21.

20. I never realized quite how widely this assumption was shared until one evening in 2003 when I was a guest on a British radio chat show, discussing U.S.-U.K. intervention in Iraq. Virtually all the calls were hostile questions directed toward what the callers took to be the hypocritical and deceptive suggestion that America and Britain might have some humane purpose in trying to change the regime in Baghdad. One man asked, voice laden with sarcasm, whether I didn't think that oil had "something" to do with America's plan to invade Iraq, to which I rather too earnestly replied, "Well, I certainly hope so."

21. See United Nations Security Council Resolution 1484, 30 May 2003 (4764st meeting).

22. Bobbitt, "What's in It for US?" In June 2004 demonstrations broke out in several cities in the Democratic Republic of Congo to protest the U.N. failure to secure the eastern city of Bukavu against dissident soldiers. In Kinshasa, U.N. troops shot and killed two looters at a U.N. warehouse.

23. The Report of the Iraq Survey Group definitively establishes—through documents, interviews with Iraqi scientists and officials of the regime, and tangible evidence such as various technologies hidden from the U.N. inspectors—that Saddam intended to ramp up his quest for WMD as soon as the U.N. sanctions were lifted. See Iraq Survey Group, *Comprehensive Report of the Special Advisor to the DCI on Iraq's WMD*, vol. 1 (2004), 34; 42–60. The full text of the report is available at http://www.globalsecurity.org/wmd/library/report/2004/isg-final-report.

24. See Paul Volcker et al., Independent Inquiry Committee into the United Nations Oil-for-Food Programme, "Comparison of Estimates of Illicit Iraqi Income During United Nations Sanctions." The document is available at http://www .iic-offp.org/documents/ComparisonofEstimates.pdf.

25. One hopes that this will be the beginning of an alliance of democracies committed to the standards set forth in the Peace of Paris that ended the Long War. See Ivo H.

Daalder and James M. Lindsay, "An Alliance of Democracies," *Washington Post*, 23 May 2004, B7. Membership in such an alliance would have to satisfy the Charter of Paris criteria:

> We undertake to build, consolidate and strengthen democracy as the only system of government of our nations. In this endeavour, we will abide by the following:

> Human rights and fundamental freedoms are the birthright of all human beings, are inalienable and are guaranteed by law. Their protection and promotion is the first responsibility of government. Respect for them is an essential safeguard against an over-mighty State. Their observance and full exercise are the foundation of freedom, justice and peace.

> Democratic government is based on the will of the people, expressed regularly through free and fair elections. Democracy has as its foundation respect for the human person and the rule of law. Democracy is the best safeguard of freedom of expression, tolerance of all groups of society, and equality of opportunity for each person.

> Democracy, with its representative and pluralist character, entails accountability to the electorate, the obligation of public authorities to comply with the law and justice administered impartially. No one will be above the law.

> We affirm that, without discrimination, every individual has the right to freedom of thought, conscience and religion or belief, freedom of expression, freedom of association and peaceful assembly, freedom of movement; no one will be: subject to arbitrary arrest or detention, subject to torture or other cruel, inhuman or degrading treatment or punishment; everyone also has the right: to know and act upon his rights, to participate in free and fair elections, to fair and public trial if charged with an offence, to own property alone or in association and to exercise individual enterprise, to enjoy his economic, social and cultural rights.

Conference on Security and Co-operation in Europe, *Charter of Paris for a New Europe*, 21 November 1990. The full text of the Charter is available at http://www.osce.org/documents/mcs/1990/11/4045_en.pdf (accessed November 7, 2006).

26. Matthew Parris, "The Right Should Oppose Bush's War on Terror," *Times* (London), 20 March 2004, 26.
27. Reisman, "Assessing Claims to Revise the Laws of War," 83.
28. Ibid., 88.
29. Rüdiger Wolfrum, "The Attack of September 11, 2001, the Wars Against the Taliban and Iraq: Is There a Need to Reconsider International Law on the Recourse to Force and the Rules of Armed Conflict?" in vol. 7 of *Max Planck Yearbook of United Nations Law*, ed. Armin von Bogdandy and Rüdiger Wolfrum (Leiden, Netherlands: Martinus Njhoff Publishers, 2004), 25.
30. Thus, Bruce Riedel has warned that the "biggest danger is that al Qaeda will deliberately provoke a war with a 'false-flag' operation, say, a terrorist attack carried out in a way that would make it appear as though it were Iran's doing. The United States should be extremely wary of such deception. In the event of such an attack, accu-

rately assigning blame will require very careful intelligence work. It may require months, or even years, of patient investigating to identify the plotters behind well-planned and well-executed operations, as it did for the 1988 bombing of Pan Am flight 103 over Lockerbie, Scotland, and the 1996 attacks on the U.S. barracks at the Khobar Towers in Saudi Arabia." Riedel, "Al Qaeda Strikes Back," 34.

31. Pew Global Attitudes Project, *America's Image Slips, but Allies Share U.S. Concern over Iran, Hamas* (Washington, D.C.: Pew Research Center, 2006). The full text of the Pew Report is available at http://pewglobal.org/reports/pdf/252.pdf (accessed November 7, 2006).

32. "The Constitutional Relationship between Rights and Powers," pp. 241 et seq.

33. See Oona A. Hathaway, "Between Power and Principle: An Integrated Theory of International Law," *Chicago Law Review* 72 (Spring 2005); see also Oona A. Hathaway, *Strong States, Strong World: Why International Law Succeeds and Fails and What We Should Do About It* (forthcoming, 2008); Oona A. Hathaway, "Why Do Countries Commit to Human Rights Treaties?" (work in progress).

34. "The Convention on the Elimination of All Forms of Discrimination Against Women, for example, has been ratified by 180 [states], and yet outright discrimination remains as rampant as ever in many of those states—including Saudi Arabia, where women cannot drive or leave the house without a male relative. The Convention on International Trade in Endangered Species has been ratified by 167 [states], and yet only a small percentage of these states have fully complied with the straightforward reporting requirements of the treaty, much less its more strenuous protections for endangered species." Oona A. Hathaway, "Does Delegation Undermine U.S. Sovereignty?" Conference on Delegating Sovereignty: Constitutional and Politics Perspectives, Duke University School of Law, 3–4 March 2006, 3. The full text of the paper is available at http://www.law.duke.edu/publiclaw/pdf/workshop06sp/hathaway.pdf.

35. Though there may be others.

36. Hathaway, "Does Delegation Undermine U.S. Sovereignty?" 12.

37. Ibid., 5–6.

38. Rubenfeld, "Two World Orders," 32.

39. Kenneth Anderson, "Who Owns the Rules of War?" *New York Times Magazine*, 13 April 2003, 38. The essay is available at http://www.crimesofwar.org/print/onnews/iraq6-print.html.

40. Raymond Aron, *The Imperial Republic* (Lanham, Md.: Rowman & Littlefield, 1981).

41. Freedman, "The Coming War on Terrorism," in *Superterrorism*, 48. There is much to be said for seeking to establish such a norm, given that over the past century we moved from a situation where 90 percent of the casualties of war were combatants to one where 90 percent were civilians.

42. Ibid.

43. This is already becoming the case with the certification of elections by NGOs, as, for example, happened during the 2004 presidential election in Ukraine. See, e.g., National Democratic Institute for International Affairs, "Preliminary Statement of the NDI International Election Observer Delegation to Ukraine's December 26, 2004, Repeat of the Presidential Runoff Election," Press Release, 27 December 2004, http://www.accessdemocracy.org/library/1787_uk_statement_122704.html (accessed November 28, 2006); National Democratic Institute for International Affairs, "Fundamental Flaws in Ukraine's Presidential Election Process Subvert Its Legitimacy, Says NDI," Press Release, 23 November 2004, http://www.accessdemocracy.org/library/1774_uk_press_112304.html (accessed November 28, 2006).

44. Betty Sue Flowers, "The Primacy of People in a World of Nations," in *The Partner-*

ship Principle: New Forms of Governance in the 21st Century, ed. Susan Stern and Elizabeth Seligmann (London: Archetype Publications, 2004), 79.

45. Nader Mousavizadeh, "A Million Little Pieces," *New York Times*, 24 September 2005, A15.

46. Charles A. Kupchan, chair, "Summary Report of the Grand Strategy Working Group," New America Foundation Conference on Terrorism, Security, and America's Purpose: Towards a More Comprehensive Strategy, 6–7 September 2005, 4.

CHAPTER TWELVE: The Triage of Terror

1. See Mark Mazzetti, "U.S. Aborted Raid on Qaeda Chiefs in Pakistan in '05," *New York Times*, 8 July 2007, http://www.nytimes.com/2007/07/08/washington/08intel .html (accessed October 30, 2007).

2. Michael Moss and Souad Mekhennet, "Militants Widen Reach as Terror Seeps Out of Iraq," *New York Times*, 28 May 2007.

3. Ibid., quoting a "top American military official who . . . spoke on condition of anonymity."

4. James B. Petro, "Intelligence Support to the Life Science Community: Mitigating Threats from Bioterrorism," *Studies in Intelligence* 48, no. 3 (2004): 57–58, 62–63.

5. Paul B. Stares, "To Ban the Bomb, Sign the Peace," *New York Times*, 30 January 2007, http://www.nytimes.com/2007/01/30/opinion/30stares.html.

6. Quoted in David E. Sanger and Thom Shanker, "U.S. Debates Deterrence for Nuclear Terrorism," *New York Times*, 8 May 2007.

7. See e.g., Timothy Garton Ash, "A False Metaphor Has Been Written in Blood," *Guardian*, 2 November 2006, 31.

8. See Don Tapscott and Anthony D. Williams, *Wikinomics: How Mass Collaboration Changes Everything* (London: Portfolio, 2006); Yochai Benkler, *The Wealth of Networks: How Social Production Transforms Markets and Freedom* (New Haven, Conn.: 2006); Cass R. Sunstein, *Infotopia: How Many Minds Produce Knowledge* (New York: Oxford University Press, 2006); Lawrence Lessig, *Code: Version 2.0* (New York, Basic Books 2006).

9. In Alvin Toffler's words. See Alvin Toffler, *The Third Wave* (New York: Morrow, 1980).

10. See generally Godfrey Hodgson, *Woodrow Wilson's Right Hand: The Life of Colonel Edward M. House* (New Haven, Conn.: Yale University Press, 2006).

11. Dennis Patterson, "The New Leviathan," review of *The Shield of Achilles*, by Philip Bobbitt, *Michigan Law Review* 101 (May 2003): 1724–25.

CONCLUSION: A Plague Treatise for the Twenty-first Century

1. Consider this scenario involving a so-called "dirty bomb": "[F]our simultaneous attacks are made on the United States, involving three truck bombs and a bomb in a shipping container, in Newark, Detroit, Long Beach, and Miami. Fatalities are restricted to a few motorists . . . but because the bombs contain americium-241 and cesium-137 they spread panic out of all proportion to their actual damage. . . . People flee the infected cities. America closes its borders, paralyzing world trade. Supermarket shelves are emptying. There's talk of airlifting food to Hawaii. The social, economic, and political costs of the attacks (which in themselves cause no more harm than the average industrial accident) are beyond calculation." Jonathan Raban, "The Truth About Terrorism," *New York Review of Books*, 13 January 2005.

2. Which is why popularity polls and claims of popular satisfaction cannot validate a regime, e.g., Castro's in Cuba.

3. Indeed, states may achieve consensus through many forms, e.g., tribal assemblies such as the *loya jirga* that flourish in central Asia.

4. Michael Quinlan, "The Condition for Stable Deterrence," Institut Français des Relations Internationals Conference, 19 December 2006.

5. Joseph Margulies, *Guantánamo and the Abuse of Presidential Power* (New York: Simon & Schuster, 2006).

6. For example, the protests of persons in Liberia and Sierra Leone decrying U.S. reluctance to become involved.

7. Olivier Roy, "Why Do They Hate Us? Not Because of Iraq," *New York Times*, 22 July 2005.

8. Ibid.

9. Quinlan, "The Condition for Stable Deterrence."

10. "It is only aggression that calls forth defense, and war along with it. The aggressor is always peace-loving (as Bonaparte always claimed to be); he would prefer to take over our country unopposed. To prevent his doing so one must be willing to make war. . . ." Carl von Clausewitz, *On War*, ed. and trans. Michael Howard and Peter Paret (Princeton, N.J.: Princeton University Press, 1976), 370.

11. Note the Barbary pirates' declaration of war discussed in chapter 1.

12. Michael Howard, "Smoke on the Horizon," *Financial Times*, 7 September 2002, 1.

13. Don van Natta, Jr., "Blair Was Set on Path to War, British Memo Says," *New York Times*, 27 March 2006. See also Philippe Sands, *Lawless World: America and the Making and Breaking of Global Rules* (New York: Viking, 2005).

14. "International law is widely criticized and often even derided, so it should cause no surprise that many international lawyers assume that one of their primary functions is a defense of international law and a justification and endorsement of the decisions taken by its formal institutions. However well intentioned this form of professional loyalty may be, international law is the loser: One of the consequences is that appraisal, evaluation and recommendation for improvement of its performance, tasks indispensable to any purposive human activity in order to ensure that the activity is actually achieving its purpose, are left to detractors whose appetites rarely extend beyond acidic if not destructive criticism." W. Michael Reisman, "International Law in the Twenty-First Century," General Course at The Hague Academy of International Law (Summer 2007).

15. Technology and Privacy Advisory Committee, *Safeguarding Privacy in the Fight Against Terrorism* (2004). The report is available at http://www.defenselink.mil/news/Jan2006/d20060208tapac.pdf.

16. See, e.g., Matthew Yglesias, "Rogue State: Lawbreaker and Torturer—That's America, Loud and Proud," *American Prospect Online*, 26 September 2006, http://www.prospect.org/web/page.ww?section=root&name=ViewWeb&articleId=12060 (accessed April 10, 2007).

17. William Shakespeare, *King Lear*, III, vi, lines 19–21.

18. For example, Michael Ignatieff has argued, "In fact, America's entire war on terror is an exercise in imperialism. This may come as a shock to Americans, who don't like to think of their country as an empire. But what else can you call America's legions of soldiers, spooks and Special Forces straddling the globe?" Michael Ignatieff, "Nation-Building Lite," *New York Times Magazine*, 28 July 2002, 26. Cf. Chalmers Johnson, *The Sorrows of Empire: Militarism, Secrecy, and the End of the Republic* (New York: Metropolitan Books, 2004).

19. Quoted in Glennon, "Why the Security Council Failed," 19.
20. Winston Churchill is said to have advised that "[o]ne ought never to turn one's back on a threatened danger and try to run away from it. If you do that, you will double the danger. But if you meet it promptly and without flinching, you will reduce the danger by half."
21. E-mail to the author from Robert Post, 3 January 2007.
22. And it isn't just the American administration that doesn't always seem to grasp the nature of the threat posed by twenty-first century market state terrorists. Thus, in the course of a rather complacent essay about the threat of an attack on U.S. critical infrastructure, a *New York Times* writer quoted one observer who "said that he had difficulty envisioning the threat that others see from an overseas attack by electrons and photons alone. 'They unleash their deadly viruses and then they land on the beaches and sweep across our country without resistance because we're rebooting our P.C.s?' he asked." John Schwartz, "When Computers Attack," *New York Times*, 24 June 2007. Or recall those commentators discussed in chapter 2 who assured us that a "few" nuclear detonations in the American homeland could be suffered without fundamentally endangering the State.
23. See Mark Graber, "More Advice from Classical Greece," http://balkin.blogspot .com/2006/09/more-advice-from-classical-greece.html (accessed June 24, 2007).
24. The remarkable polymath Edward Binkowski has reminded me that customers might not be so forthcoming to corporations if these consumers had a clearer idea of just what they were providing and what would be done with it.

CODA

1. "We are conducting operations now as though we were on a stage. . . . There are two or more sets of players—both with a producer, the commander, each of whom has his own idea of the script. . . . At the same time, they are being viewed by a partial and factional audience, comfortably seated, its attention focused on that part of the auditorium where it is noisiest, watching the events by peering down the drinking straws of their soft-drink packs—for that is the extent of the vision of a camera." Smith, *The Utility of Force*, 284–85.
2. As Kierkegaard put it, "In the most earnest sense, God is the critical theatergoer, who looks on to see how the lines are spoken and how they are listened to. . . . The speaker is then the prompter, and the listener stands openly before God. The listener, if I may say so, is the actor, who in all truth acts before God." Søren Kierkegaard, *Parables of Kierkegaard*, ed. Thomas C. Oden (Princeton, N.J.: Princeton University Press, 1989), 90.
3. "I call heaven and earth to record this day against you, that I have set before you life and death, blessing and cursing: therefore choose life, that both thou and thy seed may live." Deuteronomy 30:19 (King James Version).
4. But recall this observation of Winston Churchill's: "If you will not fight when your victory will be sure and not too costly, you may come to the moment when you have to fight with all the odds against you and only a precarious chance for survival. There may even be a worse case. You may have to fight when there is no hope of victory, because it is better to perish than to live as slaves." Winston S. Churchill, *The Gathering Storm*, vol. 1 of *The Second World War* (Boston, Mass.: Houghton Mifflin, 1986), 312.
5. See Grant Gilmore, *The Ages of American Law* (The Storrs Lectures on Jurisprudence) (New Haven: Yale University Press, 1977), 110–11.

SELECTED BIBLIOGRAPHY

Ackerman, Bruce. *Before the Next Attack: Preserving Civil Liberties in an Age of Terrorism* (New Haven: Yale University Press, 2006).

Adams, John Quincy. *Memoirs of John Quincy Adams: Comprising Portions of His Diary from 1795 to 1848,* vol. 6, ed. Charles Francis Adams (Philadelphia: J. B. Lippincott & Co., 1874).

Albright, David, and Holly Higgins. "A Bomb for the Ummah," *Bulletin of the Atomic Scientists* 59, no. 2 (March/April 2003).

Alibeck, K. *Biohazard* (New York: Random House, 1999).

Allen, Frederick Lewis. *Only Yesterday: An Informal History of the Nineteen-Twenties* (New York: Harper & Row, 1957).

Allison, Graham T., et al. *Avoiding Nuclear Anarchy: Containing the Threat of Loose Russian Nuclear Weapons and Fissile Material* (Cambridge, Mass.: Center for Science and International Affairs, 1996).

Allison, Graham T. *Nuclear Terrorism: The Ultimate Preventable Catastrophe* (New York: Times Books, 2004).

Amar, Akhil Reed. *America's Constitution: A Biography* (New York: Random House, 2005).

Anderson, Benedict. *Imagined Communities: Reflections on the Origin and Spread of Nationalism* (Thetford, Norfolk, U.K.: Thetford Press, 1983).

Anderson, David. *Histories of the Hanged: The Dirty War in Kenya* (New York: W.W. Norton & Co., 2005).

Angell, Norman. *The Great Illusion: A Study of the Relation of Military Power in Nations to Their Economic and Social Advantage* (London: Heinemann, 1910).

"Anonymous" (M. Scheuer). *Through our Enemies' Eyes: Osama Bin Laden, Radical Islam, and the Future of America* (Dulles, Va.: Brassey's, 2002).

———. *Imperial Hubris: Why the West Is Losing the War on Terror* (Washington, D.C.: Potomac Books, 2004).

Arquilla, John, David Ronfeldt, and Michele Zanini. "Networks, Netwar, and Information-Age Terrorism," in *Countering the New Terrorism*, ed. Ian O. Lesser (Santa Monica, Calif.: RAND, 2006).

Asmus, Ronald D. *Opening NATO's Door: How the Alliance Remade Itself for a New Era* (New York: Columbia University Press, 2002).

Ball, Desmond. "Desperately Seeking Bin Laden: The Intelligence Dimension of the War Against Terrorism," in *Worlds in Collision: Terror and the Future of Global Order*, ed. Ken Booth and Tim Dunne (New York: Palgrave Macmillan, 2002).

Bamford, James. *Body of Secrets: Anatomy of the Ultra-Secret National Security Agency from the Cold War Through the Dawn of a New Century* (New York: Doubleday, 2001).

————. *The Puzzle Palace: A Report on America's Most Secret Agency* (Boston: Houghton Mifflin, 1982).

Barron, David. "Constitutionalism in the Shadow of Doctrine: The President's Non-Enforcement Power," *Law and Contemporary Problems* 63 (Winter–Spring 2000): 61–106.

Benjamin, Daniel, and Steven Simon. *The Age of Sacred Terror* (New York: Random House, 2002).

————. *The Next Attack: The Failure of the War on Terror and a Strategy for Getting It Right* (New York: Times Books, 2005).

Bergen, Peter L. *Holy War, Inc.: Inside the Secret World of Osama bin Laden* (New York: Free Press, 2001).

Bergsten, C. Fred, and Caio Koch-Weser. "The G-2: A New Conceptual Basis and Operating Modality for Transatlantic Economic Relations," in *From Alliance to Coalitions— The Future of Transatlantic Relations,* ed. Werner Weidenfeld et al. (Bertelsmann Foundation, 2004).

Berkowitz, Bruce. *The New Face of War: How War Will Be Fought in the 21st Century* (New York: Free Press, 2003).

Betts, Richard K. "Analysis, War, and Decision: Why Intelligence Failures Are Inevitable," *World Politics* 31 (1978): 61–89.

————. "Politicization of Intelligence: Costs and Benefits," in *Paradoxes of Strategic Intelligence: Essays in Honor of Michael I. Handel,* ed. Richard K. Betts and Thomas G. Mahnken (Portland, Ore.: Frank Cass Publishers, 2003).

Black, Jeremy. *The Dotted Red Line: Britain's Defence Policy in the Modern World* (London: Social Affairs Unit, 2006).

Bobbitt, Philip. "The Constitutional Canon," in *Legal Canons,* ed. J. M. Balkin and Sanford Levinson (New York: New York University Press, 2000).

————. *Constitutional Interpretation* (Cambridge, Mass.: Blackwell, 1991).

————. *Democracy and Deterrence: The History and Future of Nuclear Strategy* (New York: St. Martin's Press, 1988).

————. *The Shield of Achilles: War, Peace, and the Course of History* (New York: Knopf, 2002).

————. "War Powers: An Essay on John Hart Ely's *War and Responsibility: Constitutional Lessons of Vietnam and Its Aftermath,*" *Michigan Law Review* 92 (1994): 1364–1400.

Bobbitt, Philip, et al., ed. *U.S. Nuclear Strategy: A Reader* (New York: New York University Press, 1989).

Brooks, Rosa Ehrenreich. "War Everywhere: Rights, National Security Law, and the Law of Armed Conflict in the Age of Terror," *University of Pennsylvania Law Review* 153 (2004): 675–761.

Brown, Chris. "Reflections on the 'War on Terror,' 2 Years On," *International Politics* 41, no. 1 (March 2004): 51–64.

Brzezinski, Zbigniew K. *The Choice: Global Domination or Global Leadership* (New York: Basic Books).

————. *Out of Control: Global Turmoil on the Eve of the Twenty-first Century* (New York: Scribner, 1993).

Builder, Carl H. *The Masks of War: American Military Styles in Strategy and Analysis* (London and Baltimore: The Johns Hopkins University Press, 1989).

Bunker, R. J., ed. *Networks, Terrorism and Global Insurgency* (New York and London: Routledge, 2005).

————. ed. *Non-State Threats and Future Wars* (London: Frank Cass, 2003).

Burg, B. R. *Sodomy and the Pirate Tradition: English Sea Rovers in the Seventeenth-Century Caribbean* (New York: New York University Press, 1995).

Buzan, Barry. "Who May We Bomb," in *Worlds in Collision: Terror and the Future of Global Order*, ed. Ken Booth and Tim Dunne (New York: Palgrave Macmillan, 2002).

Byford, Grenville. "The Wrong War," *Foreign Affairs* 81, no. 2 (July/August 2002): 34–43.

Campbell, James K. "Excerpts from Research Study Weapons of Mass Destruction and Terrorism: Proliferation by Non-State Actors," *Terrorism and Political Violence* 9, no. 2 (Summer 1997): 24–50.

Campbell, Kurt M., and Michéle A. Flournoy. *To Prevail: An American Strategy for the Campaign Against Terrorism* (Washington, D.C.: CSIS Press, 2006).

Carlson, Robert. "The Pace and Proliferation of Biological Technologies," *Biosecurity and Bioterrorism: Biodefense Strategy, Practice, and Science* 1, no. 3 (2003): 203–14.

Carus, W. S. "Bioterrorism and Biocrimes: The Illicit Use of Biological Agents Since 1900," (Washington, D.C.: Center for Counterproliferation Research, National Defense University, 2002).

Cello, Jeronimo, Aniko V. Paul, and Eckard Wimmer. "Chemical Synthesis of Poliovirus cDNA: Generation of Infectious Virus in the Absence of Natural Template," *Science* 297 (2002): 1016–18.

Center for Strategic and International Studies, Global Organized Crime Project. *Cybercrime, Cyberterrorism, Cyberwarfare: Averting an Electronic Waterloo* (Washington, D.C.: CSIS Press, 1998).

Channing, Edward. *The Jeffersonian System 1801–1811* (New York: Harper & Row, 1968).

Christopher, G. W., T. J. Cieslak, J. A. Pavlin, and E. M. Eitzen Jr. "Biological Warfare: A Historical Perspective," *Journal of the American Medical Association,* 278 (1977), 412–17.

Chua, Amy. *World on Fire: How Exporting Free Market Democracy Breeds Ethnic Hatred and Global Instability* (New York: Doubleday, 2002).

Clark, Wesley K. *Waging Modern War: Bosnia, Kosovo, and the Future of Combat* (New York: Public Affairs, 2001).

Clarke, Richard A. *Against All Enemies: Inside America's War on Terror* (New York: Free Press, 2004).

Clary, Christopher O. "The A. Q. Khan Network: Causes and Implications" (thesis, Naval Postgraduate School, Monterey, California, December 2005).

Cochran, Zefram (pseudonym). "When Jack Welch Was Deputy Director for Intelligence," *Studies in Intelligence* 48, no. 3 (2004): 37–43.

Cogan, Charles. "Hunters Not Gatherers: Intelligence in the Twenty-first Century," in *Understanding Intelligence in the Twenty-first Century: Journeys in Shadows*, ed. L. V. Scott and Peter Jackson (New York: Routledge, 2004).

Cohen, Daniel. *Globalization and Its Enemies* (Cambridge, Mass.: MIT Press, 2006).

Cohen, Eliot A. *Supreme Command: Soldiers, Statesmen, and Leadership in Wartime* (New York: Free Press, 2002).

Coker, Christopher. "Cultural Ruthlessness and the War Against Terror," *Australian Army Journal* 3, no. 1 (Summer 2005–2006): 145–63.

———. "Globalisation and Insecurity in the Twenty-first Century: NATO and the Management of Risk," Adelphi Paper no. 345 (London: International Institute for Strategic Studies, 2002).

Cole, David. "Judging the Next Emergency: Judicial Review and Individual Rights in Times of Crisis," *Michigan Law Review* 101 (2003): 2565–95.

———. "The Priority of Morality: The Emergency Constitution's Blind Spot," *Yale Law Journal* 113 (2004): 1753–1800.

Coll, Steve. *Ghost Wars: The Secret History of the CIA, Afghanistan, and Bin Laden, from the Soviet Invasion to September 10, 2001* (New York: Penguin Books, 2004).

Commission on the Intelligence Capabilities of the United States Regarding Weapons of Mass Destruction, Report to the President of the United States (Washington, D.C.: U. S. Government Printing Office, 2005).

Commission on the Roles and Capabilities of the United States Intelligence Community. *Preparing for the 21st Century: An Appraisal of U.S. Intelligence* (Washington, D.C.: U. S. Government Printing Office, 1996).

Committee on Legal Affairs and Human Rights. *Alleged Secret Detentions and Unlawful Inter-state Transfers of Detainees Involving Council of Europe Member States* (Council of Europe, 2006).

Cooper, Robert. *The Breaking of Nations: Order and Chaos in the Twenty-first Century* (London: Atlantic Books, 2003).

Cordesman, Anthony H. *Terrorism, Asymmetric Warfare, and Weapons of Mass Destruction: Defending the U.S. Homeland* (Westport, Conn.: CSIS Press, 2002).

Cordingly, David. *Life Among the Pirates: The Romance and the Reality* (London: Little, Brown & Co., 1995).

Corera, Gordon. *Shopping for Bombs: Nuclear Proliferation, Global Insecurity, and the Rise and Fall of the A. Q. Khan Network* (New York: Oxford University Press, 2006).

Coyle, Diane. *Paradoxes of Prosperity: Why the New Capitalism Benefits All* (New York and London: TEXERE, 2001).

Creveld, Martin van L. *The Rise and Decline of the State* (Cambridge, U.K.: Cambridge University Press, 1999).

———. *The Transformation of War* (New York: Free Press, 1991).

Cronin, Audrey Kurth. "Behind the Curve: Globalization and International Terrorism," *International Security* 27, no. 3 (Winter 2002/03): 30–58.

———."Rethinking Sovereignty: American Strategy in the Age of Terrorism," *Survival* 44, no. 2 (Summer 2002): 119–39.

———. "Sources of Contemporary Terrorism," in *Attacking Terrorism: Elements of a Grand Strategy,* ed. Audrey Kurth Cronin and James M. Lundes (Washington, D.C.: Georgetown University Press, 2004).

Daalder, Ivo, and James M. Lindsay. *America Unbound: The Bush Revolution in Foreign Policy,* rev. ed. (Washington, D.C.: The Brookings Institution, 2005).

d'Ancona, Matthew. *Confessions of a Hawkish Hack: The Media and the War on Terror* (London: Policy Exchange, 2006).

Danzig, Richard. *Catastrophic Bioterrorism—What Is to Be Done?* (Washington, D.C.: National Defense University Press, 2003).

———. "Proliferation of Biological Weapons into Terrorist Hands," in *The Challenge of Proliferation: A Report of the Aspen Strategy Group,* ed. Kurt M. Campbell (Washington, D.C.: Aspen Institute, 2005).

Davies, Philip H. J. "A Critical Look at Britain's Spy Machinery," *Studies in Intelligence* 49, no. 4 (2005): 41–54.

———. "Ideas of Intelligence: Divergent National Concepts and Institutions," *Harvard International Review* 24, no. 3 (Fall 2002): 62–66.

David, L. M., K. J. Riley, G. K. Ridgeway, J. E. Pace, S. K. Cotton, P. S. Steinberg, K. Damphousse, and B. L. Smith. "When Terrorism Hits Home: How Prepared Are State and Local Law Enforcement?" MG-104-MIPT (Santa Monica, Calif.: RAND, 2004).

Department of Defense. *Quadrennial Defense Review Report* (Washington, D.C.: Department of Defense, 2006).

Dershowitz, Alan. "Tortured Reasoning," in *Torture: A Collection*, ed. Sanford Levinson (New York: Oxford University Press, 2004).

Dobbins, James, et al. "America's Role in Nation-Building: From Germany to Iraq" (Santa Monica, Calif.: RAND, 2003).

———. "The UN's Role in Nation-Building: From the Congo to Iraq" (Santa Monica, Calif.: RAND, 2003).

Donohue, Laura K. *Counter-Terrorist Law and Emergency Powers in the United Kingdom, 1922–2000* (Dublin: Irish Academic Press, 2001).

———. "Fear Itself: Counterterrorism, Individual Rights, and U.S. Foreign Relations Post 9–11," in *Terrorism and Counterterrorism*, ed. Russell D. Howard and Reid L. Sawyer (Guilford, Conn.: McGraw-Hill, 2003).

Dworkin, Anthony. "Military Necessity and Due Process: The Place of Human Rights in the War on Terror," in *New Wars, New Laws?: Applying the Laws of War in 21st Century Conflicts*, ed. David Wippman and Matthew Evangelista (Ardsley, N.Y.: Transnational, 2005).

Dyzenhaus, David. "Humpty Dumpty Rules or the Rule of Law: Legal Theory and the Adjudication of National Security," *Australian Journal of Legal Philosophy* 28 (2003): 1–30.

———. "The Permanence of the Temporary: Can Emergency Powers Be Normalized?" in *Security of Freedom: Essays on Canada's Anti-Terrorism Bill*, ed. Ronald Daniels, Patrick Maclem, and Kent Roach (Toronto: University of Toronto Press, 2001).

Dziedzic, Michael J. "Introduction," in *Policing the New World Disorder: Peace Operations and Public Security*, ed. Robert B. Oakley, Michael J. Dziedzic, and Eliot M. Goldberg (Washington, D.C.: National Defense University Press, 1998).

Elkins, Catherine. *Imperial Reckoning: The Untold Story of Britain's Gulag in Kenya* (New York: Henry Holt, 2005).

Ellis, Brent. "Countering Complexity: An Analytical Framework to Guide Counter-Terrorism Policy-Making," *Journal of Military and Strategic Studies* 6, no. 1 (Spring/Summer 2003): 1–20.

Elshtain, Jean Bethke. "Reflection on the Problem of 'Dirty Hands,' " in *Torture: A Collection*, ed. Sanford Levinson (New York: Oxford University Press, 2004).

Encyclopaedia Britannica, 11th ed., vol. XXI (New York: Encyclopaedia Britannica, 1911).

Evans, Gareth, and Mohamed Sahnoun, International Commission on Intervention and State Sovereignty. *The Responsibility to Protect* (Ottawa: International Development Research Centre, 2001).

Fallon, Richard H. "Legitimacy and the Constitution," *Harvard Law Review* 118 (2005): 1787–1853.

Feldman, Noah. *After Jihad: America and the Struggle for Islamic Democracy* (New York: Farrar, Straus and Giroux, 2003).

Felner, Eitan. "Torture and Terrorism: Painful Lessons from Israel," in *Torture*, ed. Kenneth Roth and Minky Worden (New York: New Press, 2005).

Fenwick, Helen. "Responding to 11 September: Detention Without Trial Under the Anti-Terrorism, Crime and Security Act 2001," in *Superterrorism: Policy Responses*, ed. Lawrence Freedman (Oxford: Blackwell Publishing, 2002).

Ferguson, C. D., W. C. Potter, A. Sands, L. S. Spector, and F. L. Wehling. *The Four Faces of Nuclear Terrorism* (Monterey, Calif.: Center for Nonproliferation Studies, Monterey Institute, 2004).

Ferguson, Charles D. *Preventing Catastrophic Nuclear Terrorism*, Council Special Report No. 11 (New York: Council on Foreign Relations, March 2006).

Ferguson, Niall. "Clashing Civilizations or Mad Mullahs: The United States Between Informal and Formal Empire," in *Terror: America and the World After September 11*, ed. Strobe Talbott and Nayan Chanda (New York: Basic Books, 2001).

———. *Colossus: The Price of America's Empire* (New York: Penguin Press, 2004).

———. *Empire: The Rise and Demise of the British World Order and the Lessons for Global Power* (London, Allen Lane, 2002).

———. *The War of the World: Twentieth-Century Conflict and the Decline of the West* (London: Penguin Press, 2006).

Fifoot, C. H. S. *Lord Mansfield* (Oxford: Clarendon Press, 1936).

Flannery, Tim. *The Weather Makers* (New York: Atlantic Monthly Press, 2005).

Flowers, Betty Sue. "The Primacy of People in a World of Nations," in *The Partnership Principle: New Forms of Governance in the 21st Century,* ed. Susan Stern and Elizabeth Seligmann (London: Archetype Publications, 2004).

Flynn, Stephen. *America the Vulnerable: How Our Government Is Failing to Protect Us from Terrorism* (New York: HarperCollins, 2004).

Forrow, Lachlan, et al. "Accidental Nuclear War—A Post–Cold War Assessment," *New England Journal of Medicine* 338 (1998): 1326–32.

Fraser, Antonia. *The Gunpowder Plot: Terror & Faith in 1605* (London: Mandarin, 1997).

Freedman, Lawrence. "The Coming War on Terrorism," in *Superterrorism: Policy Responses,* ed. Lawrence Freedman (Oxford: Blackwell Publishing, 2002).

———. ed. *War* (Oxford: Oxford University Press, 1994).

———. "The Revolution in Strategic Affairs," Adelphi Paper no. 318 (London: International Institute for Strategic Studies, 1998).

———. "Strategic Terror and Amateur Psychology," *Political Quarterly* 76, no. 2 (April-June 2005): 161–70.

———. "Think Again: War," *Foreign Policy* (July/August 2003): 16–24.

Friedman, Thomas L. *The World Is Flat: A Brief History of the Twenty-first Century* (New York: Farrar, Straus and Giroux, 2005).

Friendly, Henry J. "Some Kind of Hearing," *University of Pennsylvania Law Review* 123 (1975): 1267–1317.

Frost, Robin M. "Nuclear Terrorism After 9/11," Adelphi Paper no. 378 (London: International Institute for Strategic Studies, 2005).

Fukuyama, Francis. *The End of History and the Last Man* (New York: Free Press, 1992).

Fuller, Lon L. *The Morality of Law* (New Haven, Conn.: Yale University Press, 1964).

Gabel, Medard, and Henry Bruner. *Global Inc.: An Atlas of the Multinational Corporation* (New York: New Press, 2003).

Gall, Lothar. *Bismarck: The White Revolutionary, Volume 1: 1851–1871,* trans. J. A. Underwood (London: Allen & Unwin, 1986).

Ganor, B. *The Counter-Terrorism Puzzle: A Guide for Decision Makers* (New Brunswick and London: Transaction Publishers, 2005).

Garten, Jeffrey E. *A Cold Peace: America, Japan, Germany, and the Struggle for Supremacy* (New York: Times Books, 1992).

Garton Ash, Timothy. *Free World: America, Europe, and the Surprising Future of the West* (New York: Random House, 2004).

Garwin, Richard L., and Georges Charpak. *Megawatts and Megatons: The Future of Nuclear Power and Nuclear Weapons* (Chicago: University of Chicago Press, 2001).

Gavin, Francis J. "Blasts from the Past: Proliferation Lessons from the 1960s," *International Security* 29, no. 3 (Winter 2004/05): 100–135.

Gearson, John. "The Nature of Modern Terrorism," in *Superterrorism: Policy Responses,* ed. Lawrence Freedman (Oxford: Blackwell Publishing, 2002).

George, Alexander L. "Strategies for Preventive Diplomacy and Conflict Resolution: Scholarship for Policymaking," *PS: Political Science and Politics* 33 (2000): 15–19.

Gilbert, Paul. *Terrorism, Security & Nationality: An Introductory Study in Applied Political Philosophy* (London: Routledge, 1994).

Gilmore, Grant. *The Ages of American Law* (New Haven: Yale University Press, 1977).

Gilpin, Robert. *The Challenge of Global Capitalism: The World Economy in the 21st Century* (Princeton, N. J.: Princeton University Press, 2000).

Glennon, Michael J. "Why the Security Council Failed," *Foreign Affairs* 82, no. 3 (May/June 2003): 16–35.

Gnesotto, Nicole and Giovanni Grevi. *The New Global Puzzle: What World for the EU in 2025?* (Paris: EU Institute for Security Studies, 2006).

Goldsmith, Jack L., and Eric A. Posner. *The Limits of International Law* (New York: Oxford University Press, 2005).

Golove, David. "Military Tribunals, International Law, and the Constitution: A Franckian-Madisonian Approach," *New York University Journal of International Law and Politics* 35 (2003): 363–94.

Gompert, David C., Richard L. Kugler, and Martin C. Libicki. *Mind the Gap: Promoting a Transatlantic Revolution in Military Affairs* (Washington, D.C.: National Defense University Press, 1999).

Goodman, Martin. *Rome and Jerusalem: The Clash of Ancient Civilizations* (London: Penguin Books, 2007).

Gordon, Michael R., and Bernard E. Trainor. *Cobra II: The Inside Story of the Invasion and Occupation of Iraq* (New York: Pantheon Books, 2006).

Gorman, Siobhan. "Adm. Poindexter's Total Awareness," *National Journal* 36, no. 19 (2004): 1430–32.

Goss, Tracy. *The Last Word on Power* (New York: Currency Doubleday, 1996).

Gouré, Daniel. "Homeland Security," in *Attacking Terrorism: Elements of a Grand Strategy*, ed. Audrey Kurth Cronin and James M. Ludes (Washington, D.C.: Georgetown University Press, 2004).

Gray, John. *Al Qaeda and What It Means to Be Modern* (London: Faber and Faber, 2003).

Guicciardini, Luigi. *The Sack of Rome,* trans. and ed. James H. McGregor (New York: Ithaca Press, 1993).

Gunaratna, R. *Inside Al Qaeda: Global Network of Terror* (New York: Columbia University Press, 2002).

Gur-Arye, Miriam. "Can the War Against Terror Justify the Use of Force in Interrogations?" in *Torture: A Collection,* ed. Sanford Levinson (New York: Oxford University Press, 2004).

Guthrie, Charles, and Michael Quinlan, *Just War: The Just War Tradition: Ethics in Modern Warfare* (London: Bloomsbury Publishing, 2007).

Haass, Richard. *The Reluctant Sheriff: The United States After the Cold War* (New York: Public Affairs, 2005).

Hamilton, Alexander. "Federalist No. 1," in *The Federalist Papers,* ed. Clinton Rossiter (New York: Mentor, 1961).

Harrison, Frederic. *William the Silent* (London: Macmillan and Co., 1931).

Hathaway, Oona A. *Strong States, Strong World: Why International Law Succeeds and Fails and What We Should Do About It* (forthcoming 2008).

Hegland, Corine. "Global Jihad," *National Journal* 36, no. 19 (2004): 1396–402.

Herman, Michael. *Intelligence Power in Peace and War* (New York: Cambridge University Press, 1996).

———. *Problems for Western Intelligence in the New Century* (Norwegian Institute for Defence Studies, 2005).

Heymann, Philip B. *Terrorism and America: A Commonsense Strategy for a Democratic Society* (Cambridge, Mass.: MIT Press, 2000).

———. *Terrorism, Freedom, and Security: Winning Without War* (Cambridge, Mass.: MIT Press, 2003).

Heymann, Philip B., and Juliette N. Kayyem. *Protecting Liberty in an Age of Terror* (Cambridge, Mass.: MIT Press, 2005).

Hill, Christopher. *Liberty Against the Law: Some Seventeenth Century Controversies* (London: Penguin, 1996).

Hitchens, Christopher. *Love, Poverty, and War: Journeys and Essays* (New York: Nation Books, 2004).

Hmoud, Mahmoud. "The Use of Force Against Iraq: Occupation and Security Council Resolution 1483," *Cornell International Law Journal* 36 (2004): 435–53.

Hobbes, Thomas. *Leviathan* (Baltimore: Penguin Books, 1968 [original publication 1651]).

Hodgson, Godfrey. *Woodrow Wilson's Right Hand: The Life of Colonel Edward M. House* (New Haven: Yale University Press, 2006).

Hoffman, Bruce. *Inside Terrorism* (New York: Columbia University Press, 1998).

———. "Terrorism Trends and Prospects," in *Countering the New Terrorism,* ed. Ian O. Lesser (Santa Monica, Calif.: RAND, 2006).

Holmes, Oliver Wendell, Jr. *The Common Law and Other Writings* (Birmingham: Gryphon Editions, 1982).

Holmes, Stephen. "Al-Qaeda, September 11, 2001," in *Making Sense of Suicide Missions,* ed. Diego Gambetta (New York: Oxford University Press, 2005).

Horgan, John, and Max Taylor. "The Provisional Irish Republican Army: Command and Functional Structure," *Terrorism and Political Violence* 9, no. 3 (Autumn 1997): 1–32.

House of Commons, Report of a Committee of Privy Counsellors. *Review of Intelligence on Weapons of Mass Destruction* (London: Stationery Office, 2004).

Howard, Michael. *Liberation or Catastrophe? Reflections on the History of the Twentieth Century* (London and New York: Continuum, 2007).

———. *Empires, Nations and Wars* (Stroud: Spellmont, 2007).

———. *War in European History* (Oxford: Oxford University Press, 1976).

———. "What's in a Name?: How to Fight Terrorism," *Foreign Affairs* 81, no.1 (January/February 2002): 8–13.

Howard, R., J. Forest, and J. Moore, eds. *Homeland Security and Terrorism: Readings and Interpretations* (New York: McGraw-Hill, 2006).

Human Security Centre. *Human Security Report 2005: War and Peace in the 21st Century* (Oxford: Oxford University Press, 2005).

Huntington, Samuel P. *The Clash of Civilizations and the Remaking of World Order* (New York: Simon & Schuster, 1996).

Hutchings, Robert L., ed. *At the End of the American Century: America's Role in the Post–Cold War World* (Washington, D.C.: Woodrow Wilson Center Press, 1998).

Hutton, Lord James Brian Edward. *Report of the Inquiry into the Circumstances Surrounding the Death of Dr. David Kelly C.M.G.* (London: The Stationery Office, 2004).

Ignatieff, Michael. *The Lesser Evil: Political Ethics in an Age of Terror* (Princeton: Princeton University Press, 2004).

———. "Moral Prohibition at a Price," in *Torture,* ed. Kenneth Roth and Minky Worden (New York: New Press, 2005).

———. *Virtual War: Kosovo and Beyond* (New York: Picador, 2000).

Iraq Survey Group. *Comprehensive Report of the Special Advisor to the DCI on Iraq's WMD,* vol. 1 (2004).

Issacharoff, Samuel, and Richard H. Pildes. "Emergency Contexts Without Emergency Powers: The United States' Constitutional Approach to Rights During Wartime," *International Journal of Constitutional Law* 2 (2004): 296–333.

Jacquard, R. *In the Name of Osama Bin Laden: Global Terrorism and the Bin Laden Brotherhood* (Durham, N.C.: Duke University Press, 2003).

Jefferson, Thomas. VIII *The Writings of Thomas Jefferson,* ed. Paul Leicester Ford (New York: G. P. Putnam's Sons, 1897).

Jewett, Thomas. "Terrorism in Early America," *Early America Review* 4, no. 1 (2002).

Johnson, James Turner. *The War to Oust Saddam Hussein: Just War and the New Face of Conflict* (Lanham, Md.: Rowman & Littlefield, 2005).

Juergensmeyer, M. *Terror in the Mind of God: The Global Rise of Religious Violence,* 3rd ed. (Berkeley, Calif.: University of California Press, 2003).

Kagan, Robert. *Of Paradise and Power: America and Europe in the New World Order* (New York: Vintage Books, 2004).

Kahn, David. *The Codebreakers: The Story of Secret Writing* (New York: The Macmillan Company, 1967).

Kaldor, Mary. *New and Old Wars: Organized Violence in a Global Era* (Stanford, Calif. Stanford University Press, 1999).

Kant, Immanuel. *To Perpetual Peace: A Philosophical Sketch,* trans. Ted Humphrey (Indianapolis: Hackett, 2003 [original publication 1795]).

Kaplan, Fred M. *The Wizards of Armageddon* (New York: Simon & Schuster, 1983).

Kaplan, Robert D. *Balkan Ghosts: A Journey Through History* (New York: St. Martin's Press, 1993).

———. *The Coming Anarchy: Shattering the Dreams of the Post–Cold War* (New York: Random House, 2000).

Katona, Peter, Michael B. Intriligator, and John P. Sullivan, eds. *Countering Terrorism and WMD: Creating a Global Counter-terrorism Network* (Abingdon and New York: Routledge, 2006).

Kean, T. H., and L. H. Hamilton. *The 9/11 Report: The National Commission on Terrorist Attacks upon the United States* (New York: St. Martin's Press, 2004).

Kennan, George F. *Memoirs: 1925–1950* (New York: Little, Brown, 1967).

Kennedy, Paul. *The Parliament of Man: The United Nations and the Quest for World Government* (London: Penguin 2006).

———. *The Rise and Fall of the Great Powers: Economic Change and Military Conflict from 1500 to 2000* (New York: Vintage Books, 1987).

Kent, Sherman. "A Crucial Estimate Relived," in *Sherman Kent and the Board of National Estimates: Collected Essays* (Center for the Study of Intelligence, 1994).

———. *Strategic Intelligence for American World Policy* (Princeton, N.J.: Princeton University Press, 1949).

Kepel, G. *Jihad: The Trail of Political Islam* (London: I.B. Tauris, 2003).

Kissinger, Henry. *Diplomacy* (New York: Simon & Schuster, 1994).

———. *Does America Need a Foreign Policy?: Towards a Diplomacy for the 21st Century* (New York: Simon & Schuster, 2001).

Kitfield, James. "Anti-Terror Alliance," *Government Executive* 33, no. 2 (2001): 51–56.

Koh, Harold H. "A World Transformed," *Yale Journal of International Law* 20 (1995): ix.

Krueger, Alan B., and David D. Laitin. " 'Misunderestimating' Terrorism," *Foreign Affairs* 83, no. 5 (September/October 2004): 8–13.

Krueger, Alan B., and Jitka Maleckova. "Education, Poverty and Terrorism: Is There a Causal Connection?" *The Journal of Economic Perspectives* 17 (Fall 2003): 119–44.

Kuhns, Woodrow J. "Intelligence Failures: Forecasting and the Lessons of Epistemology," in *Paradoxes of Strategic Intelligence: Essays in Honor of Michael I. Handel,* ed. Richard K. Betts and Thomas G. Mahnken (Portland, Ore.: Frank Cass Publishers, 2003).

Kwik, Gigi, Joe Fitzgerald, Thomas V. Inglesby, and Tara O'Toole. "Biosecurity: Responsible Stewardship of Bioscience in an Age of Catastrophic Terrorism," *Biosecurity and Bioterrorism: Biodefense Strategy, Practice and Science* 1, no. 1 (2003): 27–35.

Laird, Melvin R. "Iraq: Learning the Lessons of Vietnam," *Foreign Affairs* 84, no. 6 (November/December 2005): 22–43.

Laqueur, Walter. *The New Terrorism: Fanaticism and the Arms of Mass Destruction* (New York: Oxford University Press, 1999).

LeBor, Adam. *"Complicity with Evil." The United Nations in the Age of Modern Genocide* (New Haven and London: Yale University Press, 2006).

Lederberg, J., ed. *Biological Weapons: Limiting the Threat* (Cambridge, Mass.: MIT Press, 1999).

Leebaert, Derek. *To Dare to Conquer: Special Operations and the Destiny of Nations, from Achilles to Al Qaeda* (New York: Little, Brown, 2006).

Levinson, Sanford. "Contemplating Torture: An Introduction," in *Torture: A Collection,* ed. Sanford Levinson (New York: Oxford University Press, 2004).

Lietzau, William K. "Combating Terrorism: The Consequences of Moving from Law Enforcement to War," in *New Wars, New Laws?: Applying the Laws of War in 21st Century Conflicts,* ed. David Wippman and Matthew Evangelista (Ardsley, N.Y.: Transnational, 2005).

Lind, Michael. *The American Way of Strategy* (New York: Oxford University Press, 2006).

Machiavelli, Niccolò. *The Prince and the Discourses* (New York: The Modern Library, 1950).

Macmillan, Harold. *Winds of Change 1914–1939* (New York: Harper & Row, 1966).

Malik, S. K. *The Quranic Concept of War* (Karachi, Pakistan: Wajidalis, 1979).

Mann, Thomas E., and Norman J. Ornstein. *The Broken Branch: How Congress Is Failing America and How to Get It Back on Track* (New York: Oxford University Press, 2006).

Manning, John F. "The Absurdity Doctrine," *Harvard Law Review* 116 (2003): 2387–2486.

Marx, Gary T. "Some Concepts That May Be Useful in Understanding the Myriad Forms and Contexts of Surveillance," in *Understanding Intelligence in the Twenty-first Century: Journeys in Shadows,* ed. L. V. Scott and Peter Jackson (New York: Routledge, 2004).

McDougall, Walter. *Promised Land, Crusader State: The American Encounter with the World Since 1776* (New York: Houghton Mifflin, 1997).

McGranahan, Gordon, and David Satterthwaite. "Urban Centers: An Assessment of Sustainability," *Annual Review of Environment and Resources* 28 (2003): 243–74.

Mearsheimer, John J. *The Tragedy of Great Power Politics* (New York: W. W. Norton, 2001).

Mégret, Frédéric. " 'War'? Legal Semantics and the Move to Violence," *European Journal of International Law* 13 (2002): 361–99.

Miller, Judith, Stephen Engelberg, and William Broad. *Germs: Biological Weapons and America's Secret War* (New York: Simon & Schuster, 2001).

Milsom, S. F. C. *Historical Foundations of the Common Law* (London: Butterworths, 1969).

Mitchell, Paul T. "Network-Centric Warfare: Coalition Operations in the Age of U.S. Military Primacy." Adelphi Paper no. 385 (London: International Institute for Strategic Studies, 2006).

Monbiot, George. *The Age of Consent* (London: Flamingo, 2003).

Moravcsik, Andrew. "Striking a New Transatlantic Bargain," *Foreign Affairs* 82, no. 4 (July/August 2003): 27–40.

Morgenthau, Hans J. *Politics Among Nations* (New York: Knopf, 1985).

Mueller, John. "Is There Still a Terrorist Threat?: The Myth of the Omnipresent Enemy," *Foreign Affairs* 85. no. 5 (September/October 2006): 2–8.

———. "Why Isn't There More Violence?" *Security Studies* 13, no. 3 (Spring 2004).

Napoleoni, Loretta. *Terror Incorporated: Tracing the Money Behind Global Terrorism* (New York: Penguin Books, 2003).

National Commission on Terrorist Attacks upon the United States. *The 9/11 Commission Report: Final Report of the National Commission on Terrorist Attacks upon the United States* (Washington, D.C.: U.S. Government Printing Office, 2004).

National Criminal Intelligence Sharing Plan. Executive Summary, U.S. Department of Justice, 2003.

National Intelligence Council. *Mapping the Global Future: Report of the National Intelligence Council's 2020 Project*. (Honolulu, Hi.: University Press of the Pacific, 2005).

The National Security Strategy of the United States of America (Washington, D.C.: 2002).

Neely, Mark E., Jr. *The Fate of Liberty: Abraham Lincoln and Civil Liberties* (New York: Oxford University Press, 1991).

Neumann, Peter R. "Europe's Jihadist Dilemma," *Survival* 48, no. 2 (Summer 2006): 71–84.

Nye, Joseph S., Jr. *Bound to Lead: The Changing Nature of American Power* (New York: Basic Books, 1990).

———. *The Paradox of America Power: Why the World's Only Superpower Can't Go It Alone* (New York: Oxford University Press, 2003).

Obeidi, Mahdi, and Kurt Pitzer. *The Bomb in My Garden: The Secrets of Saddam's Nuclear Mastermind* (Hoboken, N.J.: John Wiley & Sons, 2004).

O'Hanlon, Michael. *Defense Strategy for the Post-Saddam Era* (Washington, D.C.: The Brookings Institution, 2005).

Our Dumb Century: The Onion Presents 100 Years of Headlines from America's Finest News Source (New York: Three Rivers Press, 1999).

Overy, Richard. *The Dictators: Hitler's Germany, Stalin's Russia* (London: Penguin, 2005).

Pape, Robert A. *Dying to Win: The Strategic Logic of Suicide Terrorism* (New York: Random House, 2005).

Parrott, David. *Richelieu's Army: War, Government and Society in France, 1624–1642* (Cambridge, U.K.: Cambridge University Press, 2001).

Patterson, Dennis. "The New Leviathan," review of *The Shield of Achilles: War, Peace, and the Course of History,* by Philip Bobbitt, *Michigan Law Review* 101 (May 2003): 1715–32.

Penttila, Risto. "The Role of the G8 in International Peace and Security," Adelphi Paper no. 355 (London: International Institute for Strategic Studies, 2003).

Perito, Robert M. *Where Is the Lone Ranger When We Need Him?: America's Search for a Postconflict Stability Force* (Washington, D.C.: U.S. Institute of Peace Press, 2004).

Petro, James B., Theodore R. Plasse, and Jake A. McNulty. "Biotechnology: Impact on Biological Warfare and Biodefense," *Biosecurity and Bioterrorism: Biodefense Strategy, Practice and Science* 1, no. 3 (2003): 161–68.

Pew Global Attitudes Project. *American Character Gets Mixed Reviews: U.S. Image Up Slightly, but Still Negative* (Washington, D.C.: Pew Research Center, 2005).

———. *America's Image Slips, but Allies Share U.S. Concern Over Iran, Hamas* (Washington, D.C.: Pew Research Center, 2006).

———. *Views of a Changing World* (Washington, D.C.: Pew Research Center, 2003).

Pillar, Paul R. *Terrorism and U.S. Foreign Policy* (Washington, D.C.: Brookings Institution, 2001).

Plucknett, Theodore F. T. *A Concise History of the Common Law,* 5th ed. (Boston: Little, Brown, 1956).

Pluta, Anna M., and Peter D. Zimmerman. "Nuclear Terrorism: A Disheartening Dissent," *Survival* 48, no. 2 (Summer 2006): 55–70.

Pollack, Kenneth M. *The Threatening Storm: The Case for Invading Iraq* (New York: Random House, 2002).

Posner, Richard A. *Catastrophe: Risk and Response* (New York: Oxford University Press, 2004).

———. *Countering Terrorism: Blurred Focus, Halting Steps* (Lanham, Md.: Rowman & Littlefield Publishers, 2006).

———. "Torture, Terrorism, and Interrogation," in *Torture: A Collection,* ed. Sanford Levinson (New York: Oxford University Press, 2004).

Potter, William C., Charles D. Ferguson, and Leonard S. Spector. "The Four Faces of Nuclear Terror," *Foreign Affairs* 83, no. 3 (May/June 2004): 130–32.

Power, Samantha. *A Problem from Hell: America and the Age of Genocide* (New York: Basic Books, 2002).

Powers, Thomas F. "Can We Be Secure and Free?" *Public Interest* 151 (Spring 2003): 3–24.

Quinlan, Michael. "Deterrence and Deterrability," in *Deterrence and the New Global Security Environment,* ed. Ian R. Kenyon and John Simpson (New York: Routledge, 2006).

Rapoport, David C. "The Four Waves of Rebel Terror and September 11," *Anthropoetics* 8, no. 1 (Spring/Summer 2002).

Rappert, Brian. "Biological Weapons, Genetics and Social Analysis: Emerging Responses, Emerging Issues—I," *New Genetics and Society* 22, no. 2 (2003): 169–81.

Rediker, Marcus. *Between the Devil and the Deep Blue Sea: Merchant Seamen, Pirates and the Anglo-American Maritime World 1700–1750* (Cambridge, U.K.: Cambridge University Press, 1987).

Reich, W., ed. *Origins of Terrorism: Psychologies, Ideologies, Theologies, States of Mind* (Washington, D.C.: Woodrow Wilson International Center for Scholars and Cambridge University Press, 1996).

Reid, Anna. "Introduction," in *Taming Terrorism: It's Been Done Before,* ed. Anna Reid (London: Policy Exchange, 2004).

Reisman, W. Michael. "Sovereignty and Human Rights in Contemporary International Law," *American Journal of International* Law 84 (October 1990): 866–76.

Richardson, Louise. "The Roots of Terrorism: An Overview," in *The Roots of Terrorism,* ed. Louise Richardson (New York: Routledge, 2006).

———. *What Terrorists Want: Understanding the Enemy, Containing the Threat* (New York: Random House, 2006).

Riley-Smith, Jonathan. "Rethinking the Crusades," *First Things,* no. 101 (March 2000): 20–23.

Ritchie, Robert C. *Captain Kidd and the War against the Pirates* (Cambridge, Mass. & London: Harvard University Press, 1986).

Roberts, Adam. "Law and the Use of Force After Iraq," *Survival* 45, no. 2 (Summer 2003): 31–56.

Roberts, Michael. "The Military Revolution, 1560–1660," in *Essays in Swedish History* (London: Weidenfeld and Nicolson, 1967).

Rogers, James, and Matthew Jamison. "Britain and the World," in *The British Moment,* ed.

John Bew, Gabriel Glickman, and Martyn Frampton (London: Social Affairs Unit, 2006).

Rorty, Richard M., ed. *The Linguistic Turn: Essays in Philosophical Method* (Chicago: University of Chicago Press, 1992).

Ross, Philip. "Terror and Its Antidote," *Acumen Journal of Life Sciences* 1 (2003).

Roth, Kenneth. "Counterterrorism and Human Rights: An Essential Alliance," in *The Nexus of Terrorism and WMDs: Developing a Consensus* (Princeton, N.J.: Princeton University Press, 2004).

———. "Justifying Torture," in *Torture,* ed. Kenneth Roth and Minky Worden (New York: New Press, 2005).

Sageman, Marc. *Understanding Terror Networks* (Philadelphia: University of Pennsylvania Press, 2004).

Sassen, S. *Losing Control?: Sovereignty in an Age of Globalization* (New York: Columbia University Press, 1996).

Scarry, Elaine. "Five Errors in the Reasoning of Alan Dershowitz," in *Torture: A Collection,* ed. Sanford Levinson (New York: Oxford University Press, 2004).

Schelling, Thomas. *The Strategy of Conflict* (Cambridge, Mass.: Harvard University Press, 1960).

Scheuerman, William E. "Emergency Powers and the Rule of Law After 9/11," *Journal of Political Philosophy* 14 (2006): 61–84.

Schmid, Alex P. *Political Terrorism: A Research Guide to Concepts, Theories, Data Bases and Literature* (New Brunswick, N.J.: Transaction Books, 1984).

Schmidl, Erwin A. "Police Functions in Peace Operations: A Historical Overview," in *Policing the New World Disorder: Peace Operations and Public Security,* ed. Robert B. Oakley et al. (Washington, D.C.: National Defense University Press, 1998).

Sennett, Richard. *The Fall of Public Man* (New York: Knopf, 1977).

Shane, Peter M., and Harold H. Bruff. *The Law of Presidential Power: Cases and Materials* (Durham, N.C.: Carolina Academic Press, 1988).

Shawcross, William. *Allies: The U.S., Britain, Europe, and the War in Iraq* (New York: Public Affairs, 2005).

Shell Global Scenarios to 2025: The Future Business Environment Trends, Trade-Offs, and Choices (London: Shell International Limited, 2005).

Shue, Henry. "Torture," in *Torture: A Collection,* ed. Sanford Levinson (New York: Oxford University Press, 2004).

Simon, Steve, and David Benjamin."America and the New Terrorism," *Survival* 42, no. 1 (Spring 2000): 59–75.

———. "The Terror," *Survival* 43, no. 4 (Winter 2001): 5–18.

Sivard, Ruth Leger. *World Military and Social Expenditures 1996* (Washington, D.C.: World Priorities, 1996).

Slaughter, Anne-Marie. *A New World Order* (Princeton, N.J.: Princeton University Press, 2004).

Sloan, S. *Terrorism: The Present Threat in Context* (Oxford: Berg, 2006).

Smith, Rupert. *The Utility of Force: The Art of War in the Modern World* (London: Allen Lane, 2005).

Smith, Steve. "Unanswered Questions," in *Worlds in Collision: Terror and the Future of Global Order,* ed. Ken Booth and Tim Dunne (New York: Palgrave Macmillan, 2002).

Soros, George. *The Age of Infallibility: Consequences of the War on Terror* (New York: Public Affairs, 2006).

Stepniak, Sergius. *Underground Russia: Revolutionary Profiles and Sketches from Life* (London: Smith, Elder, & Co., 1883).

Stern, Jessica. "Apocalypse Never, but the Threat Is Real," *Survival* 40, no. 4 (Winter 1998): 176–79.

———. "The Protean Enemy," *Foreign Affairs* 82, no. 4 (July/August 2003): 27–40.

———. *Terror in the Name of God: Why Religious Militants Kill* (New York: Ecco, 2003).

———. *The Ultimate Terrorists* (Cambridge, Mass.: Harvard University Press, 1999).

Stiglitz, Joseph E. *Making Globalization Work: The Next Steps to Global Justice* (London: Allen Lane, 2006).

Strauss, David. "Reply: Legitimacy and Obedience," *Harvard Law Review* 118 (2005): 1854–66.

Sunstein, Cass R. *Laws of Fear: Beyond the Precautionary Principle* (The Seeley Lectures) (Cambridge, U.K.: Cambridge University Press, 2005).

Suskind, Ron. *The One Percent Doctrine: Deep Inside America's Pursuit of Its Enemies Since 9/11* (New York: Simon & Schuster, 2006).

Talbot, David. "Terror's Server," *MIT Technology Review* 108 (February 2005): 46–52.

Tenner, Edward. *Why Things Bite Back: Technology and the Revenge of Unintended Consequences* (New York: Knopf, 1997).

Thompson, Donald F., et al. *The Bug Stops Here: Force Protection and Emerging Infectious Diseases* (Washington, D.C.: National Defense University Press, 2005).

Thucydides. *History of the Peloponnesian War,* trans. Rex Warner (New York: Penguin Books, 1972).

Toffler, Alvin. *The Third Wave* (New York: Morrow, 1980).

Treverton, Gregory F. *Intelligence, Law Enforcement, and Homeland Security* (Washington, D.C.: Century Foundation, 2002).

———. *Reshaping National Intelligence in an Age of Information* (New York: Cambridge University Press, 2001).

Treverton, Gregory F., and Jeremy D. Wilson. "The Global Challenge of Operational Intelligence for Counter-terrorism," in *Countering Terrorism and WMD: Creating a Global Counter-Terrorism Network,* ed. Peter Katona et al. (New York: Routledge, 2006).

Tribe, Laurence H., and Patrick O. Gudridge. "The Anti-Emergency Constitution," *Yale Law Journal* 113 (2004): 1801–70.

Trotsky, Leon. *The Defence of Terrorism (Terrorism and Communism)* (London: Labour Publishing, 1921).

Truman, Harry S. *Memoirs: Years of Trial and Hope,* vol. 2 (Garden City, N.Y.: Doubleday & Company, Inc., 1956).

Tucker, David. "What Is New About the New Terrorism and How Dangerous Is It?" *Terrorism and Political Violence* 13, no. 3 (Autumn 2001): 1–14.

Tushnet, Mark. "The Supreme Court, 1998 Term Foreword: The New Constitutional Order and the Chastening of Constitutional Aspiration," *Harvard Law Review* 113 (1999): 29–109.

U.S. Department of State. *Patterns of International Terrorism: 1981* (Washington, D.C.: U.S. Government Printing Office, 1982).

U.S. Senate Select Committee on Secret Military Assistance to Iran and the Nicaraguan Opposition and U.S. House of Representatives Select Committee to Investigate Covert Arms Transactions with Iran. *Report of the Congressional Committees Investigating the Iran-Contra Affair, Senate Report No. 100–216 and House Report No. 100–433* (Washington, D.C.: U. S. Government Printing Office, 1987).

von Clausewitz, Carl. *On War,* trans. and ed. Michael Howard and Peter Paret (Princeton, N.J.: Princeton University Press, 1976).

Walt, Stephen M. *The Origins of Alliances* (Ithaca: Cornell University Press, 1987).

———. *Taming American Power: The Global Response to U.S. Primacy* (New York: W. W. Norton, 2005).

Walzer, Michael. *Just and Unjust Wars: A Moral Argument with Historical Illustrations* (New York: HarperCollins, 1977).

———. "Political Action: The Problem of Dirty Hands," in *Torture: A Collection,* ed. Sanford Levinson (New York: Oxford University Press, 2004).

Wechsler, Herbert. "Toward Neutral Principles of Constitutional Law," *Harvard Law Review* 73 (1959): 1–35.

Weimann, Gabriel. *www.terror.net: How Modern Terrorism Uses the Internet* (Washington, D.C.: United States Institute of Peace, 2004).

Weinberg, Albert K. *Manifest Destiny: A Study of Nationalist Expansionism in American History* (Baltimore: Johns Hopkins Press, 1935).

Weissman, Steve, and Herbert Krosney. *The Islamic Bomb* (New York: New York Times Books, 1981).

White, Jonathan R. *Terrorism: An Introduction* (Belmont, Calif.: Wadsworth, 2002), 19.

The White House. *A National Security Strategy for a New Century* (Washington, D.C.: The White House, 1997).

Wilkinson, Paul. *Terrorism Versus Democracy: The Liberal State Response* (London: Frank Cass, 2001).

Williams, Mark. "The Looming Threat," *Acumen Journal of Life Sciences* 1, no. 4 (January 2004).

Wilson, Peter Lamborn. *Pirate Utopias: Moorish Corsairs and European Renegadoes* (New York: Autonomedia, 1995).

Wohlstetter, Roberta. *Pearl Harbor: Warning and Decision* (Stanford, Calif.: Stanford University Press, 1962).

Wolff, R. P. *The Conflict Between Authority and Autonomy* (Oxford: Blackwell Publishing, 1990).

Wolfrum, Rüdiger. "The Attack of September 11, 2001, the Wars Against the Taliban and Iraq: Is There a Need to Reconsider International Law on the Recourse to Force and the Rules in Armed Conflict?" in *Max Planck Yearbook of United Nations Law,* vol. 7, ed. Armin von Bogdandy and Rüdiger Wolfrum (Leiden, Netherlands: Martinus Njhoff Publishers, 2004).

Woodcock, George. *Anarchism: A History of Libertarian Ideas and Movements* (New York: Meridian Books, 1962).

Wright, Lawrence. *The Looming Tower: Al-Qaeda and the Road to 9/11* (New York: Knopf, 2006).

Yaniv, Avner. *Deterrence without the Bomb: The Politics of Israeli Strategy* (Lexington and Toronto: D. C. Heath and Company, 1987).

Yergin, Daniel, and Joseph Stanislaw. *The Commanding Heights: The Battle Between Government and the Marketplace That Is Remaking the Modern World* (New York: Simon & Schuster, 1998).

Zakaria, Fareed. *The Future of Freedom: Illiberal Democracy at Home and Abroad* (New York: W. W. Norton, 2003).

ANNOTATED INDEX

biological weapons, 3–4, 8–9, 59, 93, 99,
101–2, 104, 119–22, 151, 209,
231–32, 236, 245, 327, 331–32, 340,
343, 424, 448, 453, 477, 479, 488,
513, 536, 538
Blackstone, William, 460–462
Blair, Tony, 77, 171–72, 176, 336, 348,
375–76, 441, 537
Bloomberg, Michael (Opportunity NYC), 89
Bremer, L. Paul (former State Department
official who was the head of the
Coalitional Provisional Authority
that directed the reconstruction and
occupation of Iraq from 2003–2004),
163, 167
Brodie, Bernard, 523
Brzezinski, Zbigniew, 482
buccaneers, 30–34
Bush Doctrine (phrase coined by the media
to describe the 2002 National
Security Strategy issued by the U.S.
administration that stressed
preemption), 433–37, 439, 449
Bush, George H. W., 438, 543
Bush, George W., 70, 82–83, 144–45, 148,
174, 208, 216, 234, 272–73, 287,
308, 316, 319–20, 348, 352, 437,
438, 439, 444, 456, 487, 489, 491,
516, 531, 537, 543
Butler Commission (official U.K.
government inquiry into the use of
intelligence on weapons of mass
destruction leading up to British
intervention in Iraq), 115

Canning, George (British Foreign Secretary
1822–1827), 429–31
Caroline, The, 434–35
Carter Doctrine (policy proclaimed by
President Jimmy Carter in the State
of the Union address January 1980,
announcing that United States would
use all necessary means to defend its
interests in the Persian Gulf), 432
Charles V, Holy Roman emperor, 27,
189–90
Cheney, Richard (Dick), 70, 476
Chirac, Jacques, 92, 487
Chyba, Christopher, 402–3

CIA (Central Intelligence Agency), 115,
118–19, 141, 166, 173, 241, 248–49,
264, 277, 292, 297–304, 312–13,
316, 318–19, 325, 331–333, 335,
337, 341, 349, 386, 393, 414, 533
Clarke, Richard, 298, 386–87
Clausewitz, Carl von, 590
claviger and steward (proposed role for
United States in twenty-first century
stressing the provision of collective
goods), 487, 497–98, 537
climate change, 87, 231, 441, 544
Clinton, Bill, 91, 139, 310, 316, 318, 386,
422, 445, 456, 489, 491, 543
COINTELPRO (1970s FBI program that
infiltrated dissident U.S. political
organizations), 248
Coker, Christopher, 143, 147, 168
collateral damage (injuries incident to, but
not the objective of, official acts of
war), 48, 533
collective goods, 126, 440, 442, 494
Columbia University, 178
commodification of WMD (the emerging
market that enables states and groups
to possess advanced weaponry
without developing it), 9, 59, 98,
471, 512, 522
compellance (the use of nuclear weapons
threats to compel a particular
political action by a state), 123, 201,
213, 236, 446, 522–23, 528–29, 545
Connectivity Paradox, 97, 401, 497
constitutional order (see also *The Shield of
Achilles: War, Peace, and the Course
of History*), 4, 8–9, 11–12, 18–20,
23, 25–27, 30–31, 34–35, 38–40,
42–44, 78, 86–87, 91–92, 94,
123–24, 126, 145, 153, 168, 180–82,
188–89, 190–92, 197–98, 212, 236,
244, 296, 338, 416, 456, 466,
482–83, 503–5, 507, 519, 523–24,
527–28, 532, 543–44, 548
Convention Against Torture or Other Cruel,
Inhuman, or Degrading Treatment or
Punishment (Torture Convention),
274, 369, 370, 385, 500
Convention on International Civil Aviation,
438
Cooper, Robert (former British diplomat
and subsequently Director-General

PERMISSIONS ACKNOWLEDGMENTS

Grateful acknowledgment is made to the following for permission to reprint previously published material.

Harcourt, Inc.: Excerpt from "Tortures" from *View with a Grain of Sand* by Wislawa Szymborska, translated by Stanislaw Baranczak and Clare Cavanagh, copyright © 1993 by Wislawa Szymborska, copyright © 1995 by Harcourt, Inc. Reprinted by permission of Harcourt, Inc.

HarperCollin Publishers: "A Poem at the End of the Century" from *Provinces: Poems 1987–1991* by Czeslaw Milosz, translated by Czeslaw Milosz and Robert Haas, copyright © 1991 by Czeslaw Milosz Royalties, Inc. Reprinted by permission of HarperCollins Publishers.

International Creative Management, Inc.: "Poem" from *The Collected Poems of Muriel Rukeyser,* copyright © 1968 by Muriel Rukeyser (University of Pittsburgh Press, 2005). Reprinted by permission of International Creative Management, Inc.

Random House, Inc.: Excerpt from "The Purse-Seine" from *Selected Poetry of Robinson Jeffers,* copyright © 1938 and renewed 1966 by Donnan Jeffers and Garth Jeffers. Reprinted by permission of Random House, Inc.

Scribner and the Estate of Marianne Moore: "What Are Years?" from *The Complete Poems of Marianne Moore,* copyright © 1941 by Marianne Moore, copyright renewed 1969 by Marianne Moore. All rights reserved. Reprinted by permission of Scribner, an imprint of Simon and Schuster Adult Publishing Group, and of Marianne Craig Moore, Literary Executor, the Estate of Marianne Moore.

Simon and Schuster: Excerpt from *Catch-22* by Joseph Heller, copyright © 1955, 1961 by Joseph Heller. Copyright renewed 1989 by Joseph Heller. Reprinted by permission of Simon & Schuster Adult Publishing Group.

PENGUIN HISTORY

THE ASCENT OF MONEY
NIALL FERGUSON

Bread, cash, dosh, dough, loot: call it what you like, it matters. To Christians, love of it is the root of all evil. To generals, it is the sinews of war. To revolutionaries, it is the shackles of labour. But in *The Ascent of Money*, Niall Ferguson shows that finance is in fact the foundation of human progress. What's more, he reveals financial history as the essential back-story behind all history.

With the clarity and verve for which he is famed, Niall Ferguson explains why the origins of the French Revolution lie in a stock-market bubble caused by a convicted Scots murderer. He shows how financial failure turned Argentina from the world's sixth richest country into an inflation-ridden basket case – and how a financial revolution is propelling the world's most populous country from poverty to power in a single generation.

Yet the most important lesson of financial history is that sooner or later every bubble bursts – sooner or later the bearish sellers outnumber the bullish buyers – sooner or later greed flips into fear. And that's why, whether you're scraping by or rolling in it, there's never been a better time to understand the ascent of money.

PENGUIN HISTORY

A HISTORY OF HISTORIES
JOHN BURROW

This unprecedented book, by one of Britain's leading intellectual historians, describes the intellectual impact that the study of the past has had in the western world over the past 2,500 years. It brings to life the work of historians from the Greeks to the present, including Livy, Tacitus, Bede, Froissart, Clarendon, Gibbon, Macaulay, Michelet, Prescott and Parkman, explaining their distinctive qualities and allowing the modern reader to appreciate and enjoy them. It sets out to be not the history of an academic discipline, but a history of choice: the choice of pasts, and the ways they have been demarcated, investigated, presented and even sometimes learned from as they have changed according to political, religious, cultural and patriotic circumstances.

Burrow argues that looking at the history of history is one of the most interesting ways we can try to understand the past. Nothing on the scale of or with the ambition of his book has yet been attempted in English.

'A triumphant success. The result is a highly enjoyable book, based on a vast amount of reading, written with attractive simplicity, brimming with acute observations, and often very witty. Anyone who wants to know what historical writing has contributed to our culture should start here' Keith Thomas, *Guardian*

'This book is magnificent: a daunting combination of vast range, profound learning and high literary art. In 500 superbly crafted pages (miraculously succinct for the task in hand), Burrow's chapters treat almost every important historian of the last two-and-a-half thousand years' John Adamson, *Sunday Telegraph*

PENGUIN HISTORY

NIXON AND KISSINGER: PARTNERS IN POWER
ROBERT DALLEK

In this epic and revelatory joint biography, one of America's most distinguished historians probes the lives and times of two unlikely leaders whose partnership dominated the world stage and changed the course of history.

Tapping into a wealth of recently declassified documents and tapes, Robert Dallek uncovers fascinating details about Nixon and Kissinger's tumultuous personal relationship – their collaboration and rivalry – and the extent to which they struggled to outdo each other in the reach for foreign policy achievements.

'Riveting ... their unlikely partnership has come under closer scrutiny than ever before' Rupert Cornwell, *Independent*

'A devastating account of irresponsibility and dysfunction within the White House ... remarkably engaging' *The New York Times*

PENGUIN POLITICS

THE LOOMING TOWER
LAWRENCE WRIGHT

'One of the best and most important books of recent years. A masterful combination of reporting and writing' Dan Rather

Brilliantly written, compelling and highly original, *The Looming Tower* is the first book to tell the full story of al-Qaeda from its roots up to 9/11. Drawing on astonishing interviews and first-hand sources, it investigates the extraordinary group of idealogues behind this organization – and those who tried to stop them.

Interweaving this story with events including the Israel–Palestine conflict, the Soviet invasion of Afghanistan and the first attack on the World Trade Center, Lawrence Wright takes us into training camps, mountain hideouts and top-secret meetings to explore how it all fed into the planning and execution of 9/11 – and reveals the real, complex origins of al-Qaeda's hatred of the West.

He just wanted a decent book to read ...

Not too much to ask, is it? It was in 1935 when Allen Lane, Managing
Director of Bodley Head Publishers, stood on a platform at Exeter railway
station looking for something good to read on his journey back to London.
His choice was limited to popular magazines and poor-quality paperbacks –
the same choice faced every day by the vast majority of readers, few of
whom could afford hardbacks. Lane's disappointment and subsequent anger
at the range of books generally available led him to found a company – and
change the world.

*'We believed in the existence in this country of a vast reading public for intelligent
books at a low price, and staked everything on it'*
Sir Allen Lane, 1902–1970, founder of Penguin Books

The quality paperback had arrived – and not just in bookshops. Lane was
adamant that his Penguins should appear in chain stores and tobacconists,
and should cost no more than a packet of cigarettes.

Reading habits (and cigarette prices) have changed since 1935, but
Penguin still believes in publishing the best books for everybody to
enjoy. We still believe that good design costs no more than bad design,
and we still believe that quality books published passionately and responsibly
make the world a better place.

So wherever you see the little bird – whether it's on a piece of
prize-winning literary fiction or a celebrity autobiography, political tour
de force or historical masterpiece, a serial-killer thriller, reference book,
world classic or a piece of pure escapism – you can bet that it represents
the very best that the genre has to offer.

Whatever you like to read – trust Penguin.

read more
www.penguin.co.uk